University of London
Institute of Latin American Studies

13

Latin America, Economic Imperialism and the State:
The Political Economy of the External Connection
from Independence to the Present

Latin America, Economic Imperialism and the State:
The Political Economy of the External Connection from Independence to the Present

Edited by

CHRISTOPHER ABEL
and
COLIN M. LEWIS

THE ATHLONE PRESS
London, and Dover, New Hampshire

Published for the
Institute of Latin American Studies
University of London

First published 1985 by The Athlone Press Ltd
44 Bedford Row, London WC1R 4LY
551 Washington Street, Dover, New Hampshire

© *University of London 1985*

British Library Cataloguing in Publication Data

Latin America, economic imperialism and the state.
—(Institute of Latin American studies
monographs; no. 13)
1. Latin America—Foreign economic relations
2. Latin America—Foreign relations
I. Abel, Christopher   II. Lewis, Colin M.
III. Series
337.8   HF3230.5

ISBN 0–485–17713–7

Library of Congress Cataloging in Publication Data
Main entry under title:

Latin America, economic imperialism, and the state.

(Institute of Latin American Studies monographs ; 13)
Bibliography: p.
Includes index.
1. Latin America—Foreign economic relations—
Addresses, essays, lectures. 2. Latin America—Economic
policy—Addresses, essays, lectures. 3. Latin America—
Dependency on foreign countries—Addresses, essays,
lectures. I. Abel, Christopher. II. Lewis, Colin M.
III. Series
HF1480.5.L384   1985   337.8   84–9260
ISBN 0–485–17713–7

Typeset by Inforum Ltd, Portsmouth
Printed by Biddles, Guildford

University of London
Institute of Latin American Studies Monographs

1. *The 'Detached Recollections' of General D. F. O'Leary*, edited by R. A. Humphreys. 1969.
2. *Accounts of Nineteenth-Century South America: an Annotated Checklist of Works by British and United States Observers*, by Bernard Naylor. 1969.
3. *Commercial Relations between British Overseas Territories and South America, 1806–1914*, by T. W. Keeble. 1970.
4. *British Nitrates and Chilean Politics, 1886–1896: Balmaceda and North*, by Harold Blakemore. 1974.
5. *Directory of Libraries and Special Collections on Latin America and the West Indies*, by Bernard Naylor, Laurence Hallewell and Colin Steele. 1975.
6. *Mexico State Paper, 1744–1843*, by Michael Costeloe. 1976.
7. *Farmers in Revolt: The Revolutions of 1893 in the Province of Sante Fe, Argentina*, by Ezequiel Gallo. 1976.
8. *Agrarian Reform and Peasant Organisation on the Ecuadorian Coast*, by M. R. Redclift. 1978.
9. *The Rise and Fall of the Peruvian Military Radicals, 1968–1976*, by George D. E. Philip. 1978.
10. *Latin America and the Second World War, Volume One, 1939–1942*, by R. A. Humphreys. 1981.
11. *Latin America and the Second World War, Volume Two, 1942–1945*, by R. A. Humphreys. 1982.
12. *British Railways in Argentina, 1857–1914: a Case Study of Foreign Investment*, by Colin M. Lewis. 1983.
13. *Latin America, Economic Imperialism and the State: The Political Economy of the External Connection from Independence to the Present*, edited by Christopher Abel and Colin M. Lewis. 1984.

CONTENTS

TABLES

MAPS

Notes on contributors

This volume is representative of scholarship undertaken in centres of Latin American studies established upon the recommendation of the Parry Committee during the 1960s, to promote further interest – principally at the level of research and postgraduate training – in Latin America at British universities. Contributors are also drawn from other institutions which developed research and teaching programmes focused upon the continent in the post-Parry era. All chapters are written either by British scholars who have worked for a substantial period in Latin America or by Latin American scholars who are, or have been, associated with British academic institutions that have a major interest in Latin American studies.

Christopher Abel is lecturer in Latin American History at University College, London, and author of *Catolicismo y conservatismo en Colombia 1886–1953* (Medellín 1984). With Nissa Torrents he co-edited *Spain: conditional democracy* (London 1983).

Marcelo de Paiva Abreu is director of FINEP, attached to the Brazilian Ministry of Planning and lecturer at the Faculty of Economics and Administration at the Federal University, Rio de Janeiro. He has studied at Cambridge and published on Brazilian financial and foreign economic policy.

Bill Albert is lecturer in Economic and Social History at the University of East Anglia. His publications include *An essay on the Peruvian sugar industry, 1800–1920* (Norwich 1976) and *South America and the world economy from independence to 1930* (London 1983).

Peter Alhadeff is Latin American research fellow at the Institute of Latin American Studies, London, and has studied at the Latin American Centre, St Antony's College, Oxford. He has published a number of articles and contributions on Argentine economic policy during the inter-war period.

M. H. J. Finch is lecturer in Economic History at the University of Liverpool where he previously taught economics in the Centre for Latin

American Studies. His publications include *A political economy of Uruguay since 1870* (London 1981) and various articles on contemporary Uruguay.

E. V. K. Fitzgerald is professor of Development Economics at the Institute of Social Studies, The Hague, and was previously assistant director of Development Studies at Cambridge. His principal publications include *The political economy of Peru, 1956–1978: economic development and the restructuring of capital* (Cambridge 1979), *ECLA and the theory of the peripheral economy* (London 1983) and, co-edited with D. Lehmann and E. Floto, *The state and economic development in Latin America* (Cambridge 1977). He has written extensively on contemporary Latin American problems and is an economic planning adviser to the government of Nicaragua.

Rhys O. Jenkins is a lecturer at the School of Development Studies, University of East Anglia, and has written many scholarly articles on transnational corporations in Latin America. His principal publications include *Dependent industrialization in Latin America: the automotive industry in Argentina, Chile and Mexico* (New York 1977) and *Transnational Corporations and Industrial Transformation in Latin America* (London 1984).

Charles A. Jones is lecturer in International Studies at the University of Warwick. He has written *The North-South dialogue: a brief history* (London 1983) and made various contributions to the debate on business imperialism and the study of business history.

Alan Knight is lecturer in Modern History at the University of Essex. He has published *The Mexican Revolution* (Cambridge 1984) and several articles on the history of Mexico during the revolutionary period.

Ernesto Laclau teaches Latin American Politics at the University of Essex. He has written *Politics and ideology in Marxist theory* (London 1977) and numerous scholarly articles on Marxism and on contemporary Latin American issues.

Colin M. Lewis is lecturer in Latin American Economic History at the London School of Economics and Political Science and at the Institute of Latin American Studies, University of London. He has written *The British-owned Argentine railways, 1857–1914: a case-study of foreign investment* (London 1983) and various articles on Latin American railway history.

Callum MacDonald is lecturer in Comparative American Studies at the University of Warwick. He has published *The United States, Britain and appeasement 1936–1939* (London 1981), *The United States, Britain and Perón, 1943–1955* (London 1983) and several articles on Anglo-US rivalry in Argentina.

Anthony McFarlane is lecturer in Latin American History at the Joint School of Comparative American Studies, University of Warwick, and was a research fellow at the Institute of Latin American Studies,

London. He has published various articles on the history of Colombia in the late colonial period and is currently preparing a book on popular movements in Spanish America during the eighteenth century.

Philip J. O'Brien is lecturer in Economics at the Centre of Latin American Studies, University of Glasgow. He has co-authored *Chile: state and revolution* (London 1977) with I. Roxborough and J. Roddick, and has edited *Allende's Chile* (London 1976). He has made many contributions to the dependency debate.

Luis Ortega is honorary research fellow at the Institute of Latin American Studies, London, and has studied at the University of London. He has published articles on Chilean economic policy and social structures during the early national period, and is now preparing a monograph on internally orientated economic activities in Chile prior to the War of the Pacific.

Gabriel Palma, sometime assistant director of Development Studies, Cambridge, and Latin American research fellow at the Institute of Latin American Studies, London, studied at Oxford. He has published several articles on dependency and is currently writing a book on the growth and structure of the manufacturing industry in Chile.

D. C. M. Platt is professor of the History of Latin America at the University of Oxford and has been director of the Latin American Centre, St Antony's College. His principal publications include *Finance, trade and politics in British foreign policy, 1815–1914* (Oxford 1968) and *Latin America and British trade, 1806–1914* (London 1972). He edited *Business imperialism, 1840–1930: an inquiry based on British experience in Latin America* (Oxford 1977) and has made numerous contributions to the debate on imperialism and dependency.

Ian Roxborough is lecturer in Latin American Political Sociology at the London School of Economics and Political Science and at the Institute of Latin American Studies, London. He has written *Theories of underdevelopment* (London 1979) and, with P. J. O'Brien and J. Roddick, *Chile: state and revolution* (London 1977). He has also published various articles on labour in Latin America.

Christopher D. Scott is lecturer in Economics at the London School of Economics and Political Science. He has published *Machetes, machines and agrarian reform: the political economy of technical choice in the Peruvian sugar industry, 1954–1974* (Norwich 1979) and various articles and contributions on aspects of Latin American agricultural economics, including colonization projects, food policy and agribusiness.

Guy P. Thomson is lecturer in History at the University of Warwick. He has published articles on the economic and social history of Mexico during the early nineteenth century and is preparing a book on industrialization and social change in Puebla, 1800–1850.

Rosemary Thorp is a fellow of St Antony's College, Oxford, and university lecturer in Latin American Economics. Her recent publications include *Peru, 1890–1977: growth and policy in an export economy* (London 1978) written jointly with Geoffrey Bertram, and *Inflation and stabilization in Latin America* (London 1981), co-edited with Lawrence Whitehead. Most recently she has edited *Latin America in the 1930s: the role of the periphery in world crisis* (London 1984).

Ernesto Tironi B., sometime visiting Latin American scholar at the Institute of Latin American Studies, London, and economic adviser to the United Nations Economic Commission for Latin America, is director of the Centro de Estudios del Desarrollo at the University of Chile, Santiago. His principal publications include *Hacia un nuevo orden económico internacional: temas principales para América Latina* (Mexico 1981) and, co-edited with R. ffrench-Davis, *Latin America and the new international economic order* (London 1982). He has also written articles on the Andean Pact and Latin American trade.

Acknowledgements

This book originates in a seminar held at the Institute of Latin American Studies some years ago. The purpose of that seminar was to examine the impact of the dependency debate, which had by that time raged for approximately fifteen years, upon Latin American scholarship. The interest stimulated by the seminar encouraged us to consider publication and subsequently to expand the scope of the investigation to include the related themes contained in this volume. In realizing this project we have accumulated many debts. The success of the original seminar owed much to the support we received from Professor John Lynch, Director of the Institute; it is his continuing encouragement that has made publication possible. We are also pleased to acknowledge the enthusiastic cooperation of contributors who not only reacted with great forbearance to our several queries and criticisms, but engaged in a lively exchange amongst themselves. The coherence of the book is due in no small measure to the willingness of contributors to respond positively to constructive comment provided by fellow authors: we are particularly indebted to Rosemary Thorp. This volume is published with financial assistance provided by the Latin American Publications Fund. We wish to thank the Fund – its officers and advisers – for their sympathetic consideration.

We are grateful to Jan Rooze who translated the chapter by Ernesto Laclau. Elizabeth Jackson helped organize the original seminar: she performed sterling service in arranging the programme and ensuring the smooth circulation of papers. Penny Ewle, Tess Truman and Cristina Weller typed much of the manuscript. They coped splendidly with contributors' idiosyncrasies and editors' anxieties. The artwork was handled by Alison Fisher, who sympathetically and faithfully translated authors' sketches into detailed maps. Gloria Jones did some typing and Daphne Rodger was involved in preparing the manuscript.

1

GENERAL INTRODUCTION

Since the 1920s Latin American diagnoses of the problems of the continent have shifted dramatically. In the first decades of the twentieth century ideologies of cultural pessimism and despair were still potent. Arguments that Latin America could never achieve parity with Western Europe or the United States of America were grounded in the assumption – widely believed to be scientifically verifiable – that Latin Americans were, as a consequence of ethnic intermixture (Iberian, black and Amerindian), congenitally incapable of achieving either a mature political democracy or sustained economic development. Although this pessimism was muted in those countries that had experienced rapid economic growth and established relatively stable quasi-representative political institutions, there was in these societies too some unease about the attainment of development goals and about external economic relations.

By the 1980s cultural pessimism had been displaced by theories of vitality and optimism. Latin American politicians and technocrats, who differ over political ideology, share a cautious confidence in the future, a belief that contemporary problems can be resolved within the present generation. Despite the reversals embodied in military rule, severe food scarcities, the oil crisis, the burden of external indebtedness and the deceleration in rates of economic growth in the 1970s, Latin American policy-makers remain convinced of the inherent resilience of the continent. Their optimism is founded upon an appraisal of its natural resources, the belief that they possess an appropriate mix of concepts and ideas specific to the requirements of the moment and, especially, a confidence in social science analysis and techniques evolved since the 1940s. This self-assurance in analysis passes over into prognosis. While the scale of the problems imparts a sense of urgency and saliency to the present situation, Latin American intellectuals retain an audacious buoyancy, a conviction that they are approaching the answers that will resolve the conundrums posed by development bottlenecks and social fragmentation, and which will yield the means of realizing the continent's potential. Many believe that Latin America now stands upon the threshold of a great transformation in which the Bolivarian ambition of equal power and status with the North Atlantic world will be belatedly and irreversibly achieved.

In part, this renewed confidence is a function of the refocusing of international attention during the post-Second World War decades upon those regions of the globe which are now collectively described as the Third World. It was a refocusing that had stimulated discussion about the determinants of growth and development and revived the debate about imperialism. In recent years controversy surrounding these issues has been fuelled by growing fears of a north-south collision. Until the Second World War it was widely held in Latin America and elsewhere that economic expansion would ultimately yield for the peoples of the region levels of material welfare equal to those enjoyed by affluent Western European countries and the United States of America. As a result of rapid population expansion and the dislocating and destabilizing impact of the events of the 1930s, there occurred during the later 1940s a questioning of prevalent expectations about the self-sustaining nature of growth, and a challenge to assumptions regarding the inevitability of economic and social development. Economic growth had been perceived as inducing development, defined in terms of sectoral diversification – or more particularly industrialization – and an improvement in living conditions which guaranteed the fulfilment of the basic wants of the majority of the population. By the 1960s economic development was portrayed as a more complex process which involved more than increasing levels of output or an expansion of foreign trade. Economic development was now measured not only in terms of per capita GDP but by reference to a scale of social and economic indicators: life expectancy at birth, literacy rates, levels of health care, conditions of housing and access to basic infrastructure. Judged by these criteria, many Latin American countries were backward in comparison with Europe and North America, though in contrast to parts of Africa and Asia there were grounds for optimism, especially in the Southern Cone countries of Argentina, Chile and Uruguay.

The obvious and growing disparities between Latin America and the countries of the North Atlantic occasioned a reappraisal of conventional liberal theories of growth: theories which had been elaborated from the historical experience of Western Europe and the United States. The impulse to formulate new hypotheses and models in lieu of the pre-Keynesian classical liberal economics which had prevailed hitherto was particularly strong in Latin America, owing to a number of post-war trends and events. It was already being observed by the 1950s that although a number of countries had experienced remarkable rates of economic growth during the late nineteenth and early twentieth centuries, development had not resulted. Many in Latin America were also influenced by the degree of government intervention taking place in

Europe. The impetus to devise an alternative to classical economic orthodoxy was subsequently enhanced by the challenge of revolutionary socialist experimentation in Cuba. However, a revival of interest in theory should not be confused with a consensus of views as to its value. Some authors search for laws, others for propensities and yet others for tendencies. Some see theory as prescriptive, others as analytical – a basis for political and/or economic action or a guide to empirical study.

The Prebisch thesis

At the heart of the debate was the theory of comparative advantage. An almost unassailable shibboleth until the foundation of the Economic Commission for Latin America (*Comisión Económica para América Latina*) in 1948, the operation of the economic laws of comparative advantage was widely accepted in the continent: the international division of labour and the specialization of production along lines of factor endowment were held to confer prosperity on trading partners. Trade was an engine of growth which permitted an escape from domestic constraints upon economic expansion. At a time when Africa and Asia were again at the centre of international attention during the late 1940s – the prelude to the Korean War, decolonization in the Indian subcontinent, turmoil in the Middle East – Raúl Prebisch*, secretary-general of ECLA (*CEPAL*), mounted a profound challenge to conventional wisdom on the nature of the links between developed and less advanced societies.

The nub of the Prebisch thesis, which was subsequently widely attacked, was that primary exporting economies would continue to experience a deterioration in their terms of trade because of changing patterns of demand in the principal markets for their exports, increasing competition amongst primary producers – given relatively inelastic demand for foodstuffs and raw materials – and mechanisms which inhibited productivity gains resulting from technological innovation (particularly in the manufacture of secondary products) being passed on to Third World consumers in the shape of lower prices. Thus the phrase 'centre-periphery' became part of the language of economics; the hypothesis of the lack of symmetry in the distribution of the gains arising from international trade between primary and secondary economies was elaborated, and the terms of trade debate came to dominate a branch of economics for several decades. The differing elasticities of demand for primary products and manufactured goods, which according to Prebisch favoured producers of the latter, subjected the countries of Latin America to a regime of weakening export prices and rising import costs. The implications for Latin America were clear: given the large size of the

---

* Authors and works cited in the General Introduction and section introductions are listed in the Bibliography.

external sector in many economies, they were likely to experience increasing difficulty in servicing external accounts – balance of payments crisis and domestic dislocation would follow.

For ECLA the solution lay, variously, in (1) import-substituting industrial expansion and export diversification, to be accomplished with government assistance, in order to maximize Latin America's advantages of an abundant supply of cheap labour, low-cost technology and wealth of natural resources, (2) agrarian reform and (3) regional integration. Prebisch did not advocate a rejection of, or withdrawal from, the international trading complex, but a 'renegotiation' of the terms under which the Latin American economies participated in world trade so that the gains could be more equitably distributed. Whereas during the 1920s an economist based in Santiago de Chile would barely have commanded a world hearing for his theories, Prebisch, a man of political dexterity as well as profound economic vision and experience, utilized the newly established interlocking agencies of the United Nations Organization to project his ideas. These views gained currency in parts of Asia and attracted attention in the United States and Western Europe. Within Latin America, *CEPAL* strategy began to obtain greater acceptance when its objectives of economic development began to be represented as inducing political stability.

The Prebisch thesis, in particular its gloomy stress upon the terms of trade debate, had aroused antagonism and unease in the United States, as had the emphasis upon government intervention and state mediation in the external sector. By the early 1960s, however, this opposition had become more muted. The elaboration of neo-orthodox modernization theories in the USA, which stressed the linkages between economic diversification and social consensus, encouraged an acceptance of ECLA mechanisms designed to promote industrialization. This convergence was formalized with the construction of the Alliance for Progress programme in the aftermath of the Cuban Revolution in 1959. Accordingly, by the early 1960s renewed United States interest in the continent had resulted in a synthesis of policies which married orthodox emphases upon administrative efficiency, fiscal responsibility and the conventional role of the state as a provider of basic services with the Commission's stress upon diversification through state-sponsored industrial expansion.

Despite this convergence, *cepalista* prescriptions continued to appeal to radicals. Marxists were sharply divided in the 1960s. Some advocated the promotion of capitalism in order to hasten the demise of feudalism; others argued that the main task lay in facilitating the transition to socialism. There was no agreement as to whether the achievement of socialism was a matter for the present generation or for the future. An equally pronounced schism arose from the Cuban revolutionary challenge to Soviet orthodoxies. Whereas the Soviet Union endorsed Latin American communist parties (and, in their absence, bourgeois nationalist parties) that sought power through the ballot box, Cuba proclaimed the view that the mainland Latin American countries, like herself, could achieve a durable socialist solution only through a violent guerrilla struggle. A Maoist alternative to both Soviet orthodoxy and Cuban dissidence served only to deepen fissiparous tendencies on the Marxist left. Radical intellectuals, unattracted by what they saw as both the grey sterility of many of the orthodox communist parties and the high-risk policies advanced by the Cuban revolutionaries, looked often for inspiration to ECLA, which promised creative vitality, intellectual innovation and ideas appropriate to Latin American circumstances within a peaceful evolutionary framework. Thus ECLA embraced both radicals and reformists within an ideologically and institutionally elastic environment.

Theories of imperialism

In one respect, however, Prebisch reflected the sharp ideological and intellectual compartmentalization of the period: in formulating notions of the links between the centre and the periphery during the 1940s, he took little cognizance of theories of imperialism. The principal focus of the debate about imperialism was then the process of decolonization taking place in south and south-east Asia, which marked the beginning of the end of what contemporaries described as the 'new' imperialism. Until the 1950s, non-Marxist, Eurocentric writing on imperialism was largely concerned with formal colonialism.

Conventionally, non-Marxist historians demarcated two periods of Western European imperial experience. First, the 'old' imperialism characterized by the zero sum game of monopoly trade and mercantilist regulation, which finally collapsed during the early decades of the nineteenth century with the successful revolutions for independence in Spanish America and the disintegration of the Luso-Brazilian connection. The crisis of 'old' mercantilist imperialism had been many decades in the making, and resulted from complex changes occurring in Western Europe associated *inter alia* with the Industrial Revolution in England. Second, the 'new' imperialism, epitomized by the late-nineteenth-century scramble for Africa and primarily characterized by strategic territorial acquisition, missionary evangelism and altruistic colonial administration, with economic interests playing a subordinate role. A Marxist-Leninist tradition of scholarship rejected this chronological schema in favour of a Leninist view that identified distinct forms of external relationships and stressed continuity in the transition from the commercial capitalism of the pre-Industrial Revolution period to a phase of industrial capitalism, and finally the age of monopoly

capitalism which dawned at the end of the nineteenth century, characterized by the concentration and centralization of capital in large
corporate institutions – the cartels and trusts – located in the advanced
economies. For writers in this tradition, the word 'imperialism' is a
strictly technical term which denotes the final stage of capitalism.
However, by the late 1940s the term 'capitalist imperialism' had already
been popularized and was held to imply an asymmetrical and often
exploitative relationship between societies.

Writing at a time when it was widely discussed whether the principal
features of imperialistic relationships would outlive the disintegration of
the 'new' empires, Gallagher and Robinson, without subscribing to
Marxist-Leninist theories, launched a challenge to accepted non-
Marxist assumptions. They rejected the view that territorial acquisition
constituted the bedrock of imperialism and that there had been a retreat
from formal empire-building between the end of the 'old' imperialism
and the beginning of the 'new'. Thus they established the hypothesis of
laissez-faire imperialism. For them the period associated with the predominance of liberal philosophy and free trade had not been an anti-
imperial epoch. On the contrary, they sought to establish a continuum
between these two phases of formal imperialism. The views of Gallagher
and Robinson were placed in sharper focus in their later works on Africa
and in Robinson's explorations of the concept of collaborative elites. In
their several works, these two authors not only rejected the chronology of
formal imperialism and diffusionist theories respecting the nature of
international economic relationships during and after the middle third of
the nineteenth century, but they also challenged elements of Marxist-
Leninist orthodoxy. Recognizing the importance of economic factors in
the process of imperialism and locating the drive to imperialize in the
central capitalist economies, they – particularly Robinson – differed
from Lenin in that they attributed to the periphery the determination of
the structure of the imperial connection. During the mid-Victorian age
of Britain's manufacturing and commercial dominance, formal colonies
were established only in those regions where indigenous interests and
institutions proved unwilling or incapable of providing an environment
suited to the expansion of trade – that is, in the absence of a compliant
collaborative elite. Gallagher and Robinson also discern in British
foreign economic policy a quest for supremacy which many scholars
would not recognize.

D. C. M. Platt answered these arguments on Free Trade imperialism
by reasserting with particular reference to Latin America the minimal
role performed by the British government in promoting trade and
finance overseas. Propounding notions of liberal political economy
simultaneously revived by participants in the anti-imperialism of Free
Trade debate, Platt reassessed the chronology of Britain's penetration of

Latin American markets between independence and the First World War. Focusing upon the period of British naval and commercial pre-eminence, he underlined the passivity of British policy in Latin America and subsequently pointed to the peripheral nature of Latin American markets (with some significant exceptions in time and space) for British traders and the exaggerated role which has been ascribed to British finance in the continent. Platt followed H. S. Ferns who, writing in the 1950s on Anglo-Argentine relations, argued that Britain's position and influence were determined by the forces of competition and the rules of the marketplace. Initially contributing to the expanding literature concerned with informal empire and economic imperialism, Platt later wrote on business imperialism and directly addressed questions of Latin American dependency. Early discussion about informal empire and economic imperialism was principally concerned with patterns of overseas investment, the structure of international trade, and the significance of connections between trade and finance within the framework of an expanding international economy dominated by the ideology of Free Trade – an environment conducive to individual maximization. For some participants in these debates the latter part of the nineteenth century was a period of rapid growth and associated socio-economic change in areas such as Latin America, which resulted from a substantial injection of capital, technology, entrepreneurship and labour that arose from progressive incorporation in a dynamic world economy unfettered by mercantilist restriction and state intervention. Accordingly, Latin America obtained the best deal possible from the international connection in the period studied.

Renewed interest in the debates on informal empire and economic imperialism gave prominence to a diversity of neglected earlier writing – by authors such as Hobson, Luxemburg and Hilferding – long eclipsed by more popular texts. These controversies, defined more narrowly than in the Latin American literature, were thoroughly explored in Roger Owen and Bob Sutcliffe (eds) *Studies in the theory of imperialism*, in which Platt launched the discussion on business imperialism. By then the concept of economic imperialism was perceived by a number of diffusionists as sterile and mechanistic: in particular much of the literature ignored the unwillingness of the British government to act in support of commerce and finance during the period addressed by these debates. Consequently, some scholars advocated a change of emphasis to micro-level studies concerned with business practices and the interaction of local groups with foreign traders and financiers. Business imperialism was essentially concerned with the issue of control: the extent to which foreigners sought to manipulate officials and politicians in Latin America, directly or indirectly constrained policy options open to Latin American governments, and denied space to domestic business groups.

Having explored these themes, the principal exponents of business imperialism found little evidence to confirm the operation of control.

Dependentistas see little significance in the distinction between business and economic imperialism. They contend that the debate is trapped within a particular conceptual and methodological ghetto of its own making. Over-concerned with direct action and explicit pressures upon Latin American governments, advocates of the concept of business imperialism are engaged in a quest for source material which, by its very nature, is unlikely to survive in archives. Indeed, the informality of agreements amongst businessmen tends to preclude the collation of documentary evidence of collusion, just as the disjuncture between business and government in nineteenth-century Britain inhibited the accumulation of material in official records. Thus empiricists have constructed a false hypothesis that cannot be validated in terms of their specific methodology. Another criticism, which is by no means peculiar to the dependency literature, stresses that notions of business and economic imperialism are over-conditioned by a North Atlantic view of international economic relations, and that there was an asymmetry in commercial and financial links between Britain and the Latin American economies which, if not perceived by modern historians, was observed by contemporary policy-makers. British scholars have thus projected North Atlantic assumptions of normal political behaviour and business practice into an alien setting. These critics maintain that, although Anglo-Latin American trade may have represented a relatively unimportant proportion of British commerce, access to the London money market and to British manufactured goods and services was vital for the Latin American economies. Contemporary Latin Americans shaped their relationship with metropolitan government and business accordingly. It is thus contended that the political economy of Latin America was distorted by the insertion of practices inimical to local needs.

The influence of the United States

Paradoxically, the business imperialism debate, which focused upon Britain's connections with the continent during the hundred years following independence and addressed the question of Great Power rivalry in Latin American markets, took little cognizance of continuing discussions conducted in the United States about the relationship between Latin America and the new metropolis.

In the 1930s the combination of the World Depression and the challenges of international fascism and communism compelled the United States to reassess its relations with Latin America. The debate about foreign policy – economic and strategic – mirrored long-standing domestic conflicts, first between isolationist and internationalist tendencies in US society, and second between conservatives, stressing the passive role of the state and dominance of market forces, and liberals, urging selective intervention for remedial purposes. These issues shaped United States policies towards Latin America, which was perceived exaggeratedly in Washington, especially in the light of the Francoist victory in Spain, as an area of possible Axis expansion. The New Deal, elaborated as a set of *ad hoc* responses to particular problems in the United States, was translated into the Good Neighbour policy in the sphere of intra-American relations: it began to emerge at the time of the abortive Cuban revolution of 1933–4, though it was not formalized until 1937–8. Advocates of the Good Neighbour strategy maintained that military intervention in the Caribbean and Central America since 1898 had been counterproductive, was costly to the United States and could not be sustained with credibility when comparable Japanese policies in Manchuria were violently opposed.

Policy-makers in Washington saw Latin America as a new frontier to be opened up with trade and investment in a concerted and coordinated fashion (in contrast to the destabilizing scramble which had occurred during the 1920s), with the backing of the federal government in alliance with its Latin American counterparts. State-sponsored institutions – the Export-Import Bank and Foreign Bondholders Council – featured amongst innovations in foreign economic policy designed to promote the co-prosperity of the Americas as a means of cementing hemispheric understanding and fostering political stability in Latin America. Claiming to have benefited from the experience of the 1920s, reformist liberals in the US foreign policy bureaucracy, encouraged by various Latin American interests, sought to secure intra-American economic relations. Alarmed by the prospect of social revolution, the formation of autarkic blocks within Latin America and the negotiation of bilateral agreements with European powers which were viewed as prejudicial to the United States, Washington directly stimulated business initiative in the continent and performed a conciliatory role in regional conflicts so as to forestall renewed German penetration and re-establish US influence. Latin American policy-makers, already imbued with a tradition of state interventionism, actively promoted and responded to US initiatives.

The liberal orthodoxy of Good Neighbour *rapprochement* has been challenged from all sides. Both Latin and North American Marxists have argued that the Good Neighbour policy represented not the rupture with the past claimed by its exponents, but a new and subtle instrument for the consolidation of US hegemony consonant with the needs of monopoly capital. The Marxist-Leninists' argument is rooted in the view that monopoly capital does not possess the internal dynamism of competitive capital; they stress that transnational enterprise required stimulation and coordination from extra-market sources – namely the state in the metropolis or an alliance between the metropolitan and the peripheral state – in order to sustain its expansionist momentum. This thesis, first elaborated in the 1930s, was presented more forcefully in the 1960s. A second line of criticism arises from a convergence in the position of Marxists and free enterprise capitalists who argue that state intervention – in the shape of reciprocal trade agreement, production quotas and price guarantees – undermined incentives, frustrated growth and locked certain Latin American economies into subordinate mono-crop dependence. Other scholars have questioned the originality – in addition to the achievements – of the Good Neighbour programme, seeing precedents for most of its features in the 1920s, and even before.

Further recent revisions have been made by authors such as J. I. Domínguez, who contend that the principal objective of US policy in the 1930s was containment and accommodation. Domínguez argues that the United States shifted from an imperialist stance – thorough supervision of policies and incumbents – between 1898 and the World Depression to hegemony – concerned only that the general direction of policy in Latin America should not be contrary to US interests. The thrust of these criticisms appears to advocate a broad continuity in US external relations from the 1880s to the present. The transformation of the United States from a continental to a world power radically changed US-Latin American relations and exacerbated Latin American fears of US intervention in the region. In contrast, another groups of historians arguing that imperialism equals territorial acquisition deny that the United States was ever imperialist. Some, like Ernest May, see US imperialism as a temporary aberration from c.1895 to c.1914, traces of which survived till the early 1930s. The major theme of this school has been the investigation of the motives underlying a US expansionist drive. Non-economic explanations range from manifest destiny to an altruistic mission to export democracy. Other interpretations have presented US expansion as having more limited goals, namely regional political stability and access to markets and raw materials. Latin American and Caribbean scholars express impatience at the narrow focus of this debate, which begs the fundamental question of the impact of US policy upon the countries of the region.

The dependency debate: origins and components

The impatience of these scholars in part reflected discussions regarding the benefits to be derived from the external connection which had been gathering momentum in Latin America since the beginning of the twentieth century, as was indicated by the writing of Encina and Bunge. This debate had been enlarged during the 1930s with the popularization of Marx among Latin Americans. Influenced by the spread of fascism in Europe and absorbing contemporary Marxist-Leninist analysis of capitalist imperialism, authors such as Mariátegui in Peru, Caio Prado

Jr in Brazil and Sergio Bagú in Argentina sharpened the focus of the discourse, challenging liberal orthodoxy. Another onslaught against the pernicious influences of external linkages was mounted by Spanish-American scholars whose writing echoed earlier *hispanista* currents of thought. They rejected a crude quest for economic expansion and ill considered attempts to emulate Anglo-Saxon socio-political models which, it was argued, undermined traditional cultural values. This writing epitomized assumptions prevalent during the 1930s concerned with the economic weakness and cultural decadence of the capitalist centre and, as reflected in the work of the brothers Irazusta and subsequently Ibarguren and Scalabrini Ortiz, pointed to a resurgence of imperialist pressure in the periphery. These intellectual traditions drawn from the right as well as the left became consolidated in nationalist schools of historiography which addressed many facets of the external nexus. It was a reappraisal that marked the degree of ideological ferment evident in Latin America during the 1930s and 1940s, and also the extent of intellectual cross-fertilization that has since prevailed amongst Latin American *pensadores*. Owing to the narrowly circumscribed group of individuals involved in these exchanges, the rupture between Marxists and social democrats to be observed in Europe did not occur to the same degree in Latin America. The contribution of this literature, which may be regarded as precursive of the dependency debate, has yet to be fully explored or acknowledged.

Thus, when theories of dependency crystallized during the 1960s in an international intellectual environment in which a renewal of interest in social and economic theory was evident, its antecedents were regarded as of more recent origin. Despite the eclecticism observable in much early dependency analysis – which drew upon both Eurocentric theories of imperialism, Marxist and non-Marxist, and upon earlier endeavours to adapt these concepts to Latin American conditions – the main focus of the initial texts was upon the shortcomings of development strategies applied during and since the 1950s. The collapse of several civilian administrations ousted by military *golpes* during the 1960s added force to the criticisms of *dependentistas*. The demise of bourgeois parliamentary instructions was held to represent the frailty of liberal democracy and the strength of authoritarian traditions in Latin America, or the inability of essentially co-optive, class-based systems to respond adequately to the pressures generated by population growth, the aspirations of enlarged urban groups and poor economic performance.

The perceived failure of ECLA-inspired *desarrollismo*, the conspicuous feature of which had been government-sponsored import substituting industrialization, attracted much odium. Forced industrialization, it was argued, had failed to effect a modernizing, secular, self-sustaining change in the structure of the Latin American economies. The narrow focus upon industrialization had induced distorted patterns of growth in the economy at large and also within the industrial sector itself. Urban industry had excessively absorbed the attention of the state to the detriment of the rural sector where, apart from the Southern Cone, the bulk of the population resided and attempted to obtain a livelihood. Except in a few cases the consequence had been a decline in rural productivity, large-scale internal migration to the cities, the exacerbation of the food crisis and, arguably, a general deterioration in living standards. Despite its favoured status and often impressive rates of expansion, industry had failed to generate anticipated employment opportunities or to demonstrate a capacity for dynamic diversification.

Indeed, in a majority of countries the industrial sector was small, fragmented and inadequately integrated into the national economy. Latin American industry had displayed little ability to establish backward linkages with other sectors of the economy. The creation of capital-intensive manufacturing units had not even resulted in the thorough modernization of the sector: on the contrary, high-technology factories existed alongside small sweatshops – a plurality of parallel structures which reflected the diversity of the sources of capital and frustrated intra-sector integration. The manufacturing sector was thus compartmentalized and isolated. Incapable of autonomous development, industrial expansion came to rely upon imported technology and inputs, access to which depended upon foreign exchange earnings generated by traditional export sectors. Yet the performance of these export sectors was eroded by industrial growth that reduced the supply of capital and labour available to them. Furthermore, expanding domestic consumption associated with the growth of the industrial and service sectors directly absorbed a portion of the surplus available for sale abroad.

In part, the structural rigidities induced by industrial expansion were a function of the concentration on the production of consumer durables. The motor, electrical and chemical industries were inherently capital-intensive and oligopolistic, particularly in those Latin American economies where the number of potential consumers of motor cars and electrical appliances was limited during the 1950s and 1960s by the relatively small size of population and also by highly skewed patterns of income distribution. Many of the firms engaged in the production of these commodities were also foreign-owned branch factories established by transnational corporations, thus further inhibiting the creation of domestic linkages whether in terms of industrial research and development or of a capital goods sector. Moreover, by the 1960s it was observed in some of the large economies that transnational enterprises were already moving into other areas of manufacturing orientated towards domestic markets, for example tobacco and food processing – areas where national capital had prevailed hitherto.

Distorted patterns of industrialization, particularly, though not exclusively, in the major economies of Argentina, Brazil and Mexico, were by the end of the 1960s held responsible for reduced flexibility in external trade and enduring balance of payments crises. Reduced rates of economic expansion, experienced as the consumer durables phase of industrialization was completed, were also noted. So too was the mushrooming of the tertiary sector, a means of generating jobs and disguising un- or under-employment.

These themes, particularly the rapid penetration by foreign capital of the most profitable areas of economic activity and enduring social inequity (often associated with a reinvigorated authoritarianism), became the principal focus of the dependency debate. Some writers stressed the inappropriateness of ECLA strategy, while another group of scholars pointed to the ineffective or partial application of *desarrollista* programmes. Yet other participants in the debate drew upon the United States Marxist tradition, notably the texts of Baran and Sweezey which insist upon the tenacity and resilience of capitalism in the periphery. The ambivalence towards ECLA manifest in the work of some scholars has occasioned confusion in terms of establishing the relationship between *cepalismo* and dependency. If much early dependency writing was projected as a criticism of *cepalismo*, recent assessments tend to emphasize the originality of ECLA's contributions to the debates about the external connection. The metropolis-satellite nexus may not be identical to the relationship elaborated in the centre-periphery concept, but the intellectual contribution of Prebisch has provided a point of departure for many subsequent essayists.

A number of authors have attempted to 'school' dependency. In his several contributions, Philip O'Brien has elaborated a schema which is amongst the more informed. O'Brien's emphasis on the significance of works published in the late 1960s – particularly that by Cardoso and Faletto – commands general agreement, as do his observations on Frank. Persuasive if dated presentations of the original *CEPAL* developmentalist thesis are to be found in Aldo Ferrer's work on Argentina, Celso Furtado's on Brazil and Anibal Pinto's on Chile. Much of the new wave of revisionist scholarship reflects the sense of acute political and economic crisis felt in Latin America since the 1960s. A moral imperative underlies the work of such authors as Nurkse, Furtado and Sunkel, whose writings combine vigour and discretion. From radically different positions, these authors share an urgency about Latin America's predicament. A similar spirit of urgency – and cautious optimism – pervades the publications of Albert O. Hirschman, who sees a bias for hope in Latin America's external connections and a revitalized form of *cepalista* industrial promotion. Many of these revisionist writers portray dependence as in part a function of internal social and institutional

structures which frustrated or distorted development strategy. By implication – and also explicitly – such scholarship is critical of the econo-
micism of early ECLA analysis, namely the failure to address political
issues and an unwillingness to stress effectively the need for social
reforms. *Desarrollismo* had naïvely assumed that social disparities and
sectoral imbalances would be resolved by economic development. Yet
many of the authors writing from a revisionist viewpoint accept a large
part of the Prebisch analysis and applaud its originality.

It is possible that the reappraisal of *cepalismo* – often sympathetic,
occasionally over-critical – tends to exaggerate the influence of ECLA.
The Commission undoubtedly functioned as a forum for a growing
intellectual interaction among Latin American policy-makers – a process that was encouraged by the observed increased influence of the
United States in the continent. And, if all *cepalista* policy prescriptions
were not new, the novelty of *desarrollismo* lay in its grasp of Keynesian
economics and its institutional basis, which made for sustained consideration of economic ideas and facilitated their practical application.
These characteristics generated kudos in a post-Second World War
milieu increasingly attuned to interventionist economics and accustomed to the policy-advisory function of international agencies.
However, international recognition did not necessarily imply enduring
and widespread influence in the continent, though *cepalismo* undoubtedly
had a profound impact in many countries at various times.

For many participants in the dependency debate the emphasis on
recent development strategy is misplaced. At best such strategies are
regarded as palliatives, more critically as a means of promoting external
dominance from the centre. For some, Latin America's current economic and social problems are the consequence of a heritage of backwardness and a growing imbalance, dating from the colonial period, in
the region's relations with the dynamic metropolitan economies. Others
writing within the dependency framework favour a wider discourse. For
these scholars the focus upon the efficacy or appropriateness of contemporary policy is not superfluous, but it lacks centrality. These writers
reject both classical liberal assumptions and the neo-Keynesian reformism of *CEPAL*-developmentalism. Frank, amongst others, attempted to
refute the basic premises upon which modernizationist and diffusionist
economic philosophy was based.

During the Cold War several neo-classical theories of growth and
development had been elaborated, popularized and transferred to Latin
America. Walt Whitman Rostow's stages of growth theory was perhaps
the best example. Drawing upon the historical experiences of Great
Britain and the United States, Rostow attempted to construct a dynamic
theory of growth rooted in liberal orthodoxy. Absorbing nineteenth-
century stage theories – many of which came from the same intellectual

tradition as Marx – and the near-contemporary scholarship of historians and economists like Schumpeter, W. A. Lewis and Gerschenkron, Rostow attempted to establish a comprehensive model which detailed the process of economic change over time and addressed related social and institutional modifications. For these authors and others of similar views, all societies over time and space may be located at different points along a continuum that stretches from a condition of backwardness at one end to a state of development at the other. An economy's progress along this curve is by no means even, nor is the process uniform for all countries. Nevertheless, irrespective of differing rates of progress between societies, these authors hold that just as all present-day advanced economies were once backward, so societies currently less developed shall ultimately achieve a state of grace – they will become developed. Movement along the curve is determined by rates of capital accumulation, the absorption and application of new technology, the transfer of resources from less- to more-productive activities and the establishment of an environment receptive and responsive to change. Although not a prerequisite, it is assumed that for certain societies the rate of expansion and development may be accelerated through international exchange – through participation in a dynamic world economy.

For Frank, the history of Latin America demonstrated the absurdity of this analysis. Since the Iberian conquest Latin America had become underdeveloped, not backward. This condition was a function of integration into the world capitalist economy: the continent's underdevelopment could only deepen over time. In effect, Frank envisaged the non-socialist economies as divided into two camps – metropolises and satellites – located not upon a single continuum but upon two divergent curves. The rate of expansion in the advanced metropolises, located upon the upper curve, is a direct function of the increasing underdevelopment of satellite economies to be found upon the lower curve. Chains of dependence link the two sets of economies and serve to transfer resources – surplus capital – from satellite to metropolis. The underdeveloping economies of Latin America can only advance by breaking the chains of exploitation which stretch from the Bolivian peasant to the Wall Street financier – a break most likely to be achieved through socialist revolution. In his volume *Capitalism and underdevelopment in Latin America* Frank brought together and synthesized *cepalista* and Marxist ideas: his book was welcomed as a breakthrough by many who questioned its originality. It was an audacious study, well timed and offering an apparently comprehensive critique that contained easily digestible ideas, employing the language of the historian and social scientist. Yet the very popularity of Frank, particularly amongst English-speaking undergraduates, tended to deflect attention from a more significant work published almost contemporaneously, namely Cardoso and Faletto's *Dependencia y desarrollo en América Latina.*

In an analysis which focused directly upon internal conditions in Latin America, Cardoso and Faletto began from a different set of assumptions: namely, that socialism was not on the immediate agenda. Thus the essential issue that they confront is how to construct a national capitalism within a framework dominated by international capital. Much of the value of their writing lies in the importance that they attach to the political, in the breadth of their canvas and in the sustained exhilaration of their presentation. The appeal of Cardoso and Faletto is probably enhanced by their commitment to evolutionary change, and a pragmatic recognition of the constraints of state power upon popular action. They also pay special attention to differences amongst Latin American societies and, like Furtado, provide a useful typology for the exploration of diverse patterns of external relationships.

Dependency and its critics

The eclecticism of dependency has attracted criticism and made for confusion. Ambivalent attitudes to the framework and the significance of the debate are reflected in this volume: for Rosemary Thorp, Frank is seminal but Cardoso barely mentioned; O'Brien accords Cardoso primacy, whereas Frank obtains but a passing respectful mention. Perhaps the influence of Frank was greater in the short term but that of Cardoso is more durable. The early writings of Frank possibly reflect the prevalent pessimism among some North American Marxists during the mid 1960s about the versatility of capitalism, which was associated with stagnation and retarded or immutably rigid structures in peripheral societies. Cardoso, by contrast, represented to some measure the optimism of the Brazilian 'miracle', which was sustainable into the late 1970s.

The writing of these and lesser exponents provoked controversy. Several scholars questioned whether dependency constituted a substantial advance upon theories of imperialism. Marxists have criticized dependency analysis for emphasizing modes of production to the exclusion of relations of production and forces of production. They have argued further that the term dependency lacks specific content to be an effective tool of analysis. Such authors as Cueva advocate that no theoretical space exists for dependency: that Latin America represents a particular case but not a unique one, that it constitutes another example of capitalism, and that the distinction drawn by Cardoso between classical and dependent capitalism confuses rather than clarifies. O'Brien, in bleak mood, has asked if dependency is no more than a manifestation of nationalism wrapped in sophisticated language. Other Marxists have found dependency wanting in its lack of an explicit theory of action. Authors writing from a US environment shaped more by sectional than class considerations have claimed that dependency writing neglects population policy, ethnicity, caste and culture – issues of growing vitality in the continent.

Frank was criticized from all sides. By Marxists for being less original than he claimed and for integrating features of US Marxist-Leninist analysis with Latin American radical thinking in a vulgarized form, and for presenting too static a picture. Frank's assertion that Latin America was capitalist from the sixteenth century onwards drew sharp rejoinders, most notably from Ernesto Laclau who castigated him for revising Lenin on the significance of finance capitalism and for equating capitalism with a money economy. Frank was lambasted for his notorious reductionism and for presenting an over-schematic analysis, and not least for a lack of differential perspective between countries, for a unilinear explanation of all imbalances and for claiming Marxist credentials when departing from Marxist-Leninist rigour by stressing external relations to the exclusion of class struggle. Frank is treated unfairly in one respect by these critics: he was not alone in his failure to discuss class struggle; neither do some of the principal Marxist authors – Althusser and Marcuse, for example – of the post-war period. Whilst Frank was censured from the left for being insufficiently Marxist, non-Marxist critics maintain that he was undiscriminating in his use of empirical evidence and, worse, that he selected evidence to suit his argument. They also stressed Frank's lack of attention to major differentials – his failure to sub-periodize the Ibero-Latin American connection and his disregard for changes in the character of the Anglo-Latin American relationship between the half century after independence and the period c.1870 to 1914.

Cardoso and Faletto have been reproached by Marxists for not paying enough attention to the class struggle (especially for assigning a passive role to the urban working class), for neglect of the extraction of surplus value by imperialist forces and for a failure to perceive that only socialism is a vehicle for genuine change. Their pursuit of objective views of society and their assumption that the future can be scientifically predicted owes as much to Comte – highly influential in Brazilian intellectual history – as to Marx, probably more. These criticisms do not disguise the fact that the initial attraction of dependency writing lay in the radical implication of its claims and the repudiation of previous orthodoxies. It thus commended itself to a wide spectrum of opinion and encouraged a mass of polemical literature that did little to further understanding of Latin America: the vitality of concepts of dependency was undermined by their simplistic and incoherent over-use.

Where does the dependency debate stand today? More coolly appraised the furore of the early years, the exaggerated claims of comprehensiveness, have been softened though rarely totally abandoned. However, it needs to be stressed that dependency analysis never became the captive of one political faction or coalition, but was sometimes translated into policy. The crisis and collapse of dependency writing, over-enthusiastically prognosticated by its most belligerent adversaries, cannot be assumed. Despite an oppressive and crabbed intellectual environment and the impact of dispersion and exile, new possibilities for dependency writing are slowly taking shape. As Laclau has indicated, the writing of Gramsci has a particular appeal in Latin America and has contributed to the renovation of Marxist-Leninist thinking on the durability of bourgeois dominance. From Marxist criticisms of dependency there may yet emerge a new and meaningful thrust, the further elaboration of the concept of hegemony, yielding on appropriate tool for an exploration of the Latin American predicament.

Further new possibilities are evident in changing economic and political circumstances. The scale of current indebtedness that threatens so many Latin American societies, from oil-exporters like Venezuela and Mexico, and those self-sufficient in oil like Argentina, to oil-importers like Brazil, may well elicit a new spurt of dependency writing. So too may the continuing ascendancy of right-wing military regimes in the southern half of the continent, and the dominance of a resurgent neo-liberalism manifest in explicit attempts to roll back the frontiers of the state, dismantle protectionist barriers and reinsert national economies within the international system. Dependency language is pervasive, as can be observed in some official rhetoric used to address the problem of external indebtedness in Mexico and Brazil during the 1980s. Indeed, *dependentista* phraseology is embodied in some of the publications of right-wing bureaucracies. However, it is both premature and facile to assert that the New Right has appropriated dependence, while it shifts uneasily from a neo-liberal internationalism to a familiar right-wing nationalism.

The line between diffusionist writing and dependency writing should not be drawn too sharply. Over-categorization has tended to obscure overlaps between them. The eclecticism and pragmatism so evident in both makes for a correspondence. Jaguaribe, for example, who postulates three possible developmental choices for Latin America – dependency, autonomy and revolution – is conventionally categorized as a diffusionist advocating autonomous national development along capitalist lines, while Cardoso – elaborating the concept of associated capitalist development – is perceived as a *dependentista*. And Cardoso has also called for a more specific consideration of detail – micro-level studies – so as better to sustain broad generalizations. Such a focus would resolve many of the early shortcomings of the debate, namely the dated criticisms of the failure adequately to define autonomy (the alternative condition to dependence) and an unsophisticated equation of dependence with underdevelopment. Cardoso's present plea for detailed historical investigation is a precise illustration of the differences that have contributed to past confusion. For many scholars, especially those trained in Anglo-Saxon empirical traditions, detailed investigations must precede generalization. Latin American exponents of dependency argued that the first task was to evolve a theory which would facilitate the elaboration and interpretation of empirical research. This contrast, and the over-use of jargon, have bedevilled the debate. A convergence of methodologies might also impart a new flourish to both the dependency and the diffusionist literature. Indeed, this process may already be observed in two major areas of current research – investigations of the state and of labour in Latin America, issues that emerge directly from the discourse.

As this volume demonstrates, numerous claims may be made for the controversy provoked by *dependentistas* and related earlier discussions. First, the more sophisticated literature has successfully challenged two established Eurocentric orthodoxies – theories of imperialism and growth. Marxism has been enriched by a stress upon the relationship between external and domestic factors in the process of imperialism. Traditional Marxist-Leninist assumptions about the role of capitalism in Third World countries have been impugned and to a degree reformulated. In questioning classical economic theory, the exponents of dependency and the associated discussion about *desarrollismo* have sharpened the focus upon the political economy of growth – in particular stressing the importance of the political – and have promoted a clearer differentiation between growth and development. The debate has revealed the shortcomings of both orthodox free market economics and development strategies. Second, the volume of dependency literature, especially some of the cruder, earlier texts, has stimulated a fruitful response amongst diffusionists and empiricists. The latter, if still disinclined to theorize, have nevertheless responded more positively to the invitation to generalize. As indicated, the discourse has encouraged exchanges among scholars of differing ideologies and methodologies, occasionally generating both heat and light.

Finally, though primarily concerned with Latin America, the issues raised in this controversy have not merely been popularized, but have achieved a multi-continental currency. The work of Amin represents a view from the periphery largely derived from the Latin American literature. Recent explorations by Africanists into the political economy of the external connection indicate the extent to which themes explored by *dependentistas* have been absorbed elsewhere. Indeed, the flow is not unidirectional. In some of its manifestations, the dependency debate reveals an increasing identification within Latin America of shared interests and concerns with other areas of the Third World or the South.

As recently as the 1960s Latin American intellectuals were barely inclined to this correspondence. The dominant Western orientation of Latin American scholars, their tendency to identify with Western Europe and the United States rather than Africa or Asia, was sustained by the view that ideas generated in Asia and Africa had little relevance for Latin America – especially the Southern Cone. Latin America was perceived as a region of higher per capita income with an established industrial sector, a long heritage of political independence and more experience in handling problems of relationships with the superpowers and transnational corporations as theoretically equal partners. *Dependentistas* have contributed to the erosion of these over-confident suppositions. In sum, it may be argued that dependency analysis, often flawed and open to misuse, provides a framework of reference, an original attempt to establish the laws of motion of non-advanced economies.

These assessments of the arguments surrounding imperialism and dependency are central to the exploration of the nature of the relationship between Latin America and the advanced economies, since independence, undertaken in this volume. Too often the discussion has taken place within an excessively narrow disciplinary framework. Accordingly, the contributors to this book have been drawn from both North Atlantic and Latin American traditions of scholarship. They have been trained in a wide range of disciplines – economic history, economics, history, philosophy and political sociology; they stress the centrality of the theme of political economy within a multi-ideological context. This choice of contributors also resolves another defect present in many early investigations of Latin America's external connections, namely an inadequate awareness of historical processes among economists and a tendency among historians to neglect relevant social science techniques. Similarly, the fusion of scholarly traditions is intended to counteract the inclination of some British scholars to underestimate the significance and vitality of recent Latin American contributions to the imperialism debate, and the reluctance of some Latin American scholars to give sufficient empirical depth to their theoretical work. It is hoped that the blend of intellectual and ideological traditions represented by the contributors will advance the investigation of the themes explored here, at both a theoretical and an empirical level. Three principal themes are dealt with in this book: the structure and complexity of external connections; the importance of the state and political economy; the emergence of organized labour and the associated processes of social differentiation.

External connections
Latin American intellectuals have always been receptive to theories that explore the external connection, because they regard it as crucial to the well-being of the continent. Since 1945 a cultural explosion in Latin

America has drawn the sustained attention of the outside world for the first time. Social scientists and historians have joined with specialists in literature and the visual and performing arts in a pursuit of cultural authenticity. Hitherto, Latin America had been perceived as the passive recipient of external influences. Now the region is acquiring a separate identity and its culture an emancipatory thrust as the continent attempts to renegotiate its external linkages. Latin American elite groups have considered themselves to be part of Western civilization. Whereas Islamic and oriental societies may be viewed as autonomous cultures, Latin America has constituted a derivative culture, open and susceptible first to European and then to US influence.

The dominance of the European image originated in the Iberian conquests and was reinforced by subsequent cycles of immigration from Southern, Central and Western Europe. Modified and invigorated by pre-columbian survivals and Afro-Asian cultural traits, the predominant culture remains syncretic. The enduring connection with Europe facilitated a rapid assimilation of political and economic ideas. Political ideologies travelled faster than technology, as was evident in the socialist mirage in Colombia in 1848, in the advent of Trotskyism in Bolivia during the 1920s, and in the plethora of constitutional documents and legal codes promulgated since independence. But the outstanding relationship, at least since c.1870, has been economic. For most Latin American countries external linkages still account for a large proportion of measurable economic activity. Taxes upon foreign commerce funded administration; capital was borrowed – and continues to be sought – abroad; various institutions emulated European and US models.

While attempts to restructure the external connection were central to ECLA's development strategy, the impetus to change was not confined to the Commission, and the debate involved more than a questioning of the laws of comparative advantage. European theories of imperialism, in addition to assessments of the likely post-war role of the United States, shaped the debate. However, the impact of these theories varied considerably. As is revealed in the sections that follow, Hobson is hardly known in the continent. He barely touched upon Latin America in his writings, making mere passing reference to US expansion. Exponents of the recent revival of interest in Hobson in Britain are careful to avoid seeing him through a prism of Leninist perceptions. The significance of Hobson for Latin America was that he underlined the capacity of capitalism to adapt to new challenges, and that he contributed to the debate on the desirability of collectivism. His influence was transmitted through later authors, especially Keynes, who was widely read by Latin American policy-makers. Lenin, by contrast, made a considerable impact through translations published in Mexico City and in Buenos Aires. His views were also transmitted to Latin America in the writing of other Europeans, like Dobb. Both admired and feared as the architect of a revolution in a country whose social and economic structure, especially in agriculture, was in the 1910s more antiquated than that of much of Latin America, Lenin was important first as a political practitioner and second as a theorist.

The state and political economy

The state is a concept which, like imperialism, is used simplistically by some Latin Americanists; its widespread adoption indicates both French and German influences absorbed since the 1840s. Rooted in mercantilist thinking, the perception of the state as performing a central function was barely touched by the nineteenth-century advocacy of liberal concepts of government. These projected the state as an active agent promoting the establishment of a *laissez-faire* environment before assuming a passive stance. During the twentieth century the state has been portrayed both as a mechanism for the defence of the status quo and as an agency for the promotion of social and economic change. In this debate the European use of the term 'the state' suggests a neutrality and technical proficiency that cannot always be attached to the government apparatus in Latin America. A tradition of interaction between private power and public authority that had its origin in the Iberian colonies became more visible with the de-professionalization of the bureaucracy after independence. More recently the term has been employed to suggest a degree of institutionalization that has often not existed in governing structures, and to dignify with a semblance of impartiality arrangements within families and factions or sectoral interests competing for influence. Meanwhile, some exponents of the concept of 'the state' have failed to differentiate between central and provincial authorities, or to distinguish the administrative role of government from full-blown interventionism.

The state has been less subject to rigorous theoretical analysis than imperialism and growth. Following conventions established in the Latin American literature, several chapters in this volume raise questions pertaining to the debate on the state. The role of government in industrial promotion is discussed throughout; so too is the interaction between the state and dominant interests – both domestic and external. Government policy towards the agrarian sector is considered in terms of land distribution and usage, food supply and exports. The competence of the state is explored with reference to the professionalism of public administration and the military, the appropriateness of domestic and foreign economic policy and relations with foreign capitalists. Furthermore, there are several detailed investigations of fiscal policy, development strategy and techniques of political control and co-option.

These explorations illuminate larger debates on the state and government in Latin America, namely:

- the autonomy of the state from class and sectional interests;
- the fragmentation of the state after independence;
- state mediation between domestic groups and external forces;
- the composition and remodelling of the state.

These debates are imbued with a notion of political economy peculiar to Latin America. Although 'political economy' has an immediate resonance for British and North American economists, the ethos of political economy influential in Britain for much of the nineteenth century is now often alleged by neo-classical and Keynesian economists to have been appropriated by Marxists. Liberal economic orthodoxy in the United Kingdom and the United States, stressing the dominance of market forces and assuming the sharp specificity of the political and the economic, shies away from this notion. Latin American scholars – Marxist and non-Marxist – exhibit no such coyness. Hence one recurring theme of this book is 'political economy' – an investigation of government policy which assumes the promotion of economic and social expansion to be a critical function of administration, and imposes the need to consider the interpenetration of sectional interests and policy determinants.

The contributors to this volume have for the most part followed conventional Latin American usage. Rejecting both the narrow economic determinism so often characteristic of European Marxist writing and an equally myopic political voluntarism frequently observed in empiricist scholarship, Latin Americans stress the intimacy and often the inextricability of the political and the economic. There are a number of reasons for this intellectual tradition. Classical economics has never enjoyed the same status in Latin America as in Britain and the United States. Other influences, for example the writings of List and Comte, and not least Spanish and Portuguese colonial traditions which antedate liberal economics, play an indisputably important but under-studied role. Another reason is the inescapable significance of the connection between political project and economic strategy in practice. This explains the space assigned in these chapters to such matters as the determination, influence and efficacy of government policy, sectional representation within the state, the relationship between specific institutions (especially the military) and society and economy, and a heavy emphasis upon non-quantifiable variables such as ideology, social differentiation and group attitudes.

Labour and social differentiation

The reshaping of the labour force to meet the requirements of an expanding capitalist system entailed the restructuring of intermediate social groups and increased state involvement. This subject is fraught with problems of categorization and conceptualization. Some authors refer to classes, others to strata, sectors or groups. Terms such as peasant, rural-urban migrant, industrial worker and lumpen proletariat are used casually by some scholars and more precisely by others. The problem of imprecision can be observed in this book where contributors examine the impact of the external connection upon occupational structure, both rural and urban; discuss the consequences of 'retarded proletarianization' and over-expansion of the tertiary sector; detail relations between labour, employers, the state and international business; consider relationships between organized and non-organized labour, and assess the significance of increased labour agitation. These issues relate to current controversy concerning:

- the role of the state in the promotion of organized labour. Such questions have been raised as (1) the concern of the state to maintain its autonomy *vis à vis* other interests and entities, (2) corporatist development strategy in which urban labour constitutes a significant consumer market, (3) frameworks of regulation designed to facilitate the emergence of a labour market suited to capitalist requirements;
- the transition from forced to free labour and the progressive incorporation of rural groups within the labour market;
- the impact of changing patterns of employment upon labour organization;
- the notion that exaggerated labour militancy has deferred and distorted capitalist development.

Industrialization, agrarian structures and periodization
The three principal themes explored in this book subsume two major issues for which the literature is large and multidisciplinary, namely industrialization and agrarian structures and change. A wide range of agrarian topics are treated by Duncan and Rutledge (eds) *Land and labour in Latin America*. Other topics, notably the recent focus upon agribusiness and food policy, and agrarian reform, are discussed by Arroyo, Goldberg, Griffin, Myint and Scott. There are also notable national studies on coffee, sugar cane, ranching and cereal production which complement themes discussed in this volume. The debate on industrialization considers scale, the consolidation of consumer markets, government promotion, foreign penetration and the definition, character and chronology of industrial expansion. Also examined here is the continuing controversy regarding the impact of wars and depressions upon the pace and direction of industrialization.

The periodization employed throughout is conventional and, while broadly appropriate for an investigation of the external connection, may be questioned. The integral unity of the sub-periods and the significance of turning-points may be challenged. Equally, a generalized chronology for the continent tends to minimize the importance of national trends: climacterics and watersheds vital for one country might have little impact elsewhere. Even events which assume a continental dimension are not necessarily of equal relevance for all societies. If the timing and scale of US penetration is taken as the principal variable, a different time schema is required for various parts of Latin America. A common chronology for the latter part of the twentieth century is particularly elusive. Nevertheless, there is a general consensus that the process of independence effected a restructuring in Latin America's relationship with external powers. Further modifications can be observed during the third quarter of the nineteenth century, though whether of a qualitative or substantive nature is disputed. Additional turning-points, of varying degrees of significance and generality, may be observed between the end of the century and the 1920s. It is sometimes asserted that the World Depression of 1929–33 and the Second World War had a momentous impact upon the continent's external linkages. Periodization is indeed part of the debate.

I

THE DEBATE

2

DEPENDENCY AND THE HISTORIAN: FURTHER OBJECTIONS

D. C. M. Platt

'De omnibus dubitandum', as Karl Marx was so fond of saying. He was right, and no end to the dependency debate is near. But reactions to an earlier article of mine in the *Latin American Research Review* suggest that much remains to be said.[1] The range of opinion within the dependency 'school' is so large, from revolutionaries to 'mildly socialistic nationalists', that it becomes difficult even to construct that convenient rhetorical device, the straw man. Cardoso had his fun with the more absurd breast-beaters of North American scholarship, sufferers from collective guilt.[2] And it is not difficult to identify (in André Gunder Frank and Immanuel Wallerstein) those 'present-day butterfly collectors' whom Cardoso describes as strolling through history 'classifying types of dependency, modes of production, and laws of development, with the blissful illusion that their findings can remove from history all its ambiguities, conjectures, and surprises'.[3] Politics, in this debate, have the priority. Dependency writers nowadays have abandoned quantitative arguments, and prefer the qualitative and intuitive. Capitalism causes underdevelopment, *tout court*. Frank has never been shy of admitting the political intentions of his rhetoric, inspired by the Cuban Revolution.[4] Yet even Cardoso, now an establishment figure, cannot rid himself of his origins; the power of attraction of dependency studies lies 'not merely' in their methodology and their opening up of a new set of themes; 'it is principally because they do this from a *radically critical* viewpoint'.[5]

Of course, history is not in evidence here, and perhaps as an historian I have no business to intervene. Nor would I think of taking up the cudgels in that delicious intra-party dispute, unhistorical as it is, between feudalism and capitalism. But 'long words bother me' (as they did the Bear of Very Little Brain), and even Cardoso clouds my mind when he refers to 'more or less abrupt "breaks" in reality [which] are reduced to "operational dimensions" which, by definition, are univocal but static'.[6]

The advantage of ideology, once the vocabulary is mastered, is that the answers come pat; further thought is unnecessary. Dubcek's minister, Zdeněk Mlynář, while a very young man and an active communist, steeped himself in the Communist Manifesto, in Engels, Lenin and Stalin. Many years later he asked (from his exile) how he could ever have 'embraced such literature as a political bible'?

> . . . only one reply seems to make sense: the ideology contained in this literature gives someone who in reality knows very little or nothing at all the self-assurance of someone who has mastered the very laws that govern the development of mankind and the world. All it demands is belief . . . with that leap of faith comes scientific knowledge . . . [you] know what is and is not scientific without having to bother with any concrete scientific research . . . you have become almost overnight a superior being with the correct views.[7]

Yet historians (and others) may occasionally feel the need for evidence: 'no investigation, no right to speak' (Mao). And it is surely suggestive that whereas I, as an historian, have been prepared to concede that, although there is little basis in history for the dependency theory, there may yet be something in the idea for the present day, students of the present day conclude that dependency, although possibly of use to historians, 'cannot be shown to be causally related to a continuance of underdevelopment'.[8] If we are both right for our own periods, there may be little left to discuss.

All the same, we are dealing with a powerful theology. Currently, 'dependent capitalism' is the explanation even for the most improbable ills, and 'structural reform' (that is, violent revolution) is the only sufficient remedy. Do we have to experience the horrors of that 'remedy' before we can proceed? 'Da mihi castitatem et continentiam, sed noli modo' (St Augustine). Give me chastity and continency, but do not give them yet. As an historian, all that I can be expected to do is to make a few suggestions for the more obvious failures in the historical approach of the dependency 'school'. History, although inadequately researched and argued, still forms a prominent element in the school's ideology. If the history is wrong, can it be that its remedies (deduced from 'history') are also misconceived?

I have mentioned elsewhere the absence of any true continuity between the overseas trading and financial connections of colonial and independent Spanish America.[9] After a burst of enthusiasm in the early 1820s, Spanish America abandoned (and was abandoned by) world markets for half a century. Furthermore, I have argued the importance of domestic resources for the last decades of the nineteenth century, at a period when the overspill of European demand had actually created a market for Spanish-American products and, with it, a supply of foreign capital. The trend in historical writing seems likely to develop ever more towards the investigation of internal, domestic development as the leading element in economic change, even for the so-called 'peripheral' countries during the nineteenth century. The trend may be expected to replace the emphasis on external trade and finance which has so pre-occupied the *dependentistas*.

It may be true that for Latin America the point has still to be established. Arthur Bloomfield has complained that too much impor-tance is attached by too many to what they have taken to be the predominant influence of exports and foreign investment on the economies of the 'newer' regions of the world during the nineteenth century: 'It may apply to some countries [but] it neglects the powerful domestic forces, on both the demand and supply sides, making for growth.'[10] Irving Kravis has challenged successfully Ragnar Nurkse's central notion of international trade as the engine of growth in the nineteenth century,[11] and has argued (for the United States) that 'the mainsprings of growth were internal; they must be sought in the land and the people and in the system of social and economic organization'.[12] Very recently Tony Smith, an Africanist, explained that the dependency theory 'in general substantially overestimates the power of the interna-tional system'.[13] My article (*Latin American Research Review* 1980) suggested that this is very evidently the case for dependency writers and Spanish America.

But if a leading target in the dependency theory has always been the foreigner (the Briton before 1914, the North American thereafter), it is true that for even the most naïve (Gunder Frank, for example), dependency has not been regarded simply as an external phenomenon: 'Dependence is also, and in equal measure, an "internal" integral element of Latin American society', in which the domestic bourgeoisie behave as full collaborators with the foreigner in exploitation.[14] The question is put, and it requires an answer. Might there have been some general understanding between foreign businessmen and *vendepatrias* by which, in their sectional interest, the rich perspectives of independent, self-sustaining, import-substituting industrial growth were sacrificed in favour of a wholly dependent economy?

The answer cannot be entirely direct, nor can it be encompassed within a single article. Obviously, monopolistic practices existed in nineteenth-century trade and finance. But so, in large measure, did fierce competition. Nor is the timing of an 'understanding' between foreign business and *vendepatrias* particularly plausible. When private business made its first important approaches to the economies of Spanish America (in the 1860s), its managers would have had to be prepared to hold their money for twenty to thirty years at low to nil interest rates if they had intended to manufacture a dependent economy and stifle the autonomous growth of local industry. And in any case, little could as yet be anticipated from a closer connection. In the late 1860s the editor of the best informed economic journal of the day, the London

Economist, did not think even to mention Argentina when he predicted that the great new suppliers of wheat for the British market would be Canada and Australia.[15]

Of course I am aware that dependency theory, except in its crudest manifestations, does not imply a simple, direct conflict between nationals ('goodies') and foreigners ('baddies'). It presupposes, in Quijano's words, a basic correspondence of interest between the dominant groups in both societies.[16] Cardoso and Faletto, in a recent reformulation of their arguments (1976), are careful to emphasize that the relationship between external and internal forces is not to be explained simply by external forms of exploitation and coercion; it is 'rooted in coincidences of interests between local dominant classes and international ones'.[17] The idea is both attractive and plausible, more particularly to Marxists (and even to Cardoso himself) for whom, in the words of the Master, 'the history of all hitherto existing society is the history of class struggle'. A common interest was surely shared by the native upper classes – the landowners, lawyers, and exporters – and the bourgeois foreigners to whom, and by whom, they exported. The same was true of the import trade. These *were* the governing groups in society, and they remained so into the twentieth century.

But the argument needs to be taken a step further. The 'collaboration' of domestic and foreign interests cannot be said to have become even relatively important within Spanish American economies until foreign trade and finance themselves had gained some stature, and this was not until the last two decades of the nineteenth century. By this time, at least in the principal republics, political power had so consolidated itself that the foreign businessman was of slight account, and it is naïve to think of the governing group as in any real sense under the control of foreigners. But in any case – and the point is surely decisive – there is no convincing evidence that the economies of Spanish America, in the half-century before the First World War, could have developed, realistically, in any direction other than they did. If some collaborative effort had indeed existed between foreigners and *vendepatrias*, it can only have confirmed a pattern of development which, for better or for worse, was already established. Other paths to development (self-sustained economic growth, import-substituting industrialization, or whatever) were implausible, and they were well known to be implausible at the time.

Dr Wenceslao Pacheco, Argentine finance minister during the great economic expansion of the late 1880s, was aware of supposedly alternative patterns of growth. Argentine industry, he said, was uncompetitive; it lacked the fundamental elements of industrialization – iron, coal and manpower. It was not wise, Pacheco added, to impose sacrifices on the people in the shape of high protective tariffs, so as to give artificial life to domestic industry. In the United States, admittedly, the government had raised tariff barriers with considerable success, but the cost to the American people had been very high, and in any case the United States possessed in abundance two of those essential elements which were missing in Argentina, coal and iron. Furthermore, by far the largest component of Argentine government income was the tariff on imports, and for Wenceslao Pacheco it was inconceivable, in a country unaccustomed to direct taxation, to abandon this resource.[18]

It is not, in fact, easy to see what any government, of whatever political complexion, could have done. Pacheco himself undertook a modest level of selective protection, in the shape of higher protective tariffs on wine, alcohol and sugar. But import duties for the period 1884–7 accounted for no less than 60.5 per cent of government revenue,[19] and higher tariffs necessarily brought lower revenue. Short of an entirely improbable revolution in Argentina's taxation system (and the same was true for the other republics), the government had no alternative to the promotion of imports and, through them, the expansion of revenues from the Custom House.

Dependency theorists, if they wish to draw sustenance from the nineteenth century, must at some point face up to the alternative strategies, if any, which were practicable for the republics. In the interests of import substitution, were the poor to pay high prices to enrich the domestic industrialist? The socialists, the unions, the anarchists, did not think so. Could there have been some plan, some alliance, between *vendepatrias* and foreigners, to make money at the expense of the rest of the community and at the cost, ultimately, of a misshapen pattern of economic development? Or was the direction of the economy simply a reflection of peculiarly favourable conditions in world markets which, if development were to proceed at all, it would have been difficult, perhaps suicidal, to replace?

The nineteenth century was not an age of planning, of model-building by more or less skilled hands. Things happened not because they were planned by finance ministers, by pressure groups, by social classes, by foreigners, by natives, but because, without intervention or planning on anything remotely resembling a twentieth-century scale, there was no genuine alternative.

The shape of Argentine economic development was rational. Argentina had industrialized to a substantial extent by the beginning of the First World War – not in capital goods, of course, but over a broad range of ordinary manufactures. 90.7 per cent of the foodstuffs consumed in the republic were locally processed. Home manufactures included 87.9 per cent of clothing, 79.9 per cent of construction materials, 70.2 per cent of furnishings, 37.9 per cent of chemical products, 33.2 per cent of metallurgical goods, 22.6 per cent of textiles, and 59.1 per cent of all other industrial products.[20] This was not, after all, an insignificant level of industrialization for an economy supposedly bent to the will of the industrialized nations of Europe and North America. Nor, as recent research suggests, was it uncharacteristic of many other parts of Latin America at the time. Argentina was superbly placed to exploit her advantages as a supplier of agricultural and pastoral products. Twentieth-century notions of planning and development – enforced industrialization, import substitution, nationalization of the command-ing heights of the economy – these were to come, but not yet. In the meantime, it is unnecessary to search for a conscious plan within such an unplanned society, or to develop theories to obscure the obvious.

Naturally, there is a problem of scale. Diminutive amounts of foreign commercial capital in small societies may have been disproportionately significant. It must be true that even a small foreign trade and small injections of foreign capital influenced disproportionately the political and economic position both of a central government and of the major towns. The Venezuelan government was dependent upon the income derived from import duties; it borrowed (when it could) abroad; government money found its way into the pockets of the governing class; and it was the governing class which both bought such imports as it could afford and then exported to pay for them. It is yet to be decided how much influence this centralized and limited activity was actually to have on the shape of the economy of nineteenth-century Venezuela.

However, there are sufficiently documented reasons to suggest that the argument for the disproportionate influence of foreign *finance* might be turned on its head. In the small economies which existed for so much of the nineteenth century – that is, before the railway boom of the 1880s – foreign capital was required only for those enterprises and undertakings which had no hope of paying for themselves, such as wars (civil or otherwise) and 'political' railways to unite the distant provinces of a republic. Where an opportunity existed to make a productive invest-ment, the securities were well taken at home. This was always the case for the great railway development of the United States. It was true of Russia once the markets of Western Europe had become saturated with Russian railway securities in the late 1860s. It became true of the better railways and public utilities of Latin America. Money was borrowed abroad to speed up productive developments which could otherwise, over a longer period, have been financed at home. Meanwhile, much foreign finance went into unproductive investment – armies and armaments, 'political' railways – so that it might well be argued that foreign finance in Spanish America was decidedly *less* effective, *less* productive for the economy, than domestic finance, dollar for dollar, pound for pound.

It is right to say that this foreign finance, largely unproductive before the 1880s, was exceptionally expensive? – Spanish America may have borrowed little, and paid too much. The evidence for the comparative cost of borrowing between nations is relatively abundant, and the conclusion can only be that the price was not unreasonably high. The arguments are complicated, but a simple answer would be that the price of borrowing before the 1860s (and really before the 1880s) was immaterial; Spanish America had no consistent access to the world's financial markets, whatever the price, and had not enjoyed such access since 1825. When the republics returned to the market in the last quarter of the nineteenth century, they found themselves able to borrow very cheaply abroad. Even in 1881, before the great boom in Argentine exports later in the decade, the bonds of the 1866/8 loans were quoted at par for 6 per cents, and they reached 104 in 1882.[21] For its ordinary needs the Argentine government, even on the domestic market, paid only 7 per cent, and on its best securities, bills on the Custom House, it paid 6 per cent and even as little as 5 per cent.[22] By 1912 it could look for money in European markets at 4.5 per cent.

Money was not expensive on international markets, and could be very cheap indeed. Cheap capital implies abundant cash in competition for an outlet, so that it was unlikely to have strings attached. Finance ministers were not afraid of borrowing abroad if they could do so for productive purposes. Juan Romero, President Roca's first finance minister, told the Argentine Congress in 1882 that 'the day that the sum of our public debt is made up of work on railways, ports, roads, etc. etc., on that day we can be sure that our country has no debts'.[23]

Robert Browning once spoke of 'the natural fog of the good man's mind'. Dependency has its nuances, but surely there must be some fault in a theory which is always proclaiming its historical roots, but which gets its history so profoundly wrong? *Some* countries in Spanish America had *some* mutually satisfactory links with external economies during the nineteenth century, but substantial and enduring links developed only during the last decades. There was no misunderstanding at the time; the governing classes were always realists. José María Rosa, Argentine finance minister shortly before the First World War, fully acknowledged that the economic growth of Argentina had been extraordinarily slow before national unification in 1862. This, in his opinion, was due above all to uninterrupted civil war and the chaotic condition of the country. Argentine imports in 1861 were worth only 22 million gold pesos (£4.4 million) and her exports $14 million (£2.8 million). The really dramatic increases occurred from the 1880s, while, as Rosa said, Argentina as a great exporter of agricultural products postdated the Baring Crisis of 1890. Argentine exports for 1889 were $90 million gold (£18 million). They rose to $134 million in 1899 (£26.8 million) and $397 million (£79.4 million) in 1909.[24]

These were important figures for the integration of Spanish America into the world economy, and they were late to develop even for the most important of Spanish American exporters, Argentina. Once, however, this integration took place, growth was rapid indeed, and it brought great wealth. Dependence is hardly adequate as a description of the position of a country like Argentina in the decade before the First World War. She was the cheapest producer of grain in the world. She was the monopoly shipper of chilled beef. She exported far more than she imported. Her politics were firmly in the hands of native Argentines. She was able instantly to raise enough money, if ever she wished, on European markets (probably in London itself) to buy up the most important foreign enterprise in the republic, the Anglo-Argentine railway system.

It was because she chose not to do so that Argentina did not buy her railways. Argentine financiers argued openly that the state should go no further with the acquisition of railways. It was wrong to tie up in public works a limited, disposable capital that might be better employed elsewhere; private enterprise must be invited to take part. This was not, said the finance minister Figueroa Alcorta in 1907, to increase the tribute to foreign capital; it was only to strengthen the national economy and to raise its productive capacity.[25] In 1911 his successor told Congress that twenty years' experience of state-owned and administered railways in Argentina had convinced both him and his colleagues that the sensible policy was to transfer them to private enterprise. Private enterprise, which was far more efficient than the state, must be associated with the national interest. In Europe, he said, the experience of state railway systems was precisely the same.[26]

Mexico adopted the opposite policy, and in the first decade of the twentieth century raised enough money on European markets to buy a controlling share in the national railway system (managed in North America). Both Porfirian Mexico and pre-war Argentina enjoyed access to cheap money where and when they chose to take it. Can either be described, realistically, as a dependency?

I do not mean that dependency never existed in any form, at any time, or in any place. All the same it may be preferable, for the nineteenth century, to start from an assumption of independence rather than dependence. Spanish America was independent, economically and politically, for by far the greater part of the nineteenth century, if for no better reason than that hardly anybody outside Spanish America cared one way or the other for Spanish American politics, trade and finance. The continuity of hegemony, between colonial Spanish America (under Spain) and the independent republics (under Northern Europe), never existed. When, at length, an interest was shown internationally in Spanish America, the political position of the principal republics was so secure that it is unrealistic to regard them as automatically the tools of foreign interests, or even automatically their collaborators. It could indeed be argued that the *vendepatrias*, so prominent in the demonology of the dependency school, were able, from their strong political base, to hold foreign business in thrall. There were corners of London, Paris, Bordeaux, Antwerp, Amsterdam, Frankfurt and even of New York, which were 'dependencies' of strong domestic interests within the Spanish American republics. I am putting it this way not because I believe it to be a valuable approach to history, but because it illustrates the limitations of an uncritical pursuit of the dependency theme.

It sounds arrogant to say so, but the whole thrust of the debate on the 'imperialism of Free Trade' has surely been diverted by mounting evidence (in my own and other publications) that neither the British government nor individual British traders were in an expansionist mood outside traditional markets during the middle decades of the nineteenth century.[27] More recently, I persuaded a group of colleagues to join me in investigating the links which, in the absence of solid diplomatic pressure, might have been expected to exist between British business and the Latin American societies within which it operated.[28] We found very little. But it was plain from our research that the nature of the business, rather than the nationality of its proprietors, provided the explanation. The merchant intermediary (foreign or native), trading between weak producers and distant markets and able (when he chose) to withdraw his capital, was in a stronger position than the great public utility company, a helpless giant, unable (if foreign) to count on diplomatic support, subject (sometimes in inflationary economies) to government-regulated rates, with its capital locked irretrievably in the country within which it chose to function.

More recently still, I took the argument further from trade to finance. The full conclusions have yet to be published,[29] but a preliminary paper in the *Economic History Review* suggested that Britain's capital exports by 1870 have been overvalued, conventionally, by as much as 100 per cent, while by 1914 they were likely still to be a third too high.[30] The effect of this research must be to take some of the steam out of the notion of a ruthless and dynamic pursuit of wealth, of economic and political control, during what amounts to the whole period from Waterloo to the First World War, and in some cases up to the World Depression. Some doubt, for example, might be cast on the theory of finance capital as the engine of imperialism, if the figure for European capital exports were found to be very substantially below the amount that Lenin had in mind. 'Conspiracy theory' is rightly scorned by all opinion, scholarly and otherwise. But it is, in fact, omnipresent, and its basis, too often, is a wildly exaggerated view of the extent and influence of international trade, investment and management in the century before 1914.

There is no reason to despair. The material for accurate research is plentiful. Most of the work still needs to be done, but meanwhile, as someone once said, 'the dust of exploded beliefs may make a fine sunset'. The need is to find an approach that can plausibly reconstruct what happened a century ago, and this can hardly be achieved outside the archives. 'Views or criticisms, which are not based on thorough investigation,' said Chairman Mao, 'are nothing but ignorant twaddle.'

Dependency is theory unsupported by fact. Argument cannot defeat dogma, and I am reminded of the third moral to be derived from Leszek Kolakowski's cautionary tale 'Balaam, or the Problem of Objective Guilt', namely, that 'it is contrary to common sense to make use of common sense in a quarrel with absolute sense'.[31] But in any case I do not mean to imply that foreign intervention, or the activities of the *vendepatrias*, had no consequences whatever; it is simply that those consequences have yet to be fully identified. Charles Jones has worked on the papers of British financial institutions and public utilities both in London and in Buenos Aires. This is the stuff of historical research, and it has brought accurate results.[32] Recently Jones published a thoughtful piece in which he concluded that British firms in Argentina, although unable to call on the power of their own government and unwilling to challenge the monopoly of coercion possessed by the Argentine state, nevertheless offended against 'the right of the State to determine the pattern of development of the national economy by control of the supply and direction of investments and determination of the exchange rate'. Furthermore, 'British enterprise undermined the Argentine State in the last quarter of the nineteenth century by impoverishing, displacing, and otherwise weakening its support.'[33] The deductions may be disputable, the conclusions disproportionately dramatic, but the *approach* is promising. Generalizations which are based on a detailed study of the evidence, which identify the elements, and which suggest the ways in which foreign business genuinely interfered with national autonomy, are obviously more fruitful than blanket theories of dependency. *De beau raisin, toujours bon vin.*

Notes

[1] 'Dependency in nineteenth-century Latin America: an historian objects' *Latin American Research Review* xv 1 (1980).

[2] I am referring to Peter Winn's exercise in 'imaginative analysis' (or do I mean 'inventive research'?): *idem*. 'British informal empire in Uruguay in the nineteenth century' *Past and Present* 73 (1976).

[3] Fernando Henrique Cardoso 'The consumption of dependency theory in the United States' *Latin American Research Review* xii 3 (1977).

[4] André Gunder Frank 'La dependencia ha muerto: viva la dependencia y la lucha de clases, una respuesta a críticas' *Desarrollo Económico* xiii (1973).

[5] Cardoso 'The consumption of dependency theory' *loc. cit.* 21.

[6] *Ibid.* 15.

[7] Zdeněk Mlynář *Night frost in Prague: the end of humane socialism* (trans. London 1980) pp. 2–3.

[8] Sanjaya Lall 'Is "dependence" a useful concept in analysing underdevelopment?' *World Development* III 11 (1975). Of anti-dependency writers for the present day, I am particularly fond of Paul Singer 'Urbanización, dependencia y marginalidad en América Latina', republished in Martha Schteingart (ed.) *Urbanización dependencia en América Latina* (Buenos Aires 1973) pp. 93–122, and David Ray 'The dependency model of Latin American underdevelopment: three basic fallacies' *Journal of Inter-American Studies* XI 1 (1973).

[9] D. C. M. Platt *Latin America and British trade, 1806–1914* (London 1972) pp. 3–61 *passim*.

[10] Arthur I. Bloomfield *Patterns of fluctuation in international investment before 1914* (Princeton 1968) p. 5.

[11] Irving B. Kravis 'Trade as a handmaiden of growth: similarities between the nineteenth and twentieth centuries' *Economic Journal* 80 (1970).

[12] Irving B. Kravis 'The role of exports in nineteenth-century United States growth' *Economic Development and Cultural Change* 20 (1972).

[13] Tony Smith 'The underdevelopment of development literature: the case of dependency theory' *World Politics* XXXI 2 (1979).

[14] André Gunder Frank *Lumpenbourgeoisie, lumpendevelopment: dependence, class, and politics in Latin America* (New York 1972) p. 3.

[15] Leading article on 'the sources of our subsistence' in *The Economist* 27 June 1868, 730.

[16] Aníbal Quijano 'Dependencia, cambio social y urbanización en América Latina' in Schteingart *Urbanización y dependencia* p. 20.

[17] Fernando Henrique Cardoso and Enzo Faletto *Dependency and development in Latin America* (trans. with new preface, Berkeley 1979) p. xvi.

[18] *Memoria del departamento de Hacienda, 1887* (Buenos Aires 1888) I 8.

[19] *Ibid.* I 28.

[20] Alberto B. Martínez 'Consideraciones sobre la fortuna colectiva del pueblo argentino' *Tercer Censo Nacional, 1914* (Buenos Aires 1917) VIII 448.

[21] *Memoria del departamento de Hacienda, 1881* (Buenos Aires 1882) p. xxiv.

[22] *Ibid.* p. xi.

[23] *Ibid.* p. x.

[24] *Memoria del departamento de Hacienda, 1910* (Buenos Aires 1911) I 83–5.

[25] Budget for 1908, printed in the *Memoria del departamento de Hacienda 1908* (Buenos Aires 1909) I, xxxv–vi.

[26] *Memoria del departamento de Hacienda, 1910* (Buenos Aires 1911) I 7.

[27] D. C. M. Platt 'The imperialism of Free Trade: some reservations' *Economic History Review* XXI 2 (1968), 'Further objections to an "Imperialism of Free Trade", 1830–60' *Economic History Review* XXVI 1 (1973), 'The national economy and British imperial expansion before 1914' *Journal of Imperial and Commonwealth History* II 1 (1973); W. M. Mathew 'The imperialism of Free Trade: Peru, 1820–70' *Economic History Review* XXI 3 (1968).

[28] D. C. M. Platt (ed. and contrib.) *Business imperialism, 1840–1930: an inquiry based on British experience in Latin America* (Oxford 1977).

[29] D. C. M. Platt *Foreign finance in continental Europe and the USA, 1815–1870* (London 1984).

[30] D. C. M. Platt 'British portfolio investment overseas before 1870: some doubts' *Economic History Review* XXXIII 1 (1980).

[31] L. Kolakowski *The devil and scripture* (trans. London 1973) p. 25.

[32] C. A. Jones 'British financial institutions in Argentina, 1860–1914' (unpubl. Ph.D. thesis, Cambridge 1973).

[33] C. A. Jones ' "Business imperialism" and Argentina, 1875–1900: a theoretical note' *Journal of Latin American Studies* XII 2 (1980).

3

DEPENDENCY REVISITED

Philip J. O'Brien

Introduction

A la Recherche du Temps Perdu
M. Proust

A revealing aspect about the debate on dependency is what it tells us, not about the past and contemporary situations of the Latin American countries, but about academics studying these problems. There can be no doubt that dependency has been a thriving business (including such articles as this, a critique revisited!). The academic business community is now clearly international; but international or not, it still suffers from limitations – in this case, serious limitations of language and communication between those writing in underdeveloped countries and those writing from the more comfortable seats of the industrialized heartland.

The original formulation of dependency in Latin America began within ECLA in the mid 1960s, although one can identify a continuity of both themes and methods long before that period in Latin American social science, for example S. Bagú *Economía de la sociedad colonial* published in 1949, and even earlier in the writings of Mariátegui, in the 1920s.[1] If there is a classic text, many people would identify it as *Dependencia y desarrollo en América Latina* by F. H. Cardoso and E. Faletto, written within ECLA between 1965 and 1967. The text is classic in the sense that it was the first clear, comprehensive, ambitious and rigorous attempt both to formulate the concept and to analyse a variety of dependency situations in Latin America. Intellectual ideas, however, are not private property, and the dependency concept did not spring fully armed from the head of a Zeus, but was part of an intellectual ferment to which many people contributed. This ferment was part of the general questioning of many of ECLA's basic assumptions about the development process, a questioning which in turn reflected the political and economic crisis in many Latin American countries. If one took the years 1967 to 1970, for example, one would find articles and books by such people as O. Sunkel, C. Furtado, T. Dos Santos and R. Mauro Marini which had the word 'dependency' in the title.[2]

In roughly the same period A. Gunder Frank's works, notably on capitalism and underdevelopment in Latin America, became well known. Confusingly, Frank himself introduced 'dependency' into some of the titles of his later works, and in English-speaking circles Frank was often taken to be the dependency theorist *par excellence*. Now there are many points of connection – not least links to the Marxist tradition, one the North American *Monthly Review* school,[3] the other more Latin American.[4] But Frank's focus has always been on the global history of capital accumulation, 'the need for the development of a theory and analysis adequate to encompass the structure and development of the capitalist system on an integrated world scale and to explain its contradictory development which generates at once economic development and underdevelopment'.[5] Outside of his polemical excursions with such catchy titles as 'Equating economic forecasting with astrology is an insult to astrologers', Frank's focus has consistently been the problem of world accumulation and the world system, as in *World accumulation 1492–1789, Dependent accumulation and underdevelopment, Crisis: in the world economy*, and *Crisis: in the Third World*.[6] The Latin American dependency writers, on the other hand, focus much more on the concrete analysis of historical and contemporary dependency situations in a variety of nation states. Dependency writers attempt to give the view from the underside of the process of capital's international expansion. So although there are many connections between Frank and dependency writers, it is perhaps more useful to place Frank with I. Wallerstein[7] and S. Amin.[8] All three emphasize dependent accumulation, but they are concerned to place it within a world system which is not really analyzed as such by dependency writers of the Latin American school.

The world system writers are difficult to locate, partly because their ambitions and far-reaching synthesis of world development have an underlying theory which is often sketchy and imprecise. There are, of course, differences of approach and analysis between Frank, Wallerstein and Amin. Nevertheless, all three insist that the processes of accumulation and development must be analysed on a world scale. This process, they argue, does not create an even, homogeneous development pattern; but rather it divides the nation states into different broad categories. For Frank 'it is capitalism, both world and national, which produced underdevelopment in the past and which still generates underdevelopment in the present'.[9] For Wallerstein, 'capitalism and a world economy (that is, a single division of labour but multiple politics) are obverse sides of the same coin',[10] and the capitalist world system is divided into core, semi-periphery and periphery states. In Wallerstein, state power is an essential means for transferring surplus from the periphery to the core. Amin lays stress on unequal specialization as being essential for the creation of the structure of peripheral capitalism: 'From the start the transition of

precapitalist formations integrated into the world system is a transition
not to capitalism in general but to "peripheral" capitalism.'[11]

Both Wallerstein and Frank tend to see monopolistic exchange as the
key to the emergence and development of a world system, and the
core/periphery bipolarity. Amin follows a more orthodox mode of production analysis, and relates the existence of peripheral capitalism to the
developments of the five main modes of production. Of these five, one,
the tribute-paying mode of production, is original to Amin. He argues
that capitalism emerged from peripheral feudalism which, in turn, was
an offshoot of the three central tribute-paying formations, China, India
and Egypt, and with the development of capitalism the former periphery
becomes 'core' and develops a world system in which core capitalism
blocks the full capitalist development of the new periphery, leaving
complex patterns of pre-capitalist modes as part of 'peripheral
capitalism'.

Amin has many useful insights into the process of the social formations
of the Third World. He also attempts a more theoretically informed
account of world accumulation than the more descriptive historical
generalizations of both Frank and Wallerstein. Nevertheless, Amin's key
theoretical account of unequal specialization based on the development
of productivity, and his analysis of wage structures, profits and surplus
absorption, are unconvincing. So even with Amin it is his insights into
historical generalizations, particularly those on class structures and
modes of production in peripheral countries, which are the most useful.

These historical generalizations have been subject to many criticisms.
Perhaps the most important is that Frank, Wallerstein and Amin exaggerate the historical importance of the Third World for the development
of capitalism in the advanced capitalist countries. Brenner, in particular,
has argued (following Marx) that capitalism has a dynamic internal to
itself which develops its forces of production through technological
development, increased productivity and profits based on relative, not
absolute, surplus value.[12] And P. K. O'Brien has argued that the size of
the surplus extracted from the Third World was largely irrelevant; 'the
"world economy", such as it was, hardly impinged . . . for the economic
growth of the core, the periphery was peripheral'.[13] These are substantial objections. But what of the obverse? Did primitive disaccumulation make a transition to capitalism in the Third World historically
problematic? It would be romantic to assume that autonomous paths for
most of the Third World would have developed their forces and relations
of production. But it is also clear that classical Marxist and neo-classical
assumptions about the impact of advanced capitalist nations on the
Third World were naïvely optimistic. Particularly in an analysis of the
Third World's historical formation, a world system framework seems
essential. For Third World nations the development of capitalism

largely came from the outside. 'The key variable was the emergence of capitalism as the dominant form of social organization of the economy. Probably we could say that it was the only mode in the sense that other "modes of production" survived in function of how they fitted into a politico-social framework deriving from capitalism.'[14] Now whether production/internal class relations are more important than how the world system creates and develops these is a substantive and not a semantic debate. Too often the criticisms of Frank and Wallerstein, in particular, as 'circulationist' rely on Marxist definitional points, when what is at issue is the analysis of historical processes and not the definition of concepts.[15]

The dependency writers have a much more modest aim. They take the world system largely as given, and analyze the specific impact of that system on local, usually ruling-class, formations. Too often this more modest, but no less important, aim was not appreciated.

Given the English bias of the English-speaking world, one problem was that, although published a decade earlier, *Dependencia y desarrollo en América Latina* was not translated into English until 1979, when the University of California Press translated the book under the title of *Dependency and development in Latin America* – an expanded and amended version of the Spanish text with an important new preface and post-scriptum. Meanwhile the dependency debate had spread around the world. It would be an interesting essay in the sociology of knowledge to trace the connections and links in this process of circulation, for particular interpretations, rather than original versions, seem to have played a key role in the spread of the concept. And all too often much of the debate concerned itself with a vulgarized version of dependency that had little to do with the classic text. Not surprisingly, just as Marx had to declare he was not a Marxist and had to attack those using 'a master key' of 'a general historico-philosophical theory, the supreme virtue of which consists in being super-historical',[16] so too did Cardoso have to distance himself from the mechanistic use of a master key, dependency, to romp through the complexities of Latin American history and its contemporary situation. Cardoso himself has given an account of some of the background to his work, simultaneously criticizing the 'consumption' of dependency which had rapidly built up its own momentum.[17]

One of the main reasons for the passion surrounding the debate on dependency theory has been the politically 'committed' stance of its principal proponents, who have set out to analyse the past and present in order to draw the kind of conclusions useful to those trying to change the future. Writers in the developed world have sometimes reacted violently to the whole school, disliking its assumption that capitalism – 'our' capitalism – has failed to develop the Third World in a satisfactory manner, and that existing relationships between developed and underdeveloped countries must be changed. On the other hand, those who share the basic political judgements of the dependency school may still want to rewrite it in terms of their own, slightly different, political programmes, dismissing other writers out of hand, not for reasons of intellectual clarity or coherence, but because of their suspicions about the 'really revolutionary' character of those involved. The dependency debate has taken place in the middle of a political minefield. But that does not mean that its writers are not serious social scientists, nor does it justify those who prefer exploding their own political passions to serious intellectual criticism, dismissing out of hand the serious work which has accumulated.

Dependency and development in Latin America is a dense and complex book which attempts to paint a broad canvas and to offer models of different varieties of dependency and their shifts over time, rather than detailed empirical evidence. Obviously the amassing and sifting of further evidence will modify and refine the models, and it may well turn out that the historical evidence contradicts some of the suggestions. If so, then the suggestions have to be modified. But it is unlikely that our ignorance of the broad canvas (although not of details) is so immense that the analysis of dependency situations will be refuted entirely on the grounds of historical evidence. Models are vital in our attempt to isolate the fundamental strands of historical causation, as opposed to the purely contingent factors (however important these may be), to our final understanding of historical events. The debate on dependency, therefore, has to concern itself with methodology and theory (hence all those long words), and with whether it is a useful or adequate approach for interpreting the Latin American social formation. In other words, *Dependency and development in Latin America* is concerned with interpretation, and can only be superseded by a better interpretation.

So where, about a decade and a half since the publication of the classic text on dependency, does the debate now stand?

Dependency refined

My first review of dependency literature, written in 1972 and one of the first critiques in English, claimed that *Dependencia y desarrollo en América Latina* 'is one of the most stimulating interpretative essays that has appeared for many years on the patterns of development in various Latin American countries'.[18] Three years later, in 1975, it was already necessary to classify the various strands within the dependency school.[19] Other English-speaking writers facing the same necessity to provide a review did likewise: Chilcote, Harding and Gabriel Palma being good examples.[20] But such classifications inevitably tend to rigidify a debate rather than develop its creative impulses, and, furthermore, they very clearly reflect the subjective criteria of the author of the critique. My own early classification was rightly criticized by C. Henfrey for over-emphasizing an author's declared political position rather than his method of reasoning.[21] Cardoso himself has poked some gentle fun at such popularizers, each of them seeking 'to locate his prophet', describe the prehistory of the 'dependency paradigm', and 'note the distinct ideological hues of the *dependentistas*'.[22]

So perhaps it is wise to steer clear of creating yet more pigeon-holes, and look at the development of the debate in the spirit of the classic text. Cardoso himself has emphasized that his work and those of others have been 'an endeavour to be *critical* and to maintain the *continuity* of previous historical, economic, sociological and political studies in Latin America'.[23] Dependency was seen as 'an attempt to revive Marxism with a new breath of life' by an effort 'to re-establish a tradition of analysis of economic structures and structures of domination that would not suffo-cate the historical process by withdrawing from it the movement which results from the permanent struggle among groups and classes'.[24] This commitment to the concrete historical process is worth remembering, given the attempt by some to hijack the concept, make it non-critical, and reduce it to a set of variables that can be subjected to statistical regressions. The dependency paradigm was originally developed to aid historical actors, not to displace them – like the original work of Marx himself – though there have always been self-styled Marxists who would prefer to recast it as a series of mechanistic formulae, and who have criticized the dependency school bitterly for its unauthorized departures from their sacred text.

That strand in the original which emphasized the dynamic and con-tradictory impact of multinational corporations on Latin American industrialization has been taken up by such works as P. Evans *Dependent development. The alliance of multinational, state and local capital in Brazil*; Rh. Jenkins *Dependent industrialization in Latin America* and *Transnational corporations and Latin American industry*; R. Newfarmer *Transnational conglomerates and the economics of dependent development*, and the many publications from the Instituto Latinoamericano de Estudios Trans-nacionales.[25] All of them demonstrate very clearly that Cardoso's original paradigm of modern 'dependent development' can be used to treat a specific area not only with adequate sophistication, but in great empirical depth.

Others have tried to fill in the gaps. One of the standard criticisms of Cardoso and Faletto has been the lack of attention they pay to labour. H. Spalding has attempted to remedy this weakness by providing a detailed analysis of urban workers in dependent societies, in his *Organized Labor in Latin America*,[26] and he and others have done much to illuminate the role played by international trade union organizations in asserting the metropolis's control. But, although some excellent studies have appeared, this area remains inadequately analyzed, and the consequences of dependent economic structures in terms of working-class formation and politics at the national level, as opposed to its local relations with foreign enterprises, still need to be properly explored. The exploration, for example, in *Las clases sociales en América Latina*[27] does little more than clear some of the ground.

In Latin America itself all of the original (that is post-1967) contributors to the dependency debate have refined and updated some of their original positions – writers such as T. Dos Santos, V. Bambirra, R. Mauro Marini, A. Quijano and C. Furtado – as indeed has F. H. Cardoso.[28] O. Sunkel, himself one of the original formulators of the concept of dependence, helped organize a project at the Institute of Development Studies at Sussex University examining situations of dependency across a wide range of countries and situations: the book edited by José Villamil, *Transnational capitalism and national development: new perspectives on dependence*,[29] gives a useful perspective on some of the results.

A clear, sympathetic review of much of the recent dependency literature can be found in R. Munck's comprehensive survey, 'Imperialism and dependency: recent debates and old dead ends'.[30] He has highlighted two new and original contributions to the debate – by Salomón Kalmanovitz, and Bernardo Sorj and Leo Zamosc.[31] Independently of each other, both introduced the problematic of the reproduction of dependent structures. Kalmanovitz takes up the idea, surely basic to all dependency writers (though with some implicit rather than explicit), that a dependency situation implies that the dependent country lacks the control to develop an internal circuit of capital accumulation. Using Marx's schema of reproduction, and inserting circuits of capital into an international circuit, both Kalmanovitz for Colombia and, particularly, Sorj and Zamosc for El Salvador, open up the possibility of insights into the subsumption of non-capitalist relations of production as well as those of dependent capitalism to the dynamic of world capitalist expansion. These two contributions are still basically economistic. As Munck says, the 'full political, ideological and social determinants remain to be incorporated'.[32]

Measured against the classic text, there are thus few comparable works in breadth of scope and in that basic ambition 'to re-establish a tradition of analysis of economic structures and structures of domination that would not suffocate the historical process'[33] nor reduce it to a mechanistic formula beyond the struggle of classes and groups. There are even fewer which attempt to deal with the kind of historical sweep of *Dependencia y desarrollo en América Latina*, outside the rather more formal analyses of the world system writers, which often seem bewildered by the significance of human activities on a more local scale. In Latin America,

Pablo González Casanova has edited an invaluable collection of essays, *América Latina, historia de medio siglo*, to which he offered a separate introductory book, *Imperialismo y liberación en América Latina*.[34] Both books have their valuable points, but they remain essentially descriptive, and do not achieve the diachronic and synchronic synthesis within a unified vision that gives *Dependencia y desarrollo en América Latina* its special quality. In the USA, Chilcote and Edelstein edited another collection, *Latin America: the struggle with dependency and beyond*,[35] with a lengthy introduction setting out the editors' view of the dependency model. But in practice, the national studies of which the bulk of the book is composed scarcely take up the problems raised, and tend to lose the clarity of Cardoso and Faletto's models in a wealth of detail on political movements. Subsequent theorists have found it extraordinarily difficult to manage that combination of theoretical model with attention to the idiosyncracies of the historical process, to see social classes as both the inevitable creations of an international capitalist system and as political personæ in their own right, which Cardoso and Faletto certainly managed, at least in the case of the Latin American bourgeoisie.

Perhaps the only really comparable work to that of Cardoso and Faletto is the ambitious essay by A. Cueva, *El desarrollo del capitalismo en América Latina*,[36] which is probably the most self-consciously Marxist text on this theme. For Cueva attempts to apply to Latin America some of Marx's thoughts about the transition to capitalism. But the application is only partial. What is needed is a creative reformulation of the whole of Marx's social circuit of capital, with each relationship having its own history. For example, one needs an historical explanation of the creation of 'free labour' in Latin America and its subsequent and perhaps only partial conversion into abstract labour power, as an immense variety of *campesinos* were dispossessed, retained or thrust off the land and reintegrated into the *sui generis* patterns of a Third World society, all within the framework of a specific state playing its own role within an international circuit of capital. The task is of course immense, but anything less may provide the odd insight but not the coherent whole.

Cueva, for example, emphasizes the 'primitive disaccumulation' of the colonial period, but without showing why it blocked the development of industrial productive forces thereafter. He takes up Marx's central concern with the appearance of free labour as the essential precondition for a transition to capitalism, without providing a convincing explanation for the stubborn persistence of pre- and non-capitalist relations of production alongside the new social patterns. Cueva would argue that the transition to capitalism in Latin America was slow and conservative, arriving only from above, under the impact of imperialist penetration, and even then under the political hegemony of a curious alliance of local landed, large commercial and foreign capitalist interests, with no revolutionary implications for older social structures. But this conclusion is static: Cueva is correctly convinced that the classic view of capitalism as a revolutionary force does not work in the context of a dependent society, but he is still not able to rework the classical theoretical models in such a way as to explain this phenomenon.

Cueva is also quite right to focus on the specificities of the transition to capitalism, and indeed one could argue that it is precisely this focus which is lacking in Cardoso and Faletto. But in his work neither the theory nor the history of these specificities have been thought through. For example, Marx argued that merchant capital 'developing on the basis of an alien mode of production which is also independent of it'[37] is an obstacle to the development of capitalism. For the independent development of merchants, capital 'stands in inverse proportion to the economic development of society',[38] as it imprisons capital within the sphere of circulation. Cueva, however, states the position without being able to use it to illuminate either the functioning of the global system and the place of a dependent economy in it, nor yet the specific historical heritage and varieties of Latin American merchant capital, and its impact on the development of a skewed productive structure and a peculiar mosaic of social classes. Nevertheless, *El desarrollo del capitalismo en América Latina* does point in the direction a fuller Marxist analysis could take.

The critics

> Cannon to right of them
> Cannon to left of them
>   Tennyson

The relationship of the dependency perspective to Marxism has produced many articles. The Marxist pedigree or lack of it shown by Cardoso and Faletto has come under close scrutiny. Cueva himself has argued that there is no theoretical space within Marxism to locate a theory of dependency, although it is, he admits, a salient feature of Latin American societies.[39] Now what is true is that there cannot be separate laws of motion of dependent capitalism, because by definition such laws cannot be separate from those of capitalism in general. But it is a closed Marxism that denies the attempt to typologize dependency situations and advance theories about them.

The problem posed by 'dependency and Marxism' has particularly vexed US Marxists with a special interest in Latin America. The first issue of their journal *Latin American Perspectives* was devoted to 'dependency theory'. The theme has continued to dominate many subsequent issues – 'Dependency theory and dimensions of imperialism', 'Views on dependency' and in 1981 'Dependency and Marxism'. This last issue, whilst containing a number of individually good articles, shows the state of confusion the debate has reached in the USA – a confusion extending not just to dependency but also to Marxism.

Summarizing the main position papers in the journal, Chilcote says:

> Jack Edelstein and Dale Johnson offer strong defences, while other contributors agree that questions of dependency in the past have assisted students in the study of Latin America, but that a new focus is now necessary. David Barkin, for example, suggests that emphasis on the internationalization of capital is the most productive framework. James Diets and Norma Chinchilla support a mode of production analysis. Colin Henfrey is critical, but sympathetic to this mode of production analysis and insists on relating a theory of imperialism to exploited classes. James Petras places attention on class and state relationships. Thomas Angotti criticizes dependency theory as idealist and leading to reformist solutions. Thus, attention must be directed to the role of imperialism in underdevelopment. John Weeks also denounces dependency theory, calling for a theory of world economy that emphasizes capitalist accumulation on an international level. Gary Howe locates the genesis of dependency in seventeenth-century mercantilist thought, whereas Carlos Johnson traces the idealist and populist notions associated with dependency to the nineteenth-century Russian Narodniks.[40]

The absurdity of this hodgepodge seems to escape Chilcote. What does it mean to have Narodniks mingling with mercantilists, with idealists, with reformists, with classes and states, with imperialism, with internationalization of capital, with exploited classes, with the world economy? Different levels of analysis, complementary and contradictory concepts, are intermingled as if it were a meaningful discourse. This is not to say that many of the articles lack merit: Howe's article on 'Dependency theory, imperialism and the production of surplus value on a world scale' is a notable and original offering within the theory of imperialism. But the North American consumption of dependency has produced a curious phenomenon: some in the belly of the beast seem determined to set themselves up as the ideological police of any deviation from a supposed historical materialism that is somehow remote from much Latin American reality. Consequently, the debate has been marred not by genuine polemical writing which is inevitable in any debate that matters, but by the pillorying and caricature of positions. Carlos Johnson, for example, not without some justification, accuses dependency of being 'an interpretative wild card',[41] an ideological construct, in which the debate over a word becomes more important than the method of reasoning. Johnson then uses his own 'wild card' of 'class struggle' and 'the realm of capitalist and socialist history' to construct a hypothesis that the dependency theses represented the needs of local competitive capital in a struggle with monopoly capital over the accumulation of surplus value in national terms. He then further, and self-contradictorily, argues that the dependency theses are a variety of Narodnikism in that they postulate the impossibility of developing capitalist relations of production in Latin America, and especially the impossibility of attaining ideal levels of capitalist production and consumption – the stagnation thesis. It is, of course, the hallmark of the ideological policy to designate a theory as 'really representing the need of'.

But what does one make of the accusation that dependency writers postulate the impossibility of developing capitalism in Latin America when the classic text, that of Cardoso and Faletto, explicitly argues the opposite? And what does one make of John Weeks' summary: 'Dependency theory explains the rise of capitalism and the division of the world into developed and underdeveloped areas by surplus transfer; this uneven development is reproduced by the continuation of such transfers (in more "purely economic form"): the analytical space in which this occurs does not involve countries except by political accident; and predicted is the flow of capital from developed to underdeveloped areas.'[42] Weeks then demolishes all the above; and in the final cut, with reference to an earlier manuscript of his, he states that 'in fact the overwhelming amount of direct investment flows are among developed countries'.[43] What has this to do with anything outside of the concoctions of the author? Similarly strange concoctions, contradicting one another, abound in the pages of *Latin American Perspectives*; which is a pity, for many of the good points and articles tend to get submerged in a flurry of wild accusations.

In Europe the Latin American dependency debate was initially absorbed and transmitted by those working on Latin America, perhaps because its framework was primarily concerned to help analyze concrete situations in Latin America. Unfortunately what tended to get absorbed in the wider left-wing circles was an essentially vulgarized version of dependency or, even more confusingly, the world system writers seen as the dependency theorists. Thus in Britain the influential *New Left Review* was capable of highlighting in its March–April 1982 issue the supposed role of Bill Warren as the leading critic of the 'dependency' stagnation or regression thesis. In their view, 'Warren's *Imperialism – pioneer of capitalism* – the most comprehensive and radical attack on dependency theory by any Marxist – argued for the dynamic and transformative role of Western imperialism in promoting capitalism within the ex-colonial economies and societies.'[44] This, in spite of the fact that ten years earlier *New Left Review* had published an article by the leading Latin American dependency theorist, Cardoso himself, arguing for capitalism's dynamic and transformative role while simultaneously giving a sophisticated and far less misleading account of its contradictions.

Anthony Brewer, in his otherwise excellent *Marxist theories of imperialism: a critical survey*,[45] also places Frank, Wallerstein and the 'dependency theorists' together in one chapter. He criticizes dependency writers for asserting that the dominant countries enjoy independent (self-sustaining) development, whereas throughout the world system one is dealing with relations of interdependence and dominance. He also criticizes them for focusing on the purely economic constraints imposed on dependent countries by the narrowness of their internal markets, balance of payments problems and technological dependence. Dependency writers would agree that these constraints are real. But Brewer's criticisms are misplaced. Dependency writers themselves argue that nations are now interdependent: their point is that this interdependence is a structurally unequal relationship. And their own original contribution is to bring into focus the consequences of this global pattern for internal class formations in the dependent nations. Brewer and the dependency writers are fighting the same battle: he would do better to pick up their new material.

The death of Bill Warren in 1978 deprived British Marxists of a stimulating and controversial writer. Warren was nothing if not a gadfly of many on the left in Britain. In a series of hard-hitting articles he attacked many conventional left positions on such topics as the EEC, Ireland, multinationals and the state. Warren's most influential writings were, however, on the problems of imperialism. In 1973 *New Left Review* published his 'Imperialism and capitalism industrialization',[46] which argued the case for the progressive role of the multinational companies in industrializing the Third World. This theme was taken up and developed in Warren's sadly influential book *Imperialism – pioneer of capitalism*.[47] A perceptive commentator, D. Seers, noticed the similarity between many of Warren's Marxist positions and those of the Chicago School of economists, and gleefully, but unjustly, pointed out that this was not too surprising as both Marxist and Chicago economists came out of the same intellectual stable.[48]

In spite of a number of valid polemical points scored off writers on imperialism and left developmental theorists, Warren's book represents a retrogressive step. Nevertheless, it is a serious book: he does, for example, give a detailed and fairly accurate account of some of the Latin American dependency views. His criticisms therefore have the virtue of tackling real writers rather than his own concoctions. These criticisms involve a series of substantial points which, if valid, would make dependency writers both empirically and theoretically wrong. With Warren one has come full circle. Cardoso and Faletto were concerned to criticize the approach of Rostow and the assumptions of a simple dichotomy between traditional and modern societies. Now in the name of a pure Marxism, Warren wants to attack the very bases of these criticisms as being romantic nationalism, at variance with reality, and not even posing the right questions.

Warren makes thirteen points in his criticism of dependency, which can be boiled down to two. First, there is a process of reciprocal interdependence with both centre and periphery influencing each other, within which dependence is declining as the geographical distribution of world economic power shifts in favour of Less Developed Countries (LDCs). Within this process the possibility of autonomous development increases as, for example, a strong LDC state can play one MNC off against another, integrating them into its own development priorities. Second, dependency assumes that there are latent suppressed historical alternatives which were somehow stifled because of external imposition – even if this imposition was mediated through internal social forces. Worse, it assumes that these alternatives might have entailed more autonomous and better development patterns.

Both elements in this critique have in fact been answered convincingly by Cardoso himself. Increasing interdependence alters the structural, not just conjunctural, power relation, as any debtor/creditor knows, and as one of the most advanced newly industrializing LDCs, Mexico, is discovering. To see LDC states integrating MNCs is to retrogress from Cardoso's more subtle analysis of the local pact of domination in, for example, Brazil between MNCs, state managers (military and technocracy) and local big capital. Warren effectively exempts MNCs from the usual Marxist rules of class analysis. Unlike local capital they do not seem to have any form of political representation within the local state. But we know from specific studies on Brazil itself that their political representation in LDCs is not only real, but often crucial in determining what strategy of development local governments adopt. This can be seen, for example, in Brazil in MNCs role in organizing the 1964 military coup,[49] and more generally their role in creating the continental model of the 'new authoritarianism'.[50] Long before Warren, Cardoso pointed out that such an alliance can produce rapid industrialization. Unlike Warren, he pointed out some of the immense costs and contradictions involved: the pressure, for example, to maintain by force an exceptionally skewed pattern of income distribution, in order to provide a dynamic market, however small, for the kind of goods the MNCs produce. The 'new authoritarianism' satisfied their needs. Warren's second point – there is no real alternative – is a return precisely to the worst forms of mechanistic and cynical Marxism, which 'suffocates' the historical process, as Cardoso has put it.

Warren's two criticisms reflect his central thesis: a refutation of the notion that imperialism is, and has been, a retrogressive force impeding or distorting Third World development. Not only does he attempt to refute this notion; he also wants to argue the opposite. To maintain this thesis Warren himself is forced to commit two cardinal sins. One is the simple reduction of everything to the crudest economism. Hence all his cheap jibes at those who do attempt to act as a force for change, even minimal change – nationalist and populist movements, movements for women's rights. What is has to be for the best: reductionism is mirrored in his panegyric to the all-embracing virtues of the expansion of capitalism over the globe. 'Capitalism and democracy are . . . linked virtually as Siamese twins'; 'the colonial record, considering the immense numbers of people involved, was remarkably free of wide-spread brutality',[51] and so on.

His other error, which flows from a similarly crude understanding of the realities of the Third World, is his assumption that imperialism not only introduces capitalist relations of production but also homogenizes the production process in terms of a cohesive, and generally beneficial, social circuit of capital. Even Warren is forced to recognize that the empirical record shows some distortions in this process. However, in his hands, the seamy and bloody underside of capitalist accumulation in the Third World becomes a temporary price for progress. LDCs are lagging behind: imperialism will speed up their advance. Meanwhile the problems of marginality, cheap female and child labour, even prostitution, are functional to the Moloch of Progress. With friends like Warren who needs enemies!

The 'suffocation' of history, indeed many of Warren's 'Marxist' points, are at bottom identical with more conventional right-wing criticisms of dependency. One of D. C. M. Platt's criticisms of dependency, for example, consists of assessing that for nineteenth-century Latin America 'there was no genuine alternative'.[52] Platt's works have the merits of a meticulous compilation of archival material concerning facts and figures.[53] However, as interpretation, they show a number of weak-nesses reflecting Platt's unwillingness to understand, or perhaps take seriously, attempts to theorize. Platt argues, for instance, that because British economic interests in nineteenth-century Latin America were constrained, given that the Latin American countries were politically independent, control was severely limited. This undoubtedly has some truth. But in whose interest were the economies of Latin America run? The market and free trade always work best when they are seemingly impersonal and neutral, and not ostensibly subject to political controls in their favour. Platt never really asks himself how, or in whose interests, 'the rules of the game' are maintained. His assumption is always that these rules are natural, and therefore for the best. Although Platt's views have evolved, he fails to recognize that men and women have always struggled to change the course of some event. They may not succeed, and one of the tasks of an historian or social scientist is to understand why sometimes they do and sometimes they do not. It is ironic that one of the theorists who placed most emphasis on the importance of human action to bring about change, Marx, has been dubbed a 'determinist', whilst those who defend the status quo can argue that things could not have developed, realistically in any direction other than they did,[54] and believe themselves to be upholders of free choice against believers in the iron laws of history.

Platt's first tilt at windmills consisted in constructing that convenient rhetorical device, the straw man.[55] Dependency, in this view, was a simple conspiracy theory which claimed that the wicked foreigner determined, dominated and exploited everything in Latin America. As an historian (a favourite phrase), Platt was able to proclaim that the emphasis on the importance of external trade, finance and investments (that is, the foreigner) was empirically wrong. Dependency defeated, QED.

In his second tilt at windmills, Platt claims he was of course 'aware that dependency theory, except in its crudest manifestations, does not imply a simple, direct conflict between nationals ("goodies") and foreigners ("baddies")' but is 'rooted in coincidences of interests between local dominant classes and international onces'[56] (a quote from Cardoso and Faletto). Nevertheless Platt still concentrates his objections on Argentina's golden export growth period, as if he were still refuting the simple formula of dependency = external domination = stagnation. For he goes on to make a general claim that dependency 'gets its history so profoundly wrong'.[57] Two assertions are made to back this statement. The first is that 'after the 1820s Spanish America abandoned (and was abandoned by) world markets for half a century'.[58] The second is that 'substantial and enduring links [with external economies] developed only during the last decades'[59] of the nineteenth century and even then domestic resources were important. Now these points may both be true: but both were already incorporated in the classic text on dependency published in 1969 – in a model possessed of infinitely greater sophistication. Cardoso and Faletto, for example, argue in their chapter on 'the period of outward expansion' that after independence 'conditions for establishing new ties with the outside were not positive' . . . that 'there was no substantial capital investment from Great Britain or Europe in newly independent Latin America', that 'to gain strength and improve trade links with the outside was a very difficult task in the first half of the nineteenth century'.[60] Similar statements abound in Furtado and Sunkel and Paz.

Cardoso and Faletto then go on to claim that in the later nineteenth century 'the Latin American countries were linked to the international market through a variety of products . . . It is interesting to note that these products could still be developed with national capital and that there were sufficient local resources to finance diversified and large-scale undertakings.'[61] However, towards the end of the nineteenth century some countries had the production of their minerals taken over by foreign firms, and Cardoso and Faletto give examples of the 'loss of control of the export sector by the national bourgeoisie' and the formation of 'enclave economies', contrasting this with situations of 'national control of the production system'. Indeed, with Argentina in mind, this is one of the substantive points Cardoso and Faletto are trying to make (against, for example, Baran) when they write that 'the existence of an important "bourgeoisie" sector was a distinctive feature of societies where production was under national control. In this type of society an expanding capitalist sector that organized output, part of marketing and in some countries, internal financing of the economy assured the formation of a national state . . . In this type of country, a national bourgeoisie was created.'[62] (Similar points, although with less emphasis on both the political factors and the political consequences, are made by Furtado and Sunkel and others.) Cardoso and Faletto go on to contrast the Argentine-type model with that prevailing in Central American 'enclave economies': Platt's history cannot encompass that kind of complexity.

To try and refute analyses of different dependency situations by concentrating solely on the period when Argentina's growth had a relatively stable duration of local accumulation, which it has never really enjoyed since, is methodologically untenable. To ignore the subtleties introduced by dependency writers when dealing with internal/external relations in different historical periods reveals a bias which conservative historians like to imagine they do not possess in their 'objective' pursuit of facts. When Professor Platt introduces his 'facts' 'as an historian', what precisely does he have in mind?

Other criticisms have involved subjecting 'dependency' to statistical tests. There is of course nothing wrong with such tests, and indeed useful empirical observations and correlations have emerged from them. Interestingly, the results of such tests, while very variable, have usually been fairly positive to some of the dependency postulates. A useful and not unsympathetic summary of some of these statistical tests, with a clear account of their assumptions, can be found in the summary by the Yale University team's S. Jackson et al. 'An assessment of empirical research on *dependencia*'.[63] Lawrence Alschuler's book *Predicting development, dependency, and conflict in Latin America: a social field theory*[64] is also positive in terms of the results he obtained by applying field theory statistically to some of the hypotheses put forward by dependency writers.

The problem, however, with these increasingly sophisticated tests is that it is difficult not to turn dependency into a formalistic, nonhistorical concept in which the historical process itself disappears. The usefulness or otherwise of the dependency concept does indeed depend on historical evidence, but such evidence has to be rich enough to encompass the dialectical movement of social classes and groups – which is after all one of the salient points dependency writers wish to emphasize.

The classic text: theory and concepts

Empirical observations must in each separate instance bring out empirically, and without any mystification and speculation, the connection of the social and political structure with production.

Marx, *The German Ideology*

The above brief examination, both of refinements to the original analyses of dependency situations and of the major criticisms of these analyses, shows that as an interpretative text, in terms both of the formulation of the concept and of the analysis of concrete situations, *Dependency and development in Latin America* has not been superseded. Serious students of dependency situations therefore have to return to this classic work. The original is still best.

Cardoso and Faletto regard themselves as working within the Marxian tradition. It is perhaps useful to see this tradition as three interrelated, but analytically distinct, aspects: the materialist conception of history, the theory of capitalist development, and the political project for socialism. Now, it is logically possible, while combining all three, to be useful on one and misleading on the others. Lenin's theory of imperialism, for example, may be misleading on, for instance, the export of capital, without invalidating his political analysis of workers' parties during the First World War – even though he himself saw them as connected.

Marx himself was sufficiently modest to describe his general method of analysis as 'the materialist conception of history'. By this he wished to emphasize that his was a method or approach and not a fully developed theory. But unfortunately, particularly from Stalin onwards, many Marxists converted the Marxist tradition into a 'science', which inevitably involved various 'isms' – historical materialism, dialectical materialism, or even scientific materialism. Marx did of course regard what he was doing as scientific. But his emphasis on a dialectical approach, on the logical historical method, on totality and on the historical nature of concepts, was always critical; and although he frequently, and understandably, made prognoses – such as the overthrow of capitalism – he usually refused to give any iron-clad guarantees concerning the future: and indeed how could he, given the emphasis he always placed on the importance of human action?[65] There was of course in Marx, as in nearly all nineteenth-century thinkers, a fascination with technical progress, and Marx at times slid into the mechanistic belief that technical progress led to social progress – take, for example, his belief that railways would revolutionize Indian society. This heritage of blind faith in the importance of developing 'the productive forces' (usually equated with crude indices of manufacturing production) has haunted certain Marxists, and still does, as can be seen in the later writings of Warren. Nevertheless, as long as technological determinism is avoided, an emphasis on the material conditions, the objective situation, is a healthy part of the Marxian tradition – precisely because it is so directly connected with political projects. The pessimism of the intellect is a healthy antidote to the more heady flights of voluntarism. Thus the accusation, frequently made by the more dogmatic Marxists, that Cardoso's and Faletto's concept of dependency is not 'revolutionary', that is, that its complexity may favour pessimism, does not by itself invalidate the concept. Nor indeed do the specific political positions Cardoso, in particular, may adopt necessarily make his analysis of the social formations of Latin America incorrect.

Moreover, even from the point of view of a holy script, Marx's work is very unfinished. Marx himself complained about those who wanted to change 'my sketch of the origin of capitalism in Western Europe into an historico-philosophical theory of Universal Progress, fatally imposed on all peoples, regardless of the historical circumstances in which they find themselves'. Marx's analysis of the importance of the expropriation of the peasantry, for example, is, as he emphasizes, 'explicitly restricted to the countries of Western Europe'.[66] Thus although Marx left a valuable tool-bag for understanding the dynamics of an 'ideal type' capitalism, as emerged in Western Europe, and some marvellous historical analyses, he clearly left no more than sketchy remarks on such major topics as classes, the state, the international economy and imperialism, and very little on nationalism ('the theory of nationalism represents Marxism's great historical failure').[67] Later writers have enriched and added to the body of Marxist theory. However, it should by now be clear, particularly after the disastrous experiences of Stalinist Russia, the dubious record of all regimes calling themselves communist, and failure of many Marxist prognoses concerning the development of capitalism (and even more disastrously the turning of prognoses into predetermined predictions which then have to be explained away because of 'betrayals' or whatever), that there is a crisis of Marxism. There are, and should never be, sacred texts. Nevertheless there is also no point in abandoning the Marxian tradition. That tradition is an invaluable guide for trying to understand historical processes, and it is a useful exercise to evaluate the analyses of dependency in the light of it. One should, after all, set high standards.

What then is the object of analysis, the methodology, theory and concepts employed by Cardoso and Faletto to analyze the concrete realities of Latin America? There has, of course, been an evolution in the thinking of Cardoso and Faletto, with respect to their original draft.[68] The preface to the English edition of their book is much more explicit about their proposed object of analysis and methodology than the earlier Spanish editions. It could be argued that what is explicit in 1979 was only partially so in 1969. But it is surely unfair to restrict criticisms to an initial position (as so many critics do with A. G. Frank, and thus ignore his later, and improved, writings). So this critique and appreciation will concentrate on the English edition of *Dependency and development in Latin America*.

The object of analysis, methodology, theory and concepts here proposed all place strong emphasis on the problem of the need to attain a dialectical, global and dynamic understanding of social structures in Latin America. Yet invariably in the sentence following such an emphasis Cardoso and Faletto stress that the basic aspect of such a task is 'to determine what forms the structures of domination will adopt'.[69] This changing focus is important because, although Cardoso and Faletto state that they are analyzing 'how social, political, and economic development are related in Latin America',[70] explaining 'exploitative processes' and 'the system of production and the institutions of appropriation' and 'the possibilities for change',[71] in practice all this is equated with analysing the 'process of domination through which existing structures are maintained'.[72] This is an important shift, and one which dominates the substantive analysis of the concrete situations.

In view of ECLA's own exclusive emphasis on economics, there may have been a case for bending the stick in the direction of the political; after all, as Cardoso and Faletto point out, ECLA's critical view of comparative advantage managed to avoid an analysis of social processes, imperialism and classes. But for the political economy tradition which Cardoso and Faletto claim to represent, an exclusive emphasis on domination is strange and somewhat paradoxical.

It is somewhat paradoxical given that their key concept, dependency, is meant to help explain class formations and domination. Cardoso and Faletto define dependency thus: 'a system is dependent when the accumulation and expansion of capital cannot find its essential dynamic component inside the system'.[73] In a later article Cardoso explained this as follows: 'the production goods sector (Department I) which is the centre pin of accumulation in a central economy does not develop fully'.[74] Thus though all economies nowadays are highly 'interdependent', this interdependency is not equal, for peripheral economies do not have capital goods sectors strong enough to ensure continuous advance, in financial, technological and organizational terms, so they have to obtain them elsewhere and face rules of domination. Whereas developed capitalist countries face rules of competition, underdeveloped countries face, and have always faced, rules of domination. Dependency therefore is introduced to emphasize the difference between a developed capitalist nation and an underdeveloped one, and hence, presumably, the way in which internal relations of dominance express themselves differently in each case.

Both Cardoso and Faletto emphasize that they are not proposing 'a theory of dependent capitalism' because by definition there cannot be such a theory without some treatment of the global dynamics of capitalism. They are, they state, referring to 'situations of dependency'. This is a valid point if they wish to emphasize that there is no simple unilinear theory applicable spatially and temporarily, and that what are important are 'concrete analyses of concrete situations' (Lenin). But Cardoso and Faletto are being excessively evasive – the frequent criticisms made of their open-endedness, a virtue, can justifiably be made of a certain evasiveness and even slipperiness in their writings – in maintaining that all they are doing is proposing a series of empirical analyses giving specificity and bringing up to date 'the analysis of a general economic theory of capitalism'. For the very concept of dependency must cast doubt on that general economic theory as it has usually been propounded. The concept of dependency was introduced precisely because the theories of imperialism were considered inadequate. For these theories not only failed in their explanation of the dynamics of capitalist expansion (for instance, Lenin's 'last stage of capitalism', 'overripeness'), but also, and more crucially for dependency writers, they failed in their analysis of both the political and economic consequences of the expansion of capitalism in imperialized countries.

There is of course no preordained reason why a developed capitalist country cannot slip into the category of underdeveloped nor an underdeveloped one become developed. What is unlikely, however, is a process of convergence, a global shift in economic power to the LDCs as a whole, which is Warren's thesis. There may be conjunctural shifts for a whole group because of favourable monopoly prices, for example in the case of the oil-exporting countries – conjunctures not unknown in the history of LDCs. But evidence of a structural shift even among the newly industrializing LDCs remains unconvincing.

This is really the heart of the argument. One could well argue that the rules of capital accumulation which have prevailed in developed capitalist countries are now in the process of breaking down. Nevertheless, since the end of the Second World War the process of capital accumulation, the totality of the social circuit of capital in developed capitalist countries as a whole, has operated within a pattern which some French Marxists have called 'central Fordism', by which they mean two interlinked phenomena: first, a mode of capital accumulation, a system of intensive accumulation combining a rise in labour productivity with an increase in per capita fixed capital (the technical composition of capital), and second, a continual adjustment of mass consumption to this increased productivity so that wage-earners, and through them virtually the whole of society, were integrated into the process of capital accumulation.[75] Naturally, central Fordism, Keynesianism and the social democratization of all workers' parties went together.

It is this pattern which many people mean when they talk about industrialization or even development. And this was clearly behind ECLA's views of the potential role of industrialization in Latin America. It would be dangerous to idealize a package with such a brutal exploitative underbelly. Nevertheless as a process, and particularly when compared to the real experiences of the USSR and Comecon countries, it had its attractions.

The question remained: could such a 'central Fordist' package be exported to the Third World or even, if this was unrealistic, could the processes of establishing such a package be exported? Contrary to Warren, it seems this was never exported as a package to under-developed capitalist countries. Their lack of a Department I meant that their integration into the social circuit of capital was only partial, and they were unable to integrate mass consumption into their internal social circuit even when, as in Brazil, intensive accumulation did lead to the mass production of technically sophisticated goods for the internal market. Capital, therefore, has never been constantly expanding value internally in the Third World. This is not to deny the rapid growth of local capitalism in some LDCs. Such a growth, largely financed through foreign debt, has indeed taken place and has dramatically altered the political, social and economic situation in these countries. It is precisely on the analysis of these situations that the 'new dependency' theory has focused – for this pattern of accumulation, this rapid development of the forces of production, does not imitate the patterns of the centre. Both the dissolution of the old and the reconstruction of the new in the periphery remain highly fragmented. Hence, to return to Cardoso's and Faletto's concern, the internal relations of dominance are different.

But having reached the nub of the problem, and having indicated its essence, Cardoso and Faletto back away from analyzing in depth the ways in which the rules of domination have operated, and the whys and wherefores of their changes in relation to the key concept of dependency. For having defined dependency, Cardoso and Faletto then correctly observe that, for rules of domination to operate effectively, internal allies are needed to operate them. Thus any analysis of dependency situations requires a dialectical analysis of the relationship between the internal and the external. 'We conceive the relationship between external and internal forces as forming a complex whole whose structural links are not based on mere external forms of exploitation and coercion but are rooted in coincidences of interests between the local dominant classes and on the other side are challenged by local dominated groups and classes.'[76] Thus there is a need to 'elaborate concepts and explanations able to show how general trends of capitalist expansion turn into concrete relations among men, classes and states in the periphery',[77] that is, a methodological movement from an abstract style of analysis into a concrete form of historical knowledge. This indeed is an admirable statement. But in practice Cardoso and Faletto apply neither their key concept of dependency, nor the general methodology proposed, to their analysis of the general social formations of Latin America. For the nature of Department I goods in the world system, and in turn the lack of them, has consequences for the rules of domination both internally and externally.

One would thus have expected Cardoso and Faletto to analyse these changes in relation to different periods in the social formations of Latin America. Instead they return to domination as being political, and concentrate on groups and classes and their factions in the pact of domination at the level of the state, linking this to changes in some characteristics of the system of production. This seems to be what C. Henfrey is getting at (somewhat obscurely) when he writes, 'Cardoso and Faletto do nothing to theorize this dominance (or dominances) of the political in the history of dependent social formations . . . In effect, the internal becomes the political – as opposed to the primarily political expression of latently economic variables – and the external the economic.'[78] But Henfrey's point is obscure because in his article he does not focus on Cardoso's and Faletto's key concept of dependency, but instead concentrates on the less crucial issues of the stagnation theses – less crucial because the debate should have been about the nature and causes of the cyclical patterns of both growth and crises.

There is nothing wrong with focusing on the political level nor, indeed, particularly given the history of Latin America, with concentrating on the concrete processes of domination. Such a concentration could still have used 'dependency' to bring out empirically the specificity of 'the connection of the social and political structure with production', as Marx argued, and to give a 'global and dynamic understanding of social structures'. But in Cardoso and Faletto the dialectical and contradictory process becomes too one-sided, and the specificity of changing class structures in Latin America becomes in practice varieties of ruling-class domination – leading to a focus not on class relations, but on the internal structures of the ruling class. This problem of class analysis is developed in the next section.

History as the past: the present as history

> The un- and anti-historical core of bourgeois thought appears in its most glaring form when we consider the problem of the present as an historical problem.
>
> G. Lukacs

Most historians tend to eschew explicit theory. This seems to be particularly true of Anglo-Saxon and Latin American historians who for different reasons tend to be conservative – although each includes in its number Marxist and radical historians.

This aversion to theories and models partly stems from the justifiable feeling that theories and models cannot cope with the complexity of historical reality. All models are abstractions, simplifications of reality. John Womack, for example, in his fine piece of historical writing, *Zapata and the Mexican Revolution*, claims, 'this is a study not in historical sociology but in social history. It is not an analysis but a story because the truth of the revolution in Morelos is in the feeling of it, which I could not convey through defining its factors but only through the telling of it. The analysis that I could do, and that I thought pertinent, I have tried to weave into the narrative, so that it would issue at the moment right for understanding it.'[79] But the facts, the story, the feeling necessarily relate one thing to another and therefore depend on theories, however implicit. Even with John Womack, the feeling of the Revolution in Morelos depends upon theories of rural class structure, the nature of power, mass social movements and resistance and so on.

But all too often the conservatism of historians hides an unwillingness to examine assumptions, and thus explicitly face up to the models and the views of society and change underlying those assumptions. The historical sociology approach, of which Cardoso and Faletto are supreme examples, tries to make explicit their theories and models. If too crude, models may convey the impression that they are imposing themselves on the infinite complexity of historical processes. But, if handled sensitively, as I have argued Cardoso and Faletto do, then models may illuminate and help interpret these complexities. I will leave it to historians to judge the accuracy or otherwise of Cardoso's and Faletto's historical 'facts': it would be useful for an historian who wants to object to show where they may be misleading. What is of concern here is the method of interpreting different dependency situations in Latin America. This method, the 'historical-structural' method, emphasizes 'not just the structural conditioning of social life, but also the historical transformations of structures by conflict, social movements and class struggles'.[80] In dependent social formations such as those of Latin America, structural conditioning and transformation require an understanding 'of the way internal and external structural components are linked' in which 'the external is also expressed as a particular type of relation between social groups and classes':[81] hence the emphasis on 'the internal manifestations' of dependency. This approach must be difficult to grasp if one comes to dependency with the prejudices of those who have always criticized its supposed emphasis on external factors.

Using this method, Cardoso and Faletto identify three essential dependency situations in Latin America. The first are enclave economies in which 'foreign invested capital originates in the exterior, is incorporated into local productive processes',[82] and the goods produced are sold in the external market. The second are nationally controlled economies in which a local bourgeoisie originates a process of internal capital accumulation, but in which the goods produced are realized in the international market. And the third is the case of dependent industrializing economies in which initial accumulation results from investments by multinational corporations (often using local funds for part of the investment), and in which a substantial part of the goods produced is sold in the internal market. These different forms of dependency situations imply different class formations, forms of state, ideologies and so on. Using the social circuit of capital concretely (and thus avoiding the misleading production and circulation debate), and from there analyzing the social classes and political context 'that allow or prevent the actualization of different forms and phases of capital accumulation',[83] is an approach that I have defended earlier as most promising.

Promising or not, it is an approach which *in practice* Cardoso and Faletto do not employ. Instead of building up a complex pattern of class and groups relations, state forms and regimes and ideologies based on the varieties of surplus production, extraction and appropriation in Latin America, Cardoso and Faletto offer illuminating characterizations, and at times brilliant insights, into the development of their dependency situations. Nevertheless these characterizations remain at the level of typologies drawn from empirical observation, rather than theoretical determinations. For example, the specificity of the production process, and hence the immense complexity of relations of production in Latin America, hardly appear. This is not just important for the formation and development of rural and urban working classes, but also for explaining domination itself. Even in the twentieth century the varieties of wage labour and non-wage labour not only pose problems for the formation of a national labour movement (hence the emphasis in Latin America on social movements), but also pose problems for a stable, hegemonic dominant-class rule. But posing the problem in terms of enclave and nationally controlled production dependency situations, it is difficult to understand the problem of the formation of a ruling class in Latin America.

Alavi, for example, has argued that the structural dynamics of dependent capitalism makes the formation of a ruling class unlikely.[84]

He claims that the specific situations of dependency lead to three separate dominant classes: landowning, local industrial bourgeoisie and metropolitan bourgeoisie, which coexist as competing, exclusive interests, without a structural contradiction. This lack of a ruling class in dependent capitalist nations allows the development of an overdeveloped, autonomous state whose practice is 'to maintain a system of domination' with relatively ineffective representative political institutions. Alavi's point may be over-schematized and somewhat static, but he does pose the problem of domination in relation to the structural characteristics of dependency and its consequences for class formations. Cardoso and Faletto hint at this, but do not really pose or analyze the problem.

This lack of analysis of class relations in *Dependency and development in Latin America* has been widely criticized.[85] Such a lack weakens the historical analysis; it is more damaging for the present as history where actual political practices are involved. Cardoso and Faletto, for example, emphasize that now 'what is specific in the Latin American situation of dependency is the difficulty in conceiving of a political passage to socialism by a strictly proletarian route, given the structural conditions of industrial capitalism in the periphery'.[86] However, they fail to analyse and even relate such a crucial point to their concept of dependency, so why such a view may or may not be valid is not specified.

It is noticeable that although written after the Cuban Revolution, *Dependency and development in Latin America* nowhere analyzes the Cuban experience. This experience is only mentioned in the post-scriptum. But the complexities of dependency situations in a world in which the socialist bloc and Cuba form a part are conveniently overlooked. Such an omission is damaging within the very concept of dependency, for the presence of such a bloc alters the rules of domination.

This failure to analyze any experience of radical change in dependent social formations may account for the deliberate vagueness concerning class and group movements and programmes for change in Latin America. Both the experience of achieving radical change in the Third World and the consequences of such change have been highly complex – and problematic for Marxists. Successful revolutions have by and large not followed the Russian Revolution, where the industrial proletariat did play a key role. Elsewhere the radicalized intelligentsia, not only as leaders but also as an important part of the cadres, together with *campesinos*, to use as neutral a term as possible, have been the main social force. Radical changes have achieved tremendous advances in education, health and basic necessities. There has been a break with an existing dependency situation as classically defined. (Those writers attempting to portray Cuba as having exchanged one dependency for another confuse the inability of a small, blockaded nation with a specific natural resource base to change that base in the short and medium run with the exploitative rules of domination of the prior dependency situation.) But the changes have also not dramatically increased levels of labour productivity. At best the changes have introduced a participatory political and social system, but hardly a democratic one; and at worst the participatory system has been replaced by an authoritarian, bureaucratic and repressive one. Faced with these complexities, Cardoso and Faletto tend to retreat to vague ideological appeals concerning the popular classes and the nation. The emphasis on the dominant classes and their internal conflicts is still really there. What is clear is that the assumption in Cardoso and Faletto that politics does not really require an analysis of the political economy of class relations is misleading – in its own way as misleading an assumption as the 'economism' of the Second International. *Dependency and development in Latin America* was and still is an invigorating breath of fresh air. It has major flaws, and can and should be criticized. But the baby should not be thrown out with the bathwater. Given a revival of a 'realistic productionist' Marxism as in Warren and others, then it is clear that the basic creative insights of the dependency framework have to be defended and advanced.

Notes

[1] José Carlos Mariátegui (1894–1930), described by Fredrick B. Pike, an anti-Marxist, as 'perhaps the only original Marxist thinker that Latin America has so far produced', played a key role in the theory and practice of the early formation of the Latin American communist movement. His major book, *7 ensayos de interpretación de la realidad peruana*, Biblioteca Amanta, Peru, was published in 1928. Mariátegui's role in the Peruvian general strikes of 1919 led to his exile to Europe. In Europe he met many of the European intellectuals of the left, and was in Italy at the time of the factory occupations of 1920 and the founding of the Italian Communist Party at Livorno in 1921. From 1923 onwards, on his return to Peru, Mariátegui was actively involved in the struggle of the Peruvian working class, and he played an important role in the establishment of the Peruvian Socialist Party. Like many 'classical' Marxist writers, Mariátegui combined 'theory and practice', and it was this which gave his writings a creativity lacking in later Marxist scholastics. An excellent brief summary of works by and on Mariátegui can be found in Harry F. Vanden 'Mariátegui: marxismo, comunismo, and other bibliographic notes' *Latin American Research Review* xiv 3 (1979).

The Argentine author, Sergio Bagú, has been considered by some as the father of dependency, in that his *Economía de la sociedad colonial*, El Ateneo, Buenos Aires 1949, expressed many of the later well known formulations on dependency.

[2] To take just some examples:
O. Sunkel's and P. Paz's useful and stimulating textbook, *El subdesarrollo latinoamericano y la teoría del desarrollo*, was published by Siglo xxi Mexico City, in 1970. This text was one of the most ambitious attempts to reinterpret Latin American underdevelopment from the colonial period onwards within a dependency framework. About the same time, Sunkel had been developing the concept of dependency in a series of articles, some of which appeared early on in English, e.g. 'National development policy and external dependence in Latin America' *Journal of Development Studies* vi 1 (1969), 'Capitalismo transnacional y desintegración nacional' *El Trimestre Económico* xxxviii 2 (1971). C. Furtado's *Teoría e política do desenvolvimento econômico* was published in 1967 by Editora Nacional, São Paulo,

Dialéctica del desarrollo in Mexico City in 1969. And his well known and popular *Economic development of Latin America* was first published by Cambridge University Press in 1970, translated from the original text *Formação econômica da América Latina*, published a year earlier. Numerous articles by Furtado were published in the same period, e.g. 'La concentración del poder económico en los Estados Unidos y sus proyecciones en América Latina' *Estudios Internacionales* 1 3 (1967/8) and 'Dependencia externa y teoría económica' *El Trimestre Económico* xxxv 2 (1971).

Rui Mauro Marini's book *Subdesarrollo y revolución* was published by Siglo xxi, Mexico City, in 1969. Theotónio Dos Santos published three of his works in 1969 and 1970: 'El nuevo carácter de la dependencia' in José Matos Mar (ed.) *La crisis del desarrollismo y la nueva dependencia* (Buenos Aires 1969), 'La crisis de la teoría del desarrollo y las relaciones de dependencia en América Latina' in H. Jaguaribe *et al. La dependencia político-económica de América Latina* (Mexico City 1970) and *Dependencia y cambio social* (CESO, Santiago 1970).

[3] The US journal *Monthly Review* has had considerable impact in Latin America, not least because for some time selections from it were published in Spanish and fairly readily available throughout Latin America. The writings of the three editors of *Monthly Review*, Paul Sweezey, Harry Magdoff and Leo Huberman, and a host of other people including Paul Baran, James Petras and A. G. Frank, were often published by Monthly Review Press and translated and distributed fairly widely throughout Latin America. The *Monthly Review* Marxist tradition has generally put a lot of emphasis on the importance of 'underconsumption' and the problem of the 'surplus'.

[4] The Latin American Marxist tradition has also been very eclectic, both politically and intellectually. It is not unusual to find a hodge-podge of contradictory theories and positions merged into a common discourse. Partly because of the speed with which foreign texts are translated into Spanish, the Latin American left has been able to draw on a variety of Marxist authors. Unfortunately at times this may have hindered rather than assisted the development of a Latin American Marxist tradition creatively analyzing the concrete situations of Latin America. Mariátegui was an obvious exception. And I would argue that the Marxist dependency writers are another exception. The eclecticism may still be there, but at least they attempt to use some Marxist concepts creatively in an analysis of Latin America.

[5] A. G. Frank *Capitalism and underdevelopment in Latin America: historical studies of Chile and Brazil* (New York 1967).

[6] A. G. Frank *World accumulation 1492–1789* (London 1978), *Dependent accumulation and underdevelopment* (London 1978), *Crisis in the world economy* (London 1981), *Crisis in the Third World* (London 1981), *Reflections on the world economic crisis* (London 1981).

[7] A useful summary of some of Wallerstein's definitions can be found in Immanuel Wallerstein 'The rise and future demise of the world capitalist system: concepts for comparative analysis' in his *The capitalist world economy*. His analyses are contained in I. Wallerstein *The modern world system* (2 vols, New York 1974–80), *The capitalist world economy* (Cambridge 1979).

[8] S. Amin's writings are voluminous. In addition to his empirical studies of Africa, he has written a number of major theoretical works including *Accumulation on a world scale* and *A critique of the theory of underdevelopment*, published as a combined two-volume study by the Harvester Press (Hassocks 1974). Much of this is also contained in S. Amin *Unequal development* (Hassocks 1976) and *Imperialism and unequal development* (London 1977). A useful summary of Amin's basic position can be found in 'The end of a debate', incorporated in the latter volume. Amin's methodology has been developed in S. Amin *The law of value and historical materialism* (New York 1978).

[9] Frank *Capitalism and underdevelopment*.

[10] Wallerstein *The capitalist world economy*.

[11] Amin *Accumulation on a world scale*.

[12] R. Brenner 'The origins of capitalist development: a critique of neo-Smithian Marxism' *New Left Review* no. 104 (1977).

[13] P. K. O'Brien 'European economic development: the contribution of the periphery' *Economic History Review* xxxv 1 (1982).

[14] Wallerstein *The modern world system.*

[15] In spite of many valid points, this remains largely true of the criticisms of Frank and Wallerstein in R. Brenner *op. cit.* and E. Laclau *Politics and ideology in Marxist theory* (London 1977).

[16] S. Avineri (ed.) *K. Marx on colonialism and modernization* (New York 1968).

[17] F. H. Cardoso 'The consumption of dependency theory in the United States' *Latin American Research Review* xii 3 (1977).

[18] P. J. O'Brien 'Dependency: the new nationalism?' *Latin American Review of Books* no. 1 (1973).

[19] P. J. O'Brien 'A critique of Latin American theories of dependency' in I. Oxaal *et al. Beyond the sociology of development: economy and society in Latin America and Africa* (London 1975).

[20] R. H. Chilcote 'Dependency: a critical synthesis of the literature' *Latin American Perspectives* (hereafter *LAP*) i (1974); T. H. Harding 'Dependency, nationalism and the state in Latin America' *LAP* iii (1976); G. Palma 'Dependency: a formal theory of underdevelopment or a methodology for the analysis of concrete situations of dependency' *World Development* vi (1978).

[21] C. Henfrey 'Dependency, modes of production and the class analysis of Latin America *LAP* viii 30, 31 (1981).

[22] Cardoso 'The consumption of dependency'.

[23] *Ibid.*

[24] *Ibid.*

[25] P. Evans *Dependent development. The alliance of multinational, state and local capital in Brazil* (Princeton 1979); Rh. Jenkins *Dependent industrialization in Latin America* (New York 1977), *Transnational corporations and Latin American industry* (London 1983); R. Newfarmer *Transnational conglomerates and the economics of dependent development: a case study of the international electrical oligopoly and Brazil's electrical industry* (Greenwich, Conn. 1980). The ILET publications appear in book form as coeditions of ILET and Editorial Nueva Imagen, Mexico.

[26] H. Spalding *Organized labor in Latin America: historical case studies of urban workers in dependent societies* (New York 1977).

[27] Instituto de Investigaciones Sociales, UNAM *Las clases sociales en América Latina* (Mexico 1973).

[28] For example, T. Dos Santos *Imperialismo y dependencia* (Mexico 1978); V. Bambirra *Teoría de la dependencia: una anticrítica* (Mexico 1978); R. Mauro Marini 'Las razones del neodesarrollismo' *Revista Mexicana de Sociologia* xl 4 (1978); F. H. Cardoso and José Serra 'Las desventuras de la dialéctica de la dependencia' *Revista Mexicana de Sociología* xl 4 (1978).

[29] José Villamil (ed.) *Transnational capitalism and national development: new perspectives on dependence* (Hassocks 1979).

[30] R. Munck 'Imperialism and dependency: recent debates and old dead ends' *LAP* viii 30, 31 (1981).

[31] S. Kalmanovitz 'Teoría de la reproducción dependiente' *Críticas de la Economía Política* ii (1980); Bernardo Sorj and Leo Zamoso 'La reproducción del capitalismo periférico: estructura y contradicciones' *Caderno do Departamento de Ciencia Política* 4 (1977).

[32] Munck *op. cit.*

[33] Cardoso 'The consumption of dependency' *op. cit.*

[34] Pablo González Casanova *Imperialismo y liberación: una introducción a la historia contemporánea de América Latina* (Mexico 1979), (ed.) *América Latina: historia de medio siglo* (Mexico 1977).

[35] R. Chilcote and J. Edelstein (eds) *Latin America: the struggle with dependency and beyond* (New York 1974).

[36] A. Cueva *El desarrollo del capitalismo en América Latina* (Mexico 1978).

[37] K. Marx *Pre-capitalist economic formations* (London 1978).

[38] *Ibid.*

[39] A. Cueva 'A summary of "problems and perspectives of dependency theory" ' *LAP* III (1976).

[40] R. H. Chilcote 'Issues of theory in dependency and marxism' *LAP* VIII 30, 31 (1981).

[41] C. Johnson 'Dependency theory and processes of capitalism' *LAP* VIII 30, 31 (1981).

[42] J. Weeks 'The differences between materialist theory and dependency theory and why they matter' *LAP* VIII 30, 31 (1981).

[43] *Ibid.*

[44] *New Left Review* no. 132 (1982).

[45] A. Brenner *Marxist theories of imperialism – a critical survey* (London 1980).

[46] B. Warren 'Imperialism and capitalist industrialization' *New Left Review* no. 81 (1973).

[47] B. Warren *Imperialism: pioneer of capitalism* (London 1980).

[48] D. Seers 'The congruence of Marxism and other neoclassical theories' in K. Q. Hill (ed.) *Towards a new strategy for development* (New York 1979).

[49] R. Dreifuss *1964: A conquista do estado* (São Paulo 1981).

[50] P. J. O'Brien 'The emperor has no clothes: class and state in Latin America' in O'Brien (ed.) *The state and economic development in Latin America* (Cambridge 1977).

[51] Warren *Imperialism: pioneer of capitalism.*

[52] D. C. M. Platt 'Dependency and the historian: further objections' q.v.

[53] D. C. M. Platt *Finance, trade and politics in British foreign policy, 1815–1914* (Oxford 1968), *Latin America and British trade, 1806–1914* (London 1972), (ed.) *Business imperialism, 1840–1930: an inquiry based on British experience in Latin America* (Oxford 1977), 'Economic factors in British policy during the "New Imperialism" ' *Past and Present* no. 39 (1968), 'The imperialism of free trade: some reservations' *Economic History Review* XXI 3 (1968).

[54] Platt 'Dependency and the historian: further objections' q.v.

[55] Platt 'Dependency in nineteenth-century Latin America: an historian objects' *Latin American Research Review* XI 1 (1980).

[56] Platt 'Dependency and the historian: further objections' q.v.

[57] *Ibid.*

[58] *Ibid.*

[59] *Ibid.*

[60] F. H. Cardoso and E. Faletto *Dependency and development in Latin America* (Berkeley 1979).

[61] *Ibid.*

[62] *Ibid.*

[63] S. Jackson 'An assessment of empirical research on *dependencia*' *Latin American Research Review* XIV 3 (1979).

[64] L. Alschuler *Predicting development, dependency and conflict in Latin America: a social field theory* (Ottawa 1978).

[65] This is, of course, an interpretation of the balance of Marx – an 'open' Marx. There are other interpretations of a 'closed' Marx with no shortage of quotations, not least Marx's own references, in his first preface to *Das Kapital*, to 'the natural laws of capitalist production . . . tendencies working with iron necessity towards inevitable results'.

[66] K. Marx and F. Engels *The Russian menace to Europe* (London 1953).

[67] T. Nairn *The break-up of Britain* (London 1982).

[68] This has been more noticeable in the case of Cardoso than of Faletto who, particularly since the Chilean coup of 1973, has tended to withdraw to his earlier interests in anarchism in Latin America.

[69] Cardoso and Faletto *op. cit.*

[70] *Ibid.*

[71] *Ibid.*

[72] *Ibid.*

[73] *Ibid.*

[74] F. H. Cardoso 'Som new mistaken theses on Latin American development and dependency', mimeo (October 1973).

[75] Cf. A. Lipietz 'Towards global Fordism?' *New Left Review* no. 132 (1982).

[76] Cardoso and Faletto *op. cit.*

[77] *Ibid.*

[78] Henfrey *op. cit.*

[79] J. Womack *Zapata and the Mexican Revolution* (London 1972).

[80] Cardoso and Faletto *op. cit.*

[81] *Ibid.*

[82] *Ibid.*

[83] *Ibid.*

[84] H. Alavi 'State and class under peripheral capitalism' in H. Alavi and T. Shanin (eds) *Introduction to the sociology of developing societies* (London 1982).

[85] Such criticisms have usually taken two forms. One is to criticize the emphasis on 'nation'. But given the fragmentation of a dependent capitalist society, is this emphasis misleading? The second criticism is to prioritize the 'experiences' to the working classes. Such experiences are crucial, but it is politically dangerous to do this without analyzing class relations and complementing any history 'from below' with one 'from above'. The material bases for particular experiences can be dramatically shifted, as in Pinochet's Chile.

[86] Cardoso and Faletto *op. cit.*

4

THE HEGEMONIC FORM OF THE POLITICAL: A THESIS

Ernesto Laclau

A Concepts and problems of a theory of hegemony

1 'Hegemony' is the basic concept of Marxist political theory. It is the key to understanding the dimensions and limits of the political, as well as the basic assumptions of socialist strategy.

This approach to the formulation of Marxist political theory, however, means a departure from a long tradition of interpreting politics and the state – running back to the Second International, or even before. The divergence stems from a number of preliminary theoretical decisions:

a) to eliminate class reductionism as the basic assumption of political theorizing;

b) to break with empiricist and rationalist conceptualizations of social class;

c) to adopt 'superdeterminism' and 'articulation' as basic concepts of political analysis;

d) for a fuller understanding of social antagonisms, to introduce the concepts of democratic and popular 'positionality'.

2 Class reductionism mainly results from three basic premises:

a) the view of a rigid separation between basis and superstructure;

b) the *overriding* identification of classes at the level of the basis, i.e. by their role in the production process, with clearly separate 'class interests' as a result;

c) the conviction that the forms of consciousness and political expression of social agents logically sprout from their own class nature.

Whether these 'superstructural' forms are defined as epiphenomena (as in classical economism) or as the highest instance in the process of class formation (Lukacs), class appurtenance remains a constant assumption in any approach.

There are only two conceptions where hegemony seems compatible with class reductionism:

a) in the notion of *class alliance*, where classes with diverging interests, ideologies and forms of organization, agree on common tactical and strategic objectives, and unite under the political leadership of one of the classes;

b) in the conception of a dominant class pervading society with its own ideas, values or forms of consciousness; in this case, hegemony is inseparable from the notion of 'false consciousness' with regard to the subordinate groups.

3 At the root of this reductionist view of society lies an empiricist assumption according to which classes correspond to social groups which are empirically *given*. If this were true, then of course the class character of all features and positionalities of the social agent would be a real tautology. The view is, however, hardly compatible with the identification of classes according to their role in the production process – as it derives the class identity of the agent from one of its positionalities rather than from all of them. Traditionally, this obstacle was removed by adding a rationalist dimension to the empirical analysis: that other features of the agent, such as family, the political, or ideology, are logically *derived* from his class position.

In this sense, defining class according to their economic positionalities is perfectly consistent with identifying them as social agents which are empirically given.

In practice, the empirical and rationalist conceptions of social classes are represented in a theoretical approach which regards them as *the ultimate units* of historical analysis, and which seeks to understand a social phenomenon by the way it is linked with certain social classes. (Well known examples are characterizations such as 'petty-bourgeois deformation', 'vices of feudal ideology'.)

4 The foregoing suggests that the notion of hegemony can hardly be approached with a reductionist version of Marxism.

If classes are viewed as constituted around specific and inalienable interests, and furthermore as organized on the basis of narrow 'cosmovisions', then the only type of relationship they are able to establish between them is some kind of alliance with precise objectives. But as soon as an alliance asserts a common identity or an ideology shared by the participating groups, then reductionism would brand the ideology as proper to the leading class of the alliance. Its adoption by part of the other class, therefore, can only represent a case of 'false consciousness'. (For example, nationalism has often been pictured as bourgeois ideology.) This reductionist focus cannot be upheld, as will be shown in summarized form in theses 5, 6, and 7. At the same time, we will attempt to provide the basis for an alternative approach, via the notion of hegemony.

The fundamental assumptions of this approach are as follows:

a) No automatic relationship between the different positionalities is implied. (For example, there is no necessary relationship between the worker's ideology in a family context, and his role in the production process.) By accepting this, the correspondence between social class and a group empirically *given* can be rejected – unless a class approach can only nominally be adopted.

This leaves two possible routes: on the one hand, to identify classes according to the economic positionalities of the agents. This requires alternative forms of conceptualization, based upon sets of articulations which embrace all positionalities, not merely the economic ones. On the other hand, social classes can be viewed as precisely these sets of articulations. This involves the conceptualization of social classes in a much more concrete and historical way than Marxism has produced until now. From a theoretical standpoint, both routes are equally valid.

b) The historic form of how the ensemble of positionalities is articulated in society is precisely what constitutes its hegemonic principle. And this hegemonic principle requires power and domination. Hegemony is therefore not an alliance between already constituted social agents, but it is the principle itself of the formation of these social agents. In as far as there are hegemonic transformations in society, the identity of the social agents also changes. This is the Gramscian principle of the *war of position*, which refers to the historical formation of the very social agents in their process towards becoming a state.

c) Therefore, the unit of the agent is not a unit *a priori*, but it is *superdetermined*, as a consequence of the historical articulation of a hegemonic principle.

d) Along this line of thinking, the starting-point of all concrete social analysis is to identify its hegemonic structures: it is only through this hegemonic principle, as the specific form of the articulation of positionalities, that the different social agents can be integrated.

5 As discussed, the hegemonic form of the political requires the disarticulation and rearticulation of the positionalities. Beyond the general form under which it presents itself, namely the war of position, we must now consider the specific conditions as well as the historical limits of politics based on hegemonic forms.

A first condition is that there must be a certain distance between different levels of social reproduction. This allows a margin of flexibility, and at the same time it creates possibilities of differential articulation between levels. For example, in a capital accumulation model with wages constrained at subsistence level, the hegemonization of wage demands cannot be part of the power discourse. By contrast, the social policy of Disraeli in England was hegemonic, as it succeeded in disarticulating a number of mass demands from the radical popular discourse where they had until then found expression. Next, the demands were rearticulated within an alternative conservative discourse. A similar approach can be observed with the social policy of Bismarck in Germany.

At the other extreme, a medieval peasant community reproduced itself on the basis of a very rigid articulation of positionalities, which precluded any reshaping or rearticulations. The hegemonic form of the political was absent. In fact, we have witnessed a progressive shift of social reproduction towards more hegemonic forms. This is because social reproduction came to rely less upon ancestral practices of simple communities, and more upon political decisions affecting society as a whole. So hegemony presupposes the growing primacy of the political in as far as it creates the conditions from social reproduction. In this sense, 'the political' refers to forms of articulation which allow a fair degree of flexibility. Consequently, the process of formation of the modern state should not only be seen as one of decision centres, embracing even larger communities, but also as the process of a growing distance between the material reproduction of society and the existential conditions of this reproduction. It is precisely this historical hiatus which the concept of hegemony seeks to explain. If the medieval peasant community represents the extreme form of social reproduction without hegemony, then the other extreme would be the myth of modern 'totalitarianism', a leviathan state capable of rearticulating all the aspects of life of a community.

But this capacity for rearticulation can only assume a hegemonic form if the process of articulation and rearticulation of positionalities takes place along *consensual* lines, i.e. as an objective process of the formation of new subjects. Thus, there are two possible limits to the hegemonic transformation in a given historical situation: on the one hand, there are areas in the life of a community which the hegemonic form has as yet left untouched; on the other hand, for the process of transformation to be really hegemonic (i.e. so that it operates by forming new subjects, rather than by pure and simple coercion), the historical rearticulations which are possible at a given moment will have to be taken into account. In fact, they must form a war of position. This highlights the serious problem we encounter when studying the state in Third World countries: the state has often assumed its form through the process of decolonization, following an external logic, and not as a response to the internal growth of centres of hegemonic decision. The state, therefore, is weak – as it possesses only a limited capacity to intervene in the process of social reproduction.

6 From the above remarks we can infer that the reformulation of Marxism in terms of a theory of hegemony requires two exercises: first, to analyze which positionalities were able to articulate

themselves so as to cause the historical transformation or hegemonic structurization of society; and second, to explain these articulations as concrete and superdetermined historical forms, and not as predictable links of a paradigm.

For example, it makes no sense to ask questions like: Was the revolution in Brazil in 1930 *the* democratic-bourgeois revolution? It is impossible to construct a paradigm 'democratic-bourgeois revolution' on the basis of an articulation similar to the experiences of some Western European countries. We do know that a transition to capitalism without democracy, or implicitly without bourgeois revolution, is perfectly possible.

On the other hand, the social, political and intellectual transformations which accompanied the transition to socialism in Europe are objective, superdetermined processes – not necessary instances in the unfolding of a paradigm. In a different historical context, different articulations and combinations of positionalities are possible. Moreover, concrete positionalities cannot be considered necessary instances of a paradigm, nor can they be attributed to predetermined stages of development.

Social analysis based on a theory of hegemony presupposes precisely this: that the same elements can be articulated in a different way. If this were not the case, i.e. if each element could be defined by its position in the paradigm rather than by its concrete historical articulation, then hegemony would merely amount to pure and simple domination. By the same token, the consensual forms could then be explained by the 'false consciousness' of the dominated subjects. Also, there would not be a *production of subjects* by way of hegemonic articulations, but only forms of integrative equilibrium between already constituted subjects.

7 We have posited that the production of subjects is realized through the articulation and rearticulation of positionalities. This suggests that hegemony is affected within the discourse.

For a good understanding of this statement, three precisions need to be made:

a) To suggest that hegemony is constituted within the discursive domain does not require a superstructural conception of society; it only means that each social practice acts as a *significant practice*, which is quite different from a process of mechanical causality. In this sense, the economic practice itself forms a discourse.

b) As each social practice is significant, an ensemble of connotative articulations is created, laying the basis for hegemony and transforming social agents into subjects. There are no historical subjects prior to the discourse.

c) Each differentiation of social levels takes place within the significant practices; it does not result from the differences between significant and insignificant practices. To attribute different types of causality to different levels of society is incompatible with any notion of ensemble.

8   Until now, our analysis has not taken account of the notion of hegemony. This is, however, a central issue, as each hegemony is in fact an articulation of positionalities in land ploughed with antagonisms. Hence, if every social practice is significant, then the antagonisms cannot be taken as a *given*, but they can be organized discursively to form specific 'differences'.

Our analysis of the notion of antagonism leads to the following conclusions:

a) every antagonism is a relationship of contradiction (not contrariety), created within the discourse;
b) the discourse of rupture is a discourse of *equivalences* through which democratic subjects are formed. Thus we can speak of *democratic positionalities*;
c) a discourse can establish democratic subjects as specific positionalities in a certain social domain; but it can also divide society over fundamental antagonisms between oppressor and oppressed. In this case, the latter become popular subjects, and we can speak of *popular positionalities*. The oppressors can try to neutralize the antagonisms by reshaping them as *differences*, i.e. by reconverting contradiction in contrariety.

9   With these distinctions in mind, we now return to the problem of hegemony. Hegemony can present itself in two forms: by way of *transformism*, or by way of *popular rupture*. The first one is based on transforming antagonisms into differences; it is the basic form under which bourgeois hegemony in Europe has established itself.

The progressive democratization of the British liberal regime in the nineteenth century is the most complete and most successful case of the formation of bourgeois hegemony without popular rupture. The demands of the masses were absorbed differentially by the system, and thus positionalities were displaced which could have given rise to popular radical subjects. Giolitti's Italy or Bismarck's Germany are clear examples of the same process. Conversely, the French case represents the classic example of the formation of a new hegemony via popular rupture. The various antagonisms (or democratic positionalities) were not absorbed *differentially* by the system, and thus they were not reconverted into differences. Rather, they articulated themselves, creating a complex popular subject (a popular positionality), which proved a contradictory alternative to the *ancien régime*. Although the Jacobin discourse seemed disarticulated from a system of equivalences, yet all the terms of these equivalences symbolized domination.

10   What are the relationships between the various positionalities we have defined? In this respect, we can make the following points:

a) If each antagonism creates democratic positionalities, and if the type of mutual articulation between these depends on the hegemonic structure of society, then the positionalities do not stem from some kind of mechanical articulation existing prior to the establishment of hegemony. This means that in every historical situation there are many antagonisms, e.g. of an economic, national, sexual or institutional nature. These antagonisms do not necessarily belong to a paradigm, whether of class or any other; their articulation is the result of a war of position which establishes the hegemonic form of society. This shows the incorrectness of the traditional Marxist thesis, according to which any antagonism, directly or indirectly, is reduced to a class antagonism.

b) There is no given correlation between democratic and popular positionalities. Their relationship will depend on how varied the chain of democratic equivalences in a society is. In the process of a colonial revolution, for example, the confrontation with the imperialist powers gives rise to popular positionalities around *national* subjects. This does not mean, though, that the latter tend to establish a relationship of equivalence with all the democratic antagonisms in that society. Many of these antagonisms can remain outside the chain of equivalences, implicitly confronting them.

c) We now have two extreme situations. In the first situation the various democratic demands are translated as isolated positionalities, without being fused into one popular positionality with many equivalences. This is a frequent phenomenon in those countries which have achieved hegemony via transformism. The case of England, as we mentioned before, is a good illustration. The English political system is very sensitive to democratic demands, and it has developed a wide variety of democratic subjects. But in fact, it is weak whenever subjects are formed that threaten to divide society in two antagonistic camps. (And without popular subjects there is of course no war of position.)

On the other hand, a situation can develop where the popular positionalities are organized around a minimum of democratic equivalences. This is, for example, the case of certain national groups in Third World countries after decolonization, as they were hegemonized by conservative dominant groups. This type of popular discourse tends to present oppression as purely external, and thus it prevents the formation of a chain of equivalences which would be able to absorb the internal democratic antagonisms.

d) Between these extremes there is the more common case in which a certain number of democratic equivalences are structured around popular positionalities, whereas others remain excluded and fail to develop into popular subjects. The history of the Italian Communist party (PCI) illustrates this very neatly. At the end of the Second World War, Togliatti had a clear strategic idea of the expansion of the popular domain on the basis of a growing articulation of democratic antagonisms. For decades, the PCI understood the dialectic between popular and democratic positionalities in Italian society. In more recent years, however, the domain of democratic struggles in Italy has expanded considerably, as new subjects and antagonisms have come to the fore: for example, the women's liberation movement, the crisis of institutions, youth problems. These exceed the frame of reference of Togliatti's synthesis. The strategy of the PCI failed to hegemonize these new antagonisms, which led to a political deadlock and to a growing disorganization of the popular domain. (There can be no successful war of position if the popular subjects are unable to articulate the entire domain of democratic struggles.)

e) Finally, objective circumstances can limit the articulative capacity of certain popular positionalities. Regionalization, as well as the lack of integration of some countries, can create different forms of political culture. As a result, the ensuring chains of equivalences are fundamentally distinct, and difficult to integrate. For instance, in the current case of the Iranian Revolution, anti-imperialist popular subjects have clearly developed on the basis of Islamic fundamentalism, and in turn they have triggered off a number of democratic demands. However, other demands, like women's liberation, will be strictly excluded from this chain of equivalences. This suggests that there is some kind of dualism between popular struggle and democratic struggle: it is not the result of strategic 'inadequacies', but of objective historical limitations. Socialist political practice is often confronted with this kind of difficulties.

f) To conclude this section: what are the implications of our analysis for socialist strategy? First, it should not be a *class* strategy in the sense of a strategy built upon unique positionalities, but rather an articulation of democratic positionalities concerning popular subjects with increasing hegemonic reach. These popular subjects must wage a war of position against the power bloc.

Second, there is no *a priori* drive for unification between demo-

cratic antagonisms and popular subjects: their unity will only be
brought about through struggle and political efforts for articulation. Political mediation can only succeed when it concerns the
unity of the popular domain and the expansion of concrete democratic antagonisms. This political mediation, though, does not
require a determinate form of institution: the *party* cannot be
considered the only possible form of mediation. If socialist political objectives are seen as necessary paradigmatic instances
ensuing from unique class positionalities, then indeed the party
would seem the only form of political mediation. But if the
political mediation represents an articulation of positionalities
and antagonisms, characteristic of a particular situation and
society, the form of mediation will correspond to this particular
context, and therefore it cannot be determined in advance.

Third, as is implied in our analysis, a political strategy based
on hegemony and a war of position is clearly different from both
ultra-leftism and social democracy. Either strategy refuses to
approach the political as *articulative practice*. Ultra-leftism starts
from a revolutionary paradigm, i.e. an already constituted subject, and the system of domination is seen as a coherent ensemble
which should not be disarticulated but destroyed as a whole.
Social democracy also views the system as a coherent total; it
accepts this system, but it proposes reforms favouring certain
subjects: for example, the working class, deprived sectors. However, in both cases the alternative (revolution or reform) is cast in
non-hegemonic terms.

As our analysis has demonstrated, 'war of position', 'hegemony' and the 'formation of subject' form a trinity, an inseparable unity, and as such they represent a concept of mediation or
political struggle. Nothing can be foretold about the character of
the struggle, e.g. whether it will be peaceful or violent. The
relative weight of each of the elements of the 'trinity' will depend
on the concrete circumstances. It is important to recognize that
the struggle for the elimination of domination and the formation
of new subjects – that is, of a new social relation – stretches over
an entire epoch of history: it starts before the power is taken and
surely continues thereafter.

B The concept of hegemony and Marxist tradition

11 The theoretical space filled by the concept of hegemony has
expanded, as a result of the profound crisis of Marxist thinking in
an era of advanced capitalism and imperialism. This is because
Marxism cannot build a discourse exclusively in terms of class
struggle and class alliance. The crisis is the inevitable outcome of a

period in history, witnessing the proliferation of new contradictions, which makes it even more imperative to view the agents as complex subjects and to regard social struggle as articulative practice. Clearly, the history of Marxist thinking since the First World War is marked by an increasing awareness of this complexity.

12   The significance of these changes is shown when comparing the present-day problems of Marxism with the period of the Second International, when for the first time Marxist theory was represented as a systematic whole. Mainly thanks to Engels and Kautsky, Marx's thinking was adopted as party doctrine and accepted as an integral conceptualization of history and society. At the same time, the political practice of the new social-democratic parties extended the Marxist debate to areas and problems not tackled by Marx. This entry into new discursive domains did not, however, signal the start of Marxist forms of hegemonization and articulation of discourses: the Second International saw its theoretical and political task in the crystallization of the very paradigms of class reductionism. We shall briefly summarize the characteristics of this theoretical focus, and highlight its political and strategic consequences.

In the first place, it frustrates any articulation of positionalities, because the historical subjects are reduced to class positionalities. Classes become *subjects* of history. It is believed that the collapse of the capitalist system and the transition to socialism will come about as a result of the growing contradictions between productive forces and the relations of production, and through the progressive proletarianization of the peasant and the petty bourgeoisie – as these trends will make the working class the majority sector in society. In this way, and by pursuing its own objectives, the working class will eventually represent the vast majority of the exploited.

It is obvious that in this perspective *there are no hegemonic tasks*. The domain of Marxist discourse is seen to coincide with the domain of class discourse, and therefore it cannot be extended beyond the boundaries of the working class's own discourse. However, we have suggested that Marxist doctrine should attempt to systematize the entire social reality. If, in spite of this, the class point of view is considered the ultimate sense of direction of all social production, then the various discourses of Marxism in new social and cultural areas are the expression of other classes: one will talk of 'bourgeois science', 'bourgeois art' and 'bourgeois literature'.

(Is it necessary to recall the end to this story?) If Marxism presents itself as a global and systematic conception, and moreover as an official state doctrine, then the pervasive class approach is bound to affect the 'petty bourgeois' and 'bourgeois' discourses as

well. Thus we witness the rebuff of psychoanalysis and its replacement by Pavlovian psychology; the repudiation of the progress
made by modern logic; socialist realism; and to crown it all – the
absurd distinction between 'proletarian science' and 'bourgeois
science'.

What is important for our purposes is that this type of theoretical
perspective has constrained socialist political practice and has
prevented it from developing into hegemonic practice. These constraints were the following:

a) By universally applying the class criterion one would put a class
   label on all the political and ideological features of the social
   agents. Hence, there would be no distinct positionalities, capable
   of different forms of articulation – which is precisely what the
   politics of hegemony is all about.

b) If, with the maturing of the economic contradictions of the
   system, the socialist revolution were assured, then the socialist
   struggle should not attempt to form chains of equivalences and to
   develop new subjects. Rather, it should do the contrary: stick to
   its narrow class perspective, and watch history moving towards
   capitalism and the inevitable collapse thereof.

c) If the revolution is a necessary moment in the maturing of these
   contradictions, then the decline of feudalism, the bourgeois revolution, the development of capitalism and the socialist revolution
   are *separate and necessary historical phases in the evolution of every society*.
   At the same time, the pattern provides the conditions for a policy
   of alliances: until feudalism is rooted out, the socialist forces must
   ally themselves with the liberal bourgeoisie, to accomplish the
   bourgeois revolution, which is a more advanced historical phase.
   But obviously they cannot hope to lead the anti-feudal movement, or to advance to socialism, without passing through the
   historical process of capitalist expansion.

This 'phasism' would lead to a non-hegemonic conception of
alliances.

13 The reductionist and paradigmatic model is based upon two
unchallenged assumptions which are supposed to move its value.
The first one is the universal character of the phases and their own
way of articulating positionalities. The second is that all types of
contradiction can be reduced to a class contradiction (otherwise, it
would not be possible to regard classes as subjects of history).

Both assumptions have been seriously invalidated in a period of
historic transformations, especially during the First World War.
Leninism, then, created a theoretical and political space where, for
the first time, a hegemonic form of the political was conceivable.
Leninist theory culminated in reflections about the new contra-

dictions created by war. Indeed, these new contradictions, sprouting from a conflict of yet unknown dimensions, produced a key point of Leninism: that Marxism cannot construct its discourse exclusively on the basis of class contradictions of an economic nature, i.e. the ones inherent in the process of capitalist accumulation, but at the same time, the discourse must be founded on *the dislocation of the living conditions of the masses*, caused by new kinds of reproduction of late capitalism. This new *mass dimension* of politics has implications beyond the defence of specific interests: it means the articulation and organization of political action in vast sectors of the population, whose living conditions and forms of representation are radically transformed by late capitalism and by the war. This protagonism *of the masses* (the point has correctly been made by Giuseppe Vacca) is one of the radical new contributions of the Leninist discourse. The mass character of politics is an imperative in this new historical climate, as it concerns all classes. In Lloyd George's actions, Lenin has found a new mass form of bourgeois politics. Under the critical conditions after the First World War, the extreme application of this dimension would lead to fascism – defined by Togliatti as a reactionary mass regime. But the second vital contribution of Leninism is that this dislocation of the living conditions of the masses is not only the result of internal transformations in monopoly capitalism, but also of the worldwide articulation of capitalism. For Lenin, the world economy contains a political dimension: the chain of imperialism. Hence, the dislocation is equally caused by external contradictions. In this sense, war is little more than the freezing point of a situation which had become even more characteristic of the conditions of social reproduction and the systems of domination under monopoly capitalism.

This political and strategic focus of Leninism has a crucial implication for the theory of hegemony: that both political equilibrium and its disruption (via revolution or otherwise) are the result of *multiple* contradictions, which by their accumulation and condensation form a particular *conjuncture*.

The revolutionary strategy, therefore, cannot be based solely upon the culmination of the economic contradictions of the system, but it must represent an historical form of articulation of the various contradictions in a particular conjuncture.

There are three points to be derived from this: the priority of the political moment in the revolutionary strategy (as opposed to the approach of the Second International, which subordinated the political to the play of economic contradictions); the rejection of any mechanical or *a priori* 'phasism'; and finally, the conception of the political as articulation and hegemony. Leninism has thus incorporated the concept of hegemony in Marxist theory, as part of a *non-paradigmatic, anti-phasist* and *popular* approach to the political.

However, we should be aware of the historical limits of Leninism: in fact, Leninism represented the *difference* in the Marxist-Kautskyan discourse, i.e. it was an anti-Kautskyan discourse *within* Kautsky's intellectual horizon. For this reason, it could not entirely abandon the basic assumption of Kautsky's theory: that classes are subjects of history. For Lenin, classes remained the essential units of analysis of politics and society. Admittedly, classes in his analysis are involved in much richer and much more complex contradictions than classical Marxism would accept, but these contradictions are still *class* contradictions, and not the type of contradictions which give birth to non-class subjects.

Masses is a recurrent notion in Leninist analysis after the war; it filled a discursive vacuum in the economicist and class approach, but it never became a *theoretical* concept. This ambiguity and tension in the notion of class within Leninism would have damaging effects in the approach of the Komintern, namely by pushing to its limits the substantialist and 'militarist' approach of classes. Hence, in its conception of hegemony, Leninism is unable to convey the notion of 'class alliance'.

14   To arrive at a conception of hegemony which exceeds the limitations of the notion of 'class alliance', we must go beyond class reductionism. There are two significant instances in this process of breaking away from the narrow focus. The first was influenced by the struggle against fascism. Increasingly, democracy had come to be seen as an autonomous discourse, as a *domain* where the hegemonic-articulative practices of the classes take place, not just as the ideology of *one* class.

In this context there were a number of decisive advances towards a new interpretation of hegemony: Mao's concept of 'new democracy'; Togliatti's 'progressive democracy' in its various forms, from the Spanish Civil War to Italy's liberation struggle; or the Dimitrov Report to the Seventh Congress of the International which urged that working-class and communist parties should be viewed as the historical heirs and torch-bearers of a tradition of national and popular struggle. Above all, Gramsci's work is the most significant of all theoretical instances where the notion of hegemony exceeds the narrow frame of 'class alliance'. Hegemony is shown as the articulative principle of a new civilization, as the birth of a new common orientation for the masses. As such, it required not only a political, but a definitely intellectual and moral leadership. Hegemony is the development of new subjects, not merely the alliance between already constituted subjects. The second phase signalling scepticism towards the reductionist conception of society was a response to two basic changes taking place after the Second World War. On the one hand, there was the expansion of the domain of democratic struggle in the advanced capitalist countries. The growing bureaucratization of civil society led to new forms of struggle against the authorities: the crisis of institutions; crisis within the family; the women's liberation struggle; the emancipation struggle of national, sexual and racial minorities, and so forth. These political subjects represent new democratic positionalities, which the socialist forces must try to hegemonize by creating even more complex chains of equivalences. Clearly, this is a significant extension of the notion of hegemony *vis-à-vis* what it had come to mean during the period of anti-fascism. The domain of positionalities had become so vast that the political forms of hegemonic practice suggested by Gramsci and Togliatti needed to be reconsidered.

The other great transformation of the post-war period is the emergence of national liberation movements at the periphery of the capitalist world. This process also created new positionalities which cannot be understood solely in class terms. The dialectic between classes, the nature of accumulation, or the nature of the democratic and popular positionalities differed significantly from the characteristics of the processes of hegemonic articulation in Western Europe. Any general theory of hegemonic articulation must take these distinctive forms into account: this is only possible by breaking away from the paradigms of class reductionism.

C Problems of hegemony in Latin America

(This section is not intended as a detailed discussion of the basic forms of hegemonic articulation in Latin America, nor as a recommendation of a socialist strategy based upon these forms. We only want to highlight (1) the difficulties Latin American thinking has encountered in approaching its social and political reality in hegemonic terms; and (2) the constraints experienced by the dominant classes in establishing their politics as hegemonic practice.)

15   Differences can be viewed in two ways: either by interpreting the diversity of concrete events as a system of alternatives; or by transforming a set of concrete events in a paradigm, and then viewing other events as deviations from this paradigm. The latter is the approach of intellectual colonialism, and for a long time it has also been characteristic of mainstream thinking in Latin America: the Latin American societies were seen partly as a replica of, and partly as a deviation from, European developments. 'Civilization or

Barbarism' was the motto of several liberal generations.

For this line of thinking, a concept like 'hegemony' was absolutely inconceivable. Because if each positionality belongs, by definition, to a paradigm, then the articulation of positionalities is not a *specific historical form*, but *an essential form*. And if the articulation of positionalities is not regarded as historically specific, then hegemony is unthinkable.

We feel there are three fundamental stages in the history of the paradigms characterizing Latin American thinking. The first one is liberalism: it views the Latin American countries as incipient European societies. The coexistence of a Europeanized sector at one end, and at the other end a vast majority of regions and strata unassimilated by the model, was baptized 'transition' by liberalism, as this fits perfectly a phasist view of development. Has not Europe also gone through a process of transition, starting with backwardness and the obscurantism of feudalism and the *ancien régime*? This, undoubtedly, requires a translation: how can European feudalism be compared with the indigenous communities in Peru or with the *estancieros* in the Argentine interior? Unfortunately, the system of specific equivalences of the Latin American liberal discourse denies these differences, because it constructs society and the political as an *unthinkable*. The differences are not articulated, they are dissolved within the system of equivalences: consequently, there is no hegemony.

The second stage is the development of alternative paradigms as a response to a growing crisis of the forms of liberal discourse. This crisis resulted from the emergence of populist movements, calling for new political processes. Under these conditions, the assumptions of liberalism did not allow the development of new objects. A first alternative approach was the willingness to recognize new trends, although forms of the old discourse were used. With such an attitude, of course, it is increasingly difficult to appreciate differences in society, and hence the discourse becomes too abstract. Argentine liberalism, for example, identified Peronism with fascism. This not only showed disregard for such vital differences as the social basis of both movements, but it also implied that a very abstract, almost metaphysical, system of equivalences was used: Peronism is equivalent to fascism, to nineteenth-century *rosismo*, to medieval clericalism, and so on. A similar approach is to build concepts where the unthinkable of the political enters the discourse, but only *as* the unthinkable: the observed events are thought of as aberrations in the development process, as deviations. In the next phase, a new paradigm finally replaced the liberal paradigm: military developmentalism, for example, initiated a positive evaluation of some anti-liberal political forms, though at the cost of disregarding other differences. The military populist model, regarded as the political model of industrialization in Latin America, has given rise to new systems of equivalences: for example, the Prussian option, Nasserism.

Finally, the third phase represents a turn of 180 degrees *vis à vis* the initial position: the Latin American countries belong to the Third World. The shared positionality of Asia, Africa and Latin America as the exploited partner in the centre/periphery relationship, is seen as the essence of these societies, and therefore it must form the basis of a common political strategy: armed struggle. In this imagined 'tricontinental', the differences are overlooked just as much as in the liberal discourse. In both case, the positionalities are essential forms of paradigms, constructed between two poles. Again, there is no room for differential articulation of these positionalities, nor is there room for hegemony. The only change is that the negative pole has become positive, and vice versa.

16   The thinking of the Latin American left has been profoundly influenced (we would almost say, shaped) by the paradigms of the colonial mentality. In fact, this colonial mentality can be regarded as a system of translation based upon the construction of an unthinkable of the political. Likewise, Latin American Marxism can then be called 'metatranslation', as it reproduced, on a new conceptual keyboard, the same paradigmatic and formative oppositions as the mainstream discourse.

During the period of liberal-oligarchical hegemony, the exercise was very simple: Sarmiento's dichotomy, 'Civilization or Barbarism', or its equivalents in other Latin American countries, were translated in Marxism language by the dichotomy 'feudalism-capitalism'. Hence the extensive complicities between liberalism and Marxism in this period: in their discourse they produced the same silences, the same areas of the 'unthinkable', the same incapacity to perceive historical specificities or to design a strategy based on these specificities. Later, one started to realize that Latin America was different, and that this prevented a *direct* identification of its social and political features with similar features in Europe and with their role in the process of capitalist expansion. Marxist discourse then turned to a strategy of *reconnaissance*, for example: how to identify, in such atypical forms as *varguismo* and Peronism, the historical category of democratic-bourgeois revolution? The thinking remained paradigmatic, but now more sophisticated intellectual exercises were required, because it was felt that a series of rather accidental historical variants concealed the essential form of 'democratic-bourgeois revolution'. The historical variants are regarded as epiphenomena, relatively secondary as compared to the essential forms. And as in the final analysis the political strategy is based on these essential forms, Marxist politics tend to remain largely abstract. In very few cases, e.g. Mariátegui, the Latin American specificity is regarded as an essential factor, as the basis for a socialist strategy. The isolated incidence of these cases proves their exceptional merit.

The same comment can be made about more recent debates, like those focusing on the bourgeois-democratic or socialist character of the Latin American revolution. These debates are revealing not for their content, but for the underlying assumptions, accepted by most participants in the debates. Indeed, if the dominant mode of accumulation in a society is used as the basic criterion to determine the nature of a popular revolution; and if the strategic choices (e.g. between parliamentary road or armed struggle) depend on the bourgeois or socialist character of this revolution, then a few interesting assumptions underly these statements. These assumptions are: (a) that the mode of accumulation in a society determines which class or classes form the power bloc; (b) that classes are the only protagonists of the historical process; (c) as parliamentary forms are necessarily and inherently bourgeois, each socialist process must strive to abolish them, and therefore it must project the destruction of the state apparatus as a basic aim. Rather, the parliamentary road can only be justifiable in terms of the non-socialist character of a certain phase, or in terms of the revolutionary process as a whole. According to this perspective, it is self-evident that issues such as the viability of the parliamentary struggle in a process of popular revolution can only be assessed on the basis of the class character of the revolution.

Hegemony, conceived as we have done in terms of the articulation of a large number of contradictions and in terms of a war of position, is of course absent from this perspective. In classical Stalinism or Trotskyism we find good examples of this absence. Stalinism of the popular front period – at least in most of its pronouncements – affirmed the preponderance of the democratic elements and their bourgeois character. This gave way to a non-hegemonic politics of the right.

Trotskyism stressed the bourgeois character of democracy and the priority of the socialist struggle. This led to a non-hegemonic politics of the left. Hegemony was absent from both strategies: there was no attempt to articulate democracy within a socialist discourse. Significantly, paradigmatism and reductionism can assume both leftist and rightist forms, because they are rooted in the perspective we have described. The vicious circle can only find its answer in a

new conception of the political, based upon the notion of hegemony.
17   The foregoing shows that it is impossible to approach the political
      problems of Latin America from a perspective of hegemony, with-
      out developing new objects of discourse, i.e. without abandoning
      the reductionist view of social antagonisms. Let us give a few
      examples:
      a) An issue of current interest is the liberalization of the Brazilian
         regime. But what exactly is meant by liberalization is not at all
         clear. According to some paradigmatic images of Brazilian society,
         the coup of 1964 is a radical intervention, which entirely
         remodelled the society and installed the predominance of mono-
         poly capital. Theories like 'totalitarianism' tend to attribute an
         apocalyptic character to this intervention. But this can be dis-
         missed easily by analysis. In the first place, the military regime
         did not radically abolish the political system: the parliamentary
         system, although undergoing important changes, was maintained,
         and numerous institutions remained in old hands and continued
         to function. This was not mere window-dressing: the coup did
         radically redefine the relationship of forces in Brazil, but it was
         neither necessary nor desirable to abolish *all* the traditional forms
         of representation. It sufficed to displace and rearticulate some of
         them, whilst others were deemed to be in good hands. Conse-
         quently nobody, except for certain jacobinized groups of the
         executive, envisaged replacing them by alternative military
         forms. This is a dialectic of continuity and discontinuity, which is
         defined in terms of the articulation of positionalities. In essence:
         distinctive moments in a war of position. To understand this, one
         must analytically isolate the different positionalities, and then try
         to comprehend the historical ensemble of 1964 which was arti-
         culated on the basis of these positionalities. But to do this, one
         must abandon approaches which deny differences in the political
         structures or in social antagonisms; or approaches which des-
         cribe clearly distinct periods in slogans like 'the predominance of
         monopoly capital'. Likewise, the present 'liberalization' trend of
         the Brazilian regime should be approached in terms of the speci-
         fic factors inspiring it. The viability of the regime is threatened if
         it is unable to create a new consensus; in other words, if it cannot
         adapt itself so as to absorb a range of democratic positionalities
         which until now have been excluded from the power system. This
         is not a radical incision, but a redefinition which would broaden
         the social and political basis of the present system. The task for
         the opposition, however, is to try and construct a broader system
         of equivalences, i.e. where democratic positionalities are not
         assimilated separately, but where they can unite around new

popular subjects. Thus building a popular identity as the pole of regrouping for a project of radical democratization of Brazilian society, becomes the fundamental objective of hegemonic struggle. Therefore 'liberalization' as such does not exist; there are 'liberalizations' of fundamentally different kinds.

b) The point is often made that the Sandinista Revolution proves that the only way to power in Latin America is armed struggle. But in fact the Sandinista victory does not at all support this statement. In order to prove the point, one must show that the armed character of the struggle, which is just one aspect of the Sandinist political struggle, has brought about the victory. Rather, we believe that Sandinism is an excellent example of a war of position: around a national and popular identity, the struggle progressively creates a long chain of democratic equivalences, eventually fusing with the Nicaraguan society as a whole. Far from being a case of narrow military strategy, this is one of the finest examples of hegemonic strategy in Latin America.

c) Finally, today there is much talk of social democracy in Latin America. The proliferation of repressive regimes on the continent has revalued 'formal' liberties and democratic institutions. This is undeniably an advance on the ultra-leftism of the 1960s. There is only one problem with it: it is, again, a reductionist error to identify such an attitude with support for social democracy.

The point is not that the defence of individual liberties and democratic forms of political representation are being integrated in an alternative socialist project, but that the type of articulation represented by Western European liberties and forms of representation is being accepted. This overlooks the fact that social democracy is a concrete phenomenon, which as a successful experience was limited to particular countries of Northern Europe, having gone through a long process of industrialization and possessing a very homogeneous social structure.

In this sense, social democracy is a function of the triumph of transformism as the political strategy of certain dominant classes in Europe, and of the capacity of the parliamentary systems to absorb the democratic demand of the masses. Politically, social democracy focuses on the defence of corporative demands of certain popular sectors, demands which can be satisfied within the existing system and which are only expressed through parliamentary representation. By advocating social democracy for Latin America, one overlooks at least two things: (a) that the fusion between a liberal parliamentary system and democratic demands of the masses, as in Europe, does not exist in Latin America; (b) that there is also no social homogeneity of the popular sectors which would allow the political parties of a national dimension to represent specific interest groups, e.g. the unions. On the contrary, the popular struggle in Latin America must articulate and develop popular subjects, starting from a wide social, regional and ideological variety. Therefore, to advocate the social-democratic paradigm is to accept, once again in a reductionist way, that individual liberties and political democracy are incompatible with a project of socialist transformation of society. And this opens the door to a greater danger – namely to believe that some kind of superficial parliamentarization of the political system represents real democracy.

18 To conclude, we shall briefly discuss some fundamental problems facing any hegemonic struggle in Latin America. The first problem, as already mentioned, is the heterogeneity of the social bases and of the antagonisms which a socialist and popular strategy must attempt to articulate. The primary condition of a hegemonic strategy is to recognize the historical specificity of this ensemble, considerably more complex than the historical cleavage which Gramsci found between Northern Italy and the Mezzogiorno. There can only be hegemony if the full complexity of antagonisms, ploughing society, is acknowledged. But hegemony goes beyond the recognition of the specificity of these democratic positionalities: it is their articulation around popular positionalities. Only this articulation will transform the social agents into 'people', and the political struggle into war of position. Hence, the more heterogeneous the fronts of democratic struggle, the more instrumental will be political mediation in establishing the popular struggle. The concrete form of this mediation, however, cannot be determined in advance, as it depends on the specificity of the antagonisms it wants to articulate.

In most Latin American countries the multiplicity of antagonisms has given a great institutional variety to the struggle, ranging from the self-defence committees in the rural sector to the unions or squatter organizations in the urban centres. In this situation certain classical forms of organization are not practicable, for example a party with a class nucleus, such as the French Communist Party; a social-democratic party of corporative representation; or indeed the classical model of the Leninist vanguard. Perhaps political forms of a 'movemental' character would be most appropriate for the strategy we postulate. This we base on the need for national symbols to define the popular domain, the desirability of giving a mass character to the political action, or the large degree of local autonomy required by the heterogeneity of forces. Anyway, following our line of argument, it would be entirely wrong to recommend a recipe suitable for all situations, as this would be a relapse into a paradigmatic approach to politics.

One final essential point: the forms of popular discourse in Latin America are partly a function of the limitations the traditional classes have encountered in imposing their domination in hegemonic forms. We know that in Europe 'democracy' and 'liberalism' represented different traditions, and that for a long time they have been opposing each other. The process of consolidation of bourgeois hegemony via transformism, however, led to the progressive absorption of the former by the latter, thus closing the gap between them. The more successful transformism was, the stronger the unity between 'democracy' and 'liberalism'. In the European context, England and Italy are the extreme examples of, respectively, a successful and a failed process of progressive integration. In Latin America, on the other hand, the gap between the two has never been closed. Consequently, the liberal ideology has always been challenged by an alternative national-popular ideology – which shows the limits of absorption of the democratic demands of the masses by the oligarchical system.

If Latin American transformism was at its pinnacle with experiences like *batllismo* in Uruguay or *irigoyenismo* in Argentina, then the Chile of Ibañez, or Peru and Brazil in the 1930s, reveal its limits and signalize its collapse. Crucially, this caused a serious rift in the democratic experience of the Latin American masses. On the one hand, a series of positionalities was created, aiming at the democratization-from-within of the liberal state: for instance, the positionalities characterizing the mobilizations of the middle class in the urban areas, and the University Reform.

On the other hand, for the vast exploited sectors whose demands could not be absorbed through transformism, the democratic ideology assumed *anti-liberal* national-popular forms. The historical significance of this rift cannot be overestimated, because it led to fundamentally different and mutually opposing chains of equivalences, and this antagonistic articulation caused the weakening of the popular domain and its incapacity to design hegemonic alternatives. Liberal democratism frequently opposed popular anti-oligarchical alternatives – think of the conduct of the Partido Democrático of São Paulo in 1932, or the parties of the Unión Democrática in Argentina in 1945. But at the same time, in cases like the Estado Nôvo there can be little doubt that vast areas of democratic demands were excluded from its discourse, or that it even explicitly confronted them. This allowed the traditional dominant classes, at a crucial juncture in history, to mobilize liberal democratism against the popular regimes and to prevent them from possible hegemonic articulation of the democratic struggles.

However, very recently, this historic rift has started to narrow – which permits some optimism regarding the future of popular positionalities – i.e. of the 'people' as such, in the arena of national-populism and anti-liberal democratic traditions. This is because in Latin America, as we mentioned before, the gap between liberalism and democracy has never been entirely bridged. Therefore, the parliamentary struggle can only in a very limited way be the arena of formation of the democratic struggle, whereas deepening this struggle requires the politicization of a large variety of antagonisms as they shoot up in civil society. But, conversely, the democratic demands related to liberal forms of politics do not seem to be hegemonized, as before, by the liberal oligarchy, or confronted with the popular domain. Rather, as the tragic experience of the last twenty years has shown, the dominant classes themselves have smashed the articulations which formed the basis of that hegemony, and they have created an equivalence between the two democratic traditions, but the use of violent repression – equally affecting both traditions. For the popular domain this offers the possibility, for the first time, to hegemonize the demands related to the defence of human rights and political representation. And to hegemonize them as an important though not unique component in the war of position which the people will wage for the radical suppression of any form of exploitation and domination.

II

THE AFTERMATH OF INDEPENDENCE

5

INTRODUCTION

The visionaries of independence foresaw Latin America consisting of modern states coequal with those of Western Europe, rationally exploiting their own resources in such a way as to promote sustained economic development. These visions rapidly soured. In the half-century after independence most of Latin America was condemned to permanent stagnation, and some areas to decline. Only a few exceptional pockets enjoyed sustained or even erratic economic growth. Why did Latin America fail to achieve the dramatic change envisaged? Why did it fail to achieve during the nineteenth century the transition to a modern economy accomplished by the newly independent United States? Were the economic opportunities thrown up by independence missed? Or were there no such opportunities?

Various interrelated interpretations approach these problems radically. One – typified by the writing of Stanley and Barbara Stein – places its principal stress on the endurance of the external dominance that perpetuated underdevelopment. Scholars of this persuasion differ as to the degree of capitalist penetration of Latin America. While some contend that Latin America was only partially and incompletely incorporated within an international capitalist order, others insist that the continent was subject to a thoroughgoing capitalism. Another approach, associated with Furtado, argues that the backwardness of endogenous structures – paucity of domestic resources and institutional rigidities – precluded a speedy adjustment to the limited opportunities provided by the world economy at the time of independence. A similar approach which emphasizes, in addition, the weakness of the centre, focuses essentially upon the North Atlantic world and stresses the subordinate and geographically- and commodity-specific nature of potential linkages between Latin America and the centre. This emergent international system was further debilitated by the transition from mercantilist imperialism to the age of competitive capitalism.

Europe after the Napoleonic Wars was more concerned with the re-establishment of internal security and prosperity than with overseas adventures. In the United States an emphasis upon domestic development characterized the decades following the 1812–14 war with Britain, and tended to absorb both European attention and limited surplus resources. Efforts to emulate the North American economic model appeared doomed to failure in Latin America. Attempts to promote immigration so as to reduce reliance upon coerced labour were remarkable only for their widespread application – from Mexico to Argentina – and their lack of success (or disastrous consequences in the Mexican case). Equally unsuccessful were diverse measures to revive mining or promote industrial expansion with the use of external capital and expertise. Projects to expand foreign trade or diversify the economy were seldom fully consummated. Nonetheless, while individual Latin American economies probably did not play a large role in the evolving international order, the influence of exogenous forces was pervasive in certain regions and sectors, at policy level if not in practical achievement.

For some scholars then limited potential for cooperation with, and participation in, the world system was based upon the nature of the central economies: for others it was the backwardness of Latin America which accounted for incomplete and ineffective integration with the outside world. Whether Latin America was a marginal component of the world economy during the early nineteenth century has emerged as a pivotal issue in the debate about the external connection. It is unlikely that this controversy will be speedily resolved, in part owing to the complexity and diversity of socio-economic relations which may be observed over the period. As in evident in the chapters which compose this section, there was a high degree of plurality of modes of production in agriculture, mining and manufacturing. For Colombia Anthony McFarlane contrasts the panning of alluvial gold by families in one region with large operations using a slave workforce in another. He also illustrates the diversity of agricultural production, which ranged from export plantation agriculture and cash-crop production for domestic consumption using wage and/or forced labour, to peasant production for local markets and subsistence and semi-subsistence. Similarly, Guy Thomson, referring to textiles in Mexico, indicates the coexistence of different forms of production in manufacturing: advanced, highly capitalized factory systems and modest artisan production in urban centres, with primitive cloth-making in Indian villages.

Clearly, contemporary forms of advanced capitalism were to be observed in some areas of activity, but not in others. However, there is no precise evidence that capitalism was in the ascendance. On the contrary, in much of the continent opposite trends were in train. One principal area of scholarly neglect is the survival of subsistence and semi-subsistence economic activity, and its reinforcement as a consequence of the military and political dislocations associated with the protracted turmoil of the independence struggles. Recent research suggests that the principal economic objective of the *hacienda* in this period was self-sufficiency in the event of political disorder. The *hacienda* set out to participate in a broader cash economy while preserving the option of a retreat into local self-sufficiency. Capitalist agriculture was dependent on complex nexuses that could be seriously jeopardized by war and disorder. Equally rational were other manifestations of a retreat from capitalism. One was the corporate Indian communities, still understudied. Others – such as settlements of escaped slaves in the Caribbean or the nomadic Indian tribes of the Southern Cone – not only contained refugees from more advanced societies but constituted an alternative model. Whether or not a conscious flight from the modern order, such alternative societies revealed the frailty of capitalism in several areas of Latin America during the half-century following independence. For most Latin Americans the pace of life continued to be determined by the yearly agricultural cycle rather than the trade cycle: natural disasters – the failure of the harvest or disease – were the principal 'economic' regulators, not the performance of the external sector.

An environment conducive to dynamic individual initiative in the Rostovian sense, or likely to ensure the rapid victory of capitalism as prophesied by Marx, is difficult to discern in Latin America during these years. Luis Ortega points to the slow pace of institutional modernization in Chile; McFarlane details an even more arduous process in Colombia. In several countries in the late eighteenth century the spectacular expansion of production for the market in mining and artefacts as well as agriculture was to a significant extent the consequence of the efficacious policies of an energetic state, which during the process of independence was largely dismantled. The liquidation of peninsular interests removed expertise, which was not easily replaced, resulting in the paralysis of administration and the surfacing of regionalism. It was not surprising that, as Moreno Fraginals indicates, the country of most impressive economic growth in the period was that where colonial arrangements still existed and where, till the 1860s, regionalism was weakest – namely Cuba.

Yet if Latin America may be portrayed as disappearing beyond the edge of an economic or commercial periphery, it can hardly be said to have done so in an ideological sense. In some areas party politics barely disguised regional antagonisms, family feuding and sheer personal ambition; but elsewhere political debate was founded upon ideological commitment, and a degree of genuine experimentation was to be observed which was inconceivable in Europe even in 1848. Intellectual ferment characterized the decades around independence, as Collier, Halperín Donghi, Lynch, Safford and Skidmore demonstrate. The strength of the external connection is revealed in constitutional experiment, based upon the US model, in several polities, and the absorption of radical concepts from Europe in others. The result was a remarkable degree of pragmatism and improvisation in the shaping of political institutions. With the collapse of legitimacy in Spanish America, competing factions seized upon alternative ideologies and employed new political concepts to defend the integrity of precariously established states. While fears of mass insurrection fuelled a concern for order that made for structural continuity, the language of independence and liberal concepts of basic freedoms and equality before the law heightened popular expectations. Consisting of rigid and archaic structures upon which imported accretions were uneasily imposed, the political economies of Latin America hardly constituted the *tabula rasa* glibly portrayed by unhistorical modernization theorists writing in the 1950s.

As these chapters reveal, short-term imperatives in addition to an Iberian tradition of intervention occasioned a stress upon administration and the role of the state, notwithstanding experiments in semi-representative government and the liberal phraseology used in constitutional documents. Ortega points to the strength of conservative reaction and a successful marriage of convenience between mercantilist traditions of *fomento* and *laissez-faire* concepts of growth. Throughout Latin America the threat of social disorder triggered by the process of independence, and more prosaically the condition of state finances, occasioned a mix of responses that cannot be easily categorized as neo-mercantilist or doctrinaire liberal. While various groups assimilated classic liberal or Benthamite ideas and attempted to cast the role of government accordingly, practical considerations tempered principle. Contemporaries saw little contradiction in advocating minimal, passive state action (establishing public order, reform of the commercial code and currency, trade liberalization) and the administration of market functions through direct 'pump-priming' activity, the granting of exclusive privilege or, as became more persistent after the mid-century, the provision of loans, guarantees and financial inducements to promote entrepreneurial initiative.

Scholars have often failed to recognize the coherence (and occasionally the continuity) of these strategies, and have dismissed them as confused, contradictory manifestations of elite self-interest, or as indicating a lack of authority on the part of the state or conflict within the government apparatus. Similarly, the rationality of policy experimentation and constitutional changes in a deteriorating social and economic environment are not always observed. Protectionist tendencies and precocious manifestations of developmentalism have been disparaged as neo-mercantilist; oscillations between centralism and federalism have been pilloried as factious expediency. Such interpretations may be founded upon erroneous assumptions regarding the narrow social base of the state: Ortega and Thomson appear to argue for a broader interaction between government and society than has been allowed in some recent writing. The social composition of some post-colonial countries may be more complex than has been acknowledged heretofore. In this respect, Thomson's chapter is consonant with a small corpus of literature which argues for a significant degree of social differentiation and the early emergence of class-based interest groups during the early national period. However, these are tentative conclusions: they should not be exaggerated.

Caution must also be exercised when considering the impact of institutional experiment. An uncritical acceptance of contemporary attitudes and expectations creates a false image of surface modernity, and may also result in over-sophisticated assessments of the efficacy of government action and the coherence of administration. In Spanish America Chile was atypical and Colombia probably more representative. There were many instances when the state failed even to guarantee public order, so enhancing the attractions of political localism and economic self-sufficiency. De-bureaucratization, a dearth of skilled personnel (in the administrative and military branches of government), the local and personal focus of allegiances and inadequate means of communication, were major obstacles to the consolidation of the state. Government action was circumscribed by immunities of classes, corporations and individuals, and by a spirit of patriotism lacking a sense of nationalism. The wealth and power of the Church challenged the authority of new states seeking to dismantle colonial privileges. Indian communities constituted a society apart; slaves (and other forms of forced labour which, as Bill Albert demonstrates in Section III, persisted into the latter part of the century) were not citizens.

Nevertheless, the disarticulated state was not by definition incapable of defending national interests. In an age when the commercial house represented the face of international capital, there were also constraints upon the forces of imperialism. The commercial house might have been an appropriate means of integrating specific, isolated areas of Latin America with the North Atlantic, but the mechanism was unable to guarantee the victory of capitalism in conflicts with outmoded forms of production. The foreign merchant did not always or inevitably hold the upper hand in dealings with the *hacendado* or the state. The former was probably more susceptible to the vagaries of fortune, hence the premium placed upon liquidity and a propensity to pursue high profit in activities offering a quick turnover of capital.

The chapters that compose this section point to constraints upon both imperialism and development. Centrifugal forces – the survival of pre-capitalist modes of production, the prevalence of seigneurial social relations and regional attachments – which weakened the authority of the state also distorted the impact of the external connection and reduced the dynamism of progressive domestic interests. The experience of Colombia indicates that good intentions and government fiat were insufficient to guarantee development. For Thomson, de-linkage from the North Atlantic economy possibly fostered economic diversification and sectoral integration at a regional level, but was insufficient of itself to promote self-sustaining national development. The negative examples of Colombia and Mexico, and the positive case presented by Chile, contend that political stability rather than policy consistency was the critical factor, permitting a pragmatic response to evolving external opportunities and creating some space for domestic accommodations if not consensus. Exponents of classical diffusion theories will find scant evidence of dynamic change in Colombia's pattern of external commerce. Equally, they will gain little comfort from the Mexican case which appeared to offer the prospect of take-off from a high base. Only Chile, endowed with an administrative apparatus capable of maintaining pragmatic continuity in policy objectives, might sustain modernization hypotheses, though it hardly conforms with an orthodox liberal model.

In most cases the legacy of independence was frustration induced by unrealized expectations. Maintenance of order rather than the promotion of growth was the predominant concern of Latin American elites. The scale of the subsistence economy and the priority of forestalling class and ethnic violence constrained policy experimentation and diluted the limited potential of external linkages, at least until the last third of the nineteenth century. Patterns of external relations changed little during the decades following independence, but the structure of internal relations shifted considerably. However, the alteration of domestic institutions so as to secure internal order, and the emergence of a consensus, made it possible to seize new opportunities in the international economy which arose subsequently. When they were able, elites actively propelled their economies into the world economic system. External vulnerability was chosen even if its implications were not fully appreciated and insertion was based upon false assumptions of interdependence.

6

THE TRANSITION FROM COLONIALISM IN COLOMBIA, 1819–1875

Anthony McFarlane

The defeat of Spanish forces in 1819 at Boyacá in central Colombia both inflicted a decisive blow against Spanish power in Colombia itself, and marked a crucial stage in the war of liberation which was to destroy Spanish rule in South America.[1] For the leaders of the struggle against Spain in Colombia, political liberation cleared the way to economic progress. With the United States as a model, they foresaw a bright future for the nascent republic, now free to offer its rich resources in the markets of the world.[2] Bolívar, in particular, entertained a euphoric vision of the economic future of Gran Colombia, seeing a day when it would become 'the heart of the universe . . . the bond, the centre and the emporium of the human race'.[3] However, in the years that followed, even the modest expectations of more prosaic statesmen were to be disappointed. For most of the nineteenth century, Colombia was plagued by political and economic instability, and fell far short of the goals envisaged by the founders of the republic.

To explain how and why these early hopes were frustrated is an ambitious task, far beyond the bounds of a short essay. As yet, we know little about important aspects of economic and social life in nineteenth-century Colombia, especially at the regional level, and analysis of the interaction of economic and political life remains at a rudimentary stage.[4] Without such studies, interpretation of the forces which shaped the country's development is necessarily inconclusive, for Colombia was, above all, a highly regionalized society, exhibiting variations in economic, social and political structure seldom found within the bounds of a single nation state. Nevertheless, at a general level, the economic history of Colombia during the nineteenth century may be seen as a process of readjustment from the patterns laid down by Spanish colonialism to integration in a changing international economy, and it is this process and the problems which it entailed that are traced in this essay.

Attention will focus, first, on the structure and condition of the economy at independence, indicating the principal features of the economy upon which the political apparatus of the new republic was founded. A second section will consider the main elements of economic policy in the period up to 1850, and their impact on the economy. A final section will focus on the growth of the external sector after 1850, indicating the effects of export expansion on the domestic economy during Colombia's first commodity export cycle, up to the point where it ended with slump and political crisis in 1875.

The Colombian economy at independence

When Colombia emerged from the struggle for independence in the early 1820s, the economic life of the country had still fully to readjust to the end of Spanish domination. After the first collapse of Spanish authority in 1810, the imperial economic system was never completely recon-structed and, between 1810 and 1819, Colombia gradually formed and strengthened commercial contacts with other nations. However, in this period the potential benefits of unrestrained trade outside the Spanish monopoly were not fully realized. Politically, the country fragmented into a *mélange* of competing regional governments, creating an environ-ment of internal disorder and instability which hindered internal trade and obstructed the formation of stable external economic relations. These circumstances encouraged an exodus of Spanish merchants and capital, and commercial contacts with Europe were largely replaced by trade with British entrepôts in the West Indies. The re-establishment of Spanish government in 1815 reinstated Bourbon sovereignty, but could not restore normality in political and economic life, and the renewed struggle for independence exposed Colombia once more to the damaging effects of military conflict within her territory, to be followed by the drainage of men and money to support Bolívar's campaigns beyond her borders.

The effects of war on the Colombian economy during this period are difficult to assess. In 1824 the British consul in Cartagena stated that 'Colombia had been wasted by a sanguinary warfare of thirteen years, her population greatly diminished, her industry palsied'.[5] But the effects of war should not be exaggerated. Military operations within Colombia had been on a relatively small scale, and do not appear to have involved any large-scale destruction of assets or prolonged disruption of produc-tion. Agricultural output seems to have been maintained, as there were no serious food shortages in either urban or rural areas. In the gold-mining industry output may have fallen, but there was little permanent damage. Decentralized, lacking fixed investment in equipment, and located on the frontiers of settlement, the mining zones were much less vulnerable to the passage of arms than were the great silver mines of Mexico and Peru, and were consequently capable of more rapid recovery. The same is true of the country's most important artisan industry, that of textile manufacture. As a cottage industry based largely on female labour working within the household unit, it was much more resilient than the workshops of Ecuador and Peru, where production was imperilled by direct attack, sequestration, and the flight of labour.[6]

However, if the Colombian economy had been disrupted rather than devastated by war, and did not face a great effort of reconstruction to return to pre-independence levels of production, formidable obstacles to economic development remained. In the heady atmosphere of republican fervour which pervaded the early years of independent government, these obstacles did not distress the political leaders of the new administration, and they took an optimistic view of the country's economic prospects. Freed from the trammels of Spanish domination, they were inclined to assume that the return of peace, the opening of free contacts with other nations, and the removal of Spanish fiscal and institutional controls would provide sufficient conditions for the development of the Colombian economy. But release from the entanglements of Spanish control was not easily achieved. Although the burdens of Spanish fiscal and commercial impositions were removed, the economic and social structures evolved during centuries of colonial rule presented more enduring obstacles to change.

The economy that republican Colombia inherited from its colonial past was built around two principal axes. First, an agrarian economy which juxtaposed large estates, using Indian and mestizo labour, with peasant small holders. In this economy production was geared partly to subsistence and partly to the market. Its main centres were the long-established, more densely populated areas of settlement in the eastern and southern highlands. The other main axis of economic life lay to the west, in the mining camps of the Pacific lowlands and the province of Antioquia. In these areas, independent prospectors and slave gangs used primitive techniques to pan gold, constantly shifting their operations over the broad backlands in which auriferous deposits were found.[7]

In the principal areas of settlement, where Hispanic society had been founded on the exploitation of an indigenous peasant population, the agrarian economy was poor and backward, with limited scope for the commercialization of agricultural products. Most commodities could only be traded locally, since high costs of transport prevented them from competing with acceptable substitutes produced in other areas. Such local markets were too small to promote specialization and division of labour, and peasant agriculture was geared largely to subsistence production. In the eastern highlands, within the hinterlands of the urban centres of Bogotá and Tunja, this pattern was varied by the presence of an artisan textile industry which had emerged in the Socorro area, where the agricultural economy of poor white and mestizo farmers was supplemented by the manufacture of crude cottons.[8] Drawing on abundant local supplies of raw cotton, a cottage industry organized in peasant households produced crude cotton goods for domestic consumption, and

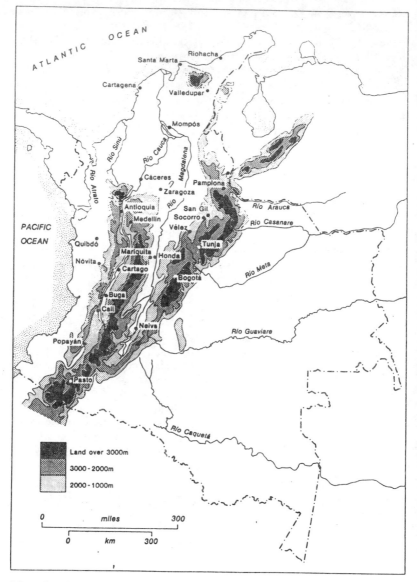

Map 1   Colombia

peasant farmers also supplemented their subsistence economy with the production of tobacco, which was marketed beyond the confines of the region. The principal market for textiles was in the eastern highland region itself and, although some part of textile production reached the mining regions and the coastal provinces, the growth of the market for domestic textiles was limited by the competition from imported cottons that were becoming increasingly cheap during the late eighteenth century.

In the agrarian economy, only the large producers, owners of haciendas producing sugar cane, cereals and livestock (in combinations which varied according to climate and topography), were able to overcome the constraints of local markets. Using combinations of free and forced labour, they engaged in the extensive production of commodities which enjoyed a more income-elastic demand than the basic foodstuffs produced by the small farmer, and which were sufficiently valuable for them to enter into inter-regional trade with the mining zones.[9] However, although the concentration of land in few hands supported a landed elite which enjoyed above-average incomes from agriculture, by itself the land could not provide the basis for large fortunes.[10] The real wealth of the territory lay not in its haciendas and farms, but in the gold mines and in the long-distance trades fuelled by their output.

In the mining sector, the principal beneficiaries of gold production were the large mine-owners and merchants connected to the transatlantic trade. The gold mines of the Pacific lowlands formed part of a network of interlocking agricultural and mining enterprises which used black slave labour.[11] By controlling production and exchange within and between the mining zones and the contiguous agricultural areas, a few great families based in the city of Popayán formed a 'slavocracy' which held sway over the economic and political life of the Cauca region of southern Colombia. Their dominant role helped to prevent the abolition of slavery in the early years of republican rule, and their power was not effectively challenged until the mid-nineteenth century.[12] In Antioquia, the other major gold mining region, labour was typically free and the returns from mining were more evenly distributed. But here too, the main beneficiaries of mining were those who controlled the trade in gold, the merchants who supplied the miners with many basic items of consumption and who took advantage of large price differentials between mining and non-mining zones.[13] Taken from the miners, gold then gravitated towards the principal urban centres, where it was used to purchase merchandise imported from Europe by merchants who, during the colonial period, were largely Spanish agents for commercial houses in Peninsular ports.[14]

During the colonial period the bulk of the surplus generated by this economy had been channelled into the hands of three main groups, which stood at the apex of the social hierarchy. First, the few great land- and mine-owners whose access to gold and contacts with mercantile capital enabled them to maintain capital-intensive enterprises based on slave labour. Another, larger but less wealthy, segment of the landed upper class attracted a more modest share of the surplus, using extra-economic coercion to obtain peasant labour. Second, the merchants – mostly peninsular Spaniards – who organized transatlantic commerce and built fortunes on the exchange of manufactured imports for gold. Third, the officers of Church and state who lived from income redis-tributed from the mass of the population through taxation. The concen-tration of income and capital in these hands did not provide a sound foundation for the development of the domestic economy. As consumers, they favoured the purchase of imports from Europe rather than goods made in the colony. As producers, their largest investments were in slave labour, also imported by Spanish merchants. And, as overseas trade was largely controlled by Spanish traders, merchant capital tended to drain back to the metropolis rather than finding productive investment in Colombia.[15]

Thus, at the time of independence Colombia inherited an economy which had been shaped by adjusting the requirements of the Spanish metropolis to the needs of colonial elites. Under these conditions, Colombia had remained at a low level of development. Most of the population lived within a subsistence or semi-subsistence economy, insulated from the effects of overseas trade. Gold provided a vital but tenuous link with the international economy, and its production for export, confined to enclaves in western Colombia, did not act as a spur to economic development. In a society organized in a hierarchy of castes, the flows of income and capital created in the external sector tended to concentrate in the hands of small groups, and was largely expended on imports. While Colombia's foreign trade rested on gold, there were few incentives to improve internal transportation, and few opportunities to commercialize agricultural production. So in the early nineteenth century Colombia was a cluster of regional economies, poorly integrated with each other, supporting a small population – about a million and a half in the 1820s[16] – and cut off from easy contact, both within the country and with the outside world, by the difficulties of transport and communication across the mountainous Andean landscape.

Economic policy and economic development, 1819–49

In economic terms, separation from Spain had several important impli-cations. As an independent nation, Colombia had direct access to foreign markets and foreign capital, economic policy was brought under national direction, and Colombian entrepreneurs could participate more fully in the country's external commerce. In the long term, the significance of these changes was considerable, permitting alterations in both the direction and composition of external trade, strengthening the domestic mercantile bourgeoisie and modifying the relative importance of groups and regions within the Colombian economy. But in the short term, during the early decades of republican government, the Colombian economy saw only minor adjustments to the patterns of economic activity characteristic of the colonial period.

The failure quickly to emerge from the chrysalis of colonial control cannot be attributed to the conservatism of government or the politicized classes which formed its constituency. Drawn from a society where even rich landowners did not disdain to engage in wholesale and retail trade, the merchants, lawyers and clerics who participated in the first republican government under Santander shared a broad consensus of attitudes towards economic policy, favouring freedom for commerce and economic enterprise. The prevailing tendency in these years was to attribute the country's economic ills to Spanish mercantilism, and to assume that the removal of institutional obstacles to private initiative was sufficient to guarantee economic recovery and to lay the foundations of future prosperity. Accordingly, among the first acts of the Congress of Cucutá – the legislature of the Republic of Gran Colombia – were measures to abolish fiscal and corporative restrictions on production and commerce, to promote freedom for foreign trade, and to encourage free markets for land and labour.[17]

The pressing financial needs of government ensured that certain vestiges of colonial restriction were left untouched. Faced with heavy charges on a national treasury depleted by war, the first Santander regime was forced to be flexible in its application of the principles of liberal economics. Indian tribute, the liquor monopoly and the colonial sales tax were removed, but the tobacco and salt monopolies, taxes on the sale of liquor, and the tithe remained. The impulse to free overseas trade from tariffs was also checked by fiscal considerations, for customs revenues had now become a major source of government income.[18] Efforts were made to reduce and to simplify duties, but throughout the 1820s duties on foreign imports remained high. However, as their main aim was to raise revenues rather than to provide protection, such duties did not conflict with a general belief that greater freedom for economic enterprise was the key to economic progress.[19]

The prevailing tendency towards a *laissez-faire* approach to economic policy was tempered by government intervention in some areas. In order to foster the growth of a national mercantile marine, national shipping and the goods which it imported were subject to lower port charges and lower duties than those imposed on foreign shipping. Attention was also given to the creation of a direct trade with Asia, and special concessions were afforded by the tariffs of 1823 and 1826 to Asiatic imports brought in national ships. Neither of these measures was successful. The advantages of national shippers were counteracted by special trade treaties, such as that made with Great Britain in 1825, while the direct traffic with Asia never became more than a dim reflection of the bright hopes of men like Bolívar who saw Colombia as a future bridge between Europe and the East.[20]

In these early years, some limited concessions were also made to encourage the application of modern techniques to Colombian resources. It was acknowledged that special privileges were permissible in areas of economic activity which required the mobilization of substantial amounts of capital or specialized technology, and where the entry of foreign investment and skill was particularly desirable. Special arrangements were therefore made to encourage foreign investment in mining, companies were given monopoly rights for the production of certain goods for stated periods and in stated areas, and monopoly contracts extended for the improvement of transportation.[21] However, such concessions yielded few positive results. Schemes for setting up ironworks and cotton and paper mills, though more serious than Cochrane's quixotic scheme to improve pearl-fishing by the use of a diving-bell, suffered the same fate as that ill conceived project. In the field of transportation also, government concessions met with disappointing results. Contracts such as that given to Juan Elbers to operate steamboats on the Magdalena River, or those drawn up for the construction of new roads and port facilities, and, most extravagant, for the construction of an inter-oceanic canal all foundered in the face of technical problems, lack of capital and insufficient government support.[22]

If economic progress in these years failed to measure up to political expectations, it was largely because the position of Colombia within the international economy remained fundamentally unchanged. Colombia's foreign trade continued to rest on gold exports, and the country was still caught in the highly specialized role in the world economy prepared by its commercial relations with metropolitan Spain. Like other Latin American countries, Colombia was exposed to a brief and intense burst of British trade and investment in the 1820s, but the boom soon burst. With British loans to the government of Gran Colombia in 1820, 1822 and 1824 went an upsurge in trade with Britain, as the loans helped to provide foreign exchange for the purchase of imports. However, when the government defaulted in 1826, the inflow of investment was stemmed and Colombia became unattractive to British enterprise and capital. Without external finance, overseas trade sank back into colonial patterns in the 1830s and 1840s, as imports were forced into line with the country's ability to provide gold in exchange.[23] As British capital turned away from Latin America, towards better opportunities in Europe and the United States, Colombia was left to vegetate on the 'old periphery' of

Hispanic American precious metal producers, awaiting the redirection of European capital and commerce.[24]

Without new sources of overseas demand or supplies of foreign capital, economic change was necessarily slow. Access to gold did allow the merchants of Antioquia to strengthen the position they had acquired as importers of British manufactures, and the capital which they accumulated in trade not only bolstered the mining industry in Antioquia itself, but also found its way into other regions.[25] However, the consolidation of domestic mercantile control over external trade and the internal accumulation of capital did not propel the economy out of stagnation. Indeed, when British investment fell off, the economy entered a phase of depression which lasted from around 1830 until about 1845.

During this period, available capital tended to gravitate towards the import trade and the financial sector, to a government laden with debts, and contributed little to the expansion of domestic production or the improvement of the domestic infrastructure. In the organization of trade, continuity with colonial patterns of commerce was apparent in the continuing predominance of Bogotá as a commercial centre, in the emphasis on importation, and in the concentration of import business in the hands of a small number of powerful wholesalers. Foreign houses had been established in the major cities, and direct relations formed with commercial centres in both Europe and the USA. But while the costs and risks of overseas commerce remained at a high level and were not offset by access to cheap credit, opportunities to engage in trade were largely restricted to those few merchants who possessed sufficient capital to organize a slow-moving wholesale trade in imports, and who used Bogotá as a centre for distribution to surrounding regions. According to a contemporary observer, Miguel Samper, the centralization of overseas commerce in Bogotá was a function of political centralization. By attracting a concourse of government employees, dependents and creditors, the centralization of government perpetuated the capital's colonial status as an artificial and parasitic centre for consumption, a position reinforced by laws which, by prohibiting the export of unminted gold, funnelled the gold trade towards Bogatá, the centre for minting.[26]

The emphasis of Colombian merchants on importing, inherited from their Spanish predecessors, had damaging effects on the domestic economy. Not only did the import of British textiles inhibit growth in domestic textile manufacture, but it also generated a balance of payments deficit which could only be covered with an outflow of circulating gold and silver currency.[27] Without a paper currency to meet domestic needs for a circulating medium, this haemorrhage of specie perpetuated the deflationary effects of overseas trade which colonial commentators had already identified as an impediment to domestic development during the eighteenth century.[28] The dampening economic effects of specie outflow were aggravated by irregularities in the organization of the internal monetary system. The circulation of many different types of coinage of varying real values, and the presence of much counterfeit money, weakened confidence in the medium of exchange and tended to drive gold and silver out of internal circulation.[29] The consequent scarcity of money not only impeded commercial transactions, but also helped to push interest rates to very high levels. High interest rates encouraged speculation in real estate, in commercial and government paper, and led in 1841 to a speculative spiral in Bogotá which, when it disintegrated into bankruptcy, further damaged the structure of public and private credit.[30]

When new opportunities in international markets failed to materialize, there was no alternative basis for growth. Although Colombian politicians recognized the need to promote economic development, they were incapable of framing policies which might effectively meet this need. With the failure of the *laissez-faire* approach followed during the 1820s, economic stasis weakened the political commitment to liberal policies. During the 1820s there had been a powerful conservative minority in the legislature which, by opposing liberal policies towards mortmain and by resisting liberal efforts to free interest rates from colonial restrictions, had voiced the dissent of those who still retained an attachment to the social organization and moral attitudes of the old order.[31] After 1830, such conservative approaches to economic policy were to play an increasingly influential part in shaping government action.

The reaction against the liberalism of the early republic has complex roots, and its social and economic dimensions are imperfectly understood. Political conflict involved much more than mere differences over economic policy and, as Frank Safford has shown, cannot be understood merely in terms of simple correlations with class or economic interest.[32] In nineteenth-century Colombia, merchants, landowners and professionals were distributed among opposing sides in politics, and the struggle between liberals and conservatives cannot be reduced to a crude dichotomy between merchants and landowners. However, Safford's analysis does indicate that the broadly conservative coalition which became the dominant force in Colombian politics during the 1830s was composed largely of landowners, merchants and professionals who were closely connected with the patterns of colonial life. They were from families which had inherited privileged positions in the established centres of colonial society, and were primarily preoccupied with preserving the existing social order. While their opponents in the peripheral provincial economies consolidated their commitment to liberalism as a means of competing with the entrenched centres of colonial society, the leading citizens of the major colonial cities adopted attitudes consonant with their desire to retain their inherited privileges and the social and economic order upon which they depended. Faced by depression and disorder in the 1830s and 1840s, and unburdened of the optimistic illusions cultivated immediately after independence, these urban elites turned towards an interventionist economic policy that was more finely attuned to their social pretensions and political instincts.

For conservatives based in the main colonial cities, especially in Bogotá with its traditional role at the heart of colonial administration, the Bourbon example of reform from above, by government fiat, was still relevant. During the late colonial period, Bourbon administrators had introduced schemes to advance the exploitation of the colony's economic resources by the introduction of modern techniques, the dissemination of scientific, practical knowledge, and the useful employment of the poor in industrial projects. Although none of these schemes was very successful, the notion that government was a crucial agency for reform and rationalization, and that scientific education and innovation were vital to economic progress, left an enduring imprint on the attitudes of the Colombian upper class. In the decade after independence, these attitudes were apparent in schemes to contract European scientists to work in Colombia, and in plans for channelling university students into the study of applied science.[33] During the 1830s and 1840s, government intervention to promote economic development also spread into other areas, as conservative statesmen flirted with neo-mercantilist solutions to the problems of economic depression and social disorder.

From their policies, two distinctive and interrelated tendencies emerge. First, in central Colombia, in the vicinity of the capital, steps were taken to encourage the development of a domestic industry through the extension of government aid to entrepreneurs. The concessions of monopoly or partial monopoly privileges made during the first Santander regime were extended under the governments of the Republic of New Granada. Between 1832 and 1844, exclusive rights for the application of new techniques were granted to enterprises producing china and porcelain, paper, glass, cotton cloth and iron. The government also offered long-term loans at low rates of interest to entrepreneurs setting up new enterprises, though the financial state of the treasury probably meant that few, if any, such loans were made.[34] In addition, it sought to encourage training in industrial skills by setting up workshops, creating apprenticeship schemes, and undertaking to instil industrious habits among the lower classes through both material incentives and coercion.[35] The second major strand of government policy designed to promote industrial growth involved the provision of tariff protection. In 1831 the *Secretario de Hacienda*, José Ignacio de Márquez, presented a series of arguments for the adoption of a protectionist policy which would prohibit the importation of foreign goods that competed with domestic products, in order to permit the development of industry which had been held back by the colonial system.[36]

However, government concern with the development of import-substitute industries was half-hearted and had no noticeable impact on the national economy. Of the various projects launched during this period, few achieved any enduring success. None was afforded adequate protection from the competition of foreign imports and, when the projects failed to make quick profits, investors soon pulled out. The ironworks of Pacho (some fifty miles from Bogotá) and the porcelain factory founded in Bogotá in 1832 were the only enterprises to survive and, after a period of losses, to bring profit to their owners. Both enjoyed some special advantages, owing to the high quality of local raw materials used in production and to the protection provided by the difficulties of carrying such goods over the mule-tracks of central Colombia.

While attempts to imitate European technical and industrial prowess foundered, the traditional cottage textile industry of the Socorro region was deprived of consistent or adequate support. Although duties on imports were increased, they did not have the effect desired by Márquez. With the elimination of costly mediation by the Spanish commercial system and the reduction in the prices of British cottons, high duties on imports did not prevent them from competing with domestic products. Only the continuing high cost of internal transport, and Colombia's inability to pay for a rapid growth of imports, prevented imports from inflicting greater damage.

However, if such indirect protection forestalled the onset of a rapid decline in Colombian textile production, it could not prevent the gradual erosion of its position in the domestic market. Although it retained a substantial share of the lower end of the market, the traditional industry was starved of the injections of capital and entrepreneurial organization required to transform it into an effective long-term competitor with foreign products. Ospina Vásquez has suggested that, although the mechanization of cotton-spinning in Europe had placed Colombian producers in a position of marked technical inferiority, the techniques employed in weaving were not so different. Hand-weaving was still widespread throughout Europe and, Ospina implies, the traditional craft industry in Colombia offered as suitable a base for modernization as did that in Europe.[37] However, if mechanization was possible, the capital and organizational skills required to carry it through were absent. Without them, in the face of competition from mechanized industries abroad, the traditional textile industry had no future. If its demise was delayed by the stagnation of the external sector before mid-century, its eventual fate was assured. After 1850 the incipient decline of the preceding decades accelerated rapidly, changing the modest prosperity of many artisans into poverty and indigence.

While the colonial pattern of trade based on the exchange of gold for manufactured imports remained intact, the pursuit of industrialization was chimerical. Mining and the import business that it supported continued to constitute the most profitable sectors of the economy, and scarce capital was either drained abroad in exchange payments or tied up in the import trade and financial sector. Under these circumstances, it was politically impossible to provide effective protection for national industry or to create the monetary institutions required to offset the shortage of capital outside the external sector. To promote the development of an autonomous national industry demanded much more than the panaceas of conservative politicians. It required support from a financially stable and prosperous government, backed and influenced by groups with economic interests in the manufacturing sector. Such groups were able to exert some pressure on government policy in Mexico, but in Colombia manufacturing interests were not represented in government.[38] The diluted, fiscally orientated protectionism of conservative administrations, their penchant for projects and monopoly contracts, their interest in 'useful knowledge', in education and in technical training, were feeble essays in economic and social reform, which eventually satisfied no one. By the late 1840s, disillusionment among both the political and economic elites and the artisans provoked a period of political ferment and confrontation. Between 1849 and 1854 a new coalition of interests, more firmly attached to the export sector and more firmly committed to *laissez-faire*, came to the forefront of Colombian politics, marking the beginning of a distinctive phase in economic policy and economic development.

The political economy of the export cycle, 1850–75

The political upheaval which affected Colombia at mid-century originated with the reassertion of liberal economic policies by a dissident faction within the ruling elite.[39] In 1847 import tariffs were drastically reduced, exposing artisans to a sudden surge of foreign competition. Faced with this threat, the artisans began to organize in political clubs, the 'Democratic Societies', and in the year before the presidential election of 1849 they joined in an unprecedented political mobilization with other opponents of the dominant conservative groups.[40] Radical liberal intellectuals, resentful of their exclusion from career opportunities and inspired by revolutionary doctrines emanating from France in 1848, gave both ideological and organizational support to the artisans.[41] Between 1849 and 1854, during the presidencies of López and Obando, these radical liberals – known as the 'Generation of 1849' – rushed through a series of reforms designed to sweep away the institutional remnants of the colonial order. These included the abolition of slavery, the separation of Church and state, and the legalization of civil marriage. Anathema to conservatives, these measures provoked a rebellion in 1851, which was quickly crushed.[42] Disillusioned by government neglect of their economic interests and political aspirations, and allied to an army faction concerned for its future, the artisans joined in an abortive military coup in 1854. They too were defeated and henceforth ceased to be an effective political force. After a brief respite, civil war broke out once more at the end of the 1850s until, with the adoption of the federal constitution of the United States of Colombia in 1863, the Liberal ascendancy was finally consolidated. Having established their influence in the early 1850s, the Liberals had gradually fused into a political party capable of fighting off all challenges to its power and of creating a political hegemony which was to endure until the late 1870s.

The Liberal ascendancy during the second half of the nineteenth century was associated in the economic sphere with the growth of Colombia's external trade. In the later 1840s, the beginnings of tobacco export and the disturbance of world gold markets by the California bonanza of 1849 signalled the onset of changes in both the composition and the scale of Colombia's exports. From mid-century until the early 1880s, the Colombian economy entered a distinctive phase of development, based on cycles of exports of tobacco, indigo and quinine, with cotton, sugar, vanilla and rubber making brief contributions in addition to the continuing outflow of gold from the mining areas. At the core of this growth in Colombian exports were increasing sales of Colombian leaf tobacco in German markets. For nearly a quarter-century after 1850 tobacco became the country's largest single export, accounting for between 70 and 90 per cent of total exports between 1852 and 1875, and involving an appreciable change in the country's position in the international economy. After the stagnation of previous decades, new contacts with overseas markets offered an escape from the constraints imposed by small domestic markets, and promised to provide the vital stimulus to domestic development that had been lacking since independence.

The Colombian bourgeoisie, particularly the rich merchants of Antioquia, seized the opportunities for profit offered by overseas demand and poured energy and capital into the development of tobacco, and later cotton and indigo plantations in the tropical frontier zones of the upper Magdalena valley.[43] New blood infused the traditional circles of upper-class society in Bogotá and new men, often from modest provincial backgrounds, extolled the virtues of dedication and discipline in the mundane travails of commerce.[44] The resurgence of liberalism which had begun in the late 1840s was now carried forward on the wave of export expansion and, as the Liberal party became the dominant force in Colombian politics, successive governments sought to clear the way for the unrestrained commercialization of the economy around the burgeoning export sector. The suppression of the state tobacco monopoly in

1850, which marked the sharp upward movement of tobacco export, was one element in a series of reforms designed to remodel Colombian economy and society. Decrees for the abolition of Indian community lands in 1850, for the abolition of slavery in 1851, for the disamortization of Church property in 1861, and the sale of government lands to private owners, all sought to remove obstacles to the free allocation of factors of production.

The power of central government was also drastically reduced. Not only was it deprived of a vital source of revenue with the termination of the tobacco monopoly, but many of its powers and functions were passed to regional state governments by the federal constitutions of 1854, 1858, and especially that of 1863. Colombian liberalism thereby sought to put into practice the central principles of classical liberal political economy, reducing the role of central government to that of a caretaker in an economy where future development was to be based on the exploitation of Colombia's comparative advantage as a producer of primary commodities. The vague and ineffective notions of industrialization current during the 1830s and 1840s were swept aside, to be replaced by a vision of the Colombian economy as an integral and complementary part of an international economy where the industrial nations would buy Colombia's primary products, while supplying the manufactured goods which they could best produce to Colombian consumers. Thus, interacting with the effects of export expansion after 1850 were domestic policies which fragmented and dispersed the power of central government, greatly modified the role of government as an agent of economic and social policy, and attacked the traditional relations of Church and state. The economic repercussions of export growth must, then, be seen against a background of political turbulence and reorganization generated by Liberal efforts to transform the nature of the Colombian state.

At first sight, the performance of Colombian exports from mid-century until the mid-1870s was impressive. In the early 1850s, the value of Colombian exports was more than double that of previous decades since independence and, with some minor interruptions, continued to increase during the 1860s and early 1870s.[45] Tobacco provided the principal impetus behind this growth, until competition from cheaper Java tobacco undermined its markets in Europe in 1875.[46] Cotton boomed briefly when US production was dislocated during the American Civil War. Exports of indigo assumed some importance in the 1870s as, in the 1850s, late 60s and finally in 1880–1, did exports of cinchona bark. Another novel export was that of straw hats, which were increasingly exported to the Caribbean in the 1850s and which, after a decline in the 1860s, re-emerged as a significant export in the early 1870s.[47] Gold, for so long Colombia's major export, was relegated to a much less important position in this period, supplying no more than about 15 per cent of the average annual value of Colombian exports.[48] Finally, coffee began to make a small contribution to exports during the 1860s, a contribution which became significant with the decline of tobacco, but which did not reveal its real potential for growth until the turn of the century.[49]

Seen within the context of the Colombian economy as a whole, the performance of the export sector becomes less impressive. Assessment of the performance of the Colombian economy during this period is hindered by the lack of both adequate official statistics and detailed regional studies. Nonetheless, Colombian historians have long recognized that export expansion was not the harbinger of prosperity and that greater dependence on foreign trade was, at best, a very insecure basis for domestic development. Indeed, in a recent analysis W. P. McGreevey has argued that, far from promoting economic growth, the cycle of primary commodity exports was associated with economic decline.[50]

McGreevey reaches this conclusion from a quantitative analysis of the net effects of trade expansion for the period 1850–70. On the side of 'gains' from trade, he estimates the amount of income earned from exports and allows for the real growth in incomes permitted by the consumption of lower-priced foreign imports. On the 'losses' side, he estimates the fall in national income provoked by the erosion of markets for domestic artisan products, the related loss of markets for domestic producers who had supplied the artisans, and the losses incurred by the peasantry as a result of Liberal policies which reduced employment opportunities and incomes in the agrarian sector. From this statistical exercise he derives the conclusion that gains to merchants, producers in the export sector and urban consumers of imports were far outweighed by the losses in income sustained by the artisans and the peasantry.[51]

There are considerable flaws in McGreevey's analysis, mainly arising from the kind of data which he deploys to demonstrate Colombian decline. His estimates of the levels of national consumption of importable products, of artisan production and its responses to import competition, and of freight rates, and his use of multipliers to calculate the costs and benefits of commercial expansion, all involve assumptions which, in the absence of concrete data, are difficult to sustain.[52] However, although McGreevey's estimates of the net impact of trade are far from conclusive, his diagnosis of decline is a forceful reminder of the flaws in the model of economic development that underpinned the economic policies of Colombia's ruling elites during the nineteenth century.

In government circles, the connection between economic progress and the expansion of trade was regarded as axiomatic. Under Spanish hegemony, trade with Europe was seen as essential both for the provision of consumer goods and, from the late eighteenth century, as a channel for exports of primary products. After independence this attitude was reinforced by liberal doctrines which, though partially eclipsed during the depression of the 1830s, seemed to be vindicated with the onset of export expansion in the late 1840s. Although they divided on other issues, there was no serious challenge from within the elite to the ideology of free trade, until the export sector collapsed in 1875. However, if the growth of the export sector was believed to be the essential foundation for both private and public prosperity, closer integration into the international economy as an exporter of tropical commodities entailed a form of development which was not conducive either to national economic progress or to political peace and stability.

The failure of export expansion to provide a base for domestic development may be attributed, in part, to the fact that export growth was insufficiently vigorous. At first, expansion was impressive, but it was not sustained. McGreevey estimates that, for the period 1845–85, exports grew at an annual average cumulative rate of 5 per cent. However, growth was concentrated in the years from 1845 to 1864. From 1866 to 1885, the overall trend in exports was towards stagnation. While Colombia became much more dependent on foreign trade, the country remained a weak exporter, with per capita export levels that were much lower than those of other Latin American countries.[53] Until coffee exports began to expand at the end of the century, exports did not keep pace with population growth.

A second problem was that the 'spread effects' of export growth were very limited. Although the volume and value of exports went through a phase of rapid growth, the area affected by export agriculture was small, and income generated in it was concentrated in the hands of a few merchants and landowners, whose consumption patterns favoured imports and had few multiplied effects on the domestic economy.[54] Rural society was largely untouched by production for export, while the release of Church and Indian lands previously held in mortmain does not appear to have had the desired effect of encouraging the commercialization of agriculture.[55] Moreover, while tobacco export improved transportation along the River Magdalena – the main artery of communication between coast and interior – neither the export of tobacco nor of other primary products did much to ameliorate the difficulties of transportation in the interior of the country.

As a source of capital available for investment in other sectors of the economy, the export economy also appears to have made only a limited contribution to domestic development. Capital from tobacco and gold-mining was both to contribute to the foundation of commercial banking during the 1870s and ultimately to provide some finance for the development of coffee cultivation.[56] However, for much of the period under consideration, it seems that capital generated in the export sector was attracted to less productive uses – in government bonds, in loans in the import-export business, in gold or in investments abroad – as merchants tried to avoid the risks arising from sharp fluctuations in export prices.[57] Indeed, it has been suggested that fluctuations in demand for export commodities encouraged Colombian capitalists to act more as speculators than as producers. When world prices for a product available for export were high, they moved to exploit it; when prices fell, they shifted their investment and enterprise into the exploitation of other exports, rather than responding to price changes by trying to become more competitive through innovations in organization, marketing or technology.[58] In view of the nature of some exports, such as cinchona bark, where the form of production was essentially extractive, and the wide fluctuations in world prices for the products which Colombia exported, such unwillingness to commit capital to long-term specialization is not surprising.

A third general problem arising from the surge of export expansion at mid-century was associated with its repercussions on the import trade. While export expansion in the years from 1845 to 1864 permitted a rapid growth of imports, the stagnation of exports after 1866 did not bring a proportionate fall in imports. To cover the persistent deficit on the balance of payments, capital was drained out of the country in exchange payments, creating downward pressures on domestic prices and incomes. From the 1870s, emissions from newly established banks helped to offset the drainage of gold specie and the liquidity problems which it caused. However, McGreevey suggests that another, more damaging, mechanism of adjustment was activated by trade deficits during the years after the mid-1860s. He argues that the burden of deflation was borne in large part by artisan groups who lost their markets to foreign textiles, and whose loss of income was multiplied downwards through the local economies of artisan regions. The effects of deflation were noticeable in the stagnation of urban areas; rapid growth in exports did not lead to the extension of employment opportunities or to greater concentration of population in the urban centres.[59]

The unequal distribution of benefits from the external sector was not necessarily an impediment to economic growth. Indeed, under 'classical' conditions for growth, the transfer of labour from traditional agricultural and artisan activities, and the depression of their consumption, have provided the cheap labour force and the capital vital for industrialization. However, in nineteenth-century Colombia the redistribution of income away from peasants and artisans did not produce savings and investment which were available to enterprises into which displaced labour might have been absorbed. Moreover, the social tensions associated with such lower-class pauperization may have been aggravated by mercantile speculation in land in some areas of Colombia. By disturbing the older, more traditional landowners and challenging their pre-eminence in rural society, the entry of new wealth into the agrarian sector may have intensified political conflict within the elite.

Throughout the nineteenth century violent conflict was a constant theme in Colombian political life, affecting the welfare of its citizens and the development of its economy. The economic costs of civil disorder are difficult to measure, but there was little doubt in the minds of contemporaries that insecurity and violence greatly damaged the economy.[60] Men and materials were poured into unproductive uses and diverted from their existing uses; commerce and production were paralyzed by conflict or the fear of conflict; capital was diverted to war financing, and government finances thrown into continuous disarray.

The origins of political instability and civil disorder defy easy definition, but the determination of the Liberals to reconstitute the Colombian state in accord with the principles of liberal political economy undoubtedly helped to deepen divisions within Colombian society, and to generate political turmoil. For even within the landed and mercantile groups connected to the external sector, there was no consensus on important political questions such as the relations of Church and state or the distribution of power between central and provincial government, and Liberal efforts to innovate in these areas were a frequent provocation to open conflict.[61] The decentralization of government power which followed the adoption of federalism, with its dispersal of financial and military resources to the provinces, may at the same time have increased the likelihood of inter-regional conflicts over such issues, while reducing the ability of central government to maintain or to re-establish public order. Equally, by transferring the responsibilities of government in such vital areas as transportation to provincial administrations, the Liberals reduced the ability of central government to pursue a coherent strategy for improving the economic infrastructure in a manner conducive to greater national political and economic integration.[62]

But perhaps the major fault of Liberalism was that, in its eagerness to purge the country of the residues of colonialism, it ignored the enduring influences of the colonial past and their capacity to resist and to mutate Liberal innovations. Assuming that the free pursuit of individual gain was synonymous with public welfare, they adopted policies which, in an economic and social system characterized by deep inequalities in the distribution of wealth and power between both classes and regions, tended to accentuate divisions. If the export sector had been a more effective 'growth-pole', then Liberal policy might have been less divisive. But while gains from the export sector were narrowly distributed, the struggle for control of government, with the perquisites of office, was aggravated by the accentuation of inequalities. This was succinctly expressed by a Liberal politician who, when relating the poverty and backwardness of Colombia to its political instability, stated that 'in

Colombia the first, if not the only industries of national, popular character have been civil war and politics'.[63]

While earnings from exports held up, the inadequacy of development based on the external sector was disguised and the ideological commitment to *laissez-faire* was sustained. But when tobacco markets collapsed in 1875, depression in the export sector precipitated an acute political crisis. Not only did government income fall drastically – a problem of export fluctuations which had caused political crises in the past – but it forced a change in tariff policy, and encouraged the critics of Liberalism to extend their resistance to Liberal policies into the economic sphere. Indeed, the Liberal party itself split, allowing Conservatives who had steadfastly opposed Liberal policies towards the Church throughout the preceding years to join with disaffected Liberals and to attack both *laissez-faire* policies and the entire ideological basis on which they rested.[64]

However, although the 1880s and 1890s saw a retreat from the political positions established by Radical Liberals, the defeat of Liberalism was neither total nor permanent. It coincided with depression in the export sector, and when that sector revived, with the expansion of coffee exports, the political fortunes of the Liberal Party were resuscitated. Although the expansion of exports from 1850 to 1875 had not succeeded in transforming the economy or in perfecting the Liberal state, it had lasting implications for the development of Colombian economy and society. The failure of liberal economic policies in the 1820s had seen a temporary shift towards a more cautious and internally orientated economic policy; the collapse of exports in the late 1870s was to provoke a similar reaction. But the underlying commitment of the landed and mercantile elites to export-based development, an orientation shaped during the colonial period, always resurfaced. If the Liberal political order proved fragile, its social basis was not destroyed. The reforms introduced during the period of Liberal hegemony may have been based on imperfect integration into the international economy, but they had gone some way towards altering the social relations of production in Colombia and to strengthening the mercantile and agrarian bourgeoisie.

Liberal policies had helped to destroy traditional ways of life and to impose the harsh realities of freedom in a market economy on peasants and artisans who had been sheltered by the slower tempo of activity in the colonial economy. They had also cleared the way for the formation of a dominant class with more clearly-defined economic interests and greater internal coherence, enabling it to exert closer control over the machinery of state.[65] Ultimately, of course, it was the renewal of growth in the export sector, based on foreign demand for coffee, which laid the foundations of a more stable order. Taking place under domestic and international conditions which were distinct from those of the first export cycle of the nineteenth century, coffee exports were to prove a more durable and effective vehicle for economic growth and political stabilization, and for the realization of ambitions frustrated during the nineteenth century.

Notes

[1] For the sake of convenience, nineteenth-century variations in the titles used to describe the modern state of Colombia are avoided in the text. Known as the Kingdom of New Granada during the colonial period, Colombia became the Republic of Gran Colombia (together with Venezuela and Ecuador) between 1819 and 1830; the Republic of New Granada between 1832 and 1857, the Granadine Confederation between 1857 and 1863, the United States of Colombia between 1863 and 1886, until finally becoming the Republic of Colombia in 1886.

[2] Javier Ocampo Lopez *El proceso ideológico de la emancipación* (Bogotá 1974) pp. 321–406, 463–82.

[3] V. Lecuna and H. A. Bierck *Selected writings of Bolívar* (New York 1951) ɪ p. 197.

[4] An outline of the problems and state of research in the economic history of Colombia is given by W. P. McGreevey in R. C. Cortés Conde and S. J. Stein (eds) *Latin America. A guide to economic history 1830–1930* (Berkeley 1977) pp. 367–82.

[5] R. A. Humphreys (ed.) *British consular reports on the trade and politics of Latin America, 1824–1826* (London 1940) p. 264

[6] There is little work on the effects of war during the Spanish reconquest and the early years of independence. José Maria Samper, writing in 1861, states that it involved the deaths of some 200,000 people and set back the growth of population. See his *Ensayo sobre las revoluciones políticas* (Bogotá 1974 edn) p. 303. But his calculations were based on flimsy data. For some further comment, see David Bushnell *The Santander regime in Gran Colombia* (Newark 1954) pp. 127–9.

[7] For a general account of the development of mining during the colonial period, see R. C. West *Colonial placer mining in Colombia* (Baton Rouge 1952) *passim*.

[8] A brief outline of the local economy of Socorro in the eighteenth century is given in J. L. Phelan *The people and the king. The Comunero Revolution in Colombia, 1781* (Madison 1978) pp. 39–44.

[9] On agriculture during the colonial period, see Juan A. Villamarin 'Encomenderos and Indians in the formation of a colonial society in the Sabana de Bogotá, 1537–1740' (unpubl. Ph.D. thesis, Brandeis University 1972), and Hermes Tovar Pinzón 'Agrarian development in New Granada during the eighteenth century' (unpubl. D.Phil., Oxford University 1978). On agriculture in central Colombia during the early nineteenth century, see F. R. Safford 'Commerce and enterprise in central Colombia, 1821–1870' (unpubl. Ph.D. thesis, Columbia University 1965) pp. 102–14.

[10] The mediocrity of creole landed fortunes during the late colonial period often drew comment from contemporary observers. See, for example, Francisco Moreno y Escandon 'Estado del virreinato de Santo Fé, nuevo reino de Granada' *Boletín de Historia y Antiguedades* xxiii (1935) 554. For a compilation of the observations of foreign travellers during the early nineteenth century, see Safford, thesis, pp. 45–8.

[11] On mining in the Pacific lowlands, see W. F. Shard 'Forsaken but for gold: an economic study of slavery and mining in the Colombian Choco, 1680–1810' (unpubl. Ph.D. thesis, University of North Carolina 1970).

[12] Michael Taussig 'The evolution of rural wage labour in the Cauca Valley of Colombia, 1700–1970' in K. Duncan and I. Rutledge (eds) *Land and labour in Latin America* (Cambridge 1977) pp. 397–409.

[13] Ann Twinam 'Miners, merchants and farmers: the roots of entrepreneurship in Antioquia, 1763–1810' (unpubl. Ph.D. thesis, Yale University 1976)

[14] A. McFarlane 'Economic and political change in the vice-royalty of New Granada with special reference to overseas trade, 1739–1810' (unpubl. Ph.D. thesis, University of London 1977) pp. 208–308.

[15] It has been suggested that the Spanish Crown made substantial transfers of revenue from Colombia to Spain during the eighteenth century, and thereby acted as a principal agent for capital export which depressed the colonial economy. See W. P. McGreevey *An economic history of Colombia, 1854–1930* (Cambridge 1971) pp. 27–8, 48. However, there is no evidence to suggest that the Crown made such large transfers of capital. Not only was the colonial treasury subsidized by transfers of revenue from Quito and Lima, but it was not until the period 1790–6 that the first remittances to Spain were made. See McFarlane, thesis, pp. 149–61.

[16] For contemporary estimates of population, see Humphreys (ed.) *op. cit.* p. 267.

[17] An account of economic policy under the first Santander regime is given by Bushnell *op. cit.* pp. 127–50.

[18] *Ibid.* pp. 76–111.

[19] *Ibid.* p. 155; Ospina Vásquez points out that the elimination of the Spanish monopoly system and the reduction of costs in Britain meant that British textiles could sustain high duties without greatly affecting the taste for such merchandise. Thus the tariff on these goods, which in 1829 stood at 18.5 and 22.5 per cent (depending on whether they were imported in national or foreign ships), did not reduce their importation, nor provide protection for domestic manufacturers: Luis Ospina Vásquez *Industria y protección en Colombia 1810–1930* (Bogotá 1974) pp. 138–40.

[20] *Ibid.* pp. 141–58.

[21] For information on these schemes, see Bushnell *op. cit.* pp. 134–43; Safford, thesis, pp. 149–50; Ospina Vásquez *op. cit.* pp. 161–2.

[22] For an account of the Elbers project, see R. L. Gilmore and J. P. Harrison 'Juan Bernardo Elbers and the introduction of steam navigation on the Magdalena River' *Hispanic American Historical Review* (hereafter *HAHR*) xxviii 3 (1948).

[23] On foreign loans, see Bushnell *op. cit.* pp. 112–26; on British trade with Colombia and the US, see McGreevey *op. cit.* pp. 35–6.

[24] The phrase 'old periphery' is Wallerstein's. See I. Wallerstein *The modern world system II: mercantilism and the consolidation of the European world-economy, 1600–1750* (New York 1980) pp. 166–7. On trends in British investment in Latin America in this period, see P. L. Cottrell *British overseas investment in the nineteenth century* (London 1975) pp. 19–25.

[25] On the characteristics of the emergent mercantile bourgeoisie of Antioquia during the late colonial period, see Ann Twinam 'Enterprise and elites in eighteenth-century Medellín' *HAHR* lix 2 (1979). There is in addition a large literature on nineteenth-century Antioquia, drawing attention to the special characteristics of the region and their relationship to its economic development. For a discussion of these themes, see F. R. Safford 'Significación de los antioqueños en el desarrollo económico colombiano: un examen crítico de la tesis de Everett Hagen' *Anuario colombiano de historia social y de la cultura* ii (1965). On the development of the Antioqueño economy after independence, see Roger Brew *El desarrollo económico de Antioquia desde la independencia hasta 1920* (Bogotá 1977). On the movement of Antioqueño capital to central Colombia, see Brew *op. cit.* p. 90; Safford, thesis, pp. 91, 392.

[26] Miguel Samper *La miseria en Bogotá y otros escritos* (Bogotá 1969) pp. 18–33.

[27] L. Nieto Arteta *Economía y cultura en la historia de Colombia* (Bogotá 1962) p. 331, shows trade balances in this period.

[28] For observations by colonial commentators on the problem of deflation, see McFarlane, thesis, pp. 198–200, 270.

[29] Safford, thesis, pp. 114–27.

[30] Safford, thesis, pp. 68–79. For a more detailed treatment see M. Deas 'Los problemas fiscales en Colombia durante el siglo XIX' in M. Urrutia (ed.) *Ensayos de historia económica colombiana* (Bogotá 1980).

31 On these factions, see Bushnell *op. cit.* pp. 52–4.

32 F. R. Safford 'Social aspects of politics in nineteenth-century Spanish America: New Granada, 1825–1850' *Journal of Social History* v (1972), 'Bases of political alignment in early republican Spanish America' in R. Graham and P. H. Smith (eds) *New approaches to Latin American history* (Austin 1974).

33 For an account of the main strands of political and social thought after independence, see J. Jaramillo Uribe *El pensamiento colombiano en el siglo XIX* (Bogotá 1974) pp. 119–49. On attitudes towards science and education, see F. R. Safford *The ideal of the practical* (Austin 1976) pp. 99–123.

34 These projects and their outcomes are described in Safford, thesis, pp. 150–75, 179–86.

35 Safford *The ideal of the practical* pp. 55–72.

36 These arguments were put forward in an address to the Convention of 1831. For a lengthy quotation from this address, showing the principal ideas of Márquez, see Ospina Vásquez *op. cit.* pp. 194–8. Also Aníbal Galindo 'Apuntemientos para la historia económica y fiscal del país' (1874) chap. 3, in Aníbal Galindo *Estudios económicos y fiscales* (Bogotá 1978) pp. 142–50.

37 Ospina Vásquez *op. cit.* pp. 171–2, 176.

38 In the textile manufacturing area of Socorro, both merchants and political representatives were committed to free trade and were among its most active protagonists. See Safford in Graham and Smith *op. cit.* p. 98.

39 For a brief survey of Colombian politics in these years, see J. León Helguera 'The problem of Liberalism versus Conservatism in Colombia: 1849–1885' in F. B. Pike (ed.) *Latin American history: select problems* (New York 1969) pp. 226–32.

40 J. Jaramillo Uribe 'Las sociedades democráticas de artesanos y la coyuntura política y social colombiana de 1848' *Anuario colombiano de historia social y de la cultura* viii (1976) pp. 5–18.

41 On the influence of French ideas, see R. L. Gilmore 'Nueva Granada's socialist mirage' *HAHR* xxxvi (1956).

42 The conservative rebellion is outlined in J. León Helguera 'Antecedentes sociales de la revolución de 1851 en el sur de Colombia (1848–1851)' *Anuario colombiano de historia social y de la cultura* v (1970).

43 A eulogy of such enterprise is found in Medardo Rivas *Los trabajadores de tierra caliente* (Bogotá 1944).

44 Marco Palacios *Coffee in Colombia, 1850–1970* (Cambridge 1980) p. 26.

45 Nieto Arteta *op. cit.* pp. 331–2.

46 J. P. Harrison 'The evolution of the Colombian tobacco trade to 1875' *HAHR* xxxii 2 (1952).

47 For a more detailed description of Colombian exports during the second half of the nineteenth century, see Safford, thesis, pp. 257–302.

48 Brew *op. cit.* p. 132.

49 Palacios *op. cit.* pp. 17–20.

50 McGreevey *op. cit.* pp. 117–41, 146–7.

51 McGreevey *op. cit.* pp. 171–81.

52 For a trenchant criticism of McGreevey's study, see F. R. Safford *Aspectos del siglo XIX en Colombia* (Bogotá 1977) pp. 201–84. For examples of the arbitrariness of McGreevey's calculations, see Safford's comments on the estimates of domestic consumption of importable goods (which is assumed to be of the order of 23 million dollars, without any supporting evidence), and on the failure to take into account the growth of artisan production for export: *ibid.* pp. 220–3.

53 Chile, Argentina and Peru had per capita export lévels which were at least three times as high as Colombia's in the second half of the nineteenth century. Safford *The ideal of the practical* pp. 43–44. On the performance of Colombian exports, see McGreevey *op. cit.* pp. 97–104.

[54] McGreevey *op. cit.* pp. 157–63, 228–30.

[55] Palacios *op. cit.* pp. 56–8, 69.

[56] Palacios *op. cit.* pp. 47–8. An excellent account of the use of capital accumulated in the export sector is found in Roger Brew's study of the regional economy of Antioquia; see Brew *op. cit.* pp. 85–125, 129–32.

[57] Palacios *op. cit.* p. 8; Deas *loc. cit.* p. 163.

[58] J. A. Ocampo, 'Desarrollo exportador y desarrollo capitalista colombiano en el siglo XIX (una hipótesis)' *Desarrollo y Sociedad* I (1979).

[59] McGreevey *op. cit.* pp. 107–11.

[60] For a classic statement of the destructive effects of war, see Samper *op. cit.* pp. 41–53. A recent survey is Alvaro Tirado Mejía *Aspectos sociales de las guerras civiles en Colombia* (Bogotá 1976). This includes comment on the costs of war: *ibid.* pp. 83–90.

[61] See, for example, Jane Meyer Loy 'Primary education during the Colombian federation: the school reform of 1870' *HAHR* LI (1971).

[62] Safford *Aspectos del siglo XIX en Colombia*, pp. 233–5.

[63] José María Quijano Wallis, cited by Charles W. Bergquist *Coffee and conflict in Colombia, 1886–1910* (Duke University 1978) p. 4.

[64] Helen Delpar 'Aspects of Liberal factionalism in Colombia, 1875–1885' *HAHR* LI (1971).

[65] Bergquist *op. cit. passim.*

7

PROTECTIONISM AND INDUSTRIALIZATION IN MEXICO, 1821–1854: THE CASE OF PUEBLA

Guy P. C. Thomson

In 1800 central and southern Mexico shared with other Spanish American provinces a large and commercially dynamic domestic and small factory (*obraje*) manufacturing industry. In that year demand greatly outstripped supply: three years of Atlantic war had blocked the dispatch of European goods. But even in the best years, Spain had been unable to supply her colonies with the cheaper or bulkier items. Since the sixteenth century American workshops had produced a wide range of manufactures. Mexico differed only in the greater scale of production (possessing a larger population than other provinces), in the dominance of urban over rural industry and in the relatively advanced technology which was being introduced into certain industries by the end of the colonial period. By 1850, thirty years after independence, Mexico was unique in Latin America in retaining intact the structure of traditional manufacturing while possessing the outlines, and some of the substance, of a modern manufacturing sector established over the previous two decades. The mid 1850s proved to be the peak in this early development of modern manufacturing, which, while still experiencing occasional short phases of expansion, declined in relative importance over the rest of the century, as opportunities for investment in mining and agriculture became increasingly important. Traditional cottage industry, it seems, declined in absolute terms from the mid-century.

A recent controversy shows the degree of divergence of opinion on the nature of the post-independence Latin American economies.[1] D. C. M. Platt and S. J. and B. H. Stein use the example of Mexico to reach opposite conclusions about the degree of autonomy/dependency of the Latin American economies in the forty or fifty years following independence. Platt asserts that the Latin American economies were inward-looking over this period, taking very little trade and finance from the more rapidly developing core economies of Western Europe and the United States, and sending back little in return. These economies, he argues, 'stood outside the currents of world trade and finance . . . their foreign trade was unimportant and stagnant'.[2] He finds this evidence alone sufficient to reject the Steins' view that the newly independent Latin American countries inherited externally dependent economic structures, and that neo-colonial informal imperialism promptly renewed and strengthened these structures. The Latin American economies, Platt argues, eventually acquired their export orientation not because of their inability to escape from the heritage of economic dependency, nor because autonomist policies of the early national period were sabotaged by European merchant financiers, not even because of pressure from imports, but because transport improvements eventually increased European demand for Latin American commodities and made production for export profitable, even natural. On the other hand, demographic and geographical handicaps provided formidable obstacles to autonomous industrial growth.

In reply, the Steins argue that their thesis of the continuity of colonial dependency stands up well to Platt's criticism. For Mexico, they see the continuing importance of silver exports after independence as exercising an insidious influence upon economic policy and behaviour. Far from being 'only an element in larger, inward-looking economies that sustained themselves almost entirely on domestic demand and production', as Platt would have it, the structural distortion occasioned by the primacy of silver-mining was a 'major factor in the containment of the Mexican artisan and fledgling industrial cotton manufacture'.[3] They reject Platt's claim that silver production had only a limited domestic impact, and insist that he has failed 'to comprehend the pivotal role of silver in economies structured . . . upon the exchange of precious metals for imported commodities which allowed colonial . . . elites to pursue a life-style and status to which they remained committed'.[4]

The purpose of this chapter is to clarify the nature of Mexico's economic predicament after the collapse of the Spanish Empire in the light of this controversy. It will be argued that, notwithstanding the continued dependence on silver as the main export, there was a considerable margin for autonomous development, that is, for growth in sectors only indirectly linked to exports. However, it will also be shown that foreign trade and finance, which Platt argues were unimportant in these decades, nevertheless exercised a critical economic and political influence, disarming protectionist economic policies and depriving entrepreneurial endeavours in the manufacturing sector of any consistent political or financial support.

The chapter is divided into three parts. The first examines the historical background to the adoption of generally protectionist and neo-mercantilist policies after independence, with accompanying investment in modern manufacturing. Why was there a predisposition towards these policies and this pattern of investment? The political implications of these developments are also assessed and discussed within the context of the nature of the neo-mercantilist state. Finally, the process of industrialization is examined both in terms of its capacity for self-sustained

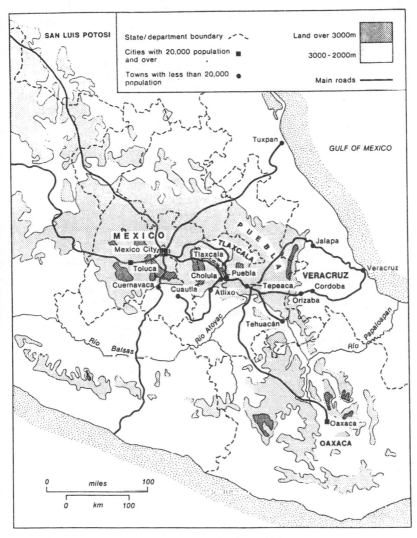

Map 2   Puebla and surrounding districts, 1850

expansion and of the relationship between domestic manufacturing and the external sector.

Colonial background and the crisis of independence

In the last decades before the Revolution of 1810, Mexico enjoyed a period of prosperity unmatched elsewhere in Spanish America. 'The gap in productivity between the Mexican economy and that of the advanced countries of the North Atlantic has never been so small' as during this period.[5] After independence knowledge of this prosperity and a determination to recover it exercised a pervasive influence upon economic policy-making and entrepreneurial behaviour.

The impressive growth of the economy of New Spain from the 1760s was caused by a combination of circumstances.[6] In certain regions, particularly northern and north-west central Mexico, population growth appears to have been the critical factor in increasing demand, permitting the expansion of the frontier of commercial agriculture while also bringing about a northward shift in the location of domestic and *obraje* manufacturing.[7] But population growth was not so obvious elsewhere. Central and southern Mexico shared only modestly in the demographic recovery of the second half of the eighteenth century. Much more important for the Mexican heartland was the high level of silver production sustained from the late 1760s. The recovery of silver-mining was a result of prudent government sponsorship. The colonial administration reduced taxes on production and on raw materials, particularly mercury and gunpowder, and encouraged a scientific approach to the industry among mine-owners. These policies, combined with tougher treatment of labour, attracted increased financial backing from merchants. Yet it is doubtful if this growth model could have been sustained indefinitely, even if the revolutions and upheavals of independence had not intervened.

By 1810, severe technical and labour problems were facing the industry, and the cost of mercury, the vital ingredient for refining silver, was rising sharply.[8] These problems hampered the industry's recovery over the thirty years following independence, so that the mining of precious metals, while remaining the principal source of exports, was no longer the engine for economic growth. Although in some years silver had accounted for from 90 to 95 per cent of exports,[9] of even greater significance for the domestic economy were the fiscal and monetary functions of the mining industry. Silver provided a firm base for government revenue[10] and ensured the availability of a circulating medium, the use of which extended to a broad spectrum of the population.[11] High levels of silver production facilitated the monetization of the economy. Mexico became noted for a relatively high level of wages matched by considerably higher prices than in Europe.[12] Over the last fifty years of the colonial period regional economies became more differentiated, and silver helped overcome the great physical obstacles to long-distance trade, permitting some degree of inter-regional specialization. Merchants had a broader field and a wider choice of investment in Mexico than elsewhere in Latin America. Investment in agriculture and manufacture for domestic consumption became popular with provincial merchants, particularly in regions close to the mining zones and in areas of rapidly expanding population.[13] Yet the primacy of mining and the great difference in the value of coin between Mexico and Europe made the accumulation of specie for export the principal concern of the great merchant houses, limiting their interest in any agricultural and industrial investment which did not swiftly contribute to this end. Most contemporaries noted a passivity in Mexico's trade, an obsession with the accumulation of coin and with commercial practices subordinate to this aim (chiefly the sale of expensive European goods).[14] Only when war interrupted Atlantic trade would leading merchants diversify on a large scale into manufacturing, permitting inter-regional trade in certain commodities, particularly textiles (Puebla's staple), to expand impressively. War-induced import-substitution occurred on several occasions during the period.

The production of Puebla textiles increased vigorously, responding to opportunities created by Spain's involvement in the wars with France (1793–5) and with Britain (1798–1801 and 1804–8). Flour exports from Puebla to the Antilles also benefited from Atlantic war, except in those years when neutral (mainly United States) shipping was permitted access to Spanish American markets. But civil war after 1810 upset both foreign and domestic trade, occasioning a significant decline in the quantity of Puebla textiles sent to the interior and presaging the eventual collapse of the region's overseas trade.

However, modern industrial processes were grafted onto this colonial manufacturing base during the 1830s and 1840s. Two assumptions are commonly made as to the nature of colonial manufacturing. One is that industry was pre-capitalist and essentially archaic: production was confined to family workshops employing obsolescent technology that required little capital investment in tools and plant and was starved of working capital.[15] The other interpretation presents the colonial artisan being displaced by both domestic Indian manufacture and the *obraje*, which has been misleadingly labelled by one historian as 'the embryo of the modern factory'.[16] The experience of Puebla over the late colonial and early independence periods suggests that both assumptions are false for this area of Mexico. In 1800 the manufacture of cotton textiles was the largest and most dynamic industry in the region, employing perhaps eighteen thousand in preparing, spinning and weaving – activities located in the capital and in the towns and villages of the central valley of

Puebla. The industry was entirely cottage-based – the *obraje* system was used only for woollen manufacture, which had undergone a steady decline in Puebla throughout the eighteenth century. Cotton weaving had become a predominantly urban industry in this area, expanding at the expense of Indian cotton production. Urban home-based cotton textile manufacture spread from Puebla in the 1760s to neighbouring zones, until the industry employed thousands in the towns and cities of Oaxaca, Mexico, Valladolid and Guadalajara by the end of the century.[17] The cotton industry was fully integrated into the structure of Mexican commercial capitalism, being financed by merchants who promoted the cultivation of raw cotton, which they purchased or supplied direct to weavers on credit. The finished products (ranging from rough unbleached cotton cloth to fine shawls) were marketed by these merchants in the fairs, mining towns and haciendas of central and northern Mexico.[18]

Before independence, Mexican manufacturers and artisans dealt chiefly in those products which merchants chose not to import because of high carriage costs and the bias of Atlantic shipping in favour of high value/low volume goods. This left the Mexican artisan and his financial backers, particularly in times of war, with a large slice of the market, between Asian and European luxuries on the one side and Indian local products on the other. With the almost continual interruption of trans-atlantic commerce during the 1790s and 1800s, the structure of Mexican industry that evolved resulted in a greater flexibility of production, closely attuned to instability in the external sector. As observed above, the principal features of this restructuring in terms of cotton textile manufacture were a growing focus upon cottage production and the decline of the *obraje*. The two developments that might have threatened the basis of Mexican manufacturing before 1810 – Catalan industrialization and direct contraband trade with the industrialized countries – were prevented by war from having a serious impact.

While Mexico was at peace and the Atlantic at war, merchants would put their coin into circulation, stimulate manufacture and even invest in commercial agriculture, given the considerable demand for foodstuffs arising from Spanish garrisons and colonies in the Caribbean cut off from the Peninsula. But rebellion in Mexico and peace in Europe had the opposite effect. By the end of the French Revolutionary and Napoleonic Wars in 1815, European producers were looking abroad for markets. However, the decline of domestic manufacture in Mexico during and after the wars of independence, though hastened by increasing imports, owed far more to the disintegration of the Spanish mercantile structure, particularly the disappearance of those 'opulent and harmonizing merchants' who had encouraged various lines of production.[19]

The insurrection of 1810–13, which was concentrated in one of the most productive regions of the country, caused a prodigious amount of damage and shattered the fragile prosperity of Mexico's late colonial silver age, upsetting in the process the entire mercantile system. The events of these years marked the beginning of a prolonged crisis from which most regions did not recover until the 1830s. At the national level, it was not until the late 1870s – with the coming of the railways – that the national market regained the degree of integration that it had enjoyed in 1800.[20] Civil war, the flooding of many of the richest mines and the increasingly unfavourable commercial environment, led to the departure of the principal merchants. Many returned to Spain, and others moved to peripheral locations such as Havana, Panama or Jamaica in order to conduct contraband trade to greater advantage. A few merchants became more directly involved with declining domestic manufacture. Vast quantities of specie were remitted abroad, producing a cash famine. Even larger quantities of bullion were exported illegally, resulting in the decapitalization of the economy.

With *de facto* independence in 1821, resuscitation of silver-mining became the major objective of official policy. Unfortunately, by the late 1820s initial enthusiasm had given way to disillusion, following the failure of several British mining enterprises during the commercial crisis of 1826, and the continuing losses (sustained by those companies that survived) that resulted from the escalating cost of mercury under the Rothschild monopoly, as well as the inability of the Mexican government to provide a suitable administrative and financial regime such as that which had made an important contribution to the silver boom of the late eighteenth century.[21] Without a buoyant mining sector, the principal stimulus to Mexican commercial capitalism (the accumulation and export of specie) was lacking. Administrative shortcomings, combined with the failure to develop a commodity to replace precious metals as an export staple, explain why the economy was so unresponsive to Liberal programmes during the 1820s, and also why protectionist strategies acquired such currency thereafter.

While it lasted, the late colonial silver cycle, in stimulating a wide range of activities, had disguised the highly regionalized structure of the Mexican economy. With the boom at an end, other forces – the fragmented pattern of settlement and the great natural barriers to trade – reasserted their influence and inhibited the integration of a national market. Thus by 1810, with the mining sector in decline and the commercial network disintegrating, the most advanced regions of Mexico became inward-looking and autarkic.[22] It is against this background, and in the further sharp deterioration in the external sector during the early 1830s, that the immediate conditions favouring industrial expansion may be found. Very similar conditions, accompanied by broadly similar responses, have been observed in Colombia at precisely the same period.[23] Monetary factors appear to have been crucial. Shortages of silver coinage had deterred importers since the late 1820s, and large issues of copper coin by the Liberal government in the early 1830s increased their disenchantment still further. The status of the copper coinage became a sensitive political question. Although a project to retire copper money was instituted in 1837, it was 1841 before the government (now Conservative) dared risk withdrawing these coins.[24] By then many owners of new spinning factories were paying wages in copper and accepting it from weavers in exchange for yarn.[25] Thus, over the crucial period of maximum industrial development (1837–42), copper money gave added protection from imports to Mexican manufacturers. The international commercial crisis of 1837 further reduced pressure from imports; French and United States import figures registered a significant drop over the late 1830s, remaining stagnant in the 1840s. The picture for British trade to Mexico is little different, registering a sharp drop after 1837 when import prohibitions were placed on ordinary cotton cloth and raw cotton.[26] The French blockade of 1838–9, lasting over twelve months, caused the greatest shortage of foreign goods on the market since the Napoleonic Wars, and should not be discounted as an important short-term factor in encouraging industrial development.[27]

Thus, most of the new industries were established over a period when the external sector was sunk in depression, if not in crisis. Much, perhaps most, of the capital invested in industry came from merchants seeking to diversify out of this unstable external sector.[28] Finding few opportunities either in mining or commercial agriculture, they turned to the resources of Mexico's cities – Mexico, Puebla, Guadalajara, Querétaro – much as the great merchants of the late eighteenth century, when war interrupted imports and bullion shipments, had fomented local manufactures.[29]

There was a political as well as an economic rationale for this renewal of interest in manufacturing. With the economic crisis, Mexico's cities, very large by pre-industrial standards, had sunk into profound social decay, which occasioned growing concern among a now precariously placed social elite, many of whom yearned for the restoration of the more tranquil and prosperous colonial order. Artisans made up a significant portion of the urban population; and because of their literacy, their strength within the army and their critical economic predicament, they represented a potentially important political constituency. For short periods during the 1820s this was acknowledged by the administrations of both Agustín de Iturbide and Vicente Guerrero, which granted temporary prohibitions against the import of cotton cloth. But for most of the 1820s and 30s economic liberalism and *laisser-faire* prevailed. Nevertheless, by the mid 1830s, after a prolonged civil war and with the urban social crisis accentuated by a cholera epidemic and a further deterioration in the country's economic predicament, protectionist and neo-mercantilist policies appeared increasingly attractive and facilitated the inauguration of the so-called protectionist era.[30]

The politics of protectionism and industrialization, 1835–54

Modern industry was born in Mexico in a period when the military and ideological struggle between Liberals and Conservatives was reaching a feverous pitch, not to be matched until the Wars of the Reform in the late 1850s. The principal bone of contention was the wealth and political influence of the Church, which the Gómez Farias government (1831–4) was determined to curtail and the Conservatives were vowed to protect.

Strategically located on the Veracruz-Mexico City road, Puebla found itself at the epicentre of this struggle: the city suffered four sieges in these years. With its powerful bishopric and numerous and active convents, which owned four fifths of the city's real estate and acted as the region's principal banking institutions, Puebla became a symbol of clerical conservatism and vested interest. Yet by 1850, while still militantly clerical, the city had become a symbol of progress and industrial innovation. And it became so over a period of Conservative rule. The Conservatives returned to power in 1835 behind Antonio López de Santa Anna who, by abandoning the Liberal cause and abolishing the 1824 federal constitution, inaugurated two decades of ineffectual and unstable Conservative, centralist and protectionist rule. Over this period the structure of modern industry was established and much of the traditional manufacturing sector was restored. Protectionism and industrialization grew to be linked in the minds of the political opponents of the Conservatives with arbitrary centralism, clericalism and class privilege.

By 1848 the young Liberals who were to lead the Reform movement a decade later, when apportioning blame for the dismal state of the republic after the catastrophic American War (1847–8), saw as one of the principal crimes of the Conservative governments of the 1840s, the policy of import prohibitions and forced industrialization. This they believed lay at the root of political instability; it had deprived the state of 40 million pesos in customs revenues and forced it into debt to unscrupulous financiers, all in favour of a small group of 'influential people (the industrialists) who became, progressively, the respectable body in society and who, in the end, could not even secure the bases of their own wealth, many suffering bankruptcies'.[31]

While it may be recognized that certain industrialists and financiers exercised an inordinate influence upon Santa Anna's various governments, it is an oversimplification to characterize the political economy of this period as the exclusive strategem of a limited group of major landowners and industrialists in the centre of the country (often residents of Mexico City) who, in alliance with the clergy and the professional army, sought to preserve or regain their privileged position, now threatened by the Liberals.[32] This interpretation is altogether too narrow, since it fails to take account of the considerable popular appeal of protectionist policies far beyond the valley of Mexico, and the significant benefits received from industrialization among broad sections of the population. Not all industrialists were plutocrats; many indeed were of modest means, artisans or shopkeepers who cooperated in industrial ventures by forming joint stock companies. The interpretation also ignores the innovative and not entirely unsuccessful mercantilist policies of certain Conservative administrations. Finally, there is an assumption in contemporary Liberal criticism and in recent historiography that a realizable Liberal alternative project lurked behind the scenes which, had it not been for the forces of Conservatism and colonial vested interest, would have provided a firmer foundation for the national economy and the nation state. The successful realization of the Liberal model, however, required a railway system, greatly increased international demand for Mexican goods, much greater availability of capital, a widespread transformation of social relations in the countryside, and a strong state. For these Mexico had to await the 1880s. During the 1830s and 40s, protectionism and a limited industrialization were a much more natural response to Mexico's past traditions, immediate economic predicament and social realities than the pursuit of doctrinaire principles of free trade urged by some Liberals.

The social, economic and spatial map of the protectionist era was taking shape by the mid 1830s. It included merchants who were becoming involved in manufacturing and developing credit links with artisans in the cities of the temperate *altiplano*, plus cotton growers, sheep raisers and their merchant allies in northern regions and in the tropical coastal areas of the south. Core zones looked to outlying areas for a renewed flow of raw materials. Indeed, given limited opportunities for export, the economic heartland of Mexico constituted the principal market for a wide range of regional commodities.

During the second half of the 1830s the lobbies of merchants, industrialists and growers favouring tariff protection shared a unanimity which disguised profound conflicts of interest that would resurface in the early 1840s. Temporary union sprang from the need to concert pressure on the government to secure full import prohibitions on raw cotton, cotton yarn and ordinary cotton cloth. Veracruz and Oaxaca were granted a prohibition on raw cotton imports as early as 1836; but the prohibition on cotton cloth – which represented a considerable sacrifice to an impoverished government – was granted only reluctantly in early 1838,[33] and rendered effective in part by the French blockade of 1838–9.[34] For two years before the final prohibition on yarn and cloth imports in 1838, handloom weavers were kept busy, as cheap British yarn was imported in record quantities, greatly expanding the country's weaving capacity in readiness for the Mexican factory spinner who was able to replace foreign yarn with his own product by 1840, as one firm after another entered production.[35] The anxiety of the handloom weavers about mechanization was calmed temporarily by a promise from the spinning factory owners that no more power looms would be set up than could consume a maximum of one half their production of yarn: the rest would be sold to weavers or exchanged for handwoven *mantas*.[36] Thus, rapid growth and an unintentionally well orchestrated staggering of import prohibitions combined with the temporary collapse of foreign trade to make 1836–9 years of some cordiality and complementarity among raw cotton growers, textile manufacturers and artisans.

After 1840 divisions emerged within and between components of the protectionist lobby. There was disagreement over raw cotton supply. Tension grew between government and industrialists regarding the application and suspension of import prohibitions, currency policy, departmental (provincial) taxation and smuggling. These conflicts reveal a high degree of regional competition, economic parochialism and widely differing assumptions about the nature of industrialization. They served to distract the state from the more ambitious neo-mercantilist economic policies designed to accompany the protectionist tariff policy and hasten economic development.

The Conservative governments of the 1830s and 40s went beyond guaranteeing tariff protection for certain industries (such as cotton and woollen textiles, paper and pottery), to engaging actively in fomenting manufacturing production. Part of the justification for the abrogation of the federal constitution in 1837, and for the more centralized government that followed, was the conviction within certain administrative circles that the state should involve itself directly in the diffusion of useful scientific knowledge, and should foster economic development through government loans, privileges, patents, tariff protection and prizes and by removing obstacles to inter-regional trade. The neo-mercantilist thread running through this period had its roots in late colonial *fomento*, of which the Mining Guild and its part in the successful recovery of silver-mining is the prime example.[37] During the 1830s the central government development bank, the Banco de Avío para Fomento de la Industria Nacional, made vital contributions to certain key enterprises and had a critical impact upon business confidence, as it convinced entrepreneurs of the state's long-term commitment to protectionism and industrialization.[38] After the demise of the Banco in 1840, government commitment to *fomento* and the central coordination of manufacturing and related development continued under the auspices of the national Junta de Industria and the Dirección General de la Industria Mexicana.

The Dirección General, which was to coordinate the activities and attend to the needs of the departmental (state) *juntas de industria*, representing both industrialists and artisans, became a fully fledged government department under Santa Anna's restored centralist administration of 1842–5. Over this period industrialists, despite all their internal divisions, enjoyed unprecedented influence upon government. It was at this point that the term 'industry' conjured up an image of exclusive sectional privilege. The import prohibitions that industrialists had won during the 1830s were written into the new ultra-Conservative constitution, the *Bases Orgánicas* of 1842 – a constitutional clause stating that no prohibited foreign goods which might prove harmful to national industry could be imported without the approval of two thirds of the departmental assemblies.[39] Increasingly, this inflexible adherence to import prohibitions, often against the wishes of the industrialists themselves and punctuated by the temporary granting of short-term raw cotton import licences to powerful merchant financiers, took precedence over any further pursuit of the broad and far-sighted industrial development plan proposed by the Dirección General de la Industria. The inflexibility can be explained by increasing government financial dependence upon *agiotistas* (financial speculators), many of whom had become raw cotton monopolists or creditors to struggling industries.[40] Under this light, strict import prohibition takes on the appearance of a guarantee provided for the benefit of *agiotistas* – a group interested in the survival if not the prosperity of the administration and of domestic manufacture – rather than a means to a greater end, namely autonomous development. The broader Colbertian aims of certain Conservative politicians, most notably Lucas Alamán, foundered eventually on the financial and political weakness of the Conservative state and the disappointing economic performance of the leading industry in the manufacturing sector, cotton textiles.

After the American war, the failure of the neo-mercantilist impulse to reappear was not greatly lamented among the industrialists. This was not simply because of their wariness of the political complications of too close an association with weak and unpopular governments and a growing preference for working through state (provincial) rather than national institutions, but also because the ambitious ideal of sustained industrial growth held during the late 1830s had everywhere been abandoned. The owners of the new enterprises, some of which had changed hands twice or three times over less than a decade, had learnt to operate fairly profitably within the limitations of a restricted market, an unstable political and a lethargic economic environment. They asked only for tariff protection from the state, and this, because of the considerable size and appreciable political weight of the new industrial sector, both Liberal and Conservative governments alike were obliged to grant.

Industrialization was not mechanically invoked by Conservative governments to shore up a tottering *ancien régime*. It grew out of an economic crisis during which investment in manufacturing production became for a time more profitable than investment in foreign trade. The choice was a risky one, and for a time government encouragement became a vital factor in building business confidence. The failure of growth in investment in modern industry to be sustained after 1842, and the serious divisions which appeared among the various lobbies, between and within regions, denied the Conservative governments of the 1840s a unified body of support which might conceivably have strengthened them against the internal and external threats that shattered the entire Mexican state between 1846 and 1848. Instead, the growing financial weakness of governments, unable to increase customs revenues because of prohibitionist legislation, forced them to raise unpopular direct taxes, even to turn to the sacred cow of Church wealth and, far more fatally, to become increasingly indebted to financiers, whose overbearing influence upon the state deprived governments of the will to innovate and of freedom to manœuvre, and robbed protectionist policies of their little remaining legitimacy and neo-mercantilist policies of any effect.

The merchant financiers of Mexico over these decades were no will-o'-the wisps. As governments became more indebted to them, they grew to control key areas of public administration and the transport and communications network, manned the customs houses, took over the repayment of foreign debts, received all the plum government contracts, and conspired against the establishment of a national bank that might reduce their private financial control over government.[41] Once new industry was established, they recognized it as a fruitful area for speculation, particularly during those periods of crisis when factories were bankrupting and the government was obliged to issue licences for importing prohibited goods. What better field for speculation? Few *agiotistas* ignored the penury of the industrial sector and its thirst for credit, several becoming industrialists as mortgages were foreclosed.[42]

It will by now have become clear that the protectionist and neo-mercantilist strategy which came to replace *laissez-faire* during the 1830s failed to serve as a recipe for greater political stability, for strengthening the state or, even less, for establishing a pattern of sustained autonomous economic development. By 1850 the economic policies of the Conservatives were as discredited as had been Liberal policies in the early 1830s.

Subsequent decades witnessed an intensification of ideological and military struggle between these two parties, during which the debate about economic policy receded in importance: two alternative economic strategies had been applied in Mexico in the three decades following independence, and had failed to broaden the country's economic options. However, despite the non-realization of the more optimistic mercantilist expectations, new industry had been established and traditional manufacture demonstrated an impressive resiliency. Indeed, it has been argued that one of the most marked characteristics of the sector during this period – of both modern manufacturing enterprises and traditional units – was adaptability. Survival depended upon flexibility of response to short-term opportunities resulting from political instability and changes in economic policy.[43]

Industrialization in Puebla: obstacles to growth

The spatial pattern of industrial investment over the 1830s and 1840s reflected the economic parochialism and inter-provincial rivalry already observed. Each department had sought to establish its own textile mill, paper factory or iron foundry. This process limited the range of the national market for those regions that attempted to specialize and were thus dependent upon extra-regional markets for their products. A certain degree of local self-sufficiency was inevitable, given the physical obstacles to trade, but the trend towards departmental autarky was accentuated by a decline in the economic importance of Mexico City, by the demonetization of the economy resulting from the stagnation of silver-mining, by civil war and by the increased incidence of banditry. These factors had a profound adverse impact upon the level of economic activity, as the experience of Puebla reveals.

The continued concentration of mercantile wealth in Mexico City in the late colonial period may have deprived peripheral locations of commercial skills, but the process had served to stimulate inter-regional exchange, sometimes over great distances.[44] After independence merchants often selected regional capitals such as San Luis Potosí, Jalapa or Guadalajara as a base of operations in place of the traditional *locus*, the national capital.[45] Puebla benefited from this trend: the city became a popular centre for merchants interested in supplying the south-east of the country. But there were negative aspects to this relocation of commercial activity. Once Mexico City ceased to act as a dynamic commercial and financial intermediary, it became more difficult for Puebla merchants and manufacturers to provision traditional markets in the interior. The scale of investments made in Puebla over the 1830s and early 1840s presupposed a national market. Although Puebla maintained its lead as Mexico's principal manufacturing centre and the city's goods continued to appear in the markets of the *tierradentro*, by the 1840s demand, particularly for textiles, was exceedingly volatile. There were repeated complaints about overproduction and the scale of contraband imports.[46]

These difficulties were compounded by currency shortage. Although a large quantity of copper coin had been issued in the early 1830s when the scarcity of coinage had been acute, copper currency, as stated above, was withdrawn from circulation in 1841. This money was sorely missed:

Puebla industrialists complained persistently throughout the 1840s that the level of coinage was inadequate even for local needs.[47] Lack of a circulating medium was particularly grave for Puebla, in that the department possessed no important silver mines. Indeed, the degree of industrial specialization for which the region was renowned had in part been perceived as a means of attracting specie from mining regions. Puebla was doubly vulnerable to the centrifugal pressures operating in Mexico at this period. Her quest for national markets antagonized interests in other departments seeking self-sufficiency; not possessing important mines or a mint, she was unlikely to find allies amongst silver-producing areas in a campaign for the restoration of copper money.

After independence, with mining depressed, the reactivation of traditional patterns of exchange between manufacturers of the south-east and the mining towns and latifundia of the north-centre and north was a slow process which disappointed many industrialists. Given the scarcity of circulating medium, large commercial operations were conducted almost entirely by means of bills of exchange, conferring great advantages upon those who possessed liquid assets, a condition enjoyed by few merchants and even fewer industrialists as the 1840s proceeded. The principal source of the economic and political power of the *agiotistas* lay in their ability to maintain liquidity when all around them – governments, traders and industrialists – were begging for money.[48] It was the *agiotistas* who frustrated currency reform and prevented the establishment of a national bank, measures which they rightly feared would undermine their monopoly of credit.[49]

Agiotistas, like their pre independence counterparts, were eager to put capital to work when local opportunities were available, but their principal interest remained the external sector where, until the late 1860s, the Mexican silver peso commanded a premium.[50] Silver continued to account for a very high proportion of Mexican exports during the mid-nineteenth century. Strategic access to silver, even when the external sector was depressed, was a source of power for the silver monopolists. They exercised a pervasive influence upon the economy and upon the character of the emerging industrial sector. The Steins' statement that the dominance of silver exports after 1821 is the key to understanding the continued economic dependence of Mexico and was a major factor in the containment of artisan and fledgling factory-based cotton manufacture is borne out by the evidence. Government policy was hamstrung by financial interests who cared little for 'national autonomy' (however that might have been conceived in Mexico during the early nineteenth century) and well appreciated that the strength of their position lay in their dominance of the means by which silver was accumulated and in their control of silver exports. For the *agiotistas* any reform – such as the reintroduction of a copper coinage – which appeared to threaten this monopoly was anathema.

Shortages of circulating medium, the disintegration of the national market and weak demand were not the only problems facing the artisanate and manufacturers in these years. Between 1840 and 1844 the high price of domestically grown raw cotton presented a serious obstacle to the development of the textile industry – imports of cotton being prohibited. The inadequate supply of Mexican cotton confounded those who had assumed that the transformation of domestic agriculture would naturally follow the modernization of national industry. Scarcity of raw material imputs threatened the stability of the local pro-industry lobby, composed of manufacturers and growers. It also reduced the credibility of government policy. Above all, the deficient supply of raw cotton made manufacturers even more dependent upon the financial sector, the *agiotistas* so firmly intent upon controlling the state, which speculated in cotton stocks. By 1841–2 Puebla industrialists were divided into two camps, one favouring the abandonment of the prohibition on raw cotton imports, the other defending its retention.[51]

This rift occurred against the background of a glut of factory-produced yarn resulting from the increased output of newly commissioned units, contraband imports and the lag in weaving capacity. The situation revealed conflicts of interest within the industry, and differing attitudes to, and expectations of, the process of industrialization. The group favouring the retention of the ban on raw cotton imports was composed of owners of small and medium-sized animal-driven Crompton spinning factories (rarely utilizing more than six hundred spindles) located within the city of Puebla, the cottage hand-loom weavers with whom these factory owners had established credit links, and neighbouring cotton growers. These interests understood industrialization to mean the restoration of the cotton weaver and his merchant backer, now turned spinning factory owner, to the position they had enjoyed before independence. In 1842, with the market glutted and raw cotton scarce, they felt that the process of industrial transformation had gone far enough. Spinning factory operators/dealers were content to take advantage of this intermediate stage of industrialization. They saw their function as essentially mercantile and little changed from the pre-factory spinning era – namely, confined to keeping cottage weavers supplied with yarn, credit and markets. Spinner/dealers were not prepared to venture into power-loom weaving, thus completing and integrating the various phases of factory production. The transformation of spinning technology which had occurred in Puebla with the introduction of the Crompton mule was basically a convenient improvement at a specific point in an essentially traditional industrial structure that was not fundamentally altered as a result of this modification.

The opposing body of industrialists and their allies who favoured the removal of the prohibition on raw cotton imports viewed the process of industrialization differently. Many were owners of large water-powered Arkwright spinning factories set up between 1831 and 1842 along the Atoyac River, beyond the boundaries of the city. Others owned Crompton factories within Puebla which had gone out of production because of the cotton famine. Linked to these spinning interests was a large body of skilled workers – foundrymen, millwrights, coopers, oil-makers, carpenters and plumbers – involved in the construction and provisioning of factories. These people were united in a commitment to a deepening and an expansion of the process of industrialization. Some of the Arkwright spinners had already introduced power-looms into their mills. They were exasperated by the stranglehold which cotton mono-polists had upon the industry. They also resented municipal taxation, which discriminated against more advanced water-driven factories in favour of those employing animal-powered machinery. Cotton shortages continued to plague the industry during the mid 1840s, despite tem-porary relaxations of the ban on raw cotton imports in 1843 and 1846. However, conflict within the industry was only resolved when the general stagnation of the Mexican economy precluded further expan-sion.

Sustained growth of cotton textile production foundered upon serious obstacles to increased domestic raw cotton supply which would have reduced raw material costs and the limited scope of the market. A few indications of the broader vision of industrial progress can also be observed in Puebla during the 1840s. An iron foundry produced the first all-Mexican steel looms and spares for imported British and United States textile machinery. Several cotton-printing, dyeing and bleaching factories were established. Product diversification was observable in the finer yarns produced by the spinning factories and the more exotic cloth woven by hand-loom operators.[52] Yet these changes may also be inter-preted as demonstrating the rigidity of constraints upon demand, rather than a commitment to, or potential for, sustained industrial develop-ment.

The evidence for Puebla over the 1830s and 1840s points to the overwhelmingly traditional character of the industrial revival that took place during these decades. The industrialists of the city did not consti-tute a coherent group. Many doubled as merchants; capital for several new enterprises came from commercial profits, often earned in the import trades. However, unlike similarly funded industrial establish-ments elsewhere in Latin America, manufacturing in Puebla during this period proved incapable of generating autonomous finance. Industry continued to depend upon the import houses and cotton monopolists for funding. Most of the dominant families of the city acquired industrial interests over these decades, if only as shareholders. Five manufacturers served as state governors and one – a Liberal – became president of the republic. But many industrialists were men and women of modest means, forming part of the large intermediate sector of urban society made up of shopkeepers, minor officials and artisans. Industrialization did not create a new class of dynamic entrepreneurs, nor did it bring about the urbanization of Mexican society.[53]

Conclusion

The term 'industrialization', because of the thoroughness of the economic transformation which it provoked in nineteenth-century Europe, the United States and Japan, carries with it ideas of sustained economic growth, capital formation around factory production, the diffusion of capital and technology to other branches of the economy and overseas, a revolution in living standards and economic independence. In Mexico during the 1830s and 40s, indeed throughout the nineteenth century, the introduction of modern industrial technology had a much more limited impact. It was successfully introduced into those industries – cotton and woollen textiles – which were time-proven and in which Mexico had certain advantages: a potential abundance of raw materials and a reasonable internal market for basic manufactures. In other industries – iron, paper, porcelain and sheet glass – shortage of cheap fuel, practical difficulties and inadequate demand sometimes proved to be insurmountable obstacles to the successful introduction of modern technology. Indeed, industries using traditional techniques often did better over this period; such was the case with Puebla's *mayolica* potteries, tumbler and bottle factories and iron foundries. Overall, the introduction of modern industrial technology and the restoration of the traditional manufacturing structure offered no keys to national economic independence or autonomous growth. Natural, spatial and physical obstacles to the growth of a national market and to the supply of raw materials to industry; the unequal nature of Mexico's economic relations with the outside world; and the secondary position of urban manufacturing within the broader social and economic structure of the country – these three factors limited the dynamism of the industrial sector and consequently its capacity to promote widespread diversification.

From the eighteenth century to the end of the period studied, Mexican manufacturing received its principal commercial stimulus when the external sector was in difficulty. In these moments industry drew much of the investment which would otherwise have gone into exports and imports; thus manufacturing production underwent a significant change both before 1810 with the commercialization and urbanization of the textile and other industries and during the 1830s and 40s with mechanization. Over these periods, as a growing number of merchants, manufacturers and artisans became involved in industry, they saw their interests as distinct from, even at odds with, those of the dominant financial interests of the country, which remained closely linked to the external sector. Before independence these interests were the great import-export merchants and silver bankers of the late colonial silver boom. During the 1830s and 40s they were the *agiotistas*, the merchant financiers to whom governments and eventually the industrialists themselves became increasingly indebted.

Entrepreneurs and artisans over the 1830s and early 1840s initially seemed to be pursuing an autonomous path of development favouring the substitution of European imports and industrial diversification, and demanding government action attuned to their peculiar currency and raw material supply requirements. The autonomist vision foundered, however, once industrial growth itself drew to a halt, when bankrupt governments abandoned mercantilist policies while maintaining only an unsteady adherence to protectionism and, most significantly of all, once opportunities for investment began to appear in mining and agriculture from the late 1840s, pointing to the external orientation of the Mexican economy over the second half of the nineteenth century. By the early 1850s the industrial sector, unable to generate its own capital, had taken its place as the poor cousin to the external sector, representing more of a complement than a challenge to it.

The mandarins of Mexican economic life in the years immediately preceding the Reform (1854–9) were the pragmatic *agiotistas* who regarded industry as a secondary area for short-term financial speculation. Their activities spanned the financing of weak governments, amassing property from weakening Church corporations, supplying and financing struggling industries, acquiring promising silver mines at low prices and investing in safe European railway stock, while keeping an eye open for every opportunity the external sector offered. Modern factories, rather like haciendas before the railway age, now possessed a certain value as rent, where money might be turned over though not accumulated, and might therefore be acquired for the purpose of short-term speculation; but they were no longer seen as symbols of economic progress. It may be concluded, therefore, that industrialization in Mexico over this period served far more as a means of keeping commercial capital alive and circulating in a country with a depressed and unstable external sector, than as a way of transforming commercial into industrial capital. For only a short period (1835–42), the recovery of urban artisanal manufacturing and the introduction of modern industrial technology appeared to be drawing Mexico onto a path of autonomous economic development. But the strength of the financial and commercial nexus linking the country to more developed areas of the world ensured that the phase was a fleeting one.

Notes

[1] D. C. M. Platt 'Dependency in nineteenth-century Latin America: an historian objects'; Stanley J. Stein and Barbara H. Stein 'The anatomy of "autonomy" ' *Latin America Research Review* xv 1 (1980).

[2] Platt *op. cit.* pp. 117 and 119.

[3] Platt *op. cit.* p. 115; Steins *op. cit.* p. 138.

[4] Steins *op. cit.* pp. 133–5.

[5] John H. Coatsworth 'Obstacles to economic growth in nineteenth-century Mexico' *American Historical Review* 83 (1978).

[6] D. A. Brading *Miners and merchants in Bourbon Mexico 1763–1810* (Cambridge 1971) pp. 156–7.

[7] Eric Van Young *Hacienda and market in eighteenth-century Mexico: the rural economy of the Guadalajara region, 1675–1820* (Berkeley 1981) pp. 11–39.

[8] Tom Cassidy discusses the impending crisis in the industry before the revolutions and the problems facing its recovery after independence. T. J. Cassidy *British capital and the Mexican silver mining industry 1820–50* (Cambridge, Centre of Latin American Studies, Working Paper no. 21, n.d.).

[9] Javier Ortiz de la Tabla *Comercio exterior de Veracruz, 1778–1821, crisis de dependencia* (Seville 1978) pp. 154–5.

[10] Brading *op. cit.* pp. 29–30.

[11] Diego López Rosado *Historia y pensamiento económico de México* (Mexico 1968–72) ii 209–10.

[12] The high wage level in Mexico was a frequent cause for complaint among British entrepreneurs after independence, while relatively high prices were the great attraction to British importers in the early 1820s. *Notes and reflections on Mexico, its mines, policy, etc., by a traveller, some years resident in that and other American States* (London 1827) p. 31. An anonymous Mexican economist argued in 1836 that, whereas in Europe the value of basic foodstuffs and clothing set the wage level, in Mexico the quantity of silver mined and in circulation had always set wages and prices which were, correspondingly, higher in Mexico than in non-mining countries to the ratio of three to one. *Algunas consideraciones económicas sobre protección de industria* (Mexico 1836).

[13] For an example of regional specialization in the Guadalajara intendency see Eric Van Young *op. cit.* For a discussion of the national livestock market see C. Harris *A Mexican Family empire* (Austin 1975) pp. 79–122.

[14] For Mexican mercantile practices see Claude Morin *Michoacán en la Nueva España del siglo XVIII. Crecimiento y desigualdad en una economía colonial* (Mexico 1979) pp. 141–208; Brading *op. cit.* pp. 95–128; Brian Hamnett *Politics and trade in Southern Mexico 1750–1821* (Cambridge 1971) pp. 95–120; Luis Chávez Orozco *Historia económica y social de México. Ensayo de interpretación* (Mexico 1938) p. 44; López Rosado *op. cit.* iv 31–97, 264.

[15] Lobato López takes this view: 'The clergy and merchants, the bankers of the colony who gave credit to shopkeepers, miners and landowners, even to the public authorities, systematically denied all credit to help manufacturers, *obrajeros* and artisans' workshops.' Ernesto Lobato López *El crédito de México* (Mexico 1945) p. 74.

[16] López Rosado *op. cit.*, iii 69–70; Luis Chávez Orozco *El obraje, embrión de la fábrica* (Mexico 1936).

[17] G. P. C. Thomson 'Economy and society in Puebla de los Angeles, 1800–1850' (unpubl. D.Phil. thesis, Oxford 1978) pp. 167–89.

[18] Thomson 'Economy and society' pp. 183–4.

[19] Mexico, Archivo General de la Nación *Consulados* vol. 463, 6 June 1816.

[20] For a succinct presentation of the economic consequences of the war, see Ciro S. Cardoso 'Latino América y el Caribe (siglo XIX): la problemática de la transición al capitalismo dependiente' in Enrique Florescano (ed.) *Ensayos sobre el desarrollo económico de México y América Latina 1500–1975* (Mexico 1979) pp. 333–7. For the impact of the wars in Puebla see Henry Ward *Mexico in 1827* (London 1828) ii 82; Joel Poinsett *Notes on Mexico*

(London 1822); Thomson 'Economy and society' pp. 192–5.

[21] For these problems and others, see Robert Randall *Real del Monte: a British mining venture in Mexico* (Texas 1972); Cassidy *op. cit.* See also perceptive contemporary analysis by 'a Resident' *Observations on foreign mining in Mexico* (London 1838).

[22] Of the five great dioceses of Oaxaca, Puebla, Mexico, Valladolid and Guadalajara, all possessed their own cotton growing zones, their own textile industries, their own commercial production of wheat and maize, their own sugar plantations and their own sheep and cattle ranges. Surpluses were sometimes exchanged between regions in certain cases of early specialization (Puebla's silk *rebozos* and sturdy cotton cloth, *manta*) or of sheer comparative advantage (the cereal harvests of the Bajío or Atlixco and Coahuila's livestock). The high degree of regional autarky and limited complementarity of Mexico's provinces lasted until the railway age, and was observed in great detail in 1800 by Alexander von Humboldt *A political essay* vols III and IV.

[23] Frank S. Safford 'Commerce and enterprise in central Colombia 1821–1870' (unpubl. Ph.D. thesis, Columbia 1965), 'Foreign and national enterprise in nineteenth-century Colombia' *Business History Review* XXXIX 4 (1965).

[24] Thomson 'Economy and society' pp. 248–58.

[25] The eventual withdrawal of copper money from circulation in 1842 caused great hardship in Puebla, where shopkeepers and industrialists were demanding compensation as late as 1849. See Thomson 'Economy and society', p. 476.

[26] *Ibid.* p. 254.

[27] E. de Antuñano *Reflexiones sobre al bloqueo y el erario de México* (Puebla 1838), *Opiniones demostrativas sobre el bloqueo de Francia a México, por lo adverso y favorable, presente y futuro para la reputación, erario a industria de México* (Puebla 1838).

[28] Safford describes similar circumstances for Colombia 'It was in this period of acute depression, just as the interest of foreign capitalists was flagging, that the Colombian upper classes took up the burden of entrepreneurial leadership.' Safford 'Foreign and national enterprise' p. 515.

[29] Robert Potash *El Banco de Avío de México: el fomento de la industria, 1821–46* (Mexico 1959); Jan Bazant 'Evolución de la industria textíl poblana, 1554–1845' *Historia Mexicana* XIII (1969); the chapters by Margarita Urias, Guillermo Beato, Rosa-Maria Meyer, Shanti Oyarzábal-Salcedo and Maria-Teresa Huerta in C. Cardoso (ed.) *Formación y desarrollo de la burguesía en México, siglo XIX* (Mexico 1978); Dawn Keremitsis *La industria textíl mexicana en el siglo XIX* (Mexico 1973); Wolfgang Muller 'El financiamiento de la industrialización, el caso de la industria textíl poblana, 1830–1910' *Comunicaciones* XV (1978), *Die textil industrie des raunes Puebla (Mexiko) im 19 jahrhundert* (Bonn 1977).

[30] Charles Hale *Mexican liberalism in the age of Mora, 1821–1853* (New Haven 1968) pp. 255–7; Potash *op. cit.* Pt I; Thomson 'Economy and society' pp. 189–225.

[31] Varios Mexicanos *Consideración sobre la situación política y social de la República Mexicana en el año 1847* (Mexico 1848) pp. 10–17.

[32] Coatsworth 'Obstacles to economic growth' p. 95.

[33] Potash *op. cit.* p. 193; Hale *op. cit.* p. 276.

[34] Potash *op. cit.* p. 197.

[35] Thomson 'Economy and society' pp. 265–6.

[36] E. de Antuñano *Economía política en México* (Puebla 1839).

[37] Hale *op. cit.* p. 269.

[38] Potash *op. cit.* pp. 219–42.

[39] Potash *op. cit.* pp. 202, 205, 208–11.

[40] Thomson 'Economy and society' p. 279; Hale *op. cit.* p. 278.

[41] On the great political influence of the *agiotistas* and on the collusion between the principal British financier and consul to Mexico City (1839–53), Ewen C. Mackintosh, and the principal Mexican *agiotista*, Don Manuel Escandón, see Barbara A. Tenenbaum "Merchants, money and mischief. The British in Mexico, 1821–1862' *The Americas* XXXV (1978–9); Margarita Urias Hermosillo 'Manuel Escandón, de las diligencias alferrocarril,

1833–1862' in Cardoso *Formación y desarrollo* pp. 25–56.

[42] For an example of a merchant financier becoming an industrialist in this way, see Guillermo Beato 'La Casa Martínez del Rio: del comercio colonial a la industria fabríl, 1829–1864' in Cardoso *Formación y desarrollo* pp. 57–107.

[43] Comments of Sergio Bagú on Guillermo Beato 'La Casa Martínez del Rio' in Cardoso *Formación y desarrollo* pp. 106–7.

[44] For Coahuila's trade with Oaxaca, made possible through Mexico City merchant intermediaries, see Harris *op. cit.* p. 109.

[45] Alejandra Moreno Toscano and Enrique Florescano 'El sector externo y la organización espacial y regional de México (1521–1910)' *Cuadernos de trabajo del D.I.H.* I (1974).

[46] Thomson 'Economy and society' pp. 285–90.

[47] *Ibid.* pp. 274–81.

[48] Cardoso *Formación y desarrollo* p. 18.

[49] Urias Hermosillo *op. cit.* pp. 41, 46.

[50] Mexico became the principal source of the world's circulating coin during the eighteenth and early nineteenth centuries. The Mexican peso was a legal medium on a par with the dollar in the United States between 1793 and 1857, acceptable in the United Kingdom during the Napoleonic Wars, the staple coin throughout Latin America for much of the nineteenth century, and one of the chief mediums of exchange in China and the Pacific through to the 1870s. See López Rosado *Historia y pensamiento económico de México* II 209–10; John McMaster 'Aventuras asiáticas del peso mexicano' *Historia Mexicana* III (1959).

[51] For conflict over the lifting of cotton prohibitions see Thomson 'Economy and society' pp. 281–9.

[52] Maria del Carmen Aguirre-Anaya and Alberto Cavabarin Gracia 'Empresarios de la industria textíl en Puebla: industria y política durante los primeros años de vida independiente' (unpubl. B.A. thesis, Puebla 1979) p. 54; Thomson 'Economy and society' p. 333.

[53] Thomson 'Economy and society' pp. 334–8.

8

ECONOMIC POLICY AND GROWTH IN CHILE FROM INDEPENDENCE TO THE WAR OF THE PACIFIC

Luis Ortega

By early 1879 Chile was facing a deep and protracted crisis that had halted the growth achieved over twenty years of vigorous economic activity. The crisis, although externally induced, tested the very foundations of the economic and fiscal systems and brought acute social unrest to the country.[1] By the end of 1881, however, Chileans had achieved a remarkable military victory over Bolivia and Peru and had relegated to oblivion the traumatic years from 1875 to 1879. The military success, territorial gains, nitrate wealth and international prestige acquired in the war restored Chilean confidence and prosperity, lost over almost half a decade. The war and its outcome marked a watershed in the evolution of the country. Thereafter, and as a result of Chile's new position with regard to the international economy, the pace of economic development changed, as did most features of Chilean society.

For the purposes of historical analysis, the outbreak of the War of the Pacific in April 1879 constitutes a useful landmark. It would be quite wrong, however, to assume that the war initiated a totally 'new era' in Chilean economic history.[2] Despite the major changes which occurred from 1880 onwards, several processes and practices were inherited from the pre-war years. The concentration of population in the Central Valley continued, the process of industrialization was accelerated by increased demand, and the railway network was further expanded.[3] There was also continuity in economic policy. The fortunes of public finances continued to be tied to those of the foreign trade sector, although ordinary revenue was almost entirely derived from taxes on exports. The taxation system underwent further modifications.

Some other elements of continuity in economic policy may be found.[4] But those mentioned below are the most significant, because they typify the economic thought behind policy-making between 1830 and 1879. Since the size of the public sector was small and the scope of government action limited, economic thinking and policies were neither complex nor elaborate. During the period studied the aims of finance ministers were basically twofold: to procure sufficient revenue to sustain the public sector, and to achieve a balanced budget. The achievement of these goals had priority over any other government action, and, at least until the mid-1850s, determined the level of public activity. In the 1860s and early 1870s, as the needs and expectations of government increased and spending grew, the level of expenditure began to determine revenue policy. But the underlying principles remained the same, according to which the fiscal component remained the central element of economic policy.

Until the early 1850s the approach of policy-makers seems to have been inspired by the kind of thought stemming from the Spanish Enlightenment. Along with pledges to economic liberalism, programmes of state-sponsored economic revival are to be found. Following the tradition started by the Economic Societies in Spain and brought to Chile by men like Cos Iriberri and de Salas, ministers and congressmen often put forward schemes for the encouragement of private initiative in local industries and for the introduction of new crops. Meanwhile government activity was carried out through the use of codes, institutions, laws and taxes inherited from the colonial period.[5] The late arrival in the country of the doctrines of classical economics[6] and the fact that the majority of ministers who held the finance portfolio during the period had no training other than that acquired serving within the administrative structure of the state, partly explain this continuity and account for the absence of radical economic and tax reform before 1879. The economic thought that developed in official circles during the fifty years under scrutiny was essentially eclectic, which perhaps explains the lack of a complete commitment to either protectionism or *laissez-faire*. This does not mean that these ideas were alien to Chile. In the 1860s a well defined group of 'liberal' economic publicists began to make their presence felt, while in the second half of the 1870s, as the country plunged into desperate difficulties, supporters of protectionism entered the economic debate. The influence of these new economic ideas was more important in an academic and journalistic sense than in actual policy. The University of Chile, newspapers and periodicals provided the main forums for the exposition of these ideas, many of which were articulated in Congress. Traditional ideas, however, were firmly entrenched both in Congress and in the executive, and no substantial reforms were undertaken. Liberal and protectionist terminology was borrowed by those in positions of power, but as late as 1878 the objectives of the reforms introduced were essentially fiscal, stimuli to internally orientated activities being 'secondary and incidental'.

Economic growth did not, therefore, appear as a direct government goal. It was seen as the task of the private sector working within a favourable legal and institutional framework provided by the government. The absence of policies of subsidy or special treatment for new initiatives, like the incipient industrial sector of the 1860s, is a reflection of that position.

Despite Chile's geographical isolation, the landowners of the Central Valley and the tiny but wealthy group of northern mineowners saw their prosperity as depending upon an early integration into the international economy. The geographical distance which separated both groups was abridged by their shared commitment to a full integration of their activities into the mainstream of the world economy. State bureaucrats held this view too, and contributed to its realization by implementing policies which resulted in a gradual and orderly opening to foreign trade. During the 1850s the process of Chilean incorporation into the world market began to gather pace; and it was to have momentous consequences. Twenty years later the use of free trade rhetoric was common practice among government officials and bureaucrats, and the establishment of Chilean links with foreign markets was regarded as a remarkable achievement.[7] Yet official policies still reflected the influence of traditional thinking.

As long as the benefits derived from trade policy were tangible, the idea of increasing Chile's links with the most advanced economies found adherents in all circles. However, when in the late 1870s the international depression and internal factors brought the country to the brink of economic and social disaster, voices questioning the system were raised. State intervention and industrial development were advocated as means of achieving autonomous economic growth. During those confused and disheartening years these views gathered support, and a new trend in economic through began to evolve. But the government's response to the problems brought about by the crisis followed the traditional line of economic management. For the 'nationalist' or 'protectionist' lobby to find an echo in official policy, some forty years had still to elapse.

The study of the economic policies pursued in Chile until 1879 provides an interesting example of the efforts made by the elite to fight the main economic problems of the country. Although a marginal component of the international economic order, Chilean achievements until the mid-1870s provide some evidence of the feasibility of economic growth based upon the development of the external sector under the guidance of the state. But the Chilean experience also shows the dangers involved in adopting such a strategy, especially in terms of exposing the country to downturns of the international economy.

The search for an expedient policy

It was only after 1830, when political and constitutional order had been restored, that the Chilean economic system could flourish in an atmosphere of stability. Economic policies were applied with determination and formed part of a coherent programme. Yet the foundations of the policies which were to prevail for the next fifty years had already been laid during the turmoil of the 1820s, a decade when short-lived governments attempted to solve acute financial problems by adopting a policy of gradual opening to foreign trade, chiefly in order to raise revenue.

Soon after Chile declared its independence in 1818, the authorities opened up the nation's port to foreign trade and made of Valparaíso an entrepôt for the Southern Pacific area. At that time Chile was facing a delicate economic predicament. Independence had raised hopes and expectations of economic growth and prosperity that had been shattered by war and social unrest. In 1818 Chile 'was passing through a painful and complex crisis which caused the justified alarm of the great majority of the citizens. Though it had been thought that the consolidation of independence would mark the beginning of an era of wealth and prosperity, Chile was in fact poorer than in 1810.'[8] The government had to act swiftly to improve the state of the economy. By opening the ports and establishing Valparaíso as an entrepôt the administration achieved partial successes in two important areas. First, the value and volume of trade expanded; and an increased availability of tonnage facilitated the export of home-produced goods. Second, customs revenue grew to become an important and stable source of income for the state, which had a substantial need for resources to finance both new military campaigns and the organization of the administrative machine. Commenting on customs revenue in 1824, the minister of finance, Diego José Benavente, told Congress: 'This is the country's most productive source of revenue',[9] a comment that might have been made by any of his successors during the next fifty years. Moreover, a growth in customs revenue permitted the postponement of the introduction of an income tax strongly resisted by the elite.[10]

By the late 1820s the new policy had shown its merits. Not only had the country improved its export opportunities, earned more foreign exchange and been able to import more, but public finances, trade and productive activities in general had experienced some benefits. Customs revenue, composed mainly of import taxes, grew by 1,360 per cent between 1818 and 1829, accounting in 1829 for 60 per cent of total public revenue.[11] Chile at the same time benefited from a considerable number of foreigners who settled in Santiago and Valparaíso and developed important commercial and productive activities.[12] In the late 1820s travellers who called at Valparaíso were witness to the commercial and material gains made by the port.[13]

Other efforts made by successive Chilean governments between 1823 and 1830 were less successful. Attempts to introduce a system of taxation failed. In accordance with the prevailing neo-mercantilist economic ideas, the government undertook to encourage the creation of manufacturing industries by granting loans and passing favourable legislation. A handful of experiments were carried out in textiles, military equipment, paper, china and the manufacturing of hemp; none achieved much success. Many projects extensively debated in Congress were never started. Thus it was left to artisans to maintain the modest manufacturing production that existed in Chile for the next four decades.[14]

The main obstacle to the success of policies introduced in the 1820s was political uncertainty. In 1830, however, the coming to power of a ruthless Conservative regime ended seven years of political experiment. Yet if the new administration showed a determination to break with the political practices of the previous decade, it continued to uphold the economic policies outlined by previous governments, especially with regard to foreign trade and taxation. What distinguished the new regime was its determination to enforce its decisions.

From the mid-1830s Chile adjusted to the conditions of the world economy, even though it was only a marginal participant. Production developed more rapidly in activities that employed intensively those factors of production which were abundant in the country, like land. Domestic output was exchanged for goods which required the application of scarce means or production, like labour and capital. Thus the country remained an exporter of foodstuffs and minerals. Its import sector consisted of numerous retail businesses and a small number of large foreign-owned commission houses which controlled the bulk of trade. These businesses also provided financial and banking services – of particular importance before 1860 because they facilitated trade and exchange in an economy characterized by monetary problems, of which a shortage of divisionary coins and notes was the most acute.

After 1830 the state provided the legal framework within which the foreign trade sector began to grow. In turn it levied import and export taxes and thereby transferred some of the wealth created by foreign trade to the rest of the economy. This system worked smoothly as long as there was sustained growth in exports. But a decline in exports had immediate and direct consequences for imports and the public sector, since it meant a shortage of foreign exchange. This meant an internalization of demand; but because the domestic supply of manufactures was inelastic, adjustments took place at the price level. Finally, a drop in imports was immediately felt by the public sector in the form of lower yields from its main source of revenue. When this occurred the state was confronted with the prospect of having to reduce its activity. From the mid-1850s when the state became more involved in the provision of services, reductions in expenditure were increasingly inexpedient, and the state therefore resorted more frequently to extraordinary sources of revenue.

Until 1879 the rate of growth of the Chilean economy was a function of the level of activity in the foreign trade sector, but the degree of correlation between external commerce and domestic growth weakened over time. From 1830 until 1860 the relationship was close: performance in

the commercial sector influenced both the general economic environment and the condition of government finances equally. The period was
one of classic export-led growth. Exports facilitated imports and, in the
absence of any autonomous basis for development (for example, manufacturing), determined the limits of fiscal intervention, particularly as
services were, in the main, provided by the state. After 1860, however,
this close relationship declined. The activities of the state continued to
increase, regardless of the evolution of foreign trade and revenue. The
public sector began to offer a wide range of services, especially in
transport and education, with public expenditure sustained during
depressive cycles by frequent and intensive use of deficit financing and
recourse to extraordinary revenue. Banking, tax and trade policy
reforms all resulted from these new trends. Thus between 1860 and 1879
the growth of the public sector became less dependent upon foreign trade
and the general level of economic activity.[15]

Economic policies from 1830 to the 1850s

The rise to power of the Conservative regime in 1830 was followed by the
adoption of more 'liberal' attitudes, especially with respect to foreign
trade. Manuel Rengifo, a talented minister of finance, began his term of
office in 1830 by introducing a *plan de hacienda*, to be implemented within
seven years. First came the elimination of tax burdens and obstacles to
trade and the granting of more guarantees to users of the Valparaíso
entrepôt.[16] Foreign trade policy was carried further in January 1834
when the first comprehensive import tariff was passed. In 1835 export
taxes were fixed, thus completing the series of measures designed to give
the most favourable facility to foreign trade, the cornerstone of Rengifo's
strategy. The average tax on most imported consumer goods was 32 per
cent *ad valorem* and that on exports 2 per cent. The import tarif was not
destined to protect industry – a superfluous function, since there was no
industry to be protected – but to raise revenue; and even raw materials
were subjected to a 10 per cent duty.[17]

On the domestic front Rengifo attempted to shrink the public sector
and gave incentives to trade and production. He reduced the size of the
bureaucracy, exempted the retail trade from the payment of the *patente* (a
licence to practise a profession or trade), abrogated the tax on the sale of
consumer goods (the unpopular *alcabala del viento*) and finally introduced
a reduction of two per cent on the stamp duty payable on sales or
long-term leases of rural property.[18] Growing foreign trade, political
stability and Rengifo's policy created a favourable climate for business,
which was reflected in public finances. Public revenue increased from
£270,506 in 1830 to £498,519 in 1840, at an annual cumulative rate of 6.3
per cent in real terms. Rengifo began to realize his aim of 'removing the
obstacles which hinder industry in general and at the same time to

increase the treasury's revenue'. He stated that 'the government, far from imposing new taxes upon the people, has eased their burdens by abolishing several of the existing ones; and furthermore the bills yet to be submitted to Parliament will be instrumental in giving more freedom and encouragement to our industry'.[19] By 1840 the economy had certainly responded.

Once legislation regulating foreign trade and domestic business had been passed, the government concentrated its activity on the reorganization of the state's economic and financial apparatus. In 1835 a thorough reform of the finance ministry was initiated, which subsequently was extended to other ministries. The completion of this reform improved public sector efficiency in terms of both policy-making and law enforcement, while also improving the state's capacity to collect revenues. Two laws further illustrate the state's new efficiency and the improved condition of the economy by the late 1830s, while shedding light on the social inspiration of the government's decisions. In 1839 the Tribunal Superior de Cuentas was entrusted with the supervision and control of all financial operations of the public sector, because its activity had expanded so dramatically. Another law, passed in 1840, introduced the first significant change in the export tariff which was intended to give a boost to the rural economy, by declaring duty-free all agricultural and pastoral products except hides. Hitherto they had been subject to taxes that fluctuated between 4 and 6 per cent.[20]

The 1840 law is of crucial importance to the analysis of Chile's economic policy throughout this period, because it best reflects the elite's attitudes in matters of taxation and economic policy. The legislation, which maintained export duties on minerals, represented not only a show of strength on the part of landowners but also their reluctance to finance the state by means of taxes that might affect them directly. Export taxes on minerals remained till 1879, though they were progressively reduced, while those on imports were always maintained above 25 per cent. These levels of taxation were tantamount to punishment of the mining sector, which was more productive and had better export opportunities than agriculture, while the use of the import tariff showed a further preference to finance the state through indirect taxes. Beyond encouraging agricultural exports, the new legislation had a special significance for other sectors of the economy. The preference for financing the public sector through import taxes, although not specifically intended to create a tax shelter in order to favour local manufacturing, was to be one of the mainstays of the growth of domestic industry from the early 1860s. In practice it amounted to an element of protection.

The tariff reform of 1840 was introduced after ten years of firm administration. During that decade Chile improved its productive and trading position significantly, mainly by recovering traditional markets like Peru, and by acquiring new ones. This was an important contribution to the nation's political success. The new economic climate introduced a mood of optimism that was reflected in government statements. In 1841, when addressing Congress for the last time as president, Joaquín Prieto stated: 'Our social edifice has serenely and majestically displayed its excellency in the midst of the storms which have wrought havoc in every other part of Spanish America.'[21] His government had consolidated the rule of law and had successfully tackled Chile's main economic problem. It had brought order to the public sector, developed a coherent fiscal system, planned the resumption of foreign debt servicing; and its foreign trade policy was rendering the desired fruits. Total public revenue, reflecting the growth in foreign trade, increased handsomely. Customs revenue, which in 1833 had accounted for 57.6 per cent of ordinary revenue, rose to 62 per cent by 1840; public enterprises and services contributed 20 per cent and other taxes 18 per cent of the revenue in 1840.[22]

Economic policy showed a marked stability and continuity in the period until 1860. Although the number of laws promulgated was modest, some of them had an important bearing on the working of the public sector and served to encourage business. During these years the first railway legislation was passed.[23] Another prominent law was the 1854 statute substituting the *contribución agrícola* for the tithe, which effectively meant the transference of tax from income to the value of the property.[24] Meanwhile an important drive towards the smelting of copper ores, which began in 1842 and rapidly exhausted the supply of wood in the mining areas, led in 1845 to the abrogation of the tax of 35 per cent levied upon imported coal; the same law declared free of duty all copper bars smelted by native coal.[25] This tariff structure was to undergo substantial modifications again in 1851.[26]

Until 1860 the austerity of government policy proved satisfactory as long as the pace of economic activity, especially that of the public sector, was kept at a modest level. Ordinary sources of revenue accounted for 94.4 per cent of total state revenue between 1840 and 1860. Moreover, public accounts for those years show only two deficits. The explanation for the success of the fiscal policy is to be found in the performance of foreign trade. Between 1845 and 1860 it grew at an annual cumulative rate of 7.9 per cent. The value of exports increased more than three and a half times; and imports, the key element in the structure of public revenue, grew at 5.7 per cent per annum, allowing public revenue to grow at 5.6 per cent per annum, whilst expenditure grew by 5.2 per cent per annum. In 1824 Diego José Benavente, the finance minister, predicted that if the country exported more 'more will be consumed, more will be imported and more imports will increase our revenue'.[27]

New problems; new policies?

The prosperous condition of the Chilean economy and of public finances in the years preceding 1860 resulted from the 'phenomenal'[28] expansion of the export sector and sound economic management.[29] But some important changes had begun to occur. A commercial crisis of some severity, but more important, changes in foreign trade patterns, made it necessary to relax economic policies. While Chile had achieved a somewhat respectable degree of externally induced growth, it still remained a marginal component of the world economic system and a small economy. However, as most Western European economies began to expand, the world demand for raw materials and foodstuffs increased sharply. For Chile this was reflected in components of demand that can be traced back to 1842[30] and that by the mid-1850s had accelerated the pace of economic activity. While from 1842 new methods in copper smelting had boosted copper and coal mining, between 1849 and 1855 the short-lived markets for wheat and flour in California and Australia stimulated agriculture.[31] An increase in demand pushed up agricultural prices and the cost of labour. Wages in the countryside rose from about 1 *real* a day in 1850 to above 2 *reales* in 1857.[32] These events had repercussions in all sectors of the economy, and brought about the first major change in economic policy and administration.

Until 1860 gold, silver and copper coins were the only legal means of payment in Chile. All evidence suggests that the monetary system was totally inadequate to meet the needs of the economy, particularly with regard to the retail trade.[33] A reform introduced in 1851 failed to improve the monetary system, and by the middle of the decade its inadequacy became a serious obstacle to growth. From about 1850 the demand for money soared, and wholesale commercial establishments further developed the existing practice of issuing their own means of payment to cover shortages. Moreover, in 1848 the establishment of a bank of issue in Valparaíso caused alarm, and rage amongst the business community of the city led the minister of finance to say in 1849: 'May we hold ourselves aloof from institutions such as banks of issue.'[34] He ordered the closure of the bank in Valparaíso, but between 1854 and June 1860 four such institutions were created, all of which issued negotiable bills which had a wide circulation.

In July 1860 the *Ley de bancos de emisión* (Law on Banks of Issue) legalized a *de facto* situation. It allowed any bank to issue negotiable bills for up to 150 per cent above their paid-up capital. The new legislation did not impose any limitations, beyond prohibiting the issue of notes of less than 20 pesos (in 1860 £1 = 5.49 pesos). There were neither regulations on the minimum amount of capital required for a bank to operate, nor limitations on the nature or maturity of loans. The law did not even mention the need for banks to keep metallic reserves against either deposits or notes issued; nor did it regulate the granting of loans to directors or establish provision for any kind of supervision or inspection on the part of the government.[35] The *Ley de bancos de emisión* was welcomed as an important progressive step by those in government and trade who only ten years earlier had been the most vociferous opponents of banks.

The formal existence of a banking system allowed a spectacular growth in the number of banks and in the quantity of money in the economy. The new institutions operated with absolute freedom, governed by a law described as one of 'the most liberal in the world' that went much further than envisaged by the contemporary theory and practice of liberalism.[36] The new banking legislation stimulated an impressive growth in financial capital. By 1876 the aggregate nominal capital of fourteen banks was £8,604,269, while their paid-up capital amounted to £2,710,273; the value of notes issued was £1,476,354. Two years later note issue rose to £2,338,709, and according to a law passed in July 1878 the notes became inconvertible. Parallel to the banks of issue there were three mortgage banks, one of which, the Caja de Crédito Hipotecario (National Mortgage Bank) had granted loans for £2,521,034 by the end of 1876. In the case of the banks of issue, their lending policy consisted only of the granting of loans for a maximum period of six months and at very high interest rates, making them unsuitable for medium- or long-term industrial projects. However, in his annual report for 1876 as finance minister, Ramón Barros Luco made special reference to the alleged benefits for the country derived from the rapid growth of the banking system. 'The banks,' he said, 'have given great impulse to industry and commerce throughout the country . . . they have spread to all the principal towns of the Republic . . . [and] have rendered important services to public and private interests.'[37]

The new banking legislation marked the first important departure from the policies introduced in the 1830s. This change was made necessary by the sudden expansion of the Chilean economy in the 1850s. There was in fact a noticeable increase in foreign trade, especially in agricultural and mineral exports, between 1849 and 1858. Increased economic activity required important sums of capital, especially for the development of infrastructure, as well as for a modicum of investment in productive activities. Thus, while the private sector began to construct railways in the northern mining districts, the state committed itself to the development of lines in the Central Valley in joint ventures with private investors. In 1852 the government began a programme of road construction and maintenance and embarked on the total transformation of the Valparaíso port facilities. The year 1852 also marked the start of a sizeable increase in public spending on services, especially education.[38] Capital requirements were considerable, and 'by its nature the system could only respond through its one recourse, the printing of money'.[39]

It was the change in the pace of economic activity which in the final analysis forced the government to relax its fiscal policy and to abandon the austere budgetary practices that had prevailed until the early 1850s. In 1858 the first deficit for twenty years appeared in the annual public accounts, and from then until 1878 deficit finance was to become an almost common feature of the budget. Furthermore, only by the late 1850s did the financing of public spending exclusively from ordinary revenue prove inadequate.

In 1858 the government resorted to the London money market for a loan of £1,034,729. The loan was used to defray the costs of the completion of the Valparaíso-Santiago railway and other public works. At a time of economic difficulties the loan had a counter-cyclical effect upon the economy and signalled the beginning of twenty years of heavy state borrowing. In this context the growth of the national debt appears as a reflection of new budgetary practices, themselves the response of the public sector to the requirements of an expanding economy. Kept at a moderate level until 1857, government borrowing subsequently accelerated, increasing at a factor of 8.5 by 1878. Domestic borrowing rose at a faster rate than external, thus representing an internalization of borrowing.

Heavy borrowing before 1878 reflected new trends in fiscal policy. Although the rate of growth of ordinary public revenue declined from 6.3 per cent per annum over the previous thirty years to 4.1 per cent between 1860 and 1878, public expenditure continued to grow at an annual rate of 5.7 per cent. This meant that extraordinary sources of revenue acquired a particular saliency in the financing of the state, to the extent that from 1860 to 1879 they accounted for 31 per cent of total public revenue. From 1858 until the outbreak of the War of the Pacific, as the state intervened more and more in the economy, the level of expenditure increasingly determined the revenue structure.

Important changes took place in the structure of ordinary revenue between 1860 and 1879. The role of customs duties declined markedly. After accounting for 61 per cent of ordinary revenue before 1860, the share of customs receipts fell to 51.2 per cent over the next eighteen years. On average, import duties accounted for 98 per cent of the revenue derived from this source. Their decline was especially marked after 1874. The profound international crisis which hit the country during the following five years eroded customs revenue, and in 1878 its share in public revenue reached its lowest point at 44 per cent. On the other hand the contribution made by public enterprises and services to ordinary revenue rose dramatically after 1860, accounting, on average, for 33.4 per cent of the monies collected.[40] Railways and post office and telegraphic services show the most important increases, with railways leading the way. In 1870 the finance minister, Melchor Concha i Toro, made one of the first official comments on the importance of the railways to the Chilean economy and finances, when in the Chamber of Deputies he said: 'Industry needs encouragement and I believe that the railway should be regarded from the point of view of the impetus it is giving and will continue to give to the country's economy.'[41] In terms of public revenue alone, the railways had already made a great impact. From 1858 to 1879 their returns formed 52 per cent of the income that the state drew from its enterprises and services. Moreover, in the six years between 1873 and 1879 the share of the railways in this revenue item rose to as much as 56 per cent. The profitable exploitation of the state-owned railways transformed the revenue item 'state enterprises and services' into the second most important source of public revenue, and it was the only one of its constituents to show an increase. In addition, this item kept a constant share of ordinary revenue between 1860 and 1879, thus indicating a growth in absolute terms. It should be noted that it grew at a similar rate to that shown by total public revenue, a fact which indicates that the consumption of goods and services provided by the state was growing. This was particularly noticeable in transport and communications, functions which gave an important boost to related activities.[42]

The third component of ordinary revenue, taxes, declined in its relative importance after 1860. From an average of 17.7 per cent between 1840 and 1860, it dropped to 14.5 per cent in the following nineteen years. The narrowing of the tax structure and the general reduction in the tax rates over the second period explain this decline. Of the six taxes which existed in 1860, only four remained in 1875,[43] and attempts to introduce a tax reform which would have included an income tax provoked a storm of protest in 1869.[44] In the Chamber of Deputies Vicente Santafuentes rose to declare: 'Only taxes needed for the functioning of the administration should be levied. Fortunate are those nations which are able to function with few taxes. For my country I would wish that industry and wealth might prosper without new and burdensome taxes, even if for this to happen it means appearing to be less civilized than other countries which do in fact pay them.'[45]

The deputy was not speaking for himself alone. Any attempts to introduce new taxes were always violently opposed, as were initiatives to raise the existing rates. In 1876, when the full effects of the economic crisis began to be felt, the government decided to resort to taxes in order to increase its revenue, 'as it [had] been absolutely impossible to rely on economies alone to compensate for the deficit'.[46] Two years were to elapse before Congress approved the new taxes, and when it did so the original rates proposed had been greatly reduced. In the case of the *contribución de haberes* (tax on capital assets and returns), which originally called for a 3 per cent levy on income derived from financial assets or real estate, the rate was reduced to 0.3 per cent. This same rate was levied upon the income of public employees and pensions, which in the original bill submitted to Congress were to be taxed at 2 per cent. The *contribución de herencias* (tax on inheritances), which fluctuated between 1 and 5 per cent, was also introduced in that package.[47]

The discussion of bills which proposed new taxes between 1876 and 1878 epitomized the attitude of the elite towards taxation. A wide range of tactics – obstruction, unnecessary prolongation of debates, lack of quorum – were used by congressmen to delay their progress.[48] Meanwhile the public sector was facing an embarrassing financial situation. Foreign observers had no doubts that the Chileans could not 'do better than turn their serious attention to one or two questions of purely internal economy, of which the most important would, perhaps, be a thorough remodelling of their antiquated system of taxation, whereby alone they can hope to increase their revenue and improve the conditions of all classes of the population'.[49] However, Chileans were not yet prepared to contemplate such an unpleasant possibility.

Meanwhile the very people who opposed taxes kept committing the state to further initiatives which demanded considerable resources. As shown above, public expenditure kept growing. By 1876 the government had invested £5,747,126 in railways alone, a sum which represented 91 per cent of the foreign debt, and a further £1,626,506 had been spent on various other public works and in strengthening national defences. These and other programmes of expenditure resulted in continuous deficits which were covered by further borrowing, especially after 1867.

The slowing-down in the growth of foreign trade, which rose at 1.5 per cent per annum between 1860 and 1879, held back the growth of ordinary revenue. The adamant refusal of Congress to discuss a complete tax reform added to the difficult predicament of the government, as alternative sources of revenue were limited or non-existent. But Congress and government had found a way round the problem.

The prevailing attitude could be summed up thus: 'If the money cannot be brought to the public coffers in any other way, indebtedness must be chosen before the introduction of taxes.'[50] The government certainly found it attractive, to the extent that between 1861 and 1879 it raised ten domestic loans totalling £3,912,837, while in London six loans were floated for the nominal figure of £7,348,074. Much of these loans, it is true, was invested in programmes of infrastructural expansion which had an important impact on Chilean development. Nevertheless, borrowing put a heavy pressure on expenditure, and from 1861 until 1879 amortization and servicing of the national debt absorbed, on average, 29 per cent of public expenditure, reaching their peak in 1877 when these payments accounted for 43.7 per cent of total expenditure.[51]

Such were the pressures which forced the government to declared the inconvertibility of bank notes in July 1878. Price inflation and currency devaluation followed, a decision to which much of Chile's economic 'frustration' has been attributed. However, there were other factors that deserve consideration.

In the first place, as indicated, foreign trade did not grow at an adequate rate to satisfy increasing public needs. In fact its growth rate declined. Second, 'large landowners, industry and most of the services sector (all of which could afford to pay)', were strongly opposed to a tax reform comprising an income tax.[52] Third, and most important, the private sector would not commit itself to the development of the infra-structure, thus forcing the government to undertake this task alone and to find the means of financing it. An outstanding example of this was the construction of the central railway network. Two companies were formed jointly by private investors and the state for the construction of lines south and west of Santiago. Eventually private investors withdrew from both enterprises, forcing the state to take over both companies.[53]

The government's only recourse was to borrow. By 1875 the burden of servicing the national debt gave Congress ammunition with which to attack the executive. The level of public expenditure was the main target and, when questioned, ministers did not deny the government's respon-sibility, although they quickly pointed out the reason. 'It is a fact which we must confess in all frankness,' one minister said, 'that we have involved ourselves in works for which our ordinary means were not sufficient and that is the reason why public finances are in disarray.'[54] However, as early as 1871, minister Altamirano had challenged Congress's caution over public spending:

> Doubtless people are right when they recommend us to be cautious in the way we use our financial credibility. However, caution cannot be applied to the point where we condemn ourselves to do nothing about those things which the country's situation urgently demands. All those things which have been done will mean further recourse to loans. This is why I say that, although it is true that our debt is already very heavy, the question is: either we bid farewell to all the advances which demand expenditure or we must resort to loans, since ordinary resources are barely sufficient to cover ordinary expenditure. Without loans there can be no railways, no ships for our Navy, there will be no money to complete the warehouses or the Congress building; there will be no bridges over our rivers, there will be no works.[55]

The stress created by spending programmes almost reached breaking-point in 1878. In June the government borrowed £411,290 to finance current expenditure. Nine of the eleven existing banks of issue made the loan in exchange for the privilege of issuing £1,629,032 in notes. This operation increased the likelihood of the introduction of paper money, as a result of which the withdrawal of deposits accelerated, and by mid-July assumed the characteristics of a run on the banks. On 23 July 1878 the government, with the approval of Congress, declared the 'inconvertibility of bank notes'.

Lack of public spirit, imagination, flexibility and courage to adopt new policies were responsible for the disastrous condition of public finances. Borrowing on a large scale was certainly not the best way to finance economic development. But were there real alternatives? Probably not, and although this policy had succeeded in pulling Chile out of the 'economic indolence in which it had hitherto lived',[56] the choice was fraught with the most explosive possibilities, as the 1878 crisis of the peso proved.

Fiscal policy and industrial expansion

Fiscal policy between 1860 and 1879 did not vary substantially from that between 1830 and 1860. But whereas in the earlier period it had led to 'a vigorous advance in our economic development, which neither has a precedent in our history nor has been continued',[57] between 1860 and 1879 fiscal policy became totally inadequate to meet the requirements of an economy in full process of growth. By adhering to established principles, Chilean governments had by 1878 put the country in an extremely dangerous and embarrassing position. Taxes introduced during that year, as well as the new import tax law, can be directly attributed to the emergency.

In July 1878 the limited but important Chilean manufacturing industry received a 'protectionist' boost from changes in the duty on imports.[58] A change which gave more effective protection to industry would by all accounts appear out of place for those times. It has been maintained that a tariff reform in 1864 signalled the start of an era of staunch liberalism in Chile, which was to lead to the country's economic frustration.[59] A common view is that until 1864 'the objective of economic policy was the development of domestic industry by means of protective tariffs and other forms of assistance', and that the previous thirty years constituted an 'era of unrelenting protectionism'. The tariff reform of 1864, it is said, 'constituted a fatal blow to the emerging and weak Chilean industry', an industry which, incidentally, has yet to be discovered.[60] In search of scapegoats, some writers have claimed that the 1864 reform marked the peak of the nefarious influence on Chilean economic policy of Jean G. Courcelle-Seneuil, a French liberal economist hired by the government as a technical adviser. Furthermore, they argued that this was the moment in which the elite abandoned sound economic practices and adopted a catastrophic *laissez-faire* policy which at a stroke destroyed the gains of the previous thirty years and halted economic development. According to some authors, the reasons for such a dramatic shift in policies seem to have been purely doctrinaire.[61] However, as recent

research shows, neither was a mythical manufacturing industry destroyed nor economic growth stopped. Furthermore, it is now clear that
Courcelle-Seneuil bears no responsibility for the tariff reform, which in
any case was applied only briefly.

In 1851 a new *Ordenanza de Aduanas* reduced the general *ad valorem* tariff
on imports from 32 to 25 per cent. Imports were taxed at rates that varied
from 30 per cent on furniture, finished garments and footware, to 6 per
cent on foods and 2 per cent on jewellery. Over one hundred items were
declared free of duty, including raw materials such as cotton, iron,
mercury, steel, tin and coal as well as machinery for agriculture, manufacturing and mining. Compared to the 1834 *Ordenanza*, the new code
gave an incentive to local production by freeing raw materials from
duties, but at the same time it introduced a new complexity by reducing
the tax rate on goods which were more likely to be produced in the
country.[62]

The 1864 law replaced this tariff structure and also opened coastal
trade to foreign vessels. The 30, 6 and 2 per cent import taxes were
abolished and a standard 25 per cent rate was introduced. The number
of articles which could be imported free of duty was reduced to twenty-
nine, though it is interesting to note that cotton was the only industrial
raw material included in that list. Machinery was taxed at 15 per cent,
but it could be imported free of duty by special government dispensation
when destined for use in agriculture, manufacturing or mining.[63] The
government defended this legislation both on principle and because of its
own financial requirements. As the minister of finance, Alejandro Reyes,
put it, the tariff essentially represented for the government a 'financial
instrument whose only objective is to provide an income without considering it as a means for achieving relief or protection'. Activities which
could not survive without a tax shelter were described as superfluous.[64]

The new customs code certainly made the prospects for the growth of
manufacturing industry more difficult. But it did not stop the creation of
new factories; in fact the favourable trade cycle 1865–73 encouraged
their creation.[65] The boom was decisive for the consolidation of the first
stages of industrialization in Chile. The increase in the level of effective
demand was directly related to the growth in national income resulting
from the expansion of foreign trade. With regard to the import tariff, the
industrialists' pressure on Congress for tax exemption on imports of raw
materials in the late 1860s and early 70s not only confirmed this, but also
resulted in the 1864 law being amended.[66] A substantial number of tax
exemptions were passed before 1872 and were codified in the duty-free
list of that year's new customs ordinance. However, most industrial raw
materials such as dyes, iron, lead, raw sugar, steel, timber and tin,
and inputs such as pipes, matrices, bolts and tools, were still charged
with a 15 per cent import tax. Only cotton and paper were exempted.

Machinery and engines for industrial purposes were included in a duty-free list which was substantially augmented but which failed to satisfy industrialists. Pressure for the elimination of the 15 per cent tax on raw materials and inputs was the main feature of the debate concerning foreign trade legislation in the 1870s, and gave rise to a protectionist tendency which was to acquire considerable strength in the following three decades.[67]

In 1877 a new law introduced a surcharge of a tenth on the existing tariff, thus raising the general import tax to 27.5 per cent. This increase, quickly voted by Congress, is best explained in terms of the mounting financial problems being faced by the state, rather than as 'a return to protectionism'. Neither can the 1878 law which raised the general import tax to 35 per cent be described as marking 'a commitment by the Chilean government to industrial development'.[68] The deep economic crisis which began in 1874, and its damaging effects on public finances, forced the promulgation of both laws. In fact, the state's financial blunders of the late 1870s were caused chiefly by the drop in the absolute value of exports, which in turn resulted in the deterioration of the balance of trade. In 1878 Chile was in the midst of an extremely grave recession; and because the state was unable to reduce its expenditure to adequate levels it had no alternative to increasing revenue. The raising of import duties in 1877 and 1878 was part of such a move.

However, the tariff reform of 1878 was not carried out at random. It was not only that the gains made by the industrialists before this law was passed were maintained, but now almost all raw materials and inputs for manufacturing were declared duty-free. Of vital importance with respect to the question of effective protection was the levying of a 15 per cent tax on imports of vehicles, machinery, engines and hardware, which previously had been free of duty because many of these goods were now manufactured in the country.[69] The 1878 import tax law favoured the consumer goods industries, particularly food, textiles, footwear, paper and furniture, as raw materials required for their manufacture were no longer taxed and a relatively high duty (35 per cent) was levied upon foreign competitors. For the capital goods industries, which were the most advanced both in terms of the number of concerns and the volume and quality of their output, the introduction of the 15 per cent tax on such foreign goods was most important, since iron, lead, steel, zinc, bolts, nuts and nails and many other inputs were now imported free of duty.[70]

The 1877 and 1878 import laws favoured the development of both artisanship and modern manufacturing industry. However, they cannot be interpreted as a shift towards protectionism, although it is true that a pragmatic commitment towards protection was gaining in popularity. These laws were rather a product of the economic emergency and were revoked once the crisis was over. It was no mere accident that the 1878 law was intended to last for eighteen months only, and it was only renewed for similar periods until 1884, when financial pressures made it necessary. Government officials were adamant that the reforms of the late 1870s were intended to solve financial difficulties of the public sector by maximizing revenue. As Rafael Sotomayor, minister of finance, put it:

> If in the course of securing a sufficient revenue one incidentally manages to give birth to or to favour an industry or craft in addition, sound economy would render a reduction or modification of the tax advisable, without, on account of this, diverging from the liberal principles which form the basis of our customs system. Without changing the fundamentals, it is necessary to make a partial and moderate revision of duties, which without reducing revenue might stimulate industry, but never losing sight of the rule that *revenue should be the prime goal, and protection, secondary and incidental.*[71]

Moreover, the contemporary attitudes towards protection indicate that it was beginning to be regarded as reaching far beyond the mere manipulation of the tariff. For some it was already clear 'that the customs ordinance is not the only appropriate means of protecting industry'. Advocates of protection also called for programmes of technical education suitable to industrial needs, and better access to credit as well as preference in the allocation of public contracts.[72] In this context there is no doubt that fiscal considerations were the principal determinant of tariff legislation. Recent scholarship, in focusing heavily upon a narrow concept of protectionism based upon tariff legislation, has overlooked the larger supportive role performed by the state as envisaged by contemporaries.

Doubtless, some of the tariff changes of 1878 favoured local producers. Pressure for such a move had been mounting since 1875, and the government finally conceded to it.[73] But even if at the time the new law was passed the declared intention of the finance ministry was 'to stimulate the development of public wealth by introducing a tax of 15 per cent on tools and machinery and relieving raw materials'[74] – a statement which resembles those of the 1820s – this was far from representing a wholehearted adoption of economic nationalism. Rather, the reform was understood chiefly as a step that would alleviate the financial constraints upon the public sector. Manufacturing industry, developed on a capitalist basis, had experienced important growth from the early 1860s. This was made possible by steady growth in the internal demand for manufactured products, which in turn was related to the country's greater interaction with the international economy from the late 1850s onwards. The tariff reforms of 1878, which should be regarded as a pragmatic commitment to protection, were a response to the pleas of substantial numbers of industrialists who were facing a difficult internal situation and intense foreign competition. In this context, these changes will be better understood if attention is paid to what was said about policy-making at the time. Marcial Martínez, a leading liberal economic publicist, claimed that although the elite belonged 'as much through temperament as conviction to the liberal school of thought . . . in all their attitudes they were partisans but not sectarian'. When having to deal with the problems of Chile's economy, they sought 'terms which might be healthy between the extremes of *laissez-faire* and protectionism'[75].

In fact, despite the rhetoric, most of the economic policies adopted by Chilean governments before 1879 had a very pragmatic character; and it is quite erroneous to label them as 'liberal' or 'protectionist'. Neo-mercantilist thought was still influential, and although politicians were not alien to new ideas their adoption was slow and never complete.

Conclusion

In 1835 Manuel Rengifo began his speech on the economy by saying:

> This is not the place and it is not my intention to contest the old theory which sees in the adoption of the 'prohibitive' system the only efficient way to improve the fortunes of people. A doctrine already discredited by experience renders superfluous the arguments which could be used to refute it. However, if the spreading of useful knowledge has served as a powerful tool in the destruction of old beliefs, the adherence to the principles of (economic) freedom, taken in their strictest sense and without regard for the peculiar circumstances of the country where they are to be applied, could, on the other hand, be highly damaging for the elaboration of a coherent plan of revenue. To give industry help and protection without the treasury suffering the effects is one of those tasks that require full understanding and wisdom on the part of legislators, a task to which no effort should be considered excessive if it contributes to its achievement.[76]

He was in fact outlining the approach to policy-making which was to prevail until the late 1870s, as Sotomayor confirmed in 1877.[77]

The policies enforced until 1879 were essentially eclectic. Until the 1850s they still reflected a strong influence of the colonial economic regime. Thereafter, some ideas derived from the theories of the classical school began to be incorporated[78] in a way which was thought adequate for the country, 'without running the risks involved in the nonsensical mania of changing everything'.[79] In the late 1850s, as a result of demands arising from an increased relationship with the international economy, the austere policies of the previous decades began to be relaxed. The state became more 'interventionist' and the revenue policies originally designed to cater only for 'needs of a strictly administrative nature' had to be replaced, as public spending began to grow autonomously. The answer of policy-makers to the new requirements consisted of heavy borrowing. But why was the state in Chile called to intervene on a much larger scale than elsewhere in Latin America during this period? What was the destiny of so much wealth created by growing exports?

There is, of course, no straight answer to these questions. There are, however, two factors that provide a partial explanation. First, the fact that by the middle of the nineteenth century Chilean entrepreneurs lost control over the export sector.[80] As a result, Chilean businessmen not only lost a substantial proportion of earnings derived from exports which might have been invested in infrastructure, but more importantly they lost to the state the direction of the economic process. Through taxes the state was able to share the profits generated by the export-import trade on a regular basis. Together with providing further intellectual and political bases for an increased participation of the state in the economic process, this situation also explains the maintenance of taxes on mineral exports until the late 1870s, and the manipulation of the import tariff for revenue purposes. Foreigners were involved in mining, and had an overwhelming control of the export of copper and the import trade; thus the levying of taxes on these activities did not carry serious political risks.[81]

Second, although in the initial stages of railway construction in the Central Valley the private sector participated in joint ventures with the state, new investment opportunities diverted the flow of capital away from public works in general. In the 1860s it became more rewarding to invest in commercial, mining and banking ventures, to the extent that by 1875 these activities concentrated 79.8 per cent of the capital of Chile's joint stock companies.[82] With the exception of some public utilities and irrigation projects, public works was not an area favoured by private investors. Moreover, the difficulties involved in port and railway construction further reduced their attraction as an investment outlet. It took, for example, eleven years to complete the 184 kilometres of track between Valparaíso and Santiago; costs exceeded estimates, dividends were low and often suspended, and the technical difficulties involved made similar projects less than attractive. Chilean entrepreneurs were not inclined to take risks and had a marked preference for investment opportunities which secured a high rate of return over the shortest period of time; activities such as railway construction failed to appeal to them. By 1872 the private sector had completely withdrawn from railway construction in the Central Valley, and certainly not because of a lack of financial resources; three years later the nominal capital of existing joint stock companies amounted to £28,493,214.

Thus the public sector was compelled to provide more services and infrastructure than had been foreseen by the architects of the republic.

That the state was able to satisfy most of the new demands was partly the result of a growth in foreign trade and sound financial management, and partly a consequence of political stability. Until 1861, the almost total exclusion of the opposition from Congress made the government's task in these matters, if not easy, at least free of major obstacles; and in the next two decades, when an enlarged role for the opposition was allowed, conflict did not involve economic policy till the late 1870s. Constitutional reform and religious affairs captured the time and energies of politicians, and neither trade nor fiscal policies were questioned.[83] Only in the crisis of the late 1870s did an open debate break out about the soundness of economic policy, and did critics of the government search for an alternative. On the other hand, the absence of major conflicts between the different regional interests contributed to taking pressure off the policy-makers. Mine-owners in the north, landowners in the Central Valley and merchants in Valparaíso shared the belief that Chilean economic prosperity depended on the success of its foreign trade. The state, which they dominated, shared this view. This consensus allowed the state to operate with a high degree of efficiency, and despite its reduced size it provided a foundation of stability, law and order upon which business could prosper.

Until the mid 1870s this approach was on the whole successful. National income grew considerably, a process of capital accumulation was started and the growth of domestic demand opened new opportunities for internationally orientated activities. The economic policy that helped to facilitate these developments cannot be defined by the use of a single concept. Economic policy was neither strictly 'protectionist' before 1864, nor was it totally *laissez-faire* thereafter. As in Britain, where such a policy was most closely followed, in the 1860s and 70s the functions of the state in the economic and social spheres exceeded those advocated by dogmatic popularizers.[84] The state spent not only what the taxpayers paid,[85] but much more, and its commitment to tax reductions forced the adoption of a borrowing policy of far-reaching consequences. The import tariff maintained its prime function as a source of revenue, and it was modified accordingly.

The success of the policies carried out in Chile until the mid-1870s was made possible partly by the favourable international economic climate and partly by the pragmatic nature of policies implemented in fiscal, monetary and trade matters. In so far as the fortunes of the Chilean economy were by the 1860s directly linked with the fluctuations of the international economy, achievements in the fiscal and productive spheres suggest that the nature of Chile's incorporation into the world economic system was crucial in the shaping of the first qualitative changes experienced by the country's economic structure. These changes implied the beginning of a process of capital accumulation primarily expressed in the development of infrastructure, manufacturing industry and various other activities that meant that a growing number of Chileans came to depend on a money wage. All these factors were part of the first stages of capitalist development in the context of a traditional society.

These changes raise questions as to the nature of the external connection enjoyed by Chile until 1880. One immediate conclusion is that the country became extremely sensitive to downturns in the economic cycle that affected the more developed economies. If in the late 1850s and early 1860s the Chilean economy suffered a severe blow as a result of the European crisis, the problems caused by the repercussions of the mid-1870s slump were many times more dramatic. The economy suffered from a loss of foreign markets, falling prices for its exports and changes in the international monetary order. Furthermore, in the public sector, falling revenues and the temporary closure of the London money market after July 1875 put the government in an extremely difficult predicament. The public sector had relied heavily on customs revenues and foreign loans for the implementation of an extensive programme of public works, as well as for financing substantial deficits in its budgets. With the deterioration of the government's main sources of income, the 'age of prosperity' of 1867–74, to which the state had contributed with high levels of expenditure, came to an abrupt end. The second conclusion is that the growth of the Chilean economy had become extremely dependent on the external connection, especially with Great Britain.

The Anglo-Chilean connection should not be seen in terms of an almighty imperial power exerting formidable pressure upon a defenceless underdeveloped country. The Chilean government and Chilean entrepreneurs always maintained a high degree of autonomy with regard to economic policy and investment strategy. It was the choice of Chileans to finance programmes of public works by borrowing heavily at home and in London, and to direct investment into commercial, financial and mining ventures rather than manufacturing, railways and port facilities. Until 1875 Chile's external connection made possible substantial economic growth and contributed to the consolidation of the country's political and social institutions. If growth did not result in self-sustained economic development, this was the consequence of decisions taken by Chileans themselves concerning the allocation of profits accumulated over several decades.

Notes

[1] William F. Sater 'Chile and the world depression of the 1870s' *Journal of Latin American Studies* xi 1 (1979); Luis M. Ortega 'Change and crisis in Chile's economy and society, 1865–1879' (unpubl. Ph.D. thesis, University of London 1979) chap. 6.

[2] Carmen Cariola and Osvaldo Sunkel 'Ensayo de interpretación in S. J. Stein and

Roberto Cortés Conde (eds) *Latin America. A guide to economic history, 1830–1930* (Berkeley 1977) pp. 277–9.

[3] On demographic changes see Carlos Hurtado *Concentración de población y desarrollo económico*. *El caso chileno* (Santiago 1966), especially chaps 1 to 4: on industrial development see Ricardo Lagos *La industria en Chile*. *Antecedentes estructurales* (Santiago 1966) *passim*; Oscar Muñoz *Crecimiento industrial de Chile* (Santiago, 2nd edn 1971) chaps 1 to 3; Henry W. Kirsch *Industrial development in a traditional society. The conflict of entrepreneurship and modernization in Chile* (Gainesville 1977) *passim*: on railway construction, Santiago Marín Vicuña *Estudios de los ferrocarriles chilenos* (Santiago 1900) *passim*; Enrique Espinoza *Jeografía descriptiva de Chile* (Santiago, 4th edn 1897) *passim*.

[4] For the 1880–1930 period see Carlos Humud *Política económica chilena desde 1830 to 1930* (Santiago 1974).

[5] Daniel Martner *Historia de Chile. Historia económica* (Santiago 1929), especially the first seven chapters.

[6] Robert M. Will 'The introduction of classical economics into Chile', *Hispanic American Historical Review* xliv 1 (1964) p. 21.

[7] See, for instance, 'Memoria del Superintendente de Aduanas, 1870' in *Memoria del Ministerio de Hacienda 1870* (hereafter *MH*).

[8] Diego Barros Arana *Historia Jeneral de Chile* (16 vols, Santiago 1884–1902) xiii 365.

[9] *MH 1824*, in *Sesiones de los Cuerpos Legislativos de la República de Chile* (hereafter *SCL*) (37 vols, Santiago 1886–1909) ix 67.

[10] John Lynch *The Spanish American Revolutions* (New York 1973) p. 142.

[11] From £8,660 to £126,393; Barros Arana *op. cit.* xiii 555 and xv 198. All monetary values in this article are expressed in pounds sterling of 1880. I am indebted to Gabriel Palma for his assistance with these calculations.

[12] Barros Arana *op. cit.* xii 375.

[13] C. E. Bladh *La República de Chile, 1821–1828* (Santiago 1951) p. 7. For a guide to travellers' accounts see Guillermo Feliú Cruz *Notas para una bibliografía sobre viajeros relativos a Chile* (Santiago 1962); Jacques Moerenhout 'Visión de Valparaíso en 1828' *Revista Chilena de Historia y Geografía* 118 (1951) p. 24.

[14] Ortega 'Change and crisis' chap. 3, where the development of modern manufacturing before the War of the Pacific is analysed.

[15] *Ibid.* pp. 320–93.

[16] The complete text of these laws can be found in Ricardo Anguita *Leyes promulgadas en Chile desde 1810 hasta el 1 de junio de 1912* (Santiago, 5 vols, 1912) i 211–12, 214, 226–8, 236–40.

[17] Anguita *op. cit.* i 240, 250, 253–4.

[18] Barros Arana *op. cit.* xvi 51.

[19] *MH 1834* in *SCL* xxii 456.

[20] Anguita *op. cit.* i 336.

[21] Message of President Joaquín Prieto to Congress in 1841, quoted in Simon Collier *Ideas and politics of Chilean independence, 1808–1833* (Cambridge 1967) p. 348.

[22] Data from *Resumen de la Hacienda Pública de Chile desde 1833 hasta 1914* (London 1914) pp. 22–6.

[23] Anguita *op. cit.* i 504–8, 516, 592, 598, 607.

[24] *Ibid.* i 616.

[25] *Ibid.* i 464.

[26] *Ibid.* i 529–86

[27] *MH 1824* p. 66.

[28] Ortega 'Change and crisis' pp. 320–93.

[29] This term is used by Markos Mamalakis *The growth and structure of the Chilean economy: from independence to Allende* (New Haven 1976) p. 28.

[30] L. Ortega 'The first four decades of the Chilean coal-mining industry, 1841–1879' *Journal of Latin American studies* xiv 1 (1982).

[31] Sergio Sepúlveda 'El trigo chileno en el mercado mundial' in *Informaciones Geográficas año VI* (Santiago 1956) pp. 34–52.

[32] On agricultural price increases see Arnold J. Bauer *Chilean rural society from the Spanish Conquest to 1930* (Cambridge 1975) p. 40 for wheat, and Appendix I for flour and beans. On agricultural wages, Sepúlveda *op. cit.* p. 44.

[33] Maria Graham *Journal of a residence in Chile during the year 1822* (New York 1969) p. 220. See also *MH 1835*, 64; Frank W. Fetter *Monetary inflation in Chile* (Princeton 1931) p. 4.

[34] *MH 1849* p. 7.

[35] Anguita *op. cit.* II 87–9.

[36] Guillermo Subercaseaux *Historia de las doctrinas económicas en América y en especial en Chile* (Santiago 1929) p. 54; Anguita *op. cit.* II 88. Emphasis added.

[37] *MH 1876* p. xxxviii.

[38] Ortega 'Change and crisis' pp. 359–91.

[39] Pierre Vayssière 'Au Chili: de l'économie coloniale à l'inflation' *Cahiers des Amériques Latines* no. 5 (1970) p. 10.

[40] Ortega 'Change and crisis' pp. 325–42.

[41] *Cámara de Diputados, Sesión Extraordinaria* 5 Jan. 1870.

[42] For their impact on urban development and manufacturing growth, see Ortega 'Change and crisis' chaps 2 and 3.

[43] *Resumen de la Hacienda Pública de Chile desde 1833 hasta 1914* pp. 20–34.

[44] *MH 1869* p. 12.

[45] *Cámara de Diputados, Sesión Ordinaria* 14 Oct. 1869.

[46] *MH 1876* p. x.

[47] Anguita *op. cit.* II 457, 472–4.

[48] William Gibbs (Valparaíso) to Antony Gibbs & Sons (London). Antony Gibbs Archive, letters (private) nos 27, 33, of 16 April and 15 July 1878 respectively, MS 11,470/2. Also letters nos 1 and 4 of 14 Dec. 1878 and 14 Jan. 1879 respectively, in MS 11,470/3.

[49] Parliamentary Papers (hereafter *PP*) 1876 LXXII 368.

[50] *Cámara de Diputados, Sesión Ordinaria* 8 June 1878.

[51] Ortega 'Change and crisis' pp. 72–102, 373, 387–8.

[52] Mamalakis *op. cit.* p. 22.

[53] Robert Oppenheimer 'Chilean transportation development: the railroad and socio-economic change in the Central Valley, 1840–1885' (unpubl. Ph.D. thesis, University of California at Los Angeles 1976).

[54] *Cámara de Diputados, Sesión Extraordinaria* 17 August 1878.

[55] *Ibid.* 27 Oct. 1871.

[56] Agustín Edwards *Cuatro presidentes de Chile* 2 vols (Valparaíso 1932) II 306.

[57] Francisco Encina *Historia de Chile* 20 vols (Santiago 1945–62) XIII 456.

[58] Ortega 'Change and crisis' chap 3 and 5.

[59] Nicolás Palacios *Decadencia del espíritu de nacionalidad* (Santiago 1908) *passim*. Palacios put forward the 'frustration theory', and was followed by, amongst others, Francisco Encina *Nuestra inferioridad económica* (Santiago 1911); Aníbal Pinto *Chile, un caso de desarrollo frustrado* (Santiago, 3rd edn 1973); Claudio Véliz 'La mesa de tres patas' *Desarrollo Económico* III 1 (1963); André G. Frank *Capitalism and underdevelopment in Latin America. Historical studies of Chile and Brazil* (New York 1967).

[60] Robert M. Will 'La política económica de Chile, 1810–1864' *El Trimestre Económico* XXVII (1960) p. 238; Lagos *op. cit.* pp. 16, 24–5.

[61] Encina *op. cit.* chap. 3.

[62] Anguita *op. cit.* I 235–9.

[63] *Ibid.* II 172–5.

[64] *MH 1865* pp. 38–9.

[65] L. Ortega 'Acerca de los orígenes de la industrialisación chilena, 1860–1879' *Nueva Historia* 2 (1981).

[66] Ortega 'Change and crisis' chaps 3 and 5.

[67] Marcello Carmagnani *Sviluppo industriale e sottosviluppo economico. El caso cileno, 1860–*

1920 (Torino 1971) chap. 3.

⁶⁸ William F. Sater 'Economic nationalism and tax reform in late nineteenth-century Chile' *The Americas* no. 33 (1976) p. 316. 'It is difficult to determine the real level of effective protection resulting from these measures. There are no systematic studies of the level of internal inflation for the period, neither is there a study of the evolution of freight rates. Palma has made some general estimates in his 'Growth and structure of Chilean manufacturing industry from 1830 to 1935: origins and development of a process of industrialization in an export economy (unpubl. Ph.D. thesis, Oxford 1979) pp. 147–50.

⁶⁹ Ortega 'Change and crisis' pp. 200–15.

⁷⁰ Anguita *op. cit.* ɪɪ 443–7.

⁷¹ *MH 1870* p. 22; emphasis added.

⁷² Mariano Egaña 'Apuntes sobre la Ordenanza de Aduanas' *Anales de la Universidad de Chile* xʟvɪɪɪ (1876) p. 231.

⁷³ Especially through the campaign maintained by the magazine *La industria chileña* between 1875 and 1876.

⁷⁴ *MH 1878* p. 11.

⁷⁵ Marcial Martínez 'La cuestión económica. Cartas relativas a la materia' *Obras Completas* 3 vols (Santiago 1919) ɪ 19.

⁷⁶ *MH 1835* p. 507.

⁷⁷ See above, note 70.

⁷⁸ Will 'The Introduction of classical economics into Chile' p. 21.

⁷⁹ *MH 1835* p. 507.

⁸⁰ In 1849 63 per cent of the wholesale merchants established in Valparaíso were foreigners. 24.5 per cent of the total were British: Bauer *op. cit.*, table 4, p. 38.

⁸¹ Ortega 'Change and crisis' chap. 4, for exports of copper.

⁸² Luis Escobar *El mercado de valores* (Santiago 1959), p. 137.

⁸³ Ricardo Donoso *Desarrollo político y social de Chile desde la constitución de 1833* (Santiago, 2nd edn 1942) *passim*; Harold Blakemore *British nitrates and Chilean politics. Balmaceda and North. 1886–1896* (London 1974), especially chap. 1.

⁸⁴ Tom Kemp *Historical patterns of industrialization* (London 1978) p. 83.

⁸⁵ Manuel A. Fernández 'El enclave salitrero y la economía chileña, 1880–1914' *Nueva Historia* 3 (1981) p. 20.

III

THE CLASSICAL AGE OF IMPERIALISM

9

INTRODUCTION

The period *c.* 1870 to the First World War brought a new phase in the evolution of the Latin American economies and polities. A dramatic transformation in the international economic order led to the crystallization of a world economy which superseded an earlier focus upon the North Atlantic. For scholars writing from a European perspective, particularly those indebted to Hobson and Lenin, this was the classical age of imperialism in which the rapid growth of international trade, expanding opportunities for investment overseas and large-scale migration were to be observed. Scholars writing from a US environment have tended to stress the restructuring of capitalism during this period – a discussion which features the appearance of corporate entities and is projected into the incipient activity of multinational corporations in export agriculture, mining, oil and banking. By contrast, Latin American scholars have stressed domestic economic activities; the concept of political economy; the role of the state and its significance in the reorganization of the Latin American economies and the promotion of growth; the social formation and autonomy of the state, and its emphasis upon centralized political and social controls. Latin American writers have been prone to study this period in order to explain contemporary dilemmas, and are inclined to regard it as precursive of a more thorough imperial penetration after 1945. Thus scholars disagree even over the dating of the classical era of imperialism.

The European connection and the US challenge

Latin America's external linkages were for most of this period concentrated upon Great Britain. London was the world's principal financial market. Britain produced much of the continent's manufactured imports, and purchased or commercialized a substantial part of the region's exports. British commercial connections with Latin America multiplied, and there was a proliferation of London-registered railway companies, banks and utilities operating in the region. These were the mechanisms that feature in the debates about the imperialism of Free Trade and business imperialism.

An understandable concern to study the British connection neglects, however, processes of immigration which some writers have represented as even more effective conduits of external influence. While there were large currents of migration from Asia to the continent and early movements of return migrants from the United States to Mexico, the most important flow of migrants originated in Western Europe, principally Italy and Iberia. Immigrants transmitted to Latin America the ideas of the Paris Commune, Italian radicalism and Spanish anarchism. They also formed captive markets for European exports and eased the penetration of Latin American countries by the continental powers, notably Germany, France and, to a lesser extent, Italy. Germany and France began to rival British pre-eminence: the emergence of the Paris and Berlin bourses challenged the hegemony of the London money market, particularly for government paper. Another challenge was contained in the expansion of manufactured exports from Germany and the United States, countries characterized by a more dynamic capitalism than Britain, which progressively undermined the British commercial position in many parts of the region. These rivalries, and Latin American responses to them, are eminently documented for Mexico in the writings of Katz.

Why was the British ascendancy of the 1860s seriously challenged in most of the continent by 1914? Some historians maintain that British resources were over-extended, that Britain retreated into safer, easier markets and outlets for investment in the British Empire and the Far East. Others contend that British capitalism was outmoded, insufficiently resilient to meet the challenges posed by her more forceful competitors. According to these scholars, the backward nature of British capitalism was reflected in the delayed emergence of large-scale units of production in Britain itself, and in the tardy evolution of 'big business' practices in the United Kingdom. These problems were compounded by the compartmentalization of administration and business in Britain, which stood in sharp contrast with the close relationship between political and business decision-making that prevailed in Germany in particular, and also perhaps in the United States.

The literature surrounding the British connection with Latin America mainly concerns economic matters; that spawned in the United States deals principally with the motives behind US expansion. Competing interpretations vie for pre-eminence. One stresses US aspirations to world power status, and perceives her participation in the Spanish-American-Cuban War (1895–8) as an assertion of rank in both the Far East and the Caribbean/Latin America. Historians examining the political and military components of US expansion differ about the weighting to attach to the higher echelons of the federal administration, the naval-industrial lobby, the popular 'yellow' press and progressive Protestant evangelism. Some authors also emphasize a mission to export political democratic stability and capitalist growth on a Washington model. Other writers see US expansion as a continuing process of 'frontier' consolidation – a southward movement following the completion of the drive to the west. A further group of scholars, who emphasize economic factors in US penetration, lay stress upon the pursuit of export markets for manufactured goods and foodstuffs. Some underline a long-term strategic aim to secure access to raw material supply so as to guarantee future US economic growth, others attach importance to the carving out of spheres of influence. A number of historians pin principal responsibility for US imperialism upon irrationality. The debate about US expansion, though provocative, is rarely illuminating about the impact of US penetration in Latin America. The writing of Benjamin well illustrates potentially fruitful lines of inquiry that the literature might take.

Frequently North American scholars involved in this discourse have demonstrated scant awareness of Latin American historiography. Perhaps this literature also attaches insufficient significance to other features of the external connection, in particular the European presence in Latin America, notably the selective assimilation of French ideas – *la mission civilisatrice* – and also the response to German influence. Of paramount importance were French and German influences upon changing views of the role and functioning of the state, and the interrelationship between government and society. These manifestations of cultural imperialism have absorbed the attention of Latin American writers. In this context it must be remembered that state structures established during the third quarter of the nineteenth century survived in the main until the inter-war years, that government action was related to the process of incorporation within the world economy, and that external linkages influenced the structure of administration in Latin America.

Endowed at an early stage with an effective administration, by 1880 the writ of central government in Chile ran throughout the territory approximately encompassed within current national frontiers, following successful Indian campaigns in the south and a war against Bolivia and Peru in the north. Recrudescent *porteño* sectionalism was finally defeated in 1880 after the last vestiges of nomadic Indian tribes had been cleared from Patagonia, thereby completing the consolidation of Argentina's frontiers. While Chilean and Argentine governments overcame the opposition of aboriginals who had resisted the onslaught of Europeanization since the Iberian conquest, elsewhere – especially in Mexico and the northern Andean countries – nation-building between the 1850s and 1890s was accomplished in classic liberal fashion, by dismantling institutions that challenged the supremacy of state authority. In the Empire of Brazil the centralized state was firmly established by mid-century, and survived intact until the end of the 1880s.

Sustained access by government to external borrowing and direct investment in social overhead projects hastened the process of national integration. New resources arising from tariff revenues gave central government an added strength *vis-à-vis* regional and municipal government, thus reinforcing the power of the centre at the expense of the regions and localities. Great Power rivalry and border disputes made it essential for Latin American countries to conduct an efficient and effective international diplomacy. Hence further emphasis upon the consolidation of the central state.

Three major features accompanying these readjustments in Latin America's external relations can be identified. First, there were significant locational shifts: a tendency towards the concentration of investment in the larger countries of the continent and in the Southern Cone. Second, there was the spread southwards of US influence by dint of proximity to Mexico, the Caribbean and circum-Caribbean – and also Chile. Third, a gradual restructuring in flows of foreign capital is evident: from portfolio to direct investment; from lending to governments to direct investment in plantation agriculture, non-ferrous metals, oil and ultimately manufacturing. These processes were reflected in modifications in the commodity composition of Latin America's external trade. Diversifying export profiles were closely linked with the changing nature of capitalism at the centre – notably a growing demand for minerals and an expanding mix of tropical and temperate agricultural commodities. The increasing volume of imports of intermediate products and capital goods – especially from Germany and the United States – indicated a trend towards economic diversification in certain republics. Thus, with the gradual percolation of US influence through the continent, an enlarged German presence (temporarily eclipsed during the First World War) and also the French challenge to the British position, there evolved a disputed and unresolved external ascendancy, as well as possibilities for Latin American elites to exploit differences among the Great Powers. Meanwhile a minor rival, Spain, was finally removed from Latin America with the loss of her last colonies, Cuba and Puerto Rico, in the war of 1895–8.

Imported ideologies and the adaptation of domestic structures

Even before new opportunities were proffered by the emergent world economy, the state in Latin America sought to promote the consolidation of national markets and to facilitate factor mobility by reducing the privileged position of the Church, by destroying the protected status enjoyed by Indian communities, and by abolishing state monopolies. Having dismantled mercantilist survivals, the state liberalized banking and mining legislation and regulations governing foreign and domestic trade, and endeavoured to stabilize national currencies so as to create an environment congenial to national and foreign entrepreneurs. Further positive action can be seen in the granting of bounties and guarantees to encourage initiative in specific sectors. A near-consensus prevailed until the 1890s, which applauded and supported external investment in key sectors of the economy. State borrowing for capital projects (as opposed to the financing of military expenditure and current consumption in previous decades), and the allocation of franchises to domestic and foreign interests, indicated both a desire to foster economic expansion and possibly a perception of backwardness. Influenced by events in the United States and Europe, elite groups were anxious that contemporary aspects of modernity should be seen to function within Latin America. Perhaps the attachment to railways and liberal constitutions was a manifestation of cultural underdevelopment.

Intervention was not passive. In Latin America, as elsewhere, it was acknowledged that public utilities – the railways, tramways, gas, electricity, water and drainage companies associated with urbanization and export expansion – necessitated government regulation. Reforms in economic policy were prefaced by attempts to raise the efficiency of the state apparatus. An influx of foreign technical personnel intended to advise on fiscal reform, engineering projects and the professionalization of the military was complemented by the growth of a small circle of national *técnicos*. Their influence derived not from a national or regional power base, but from the scarcity of expertise acquired through training abroad and of the pragmatic accumulation of empirical experience obtained in ministries and state regulatory bodies. These proto-technocrats were often considered valuable to government because they were thought to be independent of entrenched regional faction or vested sectional interest.

It was generally assumed that institutional modernization would facilitate rapid economic expansion. Rarely was this expectation realized. The divergence between assumption and experience has encouraged some scholars to stress the disjunction between the North Atlantic liberal model and Latin American practice. Writers point to Indian alienation, the adverse effects of land policy, and uneven nature of territorial consolidation that came with railway construction, and specific patterns of enclave development fostered by the rapid growth of foreign trade. The process seemed to offer greater facilities to foreign than to domestic capitalists, or rather to resident foreigners closely tied to elite groups, who enjoyed easier access to finance and technology than national entrepreneurs. Some scholars have also emphasized the role of Free Trade in demolishing artisan units of production and suffocating manufacturing potential. But this view ignores the primitive character of much manufacturing and the limited size of domestic markets. Such scholarship over-plays passivity and understates the active participation of Latin American governments in the economy. *Laissez-faire* tenets were honoured more in the breach than in the observance. The state was prepared to assume an entrepreneurial role in the face of the reluctance of local capitalists to venture funds beyond a circumscribed mix of highly remunerative activities and the selectiveness of foreign investors' preferences.

By 1914 the government owned or operated approximately two thirds of the national railway network in Brazil, Chile and Mexico: elsewhere state supervision was becoming increasingly common. The trends which Henry Finch outlines for Uruguay were visible in other countries. Uruguay was exceptional only in the scale and precociousness of state intervention, notably attempts to domesticize the financial operations of foreign-registered banks and insurance companies. As Charles Jones indicates, this was a sensitive area that required a delicacy of touch and a degree of precision often lacking in state bureaucracies. Nevertheless, government-run commercial banks were an established feature of the Southern Cone economies by this time; and in Argentina the federal government had initiated a policy which would lead ultimately to a state monopoly in the exploitation of national oil deposits. Contemporaries saw no contradiction in government intervention or regulation and an avowal of liberal intentions. The state complemented rather than compromised individual initiative. Profit guarantees, subventions, the conferment of monopolies and the waiver of tax liabilities were accepted as appropriate to the role of the state, commensurate with the maintenance of order.

Passivity hardly characterized government action in the labour market. A perception of chronic labour scarcity pervaded official thinking, engendering attempts (attuned both to domestic circumstances and to evolving international opportunities) to assist local capitalists in their quest for workers. In areas of relatively dense indigenous settlement – parts of Mexico, Central America and the Andean countries – several mechanisms were devised to push Indians into the labour market. Elsewhere governments encouraged an inflow of foreign workers. Albert points to Peruvian experiments with semi-servile forms of labour recruitment and measures to force upland Indians into the wage sector. Oriental indentured labour was imported into Peru and the Caribbean. Forced labour gangs composed of political dissidents, common criminals and marginal elements of society, supervised by the army and employed upon an array of public or private projects, were not peculiar to dictatorial regimes sheltering behind a façade of liberal parliamentary institutions, like the Mexico of Porfirio Díaz or the Venezuela of Juan Vicente Gómez. Indebtedness, the denial to workers of the right of freedom of association, and state sanction of the private use of violence by employers were widespread and regarded as legitimate means of coercing and disciplining the workforce in countries enjoying semi-representative presidential government. Brazil and Argentina, in particular, strove to overcome the problem of labour shortage by promoting European immigration through assisted sea passages, officially sponsored advertising campaigns, the issue of free railway tickets to up-country destinations, and state financial aid to colonization companies. Further devices to foster migration were applied within Latin America itself. As Ospina Vásquez and Palacios demonstrate, in Colombia both central and regional government provided inducements for labour to move from areas of economic stagnation and decline to the increasingly prosperous coffee-producing regions. Similarly, on the West Coast migrant labour was attracted across departmental boundaries and national frontiers, from over-populated regions to the nitrate fields.

Long before 1900 the rhetoric of immediate post-independence settlement schemes, cast in terms of rural colonization projects and the disposal of government land in medium-sized parcels to immigrant farmers, had given way to a quest for labour – field hands to meet the requirements of export agriculture and urban workers to service the requirements of growing cities. Labour codes were decidedly illiberal and draconian measures to discipline itinerant workers, and social groups perceived as peripheral owed more to colonial regulation than to *laissez-faire*.

Controversy surrounding the consequences and effectiveness of labour and immigration policies is reflected in this section. Albert observes variations by crop in the sequence of transitional stages from forced to wage labour and the consolidation of capitalist relationships in the labour market. Finch and Colin Lewis illustrate examples of social differentiation, and hint at more sharply defined class differences. By the end of the nineteenth century a greater heterogeneity of class structure had emerged: societies remained fragmented but could no longer be simply categorized in terms of master and slave, *hacendado* and Indian villager. In Section II McFarlane and Thomson confirm recent revisionism that questions earlier dichotomized social stereotypes attributed to the late colonial period. The chapters which compose this section confidently discuss the proletarianization of rural and urban labour, and indicate the emergence of clearly recognizable intermediate social groups and the proliferation of political interests contending for power. A more complete integration within the world economy also occasioned potential for intra-elite conflict, as several of these chapters demonstrate. Yet the external sector is already portrayed as an integral part of the support base of authoritarianism. International forces are open to the charge of compliance with, or being the beneficiaries of, authoritarian regimes.

Diversification and insertion within the world economy

Another area of controversy, and one that has received much attention in the dependency literature, concerns the degree of dynamic domestic diversification associated with the consolidation of external linkages. Albert and Lewis advance an optimistic evaluation of the potential for endogenous expansion. Taking issue with Furtado, Albert details the backward linkages associated with sugar cane in Peru. He also arrives at less negative conclusions than have been reached elsewhere regarding the impact of export production upon domestic food supply. For Lewis, as for Ortega in Section II and Gabriel Palma in Section IV, state-sponsored public works projects facilitated national integration, promoting industrial expansion in an environment of export-led growth. The favourable assessment of the efficacy of government policy implicit in much of this analysis may be disputed, particularly for areas other than the Southern Cone.

Adverse features arising from the external connection are also described in this section. Several sharp crises occurred during the period dealt with by these chapters. Integration into the world order made the Latin American economies more susceptible to externally induced cyclical fluctuations. The 1873 crisis which marked the onset of the so-called 'Great Depression' was probably the first to have a generalized impact upon the continent. The Baring Crisis of 1890 had widespread effects. These and milder dislocations which brought a contraction in export earnings, reduced access to external borrowing and precipitated exchange depreciation. They were accompanied by financial stringency, bankruptcy, unemployment, hunger and social discontent – strikes and urban demonstrations, popular agrarian protest, banditry and messianic movements.

Such crises occasioned a reconsideration of the vitality of the external connection, further elaborated during the First World War and the World Depression of 1929–33. The events of 1873 and 1890 provide a neglected opportunity to test the exogenous-shocks hypothesis popularized at the outset of the dependency debate. For some Latin American economies, de-linkage from the central economies was more complete in these years than in 1914 or 1929. Finch and Jones approach several aspects of this debate. They also discuss the dynamism of the connection with Britain. Like others, Finch emphasizes the relative decadence of British capitalism and the negative nature of resurgent British influence in Uruguay; for Jones, British business practice was inappropriate to Argentine requirements. Both stress disjuncture between economic and political decision-making, and point to the inevitability of conflict with foreign capital. All chapters identify areas of potential conflict and compact between domestic and external interests: some also indicate limits to foreign control.

The contributors to this section refer to the principal themes raised by the external connection during the late nineteenth and early twentieth centuries. One inescapable issue was the restructuring of capitalism at the centre. The stress laid by some authors on the fragility of capitalism in Latin America during this period has possibly been overstated because it neglects the weakness of alternatives to it. Mercantilist policies still exerted some influence, but retreat into isolation or self-sufficiency was no longer a viable option, as political decomposition in some Andean countries indicated. Nevertheless, the US model of capitalism was probably more alluring than the British to Latin American entrepreneurs; French and German influences – particularly concepts of the state – were more appropriate in securing an institutional climate conducive to prosperity, and were more effective in assuring the victory of capitalism in Latin America. Whether restructuring at the centre created opportunities for greater autonomy in the periphery is less obvious.

To date this debate has been largely confined to the 1930s, though much of it appears equally apposite to pre-1914 rivalry in the continent. The consolidation of the state is another theme of crucial importance. Centralization of government authority was often a prerequisite for successful insertion within the world economy; sometimes the processes of centralization and insertion were concurrent. The resultant composition of the emergent state established the parameters within which reformist policies might be applied, and determined the potential for progressive social differentiation or for the consolidation of authoritarianism. Finally, these chapters demonstrate, as do those in Section IV, the problems of establishing a generalized chronology for Latin America during the early twentieth century. Incorporation within the world system and contrasting manifestations of the external connections had produced by 1914 possibly greater disparities within and between Latin American societies than had existed previously or would be identified subsequently.

10

THE STATE AND BUSINESS PRACTICE IN ARGENTINA
1862–1914

Charles Jones

Following the unification of Argentina in 1862, substantial sums of money were raised in London for investment in the republic. The greater part of these funds went to the national government and to the leading provinces and municipalities, or else was invested in major railways enterprises such as the Central Argentine or the Buenos Ayres Great Southern. Although shares in these companies represented equity, some had in effect the character of fixed-interest securities, since a minimum dividend was guaranteed by the state. So long as the federal government continued to meet its obligations, it was therefore to perhaps no more than an eighth of Anglo-Argentine securities that substantial risk attached. These were the ordinary and, to a lesser extent, the preference shares of the banks, mortgage and investment companies, land and raw materials processing companies, urban utilities, and a small number of non-guaranteed railways.[1] Possibly the more exposed position of these smaller Argentine ventures on the London market provided an incentive to thorough management, and contributed to the high quality of their systems of communication. Certainly by the 1970s the surviving documentation of the more important of the smaller Anglo-Argentine companies was relatively superior to that of the larger railway companies and to remaining European records of the Argentine external debt. In particular the records of the several British banks eventually absorbed into the Bank of London and South America, and of the substantial number of mortgage, land, railway, and urban utility companies overseen by the River Plate Trust, Loan and Agency Company, together provide a most valuable commentary on the activities of the firms themselves and their relations with government.

Two principal themes of public concern emerge from these records. First, there is the question of the appropriateness of business practices and priorities developed in Britain to the very different circumstances prevailing in Argentina – a question which arose most clearly and controversially in relation to the lending policies of banks and mortgage companies and the investment policies of insurance companies. A second question, more general in scope, concerns the effect of a gradual concentration of managerial power within Anglo-Argentine firms, and the impact of increasing centralization of authority in London on responsiveness to Argentine needs. Both are recognizably related to preoccupations of the literature on contemporary multinational firms, a not inconsiderable part of which continues to be addressed more to the institutional and structural effects of direct foreign investment upon host economies than to net flows of surplus between economies – to microeconomic rather than macro-economic questions.

A further reason for considering the political aspects of British investment in economic enterprises is that some social scientists working on multinationals have recently exhibited confusion about the comparability of the British and United States experiences in Latin America.[2] While much British investment was indeed portfolio investment of a passive character, much was in firms which were managed from London and had a relatively concentrated ownership structure giving considerable power to very small numbers of very large shareholders.[3] This sort of firm, though commonly active in only one or at most in a handful of foreign countries, though operating through branches rather than locally registered subsidiary companies, and though active in infrastructure rather than manufacturing, had much more in common with modern direct foreign investment than has sometimes been supposed.

British banking policy in theory and practice

British financial institutions undoubtedly projected a conservative, cautious image, thereby laying themselves open to the charge of starving remote provinces, small borrowers, and agricultural and industrial entrepreneurs of credit in order to satisfy the needs of established international merchant houses. London directors and managers of the commercial banks clearly saw this as their proper function and left their branch managers in no doubt. 'Safety before profit is our home maxim,' declared the head office manager of the London and River Plate Bank in 1866, a view seconded by John Morris, for many years chairman of the leading Anglo-Argentine mortgage companies, when he affirmed that 'banks are not leaders, but followers'.[4]

In practice this policy took the form of a constant flow of injunctions from head office to the branches. For the commercial banks mortgage lending was to be avoided, as also was lending to government, to senior politicians, to direct competitors of the bank, and to mercantile firms which were known to be tying up funds in long-term or speculative ventures.[5] In the mortgage companies too, leading politicians were generally unwelcome clients. When former president of the republic Julio A. Roca applied to the River Plate Trust, Loan and Agency Company for a loan in 1894 he was turned down because, in the words of the London general manager, 'If we once granted him a small loan it would be all the more difficult for us to refuse if he came to us suddenly one day for a bigger one, and he is certainly not a man that we could press for payment in the event of his interest falling into arrear.'[6] Again the Trust Company advanced only fifty per cent of the accepted valuation of any property in the 1880s, and restricted its operations, as late as 1904, to 'what might be called the inner circle: say the greater part of the province of Buenos Aires and the lower half of Santa Fé'.[7] Finally, it was only towards the end of the century that British fire insurance companies, active in Argentina for twenty years or more, were at last drawn to invest in the country by the stick of compulsory deposit legislation and the carrot of a thriving Argentine mortgage market.

Yet the claim that British firms carried some special responsibility for the lack of diversification of the Argentine economy must be qualified on three counts. First, repeated commands from London to maintain conservative standards of business practice were as often as not prompted by the misdemeanours of managers on the periphery; reality was very different from the ideal of business orthodoxy willed on managers by head offices, and peddled to shareholders, depositors and governments alike as evidence of stability. Second, by the time the directors of financial institutions founded between the 1860s and the 1880s had got their branches firmly under control, market conditions had moved decisively against the lender in a number of ways which forced significant relaxation of the controls to which debtors could be subjected. Third and last, contemporaries opposed to British financial institutions felt that their offence lay less in channelling funds into the hands of established merchants and export-orientated landowners than in denying these funds to more developmentally-minded Argentine institutions, which would have used them in ways more consistent with the long-term interests of the country and in wilfully sabotaging such institutions and the efforts of government to support them. This criticism could only be justified to the extent that local institutions tried to perform the developmentist role assigned to them by their champions.

The first of these qualifications is easily sustained. Managers certainly did break the rules continually; they had to if they were to make any money. The extreme seasonal variation in demand for money, which marked the wool-exporting Buenos Aires economy of the 1860s and 1870s, left the banks with funds on their hands in the dull season, which they could only employ by granting unsecured overdrafts to local merchants.[8] By 1866, four years after it was established, the Buenos Aires branch of the London and River Plate Bank was operating with a capital of £250,000. Assets included £150,411 owed by thirty-three clients on unsecured overdraft, and substantial further sums secured by mortgages or by credit balances in a currency other than that of the debt. The smaller Rosario branch of the bank was badly caught out by the failure of its competitor, the Banco Comercial, in 1868. Mariano Cabal, proprietor of the Banco Comercial, owed the London and River Plate Bank just short of £60,000.[9] Not only had too much been advanced to one man, but it had been secured by mortgages, had been applied to the support of a direct competitor, and had been loaned to a man who happened also to be the current governor of the province of Santa Fé.

Again, in 1880, in order to avert the failure of S. B. Hale & Co., the London Bank was obliged to take over as a going concern the Tatay *estancia*, valued at little short of £100,000.[10] No wonder Nicholas Bouwer, Baring Brothers' agent, found the annual report of the London Banks for 1876 entertaining. The chairman, George Drabble, announced losses and a transfer of £80,000 from the reserve fund, blaming this squarely on the national government for floating the peso and on the government of Santa Fé for bringing about a temporary closure of the Rosario branch. Bouwer, who knew better, observed that 'it is a well known fact that the Bank has made money out of both these events . . . There is no doubt that the profits of the bank and . . . the reserve fund have gone to wipe off bad debts of many years' standing which up to now the directors had never dared touch.'[11] So, while its London directors constantly envisaged the London and River Plate Bank as a single-minded auxiliary of international commerce, the need for profit led it into financing a wider range of activities across a broader geographical field than had been intended, and this was even more true of the lesser British banks, late-coming competitors of the London Bank, which lacked the firm local deposit base of the London Bank.[12]

It is true that City control of the branches was gradually increased, with the removal of a number of early managers and their substitution by company men equipped with the mental set of head office. The creation of inspectorates within the banks also helped. Yet these moves, completed before 1890, were overtaken by decisive changes in economic conditions leading to a more competitive credit market. From the late 1870s regular steamship services, improved banking facilities, and telegraphic communications led a number of the larger European manufacturers to internalize overseas marketing and the purchase of raw materials by sending out travelling salesmen or buyers to markets such as Argentina, so cutting out the old-established international merchant houses which had formerly earned commission on these operations.[13] Furthermore, many of these salesmen and buyers, scenting opportunity in the growing Argentine economy, soon went freelance. The banks suddenly found that they were having to deal with all sorts of small clients of whose creditworthiness they could discover little.[14] To make matters worse, some of the international houses, most notably Ernesto Tornquist & Co. and S. B. Hale & Co., had responded to this pressure on their traditional mercantile business by themselves diversifying into banking.[15]

Growing competition in the exchange market provided the point of leverage. If a banker wanted the exchange of the new firms, they could press him to grant easier borrowing terms or else go past him and deal with firms like Tornquist's or Hale's. Brokers fostered this process by carrying information to clients and by aggregating their (the clients') bargaining power, and the banks were increasingly obliged to make concessions. All this came to a temporary halt at the end of the 1880s when the Argentine economy was thrown into crisis by the cessation of foreign lending, but as the economy recovered after 1895 it became clear that there was such a plenteous supply of money – local and European – that the old criteria would have to be relaxed still further if the existing banks were not to be entirely outflanked by new institutions. In the winter of 1904 the Buenos Aires discount rate sank below 4 per cent. At the close of 1903, Argentine banks were lending freely at 6 per cent for six months on single signature, and total renewals were commonplace.[16] In England, too, a glut of money expressed in the rising ratio of bank deposits to advances and discounts and in low interest rates was leading to liberalization; practices once condemned as unsound were now openly resorted to.[17] To the overseas banks this meant that they no longer had to fear that the extensive use of overdrafts, financing, and the rediscounting of bills on the London market would act as alarm signals, adversely affecting their credit in the metropolis.[18]

Competition and the removal of old restraints led the banks into new fields. Three British banks together provided more than £100,000 in advances against the 1897 Argentine sugar crop.[19] But the most tempting plum of all was the lucrative medium-term mortgage market, which had formerly been left pretty much to a handful of specialist British firms of which the River Plate Trust, Loan and Agency Company and the Mortgage Company of the River Plate were by far the most important. From 1896 new lenders emerged: the Anglo-Argentine Bank with Belgian funds, Tornquist's with German savings, the British Bank of South America for the account of the Scottish Widows' Fund, Moore & Tudor for Standard Life, and Krabbe King & Co. for the Law Union and Rock Insurance Company.[20] By 1901 Francis Chevallier Boutell of the River Plate Trust, Loan and Agency could write with little exaggeration that 'there is not an English firm of any importance that is not engaged directly or indirectly on mortgage business'.[21] Not surprisingly rates for new hard-currency mortgage loans fell from 10 per cent in 1895 to 7 per cent by 1905, never again rising beyond 8.5 per cent before 1914 except, very briefly, late in 1912.[22]

British banks, state banks and public service banking

It appears that British financial institutions were never as conservative as their London directors would have wished. Nevertheless, there is evidence to suggest that some – most notably the London and River Plate Bank and the River Plate Trust, Loan and Agency Company – were considerably more cautious than a majority of their Argentine contemporaries. The Trust Company, raising funds in Britain, largely escaped criticism, but the London Bank and other more or less orthodox private banks were constantly attacked by local politicians on the ground that their success in attracting deposits made it difficult for the official banks to carry out public service banking functions.

The largest and most prestigious by far of the official banks was the Banco de la Provincia de Buenos Aires. Established in 1854, the Banco de la Provincia grew rapidly. In the late 1870s its assets averaged about seven times those of the next largest bank in Buenos Aires, the London and River Plate Bank. In an advertisement of 1869 the Banco de la Provincia offered 'loans to the working classes', explaining that 'the Bank lends to artisans and operatives sums from three to twenty thousand dollars on their own signature taking as security a document with any well-known signature'.[23] Numerous later commentators would look back on the Bank, which failed in 1891, as a major factor in Argentine development.[24] But contemporaries recognized that there were strict limits to the developmental role of the Bank. In spite of the wishes of provincial minister of finance Rufino Varela, the Bank refused to assist the first Argentine woollen mill in the mid-1870s.[25] In the depths of the 1870s recession, when the Bank had to choose between its two main classes of clients, there was no hesitation. In spite of renewed opposition from Varela, the Bank instituted a review of all private accounts, raising a storm among landowners who had come to look on the bank 'as an institution specially created to supply them with funds without their being compelled to refund in due course'.[26] In the last resort the Provincial Bank would always sacrifice private clients in order to sustain its major client, the provincial government; its idea of development banking was simply to lend to producers rather than to merchants, but without any serious attempt to encourage new or more wide-ranging kinds of economic activity. Finally the Bank became more and more a creature of the incumbent faction. Thus, in 1887, the incoming administration discovered that a staff of twenty-eight clerks had been maintained by the Bank solely for electioneering purposes, and that something in the region of $8 million *moneda nacional* (about £1,185,000) had been siphoned off to cover the election expenses of the outgoing administration.[27]

The London Bank undoubtedly competed with considerable success against the Banco de la Provincia and its lesser imitators, the Banco Nacional and the Banco Provincial de Santa Fé. Equally certainly, this competition was interpreted as deliberate hostility by governments, leading to a long campaign against the Rosario branch of the London

Bank by the government of Santa Fé, in which both sides resorted to unconstitutional measures.[28]

It has been argued above that if British banks were responsible in some degree for the failure of Argentina to develop a more diversified economy less heavily reliant on exports of unprocessed primary commodities, the responsibility did not arise from their own lending policies nor from the impediment they presented to official banks with a clear commitment to some coherent long-term plan for the structural development of the economy. Was it, perhaps, through the influence they exerted on banking and monetary policies that British banks helped shape the future of the Argentine economy? A case can be made, based on two aspects of the period 1887 to 1914.

First, it is probable that the banking system embodied in the Guaranteed Banks Law of 1887 would have come into being much more quickly and have stood a much better chance of weathering the crisis at the end of the decade, had it received the wholehearted support of the private banks. The law was designed to create not a multiplicity of banks of issue, but a standard federal emission. Banks coming into the system were to buy national government bonds. The bonds were to be deposited with the Banco Nacional in exchange for banknotes, and the gold which had been paid to the government in exchange for the bonds was also to be placed on deposit with the Banco Nacional for two years before being applied to the amortization of the national external debt. In this way it was hoped that the supply of money and credit in Argentina and, in so far as these factors influenced it, the national economy as a whole, could be insulated from the sharp fluctuations in the London capital and money markets which Argentine governments were quite powerless to control and which had so considerably exacerbated the economic difficulties of the republic in the 1870s.[29] In addition, it was widely supposed that the law would stimulate a growth in the banking system and in money supply which would itself stimulate real economic growth. This side of the policy, if irresponsibly conducted, could all too easily result in inflation and unsound banking, so precautions were included in the draft law, some of which unfortunately failed to survive the debate in Congress. Banks within the system were to be subjected to inspection and would be guaranteed, in that the government undertook to make good to creditors any deficit remaining after the sale of the bonds covering its emission in the event of the failure of a member bank.[30]

Instead of support, the scheme encountered sustained resistance from the private banks. Typical was the reaction of Thomas Jones, Buenos Aires manager of the English Bank of the River Plate. Jones agreed that internalization of the external debt was a laudable objective; he felt that so long as the scheme was executed with efficiency and honesty, there was every possibility of its success, but he trusted neither the Banco

Nacional nor the government. He suspected that gold might be diverted for purposes other than extinguishing the external debt, and that information obtained by the guaranteed banks inspectorate would be misused for speculative purposes by officials and ministers.[31] Others felt the same, quite understandably in view of prevailing standards of public conduct. Thus began a battle of four years' duration between idealist ministers of finance – Wenceslao Pacheco, Rufino Varela and Vicente F. López – and realist bankers: a battle which ended in ignominious defeat for the government in 1891, with the failure of the official banks and the almost simultaneous merger of the London Bank and the Banco Carabassa, to form a private colossus amidst the ruins of the 1887 law.[32]

To regard the forebodings of Jones and other bankers in 1887 as self-fulfilling prophecies would be to exaggerate their contribution to the fiasco of 1891. More important in the long term was the illusion, to which the polarization of conflict between the public and private banks at this time doubtless contributed, that the private banks survived the crisis because they were conservatively managed, while the public banks failed in part because of their supposedly developmental orientation. In fact the central reason that the public banks failed was that they were bankers to government, and it was the effect on public finance of the drying-up of new European funds for investment in government bonds that provided the immediate cause of the crisis. Those close to government went down with government. Their failure had little to do with the private sector lending policies of the official banks. Indeed, it took place at a time when exports, on which the private debtors of the official banks chiefly depended for their income, were quite buoyant, and receipts from exports measured in paper pesos (in which many loans were denominated) were soaring.[33] But the myth of differences in private lending policies being the key to survival or failure became accepted, and was a powerful influence in shaping the new Banco de la Nación to be more or less independent of the government, 'treating financial questions, as far as they can, in a more commercial and prudent spirit than was the case formerly'.[34]

The chief unforeseen consequence of this aping of the supposed practice of the British banks was that nothing was done before 1914 to tackle the problem of general illiquidity in the Argentine banking system. The absence of any rediscounting facility was a serious technical weakness which meant that Argentine bankers, unlike their European counterparts, could not count their entire holdings of bills as a reserve against sight liabilities, but only those falling due over the next day or two. So the Banco de la Nación was obliged to hold an average of 40 per cent liquid assets against sight deposits in 1912, while comparable ratios in England and Germany were 15.5 and 6.5 per cent respectively.[35] The conservatism of the Banco de la Nación, coupled with scars inflicted on the official

mind by the disaster that had befallen the expansionary monetary policy
pursued under the Guaranteed Banking Law at the end of the 1880s,
ensured that proposals to reduce the external debt and introduce greater
flexibility into the banking system by applying the now very substantial
Argentine gold reserves to the rediscounting of commercial bills met
with a consistently frosty response; an opportunity to redirect some of
the substantial export surpluses of the period after 1890 towards a
broadening of the economy was lost.

So it was more through the influence of their misleading public image
of conservatism on Argentine government policy after 1890, than by any
direct action in the economy, that British banks contributed to the
over-specialization of the Argentine economy. The entire public debate
over the merits of public service or development banking, the impedi-
ments placed in the way of the official banks by the British, and the
narrowness of the lending policies of private and foreign institutions,
were in large measure spurious. None of the participants conformed in
reality to the role in which he was cast. A more careful political analysis
of lending policies, if the evidence were available, would probably
support more sordidly factional differences between institutions.
Economic debate provided a convenient cipher to conceal and dignify
more squalid conflicts.

Corporate control and local decision-making
If the charge of importing inappropriate techniques and business practices falls, one other principal cause of conflict between British firms and
Argentine authorities remains. This is that British firms in the republic
increasingly took on an absentee, rentier quality. The implications are
that the British gradually became more distant, less easy to negotiate
with and more inclined to turn to their own government for support, and
that they ceased to act in a vigorous, entrepreneurial way and so
acquired more and more the character of a profitable but static island in
a dynamic economy, ultimately anachronistic and expendable.

At the root of this line of thought are numerous instances of the
dismissal of Argentine or Anglo-Argentine staff by British firms, the
removal to Europe in the later years of the century of capitalists who,
though foreign-born, had appeared permanently committed to Argentina, and the sale to British and European capitalists of ventures
initiated by local entrepreneurs.

Attention has already been drawn to the sharp policy divisions within
the London and River Plate Bank in its early years. The initial policy was
to appoint merchants with local experience to manage branch banks,
sometimes on a profit-sharing basis, under the supervision of senior
members of the local business community who, if not themselves politicians, had the ear of government. Management teams of this sort

proved to be hopelessly risk-loving and entrepreneurial, however, and had either to be sternly disciplined or else replaced by men who had had no previous exposure to the temptations of a fast-growing export economy. That similar schisms occurred within other Anglo-Argentine companies suggests that this sort of conflict may have had more to do with the joint stock company as an institution or with problems of management at a distance than with banking as such. Within a few years of its registration in 1881, Murray Wilson,' one of the managers of the River Plate Trust, Loan and Agency Company, observed that most mortgage business came to the firm through brokers who were also mercantile agents, representing the only link between many *estancieros* and the credit market. Why not internalize this evident market imperfection by going into the mercantile agency business in order to gain direct access to potential clients? Reginald Nield, an Anglo-Argentine merchant taken on to advise management of the Trust Company in the early days, tempted the board with ambitious colonization schemes.[36] Nield and the Buenos Aires managers – Wilson, Cox and Chevalier Boutell – pressed to be allowed to lend against harvested grain, to carry on a foreign exchange business, to accept deposits and to act as estate agents.[37] But the drift into vertical and horizontal integration was firmly resisted by London. The mercantile agency scheme, which would have required the acquisition of the goodwill of an established firm to have stood any real chance of success, was begun from scratch in a halting, capital-starved way and soon abandoned.[38] The other proposals came to nothing.

More acrimonious and of greater political consequence were those instances where intra-firm struggles masked an effective transfer of control from Argentina to London. This happened in a number of enterprises of which the Argentine founders thought they could enlist British capital without conceding any significant measure of managerial power to the City of London. The Wanklyn brothers, Frederic and John, sold their established Buenos Aires private banking firm to a new British-registered company, the Commercial (later the Mercantile) Bank of the River Plate in 1873.[39] Frederic Wanklyn in Buenos Aires retained control over a weak London board as managing director, and bent the bank very much towards the schemes of his long-time friends and associates Ambrosio Lezica, Samuel Lafone, Enrique Fynn and S. B. Hale. Whether by accident or design, the position of the Wanklyns appeared to be further strengthened by the dispersal of the larger shareholders of the bank across a number of centres: London, Paris, Liverpool, Manchester, Vienna and Buenos Aires. Yet when the new venture ran into trouble after 1874 and Frederic Wanklyn died, it was City capital under the leadership of Charles Morrison that moved in to liquidate the business, establishing from its remains two of the most profitable of all

Anglo-River Plate ventures, the River Plate Trust, Loan and Agency Company and the Montevideo Waterworks Company.[40] In much the same way the Anglo-Argentine Cassels brothers hoped to control and even outwit the London board of the River Plate Electricity Company, founded in 1889 to take over their existing partnership, the Empresa de Luz Eléctrica de la Plata. As managing director in Argentina, Walter Cassels appears to have conspired to drive the company into liquidation, hoping to buy back the enterprise he had sold, together with the substantial additions to fixed assets made with the proceeds of the London flotation, at very little more than had been paid for it in 1889.[41] Substantial disagreements led to Cassels' dismissal in 1898.[42]

The very different milieux in which they found themselves – the directors in close proximity to shareholders, ever conscious of the fluctuations of the stock market value of their enterprise, the managers in Argentina face to face with new opportunities – served to make even more abrasive than usual the naturally conflictual relationship between ultimate financial controllers and day-to-day executives within these firms. In short, the mind of the City of London, risk-averse, logical, relatively unsentimental, influenced business policy in Buenos Aires through the hierarchical structure of the joint stock company, effecting a gradual accumulation in London of power over the Argentine economy which was carried still further by straightforward arms-length sales of Argentine enterprises such as the Carabassa Bank, Bieckert's Brewery, and of the state-owned Buenos Aires and Entre Ríos railways to British and continental capitalists.

It is very hard indeed to evaluate this shift of control to London. The early Anglo-Argentine enterprises of the 1860s and 1870s were undoubtedly assisted in their dealings with government, as much as they were put at risk in their commercial dealings, by the fact that they were 'essentially an expression of the faith of British merchants and capitalists with prior personal experience . . . in the country's natural potential . . . [who] were generally men who had been prominent . . . for many years, [and whose] new entrepreneurial activities grew out of their earlier commercial connection with the region'.[43] The words are those of Peter Winn, writing of Uruguay, but they describe exactly the degree of moral association of British capital with the liberal regimes which ruled in Buenos Aires after the fall of Rosas, and in Argentina from 1862. By 1890 this generation of Anglo-Argentines had either been ousted from management by City men and had declared unequivocally for the republic, or else had been coopted, like Reginald Nield or George Drabble, on to the London boards, leaving Argentina for good. It is true that some of the men put in by London boards to curb the waywardness of local management themselves became absorbed into Argentine society. It is true that easier transport and the sheer scale of the assets owned by some

British companies in Argentina drew directors out to the River Plate on tours of inspection with growing frequency after 1890. Yet it is hard to resist the conclusion that the lines of cleavage between settled Anglo-Argentines, expatriate British, and City men were clearer by the turn of the century than they had been thirty years before, and that the easy cosmopolitanism of the 1860s had perished.

It is tempting to conclude that this polarization made high-level political negotiations between Anglo-Argentine firms and Argentine governments more difficult because of the constant need to refer matters to London for decision, and this was certainly the case on occasion. It may even be that the Argentine ruling class was in some way rendered less flexible and less able to meet the challenges of the new century by the feebleness of domestic finance capital and the lack of adequate and legitimate representation in its counsels of British finance capital. These are hypotheses that may only be tested against twentieth-century events. Any weight attaching to such considerations of class-formation must, however, be balanced against the undoubted strength of quite discrete tendencies in the world economy working against the continued co-operation of metropolitan and peripheral elites, even in the absence of distinctly social cleavages. When Farquhar Macdonald, manager of the Rosario Drainage Company, observed in his report for 1890 that 'a feeling inimical to residence in Europe of the head office of these companies is gaining ground', he was not recording reasonable elite objections to the difficulty of doing business with absentee principals, but rather the unreasoned expression of the objections of the mass of rate-payers and consumers of services provided by British-owned urban utilities to the fact that the prices of these services were tied to gold, while their own incomes were in rapidly depreciating paper currency.

Probably no one would have cared very much about the British had they not moved from the provision of intermediate financial and commercial services into a direct market relationship with the growing number of politically articulate Argentines. This is why 1890 was crucial. It was the fact that world economic pressures on the Argentine economy were increasingly transmitted to the individual middle-class Argentine by the rates and prices set by explicitly British retail banks, urban utilities and railways, that created animosity against the British, and it is doubtful in the extreme whether private relations between Briton and Argentine at the elite level, even had they remained at the high level of the 1860s and 1870s, could have smoothed over these new popular perceptions of the function of British firms, or could have prevented its exploitation by populist politicians on the make. It certainly does not appear from the company records that the shift of power to London was unambiguously good or bad for the host economy. If it scotched some potentially valuable sallies into new fields of business, it also meant in the long run that these opportunities were available to local entrepreneurs instead, as the British gradually allowed their dominant position to shrink and finally vanish in one field after another.

Proto-corporate capitalism

The relatively small segment of total British capital in Argentina considered in this chapter was of particular political interest in the half-century before 1914, for a number of reasons. The kinds of infrastructure projects in which it was invested were close to the liberal hearts of the generation of politicians who dominated Argentina following the ousting of Rosas and the unification of the republic. Many of the English promoters and entrepreneurs were of some political consequence in Argentina. The new services created by them competed with local firms, both private and state-controlled, and were marketed to an ever wider and increasingly politicized public as time went by. Political relations between the Anglo-Argentine business community, various factions in the Argentine governing class, the growing body of urban middle-class consumers, the City of London, and more impersonal market forces, were complex and manifold and give the lie to the supposition that there was, as Peter Evans has recently hypothesized, an age of classic dependence before 1914 in which direct foreign investment was negligible and 'foreign ownership did not necessarily imply the ability to control what went on in the Brazilian company'.[44] Important, if quantitatively small, amounts of British capital in the southern-zone countries of Latin America, frequently and misleadingly classified as portfolio investment, went into economic enterprises directly controlled from London, which raised very much the same problems of conflicting economic objectives, ideology, and practice that stand at the heart of the current debate on direct foreign investment.

Notes

[1] On the difficulties of classifying foreign investment (portfolio, expatriate, direct) see Irving Stone 'British direct and portfolio investment in Latin America before 1914' *Journal of Economic History* XXXVII 3 (1977) and John M. Stopford 'The origins of British-based multinational manufacturing enterprise' *Business History Review* XLVIII 3 (1974).

[2] Peter Evans *Dependent development. The alliance of multinational, state and local capital in Brazil* (Princeton 1979) p. 77 *et. seq.*

[3] Charles A. Jones 'Great capitalists and the direction of British overseas investment in the late nineteenth century: the case of Argentina' *Business History* XXII 2 (1980).

[4] Archives of the Bank of London and South America, University College, London (hereafter BOLSA). Records of the London and River Plate Bank (D), series 1, no. 139, July 1866. See also BOLSA D94, Hackblock to Weldon, 6 Sept. 1867: 'You will bear in mind that *safety* is the *first* consideration' (original emphasis). The Morris quotation is from the Archives of Mandatos y Agencias del Rio de la Plata (Mandatos), housed at the offices of the firm in Avenida de Mayo, Buenos Aires, until their recent destruction. Records of the River Plate Trust, Loan and Agency Company Ltd (hereafter RPTLA), Morris to Boutell, 17 July 1889.

5 On mortgage lending see BOLSA D91, Bruce to Green, 23 Dec. 1862 and 7 March 1864; D1, 22 April 1865; D95, Hackblock to Weldon, 6 Sept. 1867. On lending to government and politicians see BOLSA D91, 23 April 1863 and 25 May 1864; D1, 8 Jan. and 8 Oct. 1866. On lending to competitors see D94, Hackblock to Weldon, 8 Jan. and 22 Feb. 1868. On accommodation paper and kindred subjects see BOLSA D91, Bruce to Green, 8 April 1863.

6 Mandatos, RPTLA, 'Letters to Mr. Toso', Anderson to Toso, 12 July 1894. Of the not dissimilar case of Manuel Quintana, Anderson remarked curtly, 'We object to loans to big men and politicians', *ibid.* 10 Sept. 1894.

7 Mandatos, RPTLA, Anderson to Boutell, 1 June 1898; Anderson to Branwell, 21 Dec. 1904.

8 BOLSA D95, 8 June 1866.

9 BOLSA D94, head office to Weldon, 23 Nov. 1868.

10 BOLSA D1, 3 April 1880; D35 24 April 1880.

11 Archives of Baring Brothers Ltd (hereafter BA), HC4.1.65, 31 Jan. 1877.

12 BOLSA Records of the London and Brazilian Bank (G), series 11, 17 Oct. 1894, 13 Feb., 13 March and 30 Sept. 1896, 8 April 1897, 7 April 1899 and 8 June 1900; Mandatos, RPTLA, 19 Aug. 1897.

13 On the effects of the telegraph see PP 1878 LXXIII, Report by Consul Murray for the year 1876, and William Hadfield *Brazil and the River Plate 1870–76* (London 1877) p. 277.

14 BOLSA D35, 14 Nov. 1879, D1, 18 Dec. 1879, 9 March 1882.

15 On Hales see BA HC4.1.65, 3, 7, 11, 14 July 1882, 20 March 1883, Nov. 1884; on Tornquist's, Mandatos, Records of the English Bank of the River Plate (hereafter EBRP), 10 Oct. 1885; BOLSA D35, 4 Jan. 1894 and 12 May 1899.

16 Mandatos, RPTLA, Boutell to Anderson, 19 Nov. 1903.

17 Shizuyu Nishimura *The decline of the Inland Bill of Exchange, 1855–1913* (Cambridge 1971) pp. 55–64.

18 BOLSA G11, 15 Aug. 1896.

19 Mandatos, RPTLA, Boutell to Anderson, 0 Aug. 1897.

20 Mandatos, RPTLA, Boutell to Anderson, 21 Aug. 1895, 25 Sept. 1896, 10 Nov. 1898, 7 July 1899, 18 and 24 Oct. 1901, 9 Jan. 1902; BOLSA D35, 21 Jan. 1899.

21 Mandatos, RPTLA, Boutell to Anderson, 18 Oct. 1901.

22 Mandatos, RPTLA, Managers' Monthly Reports.

23 M. G. and E. T. Mulhall (eds) *Handbook of the River Plate* (Buenos Aires 1869).

24 Norberto Piñero *La moneda, el crédito y los bancos en la Argentina* (Buenos Aires 1921) p. 209; *South American Journal* 7 April 1894, p. 375, letter reprinted from *Pall Mall Gazette* and dated Buenos Aires, 10 March 1894; US Consular Despatches, W. J. Buchanan to State Department, 162, Enclosure 1, 21 Oct. 1895; José Terry *La crisis, 1885–1892* (Buenos Aires 1893) p. 269, quoted by Orlando Williams Alzaga 'La ganadería argentina, 1862–1930' *Historia Argentina Contemporanea* III p. 413.

25 José C. Chiaramonte *Nacionalismo y liberalismo económicos en Argentina, 1860–1880* (Buenos Aires 1971) p. 240; BA, HC4.1.65, Bouwer to head office, 31 Aug. and 8 Sept. 1877.

26 BA, HC4.1.65, Bouwer to head office, 1 May 1877.

27 BOLSA D35, 3 Sept. 1887.

28 Accounts of the Rosario affair of 1876 are to be found in A. J. S. Baster *The international banks* (London 1935) pp. 131–7; H. S. Ferns *Britain and Argentina in the nineteenth century* (Oxford 1960) pp. 381–6; David Joslin *A century of banking in Latin America* (Oxford 1963); Ezequiel Gallo 'El gobierno de Santa Fé vs. el Banco de Londres y Río de la Plata, 1876' documento de trabajo, agosto de 1972, Instituto Di Tella, Centro de Investigaciones Sociales, Buenos Aires, mimeo. The undoubtedly unconstitutional behaviour of the provincial government may have been sparked off partly by the passive involvement of the Rosario manager of the London and River Plate Bank in the coup which the Cullen brothers of Santa Fé were preparing. See BOLSA D35, Maschwitz to Smithers, 10 March 1876; D35a, Behn to Smithers, 14 March 1876, and Treacher to Smithers, 12 Feb. and 29 March 1877.

[29] BOLSA D1 29 June 1876, pp. 2–3.

[30] Angel M. Quintero Ramas *A history of money and banking in Argentina* (Río Piedras, Puerto Rico 1965) pp. 85–91.

[31] Mandatos, EBRP, Jones to head office, 16 Sept. 1887.

[32] Argentine Senate *Diario de sesiones*, 4 Nov. 1891, p. 863; exchange between V. F. López and D. Rocha. For a detailed account of the events of 1887 to 1891 see C. A. Jones 'British financial institutions in Argentina, 1860–1914' (unpubl. doctoral dissertation, Cambridge 1973) pp. 241–66.

[33] J. H. Williams *Argentine international trade under inconvertible money 1880–1900* (Cambridge 1920); M. G. and E. T. Mulhall *Handbook of the River Plate* (Buenos Aires 1892) p. 43, provide contrasting figures. The Mulhalls' are probably more reliable than the official figures. The average gold premium in 1891 was 274.

[34] BOLSA D35, 15 June 1897.

[35] R. A. Ramm Doman *Política monetaria y bancaria en la Argentina* (Buenos Aires 1914) p. 9.

[36] Mandatos, RPTLA, Nield to Preston, 29 July and 23 Sept. 1882, 17 Jan. 1883.

[37] Mandatos, RPTLA, Wilson to head office, confidential, 6 March 1886, 16 Jan. 1886; Chevallier Boutell to Anderson, 27 July 1888.

[38] Mandatos, RPTLA, Wilson to head office, confidential, 21 and 28 Oct., 12 Nov. and 7 Dec. 1885, 17 March and 31 Dec. 1886.

[39] Public Record Office (London) Board of Trade Papers 31–1736/6406.

[40] Charles A. Jones 'Great capitalists and the direction of British overseas investment'.

[41] Mandatos, Records of the River Plate Electricity Company (hereafter RPEC) J. J. Wilson to head office, 1 March 1891.

[42] Mandatos, RPEC, Von Chauvin to Boutell, 18 March 1898.

[43] P. E. Winn 'Uruguay and British economic expansion, 1880–1893' (unpubl. doctoral dissertation, Cambridge 1971) p. 16.

[44] Peter Evans *Dependent development* p. 77 *et. seq.*

11

RAILWAYS AND INDUSTRIALIZATION:
ARGENTINA AND BRAZIL, 1870–1929

Colin M. Lewis

Before the emergence of the 'new' economic history, more particularly the application of counterfactual analysis and the concept of social savings to the study of railway history, it was a commonplace that the financing, construction and operation of railways occasioned a profound impetus to economic expansion. Writing in the 1940s, Jenks portrayed railways as the essence of modernization.[1] Railways epitomized innovation: they were the manifestation of revolutionary technology, encouraging initiative, fostering an environment conducive to the application of novel concepts and stimulating widespread experimentation. Many scholars, of various ideological persuasions, subscribed to this view. The appearance of railways, it was argued, resulted in the restructuring of capitalism, effected and/or resolved progress-inducing bottlenecks, and directly promoted the expansion of basic industries. If the greater part of this debate evolved within the context of the study of the history of the North Atlantic economies, the primacy of railways in the mix of factors tending to promote development was held to apply universally.[2] Such assertions constituted a major problem for students of Latin American economic history, in part because much of the literature emanating from the USA was located within the areas-of-recent-settlement school of historical analysis. As railways had proved a stimulant to growth in the northern portion of the hemisphere, why had they not done so in those parts of Latin America which most approximated to the USA in terms of resource base, notably in the frontier zones of the Southern Cone endowed with reserves of hitherto unexploited fertile land?

Traditional interpretations, which posed a conundrum for diffusionists (usually resolved by reference to the late start of rail projects or the inadequate volume of construction), constituted little difficulty for authors writing from dependency perspectives. Referring to an earlier nationalist historiography, and implicitly acknowledging orthodox interpretations of railways as agents of a profound secular change in the pace and direction of economic activity in advanced economies, *dependentistas* argued that railways had failed to perform this role in the countries of Latin America because of the external animus underlying construction (occasioning a reliance upon foreign funding and equipment

supply), and the structuring of networks in conformity with the requirements of international trade.

The elaboration of a new methodology added further confusion to the
dispute. Recourse to social savings analysis and counterfactual hypo-
thesizing indicated that railways were significant, rather than dominant,
as proponents of economic change. A consensus emerges from several
studies which indicates that the savings produced by rail transport
(when compared with the next most efficient means of communication)
were relatively small – a generalization which applied both to advanced
and to less developed economies.[3] The impact of railways (as revealed in
terms of social savings) appeared to be greater in those countries where
topography – rather than the degree of backwardness *per se* – precluded
the application of pre-rail forms of internal transport innovation and
consequent dependence upon roads or tracks.[4] Nevertheless, even substantial social savings are not held to impart a dynamic developmental
impulse – quite the contrary. Moreover, rigorous testing of qualitative
assumptions regarding the strength of backward linkages to basic industries demonstrated those assumptions to be often ill founded. And the
weakness of linkage effects was exacerbated in many less advanced
regions by the availability of imports, especially during the formative
stage of the rail age. The significance of this apparent convergence
between dependency scholarship and cliometrics regarding the impact
of railways in Latin America is enhanced by sharp differences in almost
all other respects between these two frameworks – one imbued with the
language of Marxist-Leninism, the other taking little cognizance of
Marxian economics.

Despite this concurrence, much of the literature fails to address a
number of themes pertaining to wider connections between railways and
industrial expansion, particularly in relation to the regions which form
the focus of this chapter, the economic zone centred upon São Paulo and
the Argentine pampas. *Dependentistas* are too much concerned with railways as an exogenous device linking Latin American markets to the
centre: they often fail to contemplate domestic integrating functions.

More critically, works written from a dependency standpoint rarely
differentiate between railways as providers of transport services and
effects associated with the physical construction of railways. In the
debate relating to industrialization both cliometricians and *dependentistas*
have, with few exceptions, neglected the extent to which railways were
themselves expressions of industrialism. From an early phase British
railway companies tended to internalize operations, inevitably curtail-
ing some spin-offs. Similar characteristics can be observed amongst
British-owned companies functioning in Latin America. These themes
form the core of this chapter. A consideration of the consequences of
market integration is prefaced by a discussion of the motives promoting

construction. Related topics such as the formation of a labour market and railways as expressions of corporate capitalism are also addressed. The extent to which railways facilitated the diffusion of new and institutional capital-mobilizing mechanisms is elemental, but one which requires further elaboration, although the evidence for Brazil is already persuasive.

The formation of a 'national' network

Most mid-nineteenth-century Latin American governments were anxious to upgrade the quality of social overhead capital, even if few states went so far as Argentina, whose 1853 constitution incorporated an obligation to construct railways. The impetus to foster railway building emanated from several sources. Consolidation of national territory was paramount, particularly in regions where international boundaries were ill-defined or where vast tracts were ravaged by marauding Indians. Security, however, was not merely conceived in terms of the threat of external aggression: domestic instability, and regional rivalries and antagonisms were equally potent forces confronting central governments. Order-inducing trunk line construction was viewed as essential to the application of national authority in factious provinces. Invariably, such strategic considerations were cast in elegantly phrased liberal senitments popular at that period, or conveyed in sophisticated expressions of the fomentative power of railway building. It is not difficult to discover emphases upon strategic considerations in the writings of Argentine statesmen or Brazilian parliamentarians. Trenchant observations regarding the interrelationship of infrastructural development and the consolidation of the state abound in the works of Sarmiento and Alberdi.[5] Public figures, many of whom had first-hand knowledge of the situation, were aware of events in North America and Europe, where railways were increasingly regarded as essential adjuncts of modernity and a sector of the economy in which government should play an active role.[6]

Following the War of the Triple Alliance, the Imperial Government embarked upon a large-scale programme of construction in southern Brazil designed to remedy the inadequate state of communications in the region revealed by the war. Railway building along the southern and western frontiers in Rio Grande do Sul, Santa Catarina and Pananá was also intended to reinforce Brazil's geopolitical hegemony in this sensitive border zone, and facilitate the provisioning of the area's large garrison.[7] The Argentine federal government needed no lessons in the military significance of railways: the prompt despatch of troops by rail had pre-empted a serious challenge to the authority of the newly installed administration, following the 1874 presidential elections.[8] Subsequently, railways contributed to the pacification of the southern pampas during the Indian campaigns of 1879/80.[9] And, towards the end of the century, when relations with Chile reached a low point, the government in Buenos Aires granted a particularly favourable franchise to a British-owned company to build towards the frontier in northern Patagonia.[10]

Nevertheless, if railway construction was sometimes conceived in essentially political terms, as a means of securing sensitive frontier zones or imposing central authority upon recalcitrant provinces, much building was undoubtedly regarded as economically regenerative, demonstrating not merely coercive intentions on the part of national government, but a commitment to regional welfare. During the 1860s central government support for up-country schemes was presented as *bonaresense* assistance to less fortunate areas of a recently reunited Argentina – a gesture designed to placate provincial demands for a share in 'national' resources.[11] The Central Argentine Railway Company Limited would not only hold together the scattered provinces of the Confederation, discouraging disorder, but would promote economic development in the north-west, stimulate local production and foster commercial relations with neighbouring republics. The arrival of the railway would resuscitate a previously prosperous area which had languished since independence because of inadequate means of communication.[12] Administrations at Rio de Janeiro consciously ensured a regional spread of franchises when approving early projects, providing imperial guarantees on profits for lines authorized in the sugar and coffee zones. Regional regeneration (in addition to national integration) was the principal objective of a plethora of early Brazilian lines projected to connect several zones with the São Francisco valley, a river system variously described as the Volga or Nile of Brazil.[13] The coordination and integration of inland rail and river communications would sustain the declining sugar industry of the north-east and revitalize a depressed *mineiro* economy.

Given such a diversity of emphasis, it is obvious that initial projects were not exclusively innovative in character; railways were envisaged as engendering new patterns of economic activity and also as facilitating the consolidation of existing production, permitting the recovery of regions and staple sectors dominant during the colonial epoch. Yet the extent to which pious expectations regarding regeneration, integration or national economic development were realized may be questioned. A number of authors have argued that railway construction in Latin America rarely promoted national consolidation, but rather, that the configuration of networks encouraged external economic penetration instead of endogenous diversification, and that construction was almost exclusively determined by the requirements of export production and foreign commerce.[14] An investigation of the literature produced by early Latin American railophiles during the middle decades of the nineteenth

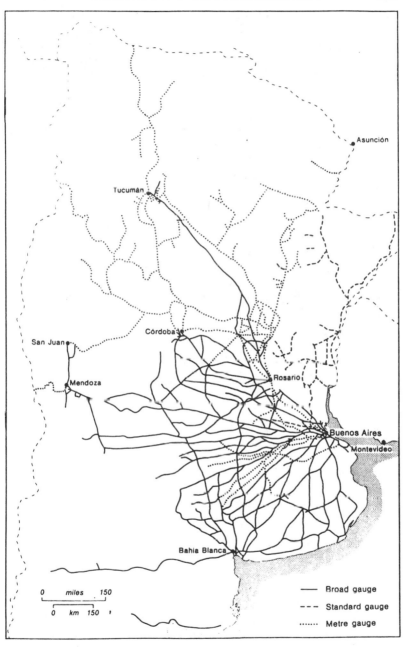

Map 3 Argentine railways, 1914

century reveals little perception of these possibilities; the focus is entirely upon the strategic or developmental properties of construction. The greater part of railway mileage planned during the late nineteenth and early twentieth centuries in the São Paulo coffee zone and the Argentine pampas facilitated the flow of exports: some lines were projected with this objective uppermost, but many were envisaged as serving primarily endogenous needs. But, irrespective of initial motivation, it can be posited that during the twentieth century national (consolidating) networks evolved which served domestic requirements as much as the demands of external trade.

The Argentine network, which stood at a little over 1200 miles in 1875, more than doubled by 1885 and doubled again by the end of that decade, doubling once more by the end of the century. In 1920 route mileage reached 21,000 miles, and in 1935, 25,000 miles.[15] A skeletal system emerged in cis-Patagonian Argentina before 1895: integrated zonal groupings were dominant by 1914, linking all major regions to the federal capital and also providing several strategic interregional trunk routes focused, in addition to Buenos Aires, upon the principal ports of Rosario and Bahía Blanca.[16] Subsequent construction yielded further interzonal connections and extra intrazonal mileage.

Table 1:   Railway density in Argentina: select provinces, 1880–1941 (square miles of territory per route mile of track)

	1880	1892	1906	1941*
Buenos Aires	84.6	46.5	27.7	14.8
Santa Fé	270.0	24.3	23.0	15.6
Córdoba	100.9	51.4	36.0	20.6
Entre Ríos	555.5	67.7	50.0	25.5

* Total route mileage in these provinces had remained essentially the same since 1930/1.
Sources: Compiled from *Railway Times* 12 July 1890 LVIII 41; República Argentina, Ministerio de Obras Públicas, Dirección General de Ferrocarriles *Estadística de los ferrocarriles en explotación durante el año 1892* (Buenos Aires, 1894), p. 9, *Estadística de los ferrocarriles en explocation, Tomo XV, año 1906* (Buenos Aires, 1907) p. 37, *Estadística de los ferrocarriles en explotación, Tomo XLIX, ejercicio 1940/41* (Buenos Aires, 1943), p. 86.

As Table 1 demonstrates, although more dramatic relative growth rates occurred during the 1880s, post-Baring Crisis construction increased the degree of effective communication in Argentina, particularly in those littoral and riverine provinces listed, where the greater part of the population resided. Brazilian railway expansion was less dramatic, standing at 1100 miles in 1875, 17,720 miles in 1920 and approximately 20,700 in 1939.[17] At the fall of the Empire only central – mainly coastal – Brazil possessed an effective rail network, though there were regional groupings in the north-east and south. Not until the 1920s were the western coffee districts of the state of São Paulo linked into this system, and a relatively dense network did not exist before the 1940s.

But by this date the continuing expansion of the *EF Mogiana*, the revitalization of the *EF Sorocabana*, and the extension of affiliated lines during the inter-war period ultimately provided through services from São Paulo to the far south and westwards towards the frontier with Bolivia, thus establishing a sub-national system south of Belo Horizonte.[18] Consequently, a large part of Brazil was linked to the Rio-São Paulo rail axis by 1929, while specifically orientated towards São Paulo markets were the greater part of the south and west of the state of Minas, much of southern Mato Grosso and Goiás. Similarly focused upon the *planalto* was northern Paraná. Even the southern littoral was partially incorporated within the São Paulo web of communications and distribution. In this manner, central and southern Brazil obtained an infrastructure of the quality and complexity (even allowing for breaks of gauge) which had prevailed in Argentina north of the Río Negro since before the First World War. Physically these regions constituted integrated economic zones, welded together by various trunk lines and an extensive system of branches and secondary routes.

Market integration

Trunk line building resulted in the physical integration of southern and central Brazil and the Argentine pampas by the inter-war years. But market homogenization was as much a matter of cost-reducing rail freights and the structure of tariff schedules as an aggregation of route mileage. Despite the rhetoric of promotional literature, few early enterprises applied obviously developmental tariffs, nor did railways necessarily facilitate sudden or dramatic savings in transport costs. Foreign-owned companies (anxious to secure access to European capital markets) usually charged what the market would bear in order to ensure the prompt service of scrip, or depended upon state assistance to satisfy the aspirations of investors. For much of the nineteenth century, opinion was also divided concerning the public service function of railways: fiscal constraints limited the extent of official subvention. Periodically the burden imposed upon impecunious provincial and central governments by social overhead provision caused alarm.[19] But, and notwithstanding these considerations, most concessions granted by various Argentine administrations before 1890 carried a profit guarantee. Until the Second World War similar guarantees were offered by Brazil to privately financed railway companies (whether funded by domestic or foreign interests) and to lessees operating government-owned track. Moreover, financial caution was often subverted by political expediency: governments franchised and guaranteed companies which had little prospect of

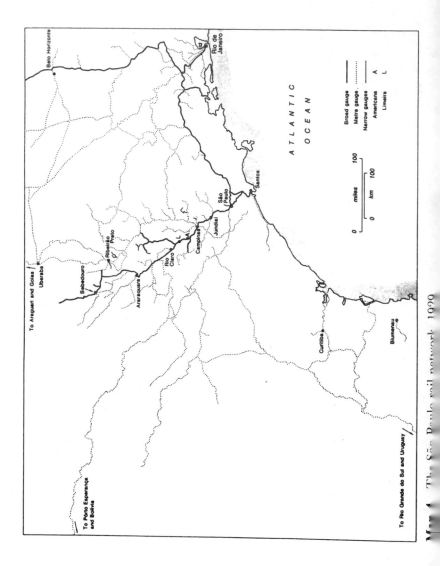

Map 4. The São Paulo rail network, 1909

ever covering operating costs from revenue; government-owned lines operated at lower profit margins (questions of efficiency apart) than would be tolerated by private enterprises, and were subject to political interference.

Comparable data is almost impossible to obtain, but it would appear that during the early phase of railway development some state systems, while not specifically applying 'cheap' tariff regimes, levied lower charges than private (particularly foreign-registered) companies. Generally acknowledged as an efficiently managed entity, the provincially owned *FC Oeste* often charged lower freight rates than the London-based Buenos Ayres Great Southern Railway Company Limited (BAGS). Operating in almost identical zones of the province of Buenos Aires, these not dissimilar networks handled several common categories of traffic between the late 1860s and early 1880s and, despite more moderate charges, the *Oeste*'s gross return on capital did not contrast unfavourably with that of the BAGS.[20] Reference to crude operating ratios may support a similar argument for some Brazilian coffee lines during the period.[21] Elsewhere mounting operating deficits and long-term dependence upon state aid would appear to indicate various forms of indirect subsidies for rail users. There is evidence – though by no means unambiguous – by the beginning of the twentieth century, of fairly frequent and successful attempts to manipulate state railway freight rates in Brazil.[22]

Irrespective of whether profit guarantees and government-funded operating deficits provided artificially cheap transport facilities, or whether railways in fact constituted an heroic, cost-reducing innovation, it is evident that in the coffee zone the coming of railways represented a marked economy on traditional means of communication.[23] Indeed, the savings effected by coffee lines contrast with the situation prevailing in other regions, for example north-eastern sugar-producing provinces, where railways do not appear to have had such a dynamic impact and where pre-modern forms of transport (even for long hauls) survived into the age of steam power.[24] And sharp falls in freights were not the only direct results attributed to the onset of the railway age. Hitherto much capital, in the form of slaves, had been tied up in shipping coffee.[25] Railways permitted the more effective utilization of a scarce resource which could be relocated in favour of production. If the state or foreign investors could be persuaded to subscribe to new forms of transport, the capital saving for *fazendeiros* would be even more substantial. Little wonder planters in the lower Paraiba valley sought to promote railways with alacrity, but would not venture funds beyond initial flotation. The rapid demise of traditional means of moving goods, following the arrival of railways, is further indication that the differential in freight charges must have been large.[26] The position is less clear-cut in Argentina. While some authors claim a dramatic saving, other assessments are more modest.[27] Moreover, competition from traditional means of transport plagued the early railway companies, whose Annual Reports are replete with guarded references to the continued vitality of carting.[28] Cart competition was an enduring feature of Argentine railway history during the third quarter of the nineteenth century, and tended to respond vigorously in the face of increases in rail freights.[29]

Undoubtedly, topographical factors partly explain the rapid dominance of railways in coffee areas, and the survival of more traditional means of transport, particularly for hides, wool and a range of animal products, in Argentina, though the nature of this traffic was also important. Primitive pastoral commodities, which were slow to deteriorate, did not require speedy, reliable shipment. However, the determination of rail operating costs was probably the most significant factor that sustained cart competition in Argentina. Large fixed charges meant high tariffs when the volume of traffic was limited – hence the dependence upon state aid. But as the marginal costs of railway operating were relatively low, tariffs could be reduced dramatically when the volume of freight increased. If for structural reasons the potential for traffic expansion was small, rail tariffs were likely to remain high, and pre-modern forms of transport, which did not have to carry heavy fixed costs, could continue to compete successfully with railways. Thus, by the end of the century, when the pampas were producing a rapidly expanding volume of grain and prime cattle, Argentine railways had little to fear from cart competition. Even if the coming of the railways did not necessarily imply an immediate, sharp, universal reduction in transport costs, it is clear that in both Argentina and Brazil only rails, not mules or bullock carts, could have forged a truly national market.

Market expansion: monetization and the purchasing power of railway labour

By the turn of the century the pampas and *planalto* possessed expanding regional networks which integrated local markets. Subsequent construction would, in the main, serve to enhance the scale and density of these rail systems. Yet even before this period railways had already brought about qualitative modifications in market structures: railway construction had increased effective demand, undermining subsistence activities at a regional level.

From the 1870s until the early 1910s, and again during the later 1920s, the physical expansion of the railway network had a profound effect upon the rural economy, not merely in terms of the expansion of the frontier of profitable agricultural exploitation, but directly stimulating the monetization of the economy. The great cycles of railway building, which occurred during the early 1870s, the decade or so following 1883 and the years between c.1907 and 1914, saw gangs of navvies toiling in the pampas and the coffee zone.[30] Railway labourers inundated small rural townships with their purchasing power; the scale and duration of these construction waves – even during the trough of a depression the momentum of construction work rarely came to an absolute halt – ensured that at a regional level the consequences were not transient. After the armies of navvies had passed, at intermediate points along the line, especially major junctions, local distribution centres remained. Breaks of gauge often represented a positive gain for up-country towns, generating even greater post-construction employment opportunities than might otherwise have been the case, as was revealed by the nature of the network in São Paulo, where gauge diversity was a particularly prevalent feature of the railway system.[31]

Early lines were constructed by British contractors, normally employing British labour. The initial period of railway building may be represented as a direct stimulus to immigration at a time when the absolute flow of migrants was small. The Brazilian authorities certainly viewed the original companies as mechanisms promoting immigration and the development of a free labour market. To this end railways were precluded from employing slaves, in part to inhibit competition with agriculturalists for labour, but also in anticipation that companies would be forced to recruit abroad.[32] When the company was first established, and before the difficult work of ascending the *serra* had commenced, the San Paulo offered employment to several hundred labourers: when this task was in hand the company had over five thousand on its pay roll.[33] At much the same time, the Bahia railway, already well advanced upon the construction of its main line, was employing some three thousand men – a labour force which local interests were concerned should remain in the province after the completion of construction work.[34]

In addition, railway construction gangs were notoriously 'difficult', hardly constituting a docile labour force. During periods of rapid and extensive building, navvies demonstrated a proclivity to use their bargaining power to improve working conditions and settle wage claims. Consequently labourers were often viewed as a threat to the prevailing order in the countryside – a necessary evil, tolerated, but treated with circumspection and apprehension.[35] Railway navvies, prone to spasmodic bouts of self-assertiveness, facilitated the demise of archaic patterns of employment. As one element in the emerging wage-labour force, they contributed to that mix of factors making for the suppression of pre-capitalist structures. Clearly, the purchasing power and influence of construction gangs (as distinct from workers employed in operating railways) were direct functions of the building cycle and supply of labour in regional markets. Exact figures are almost impossible to obtain but it has been estimated that, depending upon terrain, the cost of materials (rails, rolling stock, and so forth) rarely absorbed more than 25 per cent of total expenditure on construction, the major item being labour costs.[36] Sums expended upon extension building by the two major lines in the province during 1874 and 1875 were equivalent to one third of Buenos Aires tax receipts, and represented a significant increase in local purchasing power.[37] In 1913 the wages and salaries bill for the total network was equivalent to 28.8 per cent of national government revenue, or 3.6 per cent of national product.[38] When armies of construction workers were employed laying track, the flow of money into the economy must have been considerable. Railway labour – whether immigrant or native – depended upon the market for basic necessities, creating an upsurge in effective demand throughout the economy.

With the passage of the gangs, the permanent way remained to produce a demographic revolution, drawing immigrants into the countryside and effecting modifications in the existing social order. The spread of coffee cultivation in Brazil and (to a lesser extent) cereal-growing in the Argentine peopled rural zones.[39] Attracted first to the agricultural colonies of the province of Santa Fé, immigrants later flocked to the new pampas grain belt where, even if transient, the sheer scale of numbers augmented population. Qualitatively, the demographic consequences of coffee cultivation were more profound: the process of land clearance and the cycle of cultivation resulted in the adoption of the *colonato*, a form of labour management which favoured the contracting of immigrants in family groups and long-term settlement in rural areas. In both cases a money economy rapidly emerged.

Whether the coming of the railways occasioned changes in wage levels or the social position of labour generally is less unambiguous. Moreover, much depends upon assessments of the strength and degree of organization prevalent amongst railway workers, and the extent to which labour was able to articulate demands coherently. In addition, it is a debate which focuses upon the regular employees of railway companies. Structured organizations, railways offered a multiplicity of employment activities, from senior administrative posts to a range of unskilled jobs. Nevertheless, during the formative phase, too much stress should not be placed upon the degree of social differentiation induced by the companies. Railway employees and workers often demonstrated a strong sense of corporate loyalty which transcended obvious differences of social position and origin. Mattoon has shown that, especially – though not exclusively – for skilled labour, company loyalty made for upward social mobility.[40] At the other end of the social spectrum, technical and administrative personnel might aspire to a shareholding in the company which employed them. Approximately a dozen years after incorporation, the share lists of the *Companhia Paulista* (*CP*) reveal modest holdings by several senior officers and even a number of skilled employees.[41] It was fairly common practice amongst the British-owned Argentine railway companies to second head-office administrators or Buenos-Aires-based managers to London boards of directors.[42] Nor was it unusual in either Brazil or Argentina for officials of one company to place capital in another. The line of demarcation between senior employee and owner was decidedly blurred. If the coming of the railways created new highly remunerative openings for individuals possessed of technical or managerial skills (either in railway administration *per se* or within state regulatory bodies established subsequently), these professional positions were filled by immigrant technocrats who blended easily into the existing social environment or by individuals drawn from the ranks of the local landed interest.[43] There was little difficulty in recruiting suitably qualified legal representatives from the ubiquitous gaggle of *bachareis*.

To present railways as an effective force promoting social stratification and social 'improvement' requires evidence of mass mobilization rather than individual upward mobility. Taking unionization and cooperation amongst groups of workers as a coefficient, it may be argued that railway workers in Argentina were a more cohesive body than their Brazilian counterparts. Argentine railwaymen demonstrated the capacity to forge a common identity and advance sectional interests in the face of conflicts with employers and principal consumers of railway services. In Brazil railway labour was less able to overcome the traditional divisions that sundered the railway community. Notwithstanding the position achieved by *CP* workers during the early twentieth century, the environment within which workers operated was traditional and paternalistic.[44] Despite violent strikes, and struggles to improve working conditions and wages, railwaymen in São Paulo were in essence a passive, though undoubtedly privileged, group. While in both countries the years immediately prior to the First World War constituted a period of growing labour unrest, disputes in Brazil rarely extended beyond the confines of one system, and only exceptionally outside the sector. The 1920 strike on the Leopoldina Railway caused much consternation when railway workers were able to mobilize sympathetic action amongst other groups in the Rio area.[45] The contrast with labour disputes in Argentina is marked. Although the early history of railway unionization on the River Plate reveals the movement to be riven with ideological factionalism, inter-company indifference, and the tendency of locomotive drivers and footplate men to distance themselves from other groups of workers in the industry, unity was precariously forged between 1907 and 1922.[46] In addition, rail labour promoted the growth of, and fostered cooperation amongst, unions in other sectors, serving as patron to the organization of a national movement.[47] By the 1920s railway unions in particular, and also some other sectors of the urban labour force which were effectively unionized, had achieved a position of influence. They constituted a force which successive administrations sometimes tolerated, and occasionally attempted to cow or coopt. At least until 1929 organized labour was able to maintain a degree of independence in Argentina.

This difference between the two countries may be explained by the political environment within which the proletariat operated. Universal male suffrage, reinforced with the establishment of a secret ballot in 1912, placed additional power in the hands of the Argentine labour movement. Radical administrations during the 1920s occasionally courted railway workers, as indeed had earlier governments.[48] But the mellowing attitude of the state to railway unions was essentially *post hoc*. Of greater significance was the physiognomy of the network. By 1914 most major companies had obtained an entry into the federal capital, thus facilitating contact amongst various sections of the union movement. In addition, Argentine networks were substantially larger than their Brazilian counterparts. Notwithstanding the fragmented nature of the Brazilian system at this juncture, given the size of the country, many companies were fairly small concerns.

Taking route mileage as a guide, Brazil's most extensive system in 1879 was the *Estrada de Ferro Dom Pedro Segundo* (*EFDPII*), operating some 389 miles of track, followed by three other entities extending between 126 and 138 miles. The vast majority of the remaining companies operated networks considerably less than one hundred miles.[49] At the same time, the longest Argentine system possessed 340 miles, and three other companies ran from 201 to 246 miles of rails.[50] Many decades later the four largest Brazilian systems were 2,416, 2,087, 1,970, and 1,914 miles respectively: the 'big four' pampean systems boasted track of 5,072, 3,722, 2,810 and 1,924 miles. The largest Brazilian grouping accounted for only 11.4 per cent of total national mileage; the principal Argentine company represented almost double that proportion of a greater aggregate federal route mileage. By 1914 the network of Argentina embraced basically six large zonal systems, while the Brazilian structure – notwithstanding a few exceptions – was fragmented, the cohesion of the network disrupted by conflicts of jurisdiction between federal and state authorities and the sub-regional focus of smaller companies.

Argentine railwaymen were grouped in large, company-structured organizations, often employed in massive factory-style workshops and depots. In contrast, Brazilian labour was scattered over the railway system, isolated in smaller groups, less amenable to effective organization and beyond an integrated chain of communication. Although the workshops of the *Sorocabana* and *Paulista* might be compared with those of the Buenos Ayres Western Railway Company Limited, or the Buenos

Ayres & Pacific Railway Company Limited, the number of workers employed therein represented a much smaller proportion of the total labour force, and were not on a par with the vast agglomerations to be found in the railway towns of the Central Argentine or BAGS. The size of Argentine railway companies, the sheer scale of operations, the concentrations of labour in the federal capital and major regional junctions such as Pergamino, Rosario, Córdoba and Bahía Blanca where the various zonal systems impinged one upon the other, provided the focus for inter-company contact and intra-union solidarity that was lacking in Brazil. The history of railway unionization in the two countries reflects the differences in the evolution of their respective labour movements.

In a pre-industrial economy, the role of public utility workers in the formation of a national labour movement was likely to be of particular significance, because of the absence of other sectors capable of effective organization. Large-scale enterprises made for a concentration of labour. Until the emergence of an industrial sector, the large utility corporations constituted major employers of labour in Argentina. If effective unionization implies improved working conditions and higher wage rates than might otherwise have prevailed, then it may be argued that the activities of the early rail unions made for an improvement in incomes, both for their own members and, via the institutionalization of a national trade union movement, for a broader spectrum of wage-earners. Labour organizations facilitated the integration of immigrants into the ranks of the working classes, and imparted a greater degree of cohesion to less privileged strata of society. Despite deficiencies in the data, the fragmentary state of comparable time series and the conflicting interpretations that may be placed upon qualitative evidence, it would appear that real wages in Argentina were, on the whole, relatively higher than those prevailing in Western Europe, and that the standard of living of urban workers was possibly higher than in some other areas of recent settlement during the first three decades of the twentieth century, a period when real incomes registered a steady, though not uninterrupted, increase.[52]

Migrants certainly perceived Argentina as a more attractive land of opportunity than Brazil, a view no doubt strengthened by the occasional bans imposed by several European governments upon emigration to the latter. Of the two principal currents of migrants which flowed to southeastern Latin America during these years, Italians exhibited a clear preference for Argentina from 1899 until 1910, when registered departures for Brazil yielded a slight relative increase: Spaniards consistently favoured Argentina over Brazil from 1897 until the First World War.[53] Indeed, only during the period of the Baring Crisis had Brazil displaced Argentina as the principal South American destination for these emigrants. Portuguese emigrants favoured Brazil.

Diversification and industrialization

Consequent upon the integrating effect of railway building, migration and the resultant expansion of income-generating rural activities, regional market growth accelerated with the diffusion of a cash economy and increased domestic purchasing power. The extent to which these processes sponsored domestic industrialization has, nevertheless, been questioned, both in general terms and specifically with regard to the railways. Much stress has been placed, in the traditional historiography, on the backward linkages established by railway construction and operations. For the dependency school, the obvious lack of railway-orientated supply industries in Latin America, or the ephemeral nature of such ventures, appears to confirm the weakness of railways as stimulants of specific basic industries and possibly of industrialization *per se*. A narrow focus upon backward linkage tends, however, to ignore the positive diversifying impulses associated with the provision of transport services. By the early twentieth century, the *planalto* and pampas possessed (as has been argued above) extensive, and increasingly intensive, rail networks affording local distribution services – equally available to national industry and importers. Even before the turn of the century, local manufacturers responded to the pull of the home market. Cheap transport facilities, the modernization of the rural economy and increased domestic demand were strong impulses when linked to the growth of population, in economies already endowed with a proto-industrial base.

Cotton textile manufacturing in Brazil predates the railway age: by the 1860s an infant industry, centred mainly on slave markets in the north-east, had achieved a viable level of output.[54] Given a favourable exchange and tariff environment, the survival of the industry was reasonably secure, but dynamic development depended upon large, discriminating markets which were emerging in the centre-south. One of the heroic tales of the history of Brazilian industrial development points to railways as a causal factor in the relocation of the cotton textile industry. The modern cultivation of raw cotton in the province of São Paulo dates from the arrival of the San Paulo Railway, which sponsored the planting of cotton seeds in an attempt to diversify traffic.[55] In the heady days of the US Civil War it appeared that cotton might rival coffee as an export crop. Even when the boom burst there were those associated with railways who continued to argue enthusiastically in favour of cotton-growing.[56] Gradual decline, as the United States reasserted its primacy in world markets, was not without benefit to local manufacturers. The collapse in exports was not matched by a correspondingly severe contraction in raw cotton output, despite the loud complaints of producers (who sometimes diversified into manufacturing) over falling prices.[57] The volume of cotton traffic on the *EFS* (which served the principal growing area) fluctuated violently, but remained surprisingly large from the mid 1870s to the mid 1880s, a period of acute depression in the export trade.[58] An expanding railway network, which gave access to growing domestic markets and integrated manufacture with cheap raw material supply, constituted a further advantage to an industry already enjoying tariff protection in the order of from 50 to 80 per cent, and whose locally distributed goods did not have to bear heavy port ware-house fees, brokerage and international freight charges. Small wonder that textile manufacturing might yield profits of 30 and 40 per cent.[59]

Textile production epitomized the form of 'industrialization' which early promoters of railways most appreciated; it was directly related to the diversification of rural production, as much for domestic consumption as for export. During the nineteenth century, when Brazilian and Argentine statesmen spoke of industry, and prospects for the development of industries, they referred invariably to 'natural' industries – the processing of locally derived, rural-based raw materials. Brazilian legislators were most precise in the anticipated spread effects of transport innovation. Discussions of railway projects were associated with the stimulation of agricultural production, commercial expansion and industrial progress: the three areas of activity were but various facets of one process.[60] Many of these assumptions and expectations might have been optimistic, but they were not fundamentally erroneous. In Argentina, late-nineteenth-century controversy concerning the small size and efficiency of the industrial sector was centred upon agropecuarian diversification.[61] It is hardly exceptionable that two of the most spectacular examples of modern, large-scale Argentine industrial expansion prior to 1900 are encompassed by the wine and sugar processing complexes.

The formation of a national railway system linked main producing zones located in Cuyo (wine) and the north-west (sugar) with burgeoning littoral markets. Although of colonial origins, both industries were transformed with the arrival of railways.[62] When trunk lines penetrated the Argentine west and north-west during the penultimate decades of the century, both industries underwent a major restructuring: output rose dramatically, small artisanal production units were superseded by large, capital-intensive, vertically integrated organizations which controlled raw material cultivation, elaboration and marketing. Sugar output, for example, increased by a factor of 21 between 1876 (the year when railheads were pushed into the cane fields) and the Baring Crisis, and grew by a further 250 per cent by the First World War.[63] Railways facilitated a process of technological innovation and institutional reorganization, permitting the concentration of production at the source of raw material supply. Before 1929 sugar and wine were virtually the only major domestic industries to develop outside the metropolitan area, the principal market for all products. Luxury alimentary commodities did not, however, constitute the principal form of rail traffic diversification between the 1870s and 1930.

Table 2: Coffee tonnage as a percentage of total freight on main coffee-carrying lines, Brazil, 1876–1930 (annual averages)

	EF Paulista (percentage)	EF Mogiana (percentage)
1876–80	n.a.	50.0
1881–5	63.2	63.9
1886–90	50.2	43.4
1891–5	37.5	37.2
1896–1900	43.3	41.9
1901–5	52.1	49.2
1906–10	52.2	43.6
1911–15	37.3	26.8
1916–20	27.8	22.0
1921–5	23.4	18.1
1926–30	22.3	16.2

Source: F. A. Marqués De Saes 'Expansão e declino das ferrovias paulistas, 1870–1940' in C. M. Pélaez and M. Buescu (eds) *A moderna história econômica* (Rio 1976) p. 79.

The relative decline in coffee traffic registered in Table 2 is even more startling when set against the vast absolute increase in coffee production and volume of freight generated, given that the configuration of the railway network ensured that newly planted areas in western São Paulo, southern Minas and northern Paraná shipped the bulk of their coffee over the two lines referred to in the table. Coffee became relatively less significant because of the increased volume of commodities directed towards the domestic market, particularly locally produced foodstuffs, but also industrial raw materials, construction material and manufactures.[64]

While the *paulista* coffee lines underwent freight diversification, a reverse tendency was manifested by the principal Argentine networks. The zonal structure of the national system ensured a shifting pattern of product primacy, with change over time a function of parallel and related movements of the grain and prime cattle frontiers. The tendency was for increasing specialization between 1880 and 1930. With few exceptions, by 1914 the *freight* schedules of each of the major companies were dominated by a narrow list of commodities. Diversification was revealed in a widening range of rural products at the national level. Argentina's expanding mix of temperate arable and pastoral commodity production correlates with the expansion of the rail network, its degree of density and the nature of regional product specialization thereby engendered.

Although the coming of the railways might have had little impact upon traditional pastoral activities or even wool production, bulk cereal cultivation and high-quality stock raising were more responsive. Before the arrival of the railways, Santa Fé agricultural colonies had languished, a prey to Indian raids; they were islands of subsistence in the desert awaiting salvation by the Central Argentine. Once endowed with rails, *santafesino* grain lands and the Buenos Aires cereal belt flowered; initially catering to domestic demand (substituting imports from the USA and Chile), production later responded to world market stimulus.[65] For Argentina, export production was closely related to domestic market supply. Notwithstanding the vast increase in cultivation during the first three decades of the twentieth century, internal consumption began to absorb a growing proportion of total output. By the First World War some 60 per cent of total meat output was consumed domestically, approximately one half of the wheat harvest was directed towards the home market (though the proportion was liable to violent fluctuation because of the volatility of annual production), and a substantial volume of other cereals was also retained for domestic use.[66]

The impact of post-1880 *paulista* and Argentine railway construction was probably the most important factor directly encouraging domestic industrial growth. The productive use of new exploitable pampean lands occasioned by the westward race of the grain and cattle frontiers yielded a supply of cheap foodstuffs which underwrote the consumption of wage goods. In São Paulo the cultivation of domestically demanded staples, on lands vacated by the movement of coffee cultivation to the south and west, was possible because the rail system which had been constructed with coffee profits shipped flour, wheat and other items of prime necessity at lower freights than were applied to coffee itself. Indeed, the central districts of the state of São Paulo were to emerge as a food-producing zone not only for the city but for up-country coffee regions.[67] The derived consequences of railway construction were to be observed not so much in the dynamics of luxury primary product processing industries, or in the grain-based industries of milling and brewing, but in the broad effect upon mass disposable incomes.

The positive impact upon endogenous industrialization resulting from the forward linkages effected by railway consolidation and associated income expansion following the modernization of rural production may be observed, for Argentina, in the restructuring of the import schedule. Increased domestic manufacturing capacity before 1914 resulted in a relative decline in imports of finished products and a shift towards intermediate products, raw materials and capital goods: by 1929 approximately one half of all manufactured products consumed in the

Argentine were locally produced.[68] Pre-inter-war Brazilian industrial expansion is well documented, though the significance of railways in consolidating a regional market is less directly addressed or acknowledged.[69]

In contrast, backward linkages *were* weak. As was the case at the outset of the railway age in the USA, most railway iron was imported, and so was fuel (local coal deposits being virtually unexploitable). However, unlike the USA, independent engineering complexes did not subsequently expand capacity to supply Argentine and *paulista* companies during post-formative periods. By the end of the nineteenth century, despite some specifically regional purchases of stone, water and so forth, quebracho wood for sleepers represented the only endogenously derived input organized on a national scale in Argentina: a product which subsequent legislation required all companies to buy domestically.[70] Locally procurable inputs were more readily available in Brazil, where there were also more explicit attempts to harness railway development to industrial promotion after the fashion of czarist Russia.[71] Yet, in spite of the preference accorded to the São Paulo iron industry, technical difficulties and the high cost of domestically produced material undermined an interesting experiment in sponsored industrialization, which was relegated to a mere episode in *paulista* railway history.

More positive, and independent of official intervention, was the stimulant to the timber trade. After 1870, with the laying of rails in the new coffee districts, a symbiotic relationship emerged between these two branches of agriculture. *Paulista* railways became avid consumers of timber cleared from virgin forests preparatory to coffee planting. Large quantities of wood were used in the laying of permanent way and for fuel. The poor quality and inadequate preparation of the wood initially utilized resulted in the rapid deterioration of sleepers; subsequently the rapid expansion of the system sustained demand.[72] Substituting for imported coal, wood was burnt extensively by the coffee lines, and the *fazendeiros* retained stands of timber for this purpose.[73] Given that many coffee planters were railway shareholders, the directness of these linkages is hardly surprising. Nevertheless, such a substantial regional demand for wood undoubtedly valorized what would otherwise have been a worthless by-product of land clearance, so reducing the burden of plantation preparation costs.

Finally, railway building provided further openings for the São Paulo civil engineering industry. Topography (as much as domestic ownership) probably explains the larger role performed by native subcontractors in Brazilian railway construction than in Argentine. From an early stage local firms tended to predominate in permanent way-laying and related engineering projects. The 'technology gap' between corduroy road building in the *serra* and the primitive North American style of railway construction favoured by some *paulista* lines was narrow. Indeed, costs of construction do not appear to have been dissimilar.[74] This factor may account for the enduring romance between railways and the coffee elite, and the assiduity with which provincial administrations granted concessions during the 1870s. Corporate financing of railways represented a privatization of overhead costs hitherto borne by the state. Little wonder that an impecunious province like São Paulo was so profligate with profit guarantees and promises of subventions during the decade following the war against Paraguay. The 'cost' of guarantees, and subsidies for unprofitable lines, should be set against savings effected in the highway maintenance and construction budget. The coming of the railways resulted in a speedy curtailment of expenditure under these heads.[75]

Yet, as has been related above, the force of backward linkage was not strong, particularly in the Argentine. Foreign ownership, the location of boards of directors in London, and franchises providing for duty-free importation of equipment and materials were powerful influences making for the external provisioning of stores, locomotives and the whole paraphernalia of railway operations. But the propensity to import was not peculiar to externally registered entities, as the experience of Brazilian coffee lines demonstrates. At the beginning of the railway age, technological and financial considerations promoted dependence upon external supply. An equally significant inhibitor to the creation of dynamic backward linkage with other sectors of the economy in the long term was a tendency for companies to internalize a range of ancillary activities through vertical integration. Horizontal expansion (whether by means of amalgamation or physical extension) increased the scale of corporate operations, thereby encouraging vertical growth, which frustrated the elaboration of extra-sectoral connections. Nevertheless, from a comparatively early stage the companies represented a relatively large element of industrialism in essentially non-industrial economies, notably in the shape of their workshops and repair depots.[76] Even small companies, serving circumscribed zones, required a basic minimum of repair and service capacity; major industrial complexes evolved around larger systems.

Already in 1882 railway companies operated the largest industrial workshops in Argentina.[77] While the data pertaining to industrial units does not distinguish between labour-intensive artisanal establishments and modern factories, it is clear that railway locomotive and carriage shops constituted the most significant concentrations of labour in the province of Buenos Aires. The workshops of some small provincial lines employed more individuals than the average-sized manufacturing firms in an admittedly rural-based economy. At the *Oeste* and BAGS machine shops, on the other hand, were concentrations of 292 and 403 workers respectively at a time when total company workforce exceeded 1,500. Moreover, as companies grew, so these facilities were extended and modernized. When completing a major extension to Bahía Blanca in 1884, the Great Southern relocated and expanded the locomotive shops.[78] Successive waves of extension building witnessed additional improvements. Although on a somewhat smaller scale, a similar situation prevailed on the coffee lines. At this period the *CP* had already established carriage and engine shops in Jundiaí – a factory complex that would grow to become one of the largest in the state during the next fifty years.[79] By the mid 1880s even medium-sized Argentine networks possessed the capacity to manufacture wagons and assemble imported equipment.[80]

With the pre-war extension-building boom which occurred at the beginning of the new century, the scope of rail networks increased, generating extra work for the shops. At this juncture major companies in Argentina allocated substantial proportions of new capital for the conversion of shops and depots into manufacturing units.[81] After network refurbishment during the 1920s, the Sorocaba shops and depots of the *EFS* were the largest and most modern in Latin America for a metre-gauge railway. The locomotive machine shop was capable of handling the largest engines then produced.[82] As befitted their position, the broad-gauge pampean lines possessed even more extensive facilities, which had also been extended and updated during the 1920s. At Remedios de Escalada, some seven miles out of Buenos Aires, the BAGS *talleres* provided employment for 2,700. All the company's coaching stock was by this time being manufactured in Argentina, and the locomotive shops were capable of providing every component required to construct engines, save only boiler shells and cast steel parts.[83] Located on separate sites, Central Argentine engine and carriage shops employed a total of over 3,300 and were equipped to manufacture all items required to produce engines, coaching stock and wagons.[84]

These capital-intensive manufacturing complexes were supplied with modern machinery; they contained foundries, forges, gas-making plant and electricity-generating power stations. The provision of capacity on such a scale was an indication of a commitment to manufacture locally, even if purchases of equipment from abroad did not cease. Workshop modernization and reconstruction effected a restructuring of British-owned Argentine railway imports. Whereas at the turn of the century Annual Reports referred to the placing of orders in Britain for locomotives and rolling stock, by the 1920s the emphasis was upon semi-finished products, raw materials and items for workshop assembly (in addition to sophisticated equipment) – a process precursive of post-Second World War patterns of industrialization.[85]

The spread effect of these establishments is difficult to assess. Most of the plant and much of the materials were imported or recycled. Yet they must have assisted in the creation of a technically skilled segment of the labour force which probably benefited other industries. Moreover these units manifest the potential for indigenous industrial consolidation. In this context it is not without significance that Jundiaí was to emerge as an important up-country heavy industrial centre by the inter-war period, or that other focuses of *paulista* industry were to be found at Sorocaba, Campinas and Limeira, major conurbations that were often the site of railway workshops and strategic junctions. The Argentine motor-mechanical industry expanded in Córdoba where – apart from locational advantages – the Córdoba Central workshops were housed, containing the largest forges and some of the finest boiler and erecting shops in the republic.[86] The railway ensured that the area contained a stock of skilled labour which antedated the arrival of car and lorry manufacturers.

Of a more qualitative nature were innovations in corporate practices introduced by railway companies. It is now widely acknowledged that the coming of railways inculcated new commercial attitudes, and established new structures, in Brazil. Little distinction is made between foreign-financed and locally registered concerns. Both served as a model for institutional modernization in other sectors of the economy, encouraging a vogue for limited liability, specifically amongst the planter aristocracy, and a high degree of pragmatism on the part of local capitalists.[87] In addition, domestically funded entities not only served as vehicles for entrepreneurial initiative, but also facilitated the institutionalization of capital flows and savings nexus on a regional basis: good quality railway paper was always absorbed with alacrity by the local market.[88] Argentine companies were possibly, by the 1920s, an even more effective manifestation of corporate capitalism, given a demonstrable proclivity for diversification. Having completed the phase of horizontal integration by 1914, many British-owned lines diversified vertically thereafter, one of the most successful ventures being the expansion of oil production and exploration undertaken by a consortium of three companies.[89] Originally stimulated by the instability of fuel supplies, the conversion of steam locomotives from coal to oil burners not only afforded economies in working but also revealed potential for import substitution. By 1926 over one half of the Great Southern's fuel requirements was met from oil, a remarkable turn-around since 1916, when oil had been introduced as an emergency, wartime 'second string'.[90] Oil surplus to requirement was disposed of on the local market.[91] The switch to oil during the 1920s contrasted sharply with the high degree of dependence upon coal prior to the First World War. Between 1908 and 1913 coal represented some 72.5 per cent of the railways' fuel requirements, with a tendency to increase over time.[92]

Lacking readily obtainable timber, Argentine companies had always been more firmly wedded to coal than their Brazilian counterparts.

Diversification into oil prospecting was not the only departure from simple railway operation undertaken by the Anglo-Argentine lines. Several companies operated docks and elevator firms (jointly and individually) others diversified into urban utilities – water, lighting, electricity generation – and tourism.[93] Four companies operated a fruit marketing and distribution enterprise: many were involved in crop promotion and experimentation.[94] Some of these activities were fairly closely related to railway operations, others less so, but there is little doubt that the 1920s witnessed a marked acceleration in the pace of diversification amongst British-owned railway concerns based in Argentina.

Railways and domestic diversification

It is tautological to argue that speculation concerning the impact of railway construction on the *planalto* and in the pampas must take cognizance of the rural bias of economic activity in these regions. The dominant nature of agrarian pursuits tends to over-emphasize the importance of railways as expressions of industrialism, given that the linkages between railways and industry were of a predominantly passive form. Railways did not directly activate the expansion of a large and dynamic manufacturing sector. An improving and expanding system of transport, railways served to integrate – at the provincial, regional or sub-national level – the market. Consequently, although specific locational advantages were thus conferred upon a limited number of industries, the significance of railway development must be sought in the distributive function of intensive railway networks – facilities which encouraged the shipment of manufactured products. Sheltered behind tariff barriers and enjoying the advantage of currency depreciation (coupled with occasional preferential exchange treatment), *paulista* industry expanded. In as much as the major markets for (and often centres of production of) manufactures were located in up-country conurbations (usually important junctions or the site of workshops) in addition to the city of São Paulo, industrialization implied dependence upon the railway system. The lie of the terrain and only partially successful schemes to improve river communications confirm the evidence provided by freight differentials that there were no practicable alternatives to railways.

Argentine markets were more concentrated than Brazilian, and were thus possibly easier to provision by means of imports. Yet even here, in addition to the examples provided by wine and sugar processing, the deepening of the market owed much to the railway age. The large-scale shipment of basic foodstuffs was only feasible by rail, though the savings compared with carting might not have been great for traditional pastoral commodities. Cheap food freights and the introduction of wage labour into rural areas stimulated the monetization of an emerging mass market, and made for increases in disposable income which underwrote the expansion of demand for manufactures. A substantial proportion of this consumption was already domestically supplied in 1914: indigenous manufacture would achieve an even larger percentage by 1929.[95]

It was the coming of the railways which brought about this situation and which, in Argentina, was also responsible for a relative improvement in the position of some segments of the labour movement. In absolute terms the cash flow generated directly by railways was substantial, during both the construction and the operational phases. The money economy created by railway construction was a basic prerequisite for widespread development. Railways, however, made several direct contributions to the process of industrial expansion, notwithstanding the importance of forward linkages. The evidence for Brazil indicates that various aspects of corporate management and the institutionalization of some business practices were widespread throughout *fazendeiro* society. In Argentina, large foreign-owned companies displayed the potential for corporate diversification. Finally, railways contained within themselves manufacturing units and demonstrated the possibilities for industrial expansion which existed in agrarian economies. In these respects, rather than as a dynamic lead sector spawning a mix of backward linkages, railways may be portrayed as a force promoting industrial growth.

Dependentistas, often over-concerned with the predominance of foreign funding in the railway industry and inclined to stress the exclusiveness of connections between the supply of transport facilities and export agriculture, found implicit confirmation in a traditionalist historiography for negative assessments of the impact of social overhead modernization. Analyses focusing on the availability of transport services, and particularly the rapid expansion in the supply of such services wrought by railways, tend to enhance the importance of the latter in promoting industrial growth. Given an increasing scale of railway operations after the turn of the century and a proclivity for vertical integration, the weakness of backward linkages was sustained. Yet, paradoxically, the role of railways as manifestations of industrialism was strengthened. Increased workshop capacity promoted by the growth of individual networks emphasized the position of depots and workshops as engineering complexes, manufacturing units and employers of factory labour.

Notes

The fieldwork upon which this chapter is based was completed in Brazil during the spring and summer of 1980, thanks to financial support received from the International Centre for Economics and Related Disciplines, London School of Economics and Political Science, and the Nuffield Foundation, whose assistance is gratefully acknowledged.

¹ L. H. Jenks 'Railroads as an economic force in American development' *Journal of Economic History* IV 1 (1944).
² W. W. Rostow *The process of economic growth* (Oxford 1960) pp. 132–3, 302, *The world economy: history and prospects* (London 1978), 'The take-off into self-sustained economic growth' *Economic Journal* LXVI 1 (1956).
³ P. K. O'Brien *The new economic history of the railways* (London 1977) p. 26, 'Transporte y desarrollo económico en Europa, 1789–1914' in RENFE (ed.) *Los ferrocarriles y el desarrollo económico de Europa Occidental durante el siglo XIX* (Madrid 1981). See also G. Tortella 'Discusión y resumen de las ponencias' in RENFE (ed.) *Los ferrocarriles y el desarrollo.* O'Brien and Tortella survey the new economic history of railways which applies to Britain, France, Germany, Italy, Mexico, Russia, Spain and the USA. Both volumes also review methodological problems specific to the cliometric history of railways.
⁴ The classic studies for such economies are J. Coatsworth *Crecimiento contra desarrollo: el impacto económico de los ferrocarriles en el porfiriato* (Mexico 1976); A. Gómez Mendoza *Ferrocarriles y cambio económico en España, 1855–1913* (Madrid 1982); W. P. McGreevey *An economic history of Colombia, 1845–1930* (Cambridge 1971) pp. 262–8. See also R. Miller 'Railways and economic development in central Peru. 1890–1930' in R. Miller, C. Smith and J. Fisher (eds) *Social and economic change in modern Peru* (Liverpool 1976).
⁵ J. B. Alberdi *Obras completas* (Buenos Aires 1886) III 433; J. F. Castro *Sarmiento y los ferrocarriles* (Buenos Aires 1950) *passim*; A. W. Bunkley *The life of Sarmiento* (Princeton 1952) p. 399, cited in W. R. Wright *British-owned railways in Argentina: their effect on the growth of economic nationalism* (Austin 1974) p. 38.
⁶ Brasil, Ministério da Agricultura, Commércio e Obras Públicas (hereafter MACOP) *Relatório apresentado à assembléa geral legislativa na segunda sessão da XVa legislatura* (hereafter *Relatório . . .*) (Rio 1873) pp. 64–5, *Relatório . . . quarta sessão da XVa legislativa* pp. 71–7; Provincia de São Paulo (hereafter SP) *Annaes da Assembléa Legislativa Provincial de São Paulo: sessão de 1875* (hereafter *Annaes . . .*) (São Paulo 1875) pp. 102–9, *Annaes . . . sessão de 1876* pp. 213–14.
⁷ Virtually within months of the termination of hostilities, several surveys were undertaken in Rio Grande and the other southern provinces. Hitherto there had been little serious consideration of railway projects in this area. See MACOP *Relatório . . . terceira sessão da XIVa legislatura* pp. 135–6, *Relatório . . . terceira sessão da XVa legislatura* pp. 106–9, *Relatório . . . quarta sessão da XVa legislatura* pp. 138–41, 153–62; J. L. Love *Rio Grande do Sul and Brazilian regionalism, 1882–1930* (Stanford 1971) pp. 15, 17.
⁸ *Parliamentary Papers* (hereafter *PP*) 1875 LXXVI 316.
⁹ C. M. Lewis 'La consolidación de la frontera argentina a fines de la decada del 70; los indios, Roca y los ferrocarriles' in E. Gallo and G. Ferrari (eds) *La Argentina del ochenta al centenario* (Buenos Aires 1980).
¹⁰ *The Railway Times* (hereafter *RT*) 28 Sept. 1895 LXVIII 413; *The Times* 25 Oct. 1895 3f.
¹¹ Wright *British-owned railways* pp. 31–2, 35–6.
¹² Confederación Argentina *Mensage* [*sic*] *del Presidente de la Confederación Argentina al primer Congreso Legislativo Federal en el acto de la apertura de sus sessiones* (hereafter *Mensaje*) (Parana 1854) p. 26; J. B. Alberdi, Argentine Chargé d'Affaires, to Lord Clarendon, 29 Aug. 1856, Public Record Office, London, Foreign Office Correspondence (hereafter FO) 6/196:88–90; Edward Thornton, British Minister at Parana, to Lord John Russell, 23 Jan. 1861, FO 6/232: 29–30; William Doria, British Charge d'Affaires at Buenos Aires, to Russell, 27 March 1863, FO 6/245:54; *Brazil and River Plate Mail* 7 April 1864 I 210; P. B. Goodwin 'The Central Argentine Railway and the economic development of Argentina, 1854–1881' *Hispanic American Historical Review* (hereafter *HAHR*) LVII (1977).
¹³ A. Benévolo *Introdução à história ferroviária do Brasil: estudo social, politico e histórico* (Recife 1953) p. 17; C. B. Ottoni *O futuro das estradas de ferro no Brasil* (Rio de Janeiro 1938) p. 43.
¹⁴ A. G. Frank 'Notes on the mechanism of imperialism; the case of Brazil' *Monthly Review* XVI 5 (1964); R.M. Ortíz *Historia económica de la Argentina* (Buenos Aires 1955) I 236;

J. Fuchs *Argentina: su desarrollo capitalista* (Buenos Aires 1965) pp. 133–4, 135, 136, 138; A. Gilbert *Latin American development: a geographical perspective* (London 1974) pp. 183–6.

[15] F. Barres 'Reseña de los ferrocarriles argentinos' *Boletín de la asociación internacional permanente del congreso panamericano de ferrocarriles* (hereafter *BAIPCPF*) xxviii 86 (1944) 70.

[16] C. M. Lewis *British railways in Argentina, 1857–1914* (London 1983) chap. 8.

[17] Brasil, Ministério da Viação e Obras Públicas, Departamento Nacional de Estradas de Ferro *Estadística das estradas de ferro do Brasil relativo ao ano de 1945* (Rio de Janeiro 1952) pp. 50, 51.

[18] O. Nogueira Matos 'Vias de comunicação' in S. Buarque de Holanda and P. Moacyr Campos *História geral da civilização Brasileira, Tomo II O Brasil monarquico* (São Paulo 1974) p. 57, *Café ferrovias: a evolução ferroviária de São Paulo e o desenvolvimento da cultura cafeeira* (São Paulo 1974) pp. 119–21; J. L. Love *Rio Grande do Sul and Brazilian regionalism, 1882–1930* (Stanford 1971) p. 137, *São Paulo in the Brazilian federation 1889–1937* (Stanford 1980) p. 202; J. D. Wirth *Minas Gerais in the Brazilian Federation, 1889–1937* (Stanford 1977) pp. 46, 57. The possibility of regional hegemony on this scale had been envisaged as early as 1881, see SP *Relatório . . . 13 de Janeiro de 1881* pp. 138–9.

[19] For an expression of the undesirability of the state compromising its credit because of the promotion of railway companies applying developmental tariffs, see *Mensaje . . . 1887* p. 17. Even coffee interests in the province of São Paulo were wary of the financial implication of over-generous official support for railway projects undertaken during periods of fiscal embarrassment; see *Annaes . . . 1871* pp. 317–20. During the late 1870s would-be promoters petitioning for provincial assistance were placed in the ludicrous position of attempting to demonstrate that their railway companies would never actually have to call upon the state for the financial guarantees being requested.

[20] R. Scalabrini Ortíz *Historia de los ferrocarriles argentinos* (Buenos Aires 1958) pp. 39–40; Lewis *British railways* pp. 23, n. 85, 128–29.

[21] MACOP *Relatório . . . segunda sessão da XXa legislatura* pp. 217, 298. This report lists the working ratios (difference between gross receipts and operating expenses) of the San Paulo (Brazilian) Railway Company Limited and the *Estrada de Ferro Dom Pedro II* (hereafter *EFDPII*, respectively a British-owned company and a central government line, from inauguration until 1886. Although these networks were markedly different, both experienced severe operating difficulties due to the nature of the terrain traversed. Indeed, the costs of building and maintaining the railway through the coastal escarpment were so great that the SPR had been permitted to levy a tariff surcharge. Nevertheless, if the low working ratios of the SPR may be portrayed as resulting from onerous freights, the *EFDPII*'s comparatively high ratios can be interpreted as a subsidy to consumers.

[22] Love *Rio Grande* pp. 155, 187, 197; Wirth *op. cit.* p. 180; J. S. Duncan *Public and private operation of railways in Brazil* (New York 1932) p. 149.

[23] S. Silva *Expansão cafeeira e origines da indústria no Brasil* (Rio de Janeiro 1976) p. 57. Silva quotes several sources, including the encyclopaedic work of A. de E. Tauney *História do café no Brasil* (Rio de Janeiro 1939–43) iv 405–6, which indicates that rail freights were six times lower than rates charged by muleteers; R. Graham *Britain and the onset of modernization in Brazil, 1830–1914* (Cambridge 1968) p. 71 mentions a sharp fall in transport costs; SP *Discurso com que O Illmo. e Exm. Sr. Dr. José Antonio Saraiva, presidente da provincia de S. Paulo, abria à assembléa legislativa provincial no dia 15 de fevereiro de 1855* (São Paulo 1855) p. 42 estimates that railways would effect a 60 per cent reduction in the cost of coffee shipment.

[24] Van Ufel (pseudonym) *Ferrovia do Recife ao Limoeiro* (Recife 1885) pp. 66–7.

[25] S. J. Stein *Vassouras: a Brazilian coffee county, 1850–1900* (Cambridge, Mass. 1957) pp. 91, 108.

[26] Graham *op. cit.* p. 65.

[27] J. R. Scobie *Revolution on the pampas: a social history of Argentine wheat, 1860–1910* (Austin 1964) p. 11; J. C. Brown *A socioeconomic history of Argentina, 1776–1860* (Cambridge 1979) pp. 225–6; T. J. Hutchinson *Buenos Aires and Argentine gleanings* (London 1865) pp. 37, 60;

PP 1881 LXXXIX 433; Goodwin 'The Central Argentine Railway'.

28 Buenos Ayres Great Southern Railway Company (hereafter BAGS) *Report of the directors to the shareholders for the half-year ended June 30 1867* (hereafter *Half-yearly report* . . .) (London 1867) pp. 5–6, *Report of the directors to the shareholders and statement of the revenue and capital accounts for the year ended December 31 1867* (hereafter *Annual report* . . .) (London 1868) p. 6, *Half-yearly report* . . . *June 30 1868* p. 8, *Annual report* . . . *1868* p. 8; extract from Central Argentine report printed in *The Times* 25 March 1868 lle.

29 N. Bouwer to Baring Brothers, 8 Sept. 1877. Baring Archive House Correspondence (hereafter BAHC) 4.1.65 Pt I; *RT* 25 July 1891 p. 98.

30 República Argentina, Ministerio de Obras Públicas, Dirección General de Ferrocarriles *Estadística de los ferrocarriles en explotación, 1875–1935* (Buenos Aires 1937); Brasil, Ministério da Viação e Obras Públicas, Departamento Nacional de Estradas de Ferro *Estadística das estradas de ferro do Brasil, relativa ao ano de 1945* (Rio de Janeiro 1952) pp. 50–1.

31 Nogueira de Matos *Café e ferrovias* p. 117.

32 See Recife & São Francisco Pernambuco Railway Company *Prospectus* p. 2, copy enclosed, Consul A. Cowper, Pernambuco, to the Earl Clarendon, 15 April 1856, FO 84/996: 131–6.

33 MACOP *Relatório . . . segunda sessão da XIa legislatura* pp. 33–5; SP *Relatório que por occasião da abertura da assembléa legislativa provincial de S. Paulo no dia 3 de fevereiro de 1864 apresentado o Illmo. e Exmo. Sr. Conselheiro Doutor Vicente Pires da Motta presidente da mesma provincia* (hereafter *Relatório* . . .) (São Paulo 1864) p. 58. For an account of the company's initial expenses disbursed in connection with the recruitment of migrant labour, see SP *Documentos que acompanham o relatório que o Illmo. e Exmo. Sr. Conselheiro Doutor Vicente Pires da Motta apresentou à assembléa legislativa provincial no anno de 1863* (São Paulo 1863) p. 9.

34 MACOP *Relatório . . . terceira sessão da XIa legislatura.* See attached *Relatório apresentado ao Illm. Exm. Ministro* . . . p. 34.

35 MACOP *Relatório . . . terceira sessão de XIa legislatura* p. 31, *Relatório . . . segunda sessão da XIIIa legislatura* p. 14. During this period the San Paulo was beset with labour disputes, many of which appear to have been occasioned by the financial embarrassment of subcontractors and also by the scale of the construction works. Unlike other lines, which were built section by section, the SP Railway elected to undertake construction work on all sections concurrently. Whatever the cause, navvies employed on these works displayed a marked propensity to withdraw their labour. See also Antonio Corrêa Pacheco, Chief of Police, Itú, to Antonio da Costa Pinto, President of the Province of São Paulo, 16 Nov. 1870, Archivo do Estado de São Paulo (hereafter AESP) Ordem 1074: Lata 279: Oficios diversos – Itú, 1869–90.

36 S. Fenoaltea 'Los ferrocarriles y la industrialización italiana: analysis y reconsideración' in RENFE (ed.) *op. cit.* Although this calculation applies to Italy, the proportions are unlikely to be radically different for either the Argentine or Brazil. Sea freights would inflate equipment costs, the relative importance of which would be further enhanced by lower land prices (or the tendency for many Argentine companies to obtain possession of right of way free of charge). Wages and salaries paid to construction gangs were, nevertheless, the principal heading in the schedule of construction expenses.

37 Calculated from FFCC *Sud* and *Oeste* capitalization data in República Argentina *Segundo censo de la República Argentina, 1895* (Buenos Aires 1898) III 465–6; Province de Buénos-Ayres, Ministère de Gouvernement, Bureau de Statistique Générale *Annuaire statistique de la Province de Buénos-Ayres, 1882* (Buenos Aires 1883) p. 411.

38 Calculated from Bunge *Ferrocarriles* p. 178, *Una nueva economia* (Buenos Aires 1940) p. 187; República Argentina *Tercer censo nacional* (Buenos Aires 1917) x 389.

39 R. F. Foerster *The Italian emigration of our times* (Cambridge, Mass. 1919) pp. 230, 232, 235–8, 287–90, 297–8, 313; P. Monbeig *Pionniers et Planteurs de São Paulo* (Paris 1952) *passim*, especially pp. 100, 154–8, 173–8; T. H. Holloway 'The coffee *colono* of São Paulo, Brazil: migration and mobility, 1880–1930' in K. Duncan and I. Rutledge (eds) *Land and labour in*

Latin America: essays on the development of agrarian capitalism in the nineteenth and twentieth centuries (Cambridge 1977); Scobie, *Revolution on the pampas*, pp. 34–7, 45–50.
    40 R. H. Mattoon, 'Railroads, coffee and the growth of big business in São Paulo, Brazil' *HAHR* LVII 2 (1977).
    41 *Companhia Paulista* (hereafter *CP*) *Relatório da directoria da Companhia Paulista lido n sessão de assembléa geral em 29 de agosto de 1880* (hereafter *Relatório . . .*) (São Paulo 1880) annexo XII, *Relatório . . . agosto de 1883* annexo VIII.
    42 *Bradshaw's Railway Guide and Shareholders' Manual* 1887 XXXIX 438, 1888 XL 456, 1910 LXII 456, 1911 LXVI 461, 1915 LXVII 465; *The Universal Directory of Railway Officials, 1929* p. 265; *The Universal Directory of Railway Officials and Railway Year Book, 1934/5* p. 132, *1935/6* p. 133; D. Kelly *The ruling few or the human background to diplomacy* (London 1953) p. 293. The above references to director listings apply to the BAGS and demonstrate the tendency to transfer Buenos Aires-based general managers and London company secretaries to the board of directors upon retirement. Similar data can be provided for the other major networks.
    43 Mattoon *op. cit.*; V. B. Reber *British mercantile houses in Buenos Aires, 1810–1880* (Cambridge, Mass. 1979) p. 125.
    44 Mattoon *op. cit.*
    45 P. S. Pinheiro and M. H. Hall (eds) *A classe operária no Brasil, 1889–1930, documentos* vol. *II: contições de vida e de trabalho, relações com os empresarios e o estado* (São Paulo 1981) p. 113.
    46 A. E. Bunge *Ferrocarriles argentinos: contribución al estudio del patrimonio nacional* (Buenos Aires 1918) pp. 327–45; R. Thompson 'Organized labour in Argentina: the railway unions to 1922' (unpubl. doctoral dissertation, Oxford 1978) *passim*; D. Rock *Politics in Argentina, 1890–1930: the rise and fall of Radicalism* (Cambridge 1975) pp. 134–52. Rock and Thompson indicate the frailty of labour movement solidarity and the difficulties which had to be overcome in order to forge unity.
    47 J. de Imaz *Los que mándan* (Buenos Aires 1972) pp. 217–18; Thompson *op. cit.* pp. 280–1, 286, 288.
    48 P. B. Goodwin *Los ferrocarriles británicos y la UCR, 1916–1930* (Buenos Aires 1974) *passim*, especially pp. 32, 149–80, 219 86; Rock *op. cit.* pp. 138, 141–2, 234, 236. Rock takes a more pessimistic line, stressing the limits of official support and dangers of cooption. See also Walter Townley, British Minister at Buenos Aires, to Sir Edward Grey, 4 June 1907. FO 368/86 A102/22509/1907.
    49 *EFDPII As estradas de ferro no Brasil em 1879* (Rio 1880) pp. v–xiii.
    50 República Argentina *Segundo censo* III 463–4.
    51 Brasil, Ministéro da viação e Obras Públicas, Inspetoria des Estradas *Estatistica das estradas de ferro do Brasil relative ao ano de 1939 (Tomo XLII) Segunda Parte* (Rio de Janeiro, n.d.) p. 11; República Argentina, Ministerio de Obras Públicas, Dirección General de Ferrocarriles *Estadística de los ferrocarriles en explotación Tomo XLIX, ejercicio 1940/41* (Buenos Aires 1943) pp. 222, 226, 228, 230, 232, 234. The data and calculations relate to fiscal 1939. For an indication of divergent patterns of railway expansion in Brazil and the Argentine during the late nineteenth century, see E. A. Zalduendo *Libras y rieles* (Buenos Aires 1975) p. 83.
    52 C. F. Díaz Alejandro *Essays on the economic history of the Argentine Republic* (New Haven 1970) pp. 40–1; V. Vázquez-Presedo *El caso argentino: migración de factores, comercio exterior y desarrollo, 1875–1914* (Buenos Aires 1971) pp. 135–6. R. Córtes Conde *El progreso argentino, 1880–1914* (Buenos Aires 1979) pp. 211–40 contains a useful review of the literature and incorporates some new data.
    53 Foerster *op. cit.*, see sections on the Argentine and Brazil; V. Vázquez-Presedo *Estadísticas históricas argentinas: primera parte, 1875–1914* (Buenos Aires 1971) pp. 32, 41–4.
    54 S. J. Stein *The Brazilian cotton manufacture: textile enterprise in an underdeveloped area, 1850–1950* (Cambridge, Mass. 1957) pp. 21, 23.
    55 A. P. Cannabrava *Desenvolvimento da cultura do algodão na provincia de São Paulo* (São

Paulo 1951) pp. 9–10; Graham *op. cit.* pp. 67–8.

⁵⁶ *Companhia Ituana* (hereafter *CI*) *Relatório da directoria da Companhia Ituana apresentado à assembléa geral de accionistas em sessão de 7 de Janeiro de 1877* (hereafter *Relatório* . . .) (Itú 1872) annexo III; SP *Annaes* . . . *sessão de 1871* pp. 320–1, *Apêndice* . . . *de 1869* p. 2.

⁵⁷ *PP* 1876 LXXV 36.

⁵⁸ S P *Relatório* . . . *15 de fevereiro de 1886* p. 76; Cannabrava *Desenvolvimento* chap. 9 details the switch by cotton growers into manufacturing during the crisis of the 1870s.

⁵⁹ *PP* 1876 LXXV 36.

⁶⁰ MACOP *Relatório* . . . *primeira sessão da XIIIa legislatura* p. 99, *Relatório* . . . *primeira sessão da XVIIIa legislatura* p. 209; SP *Relatório* . . . *fevereiro de 1877* p. 54, *Annaes* . . . *1866* p. 58, *Annaes* . . . *1871* p. 220.

⁶¹ J. C. Chiaramonte *Nacionalismo y liberalismo económicos en Argentina, 1860–1880* (Buenos Aires 1971) chap. 3; C. Jones 'Ideology and the growth of the state in South America, 1860–1930' unpubl. mimeo.

⁶² E. Gallo and R. Córtes Conde *La formación de la Argentina moderna* (Buenos Aires 1967) pp. 76, 79; J. R. Scobie *Argentina: a city and a nation* (New York 1971) p. 144; Díaz Alejandro *op. cit.* pp. 213, 216, 294; Vázquez-Presedo *El caso* pp. 216–18, 220–1.

⁶³ E. C. Knight 'Cane-sugar industry' in W. Fieldwick (ed.) *Commercial Encyclopaedia* (London 1922).

⁶⁴ F. A. M. de Saes 'Expansão e declino das ferrovias paulistas, 1870–1940' in C. M. Pélaez and M. Buescu (ed.) *A moderna história econômica* (Rio de Janeiro 1976).

⁶⁵ E. Gallo 'Santa Fé en el segunda mitad del siglo XIX; transformaciones en su estructura social' in T. di Tella and T. Halperin Donghi (eds) *Los fragmentos del poder: de la oligarquía a la poliarquía argentina* (Buenos Aires 1969); Lewis 'La consolidación de la frontera'.

⁶⁶ *Revista de la economía argentina* XXI 257 (1938) 333; G. Di Tella and M. Zymelman *Las etápas del desarrollo económico argentino* (Buenos Aires 1967) pp. 237–9, 260, 281; Díaz Alejandro *op. cit.* pp. 436–7; Vázquez-Presedo *Estadísticas* pp. 83–4.

⁶⁷ Saes 'Expansão e declino'.

⁶⁸ D. C. M. Platt *Latin America and British trade, 1806–1914* (London 1972) pp. 90, 95–7; Vázquez-Presedo *Estadísticas* p. 76, *El caso* pp. 216–17; W. P. Giade *The Latin American economies: a study of their institutional evolution* (New York 1969) pp. 321, 375.

⁶⁹ A useful synthesis of the debate is to be found in F. R. Versiani *Industrial investment in an 'export' economy: the Brazilian experience before 1914* (University of London, Institute of Latin American Studies Working Paper no. 2). The classic work, however, remains W. Dean *The industrialization of São Paulo, 1880–1945* (Austin 1969). See also A. Villela Villanova and W. Suzigan *Política do governo e crescimento da econômia brasileira, 1889–1945* (Rio de Janeiro 1973).

⁷⁰ Bunge *Ferrocarriles* p. 81.

⁷¹ For differing assessments of the traffic-generating potential of the Ypanema Iron Foundry see SP *Relatório* . . . *no dia 2 de fevereiro de 1870* p. 28, *Relatório* . . . *fevereiro de 1877* p. 56, *Relatório* . . . *1878* p. 40, *Annaes* . . . *sessão de 1871* p. 3, *Annaes* . . . *sessão de 1871* p. 364, *Annaes* . . . *sessão de 1874* p. 309, *Companhia Sorocabana* (hereafter *CS*) *Relatório apresentado pela directoria da companhia Sorocobana à assembléa geral dos accionistas a 2 de janeiro do 1872* (hereafter *Relatório* . . .) (Sorocaba 1872) p. 5, *Relatório* . . . *10 de março de 1877* p. 8. See also J. Cechin 'A construção e operacão das ferrovias no Brasil no seculo XIX' (unpubl. master's dissertation, UNICAMP, 1978) pp. 83–90 for a survey of the literature pertaining to the status of the national iron and steel industry and attempts to promote its growth through the supply of railway material.

⁷² SP *Relatório* . . . *fevereiro de 1877* pp. 63–4. Most of the *paulista* railway companies' initial reports contain details of heavy expenditure on permanent way repair and renewals necessitated by rotting sleepers which resulted in frequent derailments, see SP *Relatório* . . . *5 de fevereiro de 1874* pp. 24–5.

[73] Mattoon *op. cit.*; Love *São Paulo* p. 3.

[74] SP *Relatório . . . 2 de fevereiro de 1876* pp. 34–5. The cost of a short stretch of urban highway in the Sorocaba region is shown to be approximately 70 per cent of the average mileage expenditure on building the *EFS*. See also MACOP *Relatório . . . segunda sessão da XVIa legislatura* p. 56 for average construction costs; note cheaply constructed lines in north-east and south.

[75] SP *Annaes . . . sessao de 1875* p. 409; Stein *Vassouras* pp. 106, 111; Mattoon *op. cit.* For a comparison of road and rail construction costs see SP *Relatório . . . 2 de fevereiro de 1863* pp. 7–8 and *Documentos que acompanhia o relatório que O Illmo. e Exmo. Sr. Conselheiro Doutor Vicente Pires da Motta apresentou à assembléa legislativa provincial no anno de 1863* p. 60, table IX, *Relatório . . . 2 de fevereiro de 1872* pp. 42, 46.

[76] Platt *op. cit.* pp. 90, 231–2.

[77] Province de Buénos-Ayres *Annuaire statistique* pp. 370–88.

[78] BAGS *Annual report . . . 1884* p. 16.

[79] *CP: Relatório . . . 29 de agosto de 1880* annexo xi; A. A. Pinto *História da viacão pública de São Paulo (Brasil)* (São Paulo 1903) pp. 104–11; Dean *op. cit.* p. 37 maintains that the *CP* was the largest industrial employer in the region as late as the turn of the century.

[80] *PP* 1884/5 lxxviii 160.

[81] BAW *Annual report . . . 1903*; BAGS *Annual report . . . 1904, Annual report . . . 1906; PP* 1903 lxxvi 787.

[82] SP *Mensagem apresentado ao Congresso Legislativo em 14 de julho de 1930 pelo Dr. Heitor Teixeira Penteado, vice-presidente em exercicio do estado de São Paulo* (São Paulo 1930) pp. 106–7; Duncan *op. cit.* p. 102.

[83] *The Times book on Argentina* (London 1927) p. 70.

[84] *Ibid.* pp. 80–1.

[85] Contrast the declining proportion of finished locomotives, rolling stock, etc. listed in Great Southern purchases of 'stores' and 'materials' in BAGS *Annual report . . . 1905, Half-yearly report , , . July–Dec. 1905,* and *Proceedings . . . 1927, Annual report . . . 1928, Proceedings . . . 1928.*

[86] *The Times book on Argentina* p. 92.

[87] While Mattoon *op. cit.* disagrees, most authors concur. See especially Dean *op. cit.*; Love *São Paulo* p. 55; W. Cano 'Raizes da concentracão industrial em São Paulo' (Ph.D. dissertation, UNICAMP 1975) pp. 36, 38; A. C. Castro *As ampresas estrangeiras no Brasil, 1860–1913* (Rio de Janeiro 1979) pp. 40–1, 42.

[88] *CP: Relatório . . . 26 de setembro de 1869* pp. 27–46, *Relatório . . . janeiro de 1872* pp. 33–47, *Relatório . . . fevereiro de 1876* pp. 59–64, *Relatório . . . agosto de 1880* pp. 99–128; *Companhia Mogiana* (hereafter *CM*) *Relatório da directoria provisoria da Companhia Mogyana lido em sessão da assemblea geral de accionistas no dia 30 de março de 1873* (hereafter *Relatório . . .*) (Mogi-Mirim 1873) p 11, *Relatório . . . setembro de 1873* pp. 35–51, *Relatório . . . setembro de 1883* annexo; SP *Relatório . . . 14 de fevereiro de 1873* p. 13. The share lists indicate a spread of holdings across the province, Mogi-Mirim, Campinas and São Paulo.

[89] Sir Ronald Macleay, British Minister at Buenos Aires, to the Earl Curzon, 7 March 1921, FO 371/5521, see enclosed annual report p. 24; BA&P *Annual report . . . 1920;* BAGS *Annual report . . . 1920;* BAW *Annual report . . . 1920.*

[90] BAGS *Proceedings . . . 1926.*

[91] Buenos Ayres and Pacific Railway Company Limited, meeting of chief officers: sessions 1–10, meeting held on 3 August 1928, Archivo del Ferrocarril Nacional General San Martín; Sir H. Chilton, British Ambassador at Buenos Aires, to Sir Samuel Hoare, 11 June 1935, enclosed memorandum by Lingeman dated 10 June 1935, FO 371/18633:87.

[92] Bunge *Ferrocarriles* p. 199. Coal represented an average of 80 per cent total fuel requirements in 1912–14, falling to less than half of that percentage in 1921–3 and to 31 per cent in 1936–8, see *Informes del Instituto de Estudios de Económicos del Transporte* vii (1942) 32.

⁹³ *The Times book on Argentina* pp. 70, 77, 81; E. J. Johnson *The railways of Argentina* (Washington 1942) p. 23.

⁹⁴ BA&P *Annual report . . . 1929*; BAGS *Proceedings . . . 1929*; BAW *Annual report . . . 1929*.

⁹⁵ Glade *op. cit.* pp. 321, 357, 375; Dean *op. cit.*; Vázquez-Presedo *El caso* pp. 222–5.

12

EXTERNAL FORCES AND THE TRANSFORMATION OF PERUVIAN COASTAL AGRICULTURE, 1880–1930[1]

Bill Albert

> The best lands of the coastal valleys are planted with cotton and sugar cane, not because they are suited to these crops, but because only these crops are important at the present moment [ca 1925] to English and American businessmen.
>
> José Carlos Mariátegui[2]

While there is a great deal of truth in this observation, which forms a major leitmotif in most studies of Peruvian coastal agriculture,[3] it is necessary to specify fully how and to what extent the agrarian structure here was determined by exogenous factors. It is, of course, a commonplace that the demand from Europe for primary commodities, together with European capital and credit, were influential. However, the particular structures which emerged also owed much to other external forces, including technological, political and ideological changes associated with the development of industrial capitalism in the metropolitan countries. These forces were brought into play on Peru's coast by the expansion of merchant capital, in its nineteenth-century role as the agent of industrial capital on the periphery.[4] As will be argued, the way in which merchant capital operated is of considerable importance in explaining the structural transformation of coastal agriculture. It must be stressed, however, that notwithstanding their importance, external forces played only a subordinate part in the process of change. As Marx wrote, although commerce has a powerful effect, 'To what extent it brings about a dissolution of the old mode of production depends on its solidarity and internal structure. And whither this process of dissolution will lead, in other words, what new mode of production will replace the old, does not depend on commerce, but on the character of the old mode of production itself.'[5] In order to understand the impact of outside influences on Peru, it is therefore necessary to begin with a brief sketch of the ecological peculiarities and the patterns of landholding, production, and labour supply in the coastal valleys in the early nineteenth century.

The characteristics of coastal agriculture

Describing the West Coast in 1911, James Bryce wrote, 'much of the coast of western South America as lies between the ocean and the

Cordillera of the Andes from Tumbez nearly to Valparaíso, for a distance of some two thousand miles, is dry and sterile. This strip of land varies in width from forty to sixty miles. It is crossed here and there by small rivers fed by the snows of the Andes behind, and along their banks are oases of verdure.'[6] Agriculture, confined to these oases, is entirely dependent on irrigation, and as Keith observes, 'the extent of cultivation was determined in the colonial period, as it still is, by the supply of water rather than by the availability of land'.[7] Consequently, some of the most bitter struggles in the coastal valleys were over water rights – struggles in which the owners of the large estates, who generally controlled the water-rationing system, invariably had the upper hand.[8] Further, the dependence on irrigation, combined with a relative lack of distinct seasonal temperature variation, means that on the Peruvian coast the timing of many processes of cultivation can be artificially controlled. This is most apparent in the north and, as will be shown, had extremely important implications for the employment of modern agricultural techniques, as well as for the regional concentration of particular crops. Coastal agriculturalists also benefited from the local availability of the relatively inexpensive fertilizer, guano.

The precise structure of landholding varied considerably from valley to valley, but during the colonial years increasingly it was the large estates which came to dominate in most regions.[9] It is also clear that from the early colonial period onwards commodity production had been a central feature on the coast, with plantations and small farms (*chacras*) producing cotton, sugar cane, maize, rice, wine, livestock and so on for both local and neighbouring Latin American markets.[10] The expansion of coastal exports after the mid-nineteenth century was, therefore, in keeping with the region's long-standing market orientation.

Throughout the colonial era the coastal estates had relied on slave labour, and although from independence slavery was in decline, it was not finally abolished until 1854.[11] The *hacendados*, who were generously indemnified by the government for freeing their slaves, had by this time begun bringing in indentured coolies from China,[12] a tactic adopted (often using labour from India) in many other plantation regions of the world. It was on the backs of this semi-slave labour force that the first stage of the country's agricultural modernization was carried out. The coolie traffic was ended in 1874 and from the 1880s *hacendados* once again faced the problem of labour scarcity. In the words of Juan de Arona, coastal agriculture was like the Venus de Milo, 'un cuerpo sin brazos'.[13] This was a long-term problem on the coast, where in 1876 only about a fifth of the country's population was found. Before the War of the Pacific the *hacendados* were forced to seek workers from outside the country, for despite their considerable political and economic power they were unable to force sufficient labour out of the subsistence and petty commo-

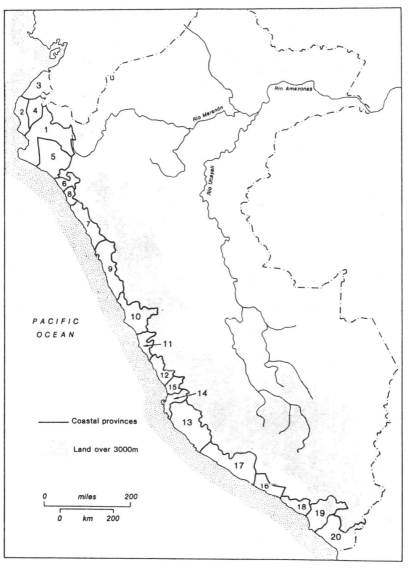

Map 5 Coastal Peru, 1880–1930*

* For names of provinces refer to p. 235.

dity sectors on the coast, and were too far away to set this process in motion in the more heavily populated *sierra*.

By the mid-nineteenth century Peruvian coastal agriculture was based on semi-servile labour and characterized by commodity production and the dominance of large estates. It is important to note that in this period, as today, because of differences in settlement patterns, soil, climate, availability of irrigation water and so forth, there was great variation in the productive structures of the individual valleys, underlining once again the importance of local factors in accounting for the specific direction of agriculture change (see Map 5 and Table 3).

External influences

Turning to the central concern of this paper – the pattern and degree of influence exercised by external factors – it is at once apparent that the revolutionary socio-economic changes taking place in Europe from the early nineteenth century had a powerful impact on the Peruvian coast. This was an inordinately complex phenomenon, and because of the limitations of space it is only possible to outline some of the more important aspects. Undoubtedly the most significant were the emergence of industrial capitalism in Europe, the accompanying rise of manufacture and increased popular purchasing power, the adoption of free trade by Britain as a means to further these developments, and revolutionary improvements in transport. All of these gave rise to a greatly increased demand for primary products. For cane growers, Britain's gradual abolition of import duties was of particular importance, as access to continental markets became increasingly restricted with the growth of protected beet sugar production.[14] While Britain's free trade policy encouraged primary producers, her efforts to end the slave trade were seen as threatening the future of many plantation areas. This trade had been an important pillar of Britain's merchant capitalism but was found to be increasingly outmoded, economically and ideologically, with the ascendancy of industrial capital.[15]

It was the general effects of Britain's anti-slavery campaign combined with the forces of nascent liberalism in Peru which undermined slavery on the coast, forcing the *hacendados* to seek a new source of labour. At the same time, Britain also indirectly helped to provide a short-term solution to this problem, as her forcible opening of China to Western commerce was an important factor contributing to the expansion of the coolie trade. There were two further related aspects of the development of productive forces in Europe which had a major impact on Peru's coast. The modernization of European agriculture was associated with both improved technology and greater attention to soil fertility. The latter gave rise to a strong demand for Peruvian guano, and it is clear that one result of the 'guano boom' was sizeable direct and indirect flows of

Table 3: Structure of Peruvian coastal agricultural production, 1929

Province (map ref)	Labour	Total cultivated hectares	Food crops	Rice	Cotton	Sugar	Cultivated pasture	Other
Tumbes (3)	1,608	1,908	807	—	—	—	—	1,101
Piata and Sullana (2 and 4)	-0,550	8,350	2,062	1,328	880	—	2,880	1,200
Piura (1)	7,294	20,078	1,381	2,864	12,997	184	2,652	—
Lambayeque (5)	10,352	26,306	11,266	11,856	127	996	1,461	600
Chiclayo (6)	19,144	41,317	10,293	10,648	10	15,205	4,604	557
Pacasmayo (8)	7,660	17,477	4,039	9,171	908	329	2,119	912
Trujillo (7)	22,267	39,237	8,126	1,519	518	21,857	5,504	1,713
Santa (9)	6,471	21,078	5,678	2,369	5,436	3,212	3,863	520
Chancay (10)	11,015	40,344	5,080	—	22,767	6,973	4,843	680
Lima (11)	10,420	38,430	6,856	114	17,723	4,217	7,562	1,958
Cañete (12)	6,724	24,714	2,879	9	18,646	808	1,817	555
Chincha (15)	3,987	19,405	4,862	—	11,434	—	1,349	1,760
Pisco (14)	6,375	13,795	2,563	—	10,340	—	823	69
Ica (13)	10,848	22,866	3,535	—	15,595	15	1,648	2,073
Camana (16 and 17)	6,880	4,933	1,712	791	985	305	905	235
Islay (18)	3,890	3,891	444	769	215	2,247	216	—
Moquegua (19)	10,344	12,889	6,260	—	937	25	4,574	1,093
Tacna (20)	2,432	3,441	501	1	1,753	3	950	232
	158,261	360,459	78,344 (21.7%)	41,439 (11.5%)	121,271 (33.6%)	56,376 (15.6%)	47,770 (13.3%)	15,258 (4.2%)
	—	—						

Notes: 'Food crops' include wheat maize, potatoes, sweet potatoes, yuca, beans. 'Other' includes grapes, coffee, olives and cocoa. Some of the provinces comprise areas which do not strictly fall within the definition of 'coastal', but the relatively small area involved does not seriously prejudice the data.

Source: Perú, Ministerio de Fomento, Dirección de Agricultura y Ganadería Estadística General Agro-Pecuaria del Perú del año 1929 (Lima 1932).

capital into cotton and sugar production.[16] This in turn allowed many *hacendados* to import new technology, that is, improved mills and processing equipment, steam ploughs, cultivators and railways, which were such an important feature of capitalist agriculture in the metropolitan countries.

Stimulated by these factors, cotton and sugar production on the coast began to rise from the 1860s. Cotton exports, which had averaged about 300 metric tons (mt) in the years 1855–64, spurred by the sharp price rises caused by the US Civil War, increased to an average of 2,700 mt in the following decade. Sugar showed a more dramatic rise, with exports climbing from 5,000 mt in 1866 to 83,500 mt by 1879. Associated with the export expansion was a stepped-up pace of land consolidation, especially by the sugar growers.[17] Fairly large-scale holdings had been the norm in most coastal valleys, but the greater attention given to export crops and the consequent need to gain more complete control of scarce irrigation water – sugar and cotton demanded greater amounts of water than other crops – accentuated this trend. While the growth in output of the two crops was dramatic, by 1875 together they still accounted for only about 15 per cent of total export earnings, the main commodities being guano and nitrates. The first period of agricultural modernization began to falter during the financial panic of the mid-70s, and finally came to an abrupt end in 1879 with the outbreak of the War of the Pacific and Chilean occupation.

Conditions facing coastal agriculturalists in the years following the war were extremely grim. Many estates had been physically devastated by the Chilean army, most *hacendados* were heavily in debt because of their pre-war modernization efforts, and the country's financial system lay in ruins. Moreover, labour supplies were unsure because the coolie trade had been stopped in 1874 as a result of US and British pressure on the Portuguese at Macao. To make matters worse, cotton prices had fallen and were to show no sustained improvement until the end of the century, and the increased dumping of bounty-fed beet sugar led to a major collapse in world sugar prices in 1883/4. From then until the First World War these prices never rose to more than half their previous levels.[18]

However, for the sugar producers the same forces of capitalist advance which underlay the growth of the beet sugar industry in Europe continued to provide a flood of technical innovations,[19] which by revolutionizing the process of cane sugar production made it possible for some cane-growing regions to compete effectively within the rapidly changing world market. This meant more than just the installation of new machinery, however. It involved changes in the organization and, eventually, in relations of production, for the technology embodied the seeds of change inherent in industrial capital and could not be totally divorced from the capitalist mode of production out of which it had arisen. This was not, however, a straightforward process. For example, the mounting cost of new equipment brought pressure on plantation owners to separate capital from labour (that is, abolish slavery). On the other hand, technical change tended to be concentrated in the processing stages of cotton and sugar production, and this gave rise to the need for more labour, particularly to harvest the expanded crop acreage required to supply the larger mills and gins. This was one reason for the planters' reluctance to abandon servile labour. They were in the end forced to, and it can be argued that although this owed much to the impact of imported European technology, it probably owed more to the related social and political changes in Europe which spawned liberalism and the anti-slavery movement.

Sugar cane: the scale and technology of production

Because of falling world prices in the last decades of the nineteenth century, Peru's sugar growers had either to adopt the new processes or go out of production. Many were, in fact, forced out, the number of *ingenios* falling from sixty-two in 1895 to only thirty-eight by 1913.[20] Production also became increasingly concentrated in the northern departments of Lambayeque and La Libertad (61 per cent by 1911/13)[21] where soil and climatic conditions were relatively more favourable for cane than in the central valleys. Moreover, the combined pressure of low sugar prices, costly new equipment, and the greater supplies needed by the larger mills, led to further land consolidation before the First World War, particularly in the Chicama valley, the country's most important producing area.[22] From the 1880s sugar was the single most important of Peru's export earners (mainly because other exports were depressed), and from the mid-1890s sugar exports rose sharply (see Table 4). By 1914 sugar provided 30 per cent of the country's exports; 40,000 hectares of coastal land was under cane, and the industry employed almost 20,000 workers [23]

Extraordinary high wartime prices brought a further expansion in cane acreage (25 per cent by 1920), production (40 per cent) and employment (30 per cent). At its high point in 1920, the sugar industry was responsible for 42 per cent of export earnings. This lofty position was not long maintained, as the steady fall in world prices from the mid-1920s made life increasingly difficult for most producers. By 1930 there were only twenty-one *ingenios* in production and the industry's export share had fallen to 10.9 per cent.[24] Although there was an increase in acreage and production in the north during the inter-war years, with the total collapse of the industry in the Lima valleys in the 1930s (there were but fourteen *ingenios* in the country by 1940), nationally there was little change.

Table 4: Peru's cotton and sugar exports: quantity and percentage of total exports 1880–1929 (ten year averages)

| | Sugar | | Cotton | | |
	Quantity (metric tons)	Share (per-centages)	Quantity (metric tons ginned fibre)	Share (per-centages)	Combined share of total exports (percentages)
1880–9	39,141	40	2,573	5	45
1890–9	64,414	32	5,918	8.5	40.5
1900–9	123,567	28	10,579	9	37
1910–9	181,404	22	21,800	14	36
1920–9	282,069	21	43,520	24	45

Sources: Shane J. Hunt *Price and quantum estimates of Peruvian exports, 1830–1962*, Discussion Paper no. 32, Woodrow Wilson School (Princeton 1973) pp. 38–40; Peru, Ministerio de hacienda y Comercio *Extracto estadístico del Perú 1934–1935* (Lima 1937) p. 135.

As suggested above, technical change in sugar-making was heavily biased towards large-scale units of production. In some countries (Cuba, Puerto Rico) this led to the formation of large mills (*centrales*) which ground the cane of independent or semi-independent growers (*colonos*), while in other regions (Peru, Hawaii), extensive enterprises controlling both cane-growing and milling came to dominate.[25] It appears that the reliance on irrigation and the need to coordinate rigorous planting, cane maturation, cutting and delivery in order to maintain an uninterrupted flow of high-quality cane to the mills – which in both Peru and Hawaii operated on a year-round basis – helps to account for the development of agro-industrial estates in both countries.[26] In Peru it was not simply that cane was grown on irrigated land, but also that the general shortage of water made producers want to monopolize as much land and the attendant water rights as possible. Finally, reliance on irrigation and the lack of distinct seasonality, especially in the northern valleys, making it possible to control the sequence of field processes and operate almost all year round,[27] was a considerable advantage. It allowed both higher cane yields and sucrose content to be realized, and the fuller utilization of the mills and factories, which in regions where the harvest was seasonally determined (Cuba) stood idle for five months a year. Ecological conditions in Peru were, therefore, extremely favourable in relation to the course of technical change, and this is important in explaining the relative success of the Peruvian industry from the late nineteenth century. For example, by the First World War cane yields on the coast matched those of the advanced Hawaian industry, and although factory methods needed to be improved, costs of production were lower than in Cuba and almost half of those in Hawaii and Puerto Rico.[28]

The rise of cotton and its domestic consequences

Although there was some recovery in cotton prices in the early 1890s, it was not until the turn of the century that this movement was sustained. Besides the effect of better prices, from the later 1890s cotton production was stimulated by the establishment of textile mills in Lima and Arequipa, by increased British demand for both cottonseed cake and Peru's Aspero cotton, and by the setting up of modern ginning facilities.[29] Cotton production began to rise, particularly from 1905, and by the First World War the volume of exports was three times its 1900 level, while the value had risen more than fourfold, rivalling that of sugar. Although estimates are unreliable, by 1915–16 about 55,500 hectares were under cotton and 20,000 workers were employed in its cultivation.[30] With the introduction of the locally developed wilt-resistant Tanguis variety and favourable prices, cotton acreage, production and employment almost doubled in the ten years to 1925.[31] At this time cotton accounted for 32 per cent of total exports – almost three times that of sugar.

The expansion of cotton from the turn of the century was particularly marked in the far north (Piura) and in the central and central southern valleys.[32] In Ica as well as many of the Lima valleys, cotton had completely displaced sugar by 1914. Cane continued to be a major crop in the valleys of Cañete, Rimac and Carabayallo, but the area under cotton here grew much more rapidly, especially during the First World War, and in the 1920s and 30s cotton entirely replaced cane in these valleys. This changeover can be traced to a number of factors. As mentioned above, compared with the north, soil and climate in the central valleys were relatively less suitable for cane, and yields were in consequence lower.[33] Wages were also higher in the central regions,[34] and because of shorter periods of high labour demand, cotton growers could more easily support high wages than could cane producers. Finally, technical change for cotton as compared with sugar was quite modest, processing could be separated from production, and capital requirements were relatively low.[35] As cotton prices moved upwards relative to those for sugar from 1900, it became increasingly attractive, particularly for the small and medium-sized landowners unable to afford the expensive and complex machinery needed to produce sugar competitively, to switch to cotton. Summing up the organization of this sector, Thorp and Bertram comment:

> In the early twentieth century cotton was grown largely by tenants and smallholders, with a few production units organized on a large scale; and consequently the owners of large areas of cotton land were often as much rentiers as capitalists. From the First World War, this situation gradually began to change, as larger and more capitalist production units became more common . . . By the end of the twenties,

however, this trend had not reached the point where it seriously modified the structure of the sector.[36]

Coastal agriculture and foreign control

Lack of adequate data makes it difficult to draw a comprehensive picture of the changing structure of coastal agriculture over this period, but a few general observations can be made. The most striking change was the massive expansion in the acreage devoted to, and the production and export of, cotton and sugar. This was associated with, among other things, greater regional specialization (see Table 3, p. 235), the import of advanced technology, the development of extensive modern integrated sugar estates, and the emergence of large concentrations of wage labour in many coastal valleys. It has also been claimed that the increased production of export crops, particularly cotton immediately after the First World War, led to a decline in food crop acreage and consequent shortages in the domestic market.[37] This widely accepted idea has recently been challenged by Bertram and Thorp,[38] who argue that in the period 1905–30 'export crops did not force an absolute contraction in the area under food crops, although export crops obviously had preferential claim on increments in cultivable area'. Notwithstanding the possible maintenance of food crop acreage, it is apparent that in these years the coastal valleys were drawn much more closely into the world market.

Assessments of the determinants and implications of the process of incorporation within the international economy vary. A commonly held view of the modernization of Peruvian coastal agriculture sees foreign control, both direct and indirect, as a pivotal factor. Dealing first with direct control, it is clearly inapplicable to the cotton sector, where estates have been owned and operated in the main by Peruvians. For sugar, however, it is generally claimed that in the difficult years after 1883 many 'traditional' *hacendados* were forced out and the industry transformed, if not completely taken over, by foreign capital.[39] If direct foreign control is judged in terms of where capital was accumulated and where economic decisions were made, the case for a substantial degree of foreign ownership is weak.[40] At a most generous estimate, foreign-owned estates accounted for no more than 25 per cent of output in 1912, and this proportion had been slightly reduced by 1930.[41]

The accusation of foreign takeover has been made primarily because many of the successful sugar producers, such as the Larco brothers, Henry Swayne and Enrique Gildemeister, were immigrants.[42] Although this in itself raises interesting questions, including the importance of capital imports, it does not represent foreign control in the normal sense. Furthermore, even the entry of new planters after the War of the Pacific has been exaggerated. In the valleys of Lambayeque, Zaña, Santa Catalina, Pativilca, Supe and Tambo, the major haciendas may have expanded in area but almost all were controlled by the same families in 1913 as they had been in 1876.[43] The principal new entrants in this period were Gildemeister, who purchased Casa Grande and Sausal from Luis Albract, another German immigrant, in 1889, and the two foreign merchant houses, W. R. Grace & Co. (Hacienda Cartavio) and Wm. and Jn. Lockett (the Haciendas San Jacinto and Santo Barbara). Both firms took over the estates in order to recover debts.[44]

The question of indirect foreign control is far less clear-cut. Both sugar and cotton producers depended on foreign merchants for the marketing of their products, as agents for the purchase of equipment, for short-term credit and for the occasional mortgage loan. From 1883, with local finance unobtainable, the merchants' position was substantially strengthened. For cotton growers the merchant link was probably more pervasive than for sugar producers, as not only were the former almost entirely dependent on loans secured against forthcoming crops – and there was no local source of this type of financial support until 1930 – but from the second decade of the twentieth century merchant houses began to set up central gins in the cotton growing regions, thereby moving towards, the control of processing as well as of financing and marketing.[45] For sugar producers the merchants were also very important, and in the period after the War of the Pacific many growers survived only by getting strong financial backing from merchant houses, for example the Aspillagas (Hacienda Cayalti) from Henry Kendall & Sons, the Larcos (Hacienda Chiclin) from Graham Rowe & Co.[46] In those cases where estates had close ties with merchant houses (and most did), this placed the latter in a position to influence decisions, if only by withholding money for new projects or by refusing to extend short-term credit. However, while they offered advice, criticized, and argued with their clients, estate correspondence suggests that their power was circumscribed and that in any case they shared an overriding common interest with local producers.[47] Moreover, from the late 1890s *hacendados* were able to raise funds from local banks, and this reduced their financial dependence on foreign merchants.[48]

Within the 'rules' of the world capitalist system, the merchants' provision of an infrastructure to link the peripheral primary producer with the metropolitan consumer was strictly legitimate. It also seems that on the whole foreign investment in the coastal export sectors was limited, and that the great bulk of the profits accrued to the Peruvian producers and not the foreign investors or merchant houses.[49] If for coastal export crops a direct drain of wealth was not a significant consideration – as it clearly *was* for mining and petroleum, both almost entirely foreign-owned by 1920[50] – what problems, if any, were caused by the undeniably strong external influences on the agrarian structures of Peru's coastal valleys?

The answer to this lies in an assessment of the argument that the effect of being drawn into the international economy through the agency of merchant capital, and having export sectors which were essentially subordinate to the interests of metropolitan industrial capital, was to forestall progressive change in Peru. This is clearly what Mariátegui had in mind: 'The landowning class has not been transformed into a capitalist middle class, ally of the national economy. Mining, commerce and transport are in the hands of foreign capital. The *latifundistas* have been satisfied to serve as the latter's intermediaries in the production of cotton and sugar.'[51] He argued that the way in which export agriculture, particularly sugar, had developed blocked progressive capital transformation in Peru. This was, he said, because of the retention, under a capitalist veneer of commodity production and the use of modern machinery, of the semi-feudal *latifundia* and its attendant servile labour relations.[52] Furthermore, for Mariátegui the town was the seedbed of modern capitalism, and the *latifundia*, because of its direct links with the world market,

> prevents the town from fulfilling the role which would maintain it and guarantee its development within the rural economy of the valleys. The hacienda by taking over trade and transport as well as the land and dependent industries, deprives the town of livelihood and condemns it to a sordid and meagre existence . . . In Peru, the meaning of republican emancipation has been violated by entrusting the creation of a capitalist economy to the spirit of the fief – the antithesis and negation of the spirit of the town.[53]

In a number of respects Mariátegui's analysis is similar to that more rigorously formulated by Geoffrey Kay.[54] The latter argues that in this period the role of primary exporters was to provide cheap raw materials and wage goods to the advanced capitalist countries, thereby contributing towards offsetting the tendency of the rate of profit to fall.[55] Merchant capital provided the means by which, through unequal exchange,[56] industrial capital could draw commodities from the periphery. He argues that, although merchant capital stimulated commodity production, because it derived its surplus in the sphere of circulation it had no inherent interest – as did industrial capital – in revolutionizing the system of production. He concludes that because of the central role assumed by merchant capital, the progressive transformation of the peripheral regions, envisaged by Marx and Lenin, was never achieved. How accurate is this line of analysis when applied to the case of Peruvian coastal agriculture? Was merchant capital able to profit by making only minor changes in existing methods of production and productive relations? Taking this a little further, did merchant capital actually retard progressive capitalist change in Peru?

Looking first at the sugar industry, it is clear that merchant capital could not profit by simply using the forms of production existing in the 1850s. As has been argued, this was made impossible by certain technological and ideological considerations contingent upon the development of European capitalism, together with the growth on the Continent of a subsidized and protected beet sugar industry. All of this had a powerful impact, completely revolutionizing the structure of cane sugar production throughout the world. In Peru these pervasive external forces, when combined with the favourable conditions and agrarian structure found in the coastal valleys, led to the emergence by 1914 of sophisticated large-scale plantations, whose production for export and use of both advanced technology and, in many cases, corporate organization, marked them as capitalist enterprises. But what of the relations of production – a major determinant of the estates' wider transforming potential? This is a key question, as critics including Mariátegui and Kay have argued that the maintenance, and even strengthening, of pre-capitalist labour relations were the result of the growth of primary export sectors and a barrier to progressive economic development.[57] To answer this question it is necessary to outline briefly the system of labour recruitment employed by the *hacendados* from the last decades of the nineteenth century.

Deprived of new inflows of Chinese coolies from the 1880s, coastal *hacendados* turned their attention to the large pool of potential workers in the *sierra*, using a form of contract labour known as *enganche*.[58] This system had a number of variants and changed over time, but essentially consisted of an agreement to work for a specified period (often ninety days) in return for a cash advance which had to be worked off on the coast. There is considerable debate as to the nature of this system. For example, Mariátegui argued that it represented 'feudal methods which persist in coastal agriculture' and that by using this form of recruitment 'the large proprietors block the appearance of free-wage contracting, a functional necessity of liberal capitalist economy'.[59] Formally, however, it can be argued that the *enganchado* was a wage-labourer, in that there was a market for the sale of his labour power and the surplus was extracted through a wage relation rather than a traditional or land-based servile obligation. Nonetheless, the fact that many of these workers retained smallholdings in the *sierra*, were only temporarily on the coast, and were subjected to coercion by the contractors and to an all-encompassing repressive paternalism on the estates, suggests that it would be incorrect to see them as a 'classic' or full-fledged proletariat. *Enganche* is more properly seen as a transitional mechanism which over time did contribute to the formation of a rural proletariat on the coast. By the early 1930s the sugar workers in the northern valleys were one of the most militant groups in the country, and provided a vital basis of working-class support for the radical Aprista Party.[60]

There is an important feature of the structure of the labour force on the sugar estates that deserves comment, for it relates to the question of the relationship of imported technology and changes in productive relations. By the First World War there was a growing number of permanent wage-labourers on the estates, in the mills and factories, operating the railways, tractors and so on. However, up to 85 per cent of the workforce remained in the field, and of these the majority were contracted workers.[61] The ratio between field and factory remained about the same into the 1930s, although there is evidence that the proportion of migrant workers declined.[62] The dual labour structure reflected to a large degree the uneven nature of technical change as between processing and growing. This in turn can be traced to the fact that improvements in cane sugar fabrication were derived in the main from European refining and beet sugar industries, in which productive priorities and relative factor costs favoured labour-saving innovations. In the cane fields, on the other hand, the new techniques used in Peru were less revolutionary,[63] borrowed from a more general pool of agricultural improvements, and harvesting, the task which demanded the greatest labour imput, was left virtually untouched until the 1950s.[64] Sugar estates, therefore, needed a relatively small number of full-time skilled workers and a much larger number of unskilled workers, whose status as part-time proletarians admirably suited the *hacendados*. As the migrant workers were not entirely wage-dependent, the *hacendados* could pay them a lower 'single wage',[65] while at the same time constant labour turnover made unionization more difficult. Notwithstanding these limitations, the fact remains that within a relatively short time a self-conscious rural proletariat was formed on the sugar estates.[66] As will be argued, because of a combination of market and technical factors it was impossible for merchant capital not to instigate a radical transformation in the sugar industry.

For cotton, unlike sugar, there were relatively few sophisticated technological developments in either growing or processing. There were, of course, some important improvements in ginning equipment, pest and seed control and in the development of new varieties, but none of these required massive capital outlay or a fundamental reorganization of production. Merchant capital could, therefore, function in a more traditional manner in this sector, controlling credit, marketing and sometimes ginning. The main change in cotton-growing in Peru, as in many other cotton producing regions, was the emergence of sharecropping (*yanaconaje*) as the principal form of productive organization.[67] This was supplemented during the short planting and harvesting seasons by contracted labour from the *sierra*. Like *enganche*, *yanaconaje* has been labelled as semi-feudal, but although it did have pre-conquest roots, it was developed on the coast as a form of direct commodity production.

Nonetheless, the productive relations on the cotton estates remained clearly non-capitalist, in contrast to those on the sugar haciendas. Merchant capital seems to have played a far more limited transforming role in cotton than in sugar.

What of Mariátegui's claim that the structure of export agriculture, dominated by large landholdings, was semi-feudal and, by stifling the growth of the towns, prevented more widespread capitalist development? Although a legacy from the colonial era, large landholding were favoured in the nineteenth century through a combination of local conditions and the exigencies of the international economy. In this sense the sugar industry can be said to have followed more or less what Lenin defined as the 'Prussian path' to capitalist development, by which 'medieval relationships in landownership are not liquidated at one stroke; they gradually adapt themselves to capitalism and for this reason capitalism for a long time retains semi-feudal elements'.[68]

With respect to the towns, the general point must be made that urbanization cannot be equated in a simple way with capitalist or industrial developments. The process was far more complex. In Peru the problem was not so much that the towns in the sugar-growing valleys were destroyed by the large estates, although some smaller ones were, but rather that their development was generally stimulated by the expansion of sugar exports, and when in the late 1920s sugar went into decline, the nearby towns followed.[69] It was not that capitalism had failed to develop. The difficulty stemmed from the fact that it had developed based on a single crop, and being totally dependent on the world market it was extremely vulnerable. This in turn limited its power to generate more widespread or sustained change in the rest of the economy. Finally, it must be remembered that unlike the primary export sectors in some countries, cotton and sugar together never reached the overall dominance in the economy as, for example, sugar did in Cuba or Hawaii.[70] While these crops may have dominated regionally, it would be wrong to see either of them as the key to the transformation or stagnation of the entire Peruvian economy, the leading sectors of which by the early twentieth century – mining and petroleum – were foreign-owned.

The transition from merchant capitalism

Although local conditions were of transcendent importance, the transformation of Peruvian coastal agriculture was profoundly influenced by, and cannot be understood except within the context of, the expansion of industrial capitalism in Europe. As the nineteenth century progressed, the coastal valleys were drawn more fully into the world division of labour, and in this process merchant capital was instrumental. But contrary to Kay's argument, there was a substantial degree of materially progressive change (that is, development of forces of production, capital accumulation, emergence of wage labour) on the coast, especially on the sugar estates. Although merchant capital may have preferred to take productive structures as it found them, as Kay admits, 'merchant capital in so far as it acts as its [industrial capital's] agent is forced to adopt a similar code', to pay more attention to the process of social reproduction.[71] This was clearly the case in the nineteenth century, as the growing demand from Europe for large and uninterrupted supplies of food and raw materials necessitated a fundamental reorganization of production in many peripheral regions.[72]

Furthermore, it seems that the impact of merchant capital in these areas was strongly conditioned by the technological imperatives of industrial capital. This is reflected in Peru not only in the different productive structures of sugar and cotton, but also in the split between field and factory on the sugar estates. Sugar was the only major tropical commodity which could also be produced in Europe. This led to both fierce competition in the world market and substantial improvements in processing which, together with the ending of slavery, forced cane producers to revolutionize their methods. In this case merchant capital could not simply take advantage of or make minor changes to existing modes of production. It had either to transform itself into industrial capital (for instance, merchants taking over sugar estates) or give encouragement to local industrial capital. This accounts to a large degree for the fact that the Peruvian sugar industry exhibited a higher level of development, in terms of both forces and relations of production, than cotton. For the latter crop technical advance was relatively slight, and merchant capital could flourish without involving itself closely with, or transforming, the process of production. Finally it must be stressed that, as important and powerful as external forces were in helping to shape the agrarian structures on the coast, the pattern which emerged (see Map 5 and Table 3, pp. 233 and 235) reflected most strongly the ecological conditions, the patterns of landholding and the historical evolution of the individual coastal valleys.

Notes

[1] I would like to thank W. M. Mathew for his most helpful comments.

[2] José Carlos Mariátegui *Seven interpretative essays on Peruvian reality* (Austin 1971) p. 68.

[3] On the history of agriculture on Peru's coast see Robert G. Keith *Conquest and agrarian change. The emergence of the hacienda system on the Peruvian coast* (London 1976); Susan Ramirez-Horton 'Land tenure and the economics of power in colonial Peru' (unpubl. Ph.D. thesis, University of Wisconsin 1977); Juan Rolf Engleson 'Social aspects of agricultural expansion in coastal Peru, 1825–1878' (unpubl. Ph.D. thesis, University of California at Los Angeles 1977); Alejandro Garland *La industria azucarera en el Perú, 1550–1895* (Lima 1895); Pablo Macera *Las plantaciones azucareras en el Perú 1821–1875* (Lima 1974); Peter F. Klarén *Modernization, dislocation and aprismo: origins of the Peruvian Aprista Party* (Austin 1973), 'Social and economic consequences of modernization in the Peruvian sugar industry, 1879–1930' in K. Duncan and I. Rutledge (eds) *Land and labour in Latin America* (Cambridge 1977); Bill

Albert *An essay on the Peruvian sugar industry 1880–1920 and the letters of Ronald Gordon, administrator of the British Sugar Corporation in Cañete, 1914–1920* (Norwich 1976); Claude Collin-Delavaud *Les régions côtières de Pérou septentrional* (Lima 1968); Manuel Burga *De la encomienda a la hacienda capitalista: el Valle del Jequetepeque del siglo XVI al XX* (Lima 1976).

    [4] See above, p. 240.

    [5] *Capital* vol. III, ch. 20.

    [6] James Bryce *South America. Observations and impressions* (New York 1912) p. 39. On the physical features of the coast, see Preston James *Latin America* (New York 1941) pp. 172–4.

    [7] Keith *op. cit.* p. 12.

    [8] Klarén *Modernization* p. 12.

    [9] Engleson claims that in the period 1824–40 a few hundred individuals owned and administered the principal coastal haciendas. Engleson *op. cit.* p. 315.

    [10] Keith *op. cit.* chap. 3; Susan Ramirez-Horton 'The sugar estates of the Lambayeque Valley 1670–1800: a contribution to Peruvian agrarian history' Land Tenure Research Paper no. 58 (Madison, Wisc. 1974) *passim*.

    [11] Macera *op. cit.* pp. xxv–xlv.

    [12] On the Chinese in Peru, see Macera *op. cit.* pp. cix–cxxi; Watt Stewart *Chinese bondage in Peru. A history of the Chinese coolie in Peru, 1849–1874* (Durham, N.C. 1951); M. J. Gonzalez 'Cayalti: the formation of a rural proletariat on a Peruvian sugar cane plantation, 1875–1933' (unpubl. Ph.D. thesis, University of California, Berkeley 1978) chaps 5 and 6.

    [13] Quoted in Macera *op. cit.* p. lxxviii.

    [14] Noel Deere *The history of sugar* (London 1950) II. 471–500.

    [15] Eric Williams *From Columbus to Castro, the history of the Caribbean 1492–1969* (London 1970) pp. 280–327; Howard Temperley 'Capitalism, slavery and ideology' *Past and Present* no. 7 (1977) *passim*.

    [16] Macera *op. cit.* pp. lxv–lxvi; Burga *op. cit.* pp. 174–8. Guano revenue allowed the government to consolidate the internal debt by selling bonds in Europe in the 1850s, and this provided the funds for the indemnification of the *hacendados* for the loss of their slaves.

    [17] Albert *op. cit.* pp. 40a–64a.

    [18] Deere *op. cit.* pp. 471–508; Williams *op. cit.* pp. 374–91.

    [19] Most of the new elaboration techniques were developed in beet production. See Deere *op. cit.* vol. II ch. *passim*.

    [20] Albert *op. cit.* p. 110a.

    [21] *Ibid.* p. 35a.

    [22] *Ibid.* pp. 40a–64a; Klarén *Modernization* pp. 3–23.

    [23] *Ibid.* pp. 28a–29a, 130a, 164a.

    [24] Perú, Ministerio de Hacienda y Comercio *Extracto Estadístico del Perú 1940* (Lima 1941) pp. 210–3, 300, 307.

    [25] US Department of Commerce, Bureau of Foreign and Domestic Commerce *The cane sugar industry. Agricultural, manufacturing and marketing costs in Hawaii, Puerto Rico, Louisiana and Cuba*, Miss. Series no. 53 (Washington D.C. 1917) pp. 26, 252. In 1914/15 88.5 per cent of cane in Hawaii was grown by the mills, while in Cuba 80 per cent was grown by *colonos*.

    [26] Gerardo Klinge *Notas sobre la industria azucarera del Hawaii* (Lima 1928) p. 15.

    [27] Douglas Horton *Haciendas and cooperatives. A preliminary study of latifundist agriculture and agrarian reform in Northern Peru*, Research Paper no. 53, Land Tenure Centre (Madison, Wisc. 1973) pp. 17–18. Mills were generally shut down for two months a year for repairs.

    [28] Albert *op. cit.* pp. 76a–9a. Lower costs in Peru were largely a function of low wages. Furthermore, the relative success of the industry may account for the fact that despite the sugar producers' powerful position in the government (through the Civilista Party) there was little direct assistance to the industry.

    [29] Rosemary Thorp and Geoffrey Bertram *Peru 1890–1977. Growth and policy in an open economy* (London 1978) p. 54.

    [30] Albert *op. cit.* p. 144a.

[31] *Extracto Estadístico 1940* p. 208.

[32] Albert *op. cit.* pp. 149a–4a.

[33] *Ibid.* p. 133a.

[34] *Ibid.* pp. 170a, 176a.

[35] Horton *op. cit.* p. 5.

[36] Bertram and Thorp *op.cit.* p. 53.

[37] Albert *op. cit.* pp. 156a–60a.

[38] Bertram and Thorp *op. cit.* p. 134.

[39] Klarén *Modernization* pp. 8–11.

[40] For an incisive counter-argument see M. Burga and A. Flores Galindo *Apogeo y crises de la república aristocrática* (Lima 1979) pp. 167–8.

[41] This figure has been calculated by including as foreign the haciendas of Cartavio (W. R. Grace & Co.), Santa Barbara and San Jacinto (British Sugar Co.), Tambo Real (Peruvian Sugar Estates Ltd), Puente Pierda (Milne & Co.), but excluding Gildemeister's Casa Grande. See Albert *op. cit.* pp. 49a–50a.

[42] Thorp and Bertram *op. cit.* p. 43.

[43] Albert *op. cit.* pp. 40a–64a.

[44] There were other ownership changes, particularly in the Lima valleys, see Albert *op. cit.* pp. 56a–61a.

[45] Thorp and Bertram *op. cit.* p. 52.

[46] Klarén 'Social and economic consequences of modernization' p. 236.

[47] Based primarily on a review of the correspondence between the Aspillagas and their British agents, Henry Kendall & Sons. Cayalti MSS, Kendall Corr. (Archivo Agraria, Lima).

[48] Albert *op. cit.* p. 82.

[49] Thorp and Bertram *op. cit.* p. 53.

[50] *Ibid.* chap. 5.

[51] Mariátegui *op. cit.* chap. 5.

[52] *Ibidl* p. 17.

[53] *Ibid.* pp. 19, 21.

[54] G. Kay *Development and underdevelopment. A Marxist analysis* (London 1975) chap. 5.

[55] *Ibid.* p. 101.

[56] Kay uses this term to denote the way in which merchant capital derives its surplus. He strongly disagrees with Emmanuel's concept of unequal exchange; see Kay *op. cit.* pp. 107–19.

[57] See also Ernesto Laclau *Politics and ideology in Marxist theory* (London 1977) pp. 30–2.

[58] There are a number of works which deal with *enganche*: see Klarén *Modernization* pp. 26–32; Albert *op. cit.* pp. 89a–102a; C. D. Scott 'Peasants, proletarianization and the articulation of modes of production: the case of sugar-cane cutters in Northern Peru, 1940–69' *Journal of Peasant Studies* III 3 (1976); Peter Blanchard 'The recruitment of workers in the Peruvian sierra at the turn of the century: the *enganche* system' *Inter-American Economic Affairs* XXXIII 3 (1979). Contracted Japanese workers were also used on the coast from 1899.

[59] Mariátegui *op. cit.* pp. 62–3.

[60] Klarén *Modernization* chaps 2 and 3.

[61] Albert *op. cit.* pp. 164a–6a.

[62] M. Gonzales *op. cit.* p. 245.

[63] The impact of the Fowler steam plough is an exception to this. It permitted a great increase in the area of land which could be profitably cultivated. This, of course, intensified demand for labour.

[64] An important reason for this was the major technological problems associated with mechanizing cane-cutting. See C. D. Scott *Machetes, machines and agrarian reform: the political economy of technical choice in the Peruvian sugar industry, 1954–74* (Norwich 1979)).

[65] Lewis Taylor 'Main themes in agrarian capitalist development: Cajamarca, Peru,

1880–1976' (unpubl. Ph.D. thesis, Liverpool 1979) p. 164.

[66] The first widespread outbreak of unrest occurred in 1912. There were other incidents during the First World War and a major confrontation in the Chicama Valley in the early 1920s. See Albert *op. cit.* pp. 178a–218a.

[67] José Matos Mar *Yanaconaje y reforma agraria en el Perú* (Lima 1976). Also Albert *op. cit.* pp. 246a–64a.

[68] Lenin 'The agrarian question in Russia at the end of the nineteenth century' *Selected Readings* vol. I (n.d.) p. 210.

[69] Albert *op. cit.* pp. 85a–7a.

[70] In 1914 sugar accounted for 77 per cent of Cuba's exports and 80 per cent of Hawaii's. US Dept of Commerce *op. cit.* pp. 96, 250.

[71] Kay *op.cit.* p. 101.

[72] Kay concedes that a new productive organization was established but argues that because of its low capitalization and dependence on large numbers of unskilled workers 'it would not be completely correct' to see them as capitalist. Kay *op.cit.* p. 102. For a criticism of this position see Henry Bernstein 'Underdevelopment and the law of value. A critique of Kay' *Journal of Political Economy* VI (1976) 57 60.

13

BRITISH IMPERIALISM IN URUGUAY: THE PUBLIC UTILITY COMPANIES AND THE *BATLLISTA* STATE, 1900–1930

M. H. J. Finch

This chapter is primarily concerned to analyze the behaviour of the largest British-owned public utility companies in Uruguay, and the relations which British interests in general enjoyed with the host country. First, however, it is necessary to indicate the general framework of the analysis.

Relations of imperialism are here assumed to exist between two countries in which the forces of production are at different levels of development, which both participate in the international capitalist system, and in which one country depends on the other as a major source of capital and as an important export market. This framework is expressed in sufficiently wide terms for the discussion of the Anglo-Uruguayan connection not to become a sterile debate as to whether or not it was 'imperialist'. Rather than seeking evidence of political interference, coercion, or a disproportionate share of the gains as evidence of imperialism, this chapter views the impact of a dominant nation on a dependent partner as structural. Financial, commercial and political dealings between two countries at different levels of development – still less the activities of individual companies – are not to be separated and analyzed for imperialist content, since they acquire their impact in a combined and complex manner.¹ Accordingly, the first section of this chapter describes briefly the determinants of the relationship between Britain and Uruguay. Subsequently a more detailed examination is made of the relations between British public utility enterprise operating in Uruguay and the Uruguayan state in the *batllista* period.

The Anglo-Uruguayan nexus and the emergence of 'batllismo'

British influence in Uruguay grew from uncertain beginnings, from a small occupying force in 1807 to a profound economic penetration by the end of the nineteenth century. By 1900, 'the economic infrastructure of Uruguay was concentrated in English hands and British informal empire had become a fact of life. British capital and enterprise dominated transportation, communications, utilities and insurance, and occupied the leading position in banking, meat processing and ranching.'² Even in 1914 almost all of Uruguay's foreign debt – in per capita terms the highest of any South American country – was held in London. The predominant position of British capital had its counterpart in the leading share of the Uruguayan import market held by British exporters before the First World War (Table 5). Although the small size of Uruguay entailed that in absolute terms the British economic interest was considerably less than in Argentina, Brazil or Chile, it also meant that British capital was advantageously placed to bring influence to bear on the Uruguayan state, whose financing so much depended on the availability of British loans.

However, by the beginning of the twentieth century British hegemony in Uruguay was under challenge, for which developments both within Uruguay and outside the country were responsible. Externally, British dominance was weakened somewhat by the growth of commercial rivals, the composition of whose exports did not display the same rigidity as those of the UK (Table 6). By the early years of the twentieth century there were German investments in banking, shipping, electric tramways and coal supply.[3] The foreign loan business was attracting the attention of Paris and New York. US interests were concerned in proposals for new railway construction. In addition, Britain's share of Uruguayan exports before the First World War was modest and substantially less than those of her two main European rivals (Table 7), and it was US corporations that held a dominant position in the meat-packing trade on the eve of the war. The combined effect of these developments, in diluting the concentration of Uruguay's external economic relationships on Britain, appeared to offer the government of Uruguay a degree of flexibility in its relations with Britain. Yet just as the ties with Britain were slackening, they were dramatically tightened again by the growth in the 1920s of the chilled and frozen beef trades, whose principal market was the UK. This export dependence endowed British interests with a new and powerful sanction, which was to find expression in the bilateral negotiations leading to the Anglo-Uruguayan Trade and Payments Agreement of 1935. Thus the 'special relationship' survived, though on a radically altered basis, until after the Second World War when most British assets were nationalized.

Domestic changes also shaped the development of British interests. In the final decades of the nineteenth century the rural sector was substantially transformed. The introduction of pedigree livestock and wire fencing by modernizing *estancieros*, and their expulsion from the land of surplus rural population, opened a rift between themselves and traditional *caudillo* landowners. Modernization was accompanied by the strengthening of the central authority of the state, particularly during the period of military government between 1876 and 1886. The ousting in 1876 of the civilian political elite, grouped in the traditional Blanco and Colorado Parties, had a special significance. The links of the elite

Table 5: Uruguayan imports, by source, 1891–1930 (five-year averages, percentages of current value*)

	1891–5	1896–1900	1901–5	1906–10	1911–15	1916–20	1921–5	1926–30
UK	31.5	26.9	25.9	29.7	24.3	18.4	18.6	15.7
France	10.8	9.4	10.4	10.3	7.6	4.0	4.8	5.0
Germany	11.0	10.9	13.3	16.2	12.6	0.9	9.1	10.8
Other European countries	23.7	23.3	20.1	20.4	28.4	9.8	14.1	16.9
US	6.2	8.0	9.1	9.7	5.2	28.2	23.8	29.1
Argentina	7.0	13.7	13.7	7.3	12.6	21.7	11.6	9.7
Brazil	8.3	6.4	6.1	5.0	7.6	14.0	10.2	6.1
Other American states	1.6	1.4	1.6	1.1	1.2	2.3	5.9	4.9
Other and unknown	—	—	—	0.4	0.4	0.8	1.9	1.9

* Before 1940 official prices were used for the valuation of imports, and infrequent changes in these prices imply that these proportions represent volume more nearly than value.
Source: Dirección General de Estadística y Censos (DGEC), Anuario Estadístico.

Table 6: Composition of British exports to Uruguay, 1891–1930 (five-year averages, percentages)

	Coal	Cottons	Woollens	Iron and steel	Machinery	Other	TOTAL	Total UK exports to Uruguay (£000)	Total UK imports from Uruguay (£000)
1891–5	10.9	38.2	10.9	8.3	3.6	28.1	100.0	1,392	304
1896–1900	16.3	34.1	10.7	9.3	2.4	27.2	100.0	1,341	359
1901–5	23.7	33.7	7.7	8.5	3.9	22.5	100.0	1,630	683
1906–10	26.5	24.0	6.7	11.8	5.2	25.8	100.0	2,602	1,149
1911–5	24.4	22.3	6.1	11.2	4.3	31.7	100.0	2,457	2,735
1916–20	10.8	37.0	10.8	8.5	1.4	31.5	100.0	3,404	6,712
1921–5	16.9	28.5	9.5	12.9	4.2	28.0	100.0	3,096	5,231
1926–30	8.8	23.8	10.4	14.3	5.7	37.0	100.0	3,185	5,838

Source: Annual Statement of the Trade of the United Kingdom.

Table 7: *Uruguayan exports, by destination,* * *1891–1930 (five-year averages, percentages of current value)*†

	1891–5	1896–1900	1901–5	1906–10	1911–15	1916–20	1921–5	1926–30
UK	14.7	7.0	8.0	7.2	13.9	20.6	26.2	24.9
France	18.8	16.7	16.4	20.1	19.3	17.8	10.9	12.3
Germany	5.6	9.9	12.0	12.9	12.1	1.7	15.3	14.9
Other European countries	17.1	21.4	22.0	21.9	22.8	21.6	17.8	18.3
US	7.1	5.7	6.5	6.4	9.1	25.2	16.5	9.9
Argentina	13.8	15.4	17.6	18.2	13.5	9.2	7.5	12.8
Brazil	20.2	21.5	13.4	9.1	5.3	2.3	3.8	4.0
Other American states	2.1	1.8	3.2	3.2	3.2	1.2	1.8	1.2
Other and unknown	0.6	0.6	0.9	1.0	0.8	0.4	0.2	1.7

* Final destinations differed somewhat from these figures, because of exports to Argentina for trans-shipment in Buenos Aires.
† Before 1925 export values were substantially affected by the use of official prices, for which no correction has been made here.
Source: DGEC, *Anuario Estadístico.*

with the dominant landowning and commercial sectors of the economy were not strong: public life had developed its own sources of financial support, while the domestic capitalist class, with a strong and significant component of immigrants, took relatively little active part in political matters. Thus the failure of the capitalist class to dominate the political system in part reflected the fact that it did not fully participate in the Blanco-Colorado tradition of the country. But in addition, a commitment to traditional party values might have clashed with the capitalist class's primary requirement of the political system, namely that the parties should abstain from armed conflict. The 'apartness' and hence autonomy which the political system thus enjoyed,[4] though far from unlimited, was in fact enhanced by the fact of divisions within the property-owning class itself. Within the urban sector, domestic producers were asserting, with some success, a claim to a protected home market in the final decades of the century, while in the rural sector the tension between the modernizing *estancieros* and the traditional *caudillo* landowners erupted in 1904 in civil war.

It was against this background that José Batlle y Ordóñez acceded to the presidency in 1903. In office (1903–7 and 1911–15), and out of office Batlle remained the dominant figure in the political life of Uruguay until his death in 1929. In view of his immense significance for the subsequent development of the country and for the course of Anglo-Uruguayan relations, it is important to stress Batlle's inheritance of 'the autonomy of Uruguayan political personnel against the strong and wealthy social classes which controlled the economy',[5] an inheritance magnified by the rapid growth by immigration of the city of Montevideo in the late nineteenth century, and by the war of 1904. Utilizing this legacy, in a period of rapid social change, Batlle was responsible for a number of radical initiatives in social and economic policy which aroused anguish and hatred among his enemies and opponents, not the least of whom were the representatives in Montevideo of British companies and the Foreign Office.

An adequate designation of *batllismo* is not easily made, but in broad terms it may be represented as urban-based, redistributive and reformist.[6] The aspect which most concerns us here, in view of the growth of the public sector in this period and Batlle's notorious support for workers in industrial disputes, is his attitude to private capital. In general it would be fair to say that Batlle sought an accommodation rather than a confrontation with capital. In relations with the rural sector, he proposed no intervention or limitation in property rights. On the contrary, though land taxes increased, this was for revenue rather than redistributive reasons (at a time of rising land prices), and the legitimacy of property rights was strengthened rather than weakened. Within the urban sector, the fundamental objective was to reconcile labour and capital. Through the formation of trade unions and left-wing parties, and the spread of anarcho-syndicalist ideology, the working class demonstrated at the turn of the century both its rising strength and the threat it posed to the traditional political parties.

If the new urban middle and working classes were to be absorbed into the Colorado Party, then the political process had to show itself responsive to their demands. Batlle had since the 1890s demonstrated a sympathy for labour's cause in industrial disputes. On the other hand, *batllismo* was not a divisive movement, employing the rhetoric of class conflict. As Batlle observed from the page of *El Día*, 'It is not true that modern societies are divided into two clearly separated classes: those of the exploiters and the exploited. Of course there are some exploiters and there are some who are exploited. But it is not true that every man is enrolled in one or other of these groups.'[7] Thus, urban capital as well as urban labour had a place in the *batllista* movement. Domestic capital was an obvious beneficiary of the pronounced growth of Montevideo in this period. It also benefited directly by specific tax concessions supplementing the protective effects of the general tariff. Moreover, the growth of the public sector, notably the state banking institutions and electricity utility, promoted rather than penalized the interests of private capital.

The attitude of Batlle to foreign capital in general, and British capital and interests in particular, was more complex. In spite of acrimonious relations with the British companies, there was certainly no general rejection of foreign capital. Proposals from the US for new railway construction were welcomed, as a means of stimulating competition to the British-owned system. In 1911 minority British participation was invited in a proposed state venture to increase the capacity of the meat-packing industry. New foreign loans were contracted, and service payments were promptly made on existing debt. And during the First World War relations between *batllista* Uruguay and the Allies – more especially France – were unquestionably close.

But Foreign Office suspicions of the dangerous radical, with his 'coarse tastes and Socialist views',[8] appeared to be substantiated by a number of earlier incidents. For example, relations with Britain were damaged during Batlle's first administration by the seizure of a Canadian sealing vessel for illegal fishing. Of more significance was the attempt to substitute a state monopoly of alcohol production in place of the effective private monopoly held by a French citizen. That case provides a close parallel with the attempt to dislodge the foreign insurance companies from their commanding position in the Uruguayan market, by the creation in 1912 of a state insurance bank. In effect, Batlle's attitude to foreign capital was the expression neither of an anti-British sentiment nor of an ideologically based opposition to imperialism, but was inspired by a determination to limit the power of foreign capital already located in the country, and to reduce the outflow of profits. It was the conduct of the British companies in Uruguay, and in particular the monopoly position of the public utilities, which were at the centre of Batlle's hostility to foreign capital.

Political attitudes and the public utilities

Some degree of friction between a foreign-owned public utility sector and the state may be regarded as almost inevitable. In general, public utilities require large fixed capital assets and are major employers of labour. They frequently operate as *de facto* monopolies, and may indeed receive concessions guaranteeing a monopoly. Their output is widely consumed within the host country, and the terms on which it is sold may have widespread effects on the efficiency of the economy or on the welfare of the society. Price and output policies may therefore have a special significance. If the price is perceived as high and/or the output inadequate or of low quality, the public criticism aroused is likely to be much greater than would be the case for a competitive industry. If, in addition, the companies are foreign-owned, claiming to incur some part of their costs in the country of origin and repatriating dividends, then government control is likely to be more difficult to effect, and public and political hostility will almost certainly be more intense.

Public utilities formed the nucleus of British enterprise in Uruguay. British companies also operated in banking, insurance, land and the meat industry, but railways alone accounted for one third of total British investment in Uruguay by 1913. The British companies, principally the Central Uruguay Railway (CUR), constituted over 90 per cent of the Uruguayan railway system. The provision of fresh water to the capital city was a monopoly of the Montevideo Waterworks Co. One of the two companies formed to build and operate an electric tramway system in Montevideo was British, and the British-owned Montevideo Telephone Co. was the larger of two companies providing a telephone service. Finally, the Montevideo Gas Co. was the only enterprise supplying gas to the capital. Not only were these companies an important bloc among British interests in Uruguay: their performance was necessarily a major influence on the development of the national economy and on the welfare of the Montevideo population.

This influence left much to be desired. Although it was Batlle who expressed public resentment and who in consequence was regarded by the companies as the source of their difficulties, it is important to recognize that the services of the various public utility companies (with the apparent exception of the Gas Co.) were both costly and deficient. All ranks of society suffered. Even the members of the British diplomatic mission privately agreed with at least some of the criticisms. The service of the Telephone Co. was 'execrable' and 'anathematized by everybody who is compelled of necessity to use it'.[9] The high tariffs and inadequate service of the railways were condemned by landowners and representatives of the foreign-owned meat packing plants, as well as by small farmers. In 1900 there were street demonstrations to protest against the charges of the Waterworks Co., which were subsequently conceded by the British Minister to be high.[10] A scrutiny by Barrán and Nahum of newspapers for the period 1885–1916 has revealed 'hundreds of furious complaints' directed at the water, tram, telephone, and in particular the railway companies.[11] Such criticisms were thus commonly made before the emergence of Batlle, and by those politically opposed to Batlle as well as by the *batllista* group, and they were evidently becoming more severe as deficiencies of service became more obvious and less tolerable during the period of rapid economic change after the turn of the century.

That the situation of the British public utilities was central to the course of Anglo-Uruguayan relations in the *batllista* period was acknowledged by the Foreign Office.[12] The assistance of the British diplomatic mission was continuously required. In 1919 the Montevideo Gas Co. was said to be 'the only one of the British concerns which had in recent years neither requested nor required in any way the intervention of His Majesty's representative'.[13] The British perception of the causes of the prevailing antagonism was that it derived from 'the feeling that nearly all the Public Utility Companies were British concerns, created and administered with a view to exploiting the country in the interests of their shareholders', a feeling that was intensified by 'a vindictive spirit on the part of Señor Batlle'.[14] Successive British ministers were certainly not unaware that many of the criticisms of the companies were justified, as we have seen, but they found it impossible not to believe in a political malevolence:

> It is obvious that so long as the 'Batllistas' can impose their will, public companies in this Country cannot expect fair treatment. I would go further and say that so long as this nationalising fanatic, Señor Batlle y Ordóñez, remains in power, no British capital should be advanced to the Government nor should British capitalists think of investing their money in Uruguay where the important British concerns, which have helped to develop the Country, are going through a process of being gradually throttled . . .[15]

In certain respects the advent of Batlle did bring the position of the companies into sharper focus. Not only were the CUR and United Electric Tramways the largest enterprises in Uruguay before the First World War, but (as with the other utilities) their labour forces were largely or wholly concentrated in Montevideo. The companies were therefore an obvious focus for trade union activity and they were greatly affected by the labour legislation of the *batllistas*. In addition the practice of reserving staff positions for British nationals became of particular concern as the ranks of the dependent middle-class population were swelled by greater educational opportunities. Moreover, the period of Batlle's influence coincided with important economic and social developments which generally implied more profitable operations for the companies but also introduced new sources of tension. Thus the arrival of the meat-freezing industry in the early years of the century prompted new investment in pedigree cattle and extensive use of the railway system for the transport of livestock for the first time. The rapid growth of Montevideo enabled the tram company to expand its services rapidly, and demand for the output of the water and telephone utilities increased as the city grew.

The political economy of conflict: franchises, tariffs and labour relations

An examination of relations between individual companies and the state[16] makes it clear that their most important determinant was the nature of the concession held (or not held). Two enterprises in fact did not hold a concession, and thus benefited from their status as near-monopolies not subject to close regulation by government. The gas company lost its street-lighting contract in 1887, but developed its supply to private consumers to such effect that its plant was modernized and capacity extended in 1916, 1920 and again in the mid-1920s. Since it did not hold a concession the company was free to adjust its tariff as necessary. In practice the price of gas was reduced three times in the twenty years before the First World War,[17] but with the rising price of coal during the war and exchange depreciation in the post-war period, the company was able to adjust its tariff rapidly. In Hanson's judgement gas was marketed at a higher price in Montevideo than generally in Europe, but at more favourable prices than elsewhere in Latin America.[18]

The Montevideo Telephone Co. also operated without the benefit of a concession, but unlike the gas company its technical backwardness attracted considerable public criticism. Not until Batlle proposed a public monopoly of the telephone service in 1913 did the company express a serious intention to modernize and amalgamate with a smaller company, in exchange for a government concession. Some agreement was reached, but wartime supply difficulties caused the plans to fall through. There was an increase in the number of telephone subscribers after the war but no improvement otherwise in the service, and the company was eventually acquired by US interests in 1927.

The railway, tram and water supply companies did hold concessions, and all gave rise to severe conflict. In the case of the railways, the crucial issue came when government sought the right to intervene in the fixing of the railway's tariff. To a considerable extent the problem of the high tariff was inherent in the nature of the railway system itself. It had been constructed in the anticipation by its promoters of a substantial traffic in transit to Montevideo from the neighbouring regions of Argentina, Brazil and Paraguay. However, this traffic failed to materialize. Uruguay thus came to possess the most intensive national rail network in South America by the beginning of the twentieth century, but the system was burdened by excess capacity[19] and consequent high costs. The physical characteristics of the system reduced the efficiency of the rail service and generated much public hostility, but it was the level of the railway tariff that was the major point of issue between the government and the CUR.

By the terms of concessions granted originally to the CUR, and later by the laws of 1884 and 1888, the state was powerless to intervene in the level at which railway tariffs were set until railway profits exceeded a certain rate.[20] Unable to show that this rate had been reached, the government could only appeal from time to time for a reduction. The issue came to a head during the First World War, when operating costs increased sharply because of the high price of coal and the effects of labour legislation. Moreover, in 1917 the forty-year concession of tax privileges and exemptions to the CUR came to an end. To meet these additional charges the CUR raised its rates, in the face of protest but at a time of export prosperity. Then, late in 1920 the company announced a further increase averaging 34.7 per cent to cover the continuing high cost of materials, but coinciding with the post-war depression in the livestock sector. The increase was almost universally condemned. In extensive debates on the issue,[21] the inadequate controls which the state could exercise over the companies were revealed in terms of the costs they declared and the authenticity of their claims for guarantee payments. Having failed in its attempt to show that freedom from state intervention in the fixing of tariffs was one of the privileges of the CUR which had expired in 1917, the government then offered a new guarantee in exchange for lower rates. The offer was rejected, leading the British minister to observe regretfully that the 'unyielding attitude of Mr. Bayne [general manager of the CUR] has not helped matters'.[22] The CUR thus retained its freedom to set its own tariff rates, even to levels 'perhaps unequalled in the rest of the civilized world'.[23]

The issues which dominated relations between the government of Uruguay and the Montevideo Waterworks Co. were the level of the water tariff and the reluctance of the company to expand its service to meet the demands of the growing urban population. As with the railway, concessions held by the company gave it bargaining strength, but in practice it was the urgent need for an improved water supply which enabled the company's interests to prevail. The original concession to provide a piped water supply was granted in 1868 to a Uruguayan syndicate, which received a monopoly concession and a subvention for twenty years. The company was acquired by British interests in 1879, and a decade later agreed to improve the quality of the water supplied in exchange for a new concession by which, essentially, the monopoly was foregone in exchange for equal fiscal treatment with any future competitor. Indeed, within a few years the company invoked this provision of the agreement to defeat a rival proposal offering a much cheaper water supply in exchange for a monopoly.

Although the possibility of a competing water supply was revived in the mid-1900s and again at the beginning of the 1920s, the company evidently believed that the technical and financial difficulties of the schemes were too great for them to be regarded as a serious threat. The company therefore concentrated on attempts to secure its future by new government guarantees, offering in return reductions in the level of the tariff, and the laying of second and third pipe mains to extend the supply. But although the company's proposals either to sell its assets to the government or to be granted a new thirty-year concession were rejected, it evidently received sufficient assurances to persuade it in 1907 to lay a second main from the source of supply, the Río Santa Lucía, sixty km. from Montevideo. At the same time the tariff was progressively reduced as the number of private services increased. Far from diminishing the profitability of operations, a dividend of 8 per cent was paid annually for twenty years after 1909.

The second pipe main ameliorated but did not resolve the problem of Montevideo's water supply. The level of demand by the early 1920s made it impossible to maintain continuous service to all consumers, and a third of the capital's population relied on collecting rainwater.[24] The company now refused to proceed with investment in additional capacity until the terms of its eventual acquisition by the government – which Batlle had long been threatening – should be guaranteed. The question was extensively debated in the legislature and not agreed until 1928. Against the opposition of the *batllistas* the company's proposal was accepted, and the third main was installed.

Whereas autonomy in setting the tariff level was essential to the railway and water companies in the successful defence of their profitable undertakings, the tram company by contrast also held a concession, but one which fixed the tariff rate. This, and a further provision in the concession which made the company ineligible to operate a motor bus fleet, greatly reduced its capacity to cope either with changes in its own costs or with competing transport systems. The United Electric Tramways (UET) of Montevideo began operations in 1906 and experienced rapid growth in its service over the next twenty years. In 1926 UET and the other, German-owned, tram company were acquired by

Atlas Electric and General Trust, and although a modest dividend was then paid annually to 1932 (only two dividends had been declared during 1913–24), the appearance of motor buses on the streets of Montevideo introduced a competition which eventually proved fatal for the trams. It was a competition made more painful by the fact that by the terms of the concessions the tram companies had been obliged to meet part of the costs of road-paving, and also by the municipal government's refusal to permit the physical integration of the two tram systems after 1926.

Relations with the municipality had long been strained. In 1911 the tram workers went on strike for two weeks in support of higher wages and shorter hours.[25] With some encouragement from Batlle, at the beginning of his second term of office, the strike was successful. But the municipality proposed to fine the tram companies for their failure to provide a normal service during the strike period. In 1918 and 1920 further strikes were met by a limited wage increase and the promise of an additional increase if the municipal government would sanction higher tram fares. Two years later, following a twenty-one-day strike, the tram companies were temporarily taken over by the municipality and a wage increase paid, though tram fares remained at the level of the original concession. In these matters the companies had redress to the local law courts, and in separate actions they defeated the municipality over the fines levied at the time of the strikes and over the intervention of 1922. These were limited victories, however, since the companies had no devices by which to meet the competition of the private bus owners.

Government regulation and intervention

Some of the weapons which the state could deploy in dealing with the public utility companies have been mentioned already. A number of them were in fact reviewed in a report of the Departamento Nacional de Ingenieros, in its attempts to enforce observance by the CUR of various regulations governing railway services.[26] The suspension of guarantee payments to the company was rejected on the grounds that not all the components of the CUR had a profit guarantee, but in any case this was an extreme measure which would undoubtedly be misrepresented as the result of financial incapacity on the part of the state. A system of fines, graduated according to the severity of the company's infraction of its contractual obligations, was a more suitable device, but the laws relating to the operation of the railways made no provision for any penalties. The report, widening its brief to take into account the 'notorious inertia of our Railway Companies' which was acting as a drag on the progress of the nation, argued that the CUR employed its monopoly powers to maximize financial returns with minimum concessions to the public. Only the reduction of the railway monopoly would enable the state to control the CUR effectively.

Indeed, apart from the abortive attempt to intervene in the fixing of the railway tariff, the stimulation of competing transport systems was the main thrust of *batllista* policy toward the railways. The only alternative, the purchase of the British-owned railways by the state, was apparently considered after the First World War and again on the eve of the Depression, but negotiations broke down on each occasion because of the deteriorating economic position. Hence, a competing railway system was envisaged with the establishment of a fund for the construction of state railways in 1912. The initiative seems to have depended on the willingness of US enterprise to become involved, but such hopes did not prosper. By 1930 only about 10 per cent of railway mileage was owned by the state, and these lines were isolated, unprofitable feeders to the CUR. Attempts to revive river shipping during Batlle's first administration had some success in reducing freight rates on the Western Extension of the CUR.[27]

But the development of road transport offered the effective challenge to the railway. Batlle proposed a national system of roads in laws of 1905 and 1912, to be built on routes parallel to the railway. During the 1920s construction was limited to the southern part of the country, such that only the short-distance traffic of the CUR was affected.[28] Nonetheless, towards the end of the decade the CUR introduced faster trains, lower tariffs, and even a fleet of motor lorries[29] – a device for meeting competition which was denied to the tram company. By 1930 it was reported that 'the road-building schemes in this Republic have assumed so comprehensive a nature, and have been pushed forward with such energy and persistence, that there is a very reason to suppose that the future will witness a rapid expansion of road transportation'.[30]

Constraints upon external control

In spite of the political hostility they encountered between the beginning of the century and the inter-war Depression, the British-owned public utilities did not fare at all badly. In Rippy's assessment, 'it is likely that [Englishmen's] investment in Uruguay yielded as high returns over the years as their capital in almost any other Latin-American country, perhaps not even excepting Argentina and Chile'.[31] In addition to the annual 8 per cent ordinary dividend of the Waterworks Co. during 1909–29, the Telephone Co. paid an annual average dividend in excess of 5.5 per cent in its last twenty years of British ownership. The Gas (later Gas and Dry Dock) Co. paid on average more than 4 per cent between 1900 and 1929. The railway investment returned rather less, but the least satisfactory performance was that of the tramways, which paid no dividend at all between 1916 and 1924.

The varying performance of the companies is not to be explained summarily, but it was clearly of critical importance to the railways to establish their right to set their tariff freely, just as the tramways were hamstrung by a concession which fixed the tariff. Both of these industries, however, were vulnerable to competing services with a very much lower fixed capital requirement provided by small-scale private interests – assisted, in the case of road transport, by a state-financed infrastructure. No such competition seriously threatened the monopoly of the Waterworks Co., which was thus in a strong position to negotiate guarantees from the government in exchange for improvements and extensions to its service. The Telephone Co., on the other hand, having failed in its first attempt to modernize its service, was apparently content to enjoy substantial profits until a proposed government monopoly threatened its existence.

Batlle was able to present a hostile attitude to the British companies for several reasons. Fundamentally, the political representation of the companies was weak, because of the lack of an effective alliance between themselves and domestic capital. Moreover, the interests of the property-owning class as a whole in Uruguay were under-represented in the political system. The companies were in any case in a vulnerable position because of the poor service they provided. This was regarded as an abuse of monopoly power, which in turn was taken by the *batllistas* to justify a strong response on the part of the state.

The weapons which the *batllista* state could deploy against the British companies were various, but none was very effective and the combined effect tended to be counterproductive. Batlle's acquiescence in strike action by the labour force, attempts to control tariffs, state assistance to competing services, the threat of new concessions, the possibility of state purchase on unfavourable terms, all created an atmosphere of considerable hostility. The effect, however, was to reveal the ambiguity of the *batllista* position. For although the deficiencies in the various services were real enough, and were conceded to be genuine by His Majesty's representatives, neither were they remedied by the *batllista* measures, nor did life become so difficult for the companies that they preferred to leave. It is true that negotiations occurred for the sale of the utilities in the 1920s, but they do not seem to have been pressed with any great urgency. On the other hand, the political uncertainty regarding their future generally discouraged the companies from undertaking substantial new investment, except where government guarantees were forthcoming (waterworks) or where competition became effective (railways), and the deficiencies of service which gave rise to much of the hostility were thus aggravated.

Only with the threat to the position of the insurance companies did Britain contemplate diplomatic action against the government of Uruguay.[32] The possibility of such an eventuality was also considered in the case of the intervention in the tramway company by the municipal government of Montevideo, but it was agreed to take the matter to the local courts. There is no doubt, though, that the defence of British capital formed a major part of the work-load of the British diplomatic mission, whose reports managed to combine righteous indignation and personal attack on Batlle with caustic comment on the inadequacy of the public utility services and the unhelpful nature of their British managements. There is no doubt either, although it required an exceptional British minister to make the point, that 'the influence of foreign public companies and the influence of foreign diplomacy does undoubtedly affect the internal policy of the country'.[33] When the Depression took hold at the end of the period, and exchange controls were introduced to complicate further the life of the British companies (and of their official defenders), it was observed with evident irritation that 'the utility companies have all experienced the fat years and cannot complain when the lean ones come round'.[34]

Notes

[1] This approach to the study of British imperialism in Latin America may be contrasted with the concept of 'business imperialism'. See D. C. M. Platt (ed.) *Business imperialism 1840–1930* (Oxford 1977) esp. pp. 8, 12.

[2] Peter Winn 'British informal empire in Uruguay in the nineteenth century' *Past and Present* no. 73 (1976) 113.

[3] Public Record Office, London, Foreign Office Correspondence (hereafter FO) 371/568, Kennedy, British Minister at Montevideo, to Foreign Office, 3 Jan. 1908, *Annual Report 1907.*

[4] Such an analysis of the political system at the turn of the century is made at length in José Pedro Barrán and Benjamín Nahum *Batlle, los estancieros y el Imperio Británico, vol. I: el Uruguay del novecientos* (Montevideo 1979) pp. 213–68, and in M. H. J. Finch *A political economy of Uruguay since 1870* (London 1981) pp. 1–4.

[5] Barrán and Nahum *op. cit.* p. 215.

[6] In an important recent contribution, Barrán and Nahum reject the use of '*batllismo*' as a designation of the policies of Batlle y Ordóñez before 1914, since at this time there was no distinct *batllista* group within the Colorado Party. They substitute the term 'reformism'. Barrán and Nahum *Batlle, vol. II: un diálogo difícil 1903–1910* (Montevideo 1981) pp. 13–14.

[7] *El Día* 21 March 1917, quoted in E. González Conzi and R. B. Giudice *Batlle y el battlismo* (Montevideo, 2nd edn. 1959) p. 390.

[8] FO 371/361, Kennedy to Foreign Office, *Annual Report 1906*, 11 Jan. 1907.

[9] FO 371/9637: A2521/2521/46, Mallet (Montevideo) to Foreign Office, *Annual Report 1923*, 12 March 1924.

[10] FO 371/161–2, Kennedy to Foreign Office, 11 Nov. 1906.

[11] Barrán and Nahum *Diálogo Difícil* p. 166.

[12] FO 371/4617: A1394/1394/46, Ricardo (Montevideo) to Foreign Office, *Annual Report 1919*, 25 Jan. 1920.

[13] *Ibid.*

[14] *Ibid.*

[15] FO 371/5720: A6329/6329/46, Michell (Montevideo) to Foreign Office, 1 Aug. 1921.

[16] The history of the railway, water and tram utilities is examined in greater detail in Finch *Uruguay* pp. 195–207.

[17] *Montevideo Times* 23 Jan. 1916.

[18] S. G. Hanson *Utopia in Uruguay* (New York 1938) p. 198.

[19] Freight traffic per route kilometre on the eve of the First World War was 45 per cent of that on the railways of Argentina. For passenger traffic the ratio was 54 per cent.

[20] The law of 1884 set the maximum rate of profit which would not attract government intervention at 12 per cent, and this was reduced for new concessions to 8 per cent in 1888.

[21] See Gámara de Senadores *La Intervención del estado en las tarifas ferroviarias* (Montevideo 1922).

[22] FO 371/5718: A1463/1463/46, Mallet to Foreign Office, 3 Feb. 1921.

[23] J. Martínez Lamas *Riqueza y pobreza del Uruguay* (Montevideo 1930) p. 227.

[24] *El libro del centenario del Uruguay 1825–1925* (Montevideo 1925) p. 737.

[25] An account of the strike is given in Milton I. Vanger *The model country: José Batlle y Ordóñez of Uruguay 1907–1915* (Hanover, N.H. and London 1980) pp. 123–32.

[26] *Memoria del Ministerio de Obras Públicas 1908* (Montevideo 1909) pp. 186–7.

[27] CUR *Report of Directors* 1906.

[28] *Economist* 17 Oct. 1925, 617.

[29] Department of Overseas Trade *Report on the Financial and Economic Conditions in Uruguay* (HMSO 1927) p. 22.

[30] Department of Overseas Trade *Economic Conditions of Uruguay* (HMSO 1930) p. 28.

[31] J. Fred Rippy *British investments in Latin America, 1822–1949* (Hamden, Conn. 1966) p. 68.

[32] See Finch *Uruguay* p. 211 and Vanger *Model Country* pp. 146–51.

[33] FO 371/2156, Innes (Montevideo) to Foreign Office, *Annual Report 1913*, 9 Feb. 1914. On the state of Anglo-Uruguayan relations, Innes also observed: 'The outstanding feature of the situation is the spirit of antagonism which reigns between the President and the British monopolies or quasi-monopolies performing public services . . . It is easy to attribute this situation, as practically the whole of the British community does, to the wrong-headedness of the President, and to call him "a damned socialist", "a public nuisance", "anti-English", "anti-foreign", etc., but such thoughtless expressions neither explain nor edify.'

[34] FO 371/15884: A1193/1193/46, Michell to Foreign Office, *Annual Report 1931*, 22 Jan. 1932.

IV

THE ERA OF DISPUTED HEGEMONY

14

INTRODUCTION

Once a neglected period, the inter-war years have become a major focus of Latin American scholarship since the 1960s. Controversy surrounds the significance of the events and processes of the 1920s and 1930s. Interest in the period has been partly triggered by the greater availability of source material resulting from the opening of official archives, and several data-collating programmes and research projects. The enthusiasm of social scientists for statistical material is given free rein in this period: reasonably reliable sophisticated statistical time series do not exist for many Latin American societies before the 1930s. Indeed, the contemporary drive to accumulate information was a manifestation of greater government involvement in economy and society. Nevertheless, the principal factors which account for the renewed scholarly interest arise from the perception that many of the continent's intractable difficulties experienced during the late twentieth century originate in these decades. Current discussion about the role of transnational corporations in Latin America compels a close examination of the patterns and processes of inter-war industrialization. Early indications of the demographic explosion which absorbed scholarly attention during the third quarter of the century, and the origins of the related phenomenon of rapid urbanization, have also been traced to this period. Another characteristic of the 1920s and 1930s is the proliferation of ideological influences upon the region.

Accordingly, for a number of scholars the inter-war decades are a period of remarkable vitality and experimentation: for others these are years of missed opportunity, leading to the pursuit of false objectives, resource wastage, distorted patterns of industrial expansion, renewed authoritarianism and ossified administrative practices. A number of writers argue that there were possibilities for radical social change in the 1930s – the socialist republic in Chile, the Cárdenas *sexenio* in Mexico, the Liberal 'revolution on the march' in Colombia, the 1933–4 revolution in Cuba, the *aprista* challenge in Peru. Other commentators, who stress the consolidation of authoritarian influences, indicate the heritage of Vargas observable in the institutional structures of post-1964 Brazil; the emergence of peronism from the economic frustrations and electoral fraud of the *década infame* (which was neither a decade nor, possibly, in the light of subsequent Argentine history, quite so infamous). Mainstream Marxists, and others, view the rise of populism as disruptive, suffocating any potential for class struggle. Thus recent major debates centred upon the period relate to the comportment and composition of the state associated with increased social heterogeneity, the opportunities presented by crisis at the centre for effective autonomy, and the extent to which industrial expansion effected social diversification.

The chapters which compose this section also reflect the problem of establishing a generalized chronology for Latin America. Exogenous shocks like the First World War and the World Depression had a continental impact. The consequences of the Depression were probably more dramatic, yet as Palma demonstrates for Chile – an economy generally acknowledged to have been one of those most adversely affected by the world crisis – the influence of the Great War could be more critical. For the countries of Central America and the Caribbean, these shocks were attenuated or exaggerated by the growing presence of the United States. Mexico is often understood to be a case apart: the forces of exogenous disturbance were experienced through the filter of revolutionary upheaval.

Political and economic ideologies: the reception of external models

The Russian Revolution probably had a more immediate impact than the Mexican. In the final stages of the First World War and during the immediate post-war cycle of collapse-recovery-boom-crisis, a combination of inflation and deteriorating living standards gave rise to violent protest from which the nascent communist parties sprang. Except in Central America, the principal impact of the Mexican Revolution was indirect – in the evolution of more modulated US responses to modest Latin American attempts to reassert a degree of national control over their economies. A secondary impact was the rise of *indigenismo* in some Andean countries, notably Peru, Bolivia and, to a much smaller degree, Colombia. Cultivating *indigenismo* as a symbol of protest against the endurance and revival of manifestations of a culture of conquest, capital-city intelligentsias perceived the rehabilitation of the Indian and progress to full citizenship as inescapable prerequisites of national integration. Social scientists in post-1945 period have given insufficient stress to *indigenismo*, and to its Caribbean counterpart, *négritude*, as early attempts to formulate a nationalist ideology, probably because they lacked economic content.

Given the scale of European immigration it is hardly surprising that Italian fascism – its trappings rather than its substance – occasioned a response in many Latin American countries. German ideological models too carried some influence; Weimar constitutionalism had an impact upon liberal circles that is sometimes underappreciated and was probably more profound than that of Nazism.

Perhaps more significant was the example of the efficient Prussian military machine, admired especially in Argentina and Chile, recipients of German military missions since the last years of the nineteenth century. Latin American militaries were particularly receptive to new ideas that justified their claim to a privileged position in the new circumstances of the early twentieth century, when *civilista*, liberal-constitutional ideas had the upper hand. Arguments that the military constituted a vanguard in the process of economic development were eagerly received by factions within some of the Latin American officer corps, for whom professionalization was not to be equated with mere technical proficiency and the assumption of a subordinate political role. These were groups who endorsed the evolution of a distinctive technocratic and meritocratic ideology within the armed forces, viewed military academies as institutions whose educational significance encompassed much more than an Anglo-US notion of military training, and saw the armed forces as examples for the organization of the remainder of society. Perceiving themselves as beau-ideals of bureaucratic organization, and envisaging their countries as continental powers in the present and world powers in the future, powerful sections of the officer corps demanded – as early as the 1920s in Argentina – a strategic diversification of the economy, especially into heavy industry, as a step towards the achievement of national ambitions. A direct continuity between these themes and the military ideologies promulgated in the 1960s, 1970s and 1980s has yet to be fully documented by historians and social scientists; but the importance of these ideas is indisputable.

The significance of German and Italian ideological models should not, however, be exaggerated. Much recent scholarship has underestimated the enduring importance attached to the Luso-Brazilian and Hispanic connections in the inter-war period by both Latin American and US policy-makers – the continuing resonance of appeals to pan-Latinism that carried prestige in an exclusive humanistic culture that rejected an emphasis upon economic growth and material welfare as evidence of degrading 'Anglo-Saxon' influences. For many conservative groups, the example of Iberian corporatism evolved by Primo de Rivera, Salazar and later by Franco provided an updated version of right-wing authoritarianism that was both better adopted to the domestic requirements of the rapidly urbanizing Latin American societies of the inter-war years, and more appropriate in forging permanent links with corporate business and its allies in the federal government of the United States. Here perhaps were the roots of later experiments with Christian democracy which proclaimed a middle way between capitalism and communism and the possibility of combining social welfare objectives with sustained economic growth, of Catholic trade unions that stressed class collaboration and mutually advantageous relationships between capital and labour, and national planning agencies that aimed at reconciling the requirements of the private sector with the priorities of the state and the public sector.

The impact of new ideologies should not be allowed to conceal the continuing vitality of liberal constitutionalism which, revitalized by the defeat of the central European autocracies by the North Atlantic bourgeois democracies, reached an apogee in the 1920s when it was embodied in the League of Nations, and was reinvigorated by the example of the New Deal in the 1930s. Positivism, with its stress on political controls and orderly growth, also continued to be influential. So too were anarchism and anarcho-syndicalism, at least during the 1920s, despite the attempts of subsequent socialist and communist historians to diminish the role of their traditional rivals in the early 'heroic' stages of worker struggles.

The principal thrust of the dominant ideological strands of the inter-war period was seldom anti-imperial. Only in the University Reform movement conceived in Córdoba (Argentina) did anti-imperialism play a significant part. In a series of international congresses held in various Latin American capitals, the movement asserted its aims of demolishing foreign influences in Latin American education, of destroying the derivative aspects of Latin American culture and of building a distinct continental identity in order to generate continental solidarity. For the most part anti-imperialism was carried over into practical policy only in countries that experienced US military intervention. It is most conspicuously evident in the *Sandinista* resistance in Nicaragua. Otherwise, as in Cuba before 1933, anti-imperialism was largely a matter of short-term factional tactics that sometimes brought it into disrepute.

The World Depression: chronology and significance

Though many accounts of the impact of the World Depression of 1929–33 upon the Latin American economies bear the mark of hindsight, it remains incontestable that governments throughout the continent were clearly compelled to project a more active public image. However, this process is often oversimplified, neglecting changes in attitudes to, and the behaviour of, the state over time. In all but the least sophisticated economies, three distinct sub-periods may be identified in terms of policy response and the restructuring of the state: the same sequence applied in most countries, but the duration of each phase was shaped by national circumstances. Initial reaction to the Depression was usually confused and occasionally apathetic; subsequent policy was characterized by pragmatism and expediency, a mix of orthodox measures and short-term experiments which reflected pressures emanating from the export sector and other dominant groups; finally, long-term strategies were evolved, often innovative, though mainly conditioned by a need to ensure flexibility rather than coherence in government policy, given the diversity of forces acting upon the state.

Looking backwards, contemporaries were inclined to view 1929 as another example of the recurrent cycle of commercial and financial crises with which they were familiar. If the events of 1929/30 were differentiated from earlier price falls and disturbances in international markets, it was in terms of severity rather than substance. Temporary disruptions in external economic relations earlier in the century had been surmounted by a combination of orthodox policies and *ad hoc* measures tempered by local circumstances – as, indeed, had the dislocation experienced at the onset of the First World War. Thus in the opening months of 1930 there was little evidence in many Latin American countries of that loss of confidence prevalent in a number of central economies, and which several US and European scholars have nonetheless sought to project into Latin American societies. It was some time before initial complacency was displaced by an awareness of the need for ameliorative action to protect primary producers, whose already deteriorating position was exacerbated by a continued collapse in export prices and the emergence of bilateralist and autarkic tendencies in world trade.

During 1930 the nature of the crisis was revealed by the increased difficulty in placing exports, the accumulation at the dockside of goods for which importers could not obtain sufficient exchange, and tightness in foreign money markets. Wider, domestic manifestations of the problem were provided by the haemorrhage of foreign exchange and the running-down of gold stocks, the depreciation of national currencies, the destabilization of the banking sector, sharp contractions in government revenue and a consequent decline in government spending. It was against this background that a clamour for government aid arose: from primary producers and exporters demanding credit and price support, and from importers fighting for access to a declining pool of exchange. Yet the contraction of government income had broader social implications, especially in those economies where the public sector was already large or responsible for a spread of essential services – for example, railways and education. Recourse to conventional budgetary programmes, ill prepared to combat repeated and sustained fiscal crises, produced a growth in unemployment amongst state functionaries, often more deeply felt at provincial level where the deteriorating financial climate was more acutely observed.

Thus, by the end of 1930 a second phase in Latin America's response to the World Depression may be discerned, partly determined by the numerous interests lobbying for assistance, though mainly explained by

increasing political instability. Mounting pressure for enlarged government action emanated from several quarters. The export sector and
various status quo groups demanded intervention to maintain both
incomes and social order. Indeed, past experience had shown that
economic dislocation was often accompanied by social protest, in both
the cities and the countryside. Unemployed bureaucrats, schoolteachers,
small businessmen and some sections of the military had also come to
question the direction of official policy which, they argued, tended to
favour foreign interests. They too demanded the maintenance of their
standard of living, the protection of their social position and a greater
participation in the state – demands which could not be easily accommodated. The generalization of the slump from the external and public
sectors to the remainder of the economy also provoked urban artisan and
working-class discontent, as employment and wage levels in export
plant, public works projects and small factories supplying the domestic
market contracted. Some students of the subject argue that the slump
strengthened the bargaining position of sections of urban labour.

These often contradictory and antagonistic pressures coalesced in
different forms across the continent. In several countries the removal of
pre-Depression regimes by 1931 encouraged innovation and permitted
the application of more considered short-term responses to the crisis.
Subsequently, during 1933–7, coherent strategies – according to some
scholars – took shape. Demand expansion was no longer envisaged as an
indirect consequence of support for the export sector, but was beginning
to be used as a mechanism to promote industrial growth and to placate a
wide spectrum of internal interests. The state became more active in
funding infrastructure (notably in those countries where it had been
dominated by private – often foreign – capital) designed both to stimulate output and raise productivity. Road-building programmes, early
experiments with aviation, irrigation schemes in Mexico, rural colonization projects and improvements in education were applied as responses
to the demands of organized pressure groups and popular discontent.
Conscious attempts to promote direct links between agriculture (or the
export sector) and domestic manufacturing, as a means of internalizing
demand and reducing reliance upon contracting foreign markets, may
be observed in the production of rural-based raw materials for industry –
especially fibres and oil seeds – and inputs for agriculture – fertilizers and
equipment. Some fiscal reforms were applied in order to finance new
obligations assumed by the state. Additional taxes upon foreign trade
were devised and a more rigorous regime of exchange control elaborated
(perhaps the most important policy measure of the decade). Innovative
direct personal and corporate taxation was implemented, credit and
currency regulatory agencies were established, and several measures
designed to promote long-term macro-economic strategy were envisaged
or applied.

The state

Assessments of the efficacy and efficiency (and indeed the novelty) of the reforms of the 1930s vary. Some authors have interpreted the developments of these years as consciously pre-Keynesian, reflecting the reconstruction of the state in accordance with a new social formation, the successor of the traditional export-based elite whose authority had been undermined by collapse at the centre. Were these changes autonomy-inducing programmes? Or were they mechanisms constructed to maximize options for domestic interests? Critics contend that to speak of a coherent strategy is unhistoric – to project phenomena of the 1950s back to the 1930s. It is maintained that too much of the 1970s literature which addresses the years from 1929 to 1939 has been over-concerned with policy-making institutions. Assumptions appropriate to the 1970s regarding the pervasiveness and effectiveness of the state are too readily observed in a very different milieu. There is an uncritical tendency to project backwards into the 1930s achievements of the post-1940 period; to confuse the existence of institutions with their effectiveness; to assume a nationwide impact for agencies with geographically circumscribed areas of operation. Scholars have been inclined to equate an increasing volume of legislation and decrees with consistent, comprehensive planning.

These critics draw support from the work of historians who perceive the inter-war period as one of gradual change, historians who do not present 1929 as a sharp rupture between phases of export-led growth and internally oriented development. Such scholars claim that many policy initiatives and devices attributed to the 1930s had been devised before 1929 or came to fruition only in the 1940s. They point to the fact that precursors of the institutions of the 1930s include:

(1) commodity producer and/or merchant groups like the Federación Nacional de Cafeteros de Colombia founded in 1927, and price support schemes such as that provided for Argentine wheat producers in 1928 or the coffee valorization programme launched in Brazil during 1907;
(2) the establishment of central banks in the 1920s, for example in Colombia; and earlier large-scale state intervention in financial markets which took place in Uruguay between 1911 and 1915;
(3) state monopolies like the YPF (Yacimientos Petroliferos Fiscales) in Argentina and the state railway corporations in Chile, Mexico and elsewhere.

Even features of exchange control policies had been anticipated in short-lived experiments in Brazil and Colombia prior to 1914. Until the age of air travel and the establishment of ECLA, intellectual exchange between Latin American countries was limited.

A further criticism of writers depicting 1929 as a watershed is that they frequently neglect the simple chronology of events and the timing of responses to the World Depression; they minimize the complacency of Latin American policy-makers and assume direct and inevitable connections between post-1936 projects and the frenetic eclecticism visible between 1931 and 1932/3 (and possibly later). Failure to distinguish accurately between time periods often compounds a parallel problem regarding continental generalization: to impute to all economies practices and philosophies evolved in the large, more advanced, countries. Whereas some governments may by 1933 have evolved coherent strategies to surmount the difficulties intensified by the Depression, others had not, or lacked the capacity to pursue such tasks to their logical conclusions.

Perhaps the debate is over-complex. Some historians argue that policy goals were much simpler and that economic objectives were subordinate to political considerations. The principal aim of strategy was to maximize employment in the bureaucracy and to cushion professional groups against job losses in the external sector. No more sophisticated construction need be placed upon the proliferation of interventionist agencies and the quest for new forms of taxation than the mere expedient of bureaucratic survival. The bureaucratic state was only interested in self-preservation. However, although this literature looks into the question of policy determination, it fails to examine the impact of strategy.

Some scholars have argued for a political transformation in the inter-war period. Their critics, presenting a more nuanced picture, argue that claims for a transformation rest upon an over-static picture of the pre-1914 period, and prefer to speak of a sequence of small shifts that had a significant cumulative impact without effecting a radical change in the social and political order. Demands for wider political participation were clearly discernible before the Crash. Challenges to the status quo took diverse forms, depending upon local circumstances. Opposition from liberal elements within the upper class, excluded from power by authoritarian right-wing regimes, was perceptible at the opening of the Mexican revolutionary upheaval and in the abortive invasions of Venezuela by enemies of the Gómez dictatorship. Violent protest among middle-sector groups is exemplified by the revolt of the *tenentes* in Brazil.

Political protest by organized labour, if not always sustained, is visible in strike activity in Argentina, Cuba and elsewhere. Yet perhaps the most salient feature of Latin American politics was the flexibility of Latin American oligarchies. The character of *batllismo* in Uruguay and the Radical ascendance in Argentina (1916–30) illustrate the malleability of governing oligarchies. Though some historians have argued

that *batllismo* and the Argentine Radical Party embodied the predominance of new social groups, especially professionals, others –
perhaps with more plausibility – retort that these were coalitions that
made possible the containment of pressures from middle-sector, and
challenges by working-class, elements. Landed oligarchies did not
relinquish effective control, but suffocated any opposition with
concessions. Colombia too provides a good example of a governing
oligarchy with a talent for trimming. During the 1920s and 1930s, the
Colombian oligarchy displayed its capacity for self-renewal by assimilat-
ing new talent and a skill in political management oiled by patronage
emanating from the gains of integration into the world economy.

Constraints upon violent opposition were considerable. One such was
ideological: the fact that most articulate Latin American groups were
imbued with a tradition of legalism and constitutionalism – an ideological constraint to which Gramscians refer. Another was economic: the
fact that in many areas this was a period of rising living standards and
improved working conditions, which no organized group was ready to
jeopardize. Third, the balance of military power had shifted. In the
half-century after independence a fragile state had no monopoly on
violence. By contrast, from the 1880s onwards the state in the large and
medium-sized countries gained the upper hand in violent confrontations
with opponents, as a consequence of trends towards military professionalization and a growth of spending on armaments made possible by
expanding import-export revenues.

The resilience, however, of traditional forces is not to be overlooked.
The resurgence of regionalism and localism is palpable in the Mexican
Revolution and the Brazilian crisis of 1930–1. Partly adapting to new
opportunities arising in an urban environment, the Church preserved
some power through accommodations with the state reached in many
countries by the 1940s. With the growth of corporatist tendencies in a
number of Latin American societies, the Church assumed the role of
mediator between government and various groups.

Social differentiation and the peripheral state
Recent Brazilian and Argentine literature has stressed the crystallization of a populist alliance, the main components of which are said to have
been forged towards the end of the period of *desarrollo hacia afuera*.
This aspect of the discourse features principally the domestic industrial
bourgeoisie and urban labour. The formation of a multi-class coalition is
sometimes argued to have fostered the growth of economic nationalism:
a function of the incorporation or conciliation of aspiring sectors in order
to defuse class, sectoral and regional conflict. It is disputed whether
industrial entrepreneurs successfully challenged the hegemony of the
primary-export complex. While for some writers industrialists merged

with dynamic elements of the landed oligarchy to form a domestic capitalist class, for others they were absorbed and emasculated in such a way as to preclude their assuming the leadership of a struggle for national autonomy.

Similarly the role of urban labour is subject to conflicting interpretations. As is revealed in several chapters here and in Section V, the history and sociology of labour organizations is one of the growth points in Latin American scholarship: the rapidly changing state of the subject permits few generalizations. Some scholars depict the increased – often state-sponsored – labour organizations of the 1930s as a logical outcome of anarchist and socialist traditions of militancy dating from the turn of the century or an earlier tradition of artisan self-help. Here was a progressive transitional stage which reflected social differentiation in some countries, and opportunities for a popular challenge to capital created by crisis at the centre. Others reject this analysis, stressing instead the authoritarian structure of state-controlled trade unions in Brazil, Mexico and other countries where ministries of labour established the framework for working conditions and wage bargaining, fixed minimum wages and administered union funds. State-sponsored unions, constituting instruments of labour management, frustrated genuine working-class aspirations and made possible the *embourgeoisement* of union bosses. These artifices anticipated features of the recent bureaucratic authoritarianism discussed in Section V. It is sometimes argued that the concessions of the 1930s directly engendered the problems of later decades.

The relationship between urban labour and external forces is a subsidiary issue in this debate. Some writers point to the unhistorical nature of 'optimistic' assessments of the labour movements, emphasizing conflicts of ideology and interest between groups of workers. They also argue that the anarchism and anarcho-syndicalism so frequently dominant among organized urban labour and mineworkers in this period originated in a hostility to the state rather than in a hostility to imperialism. Accordingly, factional struggles and cooption by the state unconsciously eased external penetration, by diverting the attention of the divided urban working class. Other issues regarding the link between urban workers and metropolitan pressures have received less attention. The impact of the growing internationalism of the US union confederation, the AFL–CIO; its commitment to class collaboration and emphasis on the restriction of trade union activity to incremental economic improvement; and the downgrading of a political component in labour activism – all remain subjects of relative scholarly neglect. So too does the influence of the International Labour Organization, which has sometimes been charged with persuading Latin American governments to enact labour legislation that was out of joint with local circumstances.

The urban focus of union activity during this period is widely acknowledged. For some scholars this confirms the pre-emptive nature of official unionism, and the defensiveness of the populist alliance constructed to protect the status quo. Industrial workers/consumers were an essential but passive element in the coalition. Non-interference in rural labour relations indicated the continuing ascendancy of the landed oligarchy within the state. Alternatively, the urban emphasis of official action can be interpreted as reflecting the urgency of urban problems and the greater competence of government in the cities. The fragility of the populist alliance, the limits imposed by the scarcity of qualified personnel, and the novelty of institutional initiative, excluded rural labour from effective incorporation.

Thus the debates about imperialism and the state involve a reassessment of the significance and of the determinants of populism. Was the populist alliance a radical departure that entailed the admission to power of new groups, reasserting national control over decision-making and facilitating economic diversification? Or did populism consist of little more than palliatives that were designed to soften the effects of the crisis and sustain existing structures? Was either of these objectives realized? Controversy surrounds the competence and effectiveness of populism as a mechanism for confronting imperialism. Was this the purpose of the populist alliance? As indicated above, there is general agreement that the state established an elastic institutional structure which did not proscribe change. But beyond that there is no scholarly consensus. For some the objective of strategy, and the achievement of policy, was economic expansion intended to promote social harmony and to forge a combative national alliance. Other scholars underscore the coexistence of innovative government agencies that formed part of the patronage network from their inception, with inefficient relics from an earlier age that were conserved as a means of rewarding clients. Practices of patron-clientage and the immobility of fossilized institutions made for weak communications between branches of government that were responsible for poorly synchronized strategies and patchily implemented programmes that inhibited economic regeneration. These exacerbated social tensions and nullified efforts to confront imperialist forces.

At another level, writers have maintained that a lack of state competence, evident in policies that were not congruent with basic structures, precipitated confusion and internal conflict that facilitated external penetration. Thus, while certain authors portray the new, aggressive, articulate state as an effective intermediary poised between internal interests and external forces, others have argued to the contrary: that the failure of the state to resolve domestic conflicts undermined its arbitrating capacity and facilitated the penetration of the state by imperialist forces. Authors of this inclination emphasize limits upon the ability of the peripheral state to intervene in the economy, and stress the influence of the metropolis in the allocation of investment, the determination of prices and production strategy. In these key areas the balance of power lay with the transnational corporation rather than with the Latin American state, whose freedom of manœuvre was circumscribed by decision-making internalized within the corporations. The basic weakness of the peripheral state was exposed in confrontations between governments and foreign corporate capital.

Related to the concept of the imperialization of the peripheral state are the debates concerning the division of the productive function within the peripheral economy and the new international division of labour. Proponents of this analysis point to the narrow concentration of state activity in the more sophisticated Latin American economies – the focus upon infrastructure, services and the production of intermediate goods – essentially productivity-raising activities which permitted the accumulation and retention of profits within those sectors of the economy (consumer durables production) dominated by private, usually transnational, corporate capital. Much of this discussion has been absorbed into the current literature dealing with the establishment of a new international economic order, which projects the role of the peripheral state as the formulation of macro-economic policy adjusted to the needs of the transnational corporation – official development strategy becomes little more than the reflection of corporate requirements. Favourable exchange regulations, the coercion of labour, tax exemptions and so forth have created an environment suited to the elaboration of cheap wage goods and producer inputs at the periphery, using low-cost technology and underpaid labour, for supply to the centre. These issues, more fully considered in Section V, raise questions both of the competence and of the survival of the nation-state, which came to be regarded in certain circles as an antiquated institution failing to meet modern needs and incapable of responding to economic challenges. In this context, the transnational corporation rather than the state is perceived as a dynamic force.

Restructuring at the centre and options for autonomy

Much of the above discussion impinges upon the options-for-autonomy debate. Those scholars who project the populist state as an aggressive institution also observe new opportunities for domestic entrepreneurial initiative and the further consolidation of the state at the periphery during periods of weakness at the centre and of intensifying rivalries among the Great Powers. For these authors international competition in Latin America during the inter-war decades, especially in the 1930s, differs from that of the immediate pre-1914 years. The earlier period, though characterized by competitive capitalism, was also an era of international economic expansion that brought in its wake the incorporation of several previously peripheral regions. Potential for effective bargaining from the periphery only occurred during a period of economic contraction that weakened the centre. Manifestations of conflict at the centre include:

(1) a partial British retreat during the First World War, which further jeopardized Britain's international competitive position as a supplier of investment funds and manufactured goods, though not necessarily as a market for Latin American primary exports. Subsequently there was a revival of British interest, mainly in traditional activities concentrated in the Southern Cone, and a vigorous expansion of earlier initiatives in oil and food processing. As areas of dynamic capitalism of strategic importance, these drew for the first time upon active government support;

(2) the consolidation of US influence in the Hispanic Caribbean and beyond, which is widely interpreted as a function of the dominance of corporate capitalism in the United States;

(3) the remarkable recovery of Germany after the First World War and attempts to regain old markets and, in the mid-1930s, to establish a sphere of German influence in certain parts of the continent;

(4) the perceived challenge of Japan, particularly in the early 1930s, whose aggressive marketing techniques resulted in the penetration of some Latin American markets and the exclusion of exports from third parties.

The successful seizure of initiatives created by acute Great Power rivalry is revealed in the accelerating pace of Latin American industrialization, notably the establishment of capital goods production in some economies and the nationalization of the oil industry in Mexico – as studied by L. Meyer.

Several authors stress too the effectiveness of Latin American international diplomacy as evidence of a growing autonomous momentum, and as exemplifying both greater state competence and a perception of national self-confidence. Intra-Latin American attempts at mediation in international conflict – for example, the Chaco War between Bolivia and Paraguay – illustrated perhaps a rejection of the conciliatory skills of the Great Powers. A brief if active participation in the League of Nations points to the persistence of an exuberant liberalism and a readiness to project Latin America into the international arena.

This debate has a particular currency in that some participants stress similarities between the 1930s and the 1980s – decades of disputed ascendancy which yield opportunities for effective Latin American bargaining. Policy-makers today may learn from the experience of their predecessors, notably the pragmatic programme of external debt management applied by successive Vargas administrations, and measures promoted in both Mexico and Brazil during the 1930s to protect vital national interests.

The opportunities-for-autonomy hypothesis has been attacked from all sides. Pursuing a recent theme in the literature, Marcelo Abreu and others deny that the 1930s were a decade of weakened or disputed hegemony in Latin America. Despite the crisis, the United States was already the predominant external influence throughout most of the continent. The resurgent British imperialism of the 1920s was a spent force: Britain was on the defensive in Latin America, her influence virtually confined to the River Plate and the Anglophone Caribbean. The German presence, though overt, was marginal. If Latin American policy-makers experienced greater room for manœuvre in relations with external interests, it was – as Callum MacDonald demonstrates in Section V – within a space created and circumscribed by Washington. These scholars, as indicated above, also deny the originality and effectiveness of state action during the 1930s. Another facet of this attack argues that those who observe greater possibilities for bargaining from the periphery misunderstand the impact and consequences of the crisis at the centre. The contraction of the world economy intensified the drive to imperialize, rather than weakening the ability of the metropolitan economies to control the countries of the periphery. A reduction in the level of international economic activity enhanced the returns from imperialism, placing a premium upon secure access to foreign markets, and encouraging the revitalization of imperial linkages at the centre and the 'reconquest' of colonial economies.

Much of the debate examines Britain's relationship with the River Plate, attempts to reconstruct complementarity in Anglo-Latin American commerce, and official British intervention in defence of sterling investments in the region. One view stresses the belated proximity of business and government in Britain during the inter-war years, and a closer supervision by the Foreign Office of Britain's commercial and financial connections with Latin America. For other scholars, however, the strengthening of Anglo-Argentine linkages was in part an example of conscious option-exercising by Argentines – a preference for the security of the old imperialism and a rejection of incorporation within the US orbit, the latter perceived as the greater threat to 'national' interests. In contradistinction, scholars who identify a quantitative retreat by the United States, or at least a hiatus in its advance, have been upbraided by others for overlooking qualitative factors, notably the attitudes of those Latin American elites who, captivated by the ideology and material achievements of the United

States, endeavoured to reorganize their economies so as to be ready to take maximum advantage of a revival in the international economy.

Few Latin American scholars, as related in the general introduction, subscribe to the neutrality or benevolence of US policy during the 1930s. At best, small Latin American victories were permitted in order to remove the last vestiges of European influence and accelerate the consolidation of US hegemony. Other writers stress US exacerbation of regional rivalries to accomplish the same objective. Where opportunities arose, effective bargaining varied according to the size and complexity of the Latin American economy; its proximity to and degree of commercial and financial dominance by the United States; the scale and scope of the presence of European powers; and the competence of the Latin American state.

The industrialization debates

Concerned principally with policy performance and conscious strategy, the discourse about options for autonomy has largely superseded and subsumed an earlier debate – the exogenous-shocks hypothesis of Latin American industrialization that featured prominently in the writing of Frank. Although by the early 1960s a respectable component of the Latin American development literature, discussion of the causes of industrial expansion served as a convenient substitute for a more thorough elaboration of autonomy in early, crude expressions of the dependency debate. Industrialization was simplistically interpreted as the internalization of the growth process, an alternative to participation in the world economy and dependence upon the foreign trade sector. The disruption of the international economic order exposed the shallowness of strategies of export-led growth, and facilitated the consolidation of a pro-industry lobby. Though the discussion presents both the First World War and the World Depression as exogenously induced shocks to Latin American export complexes (occasionally the two crises are viewed as an interrelated phenomenon), this literature centres principally upon the Depression. It depicts the Crash as a distinct watershed in Latin American history, a turning-point which marked the end of a phase of export-led growth (*desarrollo hacia afuera*) and the beginning of internally orientated development (*desarrollo hacia adentro*). Frank, in his early writing, went even further and argued that Latin American industrialization was possible only during periods of de-linkage – when the chains of dependence between satellite and metropolis were broken and the hegemony of the anti-industry alliance of landed oligarchs, merchants and agents of imperialism shattered, following collapse at the centre.

Diffusionist scholarship rebuts the uncritical identification of the process of industrialization, begun as a response to the World

Depression, with autonomous development, on the grounds that it is unhistorical. This writing, epitomized by the work of Dean and Díaz Alejandro, demonstrates the greater potential for – and actual process of – industrial expansion during phases of export-led growth. Stressing the adverse effects of exogenous shocks upon purchasing power and rates of capital accumulation in Latin America, these authors point to the transfer of export profits, and the flow of entrepreneurial expertise, from foreign commerce to domestic industry before 1914. Other writers favouring a Keynesian demand-pull explanation emphasize the percolation through society of income generated in the export sector, which underwrote the growth of purchasing power and the emergence of a money economy. All stress the importance of imported inputs – technology and equipment – during early phases of industrialization, and deny a conflict of interest between the foreign trade sector and manufacturers producing for the domestic market. They question the impact of the World Depression upon the process of industrialization, and argue further that the initial response of government to the crisis was to protect the export sector rather than promote industrial expansion. If industrial growth is perceptible in the early 1930s, it was thanks to policies of export-sector defence which indirectly extended the phase of autonomous expansion of manufacturing and eased readjustment to new world conditions. Only towards the end of the decade did government consciously pursue pro-industry programmes. This aspect of the controversy is best illustrated by the divergent positions adopted by Hilton, Wirth, and by Villela and Suzigan in the Brazilian literature.

National schools of historiography – represented in this volume mainly by the chapters on Chile – indicate the scale of pre-1929 industrial production. Writers belonging to this tradition point to scholarly output from the inter-war period and before, which both observed manufacturing growth and debated projects for industrialization, especially in the Southern Cone. In answer to exogenous-shocks hypothesists, these authors often stress the pragmatism of government policy and play down the potential for conflict between export sector interests and industrialists. Unlike Palma, who argues for 1914 rather than 1929 as the watershed in the evolution of a strategy of import substitution, some proponents maintain that the First World War was a relatively weak exogenous shock. For most countries, increased trade with the United States substituted for shortfalls in imports from European belligerents – a process that was barely disturbed by US entry into the War in 1917. Moreover, pre-war patterns of foreign commerce were rapidly re-established after 1918. Thus for most countries the First World War resulted in the restructuring rather than the rupture of external trade, and occasioned temporary difficulties rather than continuing disequilibrium in the external sector.

A focus upon national case-studies has resulted in the establishment of sharp differentials between types of exogenous shock, and amongst countries. Both world wars triggered marked increases in the prices of traditional exports and supply difficulties in the provision of imports that were resolved with varying degrees of success. Wars produced an accumulation of foreign reserves, not the total isolation of the Latin American economies. Depressions, on the other hand, were associated with the collapse of export prices, the curtailment of incomes and a reduced ability to finance imports. The responses of national manufacturing sectors to these opportunities and problems were shaped by the efficacy of government policy, the prevailing size and complexity of the sector, local resource availability – labour, capital and raw materials – and the impact of exogenous stimulants upon domestic purchasing power as much as the availability of imports. For these writers, exponents of the exogenous-shocks hypothesis have misinterpreted and have been over-selective in the use of evidence: (1) erroneously presenting an increased supply of manufactured products from existing industrial capacity as the genesis of industrialization, (2) confusing artisan output with factory production, (3) assuming naïvely that post-shock compilations of statistical data on manufacturing indicate the establishment of firms in that period, rather than the inability of government to provide such data for earlier years. Shocks may be seen as either incentive-inducing or industry-deepening episodes in the development of manufacturing, but not as the origin and the principal stimulant of industrialization.

Another attack on the de-linkage thesis of autonomous Latin American industrialization stems from that component of the dependency literature that affirms the intensification of imperialism during the 1930s. Champions of this interpretation observe the proliferation of transnational corporations in the industrial sector. Although foreign corporate capital had achieved a dominant position in most lines of export processing before 1914, production for domestic consumption was mainly – but not exclusively – organized by national or immigrant entrepreneurs. This pattern was broken during the inter-war period, particularly after 1929. Some writers present the growing participation of transnationals in more dynamic sub-sectors of manufacturing at this juncture as a discontinuum, disrupting a more 'natural' process of endogenously funded domestic industrialization, which presaged a later ascendancy. The insertion of foreign corporate capital fragmented the manufacturing sector and inhibited the consolidation of a national industrial bourgeoisie.

Thanks to this discourse, the literature on the causes and processes of Latin American industrialization has become more complex. The debate is particularly well illustrated from Brazil and Chile; there are major publications on Argentina and Mexico, and seminal works on other countries, for instance the Thorp and Bertram monograph on Peru. It is now widely held that the origins of the modern industrial sector predate the World Depression. Most authors accept an initial phase of industrial expansion associated with export-led growth, that merged, during the early decades of the twentieth century, with a phase of sponsored development characterized by pragmatic experiments in government policy, which both consciously and unconsciously strengthened or accelerated manufacturing in specific branches of industry. These phases precede the classic era of import-substituting industrialization associated with ECLA between the late 1940s and the mid-1960s. More exact definitions of industrialization have also been devised that distinguish between artisan and factory production, between processing and manufacturing. The new literature analyzes the distinct factors that account for an increase in industrial production and the installation of additional manufacturing capacity. It poses questions pertaining to the scale and composition of industrial production; the origin of capital; the relative size of the sector and its relationship with other components of the national economy.

Aspects of these debates are explored in the following chapters. All contributors consider the role of the state, and examine policy determinants and objectives. Some scrutinize sectoral diversification, others foreign economic policy, while probing issues pertaining to discussions about options for autonomy and opportunities for development. Palma and Peter Alhadeff emphasize policy initiatives and effectiveness; the former in terms of the industrialization debate, the latter contributing to recent revisionist explorations of *concordancia* development strategy, which is now depicted by scholars as less sectionally conceived than was once argued. Like Knight, they stress the growing fiscal autonomy of the state and the innovative proto-Keynesianism of economic management. Abel, Abreu and Knight look at contrasting aspects of US ascendancy. For Abreu the established reality of US hegemony precluded any fundamental or effective bargaining from the periphery. The principal differences between the Brazilian experience in the decade before 1945 and the Argentine predicament described by MacDonald in Section V was one of degree, not of substance – the options available to both countries were circumscribed and determined by US global strategy. As does Alhadeff, Abreu demonstrates the close connection between foreign economic policy and domestic policy.

These chapters warn against facile, continent-wide generalizations for the period. Even the countries of the Southern Cone exhibit vivid contrasts: Chile, on the one hand, resorted to adventurist deficit-financing and incipient autarky, Argentina, on the other, practised liberal neo-orthodoxy. For Chile monetary expansion, protectionism and developmentalist programmes served to deepen the industrial base, isolating the national economy from some adverse effects of the crisis. In Argentina, protectionism signified the defence of foreign markets and the external value of the currency. Controlled exchange depreciation, continued access to foreign money markets and the perpetuation of an image of fiscal rectitude did not, however, preclude reflation.

What was the significance of 1929? Palma is equivocal. For Mexico the inter-war Depression is portrayed as less important than the upheaval of revolution. Knight challenges the conventional view that Mexico diverged from the Latin American norm. Possibly Mexico offers the authentic Latin American option – that the continent requires violent revolution in order to accomplish the overthrow of entrenched conservative elements, and pave the way for sustained economic growth that embraces agrarian restructuring as well as industrialization – a change of gear that raises national productivity. The self-congratulatory nature of some social science literature emanating from Brazil, Argentina and Chile and emphasizing the success of industrialization in the inter-war period, stands in contrast with the miserable performance of these economies during the late 1970s and the de-industrialization strategems of extreme right-wing military dictatorship in the Southern Cone during the early 1980s. Failure to resolve agrarian problems during the period considered in this section compounded the crises of the 1980s.

15

THE POLITICAL ECONOMY OF REVOLUTIONARY MEXICO, 1900–1940

Alan Knight

This chapter presents a general interpretation of the development of the Mexican political economy in approximately the first half of the twentieth century. It sets out to do two things. First, it tries to evaluate how far Mexico's pattern of development was determined by the specific experience of the 1910 Revolution and its legacy, rather than by other factors, which may form part of a broader, shared Latin American experience. Second, it addresses itself to the particular question of economic nationalism – seen, often enough, as a manifestation of revolutionary ideology and practice – and of Mexico's economic relations with the rest of the capitalist world, notably the United States; it also considers how far the revolutionary regime sought or achieved a fundamental shift in these relations.

It may help to locate the argument within existing literature. William Glade has posed three contrasting interpretations of the Mexican Revolution and of the Revolution's relationship to the process of economic growth achieved since 1940.[1] According to the 'discontinuity hypothesis', particularly associated with the name of Frank Tannenbaum, post-1940 growth was achieved 'more or less in spite of the Revolution or, in a variant of this view, after Mexico had abandoned the Revolution, presumably at the end of the Cárdenas administration'.[2] Thus, just as 1910 marked one watershed – the popular, agrarian revolution against Díaz – 1940 marked another – the abandonment (or betrayal) of popular agrarianism in favour of urban-orientated policies of industrialization. It is a view which, *mutatis mutandis*, still commands support today.[3] A second hypothesis – the 'historic-continuity' hypothesis – has few takers, although, as Glade points out, 'it is not without a certain limited validity'.[4] According to this view, the preconditions for economic growth were established prior to the Revolution, during the Porfiriato (1876–1911). In the short term the Revolution discouraged rather than promoted growth; in the longer term it was of 'distinctly secondary importance', possibly stimulating economic growth to the extent that it followed and did not repudiate Porfirian precedents. At any rate, such an interpretation stresses the continuity of development over the last century; it indicates no great watersheds, whether 1910 or 1940; and it consequently plays down the historic impact of the Revolution.

Glade's preferred alternative combines aspects of both of these inter-pretations. For Glade, 1910 is indeed a climacteric (to this extent he subscribes to the 'discontinuity hypothesis'): the break with the Porfiriato is crucial and profound; Mexico experienced 'a revolution in the fullest sense of that word' and the Revolution, furthermore, was 'an historic social fact uniquely and intimately related to the phenomenon of economic development'.[5] 1940, however, marks no equivalent point of departure. Post-1940 growth depended upon pre-1940 policies and achievements, which were consolidated and build upon and not – as Tannenbaum argued – repudiated. Since the triumph of the Revolution, therefore, a basic continuity has prevailed. Hence, the bulk of Glade's essay is devoted to an analysis of the many ways in which the Revolution initiated and sustained economic growth: by 'internalizing' the process of development, stimulating domestic capital formation, boosting public expenditure, mobilizing human resources and encouraging innovation. The Revolution thus becomes a prodigious engine of modernization, as that process is conceived in terms of the antinomies beloved of modernization theorists: the shift from rural to urban, agriculture to industry, parochial to universal, ascription to achievement, religious to secular.[6] The history of twentieth-century Mexico is that of a (successful) 'struggle for modernity'.[7] Glade's socio-economic analysis thus com-plements Huntington's view of the Revolution's political function: it is an 'Hegelian synthesis' which conferred a 'new unifying myth and basis for legitimacy', favouring economic development, innovation and insti-tutional stability.[8] For good reason Mexico has become the 'preferred revolution' of North American observers.[9]

Economic ideology and the revolutionary upheaval

A key element within these and many other interpretations of the Revolution and of the development of the Mexican political economy is that of economic nationalism: that complex of ideas and policies designed to 'nationalize' the economy by limiting or even eliminating foreign control, promoting 'autonomous' development, and thus curtail-ing 'dependency'. Economic nationalism, of course, forms part of many varied ideologies (socialist, populist, *cepalista*), and it may assume a variety of guises (tariff protection, planning, expropriation, forced industrialization).[10] But it is a commonplace that economic nationalism was central to the Revolution, and that the Revolution in this way revealed its anti-imperialist character; disputes arise more often in discussing whether subsequent development, especially since 1940, represented the betrayal or the consummation of national aspirations for economic autonomy. Foreign penetration 'was first to provide the captal for material progress under the [Díaz] dictatorship and then to bear the brunt of xenophobia under its reform'; the Revolution was a 'sequence with reactive nationalism at its centre'; during the Revolution 'the national bourgeoisie fought to liberate the country from its economic dependence, which it could only achieve in a struggle against imperialism, especially North American imperialism'.[11] When Walt Whitman Rostow and the hacks of the Soviet Academy of Sciences are of one mind, a true broad-Church consensus may be said to prevail.

But consensuses are not necessarily correct.[12] During the Revolution of 1910–20, foreign economic interests were not conspicuously objects of nationalist or xenophobic attacks. As regards the population at large and the popular violence which was coeval with the 1910 Revolution, the chief victims were landlords, *caciques*, Porfirian (later *huertista*) officials, army officers and, to a lesser extent, Catholic priests. While some foreign groups suffered (notably the Chinese and the Spaniards – the latter being grocers, usurers, landlords and hacienda overseers), the real agents of economic imperialism – the American and European mining, oil, real estate and utility companies – emerged remarkably unscathed; on those occasions where Americans were maltreated, they generally served as scapegoats for US policy, during movements of international tension, and not as victims of a popular backlash against imperialist exploitation.[13] Some American landlords were the object of attack, even expropriation; but these were exceptional cases, and greatly outnumbered by the incidence of confiscation of Mexican and Spanish properties. They were greatly outweighed, too, by the successful survival of other American landed interests, especially those of the more prosperous, capitalist kind.[14] These interests generally paid higher wages; and they had, over the years, cocooned themselves within a web of collaboration which even the buffeting of the Revolution could not destroy. Or, rather, as soon as one collaborative relationship (for example, with Porfirian officialdom) was destroyed, another (with the revolutionary generals) took its place.[15] The same was true *a fortiori* of American and European mining and industrial interests.[16]

Smaller interests were more vulnerable. But when they collapsed it was because of problems incidental to the Revolution (the inability to get supplies, to ship out exports, or to surmount the vicissitudes of the currency), not because of deliberate nationalist or xenophobic attacks. Historically the source of higher wages,[17] jobs in the foreign export sector were at an additional premium after 1910 as unemployment, poverty and dearth became more acute.[18] Hence the frequent displays of collaboration and clientelism, which outnumbered unusual cases of 'xenophobia': in the oil fields, for example, where Mexican employees capably and conscientiously took charge after the flight of foreign staff in April 1914; or at the mining town of Cedral (San Luis Potosí) where the manager was known for his good works and, when in 1915 'revolution-

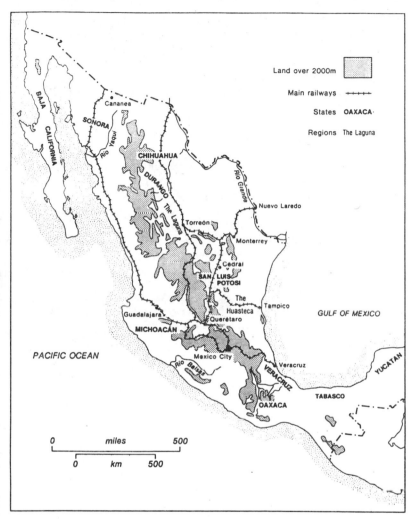

Map 6   Mexico at the time of the Revolution

aries attempted to interfere with the work . . . the women of Cedral formed a protecting posse, declaring that he had been the support and benefactor of the town'.[19] Such incidents may have indicated a lamentable false consciousness; but they were not uncommon.

There was, therefore, no generalized, popular economic nationalism, as there was a generalized, popular agrarianism.[20] On the contrary, while agrarianism welled up from the lower sectors of society, finally compelling reluctant legislators to take note, economic nationalism filtered down from the top, from an elite of educated politicians, administrators and *técnicos*. Furthermore, it did so well after the Revolution was on the march. The early programmes and manifestoes of the Revolution had little to say about the place of foreign interests in Mexico: they devoted themselves to liberal political reforms, education, vague commitments to public works (the old promise of *mejoras materiales*) and long-forgotten but contemporarily cogent denunciations of gambling, liquor, prostitution, squalor and disease. The specific abuses of some company towns were highlighted; but this was a thin plank in a broad platform, and cannot bear the weight of an economic nationalist interpretation of the early Revolution.[21]

Genuinely economic nationalist provisions – chiefly the greater taxation and regulation of foreign companies – did not become significant until the middle years of the revolutionary decade, by which time agrarian reform had already been established as a revolutionary shibboleth and a passport to power. If such provisions were indicative of deep popular resentments, they were some time a-borning. But no matter – did they not, even belatedly, denote the entry of the national bourgeoisie upon the revolutionary stage? Not necessarily. The national bourgeoisie – if by that is meant a bourgeoisie wedded to some 'project' of national capitalist development, and not supinely acting as a go-between for foreign imperialist interests – antedated the Revolution of 1910. It can be discerned – clearly, if not yet imposingly – in the diversified agricultural and industrial interests of the Creel/Terrazas clan in Chihuahua, of the Madero family in the north-east, of the *potosino* elite described by James Cockcroft.[22] As the second of these examples suggests, renegade members of the Porfirian bourgeoisie found their way into the revolutionary camp (Madero was not alone; Maytorena and the Pesqueiras of Sonora were similar cases); and below Madero there were many lesser revolutionaries who, as businessmen, shopkeepers, clerks, engineers, lawyers, foremen and workers had acted in collaboration with foreign interests. And they had done so without suffering the scars of 'affronted nationalism' or the stigma of 'status demotion'.[23]

It is a mistake, therefore, to search for the origins of their revolutionary commitment in their previous relationship with, and supposed consequential antipathy to, foreign interests. Manuel Diéguez's participation in the famous Cananea strike of 1906 would seem to make him a prime candidate for revolutionary zenophobe status; yet, commanding in Sonora ten years later, now festooned with gold braid, he was – in American eyes – a model commander, who would have no truck with working-class pretensions.[24] Obregón, Calles, Alvarado and many of the other supposed 'xenophobes' and 'Bolsheviks' also received a good press from American interests during the years of revolution. Members of the national bourgeoisie (and petty bourgeoisie) were thus to be found on both sides of the revolutionary barricades; and those who adhered to the Revolution rarely did so out of a sense of frustrated nationalism or hostility to foreign imperialist penetration.

It cannot be denied, of course, that the 1917 Constitution included a significant admixture of economic nationalism, and that the constitution in turn reflected more general trends evident in decrees, manifestoes and propaganda.[25] If economic nationalism was so marginal to the early revolution, why did it surface in subsequent years, colouring not only the constitution but also the post-revolutionary regimes of the 1920s and 30s? Certainly the triumph of the Constitutionalists – a northern group, characterized by the national orientation of its leadership – favoured such a trend.[26] Economic nationalism played no part in *zapatismo*, nor did it figure in the Plan of Ayala, the 'veritable catholicon' of the *zapatista* movement.[27] Save in two respects (to be mentioned in a moment), Madero displayed no economic nationalist tendencies, despite his northern, 'national-bourgeois' origins.[28] But the Constitutionalists transcended both their popular agrarian and their urban liberal predecessors. They were, above all, pragmatists and synthesizers: having initiated a limited, defensive states' rights rebellion against the usurper Huerta, they proceeded to improvise policy as they went along, wooing urban labour, deferring to agrarian demands, ditching (in deed if not word) the pristine liberalism of Madero. Power became the end and *realpolitik* the means.[29]

The origins and evolution of economic nationalism

Whence came their economic nationalism? Unlike liberalism or agrarianism, this was not a key attribute of original revolutionary thinking. Rather, it took seed under Díaz and fructified in the hothouse of revolution. Its pedigree was Porfirian as much as revolutionary. Thus, while agrarianism was a classic, popular demand, for which there were no Porfirian precedents (*porfiristas* like Rabasa and Limantour staunchly denied that an agrarian problem existed, rather in the manner of some recent, revisionist historians), economic nationalism drew upon clear Porfirian precedents, and even Porfirian personnel too.[30] The *científicos* (too long and too glibly portrayed as corrupt *vendepatrias*) had devised their own distinct 'project' of national development, according a prominent role to foreign investment and involving a high level of exports across a broad range.[31] This was *desarrollo hacia afuera* with a vengeance; and, as 1910 proved, it was socially and politically risky; but it would be wrong to conclude that Porfirian ideologues like Justo Sierra or policy-makers like Limantour were therefore ignorant of or indifferent to national economic needs.

Sierra, like many of his generation, was profoundly concerned by the threat of North American expansion, which had to be countered, deflected, accommodated; Limantour conceived of a sophisticated development model, whereby initially high levels of foreign investment, necessitated by Mexico's shortage of domestic capital, would eventually give way to a more autonomous, Mexicanized pattern of growth, involving industrialization and financed by export earnings.[32] In itself – *pace* Frank and the *dependentistas* – this model did not entirely lack validity: witness the experience of Argentina and Brazil (São Paulo).[33] In the Mexican context, too, it appeared to work: GDP grew at over 2 per cent per annum in 1877/8–1900/1, at over 3 per cent per annum in 1900/1– 1909/10; production for export led the way, with mining and petroleum output increasing at 7.2 per cent per annum in the last decade of the Porfiriato, while agricultural exports grew at 5.6 per cent and manufacturing at 3.6 per cent.[34] The failure of the Porfirian development model – judged according to its own capitalist criteria – did not lie principally in its encouragement of foreign investment and of the export sector; rather, as will be suggested shortly, it lay in the constraints of the domestic market, which were intimately bound up with latifundia agriculture, and in the political sclerosis of the Porfirian regime, neither of which the *científicos* were able to remedy.[35]

With regard to foreign investment, furthermore, Limantour's 'project' was flexible and evolving. By the 1900s, changes were on the agenda – some scripted in advance, some induced by circumstances. Limantour placed Mexico on the Gold Standard, restricted railway concessions, forced down railway rates, and finally achieved the merger of two thirds of the railway system in the National Railways of Mexico, which operated under government control.[36] Meanwhile, the 'Mexicanization' of the railway labour force went ahead, provoking a bitter reaction from American employees: it is ironic to note that one of the two indisputably economic nationalist policies enacted by the Madero government – the Mexicanization of the railways – was thus a continuation of Porfirian policy.[37] In addition, the 1907 recession (for recessions, great and small, cannot but call into question policies of *desarrollo hacia afuera*, and stimulate demands for protection, regulation, nationalization) prompted a vigorous debate on the Mexican mining laws, and significant changes, anticipating those of the 1917 Constitution, were only narrowly averted.[38] There were also strenuous debates over the terms of the electric power company concessions and, on the eve of the Revolution, new legislation was introduced governing hydro-electric resources; finally, as oil came on tap and the companies' large investments began to realize large profits, so voices – well modulated, articulated, Porfirian voices – began to call for greater regulation, taxation, even nationalization.[39]

The decade before the Revolution thus saw the development of a distinct 'Porfirian nationalism' which anticipated later revolutionary policies, even while it coexisted, without apparent discomfort, with the better known 'conservative' policies of the Díaz dictatorship.[40]

Economic nationalism represented a common response to external dependence, shared by regimes of different complexions and often spurred on by immediate, sobering experience: war, recession or revolution. It was hardly peculiar to revolutionary Mexico. In contrast, there was no comparable conversion to agrarian reform – of a structural, redistributive kind – outside Mexico, whose experience in this respect remained unique in Latin America prior to the 1950s. Thus even the modest reforms of the 1920s (which are retrospectively dismissed by many authorities) were exceptional; while Cárdenas' more sweeping measures beggared parallel, save for those inappropriate parallels which some, both friends and enemies, chose to draw with Soviet collectivization.[41]

Revolutionary economic nationalism in Mexico should be seen as part of a general, secular trend; and also as a response to specific circumstances – civil war, government bankruptcy, economic decline and financial collapse.[42] Through 1914–20 the foreign enclaves, especially the oil industry in the Tampico hinterland, stood out as islands of prosperity in a sea of destitution. Their very enclave character – which had excited critical comment during the Porfiriato – was thus underlined. To contemporary observers they seemed selfishly immune to the travails afflicting the rest of the country: they were seen to flirt with congenial rebels (like Manuel Peláez in the Huasteca), they were known to invoke the power of their metropolitan governments to protect their interests, and they were thought (wrongly) to be responsible for toppling and creating administrations as they saw fit.[43] Hard-pressed Mexican regimes, of different political hues, faced strong pressures to extract additional revenues from the foreign enclaves, to revise the terms of their confessions (which, where tax exemptions were stipulated, was a necessary precondition for increasing revenue) and to block the consequent appeals for redress to metropolitan governments. The Revolution thus provided a powerful circumstantial stimulus to state intervention and regulation; in addition, by bringing to power a new elite, unfettered by Porfirian *compromisos* and, indeed, rather keen to distance themselves from all things Porfirian and *científico*, it also afforded a convenient opportunity for rewriting the rules of the game. But there were contemporary parallels for much of revolutionary policy in this regard (some even emanated from the US); and Carranza's eponymous 'doctrine', which subjected foreign interests to Mexican law in defiance of extra-territorial appeals, was no more than the old Calvo clause – the creation of an Argentine jurist – writ large and proclaimed loudly and often.[44]

Nationalism, the revolutionary bourgeoisie, *la política de masas*

A general trend towards economic nationalist policies, evident in late Porfirian Mexico and in Latin America at large, thus conspired with specific pressures to produce tax increases, government regulation and state intervention in the years after 1914. These measures received their most famous – though not necessarily their most efficacious – assertion in the 1917 Constitution. Contrary to common belief, the new Constitution did not represent an enthusiastic statement of popular demands, least of all with regard to its economic nationalist provisions.[45] Rigged elections, a limited and indifferent electorate and a carefully screened attendance ruled out any such possibility. While the bulk of the nation struggled to survive, a narrow, unrepresentative and factious minority met at Querétaro to draw up the new Magna Carta – which was to be more a rhetorical declaration of intent than a cue for immediate reforms. What is more, the crucial decisions (crucial in the view of hindsight: they were often ignored at the time) were taken by a small group of backroom committee members, who shared an educated background and an enlightened, national perspective: Múgica, Rojas, Macías, Rouaix. The latter, the chief architect of Article 27, which would provide the consti-tutional basis for both the oil expropriation and the agrarian reform, was a respectable, progressive engineer, notable during his brief spell as governor of Durango for his orderly administration (a welcome change for a state accustomed to *villista* excesses, which Rouaix deplored) and for his solicitude towards foreign interests.[46]

For men like Rouaix, economic nationalism, as represented both in Article 27 and in corresponding legislative and fiscal measures, implied a gradual Mexicanization – in many respects an acceleration rather than a repudiation of Porfirian policies – and certainly not swift expropriation or socialism. And, like so much subsequent policy in this field, it was the work not of the populist demagogue (as yet, the masses were unmoved by the vision of nationalist expropriations: 1938 was twenty years and two decades of 'forging the fatherland' away) but rather of the educated *técnico*. He will appear again; he is, in some senses, the inconspicuous hero of the story.[47]

The patterns established in 1914–20 survived into the 1920s, the decade of revolutionary reconstruction and institutionalization. Allega-tions of 'Bolshevism' were wide of the mark, as Calles rightly protested: often, they emanated from companies which, when faced with increased taxation or regulation, too readily cried 'Wolf!', denouncing as 'punitive' or 'confiscatory' measures with which they subsequently came to terms.[48] The Sonorans and their allies who ruled Mexico through the 1920s were far from Bolshevist. Those of practical bent – like Calles and Obregón – gave ample proof of their attachment to free enterprise, competition and capitalism, whether as presidential candidates, presidents or businessmen.[49] Ideologues like Luis Cabrera, that barometer of revolutionary thinking, penned elegant statements to the same effect; as did Salvador Alvarado in a remarkable two-volume study which, despite its author's self-styled commitment to 'socialism' (foreigners called him a Bolshevist too), lauded social Darwinism, argued the value of foreign investment (on the right terms), and drew its basic inspiration from Samuel Smiles.[50] The Sonorans' policies built upon the precedents established in 1914–20: there was no major rupture with the fall of Carranza. They also followed, *grosso modo*, precedents established during the Porfiriato, seeking to create a powerful, centralized state (this time to be run by Sonorans rather than Oaxaqueños) and to impel the rapid development of the Mexican economy along capitalist, free enterprise lines.

Of course, while the broad objectives were familiar, some of the methods were original. But the originality – necessitated by the changes brought about by the Revolution – lay less in economic policy than in domestic political strategy.[51] This involved a battle with the Church (a battle fought with books in the schools, as well as with bullets against the *Cristeros*); it required a shift from personal, praetorian rule to the incipient party and bureaucratic structures of the late 1920s; and both processes were intimately associated with the build-up of mass clienteles through the medium of agrarian reform and organized labour.[52]

This, the new *política de masas*, represented a clear break with the Porfiriato, and obviously constituted a legacy of the armed revolution and the popular mobilization which accompanied it. But – save with respect to foreign landholdings affected by agrarian reform or to foreign companies hit by unionization, neither of which form major exceptions – these domestic innovations did not demand a major shift in Mexico's economic relations with the rest of the world. As already suggested, the Revolution prompted a redefinition but in no sense a repudiation of the role of foreign investments and foreign trade within the Mexican economy. In the case of oil, where economic nationalism was most pronounced, this redefinition involved a protracted wrangle, concerning the retroactive character of Article 27 and subsequent legislation: in 1923, with the Bucareli Treaty, and again in 1927, the Mexican government bowed to company and American pressure, not least because it hoped (wrongly, as it turned out) that this would serve to encourage production.[53]

The government also agreed to pick up the tab for damages sustained by foreign interests during the Revolution, and to resume payments on the defaulted national debt.[54] With these earnests of revolutionary good faith and with the return of political stability, foreign enterprise and investment revived. Though many small businesses, the victims of adverse circumstances rather than of deliberate hostility, had succumbed during the years of conflict, the big corporations, the real agents of economic imperialism, emerged stronger after 1920 than they had been in the days of Díaz.[55] The progressive disinvestment in the oil industry was offset by additional foreign investment in mining, which had suffered no legislative *bouleversement* as a result of the Revolution; Porfirian levels of production were attained and surpassed; and the 1920s witnessed the Indian summer of the great mining enclaves.[56] Meanwhile, the foreign electric power companies (for whom the mines were major customers) embarked on plans of expansion.[57]

As a result, foreign investment rose from 3.4 billion pesos in 1911 to 4.0 billion in 1929.[58] Porfirian trade patterns also reasserted themselves, with only limited alterations (notably the rise and fall of oil exports), and the United States remained Mexico's overwhelminlgy dominant trading partner.[59] The tariff, remaining a revenue tariff, underwent no significant changes following the Revolution; no more did financial policy, which remained strictly orthodox.[60] Here, the chief innovation was the establishment of a central bank, the Banco de México (1925): this may be seen less as an original or revolutionary breakthrough than as the final achievement of an old Porfirian objective, and part of a trend common to Latin America in the period; furthermore, the capacity of the Banco de México to influence economic performance remained exiguous until the later 1930s.[61] As for manufacturing industry, the 1920s saw significant growth, though it was growth along existing paths and in established sectors – more of the same, rather than qualitative or structural change.[62]

This clear adherence to a pattern of export-led, capitalist development in no sense represented a betrayal of revolutionary ideals, at least as those ideals were construed by the new political elite. The assurances which Obregón made to foreign capital when he bid for the presidency in 1919 were not just flannel; eleven years later the new Labour Code was drawn up with a careful eye towards foreign investors' reactions.[63] Obregón and Calles agreed in seeing foreign trade as the motor of post-revolutionary reconstruction and development; Mexico, they did not doubt, would continue to play the part of a supplier of primary goods within the world division of labour; and foreign enterprise had a crucial role to play in the revolutionary 'project', so long as it conformed to the new, carefully modified rules of the game, which gave the state an enhanced regulatory power – rules which all save the oil companies were prepared to accept, albeit in rather sulky fashion.[64] What is more, political opponents of the Obregón/Calles duumvirate often took a similar line, basing their opposition on quite different policy issues.[65]

Domestically, of course, Obregón and Calles sought to promote Mexican capitalism (as had the *científicos*). The so-called 'socialism' of the Sonorans implied the harmonization – not the elimination – of class conflict, and it required the promotion of thrift, industry and enterprise.[66] Calles lauded the virtues of individualism, placing his faith in the rural entrepreneur rather than the *ejidatario*; Pani and Montes de Oca, successive finance ministers, proclaimed the regenerative role of the Mexican middle class.[67] Hence it has become fashionable to see the Sonorans as representatives and/or servants of the Mexican national bourgeoisie, a class whose rise dominates some Mexican historiography in much the same way that the perpetually ascendant middle class dominated the old Whig interpretation of British history.[68] If this were true, it might afford some theoretical justification for the belief that the revolutionaries eagerly sought Mexico's emancipation from foreign imperialist interests.

But there are at least two major objections to this thesis. First, it overlooks the existence of a Porfirian national bourgeoisie, most of whom were anti-revolutionary: at best, therefore, the national bourgeoisie was a strangely schizoid class (hence scarcely a class 'for itself'),[69] and many of its members seemed wilfully blind to the fact that the Revolution was a vehicle for *their* 'project'. This blurring of the Revolution's subjective and objective functions is also apparent, as we shall see, in analyses of the 1930s. A second objection to the thesis is that it implies a clear antipathy to foreign interests on the part of the national bourgeoisie and its governmental agents, which is by no means evident in the time of Díaz, of Obregón or of Calles. The ambivalence of Cockcroft's Potosino bourgeoisie – an ambivalence which on close inspection seems to err much more in the direction of happy collaboration with foreign interests rather than bitter confrontation – thus recurs in the regime/national bourgeoisie of the 1920s: their prosperity is seen to be bound up with, not antithetical to, continued foreign trade and investment.[70] It was pointless, Alvarado argued, to build 'Chinese walls' against finance capital; the task was, rather, to channel its irresistible forces to mutual advantage. And, to this end, Alvarado proposed the creation of *sindicatos regionales* – regional planning, research and investment agencies, not dissimilar in function to the later Nacional Financiera – which would 'rely on private enterprise to carry out its great works . . . [so that] it would not be a question of the state managing and exploiting natural resources, but rather of a team composed of the state, Mexican citizens and foreigners'.[71] As Governor of Yucatán, Alvarado sought to convert the Regulating Commission of the Henequen Market into just such an instrument of corporate economic planning, management and development.[72]

Thus, with regard to foreign interests and their place within the Mexican economy, the changes initiated by the Revolution and evident in the 1920s did not imply a major shift in power or policy. The most important consequence was the acceleration of tendencies already apparent under Díaz. In other respects the Revolution had much more sweeping results. While economic structures remained intact, economic attitudes changed, making for greater mobility and innovation.[73] At the political level old elites were removed and revolutionary parvenus governed in their place; a new brand of mass politics came into being, characterized not by the fair and free elections promised by Madero, but certainly by a greater degree of popular mobilization and (admittedly clientelist) participation, through trade union and peasant organizations, than had been dreamed or feared in the days of Díaz. And in managing these new political forces, the state assumed a manipulative, educative and exhortatory role far beyond Porfirian precedent.[74] What James Wilkie has termed the rise of the 'active state' was therefore apparent in the political realm well before the economic; and the great innovations of the Revolution, consolidated under Sonoran rule, thus lay in the field of political mobilization – not in the field of the economy or the economy's relationship with the rest of the world[75] If, therefore, 1910–20 marked a political climacteric, continuity was much more apparent at the economic level (with the qualifications mentioned in note 73); here, the 'historic continuity' thesis has a lot to recommend it.

The 1930s: coherence, pragmatism and secular change

An important historical problem arises: how and for what reason did the ostensibly 'neo-Porfirian' political economy of the 1920s give way to the 'socialist radicalism' of Cárdenas? Was this a case of the Revolution finally delivering the goods – of the economic finally catching up with the political to effect a neat infra-/superstructural fit? Or was it, rather, the product of exogenous forces: the World Depression and its impact on Mexico? Or, finally, is the contrast an illusion, masking the 'continuity which is at the marrow of Mexican history' beneath superficially changing events and policies?[76] Clearly, each case has its merits. To the extent that there was change rather than continuity, the Depression played an important part. The forward march of the Revolution (Sonoran style) was intersected by the lateral forces of the world slump; Mexico's subsequent path of development was produced by this parallelogram of forces – the endogenous, peculiar and 'revolutionary' on the one hand, the exogenous, shared, and international on the other. The problem is to unravel the relative strengths of these forces, and the direction of the consequent diagonal of development.

The Depression affected Mexico's foreign trade severely. Imports and exports fell by two thirds between 1929 and 1932; hence federal revenue fell by a quarter and, granted the orthodox financial policies of Montes de Oca prior to 1932, federal expenditure fell roughly in proportion.[77] The economy as a whole was less seriously hit. GDP fell by some 16 per cent (sectors most closely linked to foreign trade, such as transport, were worst affected); and, though unemployment rose, aggravated by the repatriation of Mexican workers from the United States, it did not reach the levels attained in developed countries or, indeed, elsewhere in Latin America.[78] Though real wages fell, and this, combined with unemployment, injected a new militancy into the trade unions, the fall was short-lived and real wages picked up again after 1932.[79] Indeed, subsequent recovery on all fronts was notable and (compared with the US) sustained. In this, Mexico was favoured not only by the government's commitment to Keynesian monetary policies, but also by the relative diversification of the country's export base and by the fortunate upturn in oil and silver prices.[80] In severity and duration the Mexican experience of the Depression could not compare with, say, the Chilean.

The regime, however, received a severe jolt. The assumptions and expectations of the 1920s were shaken; foreign markets and private enterprise seemed to have failed as engines of sustained growth; policies of autarky and intervention acquired a fresh appeal.[81] As in the 1900s, the loss of externally induced dynamism led to a reappraisal of policy; now, however, the disillusion and consequent reappraisal were more profound, and both were further enhanced by the examples of economic action being taken in other countries: the American New Deal, the Soviet Five Year Plan, the controlled, autarkic economies of fascist Europe.[82] 'Economic nationalism', as Cárdenas pointed out to a critical foreign press in 1934, 'is a world phenomenon.'[83] A common reaction against free trade, *laissez-faire* and – in Spanish American parlance – *desarrollo hacia afuera* led to a common espousal of *dirigisme*, protection and economic nationalism, *desarrollo hacia adentro*.

Within Mexico this trend obviously antedated the coming of Cárdenas, and analyses which personalize the shift – and thereby often dramatize it in the Manichaean style beloved of historians of the Revolution – tend to miss the point. There were recent precedents, set during the Maximato, for most of Cárdenas' policies. Portes Gil had presided over a burst of agrarian reform; state governors like Tejeda (and, of course, Cárdenas himself) had mounted agrarian programmes which anticipated later national developments.[84] Cárdenas' predecessor in the presidency, the *callista* protégé and millionaire from Baja California, Abelardo Rodríguez, had established a separate Agrarian Department and promulgated both new Labour and Agrarian Codes and a Six Year Plan (endorsed by Calles), which looked to economic nationalism as a 'recourse of legitimate defence' and promised state intervention to develop Mexico's resources, to curtail foreign enterprise (for example, in the electricity industry), to combat monopolies and to promote social justice.[85] The Plan, vague and imprecise though it often was, represented a commitment to *desarrollo hacia adentro*. In 1932, furthermore, Pani replaced Montes de Oca at the treasury and embarked on consciously Keynesian, reflationary financial policies.[86]

The *cardenista* 'project' built upon these earlier initiatives, and its policies were clearly framed within the context of economic reappraisal and social conflict created by the Depression. By 1936, with the progressive strengthening of the Banco de México, a form of demand management was for the first time possible.[87] The oil and railway expropriations, following industrial disputes occasioned by falling income and unemployment, gave the state additional powers of economic control.[88] The agrarian reform, too, formed a logical part of the new, inward economic orientation: not only in terms of grand strategy (to be considered shortly), but also in terms of immediate pressures – in that the fall in agricultural exports lessened the opportunity cost of land distribution, while an expanded agricultural sector might soak up the urban unemployed and repatriated migrants.[89] No Depression, no Cárdenas. But it would be wrong to mistake a necessary for a sufficient condition, or to replace one monocausal explanation (the Revolution) by another (the Depression). For one thing, the most celebrated and decisive measures of the *cardenista* 'project' – agrarian reform (particularly the collective *ejido*) and the oil expropriation – did not take shape until the mid- and late-1930s, well after the nadir of the Depression had passed. If these were essentially responses to the Depression, they were a long time gestating: about nine years in the case of the oil expropriation. Of course, cause and effect need not be temporally juxtaposed (hence the historian's fondness for 'ultimate' effects and causes 'in the last resort'). But such a delay must imply additional intervening factors of some significance.

In fact there was both more and less to the *cardenista* 'project' than a strategic response to the Depression. His 'project' was not wholly of his own or his government's making; it evolved dialectically, that is to say, piecemeal. Ostensibly vital and distinctive elements like the oil expropriation responded as much to short-term unforeseen factors as to grand strategic designs. The exercise of greater national control over the oil industry was a long-standing revolutionary (even Porfirian) objective; but it did not require and had not required outright expropriation; expropriation, as against progressive regulation, was brought about (as the administration itself pointed out) by specific circumstances, in which the intransigence of the oil companies played a decisive part.[90] Less than a year before the expropriation, and five years after the trough of the

Depression had passed, Cárdenas approved the new Poza Rica conces-sion in favour of El Aguila, Royal Dutch Shell's Mexican subsidiary.[91] Where was the grand design, the integrated national project?

Oil tends to hog the headlines, and the oil expropriation of 1938 was dramatic, emotive and pregnant with international implications. Economically, however, and to a lesser extent fiscally too, oil was much less important than it had been back in the early 1920s.[92] The expropria-tion was more significant as an act of nationalist defiance, carrying important political consequences both at home and abroad, than as an element within some broad, integrated blueprint for national develop-ment. Oil was untypical in other respects too. Governmental attitudes towards foreign investments were – even under Cárdenas – flexible and pragmatic. In some sectors (such as the traditional mining enclaves) these attitudes were hostile or indifferent; in others, such as manufactur-ing, they were much more favourable.[93] A comparison between the oil and electricity industries helps to make the point. In the case of elec-tricity, a parallel tendency towards state regulation and intervention proceeded throughout the 1930s, building on precedents set in the previous decade; the government, concerned for the supply of cheap power to industry and to consumers, bent the companies sufficiently to its will to avoid a head-on clash; hence outright expropriation was staved off until 1960, when it was finally undertaken 'with the utmost caution', not as an emotive, nationalist issue.[94]

This case history, carefully reconstructed by Wionczek, is revealing in several respects. It illustrates the pragmatic moderation of *cardenismo*: a moderation which, in the case of oil, was converted to a more rhetorical radicalism by the brinkmanship of the companies themselves. It illus-trates too that, like both his predecessors and his successors, Cárdenas envisaged a role for foreign investment in Mexico; and foreign invest-ment indeed continued to flow into sectors where the political and economic climate was favourable.[95]

At the same time, the *cardenista* 'project' was much more than a response to the problems of the Depression, more than a series of pragmatic adjustments and innovations. This is most clearly evident in an area of overwhelmingly domestic – as against international – signi-ficance: that of agrarian reform, and of agrarian policy more generally. Structural agrarian reform, after all, played no part in the parallel responses taking place in the rest of Latin America during the 1930s; on the contrary, these policies involved, at best, a reinforcement of tradi-tional export agriculture, or, at worst, a concentration on industry and urban programmes and a transfer of resources from countryside to city, from peon and peasant to factory and white-collar worker.[96] And, though Mexico's structural agrarian reform would later be seen to fit, with almost aesthetic symmetry, into the 'national project' of the revolutionary regime and the rising national bourgeoisie, neatly complementing policies of industrialization, it does not follow that this fit was perceived at the time and planned in advance. To make this assumption is to fall prey to the teleological trap that tends to subordinate all factors (such as agrarian reform) to an overriding developmental pattern: that of authoritarian, dependent capitalism in the first case, balanced growth and 'modernization' in the second.

The historian should seek to separate the *objective* role of the agrarian reform (as perceived with the benefit of forty years' hindsight) from the *subjective* role it played during the Cárdenas *sexenio*. Then, contrary to subsequent realizations, structural agrarian reform implied a commitment to rural as against urban/industrial development; the two sectors were seen as rivals for resource allocation at a time when resources were strictly limited; furthermore, the reform carried a commitment to *ejidal*, especially to collective *ejidal*, farming.[97] In these respects the regime made a deliberate choice between alternatives and priorities, and came down in favour of a strategy which was unique in Latin America. What is more, the choice was made not so much as a calculated bid to further future balanced growth – reformed agriculture supplying cheap food for the cities, a domestic market for industry and foreign exchange for the import of capital goods and industrial raw materials – as a socio-economic end in itself, heavy with normative overtones (and, it should be stressed, carrying important political consequences).

Under Cárdenas agrarian reform was seen as the means to create a more equal, agrarian, quasi-socialist Mexico, in which the *ejido* (individual and collective) would dominate the rural sector, and the *campesinos*, not the national bourgeoisie, would be the chief recipients of government favour.[98] For its enemies agrarian reform was a reckless doctrinaire attack upon private property: again, it seems, the poor, purblind national bourgeoisie failed to recognize and endorse 'its' project.[99] For its exponents, on the other hand, the reform represented a renewal of the old revolutionary commitment to village and *campesino*, one dating from the decade of armed revolt, and now made all the more relevant and compelling, so its champions believed, by the unemployment, poverty, economic stagnation and political disillusionment which the Depression – while it had not created them – had certainly seriously exacerbated. The half-measures and compromises of the 1920s had failed; a more radical, rural-orientated revolutionary strategy was required.

This is not to deny that the reform, over and above its normative, egalitarian content, was also instrumental and manipulative; but the manipulation obeyed political rather than economic ends. The embattled *maderista* 'left' had discovered agrarian reform and *ejidal* conservation in 1912 (before long, even conservative groups took up the cry). Carranza promulgated his famous Additions to the Plan of

Guadalupe in January 1915, when *carrancista* military fortunes were at their lowest. Agrarian reform had bought off the *zapatistas* in the early 1920s, and rewarded Obregón's loyalists after the ordeal of the De la Huerta rebellion; it had helped Calles and Portes Gil defeat the *cristeros*; it had provided the rural power-base for governors like Tejeda in Veracruz, Cedillo in San Luis and, of course, Cárdenas in Michoacán.[100] Now, Cárdenas controlled the federal government's vast reservoir of patronage, vital in view of the president's conflict with Calles and the *callistas*, with Cedillo and with the *sinarquistas*.[101] Agrarian reform was, arguably, the most effective weapon in the armoury of the New Leviathan; and its extensive deployment in the 1930s, which was to have such a decisive effect on the evolution of Mexico's political economy, responded as much to political objectives as to grand economic designs.

But Cárdenas' agrarian policies went well beyond the distribution of land in *ejidal* units. As the president realized, and as other examples suggest, this alone would not have guaranteed an economic, maybe not even a political, pay-off.[102] There had also to be a real injection of resources into the rural sector, both *ejidal* and private.

In the five years following the establishment of the Banco Nacional de Crédito Ejidal (1935), 289 million pesos were lent to nearly a quarter of a million *ejidatarios*, particularly those of the Laguna collectives, and the bank further collaborated in providing an extension service which covered crop, planning, seed selection and methods of tillage and marketing.[103] Like much of Cárdenas' agrarian programme, these policies were not wholly original (Calles had established the Banco Nacional de Crédito Agricola in 1926), but under Cárdenas they were carried considerably further and faster.[104] Resources were also channelled into the rural infrastructure through the provision of roads and irrigation, thus greatly extending the improvements begun in the 1920s. Granted the high marginal productivity of these programmes, considerable external economies were achieved – chiefly to the benefit of the rural sector – as a result of fairly limited government expenditure.[105] In addition, the educational reforms of Bassols (1931–4) were continued under Cárdenas: rural schools doubled in number in the course of the 1930s, as did the number of *maestros rurales*; and, apart from the well known nationalist and 'socialist' content, rural education also embraced practical and technical training. 'The peasantry had to be made ready to receive the land.'[106]

If the rural sector in general benefited from the new infrastructure, the chief beneficiaries over time were private, commercial farmers rather than the *ejidatarios*; and it is crucial to recognize the powerful impulse which the Cárdenas regime gave to private as well as to *ejidal* cultivation in the 1930s. Particularly during the second half of his term, Cárdenas was at pains to reassure private landowners. State governors followed suit: and through the Oficina de Pequeña Propiedad (whose first director was brother to one of the founding fathers of *sinarquismo*) the regime issued certificates of *inafectabilidad*, guaranteeing properties against expropriation.[107] Throughout, the government stressed that its programme sought to boost productivity and production for the market, both domestic and foreign; hence, for example, the creation of collective (rather than individual) *ejidos* in the Laguna, at Zacatepec, Lombardía and Nueva Italia, and in Yucatán. Hence, too, the generous terms offered to the livestock business, by way of guarantee against expropriation.[108] Thus in the 1940s – when the Avila Camacho administration extended these incentives even further – commercial agriculture was well placed to respond to the mounting demands engendered by the war.[109] The dualism which observers have noted in the post-1940 agrarian system thus represented a logical consequence as much as a betrayal of *cardenista* policies.[110]

Structural agrarian reform was thus part of a more general process whereby resources were channelled into the rural sector; and it constituted a distinctly Mexican reaction to the social and economic problems of the Depression – a reaction obviously conditioned by the prior experience of the Revolution, for which there were no parallels elsewhere in the continent. The secular implications of these measures were profound, and they go a long way towards explaining the distinctive character of Mexico's political economy, as compared with other Latin American countries, in the post-war period.[111] At the political level the *campesinos* were firmly integrated into the regime by means of the governing party, the peasant confederation and the *ejidal* organizations: new, bureaucratic ties subverted and replaced the old allegiance to *cacique* and caudillo; Mexico became *un país organizado*.[112]

At the economic level investment in the rural sector soon paid dividends, as output and productivity rose. Initially, it is true, the agrarian reform seemed to depress production – though it has been argued, with some cogency, that the published figures conceal rising rural consumption through the Cárdenas period.[113] Over the medium and the long term the picture is much clearer. After 1940, as the pace of land distribution slackened – though by no means stalled – investment continued and both private and *ejidal* farms benefited from stability and rising demand. At least until the 1960s, agricultural production outstripped population growth, permitted higher levels of consumption, and made a significant contribution to export earnings.[114] Average annual growth in agriculture registered 4.9 per cent between 1935 and 1946, 7.6 per cent between 1946 and 1956 (respective figures for GDP were 5.8 per cent and 6.1 per cent); furthermore, between 1930 and 1960 some 80 per cent of increased agricultural output derived from greater efficiency rather than greater area of cultivation. This performance – to which the *ejidal* sector contributed along with the private – was not matched by manufacturing industry, where impressive growth rates were achieved with significantly lower gains in productivity.[115] Thus a declining rural population could feed the burgeoning cities, limit the upward pressure on wages and earn valuable foreign exchange.[116]

The structural agrarian reform of the 1930s made this possible as much by its effect on private capitalist farming as by its contribution to peasant productivity or peasant political quiescence. For it completed Mexico's emancipation from the constraints of latifundia production, which had constituted the biggest economic flaw in the Porfirian development strategy. *Hacendados* could no longer count on safe returns from low, inefficient demesne production, coupled with advantageous tenancy and sharecropping arrangements, both underpinned by a near-monopoly of land and labour.[117] It was not that the reform, following the destructive effects of the Revolution, overturned a 'feudal mentality'. Under the old regime landlords had maximized profits: but they had done so within the imperfect market of *latifundismo* and, with the demise of the latifundia, new economic imperatives prevailed. Extensive acres could no longer guarantee a dependent labour force. Free wage labour became the norm and, stripped of his outlying *temporal* fields, the landlord had to make his profits by more efficient demesne cultivation – not least because a display of go-ahead, commercial agriculture lessened the risks of expropriation.[118] Alternatively, denied rentier status, the landlord diverted his capital into industry, which clearly benefited by a transfer of private resources (human as well as financial) away from hacienda production.[119] In addition, rising rural consumption stimulated the domestic market which Porfirian industrialists, locked within a *latifundista* agrarian system, had chronically lacked.[120] These benefits could not have accrued while the old hacienda system survived.

The Mexican model

For Mexico, the key feature of the 1930s was neither the collapse of a single export staple nor (though this is open to some debate) an industrial breakthrough based on import substitution.[121] These trends, starkly apparent elsewhere in the continent, were more faintly traced in Mexico, where the 1930s saw only a temporary and more tolerable fall in exports, and at best a limited process of import-substitution industrialization. The latter, it is true, became more evident in the 1940s, as subsequent administrations tipped the scales in favour of industry and as agriculture adopted its more familiar role as a supplier of resources to the favoured, faster-developing industrial sector; by then, however, agriculture was better placed to perform that role without the usual problems of food shortages, balance of payments crises, and increasingly severe inflation, as happened in Argentina, Brazil and, above all, Chile.[122] ECLA was thus able to point to Mexico as one of the rare cases where agriculture 'has played the dynamic role expected of it'.[123] This economic factor, coupled with the political pay-off of the reform, sustained the generation of growth – the 'Mexican miracle' – which only showed serious signs of breakdown in the early 1970s.

The 'miracle' therefore derived from and depended upon the distinct form of economic introversion – the particular brand of *desarrollo hacia adentro* – undertaken in response to the World Depression. Mexico's peculiar response – determined by political as much as by economic considerations and conceived, we may be sure, without a full appreciation of its future consequences – provided a surer foundation for subsequent growth in the years when external stimuli revived and when a modified form of *desarrollo hacia afuera* was resumed. The distinctive and determinant features of the Mexican political economy are thus to be found in the forms of *domestic* political and economic organization, not in the field of economic nationalism nor at the 'interface' between the national and international economies – in which latter respects the Mexican case offers many more parallels with other Latin American examples.

Indeed, in these particular respects, it is the continuity of Mexico's economic relations with the outside world (chiefly the US) which is noteworthy.[124] While the domestic economy and political system have undergone formidable changes – the destruction of the traditional hacienda, the political and economic mobilization of the masses (especially the rural masses), the rise of the 'active state' and the national bourgeoisie – Mexico's place in the global economy has not been revolutionized as a result of the Revolution. It is true that foreign investment fluctuated (in response to global rather than Mexican trends), rising in the 1920s and 1950s, falling in the 1930s; it is also true that there was a secular swing away from the old export-orientated enclaves towards manufacturing, catering to domestic demand. With this process, imports switched from consumer to producer goods, domestic investment rose relative to foreign, and the latter increasingly responded to the dynamics of the domestic economy. But, to the extent that Mexico may therefore be said to have successfully 'internalized' the dynamics of growth and curtailed its dependence on external stimuli (as Glade and others argue), the same would be broadly true of other, major Latin American economies which have similarly experienced a decline of the old enclaves and a diversion of foreign investment towards manufacturing.[125] It would hardly be appropriate to infer that this trend towards 'self-generating economic expansion' or – to give it its alternative label – 'dependent development', was somehow distinct to Mexico, and attributable to the Revolution and its economic nationalist content.

On the contrary: at the level of external economic relations, it could be argued that Mexico has maintained a relatively open (and therefore 'non-nationalistic') economy, and has followed a path of development closer to that which Glade categorizes as 'neo-orthodox' (characterized by the high priority given to exports and to agricultural production and export, along the lines of comparative advantage, and by an avoidance of forced industrialization) than have many 'non-revolutionary' Latin American countries.[126]

Revolution, dependency and nationalism: some concluding perspectives

In conclusion, we can return to the original problem: the supposed climacterics of 1910 and 1940. Should they be added to the list of turning-points when history failed to turn? If the question is to be answered satisfactorily it must first be disaggregated, according to the analytical distinction made earlier. At the level of domestic social and political organization, 1910 marked a major and 1940 a minor break in continuity. The first heralded the beginning of the end for the narrow landed oligarchy of the Porfiriato and its closed, personalist politics; the second indicated (rather than determined) the priority of industrialization and capital accumulation over a more egalitarian agrarian populism. Thus far, Glade's original analysis, stressing the 1910 *point de départ* and the subsequent cumulative changes, is not wide of the mark. But in this sequential pattern of development (for, as Reynolds makes clear, the *sequence* is of central importance),[127] the dramatic changes and innovations are made at the level of the domestic political economy. Granted that the 1910 Revolution was, fundamentally, a conflict over the nature of the domestic political economy, this is both appropriate and consis tent. The middle class had sought access to political power; the peasantry fought for land and/or local autonomy.[128] Neither got quite what they wanted in the way they expected. But, by their collective efforts and the resistance they elicited, they determined the grand outlines of the Revolution and its political outcome.

But the external, international dimension was another matter. Though of consistent economic importance, foreign trade and investment did not so much dictate as respond to these domestic developments (the period of the Depression, 1929–35, marked a qualified exception); the post-revolutionary elite, broadly agreed on the need for foreign capital, decided the terms on which foreign trade and investment would operate; and, throughout the political vicissitudes of the period, there was a clear, evolving consistency in the terms which were offered – more so than in other, non-revolutionary Latin American regimes. From the economic nationalism of the late Porfiriato, through the limited disputes of the post-revolutionary decades (in which oil figures prominently but not altogether typically), to the post-1940 phase of 'preferred revolution', foreign trade and investment have played an important, increasingly regulated role, but a role less dramatic, controversial and distinctively 'Mexican' than has often been supposed. Limantour's views in the matter were not so radically different from Calles', nor Calles' from those of his successors, especially if allowance is made for the changing character of global capitalism during the century.[129] In contrast, no *científico* predicted or advocated the mass political mobilization undertaken by the governing party or the urban and rural workers' confederations, still less the sweeping agrarian reform of the 1930s. Nor were there Latin American parallels to these developments until the post-war era, by which time they had become basic landmarks of the Mexican political scene.

The reasons for this contrast – between the continuity evident in foreign economic relations and the marked discontinuity of internal socio-political development – may be traced back to the Revolution of 1910. 'The Mexican Revolution,' Lorenzo Meyer observes with a certain perplexity, 'is frequently described as an anti-imperialist struggle. To a great extent this is true, but, in the final analysis, the nature of the relationship between Mexico and the outside world has changed very little.'[130] In fact, there is no need for confusion: the 'final analysis' is correct; it is the premise which is wrong. Economic nationalism (or 'anti-imperialism') had been peripheral to the Revolution; it was not a cause eliciting the fervour of the masses; rather, it developed, in Mexico as elsewhere, as an evolutionary and elite response to practical problems of development. And, throughout, the elements of continuity were reinforced by the role of the *técnico*, whose growing importance – notwithstanding his frequent anonymity – is at once evident from a glance at dictionaries of Mexican national biography.[131] Commitment to capitalist development, even of a 'neo-orthodox' kind, represented no betrayal of revolutionary 'anti-imperialism', since revolutionary 'anti-imperialism' was largely mythical.

Thus, in common with other Latin American countries, Mexico has experienced a growth in state intervention, a shift of foreign investment from traditional enclaves to manufacturing, a phase of compulsory introversion in the 1930s, followed by renewed – and not unwelcome – extroversion since the 1940s. It would be foolish to attribute these trends, when they are encountered in the Mexican context, to the pervasive, thaumaturgic power of the Revolution. Patently, it has not required a major revolution to promote such trends elsewhere, and Glade is right to warn against a simplistic *post hoc ergo propter hoc* explanation of the Revolution's impact upon modern Mexico.[132] The Revolution has not served to revolutionize Mexico's economic relations with the capitalist world; its historic role, rather, has been to create an internal social and political environment highly favourable to the pattern of capitalist growth of which these trends form part: an environment characterized by financial and political stability, high mobility of factors of production, efficient agriculture, a coopted peasantry and a cosseted bourgeoisie. Indeed, we may go further and suggest that it has been this environment, peculiar to Mexico and directly traceable to the Revolution of 1910, which has enabled the 'revolutionary' regime – especially in the 1920s and again since the 1940s – to cleave more closely to a 'neo-orthodox' strategy of economic development, to a variety of *desarrollo hacia afuera*, than have most of its non-revolutionary, more radically economic nationalist rivals elsewhere in Latin America.

Notes

[1] William P. Glade 'Revolution and economic development: a Mexican reprise' in W. P. Glade and Charles W. Anderson *The political economy of Mexico* (Madison, 2nd edn 1968) pp. 11–22.

[2] *Ibid.* p. 11.

[3] The tendency often is to de-emphasize (even deny) the radicalism of the 1920s, to characterize 1934–40 as a phase of *sui generis* revolutionary fulfilment, and thus still to regard 1940 as a major turning-point: see, for example, Judith Adler Hellman *Mexico in crisis* (London 1978) pp. 14–54.

[4] Glade 'Revolution and economic development' p. 13.

[5] *Ibid.* pp. 9, 20.

[6] *Ibid.*, especially pp. 50–1.

[7] Charles C. Cumberland *Mexico, the struggle for modernity* (Oxford 1968).

[8] Samuel P. Huntington *Political order in changing societies* (New Haven 1971) pp. 315–24.

[9] For a sustained statement of this view see Howard F. Cline *The United States and Mexico* (Cambridge, Mass. 1963) pp. 261 ff.

[10] Harry G. Johnson (ed.) *Economic nationalism in old and new states* (London 1968).

[11] Frederick C. Turner *The dynamic of Mexican nationalism* (Chapel Hill 1968) p. 56; W. W. Rostow *Politics and the stages of growth* (Cambridge 1971) p. 75; M. S. Alperovich and B. T. Rudenko *La Revolución Mexicana de 1910–17 y la política de los Estados Unidos* (Mexico 1960) pp. 203, 237.

[12] For a divergent, correct view see Miguel S. Wionczek *El nacionalismo mexicano y la inversión extranjera* (Mexico 1967) p. 54.

[13] Alan Knight 'Nationalism, xenophobia and revolution: the place of foreigners and foreign interests in Mexico, 1910–15', unpubl. D.Phil., Oxford 1974.

[14] *Ibid.* pp. 176–97; note the example of William Jenkins analysed by David Ronfeldt *Atencingo: the politics of agrarian struggle in a Mexican ejido* (Stanford 1973).

[15] On collaboration see Knight. 'Nationalism, xenophobia and revolution' pp. 56–105. The concept derives from the work of Gallagher and Robinson: see R. Robinson 'Non-European foundations of European imperialism' in R. Owen and B. Sutcliffe (eds) *Studies in the theory of imperialism* (London 1972) pp. 117–40.

[16] Knight 'Nationalism, xenophobia and revolution' pp. 327–30.

[17] *Ibid.* pp. 85, 183; El Colegio de México *Estadísticas económicas del Porfiriato; fuerza de trabajo y actividad económica por sectores* (Mexico 1964) pp. 147–8.

[18] Knight 'Nationalism, xenophobia and revolution' pp. 324–6.

[19] Consul Canada, Veracruz, to Lansing, 21 May 1914; W. A. Thompson to Lansing, 29 May 1914, Records of the US Department of State, RG 59, microcopy 274, 812.6363/72,85; Consul Bonney, San Luis Potosí to Lansing, 30 Aug. 1915, 812.00/16135.

[20] This begs the question of popular agrarianism, the importance of which it has become fashionable to deny. Cf. Alan Knight 'Peasant and caudillo in revolutionary Mexico,

1910–17' in D. A. Brading (ed.) *Caudillo and peasant in the Mexican Revolution* (Cambridge 1980) pp. 19–27.

²¹ Stanley R. Ross *Francisco I. Madero, apostle of Mexican democracy* (New York 1955) pp. 57–64; Manuel F. Villaseñor to Madero, 26 Aug. 1911, Madero Archive, reel 20; *El Correo de Chihuahua* 27 Aug. 1910.

²² Mark Wasserman 'Oligarquía e intereses extranjeros en Chihuahua durante el Porfiriato' *Historia Mexicana* xxii (1972/3); James D. Cockcroft *Intellectual precursors of the Mexican Revolution 1900–1913* (Austin 1973) pp. 13–34.

²³ Cockcroft *Intellectual Precursors* pp. 44–5; Peter Calvert *The Mexican Revolution 1910–1914: the diplomacy of Anglo-American conflict* (Cambridge 1968) p. 287. By way of biographical evidence, note Ramon Eduardo Ruiz *The great rebellion, Mexico 1905–1924* (New York 1980) pp. 140–52, 213–38; Knight 'Nationalism, xenophobia and revolution' pp. 75–9.

²⁴ US naval report, Guaymas, 9 Nov. 1915; US army border report, Nogales, 8 March 1916, Department of State 812.00/16843,17592.

²⁵ Charles C. Cumberland *The Mexican Revolution: the constitutionalist years* (Austin 1972) p. 213.

²⁶ Knight 'Peasant and caudillo' pp. 49–58.

²⁷ John Womack Jr *Zapata and the Mexican Revolution* (New York 1969) pp. 393–404.

²⁸ Professor R. B. Brinsmade to F. Dearing, 12 Aug. 1911, Department of State, 812.50/1. On Madero's policies see Ruiz *The great rebellion* p. 386; Knight 'Nationalism, xenophobia and revolution' pp. 119–41.

²⁹ Arnaldo Córdova *La ideología de la Revolución Mexicana, la formación del nuevo régimen* (Mexico 1973) pp. 190–1.

³⁰ Cumberland *Mexican Revolution* p. 241 (Rabasa's denial); Robert F. Smith *The United States and revolutionary nationalism in Mexico, 1916–1932* (Chicago 1972) pp. 8–12; Charles W. Anderson 'Bankers as revolutionaries: politics and development banking in Mexico' in Glade and Anderson *The political economy of Mexico* p. 114.

³¹ During the Porfiriato exports grew sixfold (fourfold in per capita terms), while foreign investment rose from 110m. pesos to 3,400m., 38 per cent of which came from the US. Though certain regional monocultures developed as a result of export growth, aggregate figures reveal a tendency towards diversification, not concentration: precious metals (chiefly silver) fell from two thirds to one half of total exports, as non-precious metals and agricultural products (henequen, coffee, sugar, vanilla, chickpeas, rubber) became more important: see Fernando Rosenzweig 'El desarrollo económico de México de 1877 a 1911' *Trimestre Económico* xxxiii 1965 pp. 421–2.

³² Luis Nicolau D'Olwer 'Las inversiones extranjeras' in D. Cosio Villegas (ed.) *Historia moderna de México: el Porfiriato, la vida económica* (Mexico 1965) pp. 1171–2; Adolfo Campos 'The científicos and the Gold Standard' unpubl. Cambridge paper, 1975; Carmen Sáez 'Ideology and politics in Mexico 1879–1904: aspects of científico theory and practice', unpubl. Oxford D.Phil. 1980.

³³ H. S. Ferns *The Argentine Republic, 1516–1971* (Newton Abbot 1973) pp. 53–138; Warren Dean 'The planter as entrepreneur: the case of São Paulo' *Hispanic American Historical Review* xlvi 2 (1966); Flavio Rabelo Versiani 'Industrial investment in an "export" economy: the Brazilian experience before 1914', University of London Institute of Latin American Studies Working Paper no.2.

³⁴ Clark W. Reynolds *The Mexican economy: twentieth-century structure and growth* (New Haven 1970) pp. 21–6.

³⁵ For all their economic progressivism, the *científicos* found themselves locked within a socio-political system dominated by inefficient latifundia agriculture and peon labour on the one hand, and an autocratic, personalized, arbitrary regime on the other; institutional reforms of the latter were given up, while structural reforms of the former were scarcely considered; both conspired to inhibit sustained, stable growth. In these respects the *científicos* attempted a 'revolution from above', combining political centralization and

economic development, while 'preserv[ing] as much of the original social structure as they could': cf. Barrington Moore Jr *Social origins of dictatorship and democracy* (London 1969) pp. 433–42.

[36] John H. Coatsworth *El impacto económico de los ferrocarriles en el Porfiriato* (Mexico 1976) i 57–60.

[37] Consul Letcher, Chihuahua, to Knox, 11 April 1911, Department of State 812.00/ 1429; and Knight 'Nationalism, xenophobia and revolution' pp. 136–41.

[38] Marvin Bernstein *The Mexican mining industry 1890–1950* (Albany 1965) pp. 79–82.

[39] Wionczek *El nacionalismo mexicano* pp. 45–52; United States Senate *Investigation of Mexican Affairs, Report and Hearings before a subcommittee of the Committee on Foreign Relations* (Washington 1920) pp. 216–17; Consul Miller, Tampico, 21 Nov. 1911, 4 Oct. 1913, Department of State 812.6363/1,15.

[40] Smith *The United States and revolutionary nationalism* p. 8.

[41] Obregón distributed over a million hectares, Calles nearly three million, and the administrations of the Maximato almost three and a half million; by 1934 7.7m hectares had been distributed to three quarters of a million recipients; Cárdenas added a further 17.9m. hectares, which went to 811,000 recipients. See James W. Wilkie, *The Mexican Revolution: federal expenditure and social change since 1910* (Berkeley 1967) pp. 188, 194.

[42] I am not persuaded by recent arguments to the effect that economic collapse was less severe and sustained than previously thought. Export figures were prodigiously swollen by the oil bonanza (4m. barrels produced in 1910, 55m. in 1917, 193m. in 1921). Mining achieved a partial recovery by 1918, but domestic production agricultural and industrial, had slumped. Cf. J. Womack 'The Mexican economy during the Revolution, 1910–1920: historiography and analysis' *Marxist Perspectives* i 4 (1978).

[43] Knight 'Nationalism, xenophobia and revolution' pp. 331–5; though cf. Friedrich Katz *The secret war in Mexico: Europe, the United States and the Mexican Revolution* (Chicago 1981) which differs in important respects; Narciso Bassols *El pensamiento político de Alvaro Obregón* (Mexico 1976) pp. 162–5.

[44] Hermila Galindo *La doctrina Carranza y el acercamiento indo latino* (Mexico 1919); Smith *The United States and revolutionary nationalism* pp. 27, 44, 47, 74, 81–2.

[45] Cumberland *The Mexican Revolution* pp. 330–2, 348, 351–2.

[46] Pastor Rouaix *Génesis de los Artículos 27 y 123 de la constitución política de 1917* (Mexico 1959) Consul Hamm, Durango, to Bryan, 22 Sept. 1913, Department of State 812.00/9899.

[47] Wionczek *El nacionalismo mexicano* pp. 28, 85, 99.

[48] Smith *The United States and revolutionary nationalism* pp. 88, 99; Córdova *La ideología de la Revolución Mexicana* pp. 314–15; John W. F. Dulles *Yesterday in Mexico: a chronicle of the Revolution, 1919–1936* (Austin 1972) p. 322.

[49] Ruiz *The great rebellion* pp. 168–74, 179–81, 336–8, 387–8; Héctor Aguilar Camín 'The relevant tradition: Sonoran leaders in the revolution' and Linda B. Hall 'Alvaro Obregón and the agrarian movement 1912–20' in Brading *Caudillo and peasant* pp. 118–19, 134–6.

[50] Córdova *La ideología de la Revolución Mexicana* pp. 210–11, 245; Salvador Alvarado *La reconstrucción de México: un mensaje a los pueblos de América* (Mexico 1919).

[51] This is not to say that the Revolution had no economic impact; on the contrary, it *de facto* weakened the traditional hacienda and peonage, and it facilitated economic mobility and innovation. But these changes were not planned, decreed or legislated; they just happened. For this reason they have been underestimated by analysts who, concentrating on government policy (or the lack of it), reach the erroneous conclusion that the hacienda and rural relations of production survived the Revolution unscathed, that the 1920s represented a continuation of the Porfiriato, and that significant change had to await the *cardenista* reforms.

[52] Córdova *La ideología de la Revolución Mexicana* pp. 204ff.; Barry Carr *El movimiento obrero y la política en México 1910–29*, especially i 172–211.

[53] L. Meyer *México y los Estados Unidos en el conflicto petrolero* (Mexico 1976) pp. 27–38.

54 Though the onset of the Depression killed hopes of a settlement. See Robert F. Smith 'The Morrow Mission and the International Committee of Bankers on Mexico. The interaction of finance diplomacy and the new Mexican elite' *Journal of Latin American Studies* i 1 (1969).

55 Chester Lloyd Jones and George Wythe 'Economic conditions in Mexico' (compiled by the American commercial attachés, Mexico City, for Ambassador Dwight Morrow, 1928) State Department 812.50/161.

56 Bernstein *The Mexican mining industry* pp. 137, 143–8, 162.

57 Wionczek *El nacionalismo mexicano* pp. 45, 57–8, 72.

58 Leopoldo Solís *La realidad económica mexicana: retrovisión y perspectivas* (Mexico 1971) p. 108.

59 *Ibid.* p. 96; Reynolds *The Mexican economy* pp. 20, 205. Mexico's visible trade with the US (imports, followed by exports) as a share of total trade stood at 60 per cent and 76 per cent in 1909–10, 70 per cent and 71 per cent in 1926: *La economía mexicana en cifras* (Mexico Nacional Financiera 1978) pp. 389–92; Enrique Krauze *Historia de la Revolución Mexicana: período 1924–28, la reconstrucción económica* (Mexico 1979) p. 215.

60 G. Wythe *Industry in Latin America* (New York, 2nd. edn 1969) p. 318; Rafael Izquierdo 'Protectionism in Mexico' in Raymond Vernon (ed.) *Public policy and private enterprise in Mexico* (Cambridge, Mass. 1964) pp. 243ff.

61 Iturriaga de la Fuente *La revolución hacendaria* p. 154; Celso Furtado *Economic development of Latin America: a survey from colonial times to the Cuban Revolution* (Cambridge 1970) pp. 71–2.

62 Wythe *Industry in Latin America* p. 276; but cf. Enrique Cárdenas 'Reconstruction or development: some aspects of the Mexican economy between 1925 and 1940', paper presented at the Latin American workshop, St Antony's College, Oxford, Sept. 1981, pp. 1.2–3, 3.1, which suggests that industrial advance was rapid in the late 1920s.

63 Córdova *La ideología de la Revolución Mexicana* p. 296; Wilkie *The Mexican Revolution* p. 68.

64 Córdova *La ideología de la Revolución Mexicana* pp. 269–70; Bassols *El pensamiento político de Alvaro Obregón* pp. 132–7; Robert F. Smith 'Estados Unidos y las reformas de la Revolución Mexicana' *Historia Mexicana* xix (1969/70).

65 For example, Fransisco Serrano: Córdova *La ideología de la Revolución Mexicana* p. 312; Dulles *Yesterday in Mexico* pp.334–41. Even Vasconcelos, given to rhetorical denunciations of Sonoran *pochismo*, was ambivalent on this question: John Skirius *José Vasconcelos y la cruzada de 1929* (Mexico 1978) pp. 106–9, 197–8.

66 These themes are developed in Alan Knight 'The Mexican Revolution: ideology and practice, 1915–20' unpubl. paper given to the Society of Latin American Studies conference, Birmingham, April 1981.

67 Córdova *La ideología de la Revolución Mexicana* pp. 317–18; Nathan Whetten *Rural Mexico* (Chicago 1964) pp. 124–7; Smith *The United States and revolutionary nationalism* p. 77; Iturriaga de la Fuente *La revolución hacendaria* p. 156.

68 Albert L. Michaels and Marvin Bernstein 'The modernization of the old order: organization and periodization of twentieth-century Mexican history' in James W. Wilkie, Michael C. Meyer, Edna Monzón de Wilkie (eds) *Contemporary Mexico: papers of the IVth International Congress of Mexican History* (Berkeley 1976).

69 Karl Marx *The poverty of philosophy* (New York n.d.) pp. 145–6, *The German ideology* (New York 1939) pp. 48–9.

70 Cockcroft *Intellectual precursors* pp. 23–4.

71 Alvarado *La reconstrucción de México* i 44–5, 63, 78–84, 160, 360–1.

72 And did so with considerable success until adverse political and international market conditions terminated his project: see Gilbert M. Joseph 'Revolution from without: the Mexican Revolution in Yucatán', unpubl. Ph.D. dissertation, Yale 1976.

73 See, for example, Oscar Lewis *Life in a Mexican village: Tepoztlán restudied* (Urbana 1963) pp. 161, 178.

[74] Córdova *La ideología de la Revolución Mexicana* p. 316; David L. Raby *Educación y revolución social en México (1921–1940)* (Mexico 1974).

[75] Wilkie *The Mexican Revolution* pp. 37ff.

[76] Ernest Gruening *Mexico and its heritage* (New York 1928) p. xx. For a more recent and typically trenchant statement of the continuity hypothesis (with particular reference to the 1930s) see Jean Meyer 'Periodización e ideología' in Wilkie *et al.* (eds) *Contemporary Mexico* pp. 720–2.

[77] Solís *La realidad económica* pp. 97–8.

[78] Jean Meyer *Historia de la Revolución Mexicana, período 1928–1934: el conflicto social y los gobiernos del Maximato* (Mexico 1978) pp. 11–17; Cárdenas 'Reconstruction or development' p. 1.15 reckons repatriated workers to constitute 6 per cent of the labour force (1930–3).

[79] Jean Meyer *Historia de la Revolución Mexicana* pp. 17, 83–8; Moisés González Navarro 'Efectos sociales de la crisis de 1929 en México' *Historia Mexicana* xx 1970 pp. 536–58.

[80] Cárdenas 'Reconstruction or development' pp. 1.23, 2, 32ff.

[81] Reynolds *The Mexican economy* pp. 205–6.

[82] Albert L. Michaels 'Mexican politics and nationalism from Calles to Cárdenas', unpubl. Ph.D. thesis, Pennsylvania 1966, pp. 39–40; Wionczek *El nacionalismo mexicano* pp. 83, 85.

[83] Michaels 'Mexican politics and nationalism' p. 214.

[84] *Ibid.* p. 43; Heather Fowler Salamini *Agrarian radicalism in Veracrúz 1920–38* (Lincoln 1978) pp. 92–107.

[85] Paul Nathan 'México en la época de Cárdenas', *Problemas Agrícolas e Industriales de México* vii (1955) pp. 101–2: J. Meyer *Historia de la Revolución Mexicana* pp. 94–6; Wionczek *El nacionalismo mexicano* pp. 89–90.

[86] Cárdenas 'Reconstruction or development' p. 2.32.

[87] *Ibid.* pp. 2.37–45, 51, which notes that the Central Bank was equipped to handle the 1937 recession in a way that would have been impossible in 1929.

[88] The expropriation of the railways, though representative of a long-term trend towards the 'Mexicanization' of key sectors of the economy, aroused no furore; since the lines were all but bankrupt, the expropriation offered a relief rather than a challenge to foreign investors. See Wionczek *El nacionalismo mexicano* p. 97 and Joe C. Ashby *Organized labor and the Mexican Revolution under Cárdenas* (Chapel Hill 1967) pp. 122–41.

[89] González Navarro 'Efectos sociales' p. 541; Reynolds *The Mexican economy* p. 154; J. Meyer *Historia de la Revolución Mexicana* p. 11.

[90] Michaels 'Mexican politics and nationalism' p. 238.

[91] *Ibid.* p. 226; Townsend *Lázaro Cárdenas* p. 249.

[92] L. Meyer *México y Estados Unidos en el conflicto petrolero* p. 29–31.

[93] Blanca Torres Ramírez *Historia de la Revolución Mexicana, período 1940–1952: México en la Segunda Guerra Mundial* (Mexico 1979) p. 212.

[94] Wionczek *El nacionalismo mexicano* pp. 74–165; Timothy King *Mexico: industrialization and trade policies since 1940* (Oxford 1970) pp. 60–1.

[95] Glade 'Revolution and development' p. 75; Jean Meyer *El Sinarquismo: un fascismo mexicano?* (Mexico 1979) p.25. Between 1933 and 1940, for example, electric power output (most of which was in foreign hands) rose by some two thirds: *La economía mexicana en cifras* (Mexico, Nacional Financiera 1978) p. 73.

[96] Glade 'Revolution and economic development', *The Latin American economies: a study of their institutional evolution* (New York 1969) pp. 418, 443–4. For Latin American comparisons cf. Ferns *The Argentine Republic* p. 139; Shepard Forman *The Brazilian peasantry* (Columbia 1975) pp. 168–9; Brian Loveman *The struggle in the countryside: politics and rural labor in Chile, 1919–1937* (Bloomington 1976).

[97] Solomon Eckstein *El ejido colectivo en México* (Mexico 1966), Alicia Hernández Chávez *Historia de la Revolución Mexicana, período 1934–1940: La mecánica Cardenista* (Mexico 1979) pp. 171, 174–8.

[98] Michaels 'Mexican politics and nationalism' pp. 55–6, 83–4; Lázaro Cárdenas *Ideario político* (Mexico, 2nd edn 1976) pp. 109–64.

[99] Luis Medina *Historia de la Revolución Mexicana, período 1940–1952: del Cardenismo al Avilacamachismo* (Mexico 1978) pp. 25–32.

[100] Fowler Salamini *Agrarian radicalism* pp. 41–5; Jean A. Meyer *The Cristero Rebellion: the Mexican people between Church and state 1926–1929* (Cambridge 1976) pp. 106–10; Romana Falcón *El agrarismo en Veracrúz: la étapa radical (1928–1935)* (Mexico 1977) pp. 32–91; Nathan 'México en la época de Cárdenas' pp. 64–6.

[101] Dudley Ankerson 'Saturnino Cedillo, a traditional caudillo in San Luis Potosí 1890–1938' in Brading (ed.) *Caudillo and peasant* pp. 162–3, 167; Meyer *El Sinarquismo* pp. 188–93.

[102] Cárdenas *Ideario político* p. 119; Peter Dorner *Land reform and economic development* (London 1972) p. 66.

[103] Nathan 'México en la época de Cárdenas' pp. 113–15; Sanford A. Mosk *Industrial revolution in Mexico* (Berkeley 1954) p. 55.

[104] Medina *Historia de la Revolución Mexicana* pp. 15–17.

[105] Cárdenas 'Reconstruction of development' pp. 1.22, 25, 2.71–3; Reynolds *The Mexican economy* pp. 143, 155.

[106] Raby *Educación y revolución social* p. 42 and *passim*.

[107] Between 1930 and 1940 the number of small farms (between 50 and 1,000 hectares) grew by 11 per cent. See Cárdenas *Ideario político* p. 120; Michaels 'Mexican politics and nationalism' pp. 100–3; Medina *Historia de la Revolución Mexicana* p. 18.

[108] Dorner *Land reform* p. 48.

[109] Torres Ramírez *Historia de la Revolución Mexicana* pp. 301–29.

[110] R. Carr 'The Mexican agrarian reform 1910–60' in E. L. Jones and S. J. Woolf (eds) *Agrarian change and economic development* (London 1969) pp. 159–60; Bruce F. Johnston 'The Japanese "model" of agricultural development: its relevance to developing nations' in Kazushi Ohkawa *et al.* (eds) *Agricultural and economic growth: Japan's experience* (Princeton 1970) pp. 86–9.

[111] I risk the wrath of Professor Cockcroft, who strenuously resists any idea that 'Mexico's evolution in the twentieth century represents any form of economic development which is uniquely Mexican or *sui generis*'; but then Cockcroft's perspective takes in and blurs together the entire 'dependent' world ('from . . . Ghana to Argentina') as well as great chronological tracts (within which *Cardenismo* appears as 'a mere episode'): James D. Cockcroft 'Mexico' in Ronald Chilcote and Joel C. Edelstein (eds) *Latin America: the struggle with dependency and beyond* (New York 1974) pp. 226,261.

[112] Arnaldo Córdova *La política de masas del Cardenismo* (Mexico, 2nd edn 1976) p. 202.

[113] Reynolds *The Mexican economy* p.97; Glade 'Revolution and economic development' pp. 62–3.

[114] Nathan 'México en la época de Cárdenas' p. 117; Solís *La realidad económica* p. 112; Jesús Puente Leyva 'Acumulación de capital y crecimiento en el sector agropecuario en México' in Ifigenia M. de Navarette (ed.) *Bienestar campesina y desarrollo económico* (Mexico 1971) p. 60, notes that the average annual growth rate of Mexican agriculture was inferior only to those of Japan and Israel. By the 1970s, of course, Mexico was no longer self-sufficient in food, and the agricultural picture was looking distinctly bleaker.

[115] Solís *La realidad económica* pp. 126–7, 133; Reynolds *The Mexican economy* p. 168.

[116] Oscar Lewis 'Mexico since Cárdenas' in Richard N. Adams *et al.* (eds) *Social change in Latin America today: its implications for U.S. policy* (New York 1960) pp. 300, 312–14. Between the 1930s and the 1950s, agriculture's share of exports rose from one third to a half.

[117] Friedrich Katz *La servidumbre agraria en México en la época porfiriana* (Mexico 1980) especially pp. 34–44.

[118] Glade 'Revolution and development' p. 59; and note the successful rearguard action of William Jenkins: Ronfeldt *Atencingo* p. 20.

[119] Cárdenas 'Reconstruction or development' p.1.28; cf. Flavia Derossi *The Mexican entrepreneur* (Paris 1971) especially pp. 157, 169.

[120] Reynolds *The Mexican economy* pp. 42, 152, 176–7. The opportunities and constraints created by the level of demand in the domestic market have been the subject of frequent debate: cf. Raymond Vernon *The dilemma of Mexico's development: the roles of the private and public sectors* (Cambridge, Mass. 1963); Mosk *Industrial revolution* pp. 201–22 and Hansen *The politics of Mexican development* pp. 218–21.

[121] Solís *La realidad económica* p. 90; Reynolds *The Mexican economy* pp. 207–8, 251–2; cf. Cárdenas 'Reconstruction or development' pp. 2–5.

[122] At least until the late 1960s/early 1970s: Adriaan Ten Kate and Robert Bruce Wallace *Protection and economic development in Mexico* (Farnborough 1980) pp. 5–6.

[123] Lewis 'Mexico since Cárdenas' p. 315.

[124] Lorenzo Meyer 'Historical roots of the authoritarian state in Mexico' in Reyna and Weinert (eds) *Authoritarianism in Mexico* p. 17.

[125] Glade 'Revolution and economic development' p. 3; Enrique Pérez López 'The national product of Mexico' and Alfredo Navarrete R. 'The financing of economic development' in E. Pérez López *et al. Mexico's recent economic growth: the Mexican view* (Austin 1967) pp. 31, 111–13, 126–7; Furtado *Economic development of Latin America* pp. 171–8.

[126] Glade *The Latin American economies* pp.370–529 shoves Mexico into a 'developmental socialization' category along with Bolivia and Cuba (see pp. 483–506): an attribution which, even if it is justified with regard to domestic socio-political structures (which I doubt), is clearly inappropriate with regard to Mexico's external economic relations, where 'orthodoxy' (pp. 376–401) has better claims. On the importance of exports, especially tourism and agriculture, see Victor L. Urquidi 'Fundamental problems of the Mexican economy' in Pérez López *et al. Mexico's recent growth* p. 178 and King *Mexico: industrialization and trade policies* p. 18.

[127] Reynolds *The Mexican economy* p. 303.

[128] Knight 'Peasant and caudillo' in Brading (ed.) *Caudillo and peasant*.

[129] Cf. Limantour's presentation of the 1906–7 budget, quoted by Nicolau D'Olwer 'Las inversiones extranjeras' in Cosío Villegas *El Porfiriato: vida económica* pp. 1171–2 and the ideology and policies of Obregón, Calles and even, to an extent, Cárdenas: Córdova *La ideología de la Revolución Mexicana* pp. 296–306; Michaels 'Mexican politics and nationalism' pp. 4–7, 214.

[130] Lorenzo Meyer 'Historical roots' in Reyna and Weinert (eds) *Authoritarianism in Mexico* p. 17.

[131] Roderic Ai Camp *Mexican political biographies, 1935–1975* (Tucson 1976).

[132] Glade 'Revolution and development' p. 13.

16

EXTERNAL DISEQUILIBRIUM AND INTERNAL INDUSTRIALIZATION: CHILE, 1914–1935

Gabriel Palma

The most prominent characteristic of the conventional interpretation of the genesis of the process of industrialization in Chile, is its scepticism as to the degree of development of manufacturing before 1930.[1] It is argued that the expansion of an export economy such as that of Chile throughout the period could not but hinder the development of manufacturing in the country, that the economic policies that followed, and in particular the legendary revision of import tariffs in 1864, served only to accentuate that inherent tendency, that the presence of foreign capital and of immigrants in a number of local economic activities inhibited the emergence of local entrepreneurial initiative, and so on. On this argument, only a crisis of the magnitude of that of the early 1930s was sufficient to force a break with this pattern of underdevelopment, by compelling the local economy to industrialize.

We have demonstrated elsewhere that this conventional view misrepresented the nature of local manufacturing development before 1930, and does scant justice to its scale. Even those studies which describe the development of manufacturing before 1930 trace its origins back only to the closing years of the nineteenth century. We suggested that because of the nature of export activities, the economic policies pursued, and the structural characteristics of the international economy in the period, export-led growth in fact *stimulated* the diversification of the local economy. The origins of the resulting process of industrialization can be clearly located in the late 1860s and the early 1870s.[2] This chapter extends that analysis and further revises traditional interpretations, arguing that conventional scholarship has also exaggerated the impact of the Depression of the 1930s upon the local economy, not only because a process of industrialization had already been under way for fifty years, but also because the import-substituting phase of Chilean industrialization had begun with the First World War. This early transition was a consequence of the acute instability of the export sector after the First World War, mainly in the nitrate market. Accordingly, the World Depression does not represent so much a break with the immediate past, as far as the Chilean economy is concerned, as an acceleration of a process of transition from export-led growth to import-substituting industrialization which was already under way.

The chapter is divided into three sections. The first gives an account of the Chilean economy on the eve of the First World War. The second discusses the period from 1914 to 1929. The third, dealing with the first half of the 1930s, discusses changes taking place in the economy as a result of the Depression, and reveals continuities with the previous period.

The Chilean economy in 1914

On the eve of the First World War Chile was among the most highly developed nations of Latin America. In terms of 1980 US dollars, income per capita was approaching US $1,000, and exports per capita stood at US $330 (a figure never repeated subsequently, except in 1929), with return value at approximately US $250. Some 40 per cent of public expenditure was devoted to education or investment in physical capital, 40 per cent of the population was resident in towns of over two thousand inhabitants, and 16 per cent of the economically active population was engaged in some kind of manufacturing activity. Those employed in establishments with five or more workers provided approximately one half of the total supply of manufactures, with a volume of production 1.7 times that corresponding to a 'Chenery-normal' level. Many new manufacturing firms had been founded in the years preceding the outbreak of the War. Among those were the Compañía Industrial (1901), the Compañía Cervecerías Unidas (1902), the Sociedad Industrial de los Andes (1903), the Sociedad Nacional Fábrica de Vidrios (1904), *Cemento Melon* (1905), (destined to become the largest producer of Portland cement in Latin America and the fifth largest cement works in the world), a subsidiary of Etablissements Américaines Grety (1906), the Compañía de Molinos y Fideos Carozzi (1906), a Santiago-based subsidiary of Siemens-Schuckeet Ltd (1907), with branches opened subsequently in Valparaíso, Concepción and Antofagasta, and the Compañía Industrial el Volcán (1908).[3]

This process of economic development was, of course, very different from that of advanced capitalist countries, and manifested itself in diverse ways in various sectors of the Chilean economy; it generated inequalities at regional levels and in the distribution of income, it was accompanied by such phenomena as under-employment and unemployment, it took on a cyclical nature, and it benefited the elite almost exclusively. In other words, the development of capitalism in Chile in this period, as everywhere else and at all times, was also characterized by its contradictory and exploitative nature. Nevertheless, for the authors referred to above,[4] it seems that capitalism in Chile in this period was characterized only by these negative aspects (to the analysis of which they have made significant contributions). They have failed to see both the process of capitalist accumulation under way and modifications in the different structures of Chilean society that this process of accumulation induced as it evolved (such as modifications in the composition of productive forces, in resources allocation, in class relations and in the character of the state). Thus, they have been unable to detect the specificity of the historical progressiveness of capitalism in this period.

One of the many examples of these transformations in Chilean society in this period is the early development of the trade union movement. Under socialist, anarchist and Christian influence the Gran Federación Obrera Chileña (FOCH), led by Luis Emilio Recabarren, 'transformed itself from a mutual aid society into a revolutionary syndical organization'.[5] It provided one of the bases for the *Partido Obrero Socialista*, founded in 1912 and affiliated to the Third International in 1920.

From 1830 onward, Chile had developed as an export economy, with the 'engine' of growth provided by the exports of copper, silver, wheat and flour before the War of the Pacific (1879), and nitrates thereafter. By the First World War nitrate exports represented 80 per cent of total exports (and hence US $263 per capita), and provided half of ordinary public revenues through taxation.[6] However, by this time the absolute supremacy of nitrates within the export sector was being challenged by the initiation of large-scale copper mining. Chile had been the leading world producer of copper in the 1850s and 1860s, despite its distance from major markets and its low degree of technological development, but these factors had led to its gradual marginalization in the world market; the opening of El Teniente in 1912 and Chuquicamata in 1915 (respectively the largest underground and open-cast mines in the world) signalled the reversal of this trend. On the eve of European hostilities, then, Chilean foreign trade had reached very respectable levels, and the recent process of diversification augured well for the future.

Chile 1914–29: an economy in transition?

During the First World War (except in the first few months), the Chilean export trade continued relatively unaffected, while imports were substantially reduced. The result was hitherto unknown surpluses in the balance of trade.[7] Demand for natural nitrates, of which Chile was the only producer, increased because of its role in the production of explosives. This more than made up for decreased demand from the fertilizer industry, and led to record exports in 1916 of three million tons. Imports meanwhile fell by more than half in both value and quantum terms, with inputs into manufacturing, particularly capital goods, most seriously affected; imports of metal products, machinery and transport equipment fell to less than a quarter of pre-war levels.[8] While export activity permitted aggregate internal demand to remain relatively stable, the sharp reduction in imports channelled this demand toward the internal market. Local manufacturing activity showed an impressive ability to respond: the data provided by Muñoz suggests that during the war years manufacturing production rose by 53 per cent. Even allowing for an underestimation of the value of production in the base year of 1914, this represents a substantial achievement.[9] The Compañía de Azúcar de Viña del Mar, for example, increased production substantially and began exports to Argentina; the Compañia Industrial increased production of industrial oils by 70 per cent between 1915 and 1917; the Compañía de Tejidos and the Fábrica Nacional de Envases experienced substantial increases in sales, and the latter carried out a significant programme of expansion; and the Fundación Las Rosas produced a selection of machinery, particularly converters, for copper mining. These had previously been imported. Other foundries produced cement mixers and machinery for tanneries, again replacing former imports.[10]

Employment statistics confirm the expansion in manufacturing output.[11] Much of the capacity shown to respond to increased demand is explained by the presence of firms founded in the years preceding the outbreak of the war. Other establishments were created during the war, such as the paper factory Ebbinghaus, Haensel & Co. (1914), subsequently converted into the largest manufacturing establishment in the country, the Compañía Manufacturera de Papeles y Cartones, and the Compañia Electro-Metalurgica ELECMETAL (1917), a producer of steel and various types of metal products, machinery and transport equipment. Statistics on corporate investment in the first decade of the century reinforce the argument.[12] Nevertheless, the bonanza enjoyed by exporting and manufacturing interests during the war came to an abrupt end. In the wake of the armistice, demand for nitrates in the explosives industry fell sharply, while depressed demand for fertilizer showed no sign of immediate recovery. Indeed, increased supplies of ammonium sulphate and the rapid development of the synthetic nitrates industry spelt the irreversible decline of the Chilean nitrate sector. The immediate impact was disastrous. Nitrate exports in 1919 fell to a quarter of 1918 levels in volume, and a fifth in value. For their part, Chile's terms of trade fell by 38 per cent between 1917 and 1919. As exports represented some 30 per cent of GNP, this deterioration meant a loss of real income of around 11 per cent (assuming no changes in physical product).

Despite some recovery in the nitrate industry and the terms of trade in the 1920s, both were marked by severe instability. While the index of export prices fell rapidly and continuously throughout the 1920s, declining by 43 per cent overall, the terms of trade index behaved erratically, reflecting violent fluctuations in import prices.[13] Thus the foreign trade sector, for so long the principal motor of local economic development, became a major source of economic instability, with its principal product losing its position to natural and synthetic substitutes, the export price index falling, and the import trade subject to rapid fluctuations.

The response to these difficulties in the foreign trade sector was a relatively systematic attempt to pursue a different growth model, with the accent on production for the internal market. A more detailed analysis of the demand and supply factors behind this transition allows a better understanding of the dynamic of change. On the demand side, the essential characteristic of the period was the implementation of a number of economic policies intended to increase the proportion of aggregate demand orientated to the internal market. Between 1914 and 1929 there were several revisions of import tariffs. The first general revision took place in 1916, and provoked from the *Report on Trade* issued by the US Federal Trade Commission the complaint that the tariff on imported manufactures had risen by between 50 and 86 per cent, and that 'in various cases the increase was even greater'.[14] The *Report* calculated that, taking into account the tariff and other customs dues, American preserved foods were paying a tariff of 250 per cent.[15] The Sociedad Nacional de Agricultura achieved even more 'effective' protection for its products by blocking the completion of the Chilean section of the Salta to Antofagasta railway, and thus denying access to the nitrate zone for Argentine production.

The tariff structure was revised again several times. The 1928 revision introduced significant increases on a number of manufactured goods, and gave the president the right to increase the tariff on any product to a maximum of 35 per cent. Within two years Ibañez had used this provision to raise the tariff on the products contained in 440 customs classifications.[16] With protectionism increasing in the countries of the centre, the few remaining local critics of this policy were losing their case.

The second relevant economic policy was that of currency devaluation: between 1913 and 1929 the peso fell by 60 per cent in real terms.[17] Finally, for the first time in over half a century, there were years in which the internal rate of inflation fell below the international rate, and this also helped to direct demand towards the internal market. This and the import tariff contributed to relative increases in the prices of importables in relation to non-traded goods, and provided further stimulus to transfers of resources into import substitution. These developments helped to alter the structure of relative prices and orientate aggregate local demand towards the internal market, thus stimulating domestic production. But in addition to the more radical use of this range of policy instruments, this period was also characterized by a significant expansion in state intervention in economic activity. The internal structure of the state was redesigned, with the creation of a number of public bodies charged with promoting a range of productive activities, and the attribution to the state itself of a direct role in production.

Among the agencies which gave the state a greater degree of control over economic activity in general were the Banco Central (1925), the Servicio de Minas del Estado (1925), the Caja de Crédito Agricola (1926), the Caja de Crédito Minero (1927), the Caja de Crédito Carbonifero (1928), and the Instituto de Crédito Industrial (1928). To these should be added the Instituto de Fomento Minero e Industrial of Tarapaca and of Antofagasta, and the Caja de Colonización Agricola. These institutions provided finance, and in some cases became responsible for commercialization. For example, the Caja de Crédito Minero marketed the production of small and medium copper producers, and engaged in prospecting, infrastructural work, technical assistance and the provision of machinery. In the area of direct production, the state already possessed two manufacturing establishments, the Imprenta Nacional and the Fábrica y Maestranzas del Ejército (FAMAE), both producing exclusively to fulfil the needs of the state itself.[18] In this period, the state also began to produce inputs for private industry, steel being the most important. Despite the presence of private steel producers, established in Chile for over a decade at this time, the state took a majority share in the Compañía Electro-Siderúrgica e Industrial of Corral (1926) in order to accelerate production.

From the point of view of supply factors underlying this transitional process, one of the most significant characteristics of the period was the markedly different performances of the export and manufacturing sectors.

Table 8: Index of manufacturing and export production in Chile, 1914–1935
        (real values)   (1914 = 100)

	Manufacturing production	Exports
1914	100.0	100.0
1918	153.0	111.0
1919	153.4	39.6
1922	158.6	68.3
1925	189.1	126.1
1928/9	181.0	167.1
1932	145.5	30.6
1935	208.3	48.7

Source J. G. Palma 'Growth and structure of Chilean manufacturing industry from 1830 to 1935' (unpubl. D.Phil., Oxford 1979) Appendices 31 and 47.

As Table 8 reveals, manufacturing production grew 4.2 times more rapidly than exports during the war years, and the subsequent disparity between the two sectors was even greater. The contrast, then, dates from the war period and the years immediately following it, rather than from the 1930s as has commonly been supposed. It is difficult to reconcile this picture with the notion of an 'export' economy, in which the export sector acts as the engine of growth, and other activities move in relative harmony with it. Evidence such as this, that in the Chilean case it was the First World War which marked the beginning of the break with the 'export economy' and the start of the process of import substitution, corrects the view advanced previously by the most important accounts of the period – those of Muñoz and Kirsch – that manufacturing activities still followed the export cycle during these years.[19] In fact the performance of the two sectors could scarcely have been more in contrast.

Further information regarding the transition taking place can be derived from a detailed analysis of the structure of manufacturing production between 1914 and 1929. The most significant trend is the decline in the high share previously accounted for by current consumption goods (food manufactures, beverages, tobacco, footwear and clothing), and the corresponding increase in the significance of durable consumer goods and intermediate and capital goods (textile manufacture, paper and printing, chemical products, machinery and transport equipment).

Table 9   Production indices and relative shares in manufacturing production for current consumption goods, and durable consumer, intermediate and capital goods in Chile, 1914–1935

	(real values)		(1918 = 100)		
	Current consumption goods		Durable consumer, intermediate and capital goods		Total manufacturing production
	Index	*Relative share (percentages)*	*Index*	*Relative share (percentages)*	
1914	67.1	(82.6)	63.0	(17.4)	65.4
1918	100.0	(81.7)	100.0	(18.3)	100.0
1925	115.5	(76.3)	165.9	(23.7)	123.6
1929	107.0	(71.5)	190.5	(28.5)	122.2
1933	89.7	(68.8)	181.1	(31.2)	106.9
1935	104.4	(62.6)	278.0	(37.4)	136.1

Source   Palma 'Growth and structure' Appendices 47, 59 and 60.

As Table 9 shows, during the First World War rates of growth in each group of activities were similar; thereafter the second group experienced much more rapid growth. Between 1918 and 1929 production of current consumption goods grew at an average of only 0.6 per cent per annum, while that of the second group grew at 6 per cent per annum. Its relative share rose in consequence from 18.3 to 28.5 per cent, and the process continued after 1929.

The changing pattern described above was also reflected in the relative shares of domestic production by sector in total internal supply. On the eve of the war, manufacturing establishments employing five or more workers were providing half of total supply, but the picture in each of the two sectors examined was radically different: the local production of current consumption goods accounted for 80 per cent of internal supply, but that of the second type of goods did not account for even 20 per cent.[20] These proportions changed as a result of the war. As we have seen, the level of imports fell, while aggregate internal demand was kept up by export activities. Given the very different share accounted for by imports in the supply of the two groups examined, the falling level of imports affected them differently. In the case of current consumption goods, it was possible for domestic production to make up the difference, and in fact even increase total supply, while in the second group total supply declined by 15 per cent over four years, despite a 59 per cent increase in domestic production over the same period. At the end of the war, therefore, there were shortages of manufactures in the areas of durable consumer goods and manufactured inputs only, and it was in these sectors where import tariffs rose most substantially. Thus the strong stimulus to local production continued after the war for these products, while it did not where current consumption goods were concerned. This is reflected in the comparative production indices, as we have seen.

As a result of these changes, the share of local manufacturing production in total local supply rose from 51 to 66 per cent between 1914 and 1925; the increase for current consumption goods was from 80 to 85 per cent, and that for the second group of goods from 17 to 35 per cent.[21]

Changes in the structure of production and the local market for manufactured goods can best be appreciated from the data in Table 10, which gives production indices for the eleven activities into which manufacturing production during the period is divided.

The two activities which best illustrate this transition are those of food processing on the one hand, and metal products, machinery and transport equipment on the other. The first, which was the largest manufacturing sub-sector before the war, was relatively stagnant after it; the second grew rapidly both during and after the war, increasing by 73 per cent overall in the war years, and at a rate of 10.2 per cent per annum thereafter. Its share in total Chilean manufacturing production doubled,

Table 10   *Production indices for the different manufacturing activities in Chile, 1914–1935*
       (real values)   (1918 =100)

		1914	1918	1925	1929	1933	1935
1	Food processing	71.1	100.0	103.9	110.4	91.7	106.1
2	Beverages	68.5	100.0	135.0	94.8	78.7	91.0
3	Tobacco	46.0	100.0	159.3	125.1	92.3	106.8
4	Textiles	76.2	100.0	164.5	157.5	223.9	363.3
5	Footwear and clothing	49.1	100.0	116.9	104.9	87.6	104.4
6	Wood and furniture	90.3	100.0	140.0	107.8	98.5	124.0
7	Paper and printing	62.2	100.0	96.1	171.6	148.7	246.2
8	Leather and rubber products	63.5	100.0	122.3	103.4	85.9	99.4
9	Chemical products	73.1	100.0	151.6	192.7	144.9	200.4
10	Non-metallic mineral products	46.4	100.0	104.5	148.2	131.1	217.0
11	Metal products, machinery and transport equipt.	57.8	100.0	250.2	289.5	217.8	301.2
	TOTAL	65.4	100.0	123.6	122.8	106.9	136.1

Source   Palma 'Growth and structure' Appendix 46.

and its share in total internal supply of these products tripled.[22] The rapid growth in the production of intermediate and capital inputs, and in particular of metal products, machinery and transport equipment, reflected a clear trend towards a structure of production with a high degree of diversification and autonomy. As a consequence, some of the potential advantages for a greater degree of specialization were lost, but in any case the international economy did not display in the period the minimum levels of stability required for such potential advantages to be realized. Preliminary estimates of the share in GDP of manufactures from establishments with five or more workers place it at 9.6 per cent in 1914, 10.8 per cent in 1918 and 12.9 per cent in 1925.[23]

Along with the changes taking place in the model of growth in these years went a number of social and political developments. While economic policies were designed seeking to accelerate the growth and diversification of manufacturing production and to increase the degree of local economic autonomy, progressive social legislation was introduced, the constitution was modified, and the socio-political composition of Congress changed radically. This reflected the emergence of new groups and social forces and the destabilization of the oligarchical regime which had dominated national politics in the first century of independence. Given these changes, the country that had to face up to the crisis of the 1930s was strikingly different from that which had existed before the First World War.[24]

Before the war the export economy was relatively successful, as was its capacity to promote diversification of the local economy. Thereafter, with the crisis of the export sector, a process of transformation began. With the loss of compression in the engine of growth, as a result of export instability, there was a turn towards the manufacturing sector as a new stimulus for local development. The transition was marked by difficulties, ambivalence, political conflict, indecision and improvisation, but its central characteristic was the shift from the export economy to a process of import substitution – a process that has been examined in the literature from two perspectives. The first, related to the supply of manufactured products, concerns the increase in the proportion of total supply of manufactures met by local production. A variant of this approach, mainly focused on short-term changes, restricts attention to the local production of previously imported goods. A second approach observes the process from the point of view of demand, and distinguishes between a 'normal' process of industrialization and one that is 'forced', or based upon import substitution. The first relates to the increase in manufacturing production which would normally accompany an increase in per capita income in a country. The second, in contrast, stems from an attempt to raise the rate of growth of manufacturing activities above this 'normal' level, by introducing economic policies designed specifically for that purpose.

On any analysis, Chile was in transition between 1914 and 1929 from an export economy to one based on import substitution. The contribution of local production to the internal supply of manufactures was increasing; industrial growth was based upon the local production of previously imported goods, manufactured intermediate and capital inputs in particular; and economic policies were devised and applied in order to orientate aggregate internal demand towards the local market, and hence to accelerate the growth of manufacturing production in the country and the degree of internal economic autonomy. The efficiency of the set of policies applied may be questioned, but not its intent.

Chile 1929–35: a break with the past?

A major difference between the First World War and the crisis of the 1930s, as far as the Chilean economy is concerned, was that the former had a negative impact mainly on the import trade, whereas the latter saw the collapse of both exports and imports. In real terms, exports in 1932 stood at one sixth of their level in 1929; in quantum terms they stood at less than a quarter, while the export price index was down by half and continued to fall in 1933, reaching a third of what it had been in 1929, and a fifth of its level in 1920. This fall in the levels of exports, added to the unavailability of foreign credits and the limited stocks of gold reserves, forced imports to follow the same downward path. By 1932 these too stood in real terms at only one sixth of their 1929 levels, and fell even further in 1933. In quantum terms they also fell to one sixth of 1929 values in 1932. The import price index, however, fell far more slowly, standing at three quarters of its 1929 level in 1932 and continuing a gradual decline thereafter, but far less severe than that experienced by export prices. The terms of trade therefore moved against Chile, declining by 36 per cent between 1929 and 1932. By the same token, of course, they were moving in favour of the countries of the centre: for Britain, for example, the terms of trade reached their highest point in the whole ninety-five-year cycle covered by Feinstein.[25] According to calculations made by the League of Nations, Chile's economy was worse hit than any other in the world by the crisis. A study covering the countries accounting for 90 per cent of world trade showed Chile suffering the largest percentage decline in the value of imports and exports alike; while in quantum world trade showed a decline from 100 in 1929 to 74.5 in 1932, Chile registered an export decline from 100 in 1929 to 24 in 1932, with a low of 13 in November, and an import decline from 100 to 18, with a low of 10 in May 1932.[26]

If the balance of trade was not bad enough, the unavailability of international loans made the balance of payments worse. Chile had gone heavily into debt in the late 1920s, in particular under the Ibañez government, in order to balance its international account and service its early borrowing, but also to finance a large programme of public investment. In the United States alone Chile sold bonds to the value of US $1.76 billion during the 1920s. Foreign loans received amounted to US $338 million in 1929 and US $563 million in 1930, falling to US $53 million in 1931, and US $23 million in 1932, before disappearing altogether in 1933.[27] In these circumstances, shrinking export revenue went increasingly to service the foreign debt. This commitment absorbed US $326 million in 1929 and US $394 million in 1930, while the decline of the peso made the burden even heavier in terms of domestic currency. With Chile on the Gold Standard, the growing balance of payments deficit had to be covered by drawing on the gold reserves of the Banco Central. As gold reserves declined, the balance of payments situation became unbearable. On 17 March 1931 import tariffs on a broad range of goods were raised by 20 to 35 per cent, but despite this it proved necessary, on 15 June 1931, to declare a moratorium on the foreign debt and to impose exchange controls. This was a bid to halt the flow of gold from the Central Bank, slow the rapid decline of the peso, and ensure that essential imports would still be obtained. By this time, though, the crisis had begun to affect the political system, forcing Ibañez to resign on 26 July 1931 and thus inaugurating an eighteen-month period of greater instability than the republic had known before, marked as it was at its peak by the rise and fall of the short-lived 'Socialist Republic' of a hundred days.

With the default on the foreign debt and the introduction of exchange controls in June 1931, the deflationary process produced by adherence to the Gold Standards in conditions of crisis in the foreign trade came to a halt. Nominal money supply (M_1) had fallen by 38 per cent between September 1929 and June 1931, while over a similar period (July 1929 to November 1931) the cost of living index had fallen by 11 per cent, and the wholesale price index by 30 per cent.[28] In the meantime, the dramatic decline in revenues from export taxes had produced a substantial budget deficit. Taxes on exports produced 48 per cent of 'ordinary' public revenues before the First World War, and 28 per cent in 1925; by 1930 they contributed only 13 per cent, and by 1935 a mere 0.1 per cent. Despite drastic economies, it was impossible to balance the budget in these circumstances. The deficit in 1931 stood at 31 per cent of total expenditure (US $237 million), rising to 37 per cent in 1932 (US $189 million).[29]

The collapse of the export sector also affected production for the internal market. If we first consider the most difficult years, 1929–32 (see Table 11), it is clear that agriculture was least affected by the crisis, undoubtedly because of its reduced need for imported inputs and machinery. It is also agriculture, however, which shows the lowest growth rate throughout the rest of the decade. The experience of the mining sector was radically different. Average annual production fell to one quarter of 1929 levels in 1932, reaching its lowest point in December of that year.[30] Of the 91,000 workers employed in the sector in 1929, less than a third remained in work two years later. Mining thus accounts for fully half of the unemployment created in the period.[31] Construction, too, suffered heavily. Activity through 1932 was only a third of what it had been in 1929, and in August 1932 the number of contracts signed touched a low point of 6 per cent of the monthly average for 1929.[32] In contrast, manufacturing industry was less directly affected, reflecting the greater independence from the export cycle which resulted from the structural transformations of the 1920s, and the degrees of diversification that had been achieved. The decline in annual levels of manufacturing production was relatively slight, and by 1934 the fall had practically been made up. Furthermore, monthly production figures suggest that production continued to rise until August 1930 (to a level 11 per cent above the average for 1929), then fell for only twelve months.[33] The lowest point (August 1931) was only 25 per cent below the average for 1929, and the ground lost was recovered in only seven months. GDP fell by over one third between 1929 and 1932, largely because of the importance of mining, whose contribution in 1929 fell only 8 per cent short of those of agriculture, manufacturing industry and construction combined.

Turning now to the post 1932 recovery, we note that from the point of view of demand factors, the monetary policies pursued after the fall of

Table 11   Chilean GDP and production by activity, 1929–1940
(real value)   (1929 = 100)

	Agriculture	Mining	Manufac-turing	Construc-tion	GDP	*GDY
1929	100.0	100.0	100.0	100.0	100.0	100.0
1930	103.1	71.1	94.8	77.6	85.4	85.7
1931	83.0	48.3	76.8	34.6	64.3	68.1
1932	84.5	26.3	77.5	43.9	63.6	66.5
1933	104.8	32.8	87.1	58.0	75.3	78.1
1934	111.5	53.4	98.5	103.4	85.7	88.9
1935	97.5	61.1	111.0	110.7	87.3	90.6
1936	102.4	62.4	117.3	95.6	90.6	94.9
1937	94.0	85.8	123.5	114.6	97.5	102.6
1938	100.6	76.7	128.0	104.9	101.7	103.9
1939	109.3	75.0	130.4	133.7	98.8	100.8
1940	104.6	81.1	150.9	152.2	103.1	106.7

* GDY = GDP readjusted as a result of changes in the terms of trade
Sources   United Nations Organization, ECLA Economic survey of Latin America, 1949 (New York 1950); Palma 'Growth and structure'.

Ibañez were scarcely orthodox, particularly during the 'Socialist Republic' (June–September 1932). In fact M_1 doubled in less than two years, between August 1931 and April 1933.[34] This was not simply the result of government borrowing from the Central Bank in order to fund budget deficits. It was in part a consequence of a decree law issued by the 'Socialist Republic', instructing the Central Bank to print money in order to make loans to a number of development boards (*instituciones de fomento*) with the explicit purpose of stimulating production. The presence of activity of this kind, in addition to inevitable reactions aimed at partially compensating for falling public revenues, suggests a 'pre-Keynesian' orientation to public spending in the period. This is not to imply that those charged with shaping economic policy had a clear and coherent global alternative to the orthodox economic model. It implies that, faced with a crisis of great magnitude and having lost faith in conventional economic theory, they sought alternative ways of alleviating the chaos into which the economy had fallen. A deliberately expansionist monetary and fiscal policy was no more heretical than the new import tariffs, the default on the foreign debt, the abandonment of the Gold Standard or the introduction of exchange controls, all of which had gone before. All these policies pointed away from conventional remedies. In any case, 'flexibility' over such matters was a time-honoured custom. As a treasury minister had remarked in the middle of the nineteenth century, 'time and other circumstances modify principle'.[35]

Law 4321 of 1928 had raised tariffs, and given the president of the republic the power to introduce further increases of up to 35 per cent. The result of the use of this provision by Ibañez was that between 1928 and 1930 the tariff rose on average by 71 per cent, affecting 73 per cent of imports. Ibañez introduced further increases early in 1931, and in 1932 the short-lived government of Juan Esteban Montero imposed a further 10 per cent tariff on 'luxury goods'. In March 1933, virtually on taking power, Alessandri increased tariffs across the board by 50 per cent, and a year later that increase was replaced by a surcharge on the tariff, based upon its value in gold, of 100 per cent. In January 1935 this was increased to 300 per cent.[36]

This extraordinary increase in the tariff was in part neutralized by the rapid depreciation of the peso, but its effect, in conjunction with exchange controls and import licences and quotas, was to stimulate domestic production across the board. As a result, the tendency toward diversification noted in the previous decade and a half was accelerated. The effect on the structure of relative prices was reinforced by the behaviour of the exchange rate. Between 1930 and 1935 the peso lost two thirds of its real purchasing power; without the measures taken to save foreign exchange and reduce imports, it would undoubtedly have lost more. Between 1914 and 1935, then, the peso had seen an 80 per cent decline in its purchasing power. Furthermore, increases in the internal price index had not kept pace with the rate of devaluation. The net effect was a devaluation of 44 per cent in real terms in the period. This clearly favoured the domestic production of importables and exportables.[37]

Thus, after 1931 the combined effect of monetary and fiscal policy, import tariffs, exchange controls and devaluation of the peso was to orientate a very high proportion of existing and newly created demand to the internal market. The stimulus to domestic production that this represented was effective. Economic recovery was also encouraged by a number of acts of legislation. Law 5314 of 1933 exempted private construction started after August 1933, and finished by the end of 1935, from all taxes except those relating to paving and sewerage. It was subsequently modified to include all buildings on which the basic structural work had been completed by the end of 1935, thus extending its effective life. Within a year it had led to an increase of 77 per cent in finished construction (measured in square metres).[38] Finally, economic recovery owed much to the reactivation of the international market and the increased demand in volume terms for Chile's exports. Exports rose in value terms by 59 per cent and in quantum terms by 156 per cent between 1932 and 1935. The monthly index (1927–9 = 100) rose from 13 in November 1932 to 68 by the end of 1933; nitrate production went from 694,000 metric tons in 1932 to 1,200,000 in 1935, while production of refined and blister copper rose by 270 per cent over the same period.

Increases in the volume exported thus offset to some extent the continued decline in international prices.[39]

From the point of view of the supply side of the recovery, with the exception of agriculture, local production showed an impressive ability to respond to stimuli on the demand side. As Table 11 shows, agricultural production returned to 1929 levels by 1933 (in real value) after a shallow decline, but stagnated thereafter. Mining reached a low point in December 1932, with production standing at one fifth of 1929 levels, and recovered slowly to two thirds of 1929 levels by 1935. At this stage mining remained the most adversely affected sector, with its share in GDP reduced to 18 per cent, in comparison with 23 per cent in 1929. Given its weight in total GDP, it bore most of the responsibility for the decline in the wider measure of 12.7 per cent over the same period. The aggregation of all mining activity concealed wide variation, however. Nitrate exports in 1935 were at 42 per cent in volume terms of those of 1929, while those of copper had recovered to 86 per cent. The same trend was to continue thereafter. The level of building activity proved more sensitive to short-term fluctuations. It fell sharply before recovering rapidly. In 1935 the number of new completions in the residential sector was 5.3 times higher than in 1931, and in the industrial and commercial sector 4.1 times higher than in 1931. The recovery was such that the 1935 level of building activity was 11 per cent higher than in 1929.[40]

As we have seen, manufacturing industry experienced a rapid and permanent recovery after a relatively limited decline, to reach in 1935 the highest relative level of production of all economic activities. Important structural changes also took place during the period. A comparison of the first and second National Censuses of Industry and Commerce, made in 1927 and 1937, reveals an increase in the number of establishments with five or more workers from 8,539 to 18,328, an increase of 170 per cent. The total number employed in such enterprises increased by 83 per cent, from 82,494 to 151,157. Whereas in 1920 only a quarter of total employment in manufacturing industry was provided by such establishments, they accounted for 41 per cent in 1930, and practically 50 per cent in 1937. There was also a growing number of establishments with over a hundred workers. They accounted for substantial proportions of those workers in establishments with five or more workers: 31 per cent in processed foods, 71 per cent in beverages, 89 per cent in tobacco, 70 per cent in textiles, 36 per cent in clothing and footwear, 56 per cent in paper, 43 per cent in printing, 48 per cent in chemical products, 67 per cent in non-metallic minerals, and 60 per cent in metal products, machinery and transport equipment.[41] Figures on industrial investment reveal continued real growth despite adverse circumstances in 1930 and 1931, a decline in 1932 and 1933, and a rapid recovery in 1934 to levels above those of 1929.[42] Estimates of manufacturing production, as we have seen, show improvements from mid-1931. Once again, though, disaggregation reveals a number of contrasts.

Table 12 Indices of manufacturing production and relative shares for current consumption goods, and durable consumer, intermediate and capital goods in Chile, 1929–1940
(real values)   (1929 = 100)

	Current consumption goods		Durable consumer, intermediate and capital goods		Total manufacturing production
	Index	Relative share (percentages)	Index	Relative share (percentages)	
1929	100.0	(71.5)	100.0	(28.5)	100.0
1930	92.7	(68.9)	100.6	(30.2)	94.8
1931	76.6	(71.3)	77.1	(28.7)	76.8
1932	75.3	(69.4)	83.3	(30.6)	77.5
1933	83.8	(68.8)	95.1	(31.2)	87.1
1934	90.3	(65.4)	119.9	(34.6)	98.5
1935	97.5	(62.6)	143.9	(37.4)	111.0
1936	106.5	(64.8)	144.8	(35.2)	117.3
1937	106.2	(61.9)	163.8	(38.1)	123.3
1938	106.0	(61.1)	168.8	(38.9)	128.0
1939	108.2	(60.9)	174.1	(39.1)	130.4
1940	119.5	(59.7)	205.3	(40.3)	150.9

Sources O. Munõz Crecimiento industrial de Chile, 1914–1965 (Santiago 1968); Palma 'Growth and structure' Appendices 47, 59 and 60.

By 1935, production of current consumption goods had not yet returned to 1929 levels, while in the second group it had surpassed them by 44 per cent. Over the longer term, the first group showed a 70 per cent improvement (in real terms) over 1914, while the second group showed a 340 per cent increase. As a result, current consumption goods fell from an 83 per cent share of total manufacturing production to a 63 per cent share, with the second group gaining ground proportionately. The implicit average annual rates of growth for each group between 1929 and 1940 were 1.6 per cent and 6.8 per cent respectively; for the period 1931–40 they were 5.1 per cent and 11.5 per cent respectively.

As regards the structure of local supply of manufactures, the rapid decline in manufactured imports (from US $206 per capita in 1929 to US $26 per capita in 1934) and the rapid recovery of local production meant that by that time domestic production represented 90 per cent of total internal supply, against 60 per cent in 1928/9.[43] Per capita consumption of manufactures fell by more than one half between 1929 and 1931 (from US \$452 to US \$216), but reached US \$256 in 1934, and US \$400 towards the end of the decade.[44]

Domestic production was already supplying more than 80 per cent of current consumption goods in the 1920s. By 1935, 97.3 per cent of such goods were locally produced, but this owed more to reductions in imports than to increases in domestic production. The decline in the value of imported current consumption goods from US \$148 million in 1929 to US \$18 million in 1933 had relatively little effect upon consumption, in view of the relatively limited weight of imports in total consumption. Per capita consumption fell only from US \$194 in 1929 to US \$127 in 1932, recovering to US \$150 by 1935.[45] For durable consumer goods and intermediate and capital inputs, on the other hand, local production had been responsible for some 30 per cent of total supply in the late 1920s. With the crises, it rose to a peak of 74 per cent in 1933, and remained at 71.1 per cent in 1935. Here the rapid response of local production was as significant as the decline in imports, which slumped from US \$712 million to US \$93 million in 1933. They recovered quickly thereafter, but domestic production rose sufficiently fast for relative shares to remain virtually constant.[46]

If we return to Table 10 (p. 326), we gain a clearer view of manufacturing activity by sector in the period. In the first half of the 1930s the most outstanding performance came from textiles, which experienced a small decline in 1930, but grew thereafter at 30 per cent per annum. By 1935 real annual production grew to more than double that of 1929. Despite the sharp fall in imports, per capita internal supply in 1935 reached 80 per cent of 1929 levels. The rapid increase in textile production pushed the share of domestic production in total domestic supply from 30 per cent in 1929 to 77 per cent in 1935, and the share of textile in total manufacturing production rose from 6 per cent to 13.7 per cent over the same period.[47] Rapid increases in textile production were common in Latin America in the period.[48]

Other dynamic sectors in manufacturing in the period were non-metallic minerals, chemical products, timber and furniture, paper and printing, and metal products, machinery and transport equipment. The production of non-metallic minerals followed the fortunes of the construction sector closely, expanding at 29 per cent per annum between 1933 and 1935. Between 1929 and 1935 the share of domestic production in total supply rose from 39.5 to 86.8 per cent. In real terms, by 1935 production was over 4.6 times what it had been in 1914.[49] Production of chemicals recovered from 1933 onward, rising by 38 per cent over two years; the share of domestic production in total supply rose from 25 per cent in 1929 to 54 per cent in 1935. In real terms, by 1935 production was almost three times its level in 1914.[50] Where metal products, machinery and transport equipment were concerned, domestic production was by 1935 supplying 60 per cent of the domestic market, as against 30 per cent in the mid-1920s and 7 per cent in 1914. In relative terms, by 1935 production was 5.2 times that of 1914.[51]

Conclusions

By Latin American standards, manufacturing in Chile was relatively well advanced on the eve of the First World War. It was thus increasingly able to take on the role of the engine of local economic growth, as the export sector entered into difficulties which were to culminate in the crisis of the 1930s. The instability of the export sector would provide the stimulus, and the level of manufacturing development before the First World War the material base, for this transition from export-led development to development based upon import substitution.[52] The essential characteristic of the transition was the growing degree of autonomy of the local economy with respect to an increasingly unstable international economy. This was achieved through rapid increases in the diversification of the structure of production. Nevertheless, given the limited size of the internal market, the process of diversification inevitably brought with it significant costs in terms of the inefficiency attendant upon the lack of specialization.

However, those who would criticize the process of 'inward-orientated' development on these grounds should recall that it was precisely the instability of the international economy between the wars which led to its adoption. In the circumstances, it is hardly surprising that the form of development adopted involved some degree of disengagement from the world economy. The economic policies adopted and the changes in the structure of production during the 1920s foreshadowed the lines along which economic development would continue, not only during the 1920s but for the following four decades as well. In other words, the principal characteristics of development after 1930 were already present beforehand. Even so, the recognition that the transition towards import-substituting industrialization began early does not detract from the significance of the crisis of the 1930s for the Chilean economy. No other economy in the world suffered more acutely, and the effects were not easily borne. The point is that the two decades following the outbreak of the First World War must be seen as a single unit, whose principal characteristic was the instability of the external sector and, in response to it, an attempt to carry through a radical transformation of the economy in order to create a greater degree of local productive autonomy. The crisis which began in 1929 contributed new elements which affected the degree but not the nature of the change to a strategy of 'inward-orientated development'.

The interpretations advanced in this chapter are opposed by authors like Frank, Ramírez Necochea, Vélez, Nolff, Cademártori and Hinkelmert, who unequivocally argue for the 'positive' nature of the crisis of the 1930s. From the point of view of 'benefits', the 1930s represent no more than an acceleration and strengthening of a process of transition already under way for over a decade; from the point of view of 'costs', levels of exports per capita prevailing before the crisis have never been restored. Equally, Chile had to wait until the second half of the 1940s to reestablish the levels of per capita GDP and consumption of manufactures achieved in the 1920s. So too there were high costs of a social and political nature. Labour organization suffered a tremendous setback, with the Gran Federación Obrera Chilena (FOCH) losing three quarters of its members. Thus those authors who regard as decidedly positive the fact that the World Depression accelerated and strengthened both the transition to import-substituting industrialization and the strategy of 'inward-orientated' development, can scarcely be right to argue that the impact of the crisis was unambiguous.

Notes

An earlier version of this chapter was presented at the conference, 'The effects of the 1929 Depression on the Latin American economies', organized by Rosemary Thorp at St Antony's College, Oxford. I wish to thank the participants of that conference, particularly Marcelo Abreu, Carlos F. Díaz Alejandro, José Antonio Ocampo and Rosemary Thorp, for their comments. I am also grateful to Paul Cammack, Brooke Larson, Charles Kindleberger, Luis Ortega, Ines Sodre and Elizabeth Spillus for their contributions to the final version.

A grant from the Social Science Research Council, New York, made this research possible.

[1] For example, see M. Segall *Desarrollo del capitalismo en Chile: cinco ensayos dialécticos* (Santiago 1953); H. Ramírez Necochea *Balmaceda y la contrarevolución de 1891* (Santiago 1958), *Historia del imperialismo en Chile* (Santiago 1960); C. Véliz *Historia de la marina mercante de Chile* (Santiago 1961), 'La mesa de tres patas' *Desarrollo Económico* xxx 3 (1963); A. G. Frank 'The development of underdevelopment' *Monthly Review* xviii 4 (1966), *Capitalism and underdevelopment in Latin America: historical studies of Chile and Brazil* (New York 1967); J. Cademártori *La economía chilena: un enfoque marxista* (Santiago 1968); F. Hinkelmert *El subdesarrollo latinoamericano: un caso de desarrollo capitalista* (Santiago 1970), 'Teoría de la dialéctica del desarrollo desigual' *Cuadernos de la Realidad Nacional* vi (1970), 'La teoría clásica del imperialismo, el subdesarrollo y la acumulación socialista' in M. A. Garretón (ed.) *Economía política de la Unidad Popular* (Barcelona 1975); G. García-Huidobro 'El desarrollo económico chileno durante el siglo XX; una historia crítica' (unpubl. B.A. thesis, Santiago University 1972); H. Godoy (ed.) *Estructura social de Chile* (Santiago 1971); S. de Vylder 'The roots of Chile's underdevelopment and the factors perpetuating it; a historical interpretation' (unpubl. mimeo, Stockholm 1973); O. Sáenz 'De la Gran Depresión a la recesión actual' *Hoy* nos 297–303.

[2] J. G. Palma 'Growth and structure of the Chilean manufacturing industry from 1830 to 1935' (unpubl. D.Phil. thesis, Oxford 1979); Luis M. Ortega 'Change and crisis in Chile's economy and society, 1865–1879' (unpubl. Ph.D. thesis, London 1979), 'Acerca de los orígenes de la industrialización chilena, 1860–1879' *Nueva Historia* no. 2 (1981). By the process of industrialization is meant not only a process of simply increasing the output of

manufactures, but rather one in which an increase in the net volume of production (value added) of manufacturing activities is accompanied by a fundamental and relatively generalized transformation of the organization of production and of the complexity of the technology utilized; wage labour gradually becomes the basic relation of production and the capital equipment utilized grows not only in volume but also in range and diversity.

[3] For these calculations and statistical data see Palma 'Growth and structure'.

[4] See note 1 above.

[5] Alan Angell *Partidos políticos y movimiento obrero en Chile* (Mexico 1972) p. 23.

[6] Palma 'Growth and structure' Appendices 30, 31 and 40. 'Ordinary' public revenues were those that provided regular government income.

[7] *Ibid.* Appendix 32. In 1915 and 1916 exports were 2.3 times larger than imports.

[8] *Ibid.* Appendix 30 for nitrate exports, Appendix 31 for copper, Appendix 38 for data on imports.

[9] *Ibid.* pp. 329, 333–6; O. Muñoz *Crecimiento industrial de Chile, 1914–1965* (Santiago 1968) p. 16.

[10] Palma 'Growth and structure' pp. 33–4; H. W. Kirsch 'The industrialization of Chile, 1880–1930' (unpubl. Ph.D. thesis, Florida 1973) 85–6.

[11] Palma 'Growth and structure' p. 45. This data probably underestimates the level of production in 1914.

[12] J. Zegers *Estudios ecómicos, 1907–8* (Santiago 1908) p. 7; R. Espinoza *Cuestiones financieras de Chile* (Santiago 1908) p. 310.

[13] Palma 'Growth and structure' Appendices 20, 21, 31 and 32.

[14] US Federal Trade Commission *Report on Trade* (Washington 1916) pp. 52–3.

[15] T. Wright 'Agriculture and protectionism in Chile, 1800–1930' *Journal of Latin American Studies* XI 1 (1975).

[16] Palma 'Growth and structure' p. 284; P. T. Ellsworth *Chile: an economy in transition* (Westport 1945) p. 11. Meanwhile duties on exports fell from 46 per cent of ordinary revenue in 1910 to 39 per cent in 1915, 29 per cent in 1920, 28 per cent in 1925 and 13 per cent in 1930. Duties on imports rose from 12 per cent in 1915 and 1920 to 20 per cent in 1925 and 28 per cent in 1930. Tariff revisions may have been designed as much to restore public finances as to stimulate manufacturing. Thus the hypothesis of a deliberate stimulus to domestic manufacturing is based upon the change in the structure of effective protection for industry rather than merely upon increases in nominal import duties.

[17] Palma 'Growth and structure' Appendix 27.

[18] *Ibid.* pp. 55–7; Ortega 'Acerca de los orígenes' pp. 35–42. The first, founded in the 1850s, produced official publications; the second, established in the 1890s, provided arms and munitions for the armed forces. There existed also another interesting case, the National Foundry, founded in 1866 also for the purpose of manufacturing war materials. However, the Foundry was closed in 1874 when the diversification of its product range away from military supplies threatened firms in the private sector.

[19] Muñoz *op. cit.* pp. 44–7; Kirsch *op. cit.* pp. 46–7.

[20] Palma 'Growth and structure' Appendices 47, 59, 60.

[21] *Ibid.* Appendix 46.

[22] *Ibid.* Appendices 48 and 58.

[23] M. E. Ballesteros and T. E. Davis 'The growth of output and employment in basic sectors of the Chilean economy' *Economic Growth and Cultural Change* XI 2 (1963); United Nations Organization, ECLA *Economic Survey of Latin America, 1949* (New York 1950) p. 287.

[24] A. J. Bauer *Chilean rural society from the Spanish Conquest to 1930* (Cambridge 1975) p. 215. For the first time the great *latifundistas* no longer constituted a majority in the Senate. This social legislation concerned laws regulating labour contracts, unions and social security. The labour contract law (Law 4053) limited the working day to eight hours, and regulated also collective contracts, the employment of minors and women. To supervise the implementation of the law, the Dirección General del Trabajo was established.

[25] For Chile's terms of trade see Palma 'Growth and structure' Appendices 18 and 32; for Great Britain's terms of trade see C. H. Feinstein *Statistical tables on national income, expenditure and output of the United Kingdom, 1855–1965* (Cambridge 1972) table 139.

[26] Ellsworth *op. cit.* pp. 23–69; Palma 'Growth and structure' Appendix 31.

[27] Ellsworth *op. cit.* pp. 4 and 9.

[28] República de Chile *Estadística chilena*, see relevant years.

[29] Palma 'Growth and structure' Appendix 40. Import duties and domestic taxation rose, compensating for the fall in export revenues. In 1935 import duties provided 38 per cent of ordinary public revenue. Internal taxation, which had only represented 0.2 per cent of ordinary revenue in 1905, provided 9 per cent in 1920, 18 per cent in 1925, 30 per cent in 1930 and reached 39 per cent in 1935.

[30] República de Chile *Estadística chilena*, see relevant years.

[31] Ellsworth *op.cit.* p. 14.

[32] República de Chile *Estadística chilena*, see relevant years.

[33] Palma 'Growth and structure' Appendix 47; República de Chile *Estadística chilena*, see relevant years.

[34] *Ibid.*

[35] República de Chile *Memoria del Ministerio de Hacienda, 1849* (Santiago 1849) p. 321.

[36] Ellsworth *op. cit.* pp. 45–73.

[37] As in any 'small' economy faced with a deterioration in its terms of trade, the price of tradables rose in comparison to that of non-tradables. Thus the 39 per cent fall in the terms of trade between 1930 and 1933 was an important stimulus on the demand side to domestic production of importables. See Palma 'Growth and structure' Appendix 27 for rates of exchange; República de Chile *Estadística chilena*, relevant years, for price indices.

[38] República de Chile *Estadística chilena*, see relevant years.

[39] *Ibid.*

[40] *Ibid.*

[41] *Ibid.*

[42] Ellsworth *op. cit.* p. 21.

[43] Palma 'Growth and structure' Appendix 47.

[44] *Ibid.* Appendices 1 and 47; Muñoz *op. cit.* pp. 160–1.

[45] Palma 'Growth and structure' Appendix 56.

[46] *Ibid.* Appendix 60.

[47] *Ibid.* Appendices 46 and 51. In real terms, production in 1935 was 4.7 times greater than in 1914.

[48] C. F. Díaz Alejandro 'A América Latina em Depressão, 1929–39' *Pesquisa e Planejamento Econômico* x 2 (1980).

[49] Palma 'Growth and structure' Appendix 57.

[50] *Ibid.* Appendix 56.

[51] *Ibid.* Appendix 58.

[52] As 80 per cent of imports were manufactured goods, and these represented about one half the total internal supply, when the export sector enters a crisis this area offers the best opportunity for domestic economic expansion.

17

POLITICS AND THE ECONOMY OF THE DOMINICAN REPUBLIC, 1890–1930

Christopher Abel

Far from annexing the island, I have about the same desire to annex it as a gorged boa constrictor might have to swallow a porcupine wrong-end-to.[1]

Theodore Roosevelt

Overshadowed by an expansionist United States and the rise of a belligerent corporate capitalism, the Dominican Republic confronted changes in the international economy that were representative of those facing the small nations of the Caribbean and Central America. The Dominican Republic enjoyed few of the advantages of the larger and intermediate-size countries of Latin America in the half-century following independence. Where their elites had gained valuable experience in devising political and economic solutions appropriate to local requirements, and had evolved small nuclei of financial and technical expertise with some competence in managing the state and its economic policies, the republic was subject to a long period of Haitian domination (1822–44) which generated scepticism about the wisdom of independence and to a unique and disastrous experiment with the restoration of Spanish colonial rule (1861–5). Never forced over the edge of the periphery, the Dominican Republic remained throughout the nineteenth century weakly linked into the North Atlantic world. Her political leaders, habituated to external orientation, perceived closer links with the European powers and the United States as precautions against renewed Haitian aggression, and invoked the Great Powers to protect particular sectional interests.

This chapter examines the nature of the incorporation of a backward agrarian society into the international economy, in a period of transition from the predominance of diversified small-scale farming to near-mono-crop production concentrated in the hands of two multinational corporations (Cuban-Dominican and South Porto Rico). The same period witnesses the displacement of the ascendancy of the small trading house by that of two multinational banking corporations (National City Bank and the Royal Bank of Canada). Between 1890 and 1930 the republic experienced both direct control by the United States Marines (1916–24) and nominally independent government.

The assassination of Trujillo and the revival of democracy have given rise to a revival of intellectual activity comparable in some respects to that in Spain after the death of Franco. A *trujillista* orthodoxy that perceived the dictatorship as a welcome period of peace, prosperity, enlightened leadership and liberation from domestic chaos and external interference has been challenged by historians and social scientists in new periodicals and monographs and, not least, in textbooks designed for secondary schools and universities.[2] This chapter reviews the relationship between politics and the economy in the republic in the light of a new generation of scholarship, both Dominican and foreign.[3]

Agrarian society and the commodity export profile

The Dominican Republic was still in 1930 an overwhelmingly agrarian society. Its population, estimated by Hoetink at between 150,000 and 207,000 in 1871, rose, according to the first national census in 1920, to 895,000.[4] The level of urbanization in the republic – never a recipient of a substantial influx of European immigrants – was low by Cuban standards, and insufficient to create either a mass market or a politicized urban working class. In 1920 only 16.6 per cent of the population lived in towns of over a thousand inhabitants. The population of the capital Santo Domingo stood at 38,000, and of the second city, Santiago de los Caballeros, capital of the interior province of El Cibao, at only 20,000; only two other towns had populations of over 10,000. Only 8 per cent of the working population was classified as artisan or skilled and semi-skilled urban labour.[5]

Four export crops – tobacco, cacao, coffee and sugar cane – competed for influence.[6] Tobacco, cacao and coffee shared some common features. Each was farmed in El Cibao on small and medium-size holdings by independent peasant producers, and exported through a chain of intermediaries who furnished credit for production. Each crop had some limited multiplier effects promoting a relatively equitable income distribution that stimulated modest commercial circuits, in which locally produced foodstuffs and artisan and cottage-industry manufactures were exchanged. Each was externally vulnerable – to price fluctuations (especially the collapse of commodity prices after the First World War) and to the competition of more efficient rivals who enjoyed the advantages of economies of scale, paid greater attention to product quality and were better informed about market conditions.

In other respects, significant differences between the three crops could be observed. Excluded from the United States by a high tariff, Dominican tobacco was before 1914 marketed mainly in Germany. The determination of the United States to sever the relationship between the republic and Germany without increasing her own tobacco purchases precipitated a grave crisis in the sector during the First World War. After the war Dominican expectations of a resumption of European purchases were unfulfilled, largely because Dominican producers had failed over a long period to improve the product, because German demand had been confined to the low-quality leaf.[7] Meanwhile, challenged by a consumer preference for imported cigars and cigarettes, the tobacco sector endeavoured with some success to retrieve its domestic position through the merger of its two leading factories.[8] Unlike tobacco, the cacao sector enjoyed the advantage of access to a tariff-free US market, so that the republic emerged in 1906 as the world's fourth exporter. Cacao, however, was vulnerable in ways that tobacco and coffee were not: it was subject, above all, to a greater incidence of plant disease and a lower level of international demand. Like other Latin American producers, the republic yielded its position in the 1920s to its more efficient African competitors.[9] The coffee sector was always smaller than tobacco and cacao and never effectively challenged the leading producers. Coffee sustained a modest expansion in the 1920s mainly because, alone among peasant crops, it could be grown on land adjacent to the expanding sugar cane zone in the southern region.[10]

Sugar cane was produced principally on large estates in the south and east. Stimulated initially by a trickle of Cuban refugees from the abortive first war of independence (1868–78), sugar cane was established as a leading export in the mid-1880s, as immigrant Italian businessmen and US firms, attracted by fertile and abundant land and labour that was cheaper than in Cuba and Puerto Rico, entered the republic.

The Dominican Republic enjoyed some of the advantages of being, by Caribbean and Brazilian criteria, a latecomer to sugar cane production. A technological transition from *trapiche* production to the modern *ingenio* was achieved without the problems of seigneurial conservatism or labour resistance that were encountered elsewhere. These advantages were, however, to some extent offset by the vulnerability that arose from the scale of Dominican cane production. Because she enjoyed only a small share of the market, the republic never acquired the bargaining power exercised by Cuba in sugar cane or by Brazil in coffee. At its inception, sugar cane production was welcomed in the republic because it both raised living standards and enlarged the monetized sector, expanding possibilities for small businessmen. Subsequently, however, the positive effects of sugar cane were widely believed to be outweighed by the problems that accompanied it. Some small producers were eliminated by a price collapse and drought in 1884.[11] Others were removed when large producers, alone able to afford a costly imported technology, took advantage of political instability and falling land prices in the 1890s to buy up small holdings.

These changes were made possible by new land legislation. Disappointed by the modest results of policies to promote growth by enticing European immigrants with generous offers of public lands, the Dominican propertied classes evolved new policies based on the import of foreign capital. Arguing that the principal deterrent to growth was the scale of communal landownership, the Dominican elite introduced legislation between 1895 and 1916 that set out to release land and labour from pre-capitalist patterns of production and to smooth the entry of foreign capital. Because, however, little of the new legislation was enforced owing to political instability, it was left to the military occupation to consummate the process initiated by its Dominican predecessors. Land policy during the occupation had five principal features: an emphasis upon the redistribution of communal landholdings; the clarification and elaboration of land titles; the use of taxation as an instrument to bring unused land under cultivation; the establishment of a cadastral survey; and the formation of a land tribunal to supervise the process of distribution and to adjudicate in disputes.[12] The overall impact of these policies was ambiguous because the promise of a comprehensive policy was never acted upon. The land tax yielded little revenue; the cadastral survey was never completed; and, as late as 1925, the activities of the land tribunal did not extend beyond three provinces. The land legislation elicited the degree of adaptation required by the sugar cane corporations in order to take advantage of the limited opportunities offered by the international economy in the 1920s, while allowing pockets of pre-capitalist production to survive in much of the republic. Both reluctant to offend the external sector and afraid of promoting a peasant uprising, the Vásquez government (1924–30) introduced no substantial innovations in land policy.[13]

A trend towards concentration was accompanied by a gradual transition from national resident and family ownership to absentee corporate control. Processes that occurred slowly in the first decade of the twentieth century, when the volume of cane output stagnated because the US tariff favoured the Cuban and Puerto Rican crop, were accelerated during the First World War when the international price rose so high that it nullified the effects of the tariff. As the area of land under cane expanded – from 15,000 to 59,000 acres between 1915 and 1923 – competition for land became more fierce. The sugar cane corporations advocating private corporate ownership clashed with sections of the peasantry that adhered, often without land titles, to a tradition of communal landholding. The lands of the sugar cane corporations, enjoying superior access to legal resources, were enlarged at the expense of smallholdings by the ruthless practice of litigation, physical eviction and foreclosure upon the properties of debtors whose land had been used as collateral.

The sugar prosperity of the First World War promoted the establishment of two vast mills in the south that were owned by the corporations that dominated production. First, the South Porto Rican Sugar Corporation consolidated its stake in Central Romana, which had been purchased in 1911 as a means of maintaining a refinery in Puerto Rico at full capacity. Second, the Central Barahona, founded by the Cuban-Dominican Sugar Company, expanded at a spectacular pace to become in 1922 the second-largest estate in the republic. Whereas in 1899 Italian, Cuban, Spanish and British owners had possessed nine mills and US owners three, by 1927 US capital directly controlled the entire industry – apart from three estates owned by the Vicini family (partly domesticized Italian immigrants) and one owned by a Dominican entrepreneur who was heavily mortgaged to a US bank.[14]

From the 1890s Dominican resistance to employment on the sugar cane plantations became more militant because while daily wages fluctuated violently, real wages fell as the Dominican peso was devalued and *fichas* and *contraseñas* (tokens) were widely substituted for cash payments. Frequently preferring the independence of subsistence and semi-subsistence agriculture to wage labour, dispossessed peasants migrated to the less fertile mountain slopes of the east. The exodus of much of the Dominican peasantry and a low population density in the southern provinces persuaded the major corporations to import cheap seasonal labour from Haiti and the British West Indies from about 1900. Between 1916 and 1919 over 10,600 immigrants were registered, of whom 9,600 were contracted *braceros*. In 1919–20 a further 14,000 were registered and returned after the harvest. According to the 1920 census, foreign-born residents represented 26.3 per cent of the total population in the province of San Pedro de Macorís, the province of fastest growth in sugar cane, compared to only 5.5 per cent in the country as a whole.[15] In the mid-1920s perhaps 2,500–3,000 British West Indian *braceros* were imported annually and returned after the harvest, while a further 6,000 were settled with resident permits, especially at the Central Romana. The British Foreign Office and colonial authorities maintained an erratic supervision of the flow of migrants. While they considered living and working conditions on US-owned estates to be adequate, British officials in the island consistently condemned conditions on the Vicini estates, even recommending the governors of the Leeward and Windward Islands to withhold passports from applicants destined for them.[16]

The sugar cane boom was abruptly terminated in 1921 by falling prices associated with the post-war revival of US and European beet, and increases in the US tariff which again restricted Dominican exports. Meanwhile, the process of concentration was again accelerated as smaller operations ceased milling and were foreclosed by the banks. Gambling on a revival of the sugar cane price and alarmed by both political uncertainty in Cuba and rising costs in Puerto Rico, the large corporations chose to expand their acreage although they gained few short-term benefits. Determined not to lose a substantial capital investment, in 1926–7 the US-based corporations sought European markets for Dominican cane when none existed in the United States.

Sugar cane production brought to the republic some advantages in land sales and building materials, provided new jobs and raised income levels. It probably also provided incentives for port rehabilitation which benefited other sectors. Recent research, however, suggests a wide range of disadvantages, of which perhaps the two most damaging were a reduction in the areas of good-quality land available to domestic food crops, and an enlargement of the wage force without access to land for cultivating subsistence crops. Thus the sugar cane sector bears some of the responsibility for expanding Dominican food-import requirements – rice, beans, lard and maize – that deterred investment in other sections of the economy.[17]

Export diversification until about 1905 afforded the republic a degree of bargaining leverage with the metropolitan powers, that was well exemplified by effective resistance to attempts to enact the 1891 reciprocity treaty with the United States. Opposition to the treaty came from two sources: domestic producers who objected that items listed among duty-free US imports included such products as footwear, furniture, rice and chocolate that could be locally produced; and *cibaeño* interests that threatened armed revolt for fear that the most-favoured-nation section of the treaty would prompt German retaliation against imports of cacao and tobacco. In these years shifts in significance between export crops made for a certain tenuousness and impermanence in the external bonds of the republic, that inhibited attempts by a metropolitan power to deepen her dependency.

A gradual shift from a diversified export sector in which no one commodity predominated, to one in which the primacy of sugar cane was undisputed, occurred between 1905 and 1916. At the turn of the century export values for sugar cane and cacao were running neck and neck; and in 1913 the value of cacao exports exceeded that of sugar cane.

Table 13 demonstrates the comparative performances of the four principal export commodities between 1905 and 1930. The general trend in the value and volume of sugar cane exports was steadily upwards between 1908 and 1917; and a record production figure was achieved in 1920, although the price slumped from 12.94 cents per lb. in 1919 to 3.54 cents in 1920. The resumption of pre-war prices between 1925 and 1929 was accompanied by new production records. The performance of cacao was less dramatic, with the volume of exports growing tentatively between 1910 and 1916, reaching one peak in 1917 and another in 1921, only to fall back to pre-1914 levels and stagnate later in the 1920s. Even at its apex of the 1920s (1927), the value of cacao exports stood at much less than one half of that of sugar cane. Leaf tobacco exports behaved

	Sugar cane		Cacao		Leaf tobacco		Coffee	
	Volume in kilos (1,000s)	Value in US$ (1,000s)	Volume in kilos (1,000s)	Value in US$ (1,000s)	Volume in kilos (1,000s)	Value in US$ (1,000s)	Volume in kilos (1,000s)	Value in US$ (1,000s)
1905	48,169	3,292	13,107	2,211	5,232	480	977	157
1906	56,091	2,392	14,556	2,263	6,803	837	1,326	220
1907	49,187	2,010	10,175	2,988	9,918	1,341	1,535	252
1908	45,185	3,092	19,247	4,269	8,484	1,010	1,851	325
1909	70,599	3,395	14,820	2,759	11,259	1,239	700	128
1910	92,908	5,591	16,603	2,850	10,098	958	2,064	324
1911	85,630	4,160	19,828	3,902	13,831	1,421	1,735	319
1912	88,775	5,841	20,833	4,249	5,755	670	2,259	566
1913	78,849	3,651	19,471	4,120	9,790	1,122	1,049	257
1914	101,429	4,943	20,745	3,896	3,736	394	1,832	346
1915	102,801	7,671	20,223	4,864	6,235	973	2,468	458
1916	122,643	12,028	21,053	5,959	7,925	1,433	1,732	317
1917	131,499	13,386	23,715	4,856	8,752	1,659	1,083	228
1918	120,033	11,991	18,839	3,917	15,200	3,624	2,286	537
1919	162,322	20,698	22,418	8,011	20,302	6,661	2,209	947
1920	158,804	45,306	23,390	6,168	16,432	4,240	618	266
1921	183,611	14,338	26,574	3,083	9,172	1,609	936	241
1922	171,542	9,192	18,985	3,054	7,531	883	2,362	609
1923	169,311	18,723	19,831	2,917	16,319	1,914	1,398	428
1924	220,629	21,683	23,142	2,794	15,760	2,279	2,233	864
1925	301,106	15,447	23,482	3,875	22,260	2,765	2,666	1,295
1926	337,653	14,700	20,084	3,831	9,754	1,192	4,307	1,890
1927	295,396	16,668	26,513	7,476	20,298	2,532	4,094	1,750
1928	335,020	16,912	19,302	4,250	14,068	1,274	4,542	2,136
1929	322,088	12,259	21,322	3,870	16,454	1,381	5,508	2,444
1930	345,981	9,910	20,701	2,710	12,970	1,032	4,847	1,483

Source Paul Muto 'The illusory premise: the Dominican Republic and the process of economic development, 1900–1930, (unpubl. Ph.D. thesis, University of Washington 1976) pp. 62–5.

unpredictably. Export volume, inconsistent before 1914, fell spectacularly with the onset of hostilities, only slowly recovering until a new record of export volume coincided in 1919 with high price. A peak in export volume achieved in 1919 was never equalled in the 1920s when exports stagnated, and hopes of a recovery in 1925 when a new peak in export volume was attained were frustrated. Coffee was consistently a junior partner which performed unimpressively, except in the quinquennium 1925–9 when output surpassed past performance.

Table 14 indicates the percentage shares by value of the four principal Dominican exports in the total export of these four commodities. (No other export represented more than 3 per cent of total export volume in any one year.)

Table 14   Value of the four principal exports of the Dominican Republic as percentage shares of the total value of all four exports, 1905–1930

	Sugar cane	Cacao	Tobacco	Coffee
1905	53.6	36.0	7.8	2.6
1906	41.9	39.6	14.7	3.9
1907	30.5	45.3	20.3	3.8
1908	35.6	49.1	11.6	3.7
1909	44.5	37.1	16.7	1.7
1910	57.5	29.3	9.9	3.3
1911	42.4	39.8	14.5	3.3
1912	51.6	37.5	5.9	5.0
1913	39.9	45.0	12.3	2.8
1914	51.6	40.7	4.1	3.6
1915	54.9	34.8	7.0	3.3
1916	60.9	30.2	7.3	1.6
1917	66.5	24.1	8.2	1.1
1918	59.7	19.5	18.1	2.7
1919	57.0	22.1	18.3	2.6
1920	80.9	11.0	7.6	0.5
1921	74.4	16.0	8.3	1.3
1922	66.9	22.2	6.4	4.4
1923	78.1	12.2	8.0	1.8
1924	78.5	10.1	8.3	3.1
1925	66.1	16.6	11.8	5.5
1926	68.0	17.7	5.5	8.7
1927	58.5	26.3	9.1	6.1
1928	68.8	17.3	5.2	8.7
1929	61.4	19.4	6.9	12.2
1930	65.5	17.9	6.8	9.8

Source   Adapted from Muto *op. cit.* pp. 62–5

The crisis of 1920–1 – a crisis of market instability caused by an over-supply of primary products – served as a warning against over-reliance upon the US market and sugar cane. The Dominican elite, hoping to cushion itself against the worst effects of contractions transmitted from the United States, was deeply conscious of the removal of restrictions upon world trade after 1918. The renewed saliency of commodities other than cane encouraged Dominican merchants to seek out diversified export opportunities and to revive European ties. Shifts in the comparative strength and aggregate performance of different commodities aroused optimism regarding diversification, that was dispelled in the later 1920s when the share of sugar cane in total export values stabilized at approximately 60 per cent.

Import composition, banking and manufacturing

Before 1914 the principal sources of Dominican exports were as varied as the republic's customers: Britain and Germany exported hardware; the United States motor-cars and oil; Spain rice, clothing and general provisions; Britain re-exported oil and rice. Nevertheless the preponderance of US imports was firmly established by 1910, when US (including Puerto Rican) supplies comprised 62 per cent of total imports and the combined figure for British, French and German imports barely surpassed 31 per cent. The impulses towards heavier concentration on US supplies were already strong before the outbreak of the First World War. The United States already enjoyed significant advantages over its European competitors: the availability of investment handbooks published in English in the United States; a direct steamship route and geographical proximity which reduced transport costs; adjustment to a market that required second-quality goods; more commercial travellers; a greater proclivity to extend credit; lower prices for many manufactured goods; and better commissions for local salesmen. The ascendancy of the US importer was consolidated during the war when first the Germans were eliminated and then the position of the British and French was eroded. In 1920 the share of US importers peaked at 90 per cent.

The renewed flexibility of trading patterns after the war presented opportunities for import diversification. But few were taken up in the early 1920s, partly because the habit of purchasing from the United States had become instinctive while trading conditions were constrained; partly too because the United States enjoyed the advantage of a permanent nucleus of salesmen. But the principal reason for the slowness of European recovery was US policy calculation. On planning its withdrawal, the United States attempted to limit European options by freezing trading relations within the mould of 1922. The United States sought to preserve its lead with a most-favoured-nation trade agreement in 1924, designed to forestall a preferential trade arrangement sought by the British, who briefly displaced the United States as the principal customer for sugar cane. The British, however, failed to secure safeguards for their exports, notably Burmese rice, because the options of the Dominicans were restricted by US influence over access to credit. Only in the late 1920s did the European importers reassert themselves. By 1930 the US share of Dominican imports had shrunk to 56 per cent, a figure that it had outstripped in every previous year since 1909.[18]

Changes in the nature of metropolitan enterprise were most evident in the banking sector. In the 1890s most credit operations were still conducted by commission houses, both foreign and domestic, which reinforced low product quality by allowing small peasant producers acceptable interest rates only on short-term loans that compelled them to harvest too rapidly.[19]

The first banks in the republic were French and Dominican. The Banco Nacional de Santo Domingo, a French-owned institution, passed into US hands after US interests took advantage of a clash between the Dominican government and the bank, in which the bank invoked the protection of the French government (1903). From then on the European role in banking was negligible. The most prominent of the early Dominican banks was the Michelena Bank, which acted as depository of the receivership account. Gradually the smaller banking institutions were supplanted by transnational enterprises capable of spreading their risks by country and commodity. The commission houses now survived in a new role, as local agencies of the international banks in small towns.

Changes in the currency eased the entry of US-based banks. The future of the economy was threatened in the 1890s by reliance on the Mexican peso as circulating medium which was subject to both shortages and devaluations. And then the economy nearly collapsed owing to large emissions of paper money. In 1899, however, the custom of using the US dollar that began in the ports and seeped into the interior was legally authorized. The currency was stabilized by the use of the US dollar as the official currency, with the Dominican peso used in the interior in a subsidiary role but not accepted for exchange purposes at full face value.

Bank ownership was rapidly concentrated in few hands. The Banco Nacional de Santo Domingo was sold during the occupation to the American Foreign Banking Corporation of New York, an institution closely tied to National City of New York, to which it passed when AFBC was liquidated in 1926. Meanwhile the Michelena Bank was bought in 1917 by the International Banking Corporation, a subsidiary of National City.[20] Initially useful to the military regime because its New York office could negotiate directly with the buying agency of the military government, IBC fell out with the occupation forces, rejecting their request for a loan and demanding transition to a civilian administration on the grounds that the military government was incompetent.[21] Suffering heavy losses, IBC was handed over to National City in 1925.[22] Thus a large proportion of international and domestic banking operations were in the mid-1920s concentrated in the hands of one bank. This was closely linked through interlocking directorates to the Cuban-Dominican Sugar Company which, especially in the 1920 crisis, swallowed up the properties of small indebted *ingenios*.

The only significant competition to US-based banks came from Canadian enterprises. The first of these was the Royal Bank of Canada, established in the republic in 1912, which from its inception was involved in sugar cane transactions, mortgages and the movement of remittances of British West Indian personnel. Despite making substantial losses in 1920, the Royal Bank still made new loans in 1925 in the hope of recovering credits advanced five years earlier. The Royal Bank was followed to the republic by the Bank of Nova Scotia, which remained a minor competitor in 1930.

The position of the international banks was so strong that by 1924 no domestic bank existed. Without a national bank the state was unable to perform the intermediary role adopted in some mainland countries between the international banking system and the domestic economy. The powers of the international banks extended even to an informal surveillance of government funds, since the state relied on them to conduct government business. Abdicating a 'developmentalist' role, the international banks exerted a rigid control of credit to Dominican merchants and made none available to small farmers.[23] The only bargaining weapon open to the government was to transfer its account to the Royal Bank of Canada; but this was reputedly the most conservative of the international banks and the most hostile to proposals in 1928–9 for an agricultural mortgage bank to assist peasant producers.[24]

A manufacturing sector barely existed in the republic in the early twentieth century. Manufacturing never performed a vigorous role in the Dominican economy; and no significant changes in manufacturing activity or the substitution of new products were evident. Most manufactures, like candles and confectionery, were produced at a household level with a negligible investment and primitive technology.[25] The incomplete statistics available for 1936 suggest that industrial investment was overwhelmingly (83.5 per cent) concentrated in sugar-refining. Only electric energy represented more than 5 per cent of total industrial investment (and then only 5.2 per cent). Manufactures that in most of the mainland economies were identified with the early phases of industrial growth – brewing, cement, shoes and leather goods, non-sugar food processing and cigar and cigarette processing – each represented less than 2 per cent of industrial investment in the republic.[26]

No group articulated an ideology of industrialization; and innovation in the industrial sector was not discussed as an expedient to soften the effects of external primary product price fluctuations, even in the 1920–1 crisis. The policies of both government and opposition were predicated on the assumption that a tariff policy that curbed the flow of US manufactured imports would only hasten US reprisals against Dominican agricultural exports that would cause irreparable damage to the economy. Dominican entrepreneurs identified more profitable outlets for their savings in trade, agriculture, urban construction and government lending. Dominican policy-makers calculated that the national market was both too small to stimulate domestic industrial growth and too restricted to encourage incipient multinational manufacturers to open branch-plant operations, as happened in Mexico and Cuba during the 1920s. The state provided no incentives for domestic industrialization: no national banking system existed to assure the flow of funds to national industrial enterprise; and devaluation could not be used as a policy instrument, since the US dollar was the normal currency for business transactions.

Tariff policy reflected these attitudes. From 1891, Dominican tariff arrangements tended to favour US manufacturers. The 1891 reciprocity treaty discriminated in favour of US shoes and leather goods. The provisions of the 1909–10 tariff extended not only to machine tools and equipment (like typewriters) that could not be manufactured in the republic, but also to furniture and other items that could. The occupation tariff of 1919, merely confirming the trends established by its predecessors, was explicitly founded on the assumption that the republic should stimulate areas of comparative advantage and deny protection to infant industries, because scarce labour supplies were more effectively deployed in export agriculture and sales, repairs and servicing facilities for imports. Hence the 1919 tariff raised the number of imported items free of duty from 245 to 700. The expansion of the sugar cane sector encouraged a wave of purchases of machinery, equipment and spare parts from the United States; and the public works programme enhanced sales of US manufactures to the military government. The modification of the 1919 tariff in 1925 attempted to remedy some grievances that had arisen, by imposing duties on industrial imports destined for the sugar cane sector and giving some limited incentives to domestic manufacturing. But these were eroded by proximity to the United States: for example, the principal shoe merchant in Santo Domingo calculated that he would not have to raise his prices or reduce the quality of his merchandise in spite of the new duty on imported footwear because he could buy larger and cheaper job lots in New York.[27] In these circumstances both manufacturing and related agricultural, ranching and timber activities were inhibited.

The state, politics and economic change before 1916

The principal obstacle to the unity and consistency of Dominican policy-making before 1916 was the frailty of the state. Few permanent institutions existed. The state consisted of little more than the projection of one man. Its rudimentary apparatus was clearly inadequate to meet the new tasks required of it in a period of economic growth. The state had to conduct international diplomacy, to carve out land concessions, and maintain a military force competent to withstand a Haitian challenge. It looked to foreign assistance in the establishment of new institutions: North Americans won a contract to establish an Office of Public Works in 1908; the British were contracted to build a wireless station, and Spanish agronomists to open a school of agriculture.

The absence of clear-cut social cleavages that sharpened and clarified political alignments posed a permanent impediment to the evolution of an effective state apparatus. In other Latin American countries, diffuse and malleable political parties that claimed a permanent allegiance crystallized after independence. No such durable coalitions took shape in the Dominican Republic. Instead, there emerged temporary alliances of *jefes de compadrazgo* that embodied the attempt of a particular region or sector to impose its political ascendancy, and then crumbled in the event of a decline in the value of the export commodity upon which the political pretensions of that region or sector rested. So, for example, in the 1880s one faction – the *azules* – whose principal constituency lay in the tobacco sector, decisively displaced another – the *rojos* – whose power-base was the relatively weak timber and cattle sectors, when the sugar cane pioneers, led by Cuban refugees angered by *rojo* support for the Spanish colonial administration in Cuba, threw their weight behind the *azules*. In these circumstances a high rate of turnover in presidential office was not surprising.

The absence of social cleavages was reinforced by an absence of internally integrative factors. Dominican infrastructure was so deficient in the 1890s that the northern port of Puerto Plata enjoyed more reliable communications, through the Cable Francés, with the exterior than with the interior. Furthermore, no road connected Santo Domingo and El Cibao until the US occupation. The absence of a clear national identification among immigrants in the ports, who were subject to varying levels of social acceptance and assimilation, was matched by the localism of peasant attachments in the interior. Religion too intensified disintegrative tendencies: a formal Catholicism competed for popular support with irreligion, Protestantism (among, for example, the black US immigrants of Puerto Plata) and Afro cults. Persistent ethnic tensions, re-inflamed by the Spanish re-annexation, militated further against national integration.

Complementing the absence of internally integrative factors was the lack of permanent externally unifying forces. The principal factor that united Dominicans of all social classes and ethnic groups was Haiti – feared for its militarism and remembered for a protracted occupation when alien patterns of forced labour, landholding and military conscription were rigorously imposed. A sense of incipient nationhood, evolving in defensive response to the Haitian challenge embodied in waves of Haitian immigration in the underpopulated borderlands, was invoked by governments during both frontier disputes and insurrections by opponents who sought Haitian military support and refuge. The precariousness of this sense of nationhood was underlined by the fact that the Haitian threat provided a residual pretext for engaging ties of dependency with the metropolitan powers: foreign mediation was sought in border contests; and the threat of a Haitian invasion was used by sectional interests to contract external loans that compromised Dominican sovereignty.[28]

No opportunity existed for a national oligarchy of modern agrarian enterpreneurs to emerge. Social distinctions between *gente de primera* and *gente de segunda*, segregated in their own social clubs, posed one obstacle. But, more significantly, a precocious transnational elite without clear national allegiances began to evolve: Cuban immigrants in the sugar cane sector took the precaution of applying for US citizenship; and the Vicinis incorporated their enterprises in New York as a strategic insurance.[29]

The principal magnet of the state apparatus for competing political factions was control of the customs house revenue. Thus, in the 1890s and 1900s, a struggle that remained permanently unresolved occurred between the sugar cane sector which demanded tax exemptions and market assistance from the central government, and non-sugar agriculture which pressed for some re-allocation of wealth through export taxes on cane. For two decades, a fragile state, torn between incompatible demands that aborted any hope of evolving a long-term economic strategy, calculated its export duties only in terms of its immediate revenue needs.

The inherent weakness of the state derived partly from lack of resources. Foreign credit did not meet the same political resistance as domestic taxation, and was usually preferred to domestic credit on the grounds that *juntas de crédito* used indebtedness as a political weapon. Foreign credit was useful too in domestic financial crises when a renewed flow of government funds was imperative. Yet external indebtedness increasingly threatened the independence of the Dominican government.

In the late 1890s the lowest point of external indebtedness was reached. The crisis precipitated by the decision of the mercantile sector in 1897 to reject the paper money issued by the authoritarian regime of Ulises Heureaux (the *papeletas de Lilís*) exposed the web of indebtedness in which the state was enmeshed. In its determination to survive, the *Lilisiato* resorted to credit – both from a Dutch firm, Westendorp and Company, which in 1893 sold out to the US-based Santo Domingo Improvement Company, and from provincial *juntas de crédito* and a new group of southern money-lenders that benefited from the sugar cane prosperity. By 1900 the total external debt stood at US $24.0 millions and the total internal debt at US $2.0 millions per annum, and power became concentrated in the hands of merchants with a particular expertise in the manipulation of the debt. Their ascendancy received no coordinated challenge in the absence of a planter aristocracy.

The public debt became a central political issue. One faction arguing that Dominican external indebtedness should be diversified by balancing US interests off against different combinations of Europeans in order to assure a measure of financial independence, was pitted against another faction that asserted that the republic would receive more generous treatment in New York if its indebtedness were 'rationalized' and its European debts cancelled, so that a European role in the management of Dominican finance was removed.

External indebtedness was a major factor in the progressive involvement of the United States in the republic from the 1890s – an involvement that intensified after 1911. The conjunction of the restatement of US strategic targets with the beginnings of the sugar cane ascendancy wove a complex set of relationships. Alleging an abdication of responsibilities by Dominican governments, the influence of the federal government of the United States was exerted in diverse ways, namely:

proconsular posturings by ambassadors;
the use of US advisers to frame legislation and recommend administrative changes;
the threat of military intervention;
the accolade/withdrawal of recognition to government/rebels;
arbitration between factions and the promotion of *rapprochements* between government and opposition;
reciprocity arrangements (perceived in the United States as defensive responses to European competition);
putting pressure behind elected leaders capable of preserving political stability and providing naval support for leaders soliciting reinforcements in order to implement an agreement reached with the United States;
the withdrawal of funds from the customs house and the use of loan negotiations in order to secure a settlement of internal conflict.

The authority of all Dominican presidents was undercut: those that capitulated to US pressures lost domestic credibility; those that resisted were ousted.

Between 1905 and 1916 US involvement became more pronounced. A *modus vivendi* (1905) by which the United States took control of all internal and external debts and customs was followed in 1907 by a political protectorate imposed by the Dominican-American Convention. A series of measures culminated in 1916 in the naval occupation which the United States justified in terms of Dominican 'financial delinquency'.

One line of interpretation perceives the United States deliberately luring the Dominicans into a debt-trap that provided a pretext for naval intervention. This argument fails to explain why the United States should choose to squander naval resources in the republic during the First World War. A more plausible argument is that the United States urged the Dominicans to rationalize their external indebtedness, cancelling their European debts so that the threat of European intervention would recede, while making possible the resumption of loans in New York. Between 1904 and 1914 the threat of European intervention was real enough: France spoke of sending a squadron; a German warship made a brief appearance; Italy made demands upon Dominican customs houses.[30]

Government and opposition during the US occupation

The main and most consistently pursued objective of the United States was containment: the defence and consolidation of US interests against challenges both internal and external.

The secondary objective, pursued with vigour during the presidency of Woodrow Wilson, was the promotion of a constitutionally elected democracy. This aim stemmed from both a personal Calvinist vision of the United States as a redeemer-nation and the calculation that the promotion of democracy would serve the interests of the United States by removing the authoritarian regimes that caused rebellions that threatened foreign-owned property and personnel. The second aim was pursued less consistently than the first: partly because substantial elements in the United States deemed the 'black' peoples of the Caribbean unsuitable for democracy, and looked to stable authoritarian regimes to defend US interests; partly because the experience of attempting to impose democratic solutions from outside, rather than build democratic institutions upon authentically local traditions, proved often disastrous.[31]

In its initial phase the overriding aim of the military government was to streamline the state apparatus. The military government introduced both administrative and tax reforms in order to assure the state of a continuous flow of funds, and a military reform in order to create a professional armed force that would be neutral in clashes between Dominican factions. In the next phase the military government endeavoured to evolve an effective electoral system. The stated intentions of the occupation were clear: to impose tidy, rigid formulae, orderly procedures, a rational administration. The military government began with two advantages: boom conditions engendered by the First World War and revenues that the receivership-general had held back from the previous Dominican government when the US refused to recognize it. The economy was reactivated by external conditions and a renewal of public spending. A burst of consumer expenditure was accompanied by the creation of new jobs servicing both new imports – cars and sewing-machines – and the occupation forces.[32]

The thrust and efficiency of the intervention were blunted from the beginning by lack of unity in policy-making and incompatible interests. The absence of any comprehensive imperial strategy or even a timetable was complicated by conflicts between bureaucracies – most notably the Departments of State, the Navy and the Treasury – and the failure of the federal government to issue an authoritative statement as to whether the intervention was permanent or temporary. The confusion of responsibility among federal agencies was aggravated by uncertainty about standards of evaluation. Since the United States refused to admit that it was an imperial power, there were no familiar formulae or precedents for government – that of Magoon in Cuba was overlooked – and there hardly existed a professional group of administrators and military with colonial experience. Legislation was drafted after consulting Philippine and Puerto Rican precedents. Marines inexperienced in government were expected to interpret US policy, but received no clear directions, underwent little supervision from a federal government preoccupied with European events, and had no competence to evolve a technically equipped bureaucracy.[33] The military government was built on an ambiguity: a fiction of national sovereignty was preserved by which the US ambassador continued to represent the interests of his country to a nominally independent government led by the US naval governor. This ambiguity reinforced tendencies towards vacillation and indecision.[34]

Not only was imperial authority dispersed and fragmented, but individuals within the federal agencies who had a career stake in the consistent pursuit of a particular policy had a personal interest in perpetuating that fragmentation. Thus Ambassador Russell, an advocate of total US control from 1912, was identified with a continuous US presence, while from 1921 Sumner Welles staked his reputation upon a successful withdrawal.[35]

The Marines began by improvising an administration, and engaged in energetic public works construction and in improvements in street paving and public transport in the capital.[36] The quality of the officer corps, however, was soon diminished by the practice of the Garde D'Haiti of giving extra pay to the Marines, by the posting of officers to the Western European front in 1917, and the over-rapid promotion of NCOs discontented at their exclusion from the European theatre of war. A brief period of decisiveness and self-confidence gave way to a phase of stumbling, self-doubt and sagging morale reflected in high rates of courts-martial.[37] The advantages of accumulated experience were nullified by the decision in 1919 to withdraw the entire personnel of the military administration and replace it with inexperienced men.

As a consequence of its internal ambiguities the military government was prone to discontinuities in policy formulation. Its alternations between authoritarianism and attempts to achieve a wider degree of public acceptance were reflected in vacillation between permitting a free press and imposing censorship. Tendencies towards authoritarianism that sprang from an assumption of the right to rule by conquest were deepened by a persistent and perhaps wilful misinterpretation of the motives of the Dominican opposition. Naval personnel for whom it was axiomatic that a pre-emptive strike was imperative in order to forestall German imperial ambition, linked all forms of opposition between 1916 and 1919 with international German sabotage.[38] Throughout its existence, the military government misinterpreted delays and discontinuities in the Dominican opposition that arose from the pluralistic nature of Dominican politics as evidence of insincerity, rather than (as in Washington) as a consequence of bargaining and compromise.

Tentative attempts to draw the Dominicans into the process of shaping and implementing legislation (apart from the judiciary which remained consistently Dominican) rebounded, because the military government, afraid of yielding to what it perceived as shallow agitation, failed to compromise with any Dominican demands and thus destroyed the credibility of would-be allies. Dominican leaders were willing to endorse particular policies like the disarmament of local caudillos, but went no further. None served in any Cabinet.[39] The military government failed totally to establish a Dominican constituency by making cosmetic concessions or by putting differences among Dominicans to its own advantage.

Opposition to the military intervention was initially weak – for several reasons. Most Dominicans believed that the occupation was only temporary, and some accepted the informal paramountcy of the Great Power as realistic and even desirable. The entire Dominican elite rejected armed resistance on the grounds that they would be fighting against impossible odds. Unlike Mexico or Cuba, the republic had no earlier experience of a serious blow to national pride inflicted by the United States that might have radicalized sections of the elite. The

Dominicans resorted to some passive resistance, subterfuge and slack administration at the lower levels of the bureaucracy. Opposition was enfeebled by the fact that direct control was associated with a period of rising living standards and new employment opportunities, so that the beneficiaries of the external relationship extended to include men and women in humbler occupations – clerks, salesmen, motor-car mechanics, sewing-machine repairers and even domestic servants.[40]

In 1918–19 the Dominican elite was increasingly incensed by the military regime: by its thoroughness (even municipal police chiefs were North American), by the sacrifice of national to sectional interests, by examples of lack of respect for persons and property, and by the regime's unresponsiveness to face-saving formulae proposed by Dominicans – for example, precise constitutional recommendations worked out by members of the ousted government that were intended to preserve a certain Dominican dignity within the framework of a fiction of Dominican sovereignty. The Dominican elite was inflamed by wastefulness, by corruption in some branches of the military administration, by the failure to obtain expected benefits – like equal tariff status with Cuba – and by the high costs of a low-quality US administrative presence.[41] By 1920 there was growing elite opposition to the new pervasiveness of central authority, especially the more efficient collection of taxes that were regarded as punitive and a land policy that was considered vexatious. Above all, the Dominican elite was shocked by the incompetence of the regime. Expecting the occupying forces to be paragons of efficiency, the Dominican elite was startled by serious revenue miscalculations. In 1921 government funds were seriously depleted by the decision to place an embargo on imports of food staples in order to protect retailers and to purchase a tobacco crop for which buyers were unavailable. The military regime even undertook a public works programme without investigating either interest rates or its credit rating.[42]

Much of the peasantry in the eastern region was less cautious than the Dominican elite. Expropriation of communal lands and attempts to transform independent peasants into rural proletarians working on the sugar cane plantations had given rise to intermittent violence since 1905. During the occupation, peasant unrest erupted into the protracted guerrilla warfare of the *gavillero* revolt. Failing to recognize the presence of genuine economic and social grievances that required solution, the Marines based their policy on the assumption that the revolt was no more than an example of criminality and banditry – funded by German agents – that demanded a public order solution.

The guerrilla war gradually drove a wedge between the occupying forces and the sugar cane corporations. The Marines, on the one hand, alleged that the corporations were operating beyond the law by intimidating smallholders, making *ad hoc* payments to the guerrillas and concealing information from the government; the corporations, on the other, argued that the war disrupted the labour force and reduced the volume of food supplies available to sugar cane workers. Only after the corporations lobbied in Washington for a change in policy was one effected. The decision to provide cane-workers with small plots for growing staples, and to proscribe immigration until the sugar cane enterprises had absorbed unemployed guerrillas, made possible an effective amnesty that preluded the end of the war.[43]

In the other regions the scale and intensity of opposition varied for two reasons: namely, different levels of residual politicization and a lack of uniform practices among US commanders. The economic crisis of 1920–1 finally united disparate strands of elite opposition. Economic recession revealed both how limited the material benefits of the occupation were and that the rising living standards of the years 1916–19 were largely fortuitous consequences of the First World War which the republic would have enjoyed without the occupation. The decision of the military occupation to tie the republic to a new loan that raised the external debt to a higher level in 1921 than in 1916 united the *ayuntamientos* and chambers of commerce in unanimous opposition.

The Dominican elite was adamant that although it had retreated before the armed strength of a Great Power, it had never surrendered and had always asserted that the core of national sovereignty was non-negotiable.[44] Nationalist groups led by the brothers Henríquez y Carvajal, whose government the United States had refused to recognize, orchestrated international revulsion against what they depicted as a flagrant departure from the conventions of international behaviour which the United States professed and sought to institutionalize in the Pan-American Union. The nationalists developed lines of lateral communication with Cuba, where some press support was forthcoming and a Comité pro-Santo Domingo established. They found allies in Puerto Rico too. The success of the international offensive in Latin America – Brazil offered a tentative mediation; an Argentine warship saluted Dominican sovereignty near the port of Santo Domingo; the Colombians, still nursing the wounds of the excision of Panama, protested vigorously – raised the morale and enlarged the Dominican opposition. In Western Europe the nationalists attempted to embarrass the United States, lodging formal complaints with international bodies, but they made less headway, failing to get the issue onto the agenda of the Paris Conference of 1919.[45]

The Dominican opposition learned gradually to exploit the opportunities for manœuvre that arose from ambiguities in the military government, and came to appreciate the nature of bargaining processes in Washington. In the 1920s the United States was less internationally aggressive because it had achieved its strategic targets, principally parity with the European powers. A certain loss of didactic purpose was evident in US foreign policy; and an increasing reluctance to undertake formal imperial commitments became apparent, if only because the costs of involvement were now believed to outweigh the benefits. Furthermore, one pretext for renewed exhibitions of US resolve in the Caribbean was removed: there was no German attempt in the 1920s to extract any island from the US sphere of influence. Inquiries by the American Federation of Labour and the United States Senate in 1921 into atrocities committed by the Marines momentarily drew public attention to the island and led members of the US intelligentsia to query the presumptions upon which the intervention rested.[46]

The decisive factor in prompting the US withdrawal was the nature of US-Latin American relations. The Dominican Republic became the barometer of hemispheric relationships in the early 1920s, as Cuba was in the mid-1930s. The Dominican opposition went over the heads of the military government when it argued inflexibly that its continued presence was necessary to complete a five-year public works programme and to enforce land legislation. The Harding administration, in which the State Department regained influence from the Navy Department, was determined to restore the diminished standing of the United States in Latin America, and dissociated itself from the policy of its predecessor.[47]

The Dominican opposition responded to the more even-handed policy of the United States with a hard bargaining that angered the military regime. Determined to avoid a punitive unilateral evacuation and to secure a graduated withdrawal, the opposition adopted the tactic of taking action that prolonged the occupation, in order both to wrest favourable terms from the United States (linking the withdrawal to loan arrangements) and to ensure that the successor government should not assume office hampered by the revenue deficiencies consequent upon economic recession. Initially assuming a diehard stance and requiring an unconditional evacuation, the Dominicans softened their position when economic recovery was in prospect, when a new US loan that eased financial conditions was promised, and when attempts by the United States to tie the hands of subsequent governments to half-completed policies were partly relaxed. Thus a timetable for withdrawal was finally arranged.[48]

Domestic politics and the United States from the occupation to Trujillo

After the intervention, the United States maintained a policy of containment. A more nuanced and calculated dependence was achieved through more subtle tactics.

After a smooth transition of power to the Dominicans, the United

States chose a prudent ambassador whose behaviour reflected the growing professionalism of the State Department in the 1920s. He worked unobtrusively to promote good public relations and to preserve a practice of tutelage without the use of devices, like financial experts, that aroused public controversy. Although the ambassador scrutinized domestic legislation and concerned himself with the details of its implementation – even, for instance, the regional allocation of loan funds to irrigation and agricultural colonization schemes – he refrained from open and public pressure.[49] Working to ensure the survival of an elective regime, he was careful not to be seen selecting a successor to the occupation. Later he vigilantly supervised shifts in coalitions and configurations of domestic and international forces and, more specifically, the customs receivership, elections and the organization of the military. The ambassador used his influence to make the government of Horacio Vásquez – a man of proven malleability – palatable to the United States, and pressed for a substantial loan that would guarantee his domestic prestige and help him to co-opt supporters of his rival for the presidency, Francisco J. Peynado, and later Peynado himself.[50] Supported generously by the United States, Vásquez gave no backing to private claims against US agencies for damage caused during the occupation.

Vásquez was consolidated in power by the tax and administrative reforms of the occupation. The customs receivership achieved in eighteen years what was expected of it in fifty.[51] Thus the proportion of customs revenue turned over to the government increased dramatically after the liquidation of the 1908 and 1918 loans. The occupation was at the same time effective in assuring the state of a more broadly based income. Economic growth, more efficient tax-collection and new domestic taxes signified that, whereas in 1918 tariffs represented 88 per cent of revenues, by 1926 revenues from internal sources were not far short of those derived from external sources. This is exemplified by Table 15.

A gradual shift towards personal authoritarianism occurred. A cen-

Table 15   Sources of revenue to Dominican government (in US$ 1,000s)

	External	*Internal*	TOTAL
1924	4,284	2,920	7,204
1925	4,915	3,571	8,486
1926	4,713	4,397	9,110
1927	5,896	5,081	10,978
1928	5,290	5,134	10,424

Source   DS839.51/3119/1 April, 1929/Young to Department of State.

tralizing trend was accelerated during the occupation by the construction of an integrated road system, the disarmament of caudillos and reform of the tax and military apparatuses. Vásquez was the legatee of the atrophy of factional organization. The parties that he and Peynado led were mere networks of personal allegiance adapted to the vicissitudes of the moment, and had no deep class, sectional or territorial roots. They assumed no enduring identity and hardly won a popular following; and, in response to Vásquez's deft use of patronage, were subject to defections, multiple schisms and realignments.

Vásquez was careful not to act beyond the bounds of imperial acquiescence. His programme was explicitly bases upon external considerations:

(1) a new Convention ratified in 1925 replacing that of 1907, which restored control of tariffs to the Dominicans but authorized new external borrowing only with US approval;[52]

(2) the flotation of a large external loan to provide patronage that would consolidate the government at a regional and a local level while strengthening its international bargaining position;[53]

(3) the hiring of an advisory mission to encourage the view that the republic was fit for foreign investment.[54]

The prudence of the US ambassador and the political skill of Vásquez combined to muffle anti-imperialist feeling, except for press expressions of pro-Sandinista solidarity and praise for the Argentine exclusion of US goods in response to the protective US tariff of 1929.[55] At the same time, the conduct of the presidential elections of 1924 and the mid-term elections of 1927 conformed to the standards of cleanliness required by the United States: but, more significantly in the long term, inefficient registration and the failure of the 'democratic experiment' to secure public support were indicated by high abstention rates – 61.4 per cent in 1924.[56]

By 1927 the basis of a single party state in which the state apparatus and party organization were hardly distinguishable can be identified. Expert in exploiting the advantage of incumbency and barely restricted by institutional constraints, Vásquez established a personal ascendancy by means of cooption, in particular by selecting all employees for public posts that interested him, regardless of the rank-and-file and party committees: he set the political agenda, manipulated a consensus and decided to remain in office for a six-year period instead of four. This decision crystallized opposition that could be crushed only by prosecuting the opposition press and using techniques of coercion.[57]

The use of coercion to assure *continuismo* – the harassment and gaoling of critics – could be accomplished only with military support. Military reform embodied in legislation in 1907, 1911 and 1912 was enforced only during the occupation, when the army was reorganized as a national constabulary according to US policy objectives. The aim of the United States was to create a non-partisan constabulary that, after an effective disarmament programme, would enjoy a monopoly of violence and technical autonomy. Experienced in oppressive practices during the latter part of the occupation, the constabulary adapted willingly to the coercive tasks required by Vásquez. Sections of the officer corps, coming from an intermediate social stratum that seized new opportunities for upward social mobility when the pre-occupation elite refused to co-operate with the military reform of the occupation, felt an enduring antagonism towards critics of Vásquez who disdained them as erstwhile collaborators. In the mid-1920s Vásquez responded sympathetically to military requests for improved armaments; and the United States, equivocating between pressures to restrict arms sales to Latin America and the likelihood of British and/or German competition, opted to resume arms deliveries (suspended in 1909), accepting reluctantly the arguments of the commander-in-chief that arms-smuggling to the opposition from 1923 threatened the legitimately elected government and that Haiti would again pose a threat if the United States withdrew.[58]

In 1929 the position of Vásquez appeared impregnable. He consolidated the support of the officer corps by pampering it and enhancing its sense of power by allowing soldiers to infringe the law without fear of punishment. However, Vásquez's declining health precipitated a succession crisis. In 1930 General Rafael Trujillo, the commander-in-chief of the armed forces, seized power. Trujillo was already well known as an effective regional commander, author of a new military code and a manual of tactics, an advocate of the expansion of the medical corps and instigator of a new cadet school. A man that enjoyed close personal ties with the US Marines, Trujillo gambled that the United States would not in the crisis of the World Depression oust a military dictatorship in the Caribbean if US interests were protected.[59] Believing that the United States would never tolerate a *trujillista* coup, Vásquez miscalculated. Thus the stage was set, by a military coup astutely camouflaged as a 'civic movement' with civilian leadership,[60] for the thirty-one-year *trujillista* tyranny.

Perspectives

Between 1890 and 1930 the Dominican economy underwent a sequence of small shifts whose cumulative effect was the thorough incorporation of the republic into the international economy. The US military regime and the quasi-democratic government that succeeded it catalyzed and precipitated changes that were already under way:

(1) a drift towards export-crop mono-dependence and a failure to alter the commodity profile radically, which was compounded by a heavy reliance upon US imports;

(2) the suffocation of authentically national sources of wealth and power from which a process of development along autonomous lines could spring;

(3) a tendency towards a centralized power that shattered pre-existing regional and local allegiances and made the unfettered authority of Trujillo possible;

(4) a failure to translate an incomplete recognition of the permanent structural malaise and deep-seated weaknesses of the Dominican economy into practical policy, by giving some direction to metropolitan investment or raising the propensity to invest in sectors starved of funds.

The shift in US policy from control to containment that began in the mid-1920s and crystallized in the World Depression was often misinterpreted by Dominican politicians. Trujillo was the unintended beneficiary of changes in US strategic priorities, especially a reduction of emphasis on Germany as a genuine or perceived threat. The removal of US constraints on domestic politics gave Trujillo a freedom of movement and bargaining power that was denied to his predecessors. While internally Trujillo could turn to his advantage the inherited practice of shaping the state in the interest of particular sectors, he enjoyed the external advantage of a new relaxation in US-Dominican relations which allowed him, with a spurious and perverse credibility, to posture as the first apostle of economic nationalism in Dominican experience.

Notes

Fieldwork conducted in the Dominican Republic in Summer 1981 was financed by the British Academy.

[1] Cited in Sumner Welles *Naboth's vineyard. The Dominican Republic 1844–1924* (New York 1928) II 918

[2] See especially Frank Moya Pons *Manual de historia dominicana* (Santo Domingo 1977) and the *Revista EME–EME Estudios Dominicanos* published since 1972.

[3] Principal contributions to this new generation of scholarship within the republic include Moya Pons *op. cit.*; Wilfredo Lozano *La dominación imperialista en la República Dominicana 1900–1930* (Santo Domingo 1976); and outside it Howard J. Wiarda *The Dominican Republic – nation in transition* (New York 1969).

[4] Harry Hoetink *El pueblo dominicano, 1850–1900* (Santiago de los Caballeros 1972) p. 24; *Primer censo nacional de la República Dominica* (2nd edn Santo Domingo 1975) p. 126.

[5] *Ibid.* pp. 125–7.

[6] On the developmentalist roles of different crops, see Kenneth Duncan and Ian Rutledge (eds) *Land and labour in Latin America* (Cambridge 1977). On export crop diversification esp. Patrick Bryan 'The transformation of the economy of the Dominican Republic, 1870–1916' (unpubl. Ph.D. thesis, University of London 1977). Also Jaime Jesús Domínguez *Economía y política en la República Dominicana – años 1844–1871* (Santo Domingo

1977); Tirso Mejía-Ricart (ed.) *La sociedad dominicana durante la primera república* (Santo Domingo 1977).

[7] Hoetink *loc. cit.* p. 27.

[8] Antonio Lluberes Navarro 'El tabaco dominicano: de la manufactura al monopolio industrial' *EME–EME Estudios Dominicanos* vi (March–April 1978) 3–25; 'La economía del tabaco en el Cibao en la segunda mitad del siglo XIX' *EME–EME Estudios Dominicanos* I (Jan.–Feb. 1973) 35–60.

[9] Paul Muto 'The illusory promise: the Dominican Republic and the process of economic development, 1900–1930' (unpubl. Ph.D. thesis, University of Washington 1976) esp. p. 41; Bryan *op. cit.*

[10] Muto *op. cit.* p. 56.

[11] W. A. Lewis *Growth and fluctuations, 1870–1913* (London 1978); Bryan 'The transition of plantation agriculture in the Dominican Republic 1870–84' *Journal of Caribbean History* x–xi (1978) 82–105; Lozano *op. cit.*; José Del Castillo and Walter Cordero *La economía dominicana durante el primer cuarto del siglo XX* (2nd edn Santo Domingo 1980).

[12] The law was outlined in an explanatory pamphlet, Sec. de Estado del Interior y Policía *A los habitantes de la República Dominicana* (Santo Domingo 1919).

[13] Lozano *op. cit.*; Marlin D. Clausner *Rural Santo Domingo. Settled, unsettled and resettled* (Philadelphia 1973) esp. pp. 26–30, 201–10.

[14] Del Castillo and Cordero *op. cit.*; Bruce Calder 'Some aspects of the US occupation of the Dominican Republic, 1916–1924' (unpubl. Ph.D. thesis, University of Texas 1974) esp. p. 308; Muto *op. cit.* esp. pp. 35, 42; DS 839.61/351/3/3 Aug. 1927 Frost to Secretary of State.

[15] Muto *op. cit.* p. 42; Del Castillo 'Azúcar y braceros: historia de un problema' *Inazúcar* vi Jan.–Feb. 1981 29; Del Castillo *La inmigración de braceros azucareros en la República Dominica* (Santo Domingo 1978); *Primer censo* . . . pp. 152–7.

[16] FO A 472/25 Nov. 1919/Minutes; A 2171/2171/20/6 March 1924/Darrell Wilson to FO; A 4036/2467/20/11 July 1925/J. Bowering to FO; A 746/746/20/9 Oct. 1926/Colonial Office, memo to FO.

[17] Del Castillo and Cordero *op. cit.* pp. 18–25; Ernest Charles Palmer 'Land use and landscape change along the Dominican-Haitian borderlands' (unpubl. Ph.D. thesis, University of Florida 1976) *passim*. On food imports, especially *Listín Diario* 29 March 1924.

[18] Bryan *op. cit.* pp. 172–219; David C. MacMichael 'The United States and the Dominican Republic, 1871–1940: a cycle in Caribbean diplomacy' (unpubl. Ph.D. thesis, University of Oregon 1964) ii 589–95; Dominican Customs Receivership *Reports 1907–1930* (Washington DC 1908–31); Otto Schoenrich *Santo Domingo – a country with a future* (New York 1918).

[19] Bryan *op. cit.* pp. 173–9.

[20] De la Rosa *op. cit.* pp. 77–90; Melvin M. Knight *The Americans in Santo Domingo* (New York 1928) p. 90.

[21] 839.00/2997/3 Dec. 1921/Internal memo.

[22] 839.00/2919/1 Dec. 1925/Ewan E. Young to Secretary of State.

[23] Darrell Wilson *Report on the Economic, Financial and Commercial Conditions in the Dominican Republic* (HMSO London 1925).

[24] 839.516/19/30 April 1928/23/24 Jan. 1929/26/7 May 1929/Young to Secretary of State.

[25] Muto *op. cit.* p. 91.

[26] J. P. Perrello *Anuario comercial industrial y profesional de la República Dominicana* (Santiago de los Caballeros 1914).

[27] Knight *op. cit.* p. 127; DS 839.512/40/Consul, Puerto Plata to Dept. of State/18 Dec. 1925. On military purchases, Stephen M. Fuller and Graham Cosmas *Marines in the Dominican Republic 1916–24* (Washington DC 1974) esp. p. 31.

[28] On political narrative, Luis F. Mejía *De Lilís a Trujillo: historia contemporánea de la*

República Dominicana (Caracas 1944 and subsequent edns) is useful. Also Antonio de la Rosa *Las finanzas de Santo Domingo y el control americano* (Santo Domingo 1915).

29 Bryan *op. cit.* pp. 284–319.

30 Mejía *op. cit.*; De la Rosa *op. cit.*; Jacob H. Hollander *Santo Domingo debt* (Washington DC 1905); César Herrera *De Hartmont a Trujillo* (Ciudad Trujillo 1953). The most eminent post-1945 Dominican historian saw the internal order question as a pretext to conceal the aim of obstructing possible German use of the republic as a supply station for a submarine offensive. Emilio Rodríguez Demorizi *United States military intervention* (pamphlet, trans. Ciudad Trujillo 1958) p. 9.

31 See especially R. F. Weston *Racism in US imperialism: the influence of racial assumptions on American foreign policy, 1893–1946* and John J. Johnson *Latin America in caricature* (Austin 1980). These should be read in conjunction with R. M. Abrams 'United States intervention abroad: the first quarter century' *American Historical Review* LXXIX 2 (1974) 72–102; L. C. Gardner, W. LaFeber and T. McCormick *Creation of the American empire* (London 1973); W. LaFeber *The new empire: an interpretation of American expansion* (Ithaca 1961); E. May *Imperial democracy: the emergence of America as a Great Power* (New York 1973); T. Paterson (ed.) *American imperialism and anti-imperialism* (New York 1973); W. A. Williams *The roots of the modern American empire – a study of the growth and shaping of a social consciousness in a market place* (London 1974) and T. P. Wright Jr *American support of free elections abroad* (Washington DC 1964).

32 Calder 'Caudillos and gavilleros versus the United States Marines: guerrilla insurgency during the Dominican intervention, 1916–1924' *Hispanic American Historical Review* LVIII 4 (1978); Calder thesis esp. pp. 186–216; Del Castillo *La inmigración*; MacMichael thesis II esp. 533–4; *El libro azul* (Santo Domingo 1920, reprint 1976). The withdrawal meant a loss of £1–1½ million spent by the occupation forces on rent, servants' wages and local purchases. A 5098/752/20/7 Aug. 1924/D. Wilson to FO.

33 Especially Calder thesis p. 182.

34 Whereas the Navy Department argued that the military government functioned only by the authority of the US federal government, the State Department insisted that military government was sovereign. 839.51/2148/21 Dec. 1920/Secretary of State to Secretary of the Navy. The British endorsed the fiction partly because they hoped that outstanding British claims would be efficiently handled. 'The American Naval Officer is the duly appointed nominee of a Government regarded by us as technically sovereign and independent' A 841/428/20/7 Feb. 1921/Minutes. The occupation, however, complicated claims. When a British West Indian saddler/shoemaker issued a claim against the US Marines for destroying his house, the United States answered with a claim against the British in Ireland. The case was resolved only because the claimant accepted less than one quarter of his claim in order to pay his debts. A 5124/2576/20/14 July 1921/Minutes: A 9555/2576/20/20 Dec. 1921/Minutes. The Foreign Office was prudently noncommittal on proposals that the League of Nations should establish a protectorate, and catalogued atrocities for quotation when the New York press alleged British atrocities in Ireland, Greece, Mesopotamia and Persia. 242136/29 Nov. 1916/Minutes; A 4521/4521/10/6 July 1920/Minutes; A 5857/4521/20/21 Aug. 1920/Minutes.

35 MacMichael thesis II 415–16, 452.

36 *Memoria. Ayuntamiento de Santo Domingo 1920* (Santo Domingo 1920).

37 MacMichael thesis II 551.

38 104281/170218/6 May 1918/Godfrey Fisher to FO. Attempts to import Puerto Rican collaborators as spies and tax-collectors met with a uniform hostility. Dominicans regarded them as renegades.

39 Moya Pons *op. cit.*

40 Criticism in the United States, aimed principally at the censorship (see *New York World* 5 Dec. 1916), evaporated as the United States entered the First World War.

41 See especially 'Carta de Monseñor Nouel al Ministro Americano Russell' 29 Dec.

1920 in Antonio Hoepelman and Juan A. Senior (eds) *Documentos históricos* (2nd edn Santo Domingo 1973) pp. 16, 19, 27.

[42] Rodríguez Demorizi *op. cit.* p. 6 argues that the successes of the military administration were due principally to Dominicans who had planned reforms before 1916 but failed to implement them.

[43] Calder *op. cit.* esp. pp. 170, 186–216.

[44] Hugo Tolendino (ed.) *La información frente a la ocupación* (Santo Domingo 1922); Emilio Roig de Leuschenring *La ocupación de la República Dominicana por los Estados Unidos y el derecho de las pequeñas nacionalidades* (Havana 1919).

[45] Julio Jaime Julia *Antología de Américo Lugo* (Santo Domingo 1976) i 55–6; Hoepelman and Senior *op. cit.* pp. 281–4; *La información*, Santiago 9 Feb. 1924.

[46] Helen Leschorn 'American atrocities in the Dominican Republic' *Current History* xv (Feb. 1922) 881–2.

[47] In Ohio, a marginal state, the Republicans promised black voters that they would restore liberty to Dominican voters. A 2714/752/20/8 April 1924/D. Wilson to FO.

[48] Fabio Fiallo *La comisión nacionalista en Washington 1920–1* (Ciudad Trujillo 1939); *Memorandum del Entendido de Evacuación de la República Dominicana junio 30 de 1922* (Santo Domingo 1922). For an exercise in self-vindication, Welles *op. cit.* ii 836 ff.; and for a hostile view, José Ortega Frier (presumed author) *Memorandum relativo a la intervención del señor Benjamin Sumner Welles en la República Dominicana* (Santo Domingo 1973).

[49] DS 839.51/2942/Memo/7 May 1927.

[50] Discreet US support for Peynado was said to prejudice his chances. *La información*, Santiago 12 March 1924. The British chargé d'affaires reported that US sugar cane corporations attempted to buy peasant votes, that the peasants accepted the bribes and voted their own way. A 1779/752/20/25 Feb. 1924/D. Wilson to FO. Vásquez was advised to broaden his power-base by Welles 839.51/2575/8 April 1925/Memo of American Commissioner to Dominican Republic. Their close relationship gave rise to allegations of personal profiteering in utilities companies. Ortega Frier *op. cit.*, pp. 190–2.

[51] *Annual Report of the Chief of the Bureau of Insular Affairs 1925* (Washington DC 1925) p. 3.

[52] *Papers relating to the foreign relations of the United States*, i (1924) esp. pp. 662–6; *Informe relativo a la colaboración y canje de ratificaciones de la Convención entre la República Dominicana y los Estados Unidos de América el 27 de diciembre de 1924* (Washington DC 1926).

[53] 831.51/2621/26 May 1925/Memo of S. Welles.

[54] MacMichael thesis ii 630.

[55] See *La opinión* throughout 1928; *La información*, Santiago 26 June 1929.

[56] *La información*, 17 March 1924.

[57] E. Vega y Pagán *Historia de las fuerzas armadas* (2 vols Ciudad Trujillo 1958). Also *La opinión*, 8 March 1929.

[58] 839/24/10/23 March 1926/Memo reporting conversation with Colonel Cutts.

[59] Trujillo was criticized by the Dawes mission as a speculator in urban property and food and clothing purchases for the army. *Report on Dominican economic conditions* (Chicago 1929).

[60] Vásquez assumed that the United States would not recognize Trujillo if he seized power. Michael R. Malek 'Rafael Leonidas Trujillo Molina: the rise of a Caribbean dictator' (unpubl. Ph.D. thesis University of California, Santa Barbara 1971) pp. 118–20, 153.

18

DEPENDENCY, HISTORIOGRAPHY AND OBJECTIONS TO THE ROCA PACT

Peter Alhadeff

Fodor and O'Connell argue that the specific form of dependence of the Argentine economy in the first half of the twentieth century lay in its 'triangular' relationship with Great Britain and the United States, and that this relationship was unequal and disadvantageous for Argentina. They maintain that 1930s administrations reinforced rather than superseded this relationship, by giving preference to Great Britain, one of the sides of the 'triangle'. Above all, they take issue with the willingness of the Conservative coalition (the *concordancia*) to accept the terms of the Roca-Runciman agreement as dictated by Britain. In their view, the signature of the Roca Pact could not be defended from the standpoint of the protection of Argentina's meat exports, as the republic did not depend on them. Besides, instead of freeing private sterling remittances as contemplated in the agreement, O'Connell and Fodor suggest that the blocking of those funds should have been enforced and used as a bargaining weapon against any future restriction on exports of chilled beef to Britain (blocked sterling accounts were roughly equivalent to the chilled beef exports).[1] The implication is that the Pact need not have been signed at all – though Fodor and O'Connell do not explore what effects a unilateral seizure of sterling remittances would have had for an open economy highly dependent on its foreign trade and interested in attracting foreign capital for its future development.

In another assessment of 1930s Conservative economic policies, Gravil and Rooth[2] give an equal emphasis to the agreement – almost, it seems, to the exclusion of anything else. They describe the Pact unhesitatingly as 'the epitome and symbol of Concordancia rule',[3] and conclude that government economic management contributed to Argentina's 'acute dependence' in the period. According to them, 'Argentina's foreign trade was dragooned into the service of the British economy [by] the Concordancia's abject posture towards Britain, adopted on account of one-tenth of Argentina's export trade.'[4]

The position of Fodor, O'Connell, Gravil and Rooth is taken from a contemporary *dependentista* perspective, though there are antecedents in Argentina's historiography. A year after the agreement was signed, the brothers Irazusta published a bitter and highly charged critique of the *concordancia*'s alleged pro-British policies. The Irazustas state that the Argentine mission should never have sailed to London in the first place.[5] Moreover, from its creation in 1935 and until its dissolution in 1945, FORJA (the breakaway group of the Radical Party intent on recapturing the popular and national origins of Radicalism) regarded the production of a 'revisionist' (that is nationalist) interpretation of Argentine history as one of its fundamental tasks. According to Jauretche, its founding member and driving force, the Conservatives were responsible for sanctioning an *estatuto legal del coloniaje* by which Argentina's ties of dependence with Great Britain were wilfully strengthened. The agreement was, of course, the prominent feature of this mechanism.[6] Like the brothers Irazusta, FORJA and Jauretche believed that the Roca Pact should not have been negotiated. This impression was also conveyed by Scalabrini Ortiz, whose verbose nationalist and anti-British writings were a notorious influence on FORJA's development.[7]

The outlook of these historians, the representatives of an incipient nationalist school, came to be shared by many others after the Second World War. For Ibarguren the Roca agreement 'formalized and strengthened the old submission of the Argentine economy to the British Empire',[8] an opinion which was now held by writers to the left of the political spectrum. Thus, if for Puiggrós 'the signature of the Pact [created] new relations of dependence',[9] for Ramos it led to the acceptance of 'leonine' terms.[10] At least one writer described the clauses of the Pact as 'humiliating'.[11] In one form or another it was hinted that the agreement involved a surrender of national sovereignty to British interests.[12]

Yet it is legitimate to ask if the sound and fury raised over this event is entirely justified. Perhaps it is not, and the Conservative coalition may not have had such a strong case to answer as is generally made out. For, even though this chapter does not consider the Roca-Runciman Pact in its entirety, it appears that a lot of the writing that has singled out the agreement as a *bête-noire* may have overstated the case. It is possible to establish a direct connection between the agreement and Argentina's economic recovery from the effects of the Depression, to demonstrate that farmers and debtors in general, as well as meat producers and importers of British goods, benefited from the provisions of the agreement.

The Roca-Runciman Pact and domestic economic policy

The literature on Roca-Runciman has paid remarkably little attention to the implications of the agreement for the making of economic policy during the 1930s. Some of the financial results of the Pact have not even been explored. In particular, it is not well known that in order to carry out the *Plan de acción económica* during the latter part of 1933 and in 1934,

Finance Minister Federico Pinedo relied on the proceeds of the Roca Funding Loan, a direct result of the Anglo-Argentine negotiations in London. The *Plan de acción económica* was meant to support productive activity in the private sector by stimulating agricultural output and encouraging a downward revision of interest rates: two programmes dependent for their success upon the flotation of Roca Funding bonds. Although these schemes were devised and applied in the years 1933 and 1934, they had a lasting impact upon economic policy and performance throughout the remainder of the decade.

1 The exchange reform of 1933 and the minimum price guarantee for farmers
On 28 November 1933 the Argentine government began an active policy of supporting farmers by purchasing principal cereal crops at guaranteed minimum prices. It has not generally been recognized that the implementation of this policy was a by-product, if not a direct result, of the negotiations conducted in London between Vice-President Julio Roca (for Argentina) and Sir Walter Runciman (President of the Board of Trade, for the United Kingdom).

The sale to the Grain Regulating Board of the wheat, maize and linseed crops, whenever the international quotations of those staples fell below a stipulated minimum, afforded relief to farmers badly hit by the Depression: purchases by the Grain Board, for example, accounted for 86 per cent of the total wheat sales between December and March 1934.[13] Moreover, farmers were paid some 20 per cent above prices ruling in November 1933.[14] Given the importance of agricultural production in the national economy, the price guarantee led to a general improvement in the returns of commerce and trade, and put Argentina firmly on the road to economic recovery. The funds to subsidize cereal prices were obtained by modifying the system of exchange control so as to yield a profit: a profit derived from the difference between the rate at which the state bought foreign exchange and the rate at which exchange was sold. The price guarantee was announced as a temporary measure and, when the recovery in international grain prices rendered it useless towards the end of 1936, the guarantee was abandoned.

It is of interest here to discuss the background to this measure, in order to elucidate its connection with the Roca-Runciman agreement. In an official communiqué issued by the ministry of finance explaining the fundamentals of the scheme to support cereal crops, it was said that two conditions had to hold before the minimum price guarantee could be made effective. First, the state of national finances had to be consolidated. This had been achieved by official policies of sound financial management, practised 'relentlessly and at some effort' in the early 1930s.

Now, from a position of financial strength, the Government can tackle a vast plan to relieve the country from the weight of the economic depression. It was fundamental to get through the first stage. Nothing could actually be done under conditions of financial instability, with the Treasury choking under the pressure of unpaid commitments and with ever increasing arrears in prospect as a result of budgetary deficit.[15]

Second, and relevant to this section of the chapter, the government determined that before the exchange control system could be modified to aid agricultural producers it was necessary to secure foreign funding loans to release blocked funds in Argentina. A large and constantly increasing mass of obligations, representing the cost of imported merchandise and the profits of foreign-owned companies, could not be remitted abroad between 1931 and 1933 because of the scarcity of foreign exchange. As long as this mass of funds awaited transfer, 'a question mark [hung] over the future of the Argentine currency'.[16] The funding loans in foreign currency were intended to relieve Argentina's exchange position, and prevent pressures from building up against the peso by freeing 'the elements [that troubled] the functioning of the exchange market'.[17] This, of course, paved the way for reform in the system of exchange control, from which farmers were to be subsidized.

Given that the cereal crop purchases were to be financed from the profit made by the state by buying exchange cheap from exporters and selling it dear to importers, the reform in the system of exchange control depended crucially on a devaluation of the peso. In practice, the foreign funding loans also made the government confident that the devaluation which it was planning could be kept within control, and that the minimum price guarantee for the wheat, maize and linseed crops could be implemented without major financial disturbance. Had the government not availed itself of the funding loans, a future release of blocked remittances would probably have brought about a drastic devaluation of the peso, resulting in dire consequences for the money market, for the service of Argentina's foreign obligations and – a key consideration in the early 1930s – for the credit of the state.

As a rule, a depreciation of the peso lowered quotations of government bonds inside and outside the republic, and brought sellers on to the bond markets. Naturally, this made it relatively more difficult to raise finance by public subscription. Given that the foreign funding loans reassured holders of national bonds that there was no reason for the peso to continue sliding, the government could proceed to devalue the currency in a controlled and regulated manner, and finance the support scheme for cereal farmers without impairing its capacity to borrow in local or foreign markets.

There can be little doubt, therefore, that the foreign funding loans were necessary for the successful implementation of the measures of November 1933. No practical purpose could have been served by postponing the release of blocked funds indefinitely, as this only delayed an eventual overhaul of the exchange market. Instead, the foreign funding loans were of immediate benefit to government finances and, of course, 'allowed the execution of an economic programme'.[18]

Negotiations to secure funding loans with which to release blocked remittances began before Finance Minister Federico Pinedo took office in August of 1933. Pinedo announced his new economic measures only after concluding negotiations for a sterling funding loan and the virtual completion of arrangements for funding blockages of Swiss francs and US dollars. The most important of these funding operations was financed from the so-called Roca Funding Loan. The weight of the Loan in the sum total of the funding operations was very considerable. In December 1933, subscriptions for the Roca Loan reached 167.7 million pesos (£11.2 million), compared with 53.7 million pesos (£3.6 million) for bonds of the dollar funding loan and 51.6 million (£3.4 million) for bonds of the funding loan in Swiss francs. By May 1934, subscriptions to the Roca Loan stood at 167.8 million pesos (£11.2 million), compared with 75.9 million pesos (£5.1 million) for Swiss francs bonds, 59.0 million pesos (£3.9 million) for dollar bonds and 16.8 million pesos (£1.1 million) for bonds of a supplementary loan in pounds sterling.[19] The issue of the Roca bonds was a condition of the Roca-Runciman agreement signed in London in May of 1933.

From the start of the Roca negotiations it was clear that British commerce and banking firms, as well as the railways and other British companies in Argentina, attached great importance to the question of freeing Britain's frozen credits.[20] Following Roca's visit to Evelyn Baring on 24 February 1933, it was announced that the problem of the release of blocked funds was on the point of being resolved by a loan of about £10 million sterling. According to data gathered in London by the Board of Trade, this operation would affect approximately twenty thousand English creditors whose funds were blocked in Argentina by the Exchange Control Commission.[21] Towards the end of March, a telegram arrived in London from Buenos Aires stating that Alberto Hueyo, the finance minister, had expressed confidence in the final success of the negotiations in London concerning frozen credits. Minister Hueyo hoped that the loan could be arranged for a period of twenty years at an interest rate of 4 per cent.[22]

Negotiations over the proposed £10 million sterling loan proved to be one of the last stumbling blocks to sealing the Roca agreement. The terms of the loan were only finally agreed in April; the Pact was signed immediately after.[23] It was arranged that the Roca bonds would be issued at par, would carry interest at 4 per cent per annum, and would be redeemed within twenty years, repayment beginning after five years. The exchange rate at which the Roca bonds were to be converted, and other conditions, were to be finalized by the Argentine government and a committee representing holders of the balances concerned (Article 2, paragraph 4 of the Roca agreement).[24]

The interest rate of 4 per cent carried by the Roca bonds was attractive to the Argentine government. In 1943 Hueyo was to write that the terms of the Roca Funding Loan were the most advantageous ever to be negotiated abroad.[25] Compared to interest rates at which previous Argentine government bonds had been issued in European markets, the rate of the Roca Loan was one to two points lower, and European rates were normally below those prevailing in the United States. Undoubtedly, at a time when the foreign credit of many other nations had collapsed, the favourable terms obtained by Argentina were due to careful financial management by early *concordancia* administrations. Argentina was the first country to settle the release of blocked foreign balances with the issue of a long-term loan.[26]

The Roca agreement was signed while Hueyo headed the finance ministry. He was responsible for the bulk of the negotiations for the Roca Funding Loan. Federico Pinedo merely inherited the Roca agreement, with an undertaking to put into effect the issue of the Roca bonds. Under Pinedo, agreement was reached by October 1933 on the exchange rate at which the bonds were to be converted and on the conditions under which they were to be marketed. The conversion rate was fixed at 43d to the gold peso or 12.67 paper pesos to the pound.[27] This rate of exchange was not entirely satisfactory to holders of blocked funds, as it was a little below the average official rate of exchange prevailing during the latter stages of negotiation. Yet it was significantly better than the May rate of 13.32 paper pesos per pound sterling, operating when discussions had begun.[28] Denominated in sterling, Roca bonds were issued in Buenos Aires to holders of blocked peso accounts accumulated before May 1933. Various proportions of several series of Argentine government bonds were also set aside for blocked account holders.[29] These were the final touches stipulated in the Roca agreement.

Pinedo himself disclosed that the changes in the system of exchange control in November 1933 were announced only after the government had obtained the necessary funding loans to release the blocked foreign funds in Argentina. He added that a sharp devaluation of the peso would have ensued if the blocked remittances had been released before the funding loans were secured.[30] As the Roca Funding Loan accounted for by far the greater part of blocked remittances released at this juncture, the inevitable conclusion must be that the sterling Loan made changes in the system of exchange control possible, and that without the Loan the state might not have been in a position to guarantee minimum prices for wheat, maize and linseed. Moreover, the administration had obtained concessions from holders of blocked peso accounts which reduced considerably the costs of issuing and servicing Roca bonds.

2 The conversion of the internal public debt

Another fact which has escaped the attention of many writers is that the Roca Funding Loan was vital to the successful outcome of proposals placed before bond-holders by the government in 1933 and 1934 for the conversion of the internal public debt. These 'conversion' proposals extended the duration and the cost of government loans but resulted in diminished annual debt services, which brought immediate relief to the public and private sector at the expense, in the shortrun, of the holder of national stock.

The importance of the internal conversion operations cannot be exaggerated.[31] By the time the internal debt had been fully converted from 6 to 5 per cent, three billion pesos (£200 million) worth of bonds had been exchanged into lower interest-bearing denominations.[32] Even though the state held one third of these bonds in its coffers, and the conversion of that paper was automatic, the size of the figures involved was of the first magnitude. President Justo did not hesitate to describe the conversion of the internal debt as the biggest financial operation ever attempted in Argentina.[33]

Considerable savings were made as a result. The administration estimated that it could economize 56 million pesos in the first year of the conversion, and emphasized that this figure would eliminate the need for tax increases and ensure a balanced budget in 1933.[34] Total government expenditure for 1933 stood at 800 million pesos, so that with the internal conversion operations the government expected to save 6 per cent of its total expenditure.[35] Debt service payments in 1933 were nearly 250 million pesos, which meant that economies under this heading could be as much as 22 per cent.[36] In the event, the conversion of the internal debt saved the government 30.8 million pesos annually (£2 million) between 1934 and 1938,[37] or about 15 per cent of yearly debt service and 3 per cent of total expenditure. Yet the most important result of the conversion of the internal debt was that credit became cheaper, thus alleviating the burden on debtors throughout the country. This also had an impact on production. The conversion of mortgage bonds, for instance, afforded much relief to the 80,000 debtors of the Banco Hipotecario Nacional. The farmer who before November 1933 had to sell three hundred bags of wheat to meet one thousand pesos of mortgage payments, needed only two hundred bags to pay his mortgage arrears after the conversion of the mortgage debt, as the interest he paid on loans was reduced while the price of wheat increased.[38]

The private sector welcomed the period of lower interest rates heralded by debt conversion. As declining debt service brought down government expenditure, the likelihood of more taxation was itself reduced. Moreover, productive investment became increasingly attractive relative to bond-holding. As a result, the conversion of the internal debt had a reflationary effect on economic activity in general. This was well understood by the Confederation of Argentine Commerce and Industry, the Unión Industrial and the Sociedad Rural, who gave it their firm support.

Before the conversion of the internal debt was announced on 11 November 1933, the government took a number of steps to ensure that bond-holders subscribed to the new, lower interest-bearing issues. The success of the conversion scheme, of course, depended on the cooperation of the bond-holder. First, the government tried to bring banking interest rates down. This would obviously accelerate a general fall in interest rates and make it easier for bond-holders to accept a lower return on their investment. By November 1933, private commercial banks and the Banco de la Nación reached agreement to reduce interest charges: the banks undertook to reduce interest charges on discounts and advances by about two percentage points, while the Banco de la Nación cut the discount rate by an equivalent amount. The government also sought reductions in the interest rates paid on treasury bills (short-term promissory notes of the government, usually not extending beyond a year). Naturally, if government short-term paper paid less interest, charges on longer-term securities were bound to fall over time, and bond-holders could be expected to accommodate smaller returns in future. As a result of the concordat with bankers, the interest rate paid by the treasury for bills with a maturity of a month or longer, was cut from 5.5 to 4 per cent.[39] In addition, a short-term loan to the government of 15 million pesos (£1 million), financed by the banks at the favourable rate of 1.5 per cent, made possible the issue of new and non-renewable treasury bills payable at the same interest and within the month.[40]

This policy of reducing short-term interest rates was supported by the release of frozen funds in Argentina as a result of the Roca agreement. It was observed that the 4 per cent interest rate carried by the Roca bonds was lower than the rates paid by the government on its outstanding long-term debt in London and New York. The minimum interest rate carried by the long-dated domestic obligations in 1933 was 5 per cent. By opening the door to cheaper long-term finance, the Roca Funding Loan must have contributed to a downward readjustment of short-term interest rates. In fact, there is evidence to suggest that the Roca Loan actually helped clinch the deal between the government and the banks which, early in November 1933, inaugurated a declared policy of interest rate reductions. The series of meetings conducted by the government with representatives of private banks was called by President Justo only in October 1933, when the last details of the Roca Loan had been finally settled. Agreement on the new banking charges on discounts and advances followed swiftly.

Apart from encouraging a downward tendency in both short- and long-term interest rates, the Roca Funding Loan was important in another respect. Weeks before the conversion of the internal debt was announced, the government increased its operations in the Stock Exchange by using the bonds of the funding loans in pounds sterling, dollars and Swiss francs to boost confidence in its paper. Only the owners of blocked balances were entitled to acquire funding bonds but, as many holders of blocked remittances had temporarily taken refuge in official paper, the government accepted subscriptions for the different foreign funding bonds in national and mortgage bonds, as well as in cash and treasury bills. By May 1934, subscriptions for the funding bonds (including the bonds of the Roca Loan) reached 319.5 million pesos (£18.8 million): 291.1 million (£17.1 million) were paid for in cash and 5.5 million (£0.3 million) in treasury bills, but 19.3 million (£1.1 million) were exchanged for national bonds and 2.8 million (£0.2 million) for mortgage bonds.[41]

The funding bonds, of course, were no more than a future promise of payment in foreign currency, and the holders of blocked remittances were eager, therefore, to exchange them for government stock. This suited the government for two reasons. First, and before the conversion of the internal debt was carried out, there was always the danger that holders of blocked remittances might suddenly decide to liquidate their investments in government paper, flooding the market for government stock and depressing quotations of national and mortgage bonds. If liquidation occurred prior to the launching of the debt conversion, when confidence in government paper was needed most, the success of the entire conversion operation could be threatened.[42] The funding bonds enabled the government to buy back its securities from the holders of blocked remittances, and thus rid the market of a potential source of instability.

Second, by purchasing its stock with funding bonds, the government strengthened the market for national and mortgage bonds before disclosing the conversion operation, enhancing the attractiveness of an investment in government paper. As the planned date of the conversion offer drew nearer, the government stepped up its purchases of securities. Between 16 and 30 October 1933, it bought national bonds for 4 million pesos; between 6 and 9 November buying increased to 9.6 million; finally, between 10 and 13 November, with the conversion offer under way, 6.7 million worth of bonds were acquired. Moreover, in the six days before the operation was made public, the government accounted for an average of 77 per cent of all daily transactions on the Stock Exchange.[43] By 10 November national bonds were selling at 96 per cent of their face value – an excellent price.[44]

This activity in the Stock Exchange guaranteed the successful conversion of the internal debt. The transactions of the government, of course, were financed in their entirety by the foreign funding loans. As the Roca Loan was far and away the largest of the funding loans, its contribution to the last, preparatory stage (before the offer of conversion was put to bond-holders) cannot be in question. The value of the Roca Loan was not, however, exhausted. Bond-holders had the choice either of converting old issues into new at a lower interest rate, or simply being refunded in cash. In practice, out of 2958.8 million pesos (£197.3 million) worth of bonds negotiated, only 103 million pesos (£6.9 million) was exchanged for cash.[45] This so-called 'rescue' operation was settled with the cash proceeds arising from the sale of funding bonds, and especially from the Roca bonds.

It should be pointed out, finally, that the remainder of the sales of funding bonds in cash, that is, the difference between 291.1 million pesos and the 'rescue' operation, was used to liquidate overdue accounts of the government with its suppliers, and in the purchase of foreign exchange.[46]

The Pact and domestic recovery

The Roca Loan was only part of a more comprehensive commercial and financial agreement between Great Britain and Argentina regulating trade and commercial clearings. Yet the Roca-Runciman Pact, and the negotiations which preceded its signature, established the context within which the Loan agreement was achieved and official policy implemented. The Roca Funding Loan was essential to the application of the two most important reflationary measures of the 1930s. In addition, proceeds from the Loan facilitated the reduction of the government's floating debt and the accumulation of foreign exchange, thus providing a semblance of normality to public finance. Together with the smaller dollar and Swiss franc funding loans, the Roca bonds may be said to constitute the link between previous budget-orientated, and order-seeking, policies and more expansionist measures resorted to during and after the latter part of 1933.

Scholars have paid too much attention to the detail of the commercial provisions of the Pact (often over-emphasizing benefits accruing to cattle-breeding interests), and have ignored domestic policy implications. Argentine economic recovery after 1933 was based upon the price support scheme for agricultural producers and the funding of the internal debt, both of which were underwritten by the Roca Funding Loan. This link between the Roca agreement and Argentina's economic recovery from the Depression is not yet acknowledged in the literature. It has eluded Fodor, O'Connell, Gravil and Rooth, who have examined the agreement from a *dependentista* perspective but failed to notice the broader spectrum of policy-making. Moreover, the economic strength of the republic resulting from the Roca Loan and the operations which followed, make it difficult to see the Roca Pact and Anglo-Argentine economic relations as, in any real sense, examples of an unfavourable dependent relationship.

Even if it is debatable whether Argentine officials maximized their negotiating options in London, hostility against the Conservative coalition for signing the agreement has to be tempered. Most Argentines, not only cattlemen, derived tangible benefits from Roca-Runciman.

Notes

[1] J. F. Fodor and A. A. O'Connell 'La Argentina y la economía atlántica en la primera mitad del siglo XX' *Desarrollo Económico* xxxxix (1973).

[2] R. Gravil and T. Rooth 'A time of acute dependence: Argentina in the 1930s' *Journal of European Economic History* vii 2–3 (1978).

[3] *Ibid.*

[4] *Ibid.*

[5] R. and J. Irazusta *La Argentina y el imperialismo británico* (Buenos Aires 1934) p. 182.

[6] A. Jauretche *FORJA y la década infame* (Buenos Aires 1973) pp. 41–2.

[7] See Jauretche *op. cit.* pp. 40–1 and R. Scalabrini Ortiz *Política británica en el Rio de la Plata* (Buenos Aires 1957) p. 128.

[8] C. Ibarguren *La historia que he vivido* (Buenos Aires 1955) p. 447.

[9] R. Puiggrós *La democracia fraudulenta* (Buenos Aires 1972) p. 114.

[10] J. A. Ramos *Revolución y contrarevolución en la Argentina* (Buenos Aires 1972) pp. 193–6.

[11] J. V. Liceaga *Las carnes en la economía argentina* (Buenos Aires 1972) p. 11.

[12] Cf. D. Drosdoff *El gobierno de las vacas (1933–1956): Tratado Roca-Runciman* (Buenos Aires 1972) pp. 142–6.

[13] V. Salera *Exchange control and the Argentine market* (New York 1941) pp. 104–5.

[14] A week before the measures of 28 November 1933, 100kg. of wheat were selling spot in Buenos Aires at 4.79 paper pesos; a week later with the Grain Board, they were selling at 5.75 paper pesos.

[15] Ministerio de Hacienda 'Fundamentos de las medidas del 28 de noviembre' *Crítica Social* xii 164 (1936) 18.

[16] Ministerio de Hacienda 'Fundamentos . . ,' *loc. cit.* 10.

[17] *Ibid.*

[18] *Ibid.*

[19] F. Pinedo *En tiempos de la república* (Buenos Aires 1944) iv p. 247.

[20] *South American Journal* (hereafter *SAJ*) 25 Feb. 1933, 202.

[21] *SAJ* 4 March 1933, 230.

[22] *SAJ* 25 March 1933, 298.

[23] *SAJ* 29 April 1933, 418.

[24] *SAJ* 6 May 1933, 456.

[25] A. Hueyo 'Mirando al pasado' *La Prensa* 1 Sept. 1943, 9:7.

[26] *Ibid.*

[27] *Financial News* 30 Sept. 1933.

[28] Salera, *op. cit.*, p. 269.

[29] *The Economist* 14 Oct. 1933, 712; *The Times* 23 Oct. 1933.

[30] Ministerio de Hacienda *El plan de acción económica nacional* (Buenos Aires 1934) p. 84.

[31] C. F. Díaz Alejandro has argued that 'the remarkable 1933–39 [economic] recovery was due mainly to domestic policies'. In spite of a drop in the import quantum by more than 28 per cent, between 1925–29 and 1935–39 the real GDP expanded by 20 per cent, and by 1939 it was nearly 15 per cent above that of 1929 and 22 per cent above 1932 (in the United States, a similar comparison yields an increase of only 4 per cent between 1929 and 1939). See C. F. Díaz Alejandro *Essays on the economic history of the Argentine Republic* (New Haven 1970) pp. 95, 98 and 100. The basis of this recovery was the *Plan de aión económica* of 1933–4, and the conversion of the internal debt and the minimum price guarantee for farmers, its two key policies.

[32] 'La conversión de la deuda pública' in República Argentina *Poder Ejecutivo Nacional 1932–38* (Buenos Aires 1938) 1 n.p.

[33] 'La conversión de la deuda pública' *loc. cit.* n.p.

[34] *The Times* 14 Dec. 1932.

[35] Ministerio de Hacienda *El ajuste de los resultados financieros de 1928 a 1936* (Buenos Aires 1938) p. 146.

[36] *Ibid.*

[37] 'La conversión de la deuda pública' *loc. cit.* n.p.

[38] Ministerio de Hacienda *El plan de acción económica nacional* p. 41.

[39] Ministerio de Hacienda *Comunicado* 4 Nov. 1933 in *Crítica Social* xii 164 (1936) 7.

[40] Ministerio de Hacienda *Comunicado* 6 Oct. 1933 in *Crítica Social* xii 164 (1936) 10.

[41] Ministerio de Hacienda *El plan de acción económica ante el Congreso Nacional* (Buenos Aires 1934) pp. 17–18.

[42] In 1934 the turnover of national bonds in the Stock Exchange was 205 million paper pesos (£13.7 million). (*Economist:* Argentine Supplement, 8 Feb. 1936, 16). Given that the holders of blocked funds subscribed bonds for 19.3 millions (£1.3 million) in national paper, nearly 10 per cent of that turnover in the Stock Exchange would have been affected by liquidations, a figure that does not take into account the wider repercussions such sales would have had for the bond market.

[43] Ministerio de Hacienda *El plan de acción económica ante el Congreso Nacional* pp. 19–20.

[44] *Ibid.*

[45] 'La conversión de la deuda pública' *loc. cit.* n.p.

[46] *Ibid.*

19

ANGLO-BRAZILIAN ECONOMIC RELATIONS AND THE CONSOLIDATION OF AMERICAN PRE-EMINENCE IN BRAZIL, 1930–1945

Marcelo de Paiva Abreu

This chapter deals with the links between the consolidation of the United States' privileged position in Brazil – which eventually crystallized only during the Second World War – and the development of Anglo-Brazilian economic relations in the 1930s and early 1940s. One of the striking features of Brazil's international relations after the First World War was the relative resilience which Britain demonstrated in her role as an economic power that counted in Brazil. It will be seen that one of the important consequences of the inter-war Depression was to weaken Britain's position and, consequently, to remove one of the main obstacles to the consolidation of United States' hegemony in Brazil. Further delay in the consolidation of the foundations of *pax americana* was due to German rather than British complications.[1]

The chapter is divided into four sections. The first considers factors which sustained British hegemony in Brazil during the nineteenth century and occasioned its decline after the 1900s. The second section deals with the impact of the Depression on Anglo-Brazilian economic relations, and discusses American strategic aims in this context. The third examines the consequences of the war on relations between Britain and Brazil, and the full consolidation of America's economic and political supremacy in Brazil, which would last for at least thirty years. The concluding section discusses the meaningfulness of comparing the 1930s and the 1980s as 'unsettled' decades, that is, decades without a hegemonic power in the world economy.

Britain and Brazil

Britain's pre-eminence in Brazil, as is well known, was overwhelming in the first half of the nineteenth century and very pronounced at least until the end of the century. Transition to independence and early independent rule was marked first by the concession of preferential import duties to British goods, then by the maintenance of a very low import duty extended to all countries until 1844.[2] Britain had the *de facto* monopoly of Brazilian loans until the last decade of the century, and lost only slowly her position as the main supplier of goods to Brazil. In one important respect, however, Britain's position was not so important after the 1 given the lack of complementarity between the British Empire and Brazil, Brazil's exports tended to be absorbed by other countries, especially coffee by the United States.[3] In this sense, the Brazilian economy constituted very early a violation of the norm, as its absorption by the world economy in the scope of the so-called *pax britannica* did not depend directly on Britain's demand for its exports, as was the case, for instance, with Argentina.

From the early 1850s to the early 1900s, Britain's share of the Brazilian import trade fell from around 50 per cent to slightly under 30 per cent of the total, much of the reduction taking place before the late 1880s. As far as Brazilian exports are concerned, it would seem that by the late 1850s the United States was well established as the main customer. The importance of the British market for Brazilian trade had contracted very sharply by the end of the century, but recovered slightly in the 1900s. Immediately before the war Britain's share of the Brazilian export market was in the region of 13 per cent – slightly smaller than Germany's, in a geographically much more diversified market than hitherto.

Between the late 1880s and the beginning of the First World War a substantial amount of European – especially French – capital was invested in Brazil. This trend disturbed in a rather marginal way Britain's monopoly of the emission of Brazilian loans – as it principally involved loans to lower-grade borrowers – but seemed to be more relevant in the case of direct investments. The British were still able, in spite of keen competition from other financial markets, to maintain their hold on the borrowers who mattered most, in particular the federal government. British nervousness about the entry into the financial field of other leaders was, however, palpable. It was to be the role of the Americans in the 1920s to undermine this last pillar of British pre-eminence.

In spite of the evident erosion of her dominant economic position in Brazil, Britain in 1913 still held at least 60 per cent of total foreign capital, either in the form of direct investments or as sterling bonds; about a quarter of Brazil's imports were of British origin – slowly losing ground, it is true, to fierce German and American competition, but still maintaining quite comfortably the place of main Brazilian supplier. While the United States was the main market for Brazil, buying 40 per cent of Brazil's exports, they held only 12–15 per cent of the Brazilian market and their investments were practically negligible.

However, as the war would show, the foundations of Britain's pre-eminence in Brazil were not sound. During the 1920s British exports lost heavily as Brazil's import schedule moved away from traditional goods – whose domestic production was increasing – to modern consumer durable goods in whose production Britain did not excel. Britain's share of Brazil's exports was drastically reduced, falling from 15–20 per cent during the immediate pre-war years to 5–10 per cent in the 1920s. But, more important than trends concerning trade, the decisive new development which affected the British position was the much increased financial involvement of the United States in Brazil. Brazilian loans placed in London between 1915 and 1930 amounted to £54.3 million, while those placed in New York reached £86.5 million. This was, of course, the result of both British retraction from foreign lending, especially after 1925, and the euphoria which characterized the New York market in the second half of the decade. Britain, however, still retained an important position, since in stock terms her financial stake did not decrease much even relatively – as other stakes, like the French, shrank disastrously – and the London market still remained an alternative to be taken into consideration, particularly in the case of loans placed by the coffee valorization authorities which were banned from New York by the Sherman Act.

The maintenance of an economic counterweight to the USA was, of course, welcomed by the Brazilian authorities, who consistently searched for a 'reinsurance' policy which would make Brazil's relations with the United States less intimate. In this sense, it can be said that the existence of Britain as an alternative source of financial resources was an important explanation for the relatively tame manner in which America exercised her potentially dominant position in Brazil before 1930.

The 1930s

The interruption of the flows of foreign capital in the wake of the Wall Street crash and its European repercussions, combined with the rapid fall in international coffee prices, produced a very serious balance of payments crisis in Brazil, which led first to the exhaustion of reserves and then to devaluation and exchange control. The new policies imposed by the changed conditions in the international economy created a very marked incentive to import substitution, through the use of industrial idle capacity installed in the 1920s. Coffee sector income, on the other hand, suffered quite considerably, as devaluation did not entirely compensate for the fall in international prices.

This interruption of the flows of foreign capital resulted in a considerable weakening of an already eroded British bargaining position in Brazil. Paradoxically, in the years immediately after 1930, when the Brazilian authorities still thought that the closure of the leading financial markets – especially London – would be a temporary trend and not a structural change, Britain's leverage in Brazil in fact increased. A policy of *rapprochement* towards Britain was indeed highly favoured by those interests more intimately connected with coffee production, financing and commercialization. That this possibility could be entertained was due to the unaccommodating stand adopted by American banks in relation to Brazilian banks operating in New York, which had their credit facilities sharply curtailed in 1930, and to the State Department's erroneous assessment of the outcome of Vargas's bid for power in October of the same year.

While it is open to question whether a less orthodox man than Sir Otto Niemeyer, as leader of the financial mission which visited Brazil in the first half of 1931, would have been more effective in terms of safeguarding Britain's flagging economic influence, there is little doubt that the temporary eclipse of the United States made possible the visit of a British mission to a country which was rapidly becoming an undisputed area of American influence. In spite of the fact that practically none of the recommendations included in the mission's report were followed by the Brazilian authorities, as they were extremely orthodox, the mission prepared the ground for the negotiation of a temporary settlement of defaulted Brazilian public foreign debt in late 1931, which tended to treat more favourably Brazil's sterling loans.[4]

It was only after imperial preference had clearly shown Britain's emphasis on closer commercial relations with the Empire, and the failure of the 1933 World Economic Conference to reach agreement on a concerted move away from bilaterialism and trade control, that 'the stage was well set for the entry of Uncle Sam in a benign role, as the flow of time has wiped out of Brazilian memory his unfortunate mistakes of the 1930 revolutionary period'.[5] While it is rather unlikely that the Ottawa Agreements affected very substantially Brazilian exports to Great Britain – the British share of Brazilian exports indeed increased from around 4 per cent in 1928 to about 10 per cent in the late 1930s, as her cotton purchases shifted away from the United States – it was an important indication that the emphasis of British economic policy would be to trade with countries whose exports did not compete with Empire products.[6]

Indeed, after 1933–4 Britain's position in Brazil was considerably eroded, in comparison with the early Vargas period. Britain's policy was to concentrate her efforts on the protection of financial interests and establish a markedly lower priority for questions related to trade. This scale of priorities still paid off when the new temporary public foreign debt settlement was discussed – even if the terms partially redressed a previously unfavourable American position when compared with the 1931 agreement – but grew increasingly inefficient as it became clear to the Brazilian authorities that the maintenance of the country's financial standing was not of overwhelming importance if world financial markets remained closed. Brazil, in fact, took an increasingly pragmatic stand on the relative priorities in the distribution of foreign exchange, beginning the decade with public foreign debt service requirements very high on the list of priorities, and eventually defaulting service payments in the late 1930s.[7]

British foreign economic policy in the 1930s was, of course, realistic in a much more comprehensive way. Since it was based on an assessment of the effective bargaining power which Britain commanded in each country, it is very difficult to define a coherent strategy, as in the case of American post-1934 multilateralism. Britain's policy alternated between 'comprar a quien nos compra' or 'buy British' in Argentina or Denmark, and 'buy from whom sells you the best cheapest' in Brazil: Britain was multilaterialist where her bargaining power was weak, bilateralist where it was strong. While in Argentina the Roca-Runciman agreement of 1933 – giving in practice first priority to British foreign exchange cover requirements – was the basis of Anglo-Argentine economic relations, the most-favoured-nation clause was thought to be acceptable in countries like Brazil.[8] This policy made the British position extremely vulnerable when the Germans applied their New Plan for foreign trade in 1934, which was based on the thorough use of trade bilateralization and damaged British commerce with Brazil. With the *de facto* removal of Britain as an important contender in Brazil, it would seem that the road was open to the consolidation of American pre-eminence, based on the strong bargaining power associated with their balance of payments deficit with Brazil. But this had to wait, as the adoption by Germany of Schacht's New Plan for foreign trade made possible a fast expansion of trade between Brazil and Germany in the second half of the 1930s.

This is not the place to detail the workings of compensation trade, as it has been examined elsewhere.[9] It is enough to say that any form of trade which was based on the use of inconvertible currency *and* opened up a substantial supply of imports through the expansion of Brazilian exports, was bound to gain an important share of Brazil's foreign trade. In fact, while the expansion of the German share was not as great as suggested by Brazilian official statistics – as imports from Germany were consistently overvalued with compensation marks being taken as Reichsmarks – it is still true that the share of German imports increased from 11–12 per cent in 1934 to 19–20 per cent in 1936–8.

In spite of an American outcry over unfair competition, frequently endorsed at face value, it would seem that, *taking aggregate shares*, the increase of imports from Germany dislocated not American but British exports: the British share of the Brazilian market fell, indeed, from about 20 per cent in 1934 to 11–13 per cent in 1936–8.[10] Traditional British exports suffered most: textiles, due to increased domestic output; coal, tinplate, wire, rails, tubes and electric equipment through the competition of German goods. While American exports of consumer durable goods were obviously affected by German competition, the United States was able to recoup these losses by increasing its share in the supply of other imported goods. British industry was, on the other hand, unable to compete in the supply of more sophisticated goods, especially consumer durables.[11]

The importance of the German market as an outlet for Brazilian exports also increased very considerably in the second half of the 1930s: Germany's share of total Brazilian exports increased from 8–9 per cent in the early 1930s to a maximum of 19 per cent in 1938. This was closely associated with the increase in cotton exports at the expense of American cotton both in the German and the British markets. It may, however, be noted that even in the late 1930s the importance of the German market was not greater than it had been just before the First World War.

As Great Britain in the 1930s broke with long-established tradition in her foreign economic policy, abandoning practically all basic tenets of free trade and payments, the United States became the main advocate of a return to multilateralism. This was also, of course, a rather sharp reversal, especially in relation to traditional American trade policy, and became more defined after 1934 with the victory of the State Department's liberals over the bilateralists (led by George Peek), who proposed that the United States should adopt a policy similar to Britain's, exploiting to the end their local bargaining power with no particular qualms about the lack of a coherent general policy.[12]

Given the American commitment to multilateralism and the defensive position adopted by Britain, it is not surprising that the second half of the 1930s was marked by a continuous friction involving the American, Brazilian and German governments, concerning the expansion of the German compensation trade. The Americans exerted continuous pressure on Brazil to discontinue this trade, which started to expand very fast in 1934–5. It was held to be discriminatory, diverting trade which could generate scarce exchange cover to pay for Brazilian imports from convertible currency countries. German imports were promptly paid for and enjoyed competitive price advantages as the compensation mark was cheaper than the Reichsmark, and Germany offered generous export subsidies.

While the Brazilian authorities – keenly aware of the strength of American bargaining power – were willing to accommodate American pressure concerning other issues, the curtailment or interruption of compensation trade raised more important questions. Indeed, there was no clear alternative outlet, of the same importance for Brazilian exports, as the German market. This was particularly true of cotton, whose production was increasing very rapidly in Brazil under the umbrella of American cotton price policy. It is difficult to detect any sector of Brazilian society that did not benefit from the expansion of this trade. It favoured exporters, importers and consumers and, perhaps more important, provided much required political elbow-room for the federal government. Exports to Germany were of importance to the economies of

Rio Grande do Sul and the north-east, and made possible the acquisition of military equipment for the army.[13] Consequently, while during the second half of the 1930s Brazil yielded to American pressure and formally adopted multilateralism, at the same time she did nothing to hinder a thriving compensation trade. This has been credited as Brazilian astuteness, exploiting the advantages provided by German-American rivalry. While it is quite true that Brazil did benefit from the advantages offered by the German alternative, it is difficult to accept that the success of this ambiguous Brazilian policy can be credited to Brazil's increased bargaining power. Indeed, in many instances during the 1930s the United States tended to adopt a moderate stand, abstaining from full use of her strong position *vis à vis* Brazil. This was true in the case of the public foreign debt, of commercial arrears, of the compensation trade and even of the 1935 Trade Agreement. In almost every case American strategic aims prevailed over short-term considerations, in sharp contrast with British policy. In fact America's attitude to Brazil in the 1930s – not unduly pressing Brazil on the compensation trade and considering Vargas's regime as 'a dictatorship more acceptable than others' – was a policy of enlightened self-interest, having as one main target the containment of Argentina, a country over which the United States had not much leverage. This policy would become even more distinct in the early war years.[14]

The relative success of Brazilian foreign economic policy in the 1930s was more a corollary of the Latin American policy of the United States than the result of Brazilian talent in creating degrees of freedom which would not otherwise exist. Therefore it is rather difficult to speak in terms of the formulation and implementation of a Brazilian strategy concerning international economic questions. If Brazil pursued a coherent line of action, it must be defined residually in relation to American strategy. To speak of a Brazilian strategy is to allow too much room for hindsight.

Recent work has tended to qualify earlier assessments of the 1930s as a decade during which only the Brazilian-American connection counted.[15] The German 'complication' was extremely important, especially between 1935 and 1938. These new interpretations, however, exaggerate either Brazil's bargaining power and negotiating abilities or the actual economic and political weight of Germany. Had the United States not been committed to multilateralism as a comprehensive solution for the problems faced by the international economy, or had Argentina's trade and payments structure made that country more vulnerable to American pressure, it is unlikely that Brazil could have played for so long an ambiguous policy. In this context, it is misleading to use terms such as 'pragmatic equidistance'[16] to define Brazil's policy during the late 1930s. The United States' economic weight in Brazil was incomparably greater than Germany's, which had only her trade as a bargaining weapon: Brazilian international economic policy was pragmatic – as any efficient policy should be – and tried to exploit in the national interest the contradictions between the United States and Germany, but was very far from equidistant, the alternative between wholly free and wholly compensation trade never being considered.

Brazilian policy respecting compensation trade has been termed by Hilton[17] an 'opportunistic response' to economic rivalry in the 1930s, maintaining American political support and increasing its German trade. Such a concept is hardly operational, since it is quite difficult to think of a country which would consider ethical arguments as of special importance in the definition of national policy. Multilateralism was defended by the United States, not because it was thought to be ethically more acceptable than bilateralism but because it best suited American national interest, possibly in the short run and certainly in the long run. Brazil's policy was similarly defined in the light of the interest of different sectors of Brazilian society. Indeed, if moral judgement provided a sound basis to assess the international economic policies followed by specific countries, what can be said of American lenience in allowing Brazil to play her ambiguous game in the name of long-term objectives? Or, how could the United States put pressure on Brazil to interrupt compensation trade with Germany when 'German-American commercial relations were . . . conducted on practically the same basis as that which the American Government was requesting Brazil to suppress.'[18]

With the growing deterioration of the international situation in 1938, the continuation of the German compensation trade was discouraged by the Brazilian authorities, who feared the accumulation of unusable blocked marks in Berlin. The road to closer collaboration with the United States was thereby open, without the interference of any European power. This new trend was made clear enough by the visit of the Brazilian foreign minister to the United States in early 1939, when, besides reaching agreement on the payment of financial arrears which had accumulated in the aftermath of a balance of payments crisis associated with the American recession of 1937, it was agreed that Brazil would considerably liberalize her foreign exchange policy and consider the resumption of public foreign debt payments.[19]

The Second World War
The first impact of the war on the Brazilian economy was, of course, the loss of important Central European markets in countries which came under German rule. The situation was further aggravated in the summer of 1940, when other traditional markets in Western Europe were lost. The importance of the American market was thus considerably enhanced, in spite of the fact that Britain increased very considerably her

purchases, especially of meat and cotton. On the supply side the impact of the war was even more pronounced, as the Anglo-Brazilian Payments Agreement of 1940 made it possible for Britain to reduce her exports to very low levels and, especially after 1941, Brazilian demand for imports of American origin had to compete with the United States' war effort.

Immediately after the outbreak of the war there was a temporary deterioration in Brazilian relations with Britain, in the wake of British unwillingness to allow military equipment purchased in Germany to pass the blockade. Many difficulties were also faced in implementing the Anglo-Brazilian Payments Agreement, as it backfired from the British point of view; the bilateral balance of payments was now favourable to Brazil, and Britain was reluctant to increase her Brazilian purchases in the short run. With the resumption of public foreign debt service in 1940 through a new temporary settlement and the acceleration of British purchases, relations improved. The British market had, of course, acquired renewed importance for Brazil, as so many of her traditional export markets were blocked. For Britain, clearing arrangements with countries such as Brazil were an important means of financing the war: they assured Britain of a supply of vital imports as well as of a flow of financial payments without entailing any obligation to supply those markets, making it possible to conduct export policy with only the war effort in mind.[20]

From 1942, however, in spite of continuous bilateral interest in the expansion of British purchases in Brazil and of the improved atmosphere created by the resumption of debt payments, Britain played a secondary role in Brazil, her aims being defined as 'if possible to intensify our existing good political, economic and cultural relations subject to the overriding necessities of the successful prosecution of the war and of the maintenance of the fullest unity and understanding with the United States'.[21] American policy in the early war years was to deal with economic problems in Latin America in the light of political considerations. This was patently the case of the Inter-American Coffee Agreement of 1940 and of the purchasing agreements of 1941 and 1942, when prices were established considerably above those ruling in the market, in sharp contrast with British procurement and pre-emption policy, which consistently struggled for the best possible prices ruling in the market.

An important American concession to Brazil in the early war period was the extension of official finance and supply priority for the construction of Volta Redonda, the first large-scale Brazilian integrated steel mill. In line with the over-valuation of Brazil's leverage in connection with the German compensation trade, recent historiography[22] has tended to stress that this was, once again, the result of Brazil's skilful exploitation of American-German rivalry, as the Germans showed a willingness to cooperate when American firms declined to get involved with the project. It is difficult to accept uncritically such an interpret-ation, because it is rather unlikely either that Germany was prepared to consider the diversion of productive capacity to the detriment of her war effort, or that the Royal Navy would allow German shipments through the British blockade. The episode must be counted as another of Vargas's negotiating ruses. What counted was not the existence of a credible German alternative, but the American policy to take into account Brazil's strategic role in Latin America, as had been the case with the German compensation trade.[23]

From 1943 American policy became rather less generous, as initial targets concerning pre-emption, procurement and political support were achieved. The Americans resisted strongly any attempt to increase Brazilian export prices, particularly of coffee, denounced Brazilian uni-lateral import controls as a breach of the 1935 Trade Agreement, resisted Brazilian attempts to develop import-substituting industries, and were unable to fulfil their promises concerning the supply of scarce materials to Brazil.

British policy, on the other hand, tended to centre on questions related to the accumulation of Brazilian sterling balances in London. British policy-makers, in fact, lived through a permanent dilemma as, while the accumulation of sterling balances was a sound objective of British policy from the point of view of war finance, the rapid increase of inconvertible balances tended to undermine sterling's credibility as a viable altern-ative key currency in peacetime.[24] The more unused sterling accumu-lated in London, the less 'sterling-minded' Brazil was likely to stay. British policy, consequently, emphasized the need to find outlets for Brazilian sterling. The main outlets proved to be the transfer of British-owned assets in Brazil to the Brazilian government, and the redemption of sterling loans as provided by the permanent 1943 public foreign debt settlement.

British direct foreign investments had been reduced by something like 20 per cent in nominal terms during the 1930s, until they reached about £100 million in 1940; in 1945 they amounted to £85 million. This reduction, which continued after the war, was at least partly associated with the sale of British assets in Brazil. While British capital was concentrated in public utilities, and therefore bound to suffer from widespread price and exchange controls in the 1930s, American invest-ments tended to be increasingly concentrated in the manufacturing sector.[25] This turned out to be an additional factor making American and British policies quite distinct. Some of the British grievances were not as strongly felt by American interests.

Brazilian public foreign debt was renegotiated in 1943, agreement being reached on a permanent settlement. The terms of the agreement underlined Britain's weak bargaining position, as many of the features

which favoured sterling loans, and which had been included under
Niemeyer's influence in the early 1930s, were dropped in favour of 'equal
treatment' to the benefit of American high-interest speculative loans
floated in the 1920s.

Thus, by 1943 the United States had consolidated beyond any doubt
her position of pre-eminence in Brazil. According to the State Department, the American ambassador to Brazil should have been regarded 'in
the same light' as HM's ambassador to Egypt.[26] Brazilian authorities
were becoming increasingly uncomfortable at the excessive intimacy of
Brazilian relations with the United States: in the words of the British
ambassador, 'the moment was ripe for Dr. Aranha to bring Great Britain
out of the bag'[27] and try to revert to the time-honoured traditional
pre-Vargas policy of using Britain as a counterweight to the United
States. But this was, of course, a wild overestimation of the real options
available to Brazilian policy-makers, as Britain had much less leverage
in Brazil than in the 1920s, providing no credibly strong alternative to
the United States such as to make 'reinsurance' a feasible policy.[28]

Indeed, the attractions of gaining politically in Latin America from
American support were very strong, as under the American umbrella
Brazil could try to restore its role of political pre-eminence in the
continent which had been lost to Argentina at the turn of the century.
The approach of peace, however, resulted in a hardening of American
policy, not only concerning economic matters, as already noted, but also
in relation to the political support of governments not elected demo-
cratically. American concern with the lack of internal democracy in
Brazil became increasingly pronounced from 1943–4, with a preference
taking shape for a 'liberal' solution which would not only remove the
contradiction between Brazil's authoritarian political regime and her
anti-Axis foreign policy, but also tend to assure the adoption of economic
policies more in line with American interests. Vargas's fall in 1945 made
possible the unchallenged continuation of American political and economic pre-eminence in Brazil, which was to last until the early 1970s. The
consolidation of the United States' position seemed, indeed, to vindicate
the emphasis placed by American policy in the 1930s and early 1940s on
long-term objectives at the expense of short-term advantages.

Crisis at the centre and autonomy at the periphery
Contrary to what is frequently implied in the literature, the exacerbation
of rivalry among the leading industrial nations in the 1930s did not
necessarily result in an increase in the degrees of freedom of the less
developed or dependent countries. While Brazil may have fared well in
this context, the reverse was true in countries where relative bargaining
positions benefited industrial nations whose international economic

policies were moving away from free trade and payments, as illustrated by the case of Argentina.

Even in the case of Brazil, it is not easy to claim clear-cut advantages as a result of greater rivalry between the main industrial nations in the 1930s. Some of Brazil's gains were direct consequences of speculative lending before 1930, in a context of much reduced export earnings by primary producer countries after the World Depression. Even then it is by no means certain that, taking the external debt as a whole, Brazil's action resulted in an overall loss to lenders; many old loans had been issued at large discounts. The mere continued existence of the German compensation trade can be taken as a gain to Brazil. What is arguable is whether this gain was the result of friction between the United States and Germany or merely a corollary of the overall American long-term Latin American policy. The second explanation is, on the basis of available evidence, much easier to accept. It would seem, consequently, that Brazil fared relatively well in her economic intercourse with the world economy in the 1930s, mainly because her weak bargaining power was in relation to the United States, the only country prepared to forgo short-term advantages in the face of a growing willingness to consolidate hegemony in Latin America.

One of the main reasons for renewed interest in the 1930s among social scientists is related, as far as international economic relations are concerned, to the alleged similarities between that decade and the late 1970s and 1980s. While, superficially at least, this view carried some appeal, many qualifications are required, some of a general nature and others specially relevant to the case of Brazil.

The unsatisfactory performance of many industrial nations, the increase in unemployment and the slackening rate of expansion of world non-oil trade cannot be compared with the impact of the inter-war Depression in terms of reduced levels of activity, increased unemployment and dislocation and reduction of world trade, especially in the more advanced economies. Even those more aligned with fashionable anti-Keynesian scepticism would agree that enough was learned about economic affairs to make a recurrence of a similar crisis rather unlikely. The main sources of instability remain: the international financial market, the lack of coordination of domestic policies which can result in sudden and competitive realignment of exchange rates, and the adoption of protectionist policies which tend to restrict trade. Perhaps more importantly, there is not a single nation which can be clearly seen as able to provide international economic leadership in the 1980s. There is no country now in the position of the United States in the inter-war period: 'able but unwilling' to lead the world economy. The 1980s are likely to be years without a clear economic – or, for that matter, political – leadership among Western countries. This situation will probably require an important overhauling of the present institutional arrangements that regulate international trade and payments.

Brazil is likely to find opportunities for 'reinsurance', but will not benefit from the studied complacency of a rising world hegemonic power, as in the 1930s. Life will be rougher in a much more complicated world economy, the increase in export earnings required by the soaring costs of servicing the debt involving in many cases tough competition and increasing political friction with the industrial nations as traditional suppliers of the world markets. In this sense the 1980s are likely to be a less sheltered decade for Brazil than the 1930s, calling for an active foreign economic policy which should at the same time assure the expansion of export markets and the continuous collaboration of foreign capital, without substantial sacrifices of national sovereignty.

Notes

[1] Many of the points discussed in this paper are addressed at greater length in Marcelo de Paiva Abreu 'Brazil and the world economy, 1930–1945: aspects of foreign economic policies and international economic relations under Vargas' (unpubl. Ph.D. thesis, University of Cambridge 1977).

[2] The classic treatment of pre-1930 Anglo-Brazilian economic relations is, of course, A. K. Manchester *British pre-eminence in Brazil. Its rise and decline: a study in European expansion* (Chapel Hill 1933). For pre-1808 Anglo-Portuguese relations see S. Sideri *Trade and power: informal colonialism in Anglo-Portuguese relations* (Rotterdam 1970).

[3] Pre-1900 Brazilian statistics are notoriously unreliable, a fact pointed out as early as 1896 by J. P. Wileman *Brazilian exchange: the study of an inconvertible currency* (Buenos Aires 1896). It is unfortunate that his plea for a 'thorough and trustworthy compilation of . . . statistics, that, embracing a long period, will afford a safe basis on which to found deductions, without which all conclusions are little better than speculations' remains unfulfilled by specialists. The general argument is not, however, affected by the poor quality of these statistics.

[4] For an analysis of Niemeyer's recommendations see M. de P. Abreu 'A Missão Niemeyer' *Revista de Administração de Empresas* July 1974; for public foreign debt questions see Abreu, thesis, chap. 3.

[5] United States Department of State *Foreign Relations of the United States 1933* (Washington 1951), pp. 30–8 and memo 16 12 32, Federal Reserve Bank of New York, no. 260, Correspondence Files, Foreign Exchange, Jan. 1931–May 1933. For results of the Ottawa Conference, see H. V. Hodson *Slump and recovery 1929–1937. A survey of world economic affairs* (1938) chap. 5 (e).

[6] Increased British imports from Brazil, however, were not sufficient to turn the balance of trade in favour of Brazil: British bargaining power remained weak. It is possible that the restriction applied to British meat imports affected Brazilian exports, as Brazil was a latecomer in this market. The considerable increase of meat exports to Britain during the Second World War tends to substantiate this, but for the fact that price considerations were very much in the background during the war.

[7] Britain's weak bargaining power in Brazil is also made explicit by the much less restrictive terms of the payments agreement signed with Brazil, compared with countries where there was effective bargaining power on the basis of bilateral trade as in the case of Argentina, as pointed out by Henry J. Tasca *World trading systems. A study of American and British commercial policies* (Paris 1939) p. 83. Tasca also stresses the 'disposition on the part of

the United Kingdom to place financial interests in a position of priority as compared with current export trade', p. 85.

[8] The ambiguity of British policy was recognized by Foreign Office officials: 'this country remains with one foot on the realm of quotas and tariffs and the other still in the realm of most-favoured-nation agreements', Mason's memo 1.8.33, Public Record Office, London, Foreign Office Correspondence (hereafter FO) 371/16534:A6417/48/2. This was, of course, strongly criticized, specially in Argentina, see *Buenos Aires Herald* 1 and 4 May 1935.

[9] See Abreu, thesis, section iv.4, specifically for the German compensation trade in Brazil. For a traditional account of German trading practices in the 1930s see H. S. Ellis *Exchange control in Central Europe* (Cambridge, Mass. 1941) especially pp. 216–21. For a recent criticism of traditional interpretations – which underlined the economic losses in clearing agreements – see L. Neal 'The economics and finance of bilateral clearing agreements: Germany, 1934–38' *Economic History Review* xxxii 3 (1979).

[10] The competitive weakness of the British 'new industries' in this period has been underlined by Alfred E. Kahn *Great Britain and the world economy* (New York 1946), chap. 6.

[11] Kahn *op. cit.* chap. 6.

[12] American policy, as opposed to Britain's 'free trade and equal treatment', had been in the past one of 'subjecting foreigners to the equal but bad treatment of a steadily increasing tariff', Carl Kreider *The Anglo-American Trade Agreement. A study of British and American commercial policies, 1934–1939* (Princeton 1943) p. 18. There were important exceptions, however, to American equality of treatment, especially in Latin America. In the case of Brazil some American imports enjoyed a discriminatory tariff for twenty years before 1923.

[13] Care must be taken not to exaggerate military influence in favour of compensation trade. It was the accumulation of unused blocked marks in Berlin that prompted the *German* suggestion that such credits should be used to purchase military equipment, and not the reverse as suggested by Stanley E. Hilton *Brazil and the Great Powers 1930–1939. The politics of trade rivalry* (Austin 1975) pp. 97, 109, 100, 130–1. See telegram 39, Berlin to Rio, 18.4.36, Arquivo Histórico do Itamaraty/Missões Diplomáticas.

[14] Memo by Spiegel and de Beers, undated, p. 3, Economic and Financial Reports, BRA/0/60, United States Department of the Treasury. It may be noted, as an illustration of American long-term priorities, that the US government consistently underlined the higher priority of commercial and direct investment questions in relation to those concerning the public foreign debt. As the treasury position became stronger in the late 1930s, the emphasis on long-term considerations became even more pronounced: Morgenthau's and White's sympathies did not lie with the widows and orphans.

[15] Stanley Hilton *op. cit.* and, more recently with emphasis on political aspects, Roberto Gambini *O duplo jogo de Getúlio Vargas: influências americana e alemã no Estado Nôvo* (São Paulo 1977), and Gerson Moura *Autonomia no dependência: A política externa brasileira de 1935 a 1942* (Rio de Janeiro 1980).

[16] Moura *op. cit.* chap. 2.

[17] Hilton *op. cit.* p. 66.

[18] Tasca *op. cit.* p. 40.

[19] Abreu, thesis, section viii.1.

[20] The aim of the payments agreements policy was to make signatory countries accept payment 'in sterling so that in the post-war period [they]come to us to use it up'. For a comprehensive treatment of payments problems see R. S. Sayers *Financial policy, 1939–1945* (London 1956).

[21] V. Perowne's printed memo on The United States and Great Britain in Latin America, 26.2.43, FO 371/33903:A2230/348/51.

[22] Perhaps the most explicit is Luciano Martins *Politique et développement économique. Structures de pouvior et système de décisions au Brésil (1930–1964)* (thèse de Doctorat d'Etat, Université de Paris 1973), pp. 295–300. A shortened version of this dissertation has

appeared in book form as *Pouvoir et développement économique: formation et évolution des structures politiques au Brésil* (Paris 1976).

[23] The lack of a credible German alternative was, in fact, well known in the State Department; see Walmsey's memo 6.3.40, 832.6511/77, National Archives: Record Group 59. Vargas started to hint that the Germans were 'interested' in Volta Redonda in early 1940, showing that his attempt to exploit German-American rivalry had little to do with an evaluation of the result of the then European War, minute, 18.1.40, Fundação Getúlio Vargas: Vargas Archives. American views on the convenience of financing Volta Redonda were, of course, conflicting. For James Forrestal, for instance, it made as much sense to produce steel in Brazil as to grow cotton in Montreal, quoted by David Green *The containment of Latin America: a history of the myths and realities of the Good Neighbor policy* (Chicago 1971) p. 44. Brazil received US $332 million worth of military equipment under Lend-Lease, another instance of American policy to strengthen Brazil in order to contain Argentina's influence in the continent.

[24] Brazilian sterling balances increased from £2 million by the end of 1941 to £15 million in 1942, £35 million in 1943 and about £50 million by mid-1945; see Abreu, thesis, chap. vii.4.

[25] Purchase of British-owned railways amounted to £22 million in the period 1945–52. This, while being on a much smaller scale than in Argentina, was not negligible if compared with Brazilian sterling balances. In 1946 total American direct investment (book value) seemed to be roughly equivalent to British direct investment (nominal value): in the region of £80 million. Investments had expanded quite substantially between 1936 and 1940 and after 1943; see Abreu, thesis, pp. 172–5 and 213–14.

[26] Charles to Scott, 5.2.42, FO 371/30365:A2674/2674/6. There are many other instances of American plain talking about their bargaining position in Brazil, especially in the late years of the war. By mid-1944, Pierson, Eximbank's president, was suggesting that his bank and the Export Guarantee Credit Department should cartelize their activities: Latin America, and specially Brazil, would be American, while Turkey and the Middle East would be British spheres of influence. This the British considered to be only a slight variation of the preferred American slogan: 'Brazil is mine.' Magowan's minute, 6.6.44, and Mather-Jackson's minute, 26.6.44, FO 371/37863:AS 3215/720/6.

[27] Charles to Eden, no. 180, 20.9.43, FO 371/33678:A 9032/2506/6.

[28] British concern not to provoke the Americans by 'interfering' in Brazil, given the vulnerability of Britain to any American retaliation, demonstrated the unsuitability of a return to 'reinsurance' by Brazil. British reluctance to implement Keynes' advice to build up a British cotton reserve in Brazil for post-war use – since Southern congressmen could behave badly in the Lend-Lease appropriation debates – is a good example of the vulnerability of Britain's position. Mather-Jackson's minutes, 10.11.42, 14.12.42 and 8.3.43, FO 371/30495:A10485/25/51, 30497:A11600/25/51, 33876:A2312/1/51; tel. 6056, Washington to London, 12.12.42, FO 371/30497:A11600/25/51.

V

THE NEW ORDER

20

INTRODUCTION

Rosemary Thorp

The changes in the last thirty-five years both in the form of Latin America's relationship with the international economy, and in our perceptions of the nature of that relationship, have been so vast and so complex that it is more than a little daunting to attempt to 'introduce' this section. A further complication comes from the fact that, not surprisingly, most of the chapters focus on the fascinating new trends of the last ten years. It is with considerable diffidence, therefore, that I shall here attempt a brief review of the events, both real and intellectual, that in some sense provide the genesis and context of the chapters which compose this section.

As of 1945 the form of Latin America's relations with the world economy was still very much that of the early twentieth-century world. The massive changes precipitated by the changing world economy between 1913 and the Second World War had not as yet fed through into major changes in the external balance. There had been a significant acceleration in industrialization, often associated with increased military and strategic interest, a growth of nationalism, a change both qualitative and quantitative in the role of the state, and a broadening of class structures.[1] But as of 1945 the Latin American economies remained still completely primary exporters: the flurry of intra-Latin American exports of manufactures during the Second World War was proving temporary, as international trade channels reopened. Although import substitution was beginning to reduce the flexibility effected by a large percentage of consumer goods imports, it was not yet a real constraint, even in the larger economies. Given the deceleration in the inflow of foreign investment since 1928, its structure had not noticeably changed, and it was still heavily concentrated in primary sectors. Perhaps the main change since the 1920s on external account was the return of the debt service burden to more reasonable levels, given the defaults of the 1930s and the dearth, since 1929, of opportunities to borrow.

What was new, however, was the degree of sensitivity to the new dominance of the United States, and a preoccupation with its implications for Latin America. While the emergence of the United States as dominant in Latin America both in trade and foreign investment had been clear well before the 1929 crisis, the effect of the war had been to make the totality of US power, both economic and political, evident in a new way. This was the context of the important contribution to the debate over Latin America's external relations which was now to be made: a major challenge to orthodoxy, though it is hard now to reconstruct the extent of that challenge.

In 1947, in the teeth of US opposition, Prebisch went to Santiago to found ECLA: the new organization had to prove itself in a short space of time if it was to stay alive at all, and the group of young economists he gathered together had to show that there was a valid 'Latin American viewpoint'. Out of this came, by 1949, the 'Prebisch thesis':[2] initially lacking in coherence, its basic argument was that the productivity gains from technical progress in industry at the centre are not reflected in lower prices but retained there, while at the periphery productivity gains in the primary sector are less significant, and wages are held down by surplus labour. The 1959 version made explicit the demand side of the model: the asymmetry of the development of income elasticities of demand for imports in centre and periphery, with consequent implications for the behaviour of the terms of trade. At the core of this approach was the analysis of why Latin American economies would not respond 'automatically' to the price signal of the terms of trade: the reason was 'structural rigidities' – market imperfections rooted in infrastructural deficiencies and in institutions and social and political systems and values. The economies therefore required the deliberate government promotion of industrialization. Foreign capital inflows were helpful to ease the overcoming of rigidities, but the ECLA of the 1950s envisaged such inflows as representing largely public capital. Thus was 'structuralism' born, subsequently to be misleadingly concentrated on the analysis of inflation. Autonomy was definitely an issue, but industrialization was to be the answer, providing independence from unstable and undynamic primary exports. No contradiction was seen in using foreign money to achieve this, channelled through government, and issues such as external constraints on policy options were not directly tackled.

By the end of the 1950s another useful concept had been contributed to the effort to conceptualize this external relation and its implications: the notion of the 'enclave'. This idea was to be taken up and refurbished in later analysis:[3] at this stage, as originally developed by Levin,[4] it analyzed the failure of primary exporting to lead to a broader-based growth process, in terms of the lack of linkages through to the rest of the economy. This was seen as no coincidence: because of the undeveloped nature of the local economy, factors of production tended to be imported and their incomes were therefore remitted abroad. The answer in principle, of course, would appear to be in government taxation, but at this stage the enclave school made no attempt to explore why governments acted or failed to act to remedy the situation.[5] As with the structuralist approach, the obstacles to some alternative path being followed were simply viewed as given, preceding the opening up to trade, and independent of the expansion mechanism, which was world trade. As a result of several important developments, this vision was soon to shift profoundly.

One major event occurred at the intellectual level: new attention was given by Marxist writers to the problem of the LDCs – and particularly noteworthy in this context is the publication of an analysis of Brazil and Chile by André Gundar Frank.[6] Classical Marxist writing had tended to see the expansion of capitalism into the less developed countries as simply the process of the destruction and replacement of the pre-capitalist system: now Frank, following Paul Baran, looked at this in more detail, and the verb 'to underdevelop' entered our vocabulary. The by now familiar analysis argued that it was not that export growth did *not* have effect: it had a *profound* effect, of such a nature as to stifle all local development, and even the possibility of development. This occurred through the introduction of monopoly elements and the consequent power relationships which effectively prevented local access to sources of income and economic opportunity. In other words, there was now a direct challenge to the perspective of ECLA and the enclave school: the obstacles were not given, did not precede trade – but were actually created by the very manner of integration into the international economy.

These ideas were violently attacked, from both right and left,[7] but whatever one's criticisms of the manner in which the ideas were developed, there is no denying the influence of this perspective. By the mid- to late 1960s, this influence was coalescing with a number of other important events at different levels.

The first of these was a growing disillusion with industrialization as a route to greater autonomy and more equal development. The expansion of industry had been looked to to give an endogenous source of stimulus to growth; to give independence from fluctuating and undynamic export receipts, by import substitution and eventually by industrial exports; and to provide employment. As of the mid-1960s, it appeared that the model was running into stagnation;[8] vulnerability to export revenue fluctuations was *greater* now that, at least in the large economies, the margin of non-essential imports was practically gone, and the contribution of the industrial sector to employment was turning out to be very disappointing, as large modern capital-intensive plants displaced small traditional labour-intensive operations. Exports, it gradually emerged, were improbable not only because of the inefficiency of the new sectors, with effective protection far higher than had been appreciated,[9] but also because of the exchange rate bias against exports inherent in the simple fact of protection.[10]

Some at least of these problems were increasingly seen as related to the next development: namely, that it was gradually becoming clear that the whole *modus operandi* of international capital was shifting. By the mid-1960s it was realized that it was no longer correct to think of direct foreign investment as concentrating on primary resource development: at the margin it was now strongly focused on the new manufacturing sectors. And by the end of the decade we were beginning to understand a great deal more about the implications and possible dangers of this process, in terms of over-pricing techniques, contracts prohibiting exports, royalties, easy importing of inappropriate technology, and so forth.

The third significant development was a growing disillusion with reformism of the Alliance for Progress type. 'Structural' reforms – in land tenure, tax and planning systems – had seemed the logical policy concomitant of structuralism, but the experience of the 1960s in this regard was totally frustrating, as the link-up between aid and reforms produced 'paper' reforms in abundance, without the necessary back-up in either technical or political terms. By the end of the 1960s structuralists were themselves disillusioned with their own approach – and all these elements came together to push them into a deeper analysis. Thus by 1969–70 we find the former structuralist writers themselves forming the core of the new 'dependency' school, in an attempt to do three things. First, and most essentially, they were determined to build political and social variables into the analysis. Second, they wanted to deepen the vision of Prebisch *et al.*, using the insights of the neo-Marxists. Third, they wanted to come to terms with the new character of international monopoly capitalism.[11]

The resulting theorizing has been much denigrated for its excessive generality and for the impossibility of reducing it to empirically testable hypotheses. (Indeed, it is so castigated within this volume.) To attempt either to expound or evaluate it would require a whole chapter, and since I have attempted this elsewhere I can validly evade the task here,[12] especially as my concern here is only to trace the evolution of ideas and of economic structures. Let me quote briefly from an earlier exposition and move on:

> Dependence is a situation which may be located at one end of a continuum, the opposite pole of which may conveniently be labelled 'autonomy'. Autonomy is not the same as total isolation, but involves rather the ability of a national economy to achieve self-sustaining growth within a capitalist framework. Among the main requirements for the achievement of autonomy are local control of the economic

surplus, local ability to innovate and to adapt technology, local ability to produce capital goods of a type appropriate to the country's resource endowment, and endogenous sources of economic dynamism (as distinct from dependence upon the growth of world markets). Dependence is not to be equated with underdevelopment; the key empirical hypothesis of the dependency writers is rather that dependent economies are particularly prone to suffer from continuing underdevelopment, or (what often amounts to almost the same thing) to undergo a distorted process of growth, the end product of which differs very greatly from the usual image of a 'developed' economy and society. Where dependence and underdevelopment coincide, mutually-reinforcing elements come into play: an underdeveloped country in the modern capitalist system tends to become dependent, while a dependent economy tends to remain underdeveloped.[13]

As with Frank, the insights of this school are surely permanent and valuable, even though detailed and convincing empirical work has not (yet) been their strong point.

First, the relationship between developed and underdeveloped economics is viewed from a very broad perspective. Rather than focusing, as we have seen earlier radical economists do, upon some specific problem such as factor movements or the terms of trade, the new approach probes all facets of the international system and its ramifications within the dependent economy, considering, for example, market relations, corporate organization, options for borrowing or bargaining, the impact of imported technology, the determinants of consumption patterns and the direction of sectional biases in policy-making.

The second feature, closely related to the first, is the emphasis placed upon the impossibility of understanding the whole by focusing on a division into neat analytical compartments, and hence upon the need for interdisciplinary research. The third contribution is that it makes intelligible the apparent paradox of countries which enjoy full political independence, yet fail to remedy the distortions induced by the inter national system. Often, indeed, policies are followed which accentuate rather than reduce these distortions. The explanation proposed is twofold: first, that in some matters the range of options open to dependent countries is artificially restricted, to the advantage of the dominant participants in the international system; while, second (and equally important), a process of 'conditioning' takes place which leads policy-makers in the dependent country to make choices which are obviously inappropriate to the 'local interest'.[14]

Whatever the value of these insights, there is no doubt that the predominance of such broad ideas in the thought and writing of those inheriting the mantle of the structuralists in the 1970s had important

and, from some points of view, unfortunate consequences. Just as structuralism had lacked short-term policy content, so now the dependency
writing hardly provided an adequate policy guide. There was as a result
something of a vacuum on the left in terms of practical policy-making,
which goes some way towards explaining the increasing strength of
monetarist views in the 1970s in Latin America, and is not unconnected
with the incoherence and contradictions of regimes such as that of
Velasco in Peru and Allende in Chile in the early 1970s. Such failures
facilitated and consolidated the major shift of this decade: the move to a
'new model' characterized by liberalization of the economy, and political
repression from the right – both playing their part in backing up and
promoting the new development (at last) of non-traditional exports, a
process which really took off with the 1972–3 boom in world trade in
manufactures. Of the countries more advanced in industrialization,
Argentina, Brazil, Colombia and Mexico had all in varying degrees
moved to incentivate non-traditional exports by the end of the 1960s; in
the early 1970s the attempts to reduce the distortions and anti-export
bias inherent in the early pattern of ISI continued. Certain countries
made a far more radical effort to eliminate distortions and resuscitate the
market – Chile and Uruguay in 1973, Argentina in 1976.

The other remarkable development of this period was in finance: with
the growth of world liquidity in the early 1970s and recession in the
industrialized countries by 1973–4, for the first time private banks began
actively to seek customers in Third World countries, in a manner
reminiscent of the 1920s. The result was the colossal rise in foreign debt
(documented in Fitzgerald's paper) and, as international market conditions worsened, what FitzGerald makes into a corollary: stabilization
and a renewed emphasis on the reinforcement of order and the depression of wages.

Where do the chapters in this section fit into this panorama? The first,
by MacDonald, on Perón and the United States in the 1940s, tells us of
what at first reading seems another world, and serves to emphasize the
changes in this span of thirty-five years. His description of the blatant
and crude imperialist policies of that period is intriguing partly because
it points up how much subtler and more complex such matters have
become. Yet at the same time it fascinates precisely because of the
parallels. It tells in detail how Washington opposed the interventionist
policies of Perón and his regime's supposed flirting with communism,
first by using Argentina's dollar shortage and then by withholding a
bilateral defence treaty, and eventually achieving success. The clarity of
the approach of those days, when no 'third position' could even be
considered and wholehearted support was expected from Washington's
allies for total free enterprise, contrasts with the way the regimes of
Allende in Chile, Velasco in Peru and Torres in Bolivia were handled in

the 1970s. But the difference is not so great – and even Argentina's fear of Brazil and need for a defence treaty are echoed in the Chile/Peru relationship and its significance for the role of US aid in relation to the two governments.

Turning to the rest, the preoccupation is, as we said before, almost entirely with the new trends of the 1970s. Scott bridges the gap, since the presence of multinationals in agriculture is a topic of more long-standing concern than manufactured exports or international bank lending, though one in which there has been much fresh interest of late. His chapter provides an overview of much recent work on agribusiness in Latin America; in the issues he deals with he identifies the questions and assumptions with great precision, showing up woolly thinking on both right and left.

The next two chapters also come well within the tradition of British empiricism. Both Jenkins and Roxborough are unhappy with the facile generalities that characterize the 'new dependency' of the 1970s. But the liberal orthodox explanation of new trends in manufactured exports is also too facile. Jenkins presents the contrasting explanations of this new phenomenon with exceptional clarity, and confronts both with the facts. The reader must find out the results for himself, but they are decidedly thought-provoking.

Roxborough takes the political dimension of the same dependency line of thought, as formulated around the experiences of Brazil and Mexico – the view that sees the state as relatively autonomous of domestic productive interests, but rather the 'executive committee' of foreign capital. The new phase of capital accumulation based on exports of manufactures in accordance with a new world division of labour, requires, so the argument goes, a restructuring of the labour force; wages must be held down and mobility increased, both of which are taken to imply political repression. But is this right, he asks. His worries are in part questions of logic, in part of fact, and all pertinent.

Tironi's chapter also comes from a good empirical tradition, non-British this time. His is the only chapter not directly concerned with the debate, and entirely non-theoretical. Nevertheless it is of considerable relevance to the evaluation of the new trends in manufactured exports and the posited 'new dependency'. To what extent, he asks, has the increase in non-traditional exports occurred at the expense of primary exports? And what are the possible implications, for example, in terms of bargaining power? The chapter makes a preliminary analysis simply in terms of trade shares, and is a tempting invitation to pursue in more depth and detail the opportunity costs of diversification.

Finally, like Roxborough and Jenkins, FitzGerald also wishes to complicate, but in his case by the introduction of neglected areas of theorizing. The new burden of debt, and the new role in this of private banks, raise enormous issues in the dependency/autonomy debate. We are dealing not merely with a triple alliance composed of multinationals based in the productive sectors, the state and the domestic bourgeoisie (the weak junior partner). Both international and domestic financial interests are also crucial, and cannot be assumed simply to align themselves with the appropriate productive interests. This is again – and perhaps more than any other – a field for much-needed work.

Notes

1 These changes are the topic of a forthcoming study: R. Thorp (ed.) *Latin America in the 1930s: the periphery in world crisis* (London 1984).

2 The principal sources are R. Prebisch *The economic development of Latin America and its principal problems* (New York 1950); ECLA *Economic survey of Latin America* (1949) and R. Prebisch 'Commercial policy in the underdeveloped countries' *American Economic Review* Papers and Proceedings (1959). For recent discussions of ECLA views see J. Love 'Raúl Prebisch and the origins of the doctrine of unequal exchange' *Latin American Research Review* xvi 2 (1981); O. Rodríguez *La teoría del subdesarrollo de la CEPAL* (Mexico City 1980).

3 For example, in analysing 'export-processing' zones and their implications.

4 For the guano economy of nineteenth-century Peru, see J. Levin *The export economies: their pattern of development in historical perspective* (Stanford 1960).

5 Another early and well known application of the framework was C. Reynolds 'Economic problems of an export economy' in C. Reynolds and M. Mamalakis *Essays on the Chilean economy* (New Haven 1965).

6 A. G. Frank *Capitalism and underdevelopment in Latin America* (New York, 1967).

7 Frank subsequently published an 'answer to critics', which had a four-page bibliography of such critics.

8 In fact this was later realized to be a statistical illusion: aggregate Latin American figures showed a slow-down, but it was due to the large weight in the total of Brazil and Argentina. The slow-down in these two countries in the early 1960s is now seen to be a complicated and interesting story, but not one in which the 'exhaustion of ISI' plays a very large role.

9 Early analyses of these problems came in ECLA *Economic Bulletin for Latin America*. 'Effective' protection is the real protection given when you allow for tariff *exemptions* on inputs; the resulting degree of protection can be far higher than the 'nominal' tariff on the final good.

10 See A. O. Hirschman 'The political economy of import-substituting industrialisation in Latin America' in A. O. Hirschman *A bias for hope* (New Haven 1971) for an explanation of this in the 'classic' article on import-substituting industrialization.

11 The dependency literature is too extensive to refer to. For an excellent discussion, see G. Palma 'Dependency: a formal theory of underdevelopment or a methodology for the analysis of concrete situations of underdevelopment?' *World Development* vi (1978).

12 R. Thorp and G. Bertram *Peru 1890–1977: growth and policy in an open economy* (London 1978) chap. 2.

13 *Ibid.* pp. 11–12.

14 *Ibid.* chap. 2.

21

THE US, THE COLD WAR AND PERÓN
Callum A. MacDonald

Introduction

During the Second World War Argentina was a major obstacle to US attempts to create hemisphere solidarity against the Axis powers. After the Rio conference of 1942, Buenos Aires maintained relations with Germany and Japan, and under the military governments which emerged after the coup of June 1943 was suspected by Washington of collaborating with Nazi interests to establish a totalitarian, expansionist, autarkic state in the western hemisphere. The US response was to attempt, through a combination of diplomatic and economic pressures, to overthrow the Argentine regime and its leading figure, Perón – a policy which reached its height in Braden's intervention on behalf of the opposition in the election campaign of 1945–6.[1]

In this period, therefore, Washington displayed open hostility to the growth of Argentine nationalism and the rise of Perón. The failure of the policy of coercion led to the adoption of a new line after 1947. The US did not abandon its hostility to Argentine nationalism, but attempted to control its effects by working with and through Perón rather than against him. This conciliatory approach was encouraged, not only by previous failures, but also because of the emergence of the Cold War with the USSR as a primary American concern. Washington did not desire a divided hemisphere in the event of a war with Moscow, nor to leave any openings which might be exploited by Soviet diplomacy. Thus there was a new emphasis on forgetting the past and incorporating Argentina, militarily and politically, into the hemisphere system. By 1947 the State Department was arguing against publication of a piece about past Argentine 'collaboration' with the Axis on the grounds that it would arouse 'memories . . . which we are all trying to forget'.[2] Washington's two main aims were to obtain Argentine cooperation against communist expansion, and to promote US economic interests in Argentina – goals which were clearly interrelated in the minds of American policy-makers.

US views of Perón, 1946–50

The new policy of working through Perón was not initiated unopposed, since until June 1947 Braden remained in charge of Latin American affairs at the State Department. Far from favouring a conciliatory line, Braden remained hostile to any *rapprochement* with Argentina. He continued to argue that Perón was an Axis sympathizer, determined to create a totalitarian, expansionist state, hostile to US economic interests and hemisphere solidarity. According to Braden, Perón's form of anti-capitalist nationalism would either pave the way for communism or provide the basis for Argentine-Soviet collaboration against the US. The Nazis had cooperated with Stalin between 1939 and 1941 and might easily do so again. Despite the election victory of February 1946, therefore, Braden remained determined to undermine Perón.[3] He argued that the poll had been rigged and was unwilling to abandon the anti-Peronist opposition. Instead Braden hoped to 'bore from within' against Perón's regime. This involved encouraging the opposition to obstruct his legislative programme in the Argentine Congress, intriguing with anti-Peronist labour leaders and alienating the army from the government by maintaining the arms embargo initiated in 1942.[4] Braden's excuse for remaining hostile towards Argentina was that the government had failed to extirpate Nazi influence as it was pledged to do by the Chapultepec resolutions. By demanding of Argentina a higher standard of compliance in controlling Axis interests than of any other Latin American state, Braden sought to ensure that the US-Argentine dispute remained unresolved.[5]

Braden's position, however, was progressively weakened because he was pursuing a line which had failed before 1946 and which took no account of the changed circumstances created by the Cold War. As the quarrel with Russia intensified, there was increased emphasis in Washington on hemisphere solidarity. Powerful elements in the Congress, the Pentagon and the State Department argued that the continuing dispute with Argentina was dividing the hemisphere, delaying the conclusion of a regional security pact and leaving a dangerous opening for Soviet diplomacy. In the event of war with the USSR, the hemisphere must not be divided as it had been after 1941. The military in particular blamed Braden for Argentine recognition of Russia, and for the presence of a Soviet trade mission in Buenos Aires in 1946.[6] It was feared that if the US remained hostile, Perón might turn to the Russians for arms and diplomatic support, and that a dangerous degree of Soviet political influence would follow. By 1947, therefore, the main priority was containing the Soviet Union, a development which made Braden's pursuit of Axis influence irrelevant.

Messersmith, the US ambassador to Buenos Aires from March 1946 until June 1947, reflected this new mood. Originally a fierce opponent of Perón, he was soon transformed into an active advocate of conciliation because of his fear of communism.[7] Messersmith, and his successors Bruce and Griffis, argued that there was no acceptable alternative to

Perón. The Radical opposition was weak, divided and bitterly nationalist. It represented the most 'irresponsible elements' in the country, and if it ever gained power was unlikely to pursue a pro-US line.[8] The only other possible government was a reactionary military regime which would pave the way for communism by attacking Perón's social programme. Perón's hold on the Argentine working class represented a valuable bulwark against the spread of communism in what might otherwise be its natural constituency. Not only was there no viable alternative to Perón, but also the Peronist programme offered a unique opportunity for the US to build a closer relationship with Argentina. Perón's industrialization policy was bound to weaken traditional ties with Europe and strengthen links with the US, the main source of the scarce capital goods and investment required by the Five Year Plan. Washington must seize this opportunity to control the effects of nationalism by working with and through Perón, guiding Argentina along the path of hemisphere solidarity. If Washington adopted a conciliatory approach, Perón would rapidly abandon his flirtation with the Russians and sign a hemisphere security pact.[9]

By mid-1947 such arguments had triumphed and provided the basis for subsequent US policy. Braden's line was clearly bankrupt and unsuited to the 'realities' of the Cold War. Moreover, it was identified with dangerously 'left-wing' elements in the US, such as the CIO unions, themselves already under suspicion of communist influence. Even Braden's own personal staff was not immune to accusations of Marxist sympathy, since one of his chief advisers, Gustavo Durán, had fought for the 'Reds' in the Spanish Civil War.[10] By June 1947, therefore, Braden was discredited and removed from office. At the Rio conference Perón was invited to join a new hemisphere security pact, and the arms embargo was removed.[11]

'Extremists' and 'moderates' in US policy

While the US recognized that Perón could be a valuable ally in the fight against communism, there were many aspects of his regime which it disliked and opposed. In particular, Washington was hostile to the 'Third Position' both at home and abroad. While Perón might assure US diplomats of his fundamental anti-communism and his readiness to align Argentina with the United States in the event of war, it was embarrassing to see a Third Position, independent of Washington or Moscow, paraded publicly, even as a rhetorical device. Moreover, Perón's attempt to develop the economy on the basis of a Third Position between capitalism and communism was regarded with disfavour. Strict bilateralism, high tariffs, state trading through the *Instituto Argentino Para Intercambio* (IAPI), and a firm refusal to join the World Bank, the IMF or GATT were not what was expected of an ally, and repudiated the US goal of an open-door world economy.[12] Washington regarded free enterprise and anti-communism as indivisible. It was impossible to run a closed economy at home and contribute effectively to containing Soviet expansion abroad. Indeed IAPI and other statist devices, by undermining the Argentine economy, weakened Argentina's value as an ally. As Bruce argued in November 1947, 'The important thing from our standpoint is for them to have an economy which is . . . stable, so that they will not only be allies, but allies sufficiently strong to be a valuable asset.'[13] While Perón himself argued that statism was merely a temporary phenomenon and that he would welcome US companies and capital to develop both Argentine industry and vital natural resources such as oil, he never seemed to fulfil his promises. A similar phenomenon was evident in Argentine foreign relations. While Perón pledged himself to hemisphere solidarity and accepted the Rio pact, the treaty remained unratified by the Argentine Congress.[14]

The forces of obstruction in both domestic and foreign affairs were identified by Washington with the 'extremist' wing of the Peronist regime, represented by officials such as Miranda, the head of IAPI, Castro, the transport minister, and Evita.[15] The most powerful figure in this group, Evita, was regarded as Perón's evil genius. Her xenophobia and her refusal to face economic realities were the source of all the shortcomings of the government. According to Griffis, she was 'by far the most radical of the two leaders', while Messersmith sourly remarked that she had 'all the sentiments . . . passions . . . and prejudices of a woman of not too great education and experience'.[16] US policy-makers believed that if the policies of the 'extremists' could be discredited and 'moderates' such as Foreign Minister Bramuglia encouraged, Argentina could be moved away from the Third Position at home and abroad and towards wholehearted alignment with the United States. As Attwood, of the Division of River Plate Affairs, remarked in May 1949, Washington must seek 'to encourage the pro-US and pro-free enterprise elements in the Argentine Government [against] the more anti-US and nationalistic groups . . . Our real hope in our US-Argentine relations is the encouragement of those elements . . . which are favourable to the United States.'[17]

Washington possessed a lever to promote such internal change without resort to open coercion. Perón had staked his political future on the Five Year Plan, but as the Argentine economy deteriorated after 1947 it was clearly unlikely to succeed without US economic support. Perón's need for external financial assistance could be used to undermine the 'extremists', erode statist experiments and push Argentina towards unequivocal alignment with the US. As Bruce argued in January 1949, the state of the economy allowed Washington to write its own 'ticket' for a settlement with Argentina.[18] This 'ticket' included restrictions on IAPI, improved conditions for foreign companies, ratification of the Rio treaty and the curbing of the 'extremists' in favour of figures such as Bramuglia.[19] Washington, therefore, was unwilling to use the economic crisis to push Perón to the wall, since there seemed to be no viable alternative in Argentina. According to the embassy, 'If the present Cabinet should fall, the Army might take over and the situation might become much worse.'[20] As Blanksten argues, US policy was to intervene in favour of Perón, but only in return for his repudiation of the Third Position.[21]

Messersmith's aim in 1946 was to steer the Five Year Plan along lines acceptable to the US by establishing close personal relations with Perón, and by providing him with US economic advisers who would provide a rational alternative strategy of industrial development to the statist model favoured by Miranda and other 'extremists'. Messersmith's influence was behind the Lord/Flannigan mission of January 1947, designed to supply technical advice on the Five Year Plan and to create openings for US business. With the assistance of these advisers, Argentine industrialization was to be promoted as a New Deal exercise in government/business cooperation, along orthodox capitalist lines rather than as an experiment in government coercion of private enterprise.[22] By the time his successor, Bruce, arrived in Buenos Aires, however, this line had clearly failed, and the statist elements which had always existed in the Five Year Plan were dominant. Under Miranda, the basis of Argentine development was hostility towards foreign companies and investors and an exaggerated economic nationalism, despite the reassuring noises made by Perón, who seemed unwilling to curb his own 'extremists'.

Bruce's strategy was to use the emerging Argentine dollar shortage to force the president's hand. Unless the Argentines abandoned IAPI and other statist devices, the Economic Cooperation Administration would refuse to authorize dollar purchases of Argentine products for the Marshall Plan. Perón, desperate for dollars, would be forced to listen to 'moderates' like Bramuglia rather than to Miranda or Evita.[23] Not only would he be forced to modify the Third Position at home as the price of US assistance, but he would also be forced to abandon it abroad and ratify the Rio pact which was languishing in the Argentine Congress. This was a strategy which at first failed to produce results, because of a failure of coordination between the State Department and ECA.

Following the sacking of Miranda in January 1949, Bruce argued that the time had come to authorize dollar expenditure in Argentina in return for limitations on IAPI and improvement in the conditions of US business. ECA remained adamant, however, apparently because of the influence of officials who wished to use the Argentine economic crisis to destroy Perón as well as the 'extremist' elements in his regime.[24] By the time the controversy was resolved in mid-1949, the European powers had little need for ECA dollars to purchase the type of agricultural surpluses produced by Argentina. As the embassy had warned, ECA intransigence forced Perón to emphasize anti-foreign nationalism in self-defence, to draw attention away from the failure of the economy.[25] ECA policy, far from curbing the influence of 'extremists' such as Evita, actually threatened to increase it, and undermined the whole strategy of forcing Perón to adopt an unequivocally pro-US position at home and abroad. Bruce, frustrated by the impasse in Washington, accused ECA of furthering the cause of communism along the River Plate.[26]

The failure of the ECA to provide dollars for Argentina forced the State Department to adopt the idea of an Eximbank loan as a lever to promote abandonment of the Third Position. By 1949 Perón was obviously desperate for US assistance, despite his earlier opposition to an American loan. Even former 'extremists' such as Cereijo, head of the Economic Council, were changing their attitude in the hope of saving the regime by an injection of US funds.[27] Argentina began to take steps to improve the position of US firms and to curb the activities of IAPI in the import trade. Simultaneously officials began sounding out Washington about the prospects of Exim funding.[28] In February 1950, Miller, Assistant Secretary of State for Latin American Affairs, visited Buenos Aires to discuss US-Argentine relations. Perón promised to ratify the Rio treaty during the 1950 congressional session, and there was talk of Argentina joining the FAO, the World Bank and the IMF.[29] A US loan was not mentioned, but a visit by Cereijo to Washington was arranged for March 1950, when financial assistance was discussed.

The State Department argued strongly in favour of Exim funding in discussions with other agencies involved. According to its representative, the group of people responsible for economic policies in the previous period had been replaced by a new group. Argentina was improving conditions for US companies and intended to join the IMF. Perón had also indicated to Miller 'that he expected the Rio Treaty to be ratified . . . This was very important in terms of hemispheric defence.'[30] The Exim loan of $125 million in May 1950, therefore, was intended to consolidate 'moderate' elements in the Peronist regime and to confirm the move away from the Third Position at home and abroad. According to the State Department, US assistance was justified because Argentina was abandoning 'erratic' nationalist policies and 'facing realistically, foreign and domestic problems'.[31] While ratification of the Rio treaty was not put forward as a formal condition of the loan, it was clearly expected by Washington as part of the 'moderate' trend which US funding was designed to encourage. The Third Position was being abandoned in favour of dependence on the US, a fact which the Argentine opposition was quick to point out.[32]

The Korean War and US disillusion

US hopes of a permanent change in Argentine policy seemed justified on the outbreak of the Korean War, since Perón publicly aligned himself with Washington. He quickly retreated from expressions of solidarity, however, towards a restatement of the Third Position at home and abroad.[33] US efforts to promote free enterprise and to guarantee Argentine support in the event of an open clash with communism had failed. Miller, Assistant Secretary for Latin American Affairs, noted bitterly in a letter to a *New York Times* journalist: 'The latest mouthings of the great leader in Argentina have left me with a feeling of nausea. You can imagine the impression made upon the American public when one of your stories appears to the effect that Perón has reiterated his third position stand on the same page with a picture of American GIs being led through Korea.'[34]

Perón's conduct in the Korean crisis, coupled with a renewed emphasis on nationalism at home, effectively terminated the 'honeymoon' of 1947–50.[35] Guarded optimism about the Peronist regime was replaced in Washington by grudging toleration of its existence. Although disappointed in Perón, however, the Truman administration did not seek to topple him from power as its predecessor had done in the Second World War, since it could see no viable alternative to his regime. Instead Washington pursued a policy of cold 'correctness', granting no special favours to Argentina. It was hoped that eventually a continuing need for US assistance would force Perón to align himself unequivocally with the United States, as he had seemed about to do in the spring of 1950. US policy was designed to prove that Perón needed the United States more than the United States needed him. As the chargé in Buenos Aires argued in March 1951, Washington should do as little for Argentina as possible: 'Allow her to become deeply concerned about supplies and materials which she needs; in short follow a policy of masterly inaction which will place us in a dominant position to the end that Argentina can realize that her own best interests are to quickly become our partner in the divided world of today.'[36]

It was hoped in the State Department that the need to conciliate the army as well as the necessity of US economic assistance would eventually bring Perón to terms. As a result of the Korean War, Washington moved to sign bilateral defence treaties with several Latin American states, which granted the signatories US financial assistance for arms purchases. Wedded to the Third Position, Argentina was not offered such an agreement, although Brazil signed a pact in March 1952.[37] Since Perón lacked dollars he could not purchase arms, and might be forced into alignment with Washington by concern in army circles about Brazil's growing military strength.

The policy of 'masterly inaction' was continued by the incoming

Eisenhower administration, which was as insistent on private enterprise as a universal development model and as hostile to any flirtation with Cold War neutralism as its predecessor. An early National Security Council (NSC) planning document emphasized that the US could use its economic strength to favour its friends in Latin America against those who failed fully to subscribe to US goals. The paper noted:

> We should make clear by our acts that cooperation begets cooperation; that the United States is capable of reacting when unfairly attacked, and that the self-interest of the Latin American countries is generally best served by cooperating with us. Our purpose should be to arrest the development of irresponsibility and extreme nationalism and their belief in their immunity from the exercise of US power.[38]

In the case of Argentina this meant a continuation of the previous line of 'watchful waiting', until Perón was forced to deal on US terms. By 1954 the policy began to produce results. In the year before his overthrow, Perón moved definitively away from statism, opening the doors to US companies and investors even in previously sacrosanct areas such as oil development. He also made overtures for a mutual defence treaty, which would allow Argentina access to US arms supplies to balance the growing power of Brazil.[39] The Third Position seemed to be finally dead, and Perón to be moving in the direction desired by Messersmith and Bruce. The growing alignment with the US was undoubtedly influenced both by the intractable economic problems of Argentina and by the death of Evita, the leading anti-American 'extremist', in 1952.[40]

Conclusions

Despite Perón's ultimate alignment with the US, there was relief in the State Department and the White House at his overthrow. Distrust of the Argentine opposition had been balanced over the years by growing impatience with Perón's equivocation. He had taken too long to fulfil the role expected of him, and his attempt to adhere to the Third Position at home and abroad after 1950 aroused hostility. As far as the Truman and Eisenhower administrations were concerned, there could be no Third Position nor any middle ground between capitalist and communist strategies of development. Washington's allies were expected to promote free enterprise at home and to emphasize anti-communism abroad. In this respect, Perón's failure to perform what was expected of him after the Exim loan of 1950, his actions during the Korean War and his renewed flirtation with the Russians in 1953, all served to make the US readier to welcome an alternative when one was presented, as it was in 1955.

Despite his apparent adherence to US goals after 1953, there was no guarantee that Perón would not again renege and take up the Third

Position if the opportunity arose. It was made clear to his successors that the price of US support would be unequivocal adherence to free enterprise and anti-communism.[41] Aramburu and Frondizi responded by closer cooperation with the OAS and by integrating Argentina fully into the world capitalist system created by the United States after the Second World War. The decision to join the IMF and the World Bank clearly implied the end of statism and the adoption of free enterprise as the strategy for Argentine development. The US responded by granting Argentina massive financial aid, both to stabilize the economy and to prevent a resurgence of Peronism.[42] In the ten years since 1946, the US had moved from intervention in favour of Perón, a policy which reached its peak with the Exim loan of 1950, towards intervention to prevent his return.

Notes

Research for this chapter was facilitated by an SSRC award and a grant-in-aid from the Truman Library.

[1] C. A. MacDonald 'The politics of intervention: the United States and Argentina 1941–46' *Journal of Latin American Studies* xɪɪ 2 (1980).

[2] American Republic Affairs memorandum, 15 Oct. 1947, ARA Reports, Box 20, National Archives of the United States, Washington DC (hereafter ARA).

[3] Braden to State Department, 8 July 1945, State Department Decimal File 711.35/7–845, National Archives of the United States (hereafter DS); Acheson to Truman, 12 July 1946, PSF, Foreign Affairs 'A', Argentina Folder 2, Box 170, Harry S. Truman Library, Independence, Missouri (hereafter HT). David Green 'The Cold War comes to Latin America' in B. Bernstein (ed.) *Politics and policies of the Truman administration* (Chicago 1970) pp. 172–3.

[4] Hadow to Perowne, 18 and 21 March 1946, Public Record Office, London, Foreign Office Correspondence (hereafter FO) 371/51810: AS1610/AS1724/235/2.

[5] Messersmith to Senator Austen, 3 Sept. 1946, Papers of the US embassy in Buenos Aires, Record Group 84, Buenos Aires 1946, file 800, Box 529, Washington National Records Center, Suitland, Maryland (hereafter WNRC).

[6] Hadow to Perowne, FO 371/51815:AS3283/235/2; Harold F. Peterson *Argentina and the United States, 1810–1960* (New York 1964) pp. 457–8.

[7] Hadow to Perowne, FO 371/44762:AS1561/235/2; Messersmith to Secretary of State, 15 Sept. 1946, WNRC, RG84, BA 1946, File 000D, Box 529.

[8] Messersmith to Salzberger, 25 Sept. 1946, George S. Messersmith Papers, File 1809, University of Delaware Library, Newark, Delaware (hereafter GMP).

[9] Messersmith to Byrnes, 15 June 1946, GMP, File 1781; Messersmith to Clayton, 31 Oct. 1946, GMP, File 1815.

[10] Hadow to Perowne, 30 March 1946, FO 371/5181:AS1978/235/2.

[11] Peterson *op. cit.* p. 458.

[12] Green *loc. cit.* pp. 173–5.

[13] Bruce to Truman, 12 Nov. 1947, HT, PSF, Foreign Affairs, File Argentina, Folder 3, Box 170.

[14] Bruce to Marshall, 3 Sept. 1947, DS 811.503/135/9–347; memo by Dearborn, 12 Sept. 1947, ARA, Box 20; Peterson *op. cit.* p. 481.

[15] Memo by Tewksbury, 14 Jan. 1949, WNRC, RG 84, BA 1949, File General Argentina Jan.–June, Box 350.

[16] Stanton Griffis *Lying in state* (New York 1952) p. 266; Messersmith's Memoir Notes, GMP, File 21010.

[17] Attwood to Daniels, 19 May 1949 *Foreign relations of the United States 1949* II 499–500 (hereafter *FR*). Ray to Secretary of State, 8 Sept. 1948, DS 835.516/9–848.

[18] Memo by Dearborn, 18 Sept. 1947, ARA, Box 20. Ray to Dearborn, 12 April 1948, DS 735.41/4–1248. Bruce to Secretary of State, 4 Jan. 1949 *FR 1949* II 473–8.

[19] Ray to Secretary of State, 24 Jan. 1949 *FR 1949* II 481–2. Ray to Secretary of State, 29 March 1949 *FR 1949* II 494–5.

[20] Ray to Secretary of State, 3 May 1949, WNRC, RG 84, BA 1949, File 273, Box 350.

[21] George I. Blanksten *Perón's Argentina* (New York 1953) p. 437.

[22] Leeper to FO, 24 May 1946, FO 371/51815:AS3053/235/2; Inverchapel to FO, 27 Jan. 1947, FO 371/61122:AS773/1/2.

[23] Bruce to Truman, 14 Nov. 1947, HT, PSF Foreign Affairs 'A', File Argentina, Folder 3, Box 170.

[24] Peterson *op. cit.* p. 476.

[25] Ray to Secretary of State, 12 Sept. 1948 *FR 1948* IX 290–2.

[26] Bruce to Truman, 17 Nov. 1948, HT, PSF Foreign Affairs 'A', File Argentina, Folder 3, Box 170.

[27] Ray to Secretary of State, 3 May 1949, WNRC, RG 84, BA 1949, File 273, Box 250. Woodward to Connelly, 13 April 1950, HT, OF, Box 366.

[28] Memo by Dearborn, 23 May 1949 *FR 1949* II 503–4; Ray to Tewksbury, 18 February 1949, WNRC, RG 84, BA 1949, File 540, Box 350.

[29] Minutes of the 156th Meeting of the National Advisory Council on International Monetary and Financial Problems, 16 May 1950 *FR 1950* II 720–1.

[30] *Ibid.*

[31] Green *loc. cit.* p. 179.

[32] Arthur P. Whitaker *The United States and Argentina* (Cambridge, Mass. 1954) p. 235.

[33] Whitaker *op. cit.* p. 234.

[34] Miller to Bracker, 14 Aug. 1950, Papers of Edward G. Miller Jnr, Box 2, Harry S. Truman Library, Independence, Missouri.

[35] Miller to Griffis, 23 April 1951 *ibid.*

[36] Mallory to Secretary of State, 6 March 1951 *FR 1951* II 1085.

[37] Memo by Schoenfield, 10 Oct. 1951, *ibid.* pp. 1110–11. F. Parkinson *Latin America, the Cold War and the world powers* (London 1974) p. 29.

[38] National Security Council, Staff Study on Latin America, 6 March 1953, White House Office, Office of the Special Assistant for National Security Affairs, Box 23, Dwight D. Eisenhower Library, Abilene, Kansas (hereafter DDE).

[39] Peterson *op. cit.* p. 489. Whitaker *op. cit.* pp. 242–4.

[40] *Ibid.*

[41] Memorandum of conversation with Gainza Paz, 10 April 1957, DDE, Ann Whitman File, International Series, Argentina, Folder 7.

[42] Dulles to Eisenhower, DDE, Central Files, OF 160, Argentina. Memo 11 Sept. 1960, DDE, Ann Whitman File, International Series, Box 1; Peterson *op. cit.* pp. 503–14.

22

LATIN AMERICA AND THE NEW INTERNATIONAL DIVISION OF LABOUR: A CRITIQUE OF SOME RECENT VIEWS

Rhys O. Jenkins

Introduction

Exports of manufactures from underdeveloped countries have grown rapidly since the 1960s, increasing by over 12 per cent per annum between 1960 and 1975 in real terms.[1] Latin American countries participated significantly in this export expansion, with an average annual growth rate of more than 16 per cent between 1961 and 1975.[2] Within Latin America the countries which have been most actively involved in this export expansion have been Argentina, Brazil, Colombia and Mexico, which between them accounted for over four fifths of total manufactured exports from the region in 1974.[3]

The now commonplace observation of rapid export growth from these countries contrasts markedly with the pessimism of as little as a decade ago regarding the possibility of expanding manufactured exports.[4] This apparently novel development has in the last few years led to a considerable literature on the growth of manufactured exports from Latin America (and of course from developing countries generally). In this chapter it will be argued that this literature has been dominated by two diametrically opposed views of the process of industrial export expansion, both of which are partial and fail to provide an adequate understanding of the phenomenon.

The first view, which is the orthodox economic approach to the question, derives from a critique of the Latin American experience of import-substituting industrialization in the 1950s and 1960s. It argues that import substitution led to major distortions within the economy because it neglected the principle of comparative advantage. By correcting these distortions and adopting a more open trade policy, the disadvantages of import substitution could be eliminated and exports of manufactures generated. From this perspective, the recent growth of manufactured exports from Latin America can be understood in terms of certain policies adopted by local governments since the mid-1960s, which have resulted in at least a partial return to specialization along the lines of comparative advantage.

The alternative view is related to the analysis of the 'new dependency' in Latin America, and the critique of import substitution developed therein. In fact it represents an extension of dependency theory (or at least one strand within it), which now locates dependence within the dynamic of world accumulation.[5] This approach, which has also been termed the 'world systems' approach, has been applied both historically to the analysis of the development of capitalism and to contemporary tendencies.[6] This view continues the emphasis of dependency theory on the penetration of the Latin American economies by transnational corporations. These corporations are now no longer solely interested in Latin America for protected markets, as in the period of import substitution, but seek to exploit cheap labour in the underdeveloped countries to produce for export to world markets. The emphasis is therefore on developments within capitalism at the centre, which lead capital to impose a 'new international division of labour' on the countries of the periphery.

These two approaches differ not only in their interpretation of the factors leading to changes in the international division of labour, but also in their assessment of the effects of these developments. Orthodox economists present an optimistic scenario of export-led growth for countries which succeed in reorientating their industrial sectors away from an excessive reliance on the domestic market to achieve international competitiveness. The world system approach, on the other hand, suggests that the new international division of labour will only lead to the deepening of dependence and a greater subordination of the peripheral economies to those of the centre. While a complete critique of these two approaches requires an analysis of these predictions, for reasons of space the present paper will be confined to the interpretations given of the growth of manufactured exports, postponing to a later date any consideration of the effects.

Two interpretations of the growth of manufactured exports

The orthodox critics of import substitution have emphasized a number of problems associated with the strategy. The fundamental criticism has been that the underdeveloped countries neglected their comparative advantage in the pursuit of industrial development. Perhaps the most influential statement of this viewpoint is the study of Little, Scitovsky and Scott and the individual country studies on which it was based.[7] In the 1970s this critique of Import-Substitution Industrialization (ISI) became a new orthodoxy in development economics, and lent support to the strategy of promoting manufactured exports adopted by a number of countries.[8]

A more open strategy of development involving the promotion of manufactured exports and a reduction in the level of protection was seen as a logical way of remedying the problems created by ISI. Since 'many of the disadvantageous effects of industrialization mentioned earlier stem from this neglect of comparative advantage'[9], a return to policies guided by considerations of comparative advantage was necessary. Exports of manufactures would perform a number of functions in this context. Limitations of market size could be overcome through gaining access to international markets, permitting greater economies of scale. At the same time international competition would force firms to be more efficient and to improve the quality of production, and provide a defence against the likelihood of oligopolistic collusion within small national markets.[10] Specialization according to comparative advantage would also lead to changes in the structure of industrial production in the underdeveloped countries, with an expansion of those industries which use the abundant factor, labour, most intensively, and a reduction in the output of more capital-intensive sectors. Thus the excessively capital-intensive pattern of production would be corrected, with beneficial effects on the level of employment.[11]

By increasing foreign exchange earnings, industrial exports would loosen the balance of payments constraint, permitting necessary imports of raw materials and intermediate products in order for existing capacity to be fully utilized. Moreover, the existence of large and growing industrial exports would improve the functioning of the balance of payments adjustment mechanism, making devaluation a more effective policy tool.[12] Finally, it is claimed that this strategy will not only contribute to increased efficiency but also to greater equity, with an improvement in income distribution being brought about by the expansion of employment.[13]

It is not surprising, in the light of this analysis, to find that recent orthodox economic writing on the growth of Latin America's exports of manufactures, when explaining the rapid growth of exports, stresses the changes in economic policy which took place in the mid-1960s. Of the four major Latin American countries, changes in policy orientation are usually identified with the beginning of the border industrialization programme in 1965 in Mexico, the generalization of indirect tax exemption for manufactured exports and duty drawbacks on imported inputs in Brazil between 1965 and 1967, subsidies for non-traditional exports introduced in Argentina in 1967, and the introduction of tax certificates (CATs) in Colombia in 1967 (although in the Colombian case the shift to export promotion had begun in a limited way with the Plan Vallejo, started in 1959).[14] In addition to tax exemption, subsidies and drawbacks on import duty, other promotional measures that have been stressed have been frequent adjustments of the exchange rates in Argentina, Brazil and Colombia to offset domestic inflation, the provision of special credit facilities to exporters (for example, FOMEX in Mexico, PROEXPO in Colombia, FINEX in Brazil), and the provision of information both to potential exporters and to customers (including trade fairs, commercial offices, and so on). The rapid growth of exports is therefore seen as a direct result of the new orientation of government policies in recent years.

In contrast to the orthodox comparative-advantage critique of import substitution, with its arguments against excessive industrialization in Latin America, dependency theory emphasized the limitations of the type of industrialization that occurred in the area in the post-war period, and in particular the domination of the dynamic sectors of the economy by foreign capital. It also pointed to the increased rigidity of imports as a result of the rising share of intermediate and capital goods in the total, and the growth of service payments related to foreign capital. Thus, despite import substitution, the traditional export sector continued to play a key role in the economy.

The recent growth of manufactured exports from Latin America and other underdeveloped countries is seen not as the result of developments internal to the peripheral economies, and more specifically not as a result of government promotion policies, but as a manifestation of a new trend in world accumulation which involves the relocation of production processes from the advanced countries to the underdeveloped areas. What are the factors which underlie this tendency towards a new international division of labour? Those most frequently emphasized are:[15]

(1) the development of the labour process in industry, which has led to the decomposition of production processes into simple units which can be carried out by unskilled labour;

(2) the development of the forces of production in transport and communications such as jet aircraft, container ships, telex and international telephone services, which significantly reduce the cost of operating over large distances;

(3) the development of international capital markets, banks and an international superstructure, e.g. IMF, GATT;

(4) the existence of a virtually inexhaustible reserve army of labour in the Third World, which can be employed at extremely low wage rates.

It is clear that, while the last of these is a vital element in the relocation of production to the Third World, the industrial reserve army did not suddenly appear in the mid-1960s, and low-wage labour has been available in the periphery for a long time. In explaining the emergence of the 'new international division of labour' in the 1960s, therefore, it is the first three aspects that must be stressed, and – since the development of international capital markets and banks has largely paralleled the relocation of production – particularly the first two. The point of this is to emphasize that the growth of manufactured exports from the Latin American countries can be seen as a response to the tendencies within central capitalism, and more specifically to the development of the forces of production at the centre. This point is made quite explicitly by Vuskovic when he states:

It would be mistaken to think that such tendencies have their principal origin in the peculiar characteristics of the underdeveloped economies . . . Rather, it must be recognized that accumulated problems, particularly obvious during the last crisis, obliged the world capitalist economy to redefine its schema of accumulation in a direction that presumes further changes in the international division of labour.[16]

In the same vein Fröbel, Heinrichs and Kreye write:

We therefore interpret the currently observable relocation of production in industry . . . as being the result of a qualitative change in the conditions for the valorisation and accumulation of capital, which is forcing the development of a new international division of labour. This new international division of labour is an 'institutional' innovation of capital itself, necessitated by changed conditions and not the result of changed development strategies by individual countries . . .[17]

The world accumulation approach to this question leads to a number of aspects of the export of manufactures being given particular emphasis.[18] The stress on the development of the forces of production in the advanced countries, and particularly the combination of the fragmentation and de-skilling of the labour process, leads to manufactured exports being largely identified with the relocation of particular production processes to the Third World. This in turn leads to an emphasis being put on ownership or, at least, effective control of exporting companies being in the hands of transnational corporations. Chossudovsky is at pains to point out that the analysis of the new international division of labour is not confined to the direct activities of transnational corporations, but extends to the subordination of national enterprises through financial, technological and other relations, and suggests 'that "national" economic categories have an entirely different meaning when applied to analysing contemporary tendencies in the internationalization of capital'.[19] This approach also tends to lead to an identification of manufactured exports from developing countries with free trade zones, that is, virtual enclaves which have little relation with the rest of the economy. As Frank states, 'Yet more often, and increasingly so, the promotion of industrial exports starts, as far as the local production area is concerned, from what is literally a *tabula rasa* . . . The new archetype of this "industrial development" are the "free production" or "export promotion" zones, which specialise in textile and electronics components production for export to the "world market".'[20]

A further aspect of this approach is that it leads to a tendency to see political developments within Latin America almost exclusively as a reflection of the logic of capital in the advanced countries. This tendency is carried furthest by Chossudovsky in his discussion of the 'peripheral state', the character of which he appears to derive from the internationalization process; 'State institutions and the various mechanisms of political and social coercion in the Third World have evolved in parallel with the underlying changes in the international division of labour.'[21] While this only emphasizes the parallel evolution of the state and its coercive mechanisms and the international division of labour, the failure to give any explanation of the former, and the frequently stressed functional relationship between the two, certainly conveys the impression that peripheral state structure can be derived from the changing international division of labour.

Some empirical considerations

As has already been hinted, the two approaches discussed make certain assumptions concerning the nature of exports of manufactures. In this section a number of these assumptions will be considered, contrasting the two positions and providing some empirical evidence. These are the type of firms responsible for exports, the kind of products exported, the institutional arrangements under which exports are made, the role of government policy, and the significance of export expansion.

1   Ownership and control of exporting firms

The orthodox approach, in so far as it is based on a neo-classical model of the Hecksher-Ohlin kind, implicitly assumes that factors of production are immobile internationally, and therefore tends to ignore the question of ownership of exporting enterprises.[22] In contrast, the world-accumulation approach stresses the crucial direct and indirect role of transnational corporations in exporting manufactures.

A first empirical question which must be answered, therefore, is the extent to which exports of manufactures from the Latin American countries are indeed under the control of the TNCs, and the degree to which the latter have participated in export growth. Table 16 shows that for the four main Latin American exporters, subsidiaries of TNCs accounted for between a third and a half of exports of manufactures in the early 1970s. As the table also shows, this was roughly the same as their participation in industrial production at this time. This proportion is at least sufficiently high to raise questions about the validity of models which assume the immobility of factors of production, and thereby abstract from the existence of TNCs.[23] On the other hand, it is clear from Table 16 that a significant proportion of exports come from national firms. Moreover, as far as can be judged, the share of TNCs in exports

Table 16   Share of foreign firms in manufactured exports and industrial production in the early 1970s: select countries

		Exports (percentages)	Production (percentages)
Argentina	(1972)	36	31
Brazil	(1974)	40	42*
Colombia	(1974)	50	43
Mexico	(1974)	50†	34‡

* 1969

† 34% excluding *maquiladoras*

‡ 1970

Sources   Argentina – exports: Instituto Nacional de Tecnología Industrial *Aspectos económicos de la importación de tecnología en la Argentina en 1972* (Buenos Aires 1974) – production: J. V. Sourrouille *El impacto de las empresas transnacionales sobre el empleo y los ingresos: el caso Argentino* ILO, WEP, 2–28/WP7 (Geneva 1976).

Brazil – exports: II. A. Garcia *La política de desarrollo de las exportaciones de manufacturas en Brazil*, E/CEPAL 1046/Add. 4 (Santiago 1978) – production: R. Newfarmer and W. Mueller *Multinational corporations in Brazil and Mexico: structural sources of economic and non-economic power*. Report of the Subcommittee on Multinational Corporations of the Committee on Foreign Relations, US Senate (Washington 1975).

Colombia – exports and production: Economic Commission on Latin America/Centre on Transnational Corporations, Joint Unit *Foreign participation in Colombian development: the role of TNCs* (Santiago 1979).

Mexico – exports: Rh. O. Jenkins 'The export performance of multinational corporations in Mexican industry' *Journal of Development Studies* (hereafter *JDS*) xv 3 (1979) – production: F. Fajnzylber and T. Martínez Tarrago *Las empresas transnacionales* (Mexico City 1976).

has not been increasing during the export boom since the mid-1960s.[24]

It is often argued, however, that formally independent exporters may be subordinated to transnationals through mechanisms of control such as technology contracts or long-term purchasing contracts. To what extent is this true in the major Latin American countries? Unfortunately there is little evidence on this. It is usually either asserted to be the case, often on the basis of comparison with subcontracting activities in the Far East, or entirely ignored. As Table 17 indicates, relatively small proportions of exports in the traditional sectors such as food, textiles, clothing, footwear, leather and furniture are accounted for by TNC subsidiaries. Is it reasonable, therefore, to suppose that these locally owned firm, which account for the bulk of these exports and which are frequently large national firms, are effectively under the control of multinational capital? Pending further investigation of relationships between these firms and their foreign customers, the question remains open.

Table 17 Share of foreign firms in exports of manufactures, by sector for Latin America, 1974 (percentages)

	Brazil*	Colombia	Mexico
Food	⎫	18.4	9.2
Drink	⎬ 22.1	—	31.1
Tobacco	⎭	36.5	0.1
Textiles		66.4†	1.4
Clothing	⎫	20.3	⎫
Footwear	⎬ 22.3	5.5	⎬ 24.2
Leather	⎭	18.3	9.9
Wood	⎫	5.5	1.1
Furniture	⎬ 0.0	18.3	2.2
		42.9	
Pulp and paper	⎫ 6.1	9.6	22.8
Printing and publishing	⎭	61.1	64.2
Rubber	⎫	12.3	38.0
Chemicals	⎬	94.4	⎫
Plastics	⎬ 42.9	86.7	⎬ 40.0
Petroleum and coal derivatives	⎭	73.6	
		—	3.1
Ceramics	⎫	35.3	⎫
Glass	⎬ 33.8	70.7	⎬ 12.0
Other non-metallic minerals	⎭	96.7	
Iron and steel		52.8	⎫ 26.4
Non-ferrous metals	⎫	75.2	⎭
Metal products	⎬ 88.6	82.3	15.4
Non-electrical machinery	76.5	29.4	33.4
Electrical machinery	85.7	87.8	90.4
Transport equipment	96.8	49.2	95.5
Scientific instruments	⎫ 0.0	45.3	⎫ 26.6
Other manufacturing	⎭	15.8	⎭
Total manufacturing	47.4	50.1	34.1

* The figures for Brazil are not strictly comparable, since they only apply to the major exporters amongst the largest 1,000 firms in the country.

† This figure exaggerates the extent of foreign control, because other sources indicate that the leading firms in this sector have a minimal foreign shareholding, but have been included because the data covers all firms with any foreign capital.

Sources H. A. Garcia *La política de desarrollo de las exportaciones de manufacturas en Brazil*, E/CEPAL 1046/Add. 4 (Santiago 1978) table F.1. Economic Commission on Latin America/Centre on Transnational Corporations Joint Unit *Foreign participation in Colombian development: the role of TNCs* (Santiago 1979) table 19. Rh. O. Jenkins, *Foreign firms, exports of manufactures and the Mexican economy*, Monograph in Development Studies no. 7 (Norwich 1979) table III.6.

2 Type of products exported

It is assumed in the orthodox approach that exports from Latin America will tend to be labour-intensive in character, since these are the products in which the countries of the region enjoy a comparative advantage. A similar implicit assumption is evident in some of the writing from a world-accumulation perspective, although here the emphasis tends to be on the relocation of labour-intensive production processes as much as products. It is therefore of interest to ask to what extent Latin American exports of manufactures are predominantly labour-intensive.

The industries usually identified as labour-intensive are textile products, apparel, wood products, furniture and fixtures and leather products (including leather footwear).[25] Table 18 shows the share of these industries in the exports of the major Latin American countries. It is clear that these industries account for a surprisingly low share of manufactured exports in Argentina, Brazil and Mexico and only in Colombia do they account for around half the total.[26] Moreover, only in Argentina has the share of these industries increased significantly between 1965 and 1974, whereas in Colombia and Mexico there have been small increases and in Brazil a decline. Nor is it possible to argue that the figures are significantly biased because they include exports generated within the Latin American Free Trade Area which would not be expected to be labour-intensive, since these countries have relatively high incomes within Latin America. Even if exports to other LAFTA countries are excluded, the same pattern exists. In 1974 less than a third of these exports were of labour-intensive products in Argentina, Brazil and Mexico.

Table 18   Exports of labour-intensive products as percentage of total manufactured exports, 1965 and 1974: select countries

	1965		1974	
	Total manufactured exports	Manufactured exports excluding LAFTA	Total manufactured exports	Manufactured exports excluding LAFTA
Argentina	3.0	3.8	15.6	27.2
Brazil	35.1	36.0	30.3	33.3
Colombia	47.5	62.3	52.6	45.7*
Mexico	18.9	22.3	20.8	23.6

* 1973

Source   Comisión Económica para América Latina *Las exportaciones de manufacturas en América Latina: informaciones estadísticas y algunas consideraciones generales*, E/CEPAL/L.128 (Santiago 1976).

3   Institutional arrangements and government policies

As already indicated, there is a tendency for writers adopting a world-system perspective to identify manufactured exports from less developed countries with the free production zones. How far does this identification fit the picture of exports from the Latin American countries under consideration?

The exports of the *maquiladoras* in Mexico, predominantly electrical products and apparel, clearly fit into this pattern. In the mid-1970s, the value added of the *maquiladoras* accounted for between 30 and 40 per cent of manufactured exports by firms other than *maquiladoras*.[27] If one considered the total value (as opposed to the value added) of *maquiladora* exports, in 1974 this came to approximately two thirds of non-*maquiladora* exports of manufactures. Thus in Mexico there is no doubt that the type of exports emphasized by this approach have been extremely significant. It is also possible that part of the exports which are not made by *maquiladoras*, especially that part made by subsidiaries of TNCs, also follow this pattern.

However, this is by no means so clearly the case when it comes to the other Latin American countries. Although free production zones have also been reported in Brazil and Colombia,[28] these do not appear to have played a major role in the expansion of exports from these countries.[29] One indication of this is the extent of US imports from these countries under Tariff Items 806.30 and 807.00, which are specifically designed to facilitate the relocation of production processes overseas for re-export to the USA. Whereas the USA imported more than $1100 million from Mexico under these headings in 1977, the corresponding figures were $121 million for Brazil, $14.7 million for Colombia and $0.4 million for Argentina.[30] Mexico accounted for 35 per cent of all US imports from underdeveloped countries under these items, while Brazil accounted for only 3.7 per cent, Colombia for less than 0.5 per cent and Argentina for only 0.01 per cent of the total. Looked at from the point of view of the exporting countries, these exports accounted for less than 10 per cent of Brazilian and Colombian industrial exports to the US in the mid-1970s. It seems, therefore, misleading to say that the free production zone is the typical case of export production in Latin America.

While the world-accumulation approach tends to prioritize the role of free production zones, the orthodox approach stresses the role of government incentives more generally, taking such zones as only one manifestation of such policies. Much of the discussion in the literature focuses on fiscal incentives, exchange rate policies, credits for export, and so on. The point here is not to question either the existence of such incentives, or the fact that they have had some effect on the decision of some firms whether to export or not. It is, however, necessary to question the sufficiency of this explanation, both in terms of its interpretation of the change in government policy and of its attempts at showing empirically the importance of these policies.

The new government policies of export promotion adopted in the mid-1960s are explained by these writers in the following terms:

> By the mid-1960s, however, the strategy (import substitution), or at least the tactics employed to pursue it, has proved unsuccessful (in terms of sustained growth, adequate expansion of industrial employment, and the removal of severe balance of payments constraints), in many instances only exacerbating the problems they were designed to cure. At the same time an exclusive group of small, developing economies was demonstrating that the classical wisdom still had some merit – trade could be an engine of growth.[31]

This type of approach raises a number of questions. Most obviously, it assumes that the state is an agent of development, above social classes, interested in growth, employment and external balance. The state is implicitly technocratic, able to make choices about the type of development strategy to be pursued in the light of past experience and alternative 'models' being followed elsewhere. Thus it is possible to view export promotion as a return to the universal and everlasting truth of the classical belief in comparative advantage and free trade. Since these principles are universally valid, it is unnecessary to look to any changes in the world economy in order to explain the new vogue for export promotion.

Attempts to explain the growth of manufactured exports purely in terms of government promotional policies have not been particularly successful. Econometric studies which relate export growth to the real effective exchange rate, taking into account the various incentives and movements in price levels, have not generally produced very strong results. In Argentina and Colombia there was no discernible effect on exports, while in Brazil there was only a very weak impact.[32] Indeed, in all three studies the level of capacity utilization in manufacturing was found to be a more significant determinant of the growth of manufactured exports than government incentives. Equations which have obtained high R^2 appear to have invariably been achieved by introducing a time trend, or some substitute for a time trend such as an index of industrial production.[33] Thus it seems that the types of variables that are specifically highlighted in this approach do not appear to have great explanatory power, while satisfactory explanation in statistical terms can only be achieved by introducing variables whose role has been inadequately theorized.[34]

4 *The significance of export expansion*

A final feature which characterizes both approaches, particularly the world-accumulation view, is a tendency to exaggerate the significance of the growth of manufactured exports and the magnitude of the change that has taken place. The emphasis on the 'new international division of labour' neglects the fact that exports account for less than 10 per cent of manufacturing output in all four countries, and that the bulk of production is still for the domestic market.[35] Even when the contribution of exports on the growth of industrial output in the period since the mid-1960s is considered, this has not been on a major scale. However, the limited extent of such exports tends to contradict the picture, which world-accumulation theorists present, of the irresistible drive of capital to fragment and de-skill the industrial process and transfer major parts of it to the Third World. In fact the tendency of these writers to focus exclusively on the production process leads them to neglect the factors which restrain and counteract the outward movement of capital towards the periphery, such as protectionist policies in the advanced capitalist countries.

Conclusion

As was suggested in the introduction to this chapter, both main approaches to the question of export promotion have been misleading because of the stress that they have placed on one particular aspect of the process. The orthodox approach, in common with neo-classical economics, generally emphasizes the sphere of exchange and the circulation of commodities. The concept of production which it employs is entirely ahistorical and asocial, involving the combination of factors of production (which are regarded as given endowments of national states) to produce commodities which then exchange through international trade. It is not surprising that this approach considers that exports from the Latin American countries will tend to be of labour-intensive products, reflecting the factor endowments of those countries. Nor is it surprising that, given the emphasis on exchange relationships, the analysis of the growth of manufactured exports should focus on exchange categories such as the exchange rate, tax rebates and subsidies.

World accumulation, on the other hand, puts an equally one-sided emphasis on the development of the capitalist labour process through fragmentation and de-skilling. Much of the argument of these writers, as far as the labour process is concerned, parallels that of Braverman and some of the criticisms that have been made of his work apply equally to their view of the new international division of labour. The major criticism of relevance in this context is the tendency to treat the working class as an object of capital, emphasizing the ability of capital to reorganize the labour process almost at will and forgetting the active role of the working class.[36] It is this absence of the working class as an active element in the accumulation process that underlies the unilineal conception of the new international division of labour that these writers present.

The emphasis on the development of the labour process in abstraction from distribution and exchange also lies at the heart of the excessive emphasis on the transfer of de-skilled production processes to free production zones as the characteristic form of export promotion. The much more complex reality of export expansion can only be understood as the product of the capitalist search for higher profits, in whatever form the opportunities may present themselves, which in turn depend on class struggle in the advanced countries and the periphery, both in production and at the political level as expressed through state intervention. The intervention of the state cannot be analysed simply in terms of the needs of multinational capital, nor in terms of a technocratic state seeking rational solutions to economic problems.

Notes

[1] H. B. Chenery and D. B. Keesing. *The changing composition of developing countries exports*, World Bank Staff Working Paper no. 314 (Washington 1979) p. 12.

[2] Comisión Económica para América Latina *Las exportaciones de manufacturas en América Latina: informaciones estadísticas y algunas consideraciones generales*, E/CEPAL/L.128 (Santiago 1976) table 1.

[3] This chapter focuses on the experience of these four countries. This should not be taken to imply that their experience is typical of Latin America as a whole, but rather that they are the most significant examples of the phenomenon under consideration, namely the expansion of industrial exports.

[4] See for instance Comisión Económica para América Latina. 'Trade in manufactures and semi-manufactures' *Economic Bulletin for Latin America* 1st half (1972).

[5] This development of dependency theory can be seen most clearly in the recent writing of André Gunder Frank. A. G. Frank *Dependent accumulation and underdevelopment* (London 1978), *World accumulation 1492–1789* (New York 1978), *Crisis in the world economy* (London 1980), *Crisis in the Third World* (London 1980).

[6] In addition to the works of Frank cited above, see I. Wallerstein *The modern world system* (New York 1974) and F. Fröbel, J. Heinrichs and O. Kreye *The new international division of labour* (Cambridge 1980).

[7] I. Little, T. Scitovsky and M. Scott *Industry and trade in some developing countries* (Oxford 1970).

[8] D. T. Healey 'Development policy, new thinking about an interpretation' *Journal of Economic Literature* x 3 (1972).

[9] Little, Scitovsky and Scott *op. cit.* p. 11.

[10] A. O. Hirschman 'The political economy of import-substituting industrialization in Latin America' *Quarterly Journal of Economics* (hereafter *QJE*) LXXXII 1 (1968) 24.

[11] Little, Scitovsky and Scott *op. cit.* p. 353.

[12] D. M. Schydlowsky 'Latin American trade policies in the 1970s: a prospective appraisal' *QJE* LXXXVI 2 (1972) 278–9.

[13] Little, Scitovsky and Scott *op. cit.* p. 353.

[14] B. Balassa 'Export incentives and export performance in developing countries: a comparative analysis' *Weltwirtschaftliches Archiv* CXIV (1978).

[15] See for instance Fröbel, Heinrichs and Kreye *op. cit.* and P. Vusković 'América Latina antes nuevos términos de la división internacional del trabajo' *Economía de América Latina* no. 2 (1979).

[16] Vuskovič *loc. cit.* 18.

[17] Fröbel, Heinrichs and Kreye *op. cit.* p. 46. See also S. Sideri 'Restructuring of the world economy and the emerging regional division of labour in Latin America' in J. Carrière (ed.) *Industrialization and the state in Latin America* (Amsterdam 1979) p.134.

[18] These points are made by the Dublin CSE Group Review of F. Fröbel, J. Heinrich and O. Kreye 'Die neue internationale arbeitsteilung' *Capital and Class* no. 7 (1979) but, as I try to illustrate below, apply more widely.

[19] M. Chossudovsky *Transnationalization and the development of peripheral capitalism,* University of Ottowa, Faculty of Social Science, Department of Economics, Research Paper no. 7903 (1979) p. 29.

[20] A. G. Frank *Third World manufacturing export production* University of East Anglia, Development Studies Discussion Paper no. 37 (1979) p. 1. al corporations in exporting manufactures, but usually in a rather peripheral way.

[21] Chossudovsky *loc. cit.* p. 2.

[22] The more empirically orientated studies do sometimes mention the role of transnational corporations in exporting manufacturers, but usually in a rather peripheral way.

[23] It is also relevant to note that exports by TNC subsidiaries are frequently to the parent company or other affiliates of the parent rather than at 'arm's length', so that 'market forces' are frequently absent. Newfarmer and Mueller indicate that 82 per cent of exports by US subsidiaries in Mexico and 73 per cent of exports by US subsidiaries in Brazil were intra-firm: R. Newfarmer and W. Mueller *Multinational corporations in Brazil and Mexico: structural sources of economic and non-economic power,* Report of the Sub-committee on Multinational Corporations of the Committee on Foreign Relations, US Senate (Washington 1975).

[24] Figures are unfortunately not available which would permit a comparison of the share of TNCs in exports of manufactures in the mid-1960s with the situation in the mid-1970s. Data on exports of manufactures by majority-owned affiliates of US firms indicates that these grew by 12 per cent for Argentina, 35 per cent for Brazil, 23 per cent for Colombia and 22 per cent for Mexico between 1966 and 1974 (US Department of Commerce figures). These compare with the growth rates of all industrial exports between 1965 and 1974 of 29 per cent for Argentina, 30 per cent for Brazil, 33 per cent for Colombia and 27 per cent for Mexico. This indicates that, at least as far as US majority-owned subsidiaries are concerned, exports have grown at below average rates in all countries except Brazil.

[25] See for instance the study by Lary where industries are classified on the basis of indicators such as value added per person employed in the USA in 1965, and it is shown that this classification is consistent across a range of countries. Although some subsectors within other industries are more labour-intensive than the average for manufacturing as a whole, they are still less labour-intensive than the average for the industries mentioned above. H. B. Lary *Imports of manufactures from less developed countries* (New York 1968).

[26] A number of authors have noted that the manufactured products exported by the major Latin American countries have often not been labour-intensive in character. See D. Felix 'Industrial structure, industrial exporting and economic policy: an analysis of recent Argentine experience' in D. Geithman (ed.) *Fiscal policy for industrialization and development in Latin America* (Florida 1974): W. G. Tyler *Manufactured export expansion and industrialization in Brazil* (Tübingen 1976): C. Díaz Alejandro *Foreign trade regimes and economic development: Colombia* (New York 1976); R. Boatler 'Trade theory predictions and the growth of Mexico's manufactured exports', Ph.D. thesis (Cornell University 1973); Rh. O. Jenkins *Foreign firms, exports of manufactures and the Mexican economy,* Monograph in Development Studies no. 7 (Norwich 1979).

[27] Comisión Económica para América Latina *La exportación de manufacturas en México y la política de promoción* CEPAL/MEX/76/10 (Mexico City 1976) table 18.

[28] Fröbel *et al. op. cit.*

[29] Díaz Alejandro *op. cit.* p. 47 states that in 1972 'export platforms' and exports from

bonded free trade zones were modest. In the 1970s the free production zones in Brazil and Colombia were estimated to employ 27,650 and 5,600 workers respectively. Fröbel *et al. op. cit.* table III 8.

[30] Data from US Department of Commerce.

[31] J. B. Donges and J. Riedel 'The expansion of manufactured exports in developing countries: an empirical assessment of supply and demand issues' *Welwirtschaftliches Archiv* CXIII (1977) 59. For similar views on the change in policy in specific Latin American countries, see L. A. Aspra 'Import substitution in Mexico: past and present' *World Development* v (1977). A. Berry and F. Thoumi 'Import substitution and beyond: Colombia' *World Development* v (1977).

[32] Felix *loc. cit.*; J. P. Wogart *Industrialization in Colombia: policies, patterns, perspectives* (Tübingen 1978). W. G. Tyler 'Manufactured export promotion in a semi-industrialized economy: the Brazilian case' *JDS* x 1 (1973).

[33] See for instance Tyler *loc. cit.*, later equations; and Donges and Riedel *loc. cit.* table 2.

[34] Faced with these problems of statistical significance, some authors resort to repeating evidence from interviews with firms where it was claimed that export incentives were significant in promoting exports. See for instance Tyler *loc. cit.* p.13 on Brazil. I found quite the opposite in interviews with TNC subsidiaries in Mexico, who in the main did not consider export incentives to have been very important. Similarly in Argentina, industrialists rarely mentioned cost competitiveness in discussing export possibilities. Felix *loc. cit.*

[35] Balassa *loc. cit.* table 2 estimates the share of exports in manufactured output in 1973 as 3.6 per cent in Argentina, 4.4 per cent in Brazil, 7.5 per cent in Colombia and 4.4 per cent in Mexico. The Mexican figure does not include the exports of the *maquiladoras*.

[36] T. Elger 'Valorization and "Deskilling": a critique of Braverman' *Capital and Class* no. 7 (1979).

23

STATE, MULTINATIONALS AND THE WORKING CLASS IN BRAZIL AND MEXICO

Ian Roxborough

In recent years, attention has been focused on two salient features of the economies of Brazil and Mexico: the size and importance of multinational corporations in these economies, and the expanded role of the state sector. The obvious corollary has been a concern for whether the 'national bourgeoisie' is about to disappear or become an appendage of the multinationals, and whether we can talk about 'state capitalism' in this context. It has also been widely claimed that the economic consequences of this new phase of development are such that the state becomes increasingly authoritarian and autonomous. This argument, which is often discussed under the heading of the 'bureaucratic-authoritarian' model and which is generally held to apply to Mexico and Brazil *inter alia*, involves a series of claims about the nature of the state, of dominant classes and of the industrial working class, which, as will be argued, are highly questionable.[1] These are, of course, some of the central questions of development theory, and have much wider implications than can be thoroughly dealt with here.

State autonomy

There are basically two views of the state: one sees it as the more or less direct expression of class interests as a consequence of the fact that the main positions in the state apparatus are staffed by personnel recruited from the dominant class(es). This is widely referred to as 'the executive committee' model. The other basic view of the state sees it as having some considerable degree of autonomy *vis-à-vis* class interests. This may be referred to as 'the relative autonomy' or 'Bonapartist' model. (Functionalist theories of the state are here treated as a version of this second view.)

Both models present certain problems. In the executive committee model, it is not always possible to demonstrate empirically any important connections between state functionaries and the dominant class, and this has led some scholars to reject this model entirely. However, while it would be correct to say that not all states are of the executive committee type, this does not, of course, imply that no state fits the executive committee model. The question then becomes one of determining the circumstances under which this model is appropriate. On the other hand, in the relative-autonomy model the question (which was implicitly solved in the executive committee model) of why the state should act in the interests of the dominant class(es) becomes a real problem.

There is, of course, no reason why the two models should not be used together. That is, it may be convenient to treat these two models as ideal-types and empirically inquire as to the degree to which concrete states approximate either ideal-type.

The prevailing position in the literature on Brazil and Mexico has been that these two states come closer to the relative-autonomy model than to the executive committee model.[2] This, at least, is the case when the relationships between the national industrial bourgeoisie and the state are examined. When foreign capital is brought into the picture a somewhat different analysis sometimes emerges, and the meaning of autonomy takes on a new dimension. Up to this point, the autonomy of the state has been taken to mean an autonomy *vis-à-vis* dominant classes within that society: the ability of the state to choose and implement policies either without the immediate 'guidance' of dominant classes or in opposition to them. But of course the policies of the state are also constrained by actors external to the society. These can take many forms. The policies of the Mexican and Brazilian states have often been constrained by a series of market pressures stemming from foreign trade and investment.[3] They have had to bargain directly with foreign investors over the conditions of entry to Mexican and Brazilian markets. And the Mexican and Brazilian state apparatuses themselves have, to some extent, been penetrated by agencies of the United States government. On all these – and other – dimensions, it is necessary to assess the degree to which states are autonomous *vis-à-vis* their external environment.

Obviously, there are complex interconnections between forms of 'external' and 'internal' autonomy. For the moment, however, they will be treated as separate dimensions and, unless otherwise indicated, whether the autonomy being discussed is 'internal' or 'external' will be apparent from the context.[4]

Dominant classes

In Mexico, the autonomy of the state from the direct influence of social classes goes back at least to the Revolution of 1910. The decade of confused and bloody conflict which was the Mexican Revolution brought to power the Sonoran dynasty: modernizing agrarian capitalists from the north and north-west of the country. Seizing hold of the remnants of the state apparatus, they set about the arduous task of solidifying and centralizing state power. Gradually the private armies of regional caudillos were subjugated by the federal army and either absorbed or disbanded. Popular discontent was mobilized in the service of this process of state-building, and the masses were brought into the corporatist control structures of the emerging state. By the end of the Cárdenas presidency (1934–40), this process of state-building had been substantially completed. Since the Second World War the *Partido Revolucionario Institutional* (*PRI*) has ruled Mexico without serious opposition.[5]

In this process of revolution and reconstruction of the state, the old dominant classes were at first disorganized and placed on the defensive (though never destroyed), and later brought under the aegis of the state in an apparently subordinate role. At the same time the holders of state power, the Sonoran dynasty and their successors, used their positions to amass personal wealth and make contacts. They then often left office to establish themselves as important members of the new industrial bourgeoisie which was growing up under the protection of the state. With the beginnings of rapid industrial growth in the 1940s, this symbiotic process of the growth of an industrial bourgeoisie dependent on the state, and a massive state apparatus dependent on continuing rapid rates of capitalist growth for its material basis, developed apace. At the higher levels of the state apparatus, many office-holders evidently planned to move into private enterprise once their political career was over. With the end in mind, office-holding served the purpose of 'primitive political accumulation', the amassing of enough capital from bribes and kickbacks to set up in business.[6]

While this flow from government to business was important in strengthening the ties between the two, so also were the responses of the private sector to the Mexican business environment. The process of import-substituting industrialization, and the key role of the state in the economy, inevitably made business highly dependent on the state. For a start, the state was a major contractor of private enterprise. Perhaps more importantly, the complex regulatory legislation which grew up during the period of import-substituting industrialization, and the large amount of discretion wielded by the state in the interpretation of this legislation, meant that the success or failure of business enterprises often depended on access to, and influence over, government decisions. It was this complex and arbitrary business environment which was a key push-factor in the growth of government-business corruption in Mexico. The result was something quite different from the organized lobbying of government by business sectors, which is characteristic of many industrial nations. Rather, the Mexican system involved efforts by *individual* firms to ensure that they were favoured by government action. The obvious way to do this was by bribing key office-holders.[7] This highly individualistic response made class unity and organization difficult to achieve, and served to reinforce the symbiotic relationship between government and the new industrial bourgeoisie.

The preceding remarks refer principally to the new sections of industry which developed in the post-war period, particularly in and around Mexico City. A rather different picture emerged in the northern industrial centre of Monterrey. By the 1890s this city had established itself as an important industrial centre,[8] much as São Paulo had done in the 1880s,[9] though unlike São Paulo, the industrial development of Monterrey was not linked with the expansion of agricultural exports. By the 1930s Monterrey was run by a closely knit industrial dynasty formed around the nucleus of the Garza-Sada families. This has always been a minority faction within Mexican capital, and the relations of this group with the state have always been strained, to say the least.[10] It was the Monterrey group which openly defied the government of Lazaro Cárdenas (1934–40), in opposition to his attempts to promote the growth of union organizations. Since then, the Monterrey industrialists have consistently fought to maintain their 'free' or 'white' unions, entirely passive company unions unaffiliated with the major union confederations in Mexico.[11] Again, during the presidency of Luis Echeverría (1970–6), the Monterrey industrialists openly attacked what they saw as the leftist orientation of the government. In political terms, the Monterrey group has always acted like an ultramontane representative of the national bourgeoisie. Possessing a high level of class integration and political consciousness, it has sought to defend the autonomy and interests of the private sector in Mexico.

Ironically, the Monterrey group is not a truly 'national' bourgeoisie, confined as it is to a specific region for its social base. The industrial interests located elsewhere in Mexico, particularly those in and around the capital, are harder to identify in terms of class cohesion. Less cohesive, they are also highly dependent on the state, and in general they have not sought to articulate a political position independent of the state, preferring to work within the complex networks of power, patronage and corruption to achieve their ends. Moreover, a question mark must now be placed over the survival in its present form of the Monterrey group. The rapid growth of the Garza-Sada complex led, in the 1970s, to its reorganization as the Grupo Alfa, with professional management committed to trimming the less profitable parts of the organization. This reorganization, together with massive expansion in some areas, was financed by heavy foreign borrowing. By mid-1982, following a major devaluation of the peso, the ability of Alfa to repay its loans was in serious doubt, and there was speculation in financial circles that the government would have to intervene to rescue the group.[12]

There seem, *prima facie*, to be good grounds for talking about a considerable degree of state autonomy in Mexico, though some analysts have argued that this autonomy is more apparent than real. We shall return to this issue shortly.

In Brazil, the beginning of an extended period of apparent state autonomy can be dated to Vargas's seizure of power in 1930. For much of the 1920s there had been movements of discontent with the old oligarchic order of the export-orientated economy, most visibly manifested in the *tenentes* revolts of 1922 and 1924. Briefly, the series of export cycles involving distinct primary products (sugar, cacao, rubber and, most importantly, coffee) had led to the emergence of a series of regional agrarian oligarchies and a relatively weak central state apparatus, whose task was primarily to hold the balance between the various regional groups and to facilitate the smoooth functioning of the export economy. In a sense, the system worked too well. The twentieth century saw an almost permanent overproduction of coffee, and the consequent attempt by the state, through a series of institutions (guaranteed prices plus stockpiling), to socialize the costs of this excess production through the economy, so that the coffee planters would continue to provide foreign exchange.[13] The World Depression of the 1930s was merely the straw that broke the camel's back. Vargas's revolt had been undertaken before the disastrous effects of the depression hit the Brazilian economy with full force.

Although industrial development had its roots in an earlier period, for a crucial fifteen years, from 1930 to 1945, Vargas oversaw the rapid acceleration of industrialization in Brazil and a significant realignment of national politics. With the creation of the *Estado Nôvo* in 1937, Vargas set his corporatist imprimatur on Brazilian political life. Since that time, it has been argued, these corporatist institutions have continued to structure state-civil society relations in Brazil, affording the state an autonomy from the direct pressures of social classes that has enabled it to oversee a process of rapid economic growth and to impose authoritarian political solutions on restive sectors, whenever necessary. 'Before the rifle butt, all classes fall silent.' In this interpretation of Brazilian history, the coup of 1964 is a mere incident, a necessary acting-out of the historical continuity of authoritarian corporatism in a context of dependent development.[14] Following these lines of reasoning, many analysts argued that, when multinational capital began to move massively into Mexican and Brazilian industry in the mid-1950s, these societies were dominated by authoritarian and autonomous states. This greatly facilitated the formation of new political alliances, of a new pact of domination.

In the extreme version of the thesis, an alliance was struck between the state and international capital. Local capital did not exist effectively as a class, or was so subordinate that it was rapidly being driven to the wall by the multinational corporations, and could be discounted as a political actor. The state became the representative of multinational capital, and its authoritarian features were necessarily strengthened. Local capital's inability to resist the incursions of the multinationals could be traced back to its own weakness *vis-à-vis* the state, itself a symptom of the structural dependency of these nations. Usually presented as an argument which would apply with equal force to all Latin American or Third World nations, it could certainly be argued in concrete historical terms for both Brazil and Mexico, as the foregoing pages have attempted to indicate.

In a weaker and more revisionist version of the thesis, the national industrial bourgeoisie is discovered to be alive and well, and a junior partner in a triple alliance with the state and multinational capital. Perhaps the best-known version of this thesis is that put forward by Peter Evans.

Arguing that reports of the death of the local bourgeoisie have been greatly exaggerated, Evans states that it has specific advantages which international capital lacks, namely a detailed knowledge of local market and production conditions.[15] Together with the existence of a strong state, this provides the conditions for the triple alliance. This is particularly the case in a situation of inter-imperialist rivalry. Evans notes that foreign direct investment in Brazil comes from a wide range of countries, and concludes that 'the overall result of the evolution is to make dependence less a question of a relationship with a particular country and more a question of a relationship with the multinationals as a collectivity ... The result of dispersion is to give the Brazilian state increased manoeuvering room.'[16] The result is the formation of joint ventures between the state and local and multinational capital. 'For multinationals asking "How can I get in?" and local capital asking "How can I survive?" the answer seems to be the same – a joint venture.'[17] In addition to local expertise, affiliation with local capital also brings with it increased political legitimacy.[18] Foreign capital is always highly vulnerable to political criticism and needs to forestall or blunt such possible attacks, a point which has also been made by Newfarmer.[19]

Although Evans generalizes from the case of Brazil to a small number of similar countries, including Mexico, he also argues that there is an important difference between the two countries. Evans believes that the nature of the Mexican state, and its relation to mass politics, means that populism is a distinct possibility in a way in which it could never be in Brazil:

> In Mexico, populism may not be a winning strategy for the state bourgeoisie, but it is a possible strategy. In Brazil it is out of the question. The possibilities for confrontation between the state

bourgeoisie and the multinationals are correspondingly greater in Mexico. At the same time, the possibility of popular mobilization creates greater impetus for alliances between local groups and the multinationals.[20]

This notion of the populist basis of the Mexican political system is a widespread one, and will be discussed below. However, before doing so, it is necessary to take up the main thread of the argument.

Sometimes the stronger version of the thesis that the state 'represents' international capital has taken the form of an argument to the effect that there has been an increasing overlapping and fusion between the personnel of the state apparatus and the managers and owners of international capital. Alonso Aguilar, Fragoso and others have put forward this thesis for the case of Mexico.[21] In Brazil, F. H. Cardoso has suggested that 'bureaucratic rings' exist which link the managers of the state apparatus and the managers of capital.[22] The evidence, however, is suggestive rather than systematic: it consists of a list of illustrative cases of such interlocks, which we may call the monopoly capitalism thesis. It focuses on the way in which the state serves to further the interests of foreign capital. The state is not independent of foreign capital; rather, it is directly subordinated to foreign capital. The autonomy of the state consists in its lack of a social base in civil society. In particular, since the national bourgeoisie does not exist as a class with its own interests opposed to foreign capital, but is (at best) a parasitic junior partner with foreign capital, there can be no question of national capital controlling the state or of (national) bourgeois hegemony; the state is merely an extension of the metropolitan apparatus of domination.

State capitalism

This perspective has been given added cogency by some recent writings on Brazil, where the importance of the direct role played by the state in the economy has been pointed out by Baer and others.[23] The discovery that the state has a directly productive role in the economy (quite apart from its role in macro-economic regulation), which makes it the most important economic factor, has led some analysts to claim that the Brazilian economy is 'state capitalism'.[24]

The state sector in Brazil in both large and growing. The state directly owns major sectors of the economy, controls most of the process of financial intermediation, and intervenes constantly in the process of price-determination, either directly or through the use of subsidies, fiscal measures, and so on. Consequently, it is claimed, any notion of a free market capitalism is inappropriate in these societies. What exists, instead, is a form of state capitalism, in which administrative prices set the parameters of economic activity, rather than competitive equilibrium prices. Beyond this, there is very little in the way of any positive analysis of the structure and dynamics of 'state capitalism'. However, the notion that a specific form of 'state capitalism' exists in Brazil needs to be treated with a certain degree of reserve. In the first place, what is important is not the absolute size of the state sector, but rather the effect the state sector has on the functioning of the rest of the economy. Although the state (if it were a unified actor) might have the power to alter the price system in a major way, it remains to be shown that this potential power is actually used. Is the behaviour of the Brazilian economy actually different from that which might be expected of a free market economy? The burden of proof, it would seem, lies with those who wish to claim that the Brazilian economy is, in some sense, not capitalist.

In the second place, Brazil's linkages with the world economy set limits on internal prices in Brazil. This is particularly the case since 1964, with the opening-up of the economy to foreign trade and investment. It was also true, however, under the protectionist regimes of the Vargas period. World prices had an indirect impact on internal prices through the distortions brought about by tariffs and quotas. This being the case, it is difficult to see how any economy can be meaningfully described as 'state capitalist' unless either all capital is state-owned or the entire economy is de-linked from the world capitalist system.

Third, to argue that, because the state sector in Brazil is important, the Brazilian economy is to be characterized as 'state capitalist', is a potentially two-edged weapon. After all, the state plays a central role in most (if not all) of the economies of advanced capitalism. Are we therefore to believe that these economies are also state capitalist? If so, why make such a fuss about the Brazilian case? To put the matter somewhat differently, it remains to be shown whether, in terms of international comparisons, there is anything unusual about the Brazilian economy.

State managers

The central question in any discussion of state capitalism must be the relationship between the state and the industrialists. This, rather than the sheer size of the state sector of the economy, must be the focus of attention. At issue is whether the functionaries of the state apparatus constitute a specific social stratum, distinct from the industrial bourgeoisie, and with their own definable corporate interests. Can they, in other words, act independently of, and/or in opposition to, the interests of the industrial bourgeoisie?

Although it may be the case in other countries, in neither Brazil nor Mexico does the industrial bourgeoisie directly control the key offices of the state. Those who run the state and those who control industry appear to be distinct groups of people.[25] This then raises the question of how and why the state acts in the interest of the bourgeoisie. There are a number of possible answers to this question. In the first place, it could be argued that there is some sort of functional constraint on the state, which ensures that it acts on behalf of capital. This functionalist approach is essentially magical and will not be pursued further in this essay. At its most extreme, this position involves a definitional tautology. One influential theorist defined the state as that which maintained and reproduced the existing system.[26] Clearly, by definition, in a capitalist society the state will further the accumulation of capital. Approaches derived from the functionalist perspective, despite their popularity, are not useful for empirical investigation.

In the second place, it could be argued that the reason why the state acts to promote the interests of a particular class is because it is subject to the pressures of various groups and organizations. This is a more reasonable approach to the problem, though it contains the difficulty variously identified as 'agenda-setting' or 'non-issues'.[27] In principle it is relatively easy to examine decisions made by the state and assess the relative impact of outside pressures.[28] What is rather more difficult, however, is to account for why some issues are debated and others are not.

A third approach would be to demonstrate that, although the personnel of the state were not recruited directly from the bourgeoisie, they were affected by various socialization experiences and came to adopt bourgeois outlooks. They might go to similar schools, live in the same neighbourhoods, belong to the same voluntary associations and intermarry. This hypothesis suggests that the state functionaries will adopt the world-view of the dominant class because they share the same lifestyle and mix together socially. Both this and the previous hypothesis are empirically testable.

A fourth approach is to suggest that state functionaries have specific interests of their own, but that these *coincide* with the interests of the industrial bourgeoisie. This view has been put forward, *inter alia,* by Fred Block. He argues that it is useful to treat the 'state managers' as a separate and distinct group with specific interests.[29]

One of the difficulties with the notion of a stratum of state managers concerns the extent to which one can, indeed, talk about them in terms of some form of class or corporate grouping. Even if we were to accept that state managers occupied roles in the state apparatus which meant that they had 'objectively' identical (or similar) interests – and this is, obviously, very questionable – it might still be somewhat premature to describe them as a class. One of the features of the class structure of capitalist societies is the degree of 'inheritance' of class position. The family and education act as mechanisms of class recruitment and, although there is enough social mobility in capitalist societies to pre-clude any notion of automatic inheritance of class position, the amount of continuity is of central importance.

Against this, it is quite correct to point out that the state managers in several non-capitalist societies have not been recruited from more-or-less stable classes. The widespread employment of eunuchs, or the educational selection mechanisms of the Chinese mandarinate, are appropriate examples of non-class forms of recruitment of state mana-gers. Nevertheless, it is unusual for state managers in capitalist societies not to be recruited from specific classes, even though these may not be the central parts of the dominant class. Hence, to talk about the interests of state managers without some prior inquiry into their class origins and affiliations seems unwarranted.

Popular representation

As Fred Block has suggested, even if there is a separate stratum of state managers, divorced from the dominant class(es), their interests are likely to converge with those of the industrialists. In a situation of international state competition, state managers need to consider how they are going to be able to maintain or expand the autonomy of their states *vis-à-vis* other states. One important dimension of such independ-ence will be economic power and autonomy. At the same time, faced with growing demands from popular classes and few adequate institu-tional means of controlling such demands, state managers, in order to head off political challenges from subordinate groups, will try to maxi-mize economic growth so as to increase the available resources for state redistribution. In the long run, and particularly in periods of stability, the interests of state managers and industrialists are likely to coincide. However, there is no necessity for this to occur, and on occasion there will indeed be significant differences between the two groups.

There are, however, important differences between Mexico and Brazil in these areas. In the first place, the Mexican state has at its disposal a set of political institutions for diffusing popular discontent which are quite unparalleled. These are, of course, the clientelistic and corporatist institutions which feed into the PRI. Not only does the Mexican state have a near-monopoly on forms of groups representation; it is also true that its coverage is extensive and quite real. This is clearly not the case with Brazil. Although the range of sectors covered by pro-government popular institutions may appear similar, both the depth of their coverage and the way in which they function seem to be quite different.

Nevertheless, despite this contrast, it would be wrong to overempha-size the 'populist' dimension of the Mexican state. It is by no means clear that the Mexican state is constrained to act in specific ways because of the importance of popular pressures. The official union apparatus, the peasant confederations and the amorphous 'popular sector' are all firmly subordinated to the political bureaucracy. This is not to say that there are no oppositional movements in Mexico, nor that the state does not need to respond to popular discontent. But this does not differentiate the Mexican state from any other state. All states need to respond, to some degree, to popular pressure. It is difficult to argue that the Mexican state is unusual in the degree to which it does this. Nor is the Mexican political system distinguished by a higher level of legitimacy or consensus than other states. Most studies of political attitudes in Mexico indicate high levels of cynicism and apathy, rather than active support for the political system.[30] What, perhaps, does distinguish the Mexican political system from others is its near-monopoly of organizational representation. The political mobilizations of the past have meant that the PRI has effectively pre-empted the organizational space that might be occupied by political challengers.

External autonomy

On the other hand, in terms of the dependency of the national economy the Brazilian state seems to have adopted a more independent posture than the Mexican state. A salient feature of the Mexican economy is the closeness of its links with the United States. Sixty per cent of foreign direct investment in Mexico is of United States origin, and 62 per cent of foreign trade is with the United States.[31] Clearly the proximity of the US and the long common border between the two countries goes some way to accounting for this (for instance, Mexican gas can easily be sold to the US, whereas the refrigeration and shipping of gas to Europe would be costly). The Brazilian state, on the other hand, seems to have pursued a policy of diversifying its foreign investments. In the early 1970s, 37 per cent of foreign direct investment came from the US and 48 per cent from Europe and Japan. Similarly, trade with the USA amounted to 29 per cent of Brazil's total foreign trade.[32]

One might speculate as to why the Mexican government has not done more to diversify the sources of its foreign direct investment. The reasons are not entirely clear. It is possible that pressure from the United States government may have played some role in preventing a more multilaterally orientated investment policy on the part of the Mexican government. The rationalization of the Mexican automobile industry may perhaps serve as an illustration. According to Bennett and Sharpe, the Mexican government had originally intended to allow a small number of automobile manufacturers to operate in Mexico. Direct pressure from the US and Japanese governments resulted in the Mexican government allowing a greater number of firms to set up than it had originally desired.[33]

This failure to diversify its economic links sharply distinguishes

Mexico from Brazil. It also suggests the need for a reassessment of Peter Evans' theory of the triple alliance as applied to Mexico. If the strength of the state derives in part from its ability to utilize inter-imperialist rivalry to pursue its own bargaining advantage, then on the basis of this theory one would expect the Mexican state to be relatively weak. Such a contention would, however, be extremely dubious. There are areas where the Mexican state is vulnerable to pressures from the US, but, *vis-à-vis* social classes within Mexico, the Mexican state is strong. It is also strong in the sense that there are few actual or potential challenges to political stability in contemporary Mexico.

The working class

Within the general context of these discussions, it is sometimes asserted that this new pattern of development based on multinational corporations and a powerful and autonomous state brings with it an increased repression of the industrial working class.[34] On the one hand, these authoritarian regimes often come to power in a crisis situation marked by high levels of working-class mobilization. An immediate task of such regimes is to remove the potential threat presented by working-class mobilization, usually through the direct repression of such movements. The military coup of 1964 in Brazil can easily be interpreted in this manner, though it is difficult to find any parallel in Mexico.[35] At the same time, it is argued, the logic of capital accumulation in this new phase requires a restructuring of the labour force. Wages have to be held down, labour mobility has to be increased and, in general, the working class has to be reshaped to fit the needs of international capital. This means policies of wage restraint or of actual drops in real hourly wage rates, and a weakening of worker control over the labour market. The aim is to enable productivity to increase faster than labour costs, so that more resources are available for capital accumulation.

A number of comments can be made. In the first place, it is by no means clear that there exists such a thing as a disembodied 'logic of capital' which provides a satisfactory causal explanation. What is involved is a conscious choice about the allocation of resources, in terms of their effects on welfare and on growth. This is hardly a new issue, and it is not confined to any particular state of development. A second comment concerns trends in real wages and earnings. At times the argument is elusive about whether real wage rates will actually decline, or whether they will merely rise more slowly than productivity. Although the difference between these two formulations in terms of rates of capital accumulation may not be particularly important, there are possibly quite substantially different implications in terms of political consequences. The argument hinges on the nature of workers' reference groups.

If real wage rates are falling, it might be reasonable to expect worker discontent.[36] Whether this was translated into industrial or political action would, of course, depend on a variety of other factors. But if real wage rates are rising, then there is no *a priori* reason to imagine that worker discontent is likely to develop. If workers make comparisons between their living situations and the rapid growth of affluence among the upper middle classes, then a scenario of rising frustration and anger is easily imaginable. But if, on the contrary, the effective comparisons that workers make are between their position now and their position at a previous time, or between their position and the situation of peers and/or rural communities of origin, then workers may well see themselves as being better off. If this is the case, then there may be no reason to expect workers to be dissatisfied.

For both Brazil and Mexico, there is considerable controversy over the facts of the matter. Most analysts agree that income distribution has worsened in both countries.[37] However, because growth rates have been high, it is quite likely that workers' real wages have increased during the post-war period. There seems to be widespread agreement that the incomes of skilled workers have risen. The controversy centres on the incomes of unskilled workers in the formal sector, and on the incomes of workers in the informal or marginal sector. Increasing infant mortality rates in the shanty-towns of São Paulo and Belo Horizonte suggest a decline in living standards for the poorer sections of the labour force in Brazil,[38] though there does not appear to be clear evidence of a similar trend in Mexico. The evidence with respect to unskilled workers in the formal sector is difficult to interpret. The incomes of this group are highly sensitive to government wage policies, and in both Brazil and Mexico there have been attempts by government to reduce wage settlements for unionized workers, which have tended to hit the unskilled sectors hardest.[39] Even so, the long-term trends suggest a secular improvement interspersed with cyclical falls.

The analysis is further complicated by the need to take account of individual job mobility. Even in a perfectly stable system, individuals can experience upward mobility through a career path as new cohorts enter at the lower rungs of the ladder, and as older cohorts leave the system. The expansion of the system, moreover, may also provide opportunities for further upward mobility. It should be stressed that we are talking about quite limited and short-distance mobility, between say, unskilled and semi-skilled. Nevertheless, limited though it may be, there is reason to suppose that such mobility is experienced as real and significant by the workers involved.

In the present state of empirical research, we simply do not know enough about workers' reference groups to make any firm statements in this area.[40] In any case, it is not likely that workers' subjective comparisons will have the kind of immediate and direct effects on political attitudes that are implied in the foregoing discussion. The links are likely to be considerably more complex. Further, the relationships between worker perceptions of relative incomes and industrial or political militancy are likely to be rather indirect.

It is often implied that this situation of declining real (absolute) or relative wages will generate worker discontent, leading to a greater potential for political or industrial militancy. This, in turn, requires some form of repression by the state, which has the exacerbating consequence of further eroding any legitimacy the regime might have. A vicious circle of repression-loss of legitimacy-militancy-repression is set up. The principal difficulty with this sort of theoretical formulation is that the links in the chain of reasoning are insufficiently specified. The causes of worker discontent and industrial militancy are highly variable. They cannot be directly 'read off' from trends in income distribution or real wages. One factor which needs to be considered is whether one response (on the part of companies and workers) to the slow growth or decline in wage rates has been an increase in the length of the working week. This might occur either through the increased use of overtime, or through an expansion in moonlighting. It may also intensify the pressures to increase the number of wage-earners in a household unit.

An increase in the hours worked by a household unit is likely to have a twofold effect. On the one hand, it will partially compensate for the low wage rate by increasing earnings. The political and attitudinal effects of this will depend on whether working-class households are concerned with absolute standards of living or whether they make comparisons with some previous time when the same standard of living could be earned with less effort. On the other hand, the increase in the number of hours worked is likely to exhaust the people involved. It may be hypothesized that this will lead to a decline in regular and routine political or industrial militancy, though it may also lead to an increased probability of explosive and 'spontaneous' outbursts of discontent. However, the usual caveat must be entered at this point: our understanding of the political processes in the working classes of Latin America is so underdeveloped that all lines of reasoning must necessarily be highly speculative and hypothetical.

The connections between the expansion of the multinational sector and the emergence or consolidation of authoritarian political forms is by no means clear-cut. The argument is premised on a number of unsubstantiated and rather dubious propositions about the likely response of the industrial labour force to changes in income distribution and/or changes in real wage rates. A somewhat different, but equally suspect, argument links the expansion of the multinationals with employment trends. Popularized by Anibal Quijano and José Nun, this line of argument claims to detect a structural dualism within Latin American industry, between the dynamic multinational sector and the 'marginal' sector.[41] This marginal sector of the economy contains nationally owned industries aimed at the low-income consumer market (textiles, food-stuffs, and so on) and artesanal industries. The capital-intensive nature of multinational investment means that employment creation is slow, probably slower than the rate of growth of the labour force. The net effect is to increase unemployment and under-employment in the economy as a whole. In the first place, it is by no means entirely clear that employment creation by multinationals is particularly slow.[42] Second, the relationship between employment and militancy is very complex. Quite what the effects are of this dualistic structure on labour militancy, and hence on the authoritarian characteristics of the regime, is not entirely clear.

In sum, it is difficult to make out a clear case to the effect that the increasing role of multinational corporations in either Brazil or Mexico (or any other Latin American country, for that matter) has any deter-minate effect on working-class politics, and through this, on the author-itarian nature of the state. This is not to say that the industrial working class is of no importance in the political life of these countries. On the contrary, in both Brazil and Mexico, organized labour is a crucial political actor. But the importance of the working class in politics derives from the industrial expansion of Brazil and Mexico in the period since the 1930s. Although multinational corporations have played a key role in the recent economic growth of both countries, there is no reason to suppose that workers employed in the multinationals will behave any differently from workers employed elsewhere. This is not the place to outline a possible sociology of the working class; nevertheless, it is clear that such a study would probably, in the present period, relegate the distinction between foreign and domestic capital to a subsidiary role in the explanation of worker behaviour.[43]

The authoritarian features in both Brazil and Mexico cannot be denied. To some extent they follow from the situation of economic backwardness which these countries confront. (At the same time, the extent to which authoritarian tendencies are present in all capitalist economies ought also to be born in mind.) But it does not thereby follow that these authoritarian features derive exclusively from the multinational-based model of economic development, nor that these political systems do not also experience pressures moving them *away* from authoritarianism and towards more open and democratic forms of politics. Signs of this are the *reforma política* in Mexico and the continuing struggle over electoral politics in Brazil.[44]

Moreover, just as the emphasis on the authoritarian features of Mexico and Brazil has drawn attention away from the democratizing pressures in those countries, so also has the attention paid to the inequalities inherent in the economic model had the effect of diverting attention away from the sheer fact of economic growth. The implications of several decades of sustained growth of GNP of between 5 and 9 per cent per annum are profound. Even after discounting for population growth rates of 3–3.5 per cent per annum, these figures are still very impressive. One of the more unfortunate heritages of certain strands of dependency theory has been an exaggerated emphasis on the *underdeveloped*, as opposed to the *capitalist*, nature of these economies. While there are undoubted (and for some countries, severe) problems associated with various aspects of the dependent and underdeveloped situation, it is by no means true that these problems are always insoluble. In the long run, as Bill Warren has argued, the Marxist prediction that the spread of imperialism would lead to the development of capitalism in the rest of the world may not be entirely implausible.[45] At any rate, there can be little doubt that the rapid industrial growth of Brazil and Mexico is producing a major transformation of the class structures of these countries.

Although the rates of new job creation have not been as rapid as planners and critics might wish, it nevertheless remains a fact that the industrial working classes of Brazil and Mexico have grown dramatically in size in the last decades. In 1950, out of a total workforce of some 17 million in Brazil, 2.4 million (14.2 per cent) were industrial workers. By 1976 the total workforce had risen to just over 40 million, and the industrial workers to 9.3 million (23.2 per cent). In Mexico over the same period, the total workforce increased from 8.3 million to 17 million and the number of industrial workers from 1.3 million to 4.2 million. This was a move from a situation where industrial workers comprised 16 per cent of the total labour force to one where they comprised 24.8 per cent.[46] And although the domestic bourgeoisie in both countries may not be as dynamic as planners and critics might hope, this class has also grown *pari passu* with economic expansion. The result is that the industrial classes have a greater weight in the social formation than previously. The question of what this means in terms of the nature of the state, and the possible implications for politics, remains an open one. Of course, there will still be enormous problems. Although population growth rates in both Brazil and Mexico appear to be dropping, it will be many years before a stable population size will be reached. If, and when, a steady state is reached, the total population is likely to be very large. Merrick and Graham, for example, estimate that Brazil's stable population might be between 300 million and 600 million, compared to a 1976 population of 110 million.[47]

Meanwhile, there remains the question of the capacity of the economies of these countries to generate sufficient employment, and hence the long-term perspectives of growth and income distribution. At the time of writing, both economies were experiencing severe recessions and high rates of inflation, and had experienced difficulties in managing their foreign debt. Although both countries have overcome similar recessions in the past, there is nothing automatic about economic growth. All that can be said is that if growth is resumed at previous rates, there is little reason to assume that employment creation will be a greater problem than it has been in the past, or that it will be dealt with any less successfully. If Mexico and Brazil continue their secular pattern of economic growth, there is every reason to expect the industrial working class to increase in size. It is likely to flex its muscles in wage bargaining in pursuit of limited gains. If regular wage increases are not forthcoming (perhaps because of anti-inflationary incomes policies), there exists the real possibility of a politically destabilizing rise in worker militancy. On the other hand, if the secular pattern of industrial development is not resumed, then we may expect a greater degree of dualism and marginality in the occupational structure.

Civil society

In Mexico, some analysts have suggested that this growth of the forces of 'civil society' heralds the demise of the autonomous and authoritarian state.[48] In this revised version of the Whig theory of history, dressed up in Gramscian terminology, the growth of civil society inevitably puts fetters on the state. The belief is that, as various classes and social forces develop, they will increasingly become autonomous from, and independent of, the state. The upshot will be the development of institutions such that many activities are no longer directly regulated by the state. In this sense, civil society refers to those aspects of the social whole which have a genuine existence independent of the state. As civil society grows, the sphere of state control diminishes. Such an outcome is indeed possible, but it only becomes inevitable if one hypothesizes an automatic negative correlation between the strength of the state and the development of civil society. Clearly, the matter is more complicated. The strength of civil society does not preclude the existence of a strong state. This said, the emphasis on civil society alerts us to the importance of an examination of the changing class structure. Such a perspective is, by and large, missing from the majority of works employing one or other variant of the 'bureaucratic-authoritarian' model.

In particular, it has been suggested that the relationship between the industrial bourgeoisie and the state might be closer than is often assumed. There might be grounds for supposing, in the case of Mexico, that the domestic bourgeoisie is attempting to take over the state apparatus, particularly in the key economic ministries. In the case of Brazil, one possible way of construing the available evidence is to emphasize the degree to which the corporatist structures of the regime have been used by the Brazilian bourgeoisie to effectively influence government policy. Given the present state of empirical knowledge, the question must remain an open one.

Similar considerations apply to the analysis of the industrial working class. It seems clear that wage policy has assumed an increasingly salient role in economic policy-making in recent years in both Brazil and Mexico. Although this is in part due to the need for stabilization programmes to deal with acute foreign debt problems, the concern with incomes policy is also a product of the size of the industrial labour force. Once again, the similarities with the political and economic problems faced by advanced industrial societies stand our.[49] 'Corporatism' may perhaps be a useful analytic category for the analysis of Mexican and Brazilian society, but it is not something which *differentiates* those societies from the societies of 'the First World', bureaucratic-authoritarian theory notwithstanding.

Clearly, the formulation of the 'bureaucratic-authoritarian' model by O'Donnell and others was an important advance in conceptualization, since it claimed to link the economic effects of development based on multinational corporations with increasing income inequalities, and hence with growing popular discontent and a repressive response on the part of the state. The upshot was, according to this line of reasoning, the emergence of a state which was increasingly authoritarian and autonomous. The notions that the economies of Brazil and Mexico could usefully be described as 'state capitalist', and that there existed a stratum of 'state managers' mediating a compromise between local and multinational capital, gave added impetus to this stress on the autonomy of the state.

Attractive though this line of argument may seem, the assumptions on which it is based are, as this chapter has attempted to show, dubious; the intermediate steps in the argument are unclear, the empirical evidence is ambiguous, and the central notion – autonomy – is more problematic than is often assumed.

Notes

[1] The bureaucratic-authoritarian model is extensively discussed in D. Collier (ed.) *The new authoritarianism in Latin America* (Princeton 1979).

[2] N. Hamilton 'The state and class conflict: Mexico during the Cárdenas period' in M. Zeitlin (ed.) *Classes, class conflict and the state* (Cambridge, Mass. 1980); P. Flynn *Brazil* (London 1978); A. Stepan (ed.) *Authoritarian Brazil* (New Haven 1973); J. Malloy (ed.) *Authoritarianism and corporatism in Latin America* (London 1977).

[3] Some of these pressures, particularly the phenomenon of capital flight, are discussed in G. Gereffi and P. Evans 'Transnational corporations, dependent development and state policy in the semi-periphery: a comparison of Brazil and Mexico' *Latin American Research Review* xvi 3 (1981). See also J. M. Connor *The market power of multinationals* (New York 1977); Rh. O. Jenkins *Dependent industrialization in Latin America* (New York, 1977).

⁴ My usage of the terms 'internal' and 'external' autonomy is somewhat similar to the distinction made by N. Hamilton between 'instrumental' and 'structural' autonomy, although her usage of 'structural autonomy' is much wider than my notion of 'external autonomy'. N. Hamilton 'State autonomy and dependent capitalism in Latin America' *British Journal of Sociology* xxxii 3 (1981).

⁵ There is a lively debate about the interpretation of the Mexican Revolution and its relationship with subsequent regimes. Useful introductions to the Marxist debate are: A. Gilly *et al. Interpretaciones de la Revolución Mexicana* (Mexico 1979); D. Hodges and R. Gandy *Mexico 1910–1976* (London 1979). A rather different perspective is presented in J. Meyer *La Revolución Mexicana* (Barcelona 1973). A wide-ranging overview of the debate is provided by O. Bayoumi 'State, society and development: theoretical considerations and a Mexican case study focusing on the current political reform', unpubl. Ph.D., London School of Economics 1981.

⁶ P. Smith *Labyrinths of power* (Princeton 1979); S. Kaufman Purcell and J. Purcell 'State and society in Mexico' *World Politics* xxxii 2 (1980).

⁷ A similar analysis for Brazil is contained in J. Foweraker *The struggle for land* (Cambridge 1981).

⁸ M. Cerruti 'Patricio Milmo: empresario regiomontano del siglo XIX' in C. F. S. Cardoso (ed.) *Formación y desarrollo de la burguesía en México* (Mexico 1978).

⁹ W. Dean *The industrialization of São Paulo, 1880–1945* (Austin 1969).

¹⁰ On the Monterrey group see, *inter alia*, M. Vellinga *Economic development and the dynamics of class* (Assen 1979); J. M. Fragoso *et. al. El Poder de la Gran Burguesía* (Mexico 1979); S. Cordero 'Concentración industrial y poder económico en México' *Cuadernos del CES* no. 8 (1977); S. Cordero and R. Santin 'Los grupos industriales' *Cuadernos del CES* no. 23 (1977). More general studies are C. Arriola *Los empresarios y el estado* (Mexico 1981); F. Derossi *El empresario mexicano* (Mexico 1977).

¹¹ On the Monterrey unions see M. Vellinga *op. cit.*; J. Rojas 'Los sindicatos blancos de Monterrey' *Memorias del Encuentro Sobre Historia del Movimiento Obrero* iii (1980).

¹² *Financial Times* 4 Aug. 1982.

¹³ The nature of the oligarchical republic is discussed in, *inter alia*, R. Faoro *Os donos do poder* 2 vols (Porto Alegre 1979, 1st edn 1957); A. Villela and W. Suzigan 'Government policy and the economic growth of Brazil' *Brazilian Economic Studies* no. 3 (1977). On the relationship between the industrial bourgeoisie and the state, see E. Diniz *Empresario, estado e capitalismo no Brasil* (Rio de Janeiro 1978); E. Diniz and R. Boschi *Empresariado nacional e estado no Brasil* (Rio de Janeiro 1978).

¹⁴ P. Schmitter *Interest, conflict and political change in Brazil* (Stanford 1971).

¹⁵ P. Evans *Dependent Development* (Princeton 1979).

¹⁶ *Ibid.* pp. 82–3.

¹⁷ *Ibid.* p. 112.

¹⁸ *Ibid.* p. 202.

¹⁹ R. Newfarmer *Transnational conglomerates and the economics of dependent development* (Greenwich, Conn. 1980).

²⁰ *Ibid.* p. 306.

²¹ J. Carrion and A. Aguilar *La burguesía, la oligarquía y el estado* (Mexico 1972); Fragoso *op. cit.*

²² F. H. Cardoso *Estado y sociedad en América Latina* (Buenos Aires 1973).

²³ W. Baer *et al.* 'The changing role of the state in the Brazilian economy' *World Development* i 11 (1973).

²⁴ W. Baer *et al.* 'On state capitalism in Brazil: some new issues and questions' *Inter-American Economic Affairs* xxx 3 (1976).

²⁵ Smith *op. cit.*; P. McDonough *Power and ideology in Brazil* (Princeton 1981). The thesis that the industrial bourgeoisie directly controls major offices in the state has been presented by R. Dreifuss *1964: A conquista do estado* (Petropolis 1981). A considerable body

of evidence is presented in this work; my assessment, however, is that the evidence does not support Dreifuss' conclusions.

26 L. Althusser *For Marx* (London 1968).

27 D. Bennett and K. Sharpe 'Agenda-setting and bargaining power: the Mexican state *versus* multinational automobile corporations' *World Politics* xxxii 1 (1979).

28 See S. Kaufman Purcell *The Mexican profit-sharing decision* (Berkeley 1975) for an interesting analysis of this type.

29 F. Block 'Beyond relative autonomy: state managers as historical subjects' in R. Milliband and J. Saville (eds) *The Socialist Register 1980* (London 1980).

30 See, for example, R. Fagen and W. Tuohy *Politics and privilege in a Mexican city* (Stanford 1972).

31 R. Newfarmer and W. Mueller *Multinational corporations in Brazil and Mexico.* Report to Subcommittee on Multinational Corporations, Committee on Foreign Relations, US Senate (Washington, US Govt. Printing Office, 1975) pp. 49 and 51; Nafinsa *La economía mexicana en cifras* (Mexico 1978) p 394.

32 Evans *op. cit.* pp. 69 and 82.

33 Bennett and Sharpe *op. cit.*; D. Bennett *et al.* 'Mexico and multinational corporations', J. Grunwald (ed.) *Latin America and the world economy* (London 1978).

34 G. O'Donnell *Modernization and bureaucratic-authoritarianism* (Berkeley 1973); D. Collier (ed.) *The new authoritarianism in Latin America* (Princeton 1979). For similar arguments vis-à-vis the peasantry, see J. Foweraker 'The contemporary peasantry' in H. Newby (ed.) *International perspectives in rural sociology* (Chichester 1978); B. Loveman *Struggle in the countryside* (Bloomington 1976).

35 On Brazil, see T. Skidmore *Politics in Brazil* (New York 1967); T. Harding 'The political history of organized labor in Brazil' unpubl. Ph.D., Stanford 1973; K. Erickson *The Brazilian corporative state and working-class politics* (Berkeley 1977); H. Fuchtner *Os sindicatos brasileiros: organização política* (Rio de Janeiro, 1980). There is no direct Mexican analogy to the 1964 military coup. In many respects, however, it could be argued that the Mexican government's response to working-class mobilization in 1948 and in 1959 was fundamentally similar. On these events, see O. Pellicer and J. L. Reyna *Historia de la Revolución Mexicana* vol. 22 (Mexico 1978); Luis Medina *Historia de la Revolución Mexicana* vol. 20 (Mexico 1979); V. Campa *Mi Testimonio* (Mexico 1978); A. Loyo *El movimiento magisterial de 1958 en México* (Mexico 1979); A. Alonso *El movimiento ferrocarrilero en México* (Mexico 1972); E. P. Stevens *Protest and response in Mexico* (Cambridge, Mass. 1974); Instituto de Investigaciones Sociales del UNAM 'El golpe al movimiento ferrocarrilero de 1948' in *Memorias del Encuentro Sobre Historia del Movimiento Obrero* (Puebla 1980); B. Hernández 'Del pacto de sindicatos industriales a la represión' in CEHSMO *Segundo coloquio regional de historia obrera* vol. 2 (1979); J. L. Reyna and R. Trejo *La clase obrera en la historia de México* vol. 12 (Mexico 1981).

36There has been considerable discussion, both in Mexico and in Brazil, about trends in real wages. For arguments that suggest a secular *rise* in real wages in both countries, see J. Wells 'Underconsumption, market size and expenditure patterns in Brazil' *Bulletin of the Society for Latin American Studies* no. 26 (1976); J. Bortz 'El salario obrero en el distrito federal, 1939–75' *Investigación Económica* no. 4 (1977). Since this is however, a highly controversial matter, I have couched my discussion in terms which are applicable to situations of either declining or increasing real wages.

37 G. Fields *Poverty, inequality and development* (Cambridge 1980); L. Taylor *et al. Models of growth and distribution for Brazil* (New York 1980); R. Tolipan and A. Tinelli *A contrôversia sobre distribuição de renda e desenvolvimento* (Rio de Janeiro 1978); T. Merrick and D. Graham *Population and economic development in Brazil* (Baltimore 1979); I. de Navarrete 'La distribución del ingreso en México' in *El pérfil de México en 1980* (Mexico 1970); Pontificia Comissão de Justica e Paz da Arquidiocese de São Paulo *São Paulo 1975* (São Paulo 1976); K. Schaefer *São Paulo: desarrollo urbano y empleo* (Geneva 1976).

[38] Merrick and Graham *op. cit.*; Taylor *et al. op. cit.*

[39] On government incomes policies see Taylor *et al. op. cit.*; J. Schlagheck *The political, economic and labor climate in Brazil*, Wharton Multinational Industrial Relations Series (Philadelphia 1977); J. Schlagheck *The political, economic and labor climate in Mexico*, Wharton Multinational Industrial Relations Series (Philadelphia 1980); C. Zazueta *et al.* 'Salarios contractuales y salarios mínimos en Mexico 1979–1981', mimeo, Secretaria de Trabajo y Previsión Social, México 1982.

[40] On social mobility see J. Pastore *Desigualdade e movilidade social no Brasil* (São Paulo 1979); J. Balán *et al. Men in a developing society* (Austin 1973); E. Contreras *Estratificación y movilidad social en la ciudad de México* (Mexico 1978).

[41] A. Quijano 'The marginal pole of the economy and the marginalized labour force' *Economy and Society* III 4 (1974); J. Nun 'Sobrepoblación relativa, ejército industrial de reserva y masa marginal' *Revista Latinoamericana de Sociología* IV 2 (1969).

[42] See, for example, O. Muñoz 'Industrialization, migration and entry labor force changes in Mexico City', Ph.D. University of Texas at Austin 1975; H. Muñoz *et al. Migración y desigualdad social en la ciudad de México* (Mexico 1977) for a less pessimistic analysis of employment generation. I should repeat, however, that as with the debate over wages and their possible political effects, my concern here is to clarify the logic of the argument and point out that there is by no means complete agreement on the empirical facts.

[43] The interested reader is referred to I. Roxborough 'The analysis of labour movements in Latin America' *Bulletin of Latin American Research* I 1 (1981); T. Skidmore 'Workers and soldiers: urban labor movements and elite responses in twentieth-century Latin America' in V. Bernhard (ed.) *Elites, masses and modernization in Latin America* (Austin 1979).

[44] McDonough *op. cit.*; O. Bayoumi *op. cit.*; H. Handelman and T. Sanders (eds) *Military government and the movement toward democracy in South America* (Bloomington 1981).

[45] B. Warren *Imperialism: pioneer of capitalism* (London 1980).

[46] IBGE *Anuario estadístico do Brasil* (Rio de Janeiro 1978); Nafinsa *La economía mexicana en cifras* (Mexico 1978).

[47] Merrick and Graham *op. cit.* p. 299.

[48] S. Zermeno *Una democracia utópica* (Mexico 1978).

[49] It is now a received orthodoxy that labour movements in Latin America differ from their European predecessors in being more political. Because of their supposed weakness in economic bargaining, they must be orientated toward the state to achieve their ends. This predisposes them to incorporation in a variety of corporatist structures. See L. Martins Rodrigues *Trabalhadores, sindicatos e industrialização* (São Paulo 1974); J. Payne *Labor and politics in Peru* (New Haven 1965); R. Katzman and J. L. Reyna (eds, *Fuerza de trabajo y movimientos laborales en América Latina* (Mexico 1979); L. Werneck Vianna *Liberalismo e sindicato no Brasil* (Rio de Janeiro 1978); J. F. Leal *México: estado, burocracia y sindicatos* (Mexico 1975). It is by no means clear, however, that this distinction is tenable; see I. Roxborough *op. cit.*

24

FOREIGN FINANCE AND CAPITAL ACCUMULATION IN LATIN AMERICA: A CRITICAL APPROACH

E. V. K. FitzGerald

Introduction

In contrast to their experience of the World Depression, the Latin American economies have maintained their respective rates of accumulation since the mid-1960s, despite the crisis at the centre of the world capitalist economy. Nonetheless, this continued growth has been accompanied by worsening trade deficits and mounting external indebtedness, highlighting the international financial relationships of the region, which have been increasingly dominated by public sector borrowing from multinational banks. The interpretation of these developments has given rise to considerable debate,[1] but it is the contention of this chapter that the relationship between foreign finance and capital accumulation on the periphery is misunderstood in that debate.

This misunderstanding arises in part from the remarkable diversity in the response of Latin American economies to changes in the world economy, in terms of both timing and form – a diversity which is clearly related not only to the objective place of each economy in the international division of labour but also to developments within the political economy itself. Our understanding of the significance of this external finance is also hampered by lack of clarity as to the role of such funds in Latin American accumulation, and the role of the state in that process. This chapter is addressed primarily to the latter question. It would appear that there are three areas of opacity – shared, incidentally by writers of both radical and conservative persuasion. First, whether savings (or 'surplus') are an *ex ante* constraint on investment in Latin America, and thus whether foreign finance can lift this constraint, albeit only temporarily. Second, whether the state has a purely instrumental role in the financing problems, responding to the requirements of the economy in some general sense, or whether its actions respond to its own 'fiscal crises'. Third, the nature of the connection between international finance and the rise of finance-capital groups to dominant positions in Latin America.

It should be stressed, however, that despite the torrent of literature on external finance in recent years, our understanding of its connection with the fundamental questions of political economy – capital accumulation and the distribution of income between classes – is still very rudimentary. In particular, the study of economic imperialism in terms of the international division of labour still needs to be extended, beyond the production and exchange of commodities, to the organization of money capital as such, in which the nation-state plays an essential role.

External finance and accumulation in Latin America

The scale of the phenomenon is clear enough: the overall external indebtedness of the main economies of the area rose from US $3.3 billions in 1955 to $7.8 billions in 1963, to $12.9 billions in 1970 and reached $74.0 billions in 1978; this debt represented, on average, 14.0 per cent of GDP in 1970 and 24.5 per cent in 1978; the average servicing of this debt rose from 16.8 per cent of exports in 1970 to 32.3 per cent in 1978.[2]

The *ex ante* relationship between net external finance and the trade gap (which are necessarily identical *ex post*, allowing for reserve variations) can be seen as involving causality in either direction. The orthodox view from the centre[3] is still that of the two-gap model where the trade gap, despite the oil problem, is fundamentally the result of domestic macro-economic imbalances (particularly fiscal deficits) where investment is higher than savings, and of a failure to adjust adequately to the changing international division of labour by abandoning 'inefficient' import subsitution and stimulating new export lines. The fortuitous availability of international finance is initially helpful, but subsequently serves only to permit a postponement of inevitable adjustment and exacerbate the problem. In contrast, the orthodox view from Latin America[4] is that the trade gap itself is the result of the turning of the terms of trade against the periphery by the centre, in order to restore its profit margin and pass on the cost of higher oil prices. The compensating finance is then seen as an additional form of exploitation within unequal exchange. As might be expected, there are monetarists who support the former view of 'financial incontinence' in a more extreme form,[5] and there are radicals[6] who stress a 'new financial dependency' as complementing and reinforcing the stranglehold of multinational corporations. However, it is interesting to note that Marxist writers tend to accept the direction of causality of the latter view; those of the world-economy school also stress the failure of Latin American bourgeoisies to adjust to the new international division of labour.[7] Scholars working on accumulation and the class struggle in Latin America[8] focus upon the internal contradictions of Latin American capitalism in determining the form of external indebtedness.

The empirical testing of these two propositions *ex post* raises serious methodological difficulties, not only because of the determination of a functional form for the separation of the trade, price and finance flows. Even if we separate out the terms of trade effect from the volumes of imports and exports, and determine the statistical contribution of each to the increased deficits, the results will not be very illuminating.[9] There is more to the problem than that trade gap 'causes' indebtedness or vice versa, although it is clear that the larger economies such as Brazil and Mexico have much greater freedom of access to international money markets than the smaller ones, whose imports are to some extent conditioned by prior availability of credit. The difficulties lie deeper.

The accumulation of capital requires the mobilization of the surplus, and thus a particular distribution of income between capital, labour and state. To achieve the realization of the surplus, bank finance is necessary in order to assure the firm control of current resources required for production. Traditionally, however, following the classical assumption in Smith and Ricardo, it has been taken as more or less axiomatic by both Marxists and non-Marxists that the availability of surplus (or profits) is a prior constraint on investment from the funding side: that, quite apart from the obvious requirement of *expected* profitability to induce investment (in the private sector, at least), the present rate of profit limits the rate of investment. For monetarists,[10] savers are distinct from investors, their savings are a stable function of income and thus dependent on income distribution.[11] For a classical Marxist, the availability of profits (arising from productivity and wage rates) determines the capacity to invest – although the role of financial intermediation is not as explicit as in the monetarist view. Amin takes the orthodox Marxist view to an extreme by suggesting that the rates of accumulation are low on the periphery as a result of a drain of surplus through unequal exchange and profit repatriation.[12] The implication of this essentially classical prior-savings approach is that banks centralize investment funds (as finance capital in the Marxist view[13] or as financial intermediaries in the monetarist one[14]) in general, and that foreign finance can relax the savings constraint in particular.

The problem with this approach is twofold. First, there is evidence that large firms that dominate production and accumulation at both centre and periphery are largely *self-financed* out of profits retained from their capital investment (that is, fixed assets), funds which are generated by monopolistic pricing practices,[15] limited to some extent by competition between firms. They act thus in order to retain corporate control of their activities, and for any one large firm or branch it is much easier to raise prices to maintain profits than to act on money wages directly. Clearly we are thinking of private manufacturing industry here. Neither small-scale competitive sectors (peasants, artisans) nor national primary commodities exporters have this power; but it is interesting to note that in both these cases the state is commonly entrusted with guaranteeing profitability by manipulating the internal terms of trade or managing the exchange rate. Multinationals engaging in intra-firm trade can largely determine their own profit margins, the location of which depends on transfer pricing practices. Similarly, state enterprise profits (except in exports) depend largely on government pricing policies. Second, the management of macro-economic policy by the state allows income distribution to be brought in line with the accumulation model, both by support of the real wage determination process (prices and supply of wage goods) and the expansion of markets for goods produced at a given profit mark-up.[16]

The role of bank finance is related to the provision of funds for circulation (working capital) rather than investment, and to the implementation of state credit policy. In Latin America personal and functional income distributions are so skewed[17] that it is implausible to claim that profits are a funding constraint upon investment. Limits upon accumulation must be sought in anticipated profitability (particularly market size and political uncertainty) or the supply of inputs (especially infrastructure and foreign exchange). Given a profit margin as a mark-up on sales, the expected profitability of investment will depend on the anticipated size of the market and the assessment of risk (both market and political) involved. We shall not discuss political risk here, although the general activities of the state in underwriting socio-economic stability are clearly crucial. The size of the market is the realization problem identified by the ECLA school,[18] although its original 'underconsumptionist' form[19] – where the personal income distribution was taken as given and the respective propensities to consume goods (particularly consumer durables) defined the market size and thus the constraint on accumulation – was unrealistic because it neglected the role of credit[20] in permitting market expansion.

The importance of retained profits as a source of investment finance is reflected in the dominance of corporate over household savings at the aggregate level.[21] Most of these savings are related to family housing, and thus have a special circuit, separate from productive accumulation.[22] The financial savings of capitalist households in the form of real estate and bank deposits do not necessarily translate into real savings for the economy as a whole.

Accumulation in Latin America is assisted by strong state support on the input side. Apart from institutions for organizing labour which vary widely between countries, there are common features.[23] The first is heavy investment in the infrastructure required to make private investment possible at all, a responsibility that now includes irrigation, energy, industrial inputs and telecommunications, as well as transport. This responsibility is due mainly to the scale of investments required, but also to the fact that prices can be set to reduce the profitability of the state sector and thus increase that of the private sector. The second common feature is increased expenditure on welfare provision, primarily for the workforce in the capitalist sector, which is in part a matter of reducing real wage costs to the capitalist, but it also responds to real gains by organized labour, and thus comes under considerable attack from business sectors and international financial institutions. The third is the expansion of state banks as a source of subsidized long-term finance, not only for state enterprises but also for strategic private firms and small enterprise. Funding for state banks comes principally from taxation which falls mainly on consumption, thus further depressing the share of wages in national income. The fact that public sector savings (that is, access to the surplus) in Latin America are generally lower than the public investment burden does not constitute a constraint, because the state can issue money in various forms in order to gain control over resources.

The effect of public deficits on the accumulation balance of semi-industrialized economies is a matter of some debate. Their inflationary effect is widely accepted – the disagreement between monetarists and structuralists is essentially over the cause of those deficits[24] – the problem being to determine where the surplus acquired by the state in this manner originates. This depends to a great extent on wages policy, for if the rate of wage increases is held below the rate of productivity growth, the effect is to increase total surplus and leave the private portion intact if not increased. The traditional monetarist view,[25] however, is that 'crowding out' takes place, where the state competes with capitalists for the available savings and thus higher public deficits lead to lower private investment. This view is unconvincing when the self-financing of firms is taken into account. Domestic 'crowding out' can plausibly occur only when tight overall credit limits are imposed (hardly a common Latin American phenomenon);[26] even then the effect would mostly be on trade (that is, consumption) credits – affecting investment through demand rather than finance. It is interesting to note that the orthodox monetarist position, as expressed in the 'monetary approach to the balance of payments', asserts that public sector deficits are reflected in the balance of payments, implying that private investment is not affected.[27]

Thus we return to the crucial interaction between domestic and foreign money. The surplus, large though it may be, cannot be fully used without conversion into foreign exchange. Directly or indirectly, both capitalist consumption and investment require foreign exchange in Latin America. Although access to foreign exchange becomes progressively less difficult as import-substitution advances and the diversification of exports allows surplus commodities to be exported more easily, the foreign exchange constraint remains – as ECLA pointed out three decades ago – the dominant restriction on continued accumulation in Latin America.[28] The problem is that foreign money cannot be generated by the state or local banks, but only by borrowing against, in effect, future exports.[29] Direct foreign investment, insofar as it involves an initial financial inflow, can be seen in the same way.

Foreign finance, therefore, permits a higher rate of surplus realization, and thus more production, investment or consumption. Despite the obvious point that loans, even if nominally related to fixed investment, are essentially 'fungible' (that is, they may merely permit existing funds to be used for other purchases), the orthodox viewpoint[30] had traditionally been that they raise the rate of investment and are thus justifiable on the grounds that they can be repaid by production and exports expanding more than the corresponding servicing costs. Despite the growing tendency in practice to describe this finance as 'balance of payments loans' and to suggest that they be used to smooth a transition to a more outward-orientated economy, the savings supplementation approach is still upheld, particularly in order to justify long-term public borrowing.

The evidence derived from the testing of 'two-gap' models in both Latin America and the periphery seems to indicate that the effect of 'external savings' on investment is not very large, the main outcome being to *reduce* domestic savings.[31] Our argument so far seems to resolve this conundrum: loans to the banking system permit greater trade credit and consumption (and thus less savings, or at least a lower savings rate), loans to state enterprises reduce the borrowing requirement (with a similar effect), while loans to the treasury reduce domestic borrowing once again, or else avoid the need to raise consumption taxes still further. This last point – the gist of Kalecki's argument – is the clue to the whole issue: the inability of the state to command sufficient control over consumption from profits and consequent misuse of foreign exchange is the real reason for recourse to external borrowing. Finally, even if it is true that the Latin American economies must import a large and crucial part of capital goods requirements, it nevertheless represents a small part of total imports.[32] In other words, foreign exchange is mainly required to sustain consumption – particularly that of the middle and upper classes – and not for fixed investment as such, although accumulation does depend to a large extent upon the expansion of consumer demand.

Finance capital in Latin America

One of the most striking features of the long post-war boom was the strengthening of transnational banking as a support to the internationalization of production. At the onset of the world recession, the role of the transnational banks grew as they recycled OPEC surpluses and the supply of dollars arising from the US fiscal deficits. At the same time, attempts by metropolitan governments to stabilize the economies and restore the rate of profit and accumulation on the basis of real wage restraint, involved the use of monetary policy to restrict consumption credit and attempts to restore the terms of trade of manufactures as against raw materials. At a world macro-economic level, therefore, there emerged from the mid-1960s onwards an increased supply of bank funds at the same time as the metropolitan demand for them declined, forcing the transnational banks outwards towards the periphery – and particularly towards the semi-industrialized countries offering a reasonable 'sovereign risk' – in search of business. This seems to be a substantially different phenomenon from the close association between transnational banks and multinational manufacturing companies in the post-war decades, and the traditional concern of the banks with the finance of international trade.[33] Unfortunately, the expansion of banks has not yet been studied as closely as that of multinationals engaged in material production. It is clear that the driving force behind the expansion of banking activity is not labour costs but the search for secure markets.

The integration of the Latin American economies into the world economy during the long boom was based on continued primary export production accompanied by rapid import-substitution in which multinational corporations were closely involved. It is also clear that this model of accumulation had, by the end of the 1960s, run into difficulties: to some extent from a lack of sufficiently large and dynamic domestic market, but primarily because of the familiar foreign exchange constraint on accumulation, combined with rising popular pressure on wages and welfare expenditure generated by the very process of industrialization. Adjustment to these problems would have been necessary even if the metropolitan economies had not entered recession; in fact growth in output and investment in Latin America was not nearly so much affected as at the centre, and much less so than in the World Depression.[34]

The policy response in the six major economies differed widely. Colombia undertook an extensive restructuring of capital in the late 1960s, involving real wage and welfare decline on the one hand, and attempts to liberalize imports and promote light manufactured exports from excess capacity on the other. Subsequent success in maintaining growth has been aided by strong agricultural exports, ranging from coffee to narcotics. Peru, by contrast, attempted at the same time a restructuring based on state investment in mineral exports and heavy industry on the one hand, and cooptation of labour through populist reforms on the other. This did not prove viable, largely because of a failure to gain fiscal access to profits and a deterioration in the terms of trade. Although an attempt was made to follow the Colombian model by cutting real wages under pressure from the international financial system, popular protest has successfully resisted the dismantling of the reforms, so that by the late 1970s a revival of accumulation again depended on mineral exports.

Both Chile and Argentina attempted – in the Chilean case more coherently but no more successfully – fundamental changes in social organization as a form of restructuring in the early 1970s. The restoration of a capitalist accumulation model required, *mutatis mutandis*, more drastic cuts of wages and welfare expenditure than in Colombia, plus the repression of organized labour. In addition, liberalization programmes in the form of cuts in tariffs, divestment of state enterprise, and monetarist demand management policies were imposed. In essence, however, the 'new' models of accumulation constitute a return to a strategy of reliance upon primary exports, in which consumer demand and imports are restricted to the requirements of the upper income strata, and industrialization is abandoned as a policy objective.

In contrast, Brazil and Mexico continued to pursue their industrialization policies, keeping constraints on wages, maintaining high rates of state investment and industrial protection, and developing exports from established manufacturing branches based on import substitution that were sustained by large domestic markets fed by consumer credit. Despite recurrent balance of payments difficulties, both Brazil and Mexico, by virtue of their size, stability and potential, could count on continued international creditworthiness, and by the end of the 1970s had accumulated between them over half of all Third World private bank debt. Such are the ironies of banking that this debt has made them preferred borrowers.

However, despite these marked differences, it is frequently suggested that 'finance capital' has become central to the Latin American accumulation model. In part, this observation is suggested by the activities of multinational banks which lend to governments and then attempt to influence state economic strategy in order to recover their loans – a tactic which has not met with much success.[35] It is also argued that financial groups become dominant in the Latin American economies in the 1970s, and forced through liberalization and stabilization policies contrary to the interests of both wage-workers and domestic industrialists.[36] It is not clear how this occurred. The inference may be drawn that the international crisis strengthened the hand of dominant groups: stabilization policies were implemented and foreign banks were able to support their peripheral colleagues. From this speculation it may be deduced that monetarist policies were somehow more quintessentially reactionary in underdeveloped countries and thus necessary for the erosion of wages, which favoured bankers.

The growth of the international banks has increasingly placed them beyond the control of national governments, while the inter-statal regulatory institutions like the IMF and the Bank for International

Settlements (BIS) have established few, if any, of the regulatory functions over private banks normal in a central bank.[37] However, the banks are not prevented from appealing to the extra-economic diplomatic power of their home governments or to intergovernmental organizations to recover their debts. It seems that not only are such banks transnationalized to a greater degree than even manufacturing corporations, but the multinational financial capital is broadly independent of firms in productive sectors. This implies that although transnational banks may own stock in many productive firms, they cannot be regarded as 'finance capital' in the sense used by Hilferding.[38] Nonetheless, at the international as at the national level, and at the centre as at the periphery, bank operations with the private sector are concerned mainly with trade credit and working capital. Financing of long-term investment projects, on the other hand, is left to retained profits or governmental development banks. Longer-term financing for Latin American governments is feasible only because better guarantees can be offered, and repayment is independent of any particular project to which funds are allocated.[39]

The place of domestic banking interests at the centre of the ownership structure in the major Latin American economies is well documented.[40] Undoubtedly domestic banks have had an increasing influence on government policy favouring monetary stabilization and trade liberalization, and in several cases (notably Argentina and Chile) appear to have become the dominant fraction of capital.[41] However, the central position of banking groups is a traditional feature of Latin American economic structure. For two centuries after independence, large commercial houses (many of them foreign), not only dominated internal trade but were also involved in manufacturing, often in close alliance with the large landowners or foreign mining companies.[42] As industrialization got under way, they became the centre of *grupos* coordinating firms in export agriculture, manufacturing, real estate, commerce and so on: groups which were, in effect, oligopolizing the corporate sector of the Latin American economies. Profits can be redeployed within the group for reinvestment; outsiders are starved of funds; one branch of production can be abandoned with relative ease in favour of another. The domestic bank operated as both cashier and manager for a cross-section of the economy, controlling both the source of deposits and the use of loans.[43] In the post-1945 stage of industrialization, these groups (each of which contained a bank) were appropriately placed to become the local partners of multinational corporations expanding into manufacturing. Own operations were sold to the MNCs, a local accommodation with the state was devised, and working capital provided in exchange for a minority share in profits. This development is to be distinguished from the subsequent arrival of the multinational banks, which tended to set up corresponding relationships with large local banks.

It could be argued that local banks cemented the three-way relationship between state, multinational firms and domestic capital which became the dominant feature of the post-war Latin American economies, allowing the traditional primary export interests to make a relatively smooth transition to modernity, and suppressing the conflict between national and international capital generated by pressure on the state from popular sectors and smaller business excluded from these arrangements.

Can these local groups be properly termed 'finance capital' in Hilferding's sense? For Brazil and Mexico, such a case can be made because the banks are closely related to production (especially manufacturing), are not dominated by another interest (such as landowners), and appear to have a coherent overall development strategy. Interestingly enough, although the Brazilian and Mexican *grupos* support stabilization policies, they have not pressed for the elimination of tariff barriers, the reduction of the state apparatus or the abandonment of wage controls. Instead, they have supported continued industrial accumulation along existing lines. However, their unwillingness to go further – for example, towards a national capital goods sector in opposition to multinational interests, greater state accumulation in productive sectors or more liberal labour remuneration policies – was demonstrated firmly and clearly in both Mexico and Brazil in the mid-1970s.[44]

Argentina and Chile seem to be quite different. While the *grupos* were developing along classical lines during the 1960s, building up links with multinationals, establishing *financieras*, shifting from agriculture to urban real estate and so on, they were rudely interrupted by threats to the social order. When the old order was re-established, the financial groups were strongly placed within the state, but the government policies and economic activities pursued by the *grupos* were not those of previous decades. Instead, the liberalization of imports and wage depression through inflation and de-unionization (rather than by state control as in Brazil and Mexico) were accompanied by bank activity in speculation. In effect, this meant a return to the traditional activities of the commercial houses of the nineteenth century, the import of luxury goods and the recirculation of rental income from primary exports. Foreign banks, while happy to lend to the new, stable governments, expressed little interest in these speculative activities, possibly because of the exchange risk involved. Curiously enough, the strength of the *grupos* has been weakened in the long term because they have been dissociated from production, and the multinationals' need for their support has been reduced with the establishment of a free market.

Colombia, it could be argued, moved smoothly into the Chilean model at the end of the 1960s. Financial groups were still closely connected to agrarian interests and had a strong interest in speculative activities and trade, as opposed to production. Foreign banks, although well represented in Colombia, have been mainly concerned with the finance of multinational affiliates. In Peru the banking sector was largely nationalized in the early 1970s, the traditional multi-sectoral *grupos* being harnessed to the needs of state capitalism. Recently, speculative finance has re-emerged in the interstices of the system, and has formed a key element in moves towards liberalization.

In sum, finance capital is central to the development of the accumulation model in Latin America, but not in a crude sense of local and foreign banks forming a 'monetarist alliance'. Rather, it appears that the financial groups have either evolved towards true finance capital (a fusion of banking and industrial interests) as part of the 'tripod' relationship, or else regressed towards commerce and speculation. Meanwhile international banks have turned towards the Latin American state as their main client, establishing a different arrangement of the tripod from that evolved in manufacturing, and one which is essentially about circulation rather than production.[45] Indeed, it could be argued that local and multinational banks are mainly concerned with two quite different commodities – pesos and dollars, so to speak – and although there is some overlap, their interests are essentially distinct. The intermediation between different currencies is the concern of nation-states through central banks.

The state and external finance
The scale of state borrowing abroad[46] and the financial consequences of the ensuing debt service become central to the Latin American accumulation model from the mid-1960s onwards. The state mediated between the domestic and the international economies. Despite the uniformity of the financial system faced by the Latin American countries and the similarity of balance of payments problems (that is, the articulation of domestic and international money), differences in the domestic accumulation models make for marked variations in the use of funds and the form of ensuing debt stabilization policies adopted. The articulation of the domestic model of accumulation with the world economy and the new set of relationships established with financial capital have both influenced the relative autonomy of the state.

Variations of fiscal expenditure have had as much to do with investment to support the private sector as with welfare expenditure. Most borrowing has been explicitly linked to the funding of state enterprise or public works. Some borrowing has been channelled through state banks to the private sector, either through the central bank in the form of foreign exchange reserves to finance private imports, or development finance for strategic sectors. Thus an expansion of state activities has occurred without any short-term need to make appropriations from the

domestic surplus. This has allowed the state to adopt a position independent of domestic capital in general and local bankers in particular.
Where the state accounts for as much as half of aggregate fixed investment and finances key private activities like peasant agriculture, construction and food imports, these investments constitute a considerable
part of the overall burden of accumulation. This has been true even in
Argentina and Chile, where many directly productive and social activities of the state have been drastically curtailed. Indirectly, external
finance serves to permit the continued realization of the domestic surplus
in the form of foreign exchange. But the connection between foreign
borrowing and the 'fiscal crisis of the state' is close, if only because the
state does not have sufficient real control of the available foreign
exchange to allocate these reserves to its own needs. It is important to
underline that this is not, in general, a distributional conflict[47] between
profits and wages. It is usually a matter of the long-term requirements of
growth and capital restructuring as against present economic stability
and business confidence. In other words, it is a problem of the relative
autonomy of the state to take action in the interest of capitalist development as a whole.

The state is responsible not only for raising and supporting the rate of
accumulation directly, but also for 'money' in its wider sense, that is,
macro-economic management. On the one hand this involves the control
of key variables like wages, credit supply and the internal terms of trade,
so as to sustain profit level and permit market expansion consistent with
the pattern of private accumulation. This alone involves considerably
more state participation in the determination of functional income
distribution in semi-industrialized than in developed economies. In the
Latin American economies, shifts in income distribution occasioned by
changes in real wage rates and the internal terms of trade have been at
times very considerable.[48] It is not surprising that these shifts, and
resistance to them, involves considerable inflationary pressure. On the
other hand, the external account must also be managed so as to
guarantee sufficient foreign exchange to realize the surplus. In practice,
this involves attempts to control imports by limiting the expansion of
domestic demand through wage and credit controls and various forms of
protection. These measures, in turn, tend to limit the rate of domestic
accumulation. The promotion of exports, therefore, in the form either of
large new natural resource projects or of substantial subsidies for
manufactured exports, also became a state responsibility in the late
1960s.

These stabilization requirements are not only difficult to reconcile in
themselves, but are upset by fluctuations in world market prices. In the
normal course of events, the Latin American economies experience
considerable variability in their international terms of trade,[49] which in

the short term the state attempts to manage by domestic stabilization policy or foreign borrowing. Domestic demand adjustments almost inevitably impede the macro-economic support policies discussed above. Indeed, this difficulty led many economics to turn 'inwards' in the first place, so that growth would be sustained by domestic (and thus potentially state-manageable) demand rather than exposed to external forces.[50] Foreign borrowing by the state to replenish reserves and ride out what is hoped to be a temporary exchange shortage is an obvious and potentially optimal policy.

The contradictory pressures of state expenditure, domestic profit maintenance and balance of payments stability can be resolved in the short run by foreign borrowing. The alternative is a further redistribution of surplus from the private sector to the state, and of income from wages to profits. Redistribution towards the state can be avoided by reducing state expenditure,[51] and a reasonable degree of balance of payments stability on capital account can be achieved by depressing domestic demand and 'opening' the economy so that this is reflected automatically on the trade balance. But in practice this amounts to the abandonment of any state role in sustaining capital accumulation or improving popular living standards.[52]

The servicing of foreign borrowing by the state places a disproportionate burden upon both the balance of payments and the public sector accounts, typically as much as one quarter of exports or one sixth of public expenditure, although as little as one thirtieth of gross domestic product.[53] Stabilization policies have become conditioned, therefore, not only by current account instability but also by debt servicing.

Thus, in contrast to the original contracting of debt, the negotiation of appropriate stabilization policies becomes a central and contentious theme in relations between state and bank consortia or international financial institutions like the IMF or the IBRD.[54] The strong position gained by the state with respect to domestic capital by external borrowing is countered by a relatively weak position with regard to international capital. Thorp and Whitehead[55] point out that it is under these conditions that orthodox (that is, monetarist) stabilization policy tends to be introduced, often imposed by force rather than by consensus in Latin America. Moreover, while the alternative non-orthodox (that is, structuralist) view offers an adequate explanation of the causes of instability, it provides no real policy measures for the short term (other than borrowing more to finance required production increases). So the form of stabilization policy, and thus the policy of accumulation and income distribution, within the particular historical context of each country, will depend to a great extent upon the dynamic of state accumulation and the specific relationship between the state and financial capital.

The relationship between the state and foreign banks is partly determined by the nature of the negotiations themselves: the desire of banks to find markets and their evaluation of the country's creditworthiness[56] on the one hand, and a government's need for further finance and willingness to adopt 'sound' economic policies on the other.[57] This varies from one case to another, but inherent economic strength (in Brazil and Mexico) and adoption of orthodox policies for political reasons (in Argentina and Chile) probably make borrowing much easier. The domestic class alliance and in particular the role of domestic finance capital clearly influence the position of the state. The IMF can only achieve acceptance and implementation of its programmes when there is sufficient domestic support for them, and this will logically come from local financial interests.

The relationship between state and local banks is complex. Financial assets are more vulnerable than fixed assets, and in a sense only exist thanks to state guarantees. They are more vulnerable than industrial assets and much more so than investments in agriculture and mining. Banks cannot operate without some form of central bank to guarantee their liabilities and assets. In Latin America, the controls of the *Superintendencia de Bancos* over lending patterns, credit volume, interest rates and disclosure of accounts would be unimaginable in manufacturing. Furthermore, the capacity of the state to change the primary money supply, vary reserve requirements and manipulate the exchange rate, directly affects the banks. However, the state must rely upon domestic banks not only to meet much of the public sector borrowing requirement, but also to implement part of its macro-economic policy through credit management, determining the volume and composition of imports and even the stimulation of different branches of production. This operational influence of banks, particularly when there are few controls on foreign exchange, can place a tight constraint upon unorthodox economic policy.[58]

The financial transnationalization of the state can restrict its negotiating power. At the level of public enterprise, increasing reliance on foreign technology and expansion into international trade[59] have increased the structural need for foreign finance. This often results in a direct engagement with foreign banks independent of overall government policy, and thus increases domestic pressure for an accommodation with them. More significantly, state bankers in public financial corporations and in central banks have strengthened their links with international banks and institutions like the IMF. This linkage has been reinforced by a common training in the United States and continuous consultation through such bodies as the Centro de Estudios Monetarios Latino Américanos.

The relationship between state and financial capital should throw light upon the concept of relative autonomy of the state, understood as the necessary freedom of action of the state from the interests of any one fraction or group of capitalists in order to promote accumulation. Relative autonomy varies, however, being affected by the degree of hegemony of different groups in 'civil society', and the internal cohesion of the state. This is particularly marked in cases of domestic class 'vacuum', combined with a high degree of nationalism (probably populist in nature) and a disciplined group of 'state managers' (such as the military in default of a party), where the space created for independent state action to promote capital accumulation is considerable.[60] The logic of relative autonomy is clearer in macro-economic management than in control of labour organization, and is more obvious still in finance, which cannot operate without constant state supervision and where stability is continually threatened by the fiscal instability of state accumulation. It is true that the relative autonomy required for an effective restructuring of capital in Latin America is unusual (a 'state of exception'); but the room for manoeuvre necessary to control the balance of payments and domestic demand levels cannot be achieved without a continual interference in the realization of profits, directing the surplus away from uses desired by the market.

Evers[61] suggests that relative autonomy from both the local and the world economy is an intrinsic feature of the peripheral state. He contends that this is a necessary premise for the fulfilment of the state's function in guaranteeing the insertion of the Latin American economies into the international division of labour. Evidently thinking of productive capital, Evers points out that the peripheral state enjoys a greater autonomy at both the domestic and international levels than does the metropolitan state – especially in matters of finance. Evers argues that the class nature of the peripheral state is essentially ambiguous, not only because of the 'incomplete' nature of the class structure in semi-industrialized countries, but also because the scope of the 'polity' and state power is essentially national, while the economy is internationalized. Again, an examination of finance tends to support this view. Our discussion suggests that the participation of the state in productive investment, and its role as the main channel for foreign finance, may well increase its relative autonomy domestically, but that inherent fiscal problems (that is, access to the surplus) and the sectional interests of 'state capitalists'[62] necessarily reduce the flexibility of monetary control and the state's ability to enforce market rules.

The requirement of private enterprise for a strong, relatively autonomous state is recognized both by the structuralist school,[63] which stresses the need for public investment and planning in order to effect the restructuring of capital, and by the version of monetarism prevalent in Latin America. This version, which owes more to 'Stanford' than to 'Chicago', incorporates aspects of the monetary approach to the balance of payments espoused by the IMF for small open economies.[64] This school of thought contrasts with metropolitan monetarism in two respects. First, it is not merely concerned with monetary stability, the reduction of rates of inflation and improved prospects for private investment. It is also preoccupied with:

(1) the alteration of supply conditions through liberalization of external trade (to encourage competitiveness and efficiency among firms);
(2) the promotion of capital markets;
(3) the restoration of investment confidence by holding down real wages;
(4) cutting back the size of the state sector.

Second, freeing the balance of payments means that both the domestic price level (for traded goods, at least) and the domestic monetary base will be effectively determined outside the economy – in other words, that domestic money will be subordinated to the dollar. This form of 'structuralist monetarism' represents a movement of the neo-classical comparative advantage school towards an explicit consideration of the problems of accumulation. The need for a strong state, firmly in control of domestic credit expansion (and thus of local financial intermediaries as well as of government borrowing), and independent of factional interests such as domestic business demanding tariff protection, is stressed. To a certain extent, state demand management is substituted for state intervention in supply in an almost Keynesian way, so that the Hayekian perception of the subordination of the state to civil society is hardly evident. In the metropolitan monetarist vision of the world, extensive foreign borrowing by the state is necessary because there are no fiscal deficits and few state enterprises. Furthermore, foreign capital enters as direct or portfolio investment, reacting to comparative interest rates. Therefore, the cause of indebtedness is the misguided intervention of the state in direct support of accumulation and wage levels. Were the state less profligate, it could regain its lost autonomy relative to international banks.

Conclusion

The three parts of our argument – the economic function of foreign loans, the place of finance capital, and the role of the state – are essential but frequently absent elements in discussions of 'the debt trap'. The weakness of this chapter has undoubtedly been its failure to integrate the three elements and to deal with a fourth: the dynamics of the worldwide expansion of metropolitan banks, of which less is understood than of their cousins in material production. Nor is the impact of attempts to establish quasi-international state institutions to control money in the

Table 19 *Annual average percentage changes in selected macro-economic variables, 1960–1978: select countries*

	Gross domestic product		Manufacturing output		Gross domestic investment	
	1960–70	*1970–8*	*1960–70*	*1970–8*	*1960–70*	*1970–8*
Argentina	4.2	2.3	5.7	2.0	4.1	1.2
Brazil	5.3	9.2	—	9.5	7.0	10.7
Chile	4.5	0.8	5.5	–2.4	3.7	–2.7
Colombia	5.1	6.0	5.7	7.0	4.5	6.3
Mexico	7.2	5.0	9.4	6.2	9.6	7.1
Peru	5.4	3.1	7.2	4.3	2.4	4.2
Unweighted six-country mean	5.3	4.4	6.7	4.4	5.2	4.5
Industrialized countries	5.1	3.2	6.2	3.3	5.6	1.5

	Export volume		Import volume		Terms of trade	
	1960–70	*1970–8*	*1960–70*	*1970–8*	*1960–70*	*1970–8*
Argentina	3.5	6.8	0.3	–0.1	–0.1	–0.6
Brazil	5.0	6.0	4.9	6.6	1.2	–1.3
Chile	0.6	6.5	4.7	–0.9	6.6	–8.2
Colombia	2.2	1.2	2.4	–0.7	1.1	–0.8
Mexico	3.3	5.2	6.4	4.0	1.4	1.0
Peru	1.9	–3.8	3.6	3.1	4.7	3.2
Unweighted six-country mean	2.8	3.7	3.7	2.0	2.5	–1.1

Notes Taking the quanta of exports (X) and imports (M), their respective prices (x,m) and the value of net external finance (F) we have, by definition:

Mm = Xx = F

which can be reset so as to give finance in 'real' terms:

$$\frac{F}{m} = M - X\,\frac{x}{m}$$

It should be noted that this net external finance is much less than the increment in debt, which must cover considerable outflows of private short-term capital and repayment of previous debt; although it might be argued that, without the additional finance, imports would be lower by the gross increase in debt.

To regress the three variables (X, M, x/m) separately on real finance does not imply any causality across the identity sign, but requires us to assume that the three variables are independent of each other and that trade volumes were not affected by prices – a point of considerable dispute. Preliminary inspection of the data indicates such an enormous variation between countries as to make cross-section analysis meaningless; variations within economies as to economic strategy, as well as the usual problems of serial correlation, make time series equally ambiguous. If the average for the six economies has any significance at all, however, it would indicate that if the 1960s and 1970s as a whole are compared, the terms of trade effect is significant and that export volume growth was higher and import volume growth lower, possibly in order to compensate.

wake of the collapse of US monetary hegemony fully understood. The central thrust of the argument here can be summarized as follows. If we agree with de Brunhoff's interpretation of Marx,[65] that there are two 'special commodities' in capitalist economies – labour and money – which the state organizes, then the study of economic imperialism cannot be concerned with the international division of labour alone but must include the organization of money in its widest sense. This includes not only monetary policy, but also fiscal structure, foreign finance and macro-economic stabilization. Whatever the organization of the new international division of labour implies in terms of less state intervention in support of wages and infrastructure, the organization of money is an intrinsic function of the state which cannot be left to market forces unless the peripheral economy is to become hopelessly unstable or integrated with a metropolitan economy in such a way as to threaten the existence of the peripheral nation-state.

Notes

[1] M. S. Wionczek (ed.) *LDC external debt and the world economy* (Mexico City 1978); A. Fishlow 'A new Latin America in a new international capital market' *CEPAL Review* x (1980); J. C. Garcia and S. E. Sutin (eds) *Financing development in Latin America* (New York 1980).

[2] International Bank for Reconstruction and Development (IBRD) *World Development Report 1980* (Washington 1980); the six economies covered here and in Table 19 account for three quarters of the population and six sevenths of the production of Latin America.

[3] IBRD *op. cit.*; Fishlow *op. cit.*

[4] That is, the ECLA view represented by P. Paz 'Causes of the external indebtedness of the Third World countries' in Wionczek *op.cit.*

[5] R. I. McKinnon *Money, capital and economic development* (Washington 1973); McKinnon (ed.) *Money and finance in economic growth and development* (New York 1976); see also S. Kalmanovitz 'Algunos elementos de la teoría y la práctica monetaristas en América Latina' *Comercio Exterior* xxxi 1 (1981).

[6] C. Payer *The debt trap* (Harmondsworth 1975); S. Griffith-Jones 'The growth of multinational banks, the Eurocurrency market and the developing countries' *Journal of Development Studies* xvii 1 (1980).

[7] F. Fröbel, J. Heinrichs and O. Kreye *The new international division of labour* (Cambridge 1980).

[8] See as examples R. Thorp and L. Whitehead (eds) *Inflation and stabilization in Latin America* (London 1979) and A. Ferrer 'El monetarismo en Argentina y Chile' *Comercio Exterior* xxxi 1 (1981).

[9] See notes to Table 19.

[10] Neo-classical economics has no theory of accumulation as such, just a concept of the supply and demand equilibrium for capital goods, savings and deposits and so on. In this sense, monetarism provides a much more satisfactory version of 'capitalist economics'.

[11] A good example of this is W. R. Cline *Potential effects of income redistribution on economic growth* (New York 1972), where the income distribution and savings propensities are held to determine aggregate savings and thus investment in Latin America.

[12] S. Amin *Accumulation on a world scale* (New York 1974).

[13] A. Brewer *Marxist theories of imperialism: a critical survey* (London 1980).

[14] McKinnon, *Money*.

[15] M. Kalecki 'Problems of financing economic development in a mixed economy' in

Essays on the economic growth of the socialist and mixed economy (Cambridge 1972); H. Flores de la Peña 'un neuvo modelo de desarrollo' *Comercio Exterior* xxvii 5 (1977).

[16] A. S. Eichner *The megacorp and oligopoly: the microfoundations of macrodynamics* (New York 1976).

[17] A. Foxley (ed.) *Income distribution in Latin America* (Cambridge 1976).

[18] C. Furtado *Teoría y política del desarrollo económico* (Mexico 1968); O. Rodríguez *La teoría del subdesarrollo de la CEPAL* (Mexico 1980).

[19] N. Lustig 'Some considerations on the theories of underconsumption and Latin American economic thought' *Review of Radical Political Economy* (1980).

[20] A point taken up to some effect, however, by M. C. Tavares 'El desarrollo reciente del sistema financiero de América Latina' *Boletín Económico de América Latina* 16 (1971) and 'El sistema financiero brasileño y el ciclo de expansión reciente' *Economía de América Latina* v (1980).

[21] W. Newlyn *The finance of economic development* (London 1977) makes this point for developing countries in general. After examining savings data for 31 such countries, he concludes that 'household savings play a minor role, with corporations generally playing the dominant role in the accumulation of the national surplus, with some tendency for government to compensate when the corporate share falls below the median' (p. 12). See also H. H. Schwartz 'Problems of industrial financing in Latin America' in J. C. Garcia and S. E. Sutin (eds) *Financing development in Latin America* (New York 1980).

[22] See, for instance, C. Lluch (ed.) *Patterns in household demand and savings* (New York 1978): the insistence of institutions such as the World Bank on studying household savings rather than that of corporations, despite the fact that their policy prescriptions are based on the need for profits as a stimulus to investment.

[23] For a development of this argument, see E. V. K. FitzGerald 'The fiscal crisis of the Latin American state' in J. F. J. Toye (ed.) *Taxation and economic development* (London 1978).

[24] R. Thorp 'Inflation and the financing of economic development' in K. G. Griffin (ed.) *Financing development in Latin America* (London 1971).

[25] As in the widely used 'Harberger model' presented in A. Harberger 'The dynamics of inflation in Chile' in C. Christ (ed.) *Measurement in economics* (Palo Alto, Calif. 1963).

[26] Except perhaps in Mexico, where the effect described does appear to take place, according to E. V. K. FitzGerald 'A note on capital accumulation in Mexico: the budget deficit and investment finance' *Development and Change* xi 3 (1980).

[27] *Ibid.*, for a discussion of the principles involved.

[28] For O. Braun *Comercio internacional e imperialismo* (Buenos Aires 1973) this 'incompleteness' of the Latin American economies is the essence of dependency: 'achieving the expanded reproduction of even the simple reproduction of capital is impeded because at least part of the machines and inputs required for production are monopolized by another country' (p. 106).

[29] We are excluding grant aid here, because whatever its implications, it has never been very important in Latin America.

[30] Although not, incidentally, in the purest form of the monetary approach to the balance of payments, which does not distinguish between forms of expenditure.

[31] K. G. Griffin *op. cit.* and L. Landau 'Savings functions for Latin America' in H. B. Chenery (ed.) *Studies in development planning* (Cambridge, Mass. 1971) confirm this position for Latin America. The data in H. B. Chenery and M. Syrquin *Patterns of development 1950–70* (New York 1975) indicates that for developing countries as a whole as little as a quarter of increases in net external funding go into investment.

[32] According to IBRD *op. cit.*, the share of machinery and equipment in total imports of our six countries averaged 42 per cent in 1960 and 36 per cent in 1977.

[33] See D. Joslin *A century of banking in Latin America* (Oxford 1963) and C. Marichal 'Perspectivas históricas sobre el imperialismo financiero en América Latina, 1820–1930' *Economía de América Latina* v (1980) for contrasting views.

[34] See Table 19.

[35] Thorp and Whitehead *op. cit.*

[36] S. Lichensztejn 'Notas sobre el capital financiero en América Latina' *Economía de América Latina* v (1980) has a simple dependency view.

[37] F. L. Block *The origins of international economic disorder: a study of United States international monetary policy from World War II to the present* (Berkeley, Calif. 1977); R. Cohen *Transnational banks: operations and strategies and their effects in developing countries* (Berkeley, Calif. 1979); J. Aronson *Money and power: banks and the world monetary system* (Beverly Hills, Calif. 1977)

[38] It is unfortunate that Fröbel *et al.* and similar researchers have not produced a structural analysis of the dynamics of the international expansion of banks. But see D. M. Kotz *Bank control of large corporations in the United States* (Berkeley, Calif. 1978).

[39] T. H. Donaldson *International lending by commercial banks* (London 1979). It may well be, however, that the entry of Japanese and German banks into the Latin American market, with their tradition of direct investment finance, will change this.

[40] For example, P. Evans *Dependent development: the alliance of multinational, state and local capital in Brazil* (Princeton 1979); J. M. Fragoso *El poder de la gran burguesía* (Mexico City 1979); E. V. K. FitzGerald *The political economy of Peru 1966–1978: economic development and the restructuring of capital* (Cambridge 1979).

[41] Ferrer *op. cit.*, for instance.

[42] R. Thorp and I. G. Bertram *Peru 1890–1977: growth and policy in an open economy* (London 1978), for instance; similar historical evidence for other economies abounds.

[43] N. H. Leff 'Capital markets in less-developed countries: the group principle' in McKinnon *Money* and P. J. Drake *Money, finance and development* (Oxford 1980) for wider discussions of these groups.

[44] See FitzGerald and Wells in Thorp and Whitehead *op cit.*

[45] Interest in production appears to be confined to the (more reliable) primary export capacity and import restraint required to service loans; see Garcia *op. cit.* and Donaldson *op. cit.*

[46] Our six economies borrowed a total of some $66 billions from the prime Euromarket (Eurobonds, Eurocredits and foreign bonds) between 1970 and 1979, of which Mexico and Brazil accounted for $63 millions. Although this represents 55 per cent of all non-OPEC developing country borrowing in the period, it is only 13 per cent of total borrowing from that market: in other words, Latin American borrowing was probably marginal to the overall recycling process, however central it was to the six economies themselves or to the profitability of certain banks. *Source*: IBRD *Borrowing in International Capital Markets* (various issues), calculated by J. Nicolini.

[47] In contrast to the argument put forward for developed capitalist economies by J. A. Kregel *The reconstruction of political economy: an introduction to post-Keynesian economics* (London 1973) p. 183.

[48] For example, note the halving of real wage levels not only in Chile 1974–8 but also Peru 1975–80.

[49] To the extreme that, between 1970 and 1975, the terms of trade for Argentina rose from 100 to 117 and fell to 71; those for Brazil rose from 100 to 109 and fell to 91.

[50] M. Kuczinski 'Semi-developed countries and the international business cycle' *BOLSA Review* (1976).

[51] But as Ferrer *op. cit.* points out, even the Videla and Pinochet administrations were not able to achieve budget equilibrium and thus make monetary policy independent of fiscal problems.

[52] And thus the legitimation of the state itself in this role.

[53] For our six economies in the period 1970–8, exports averaged 14 per cent of GDP, debt service 24 per cent of exports, and public expenditure (defined as government current expenditure plus public fixed investment) 25 per cent of GDP. *Sources*: IBRD *op. cit.*, FitzGerald 'The fiscal crisis'.

[54] B. Stallings 'Bancos privados y políticas nacionalistas: la dialéctica de las finanzas internacionales' *Economía de América Latina* v (1980), J. Quijano 'El Euromercado y la nueva

relación entre el estado y la banca privada' *Economía de América Latina* v (1980). The IMF, and IBRD (through the 'Club of Paris'), effectively negotiate on behalf of multinational banks in the sense that they are attempting to guarantee repayment of loans, but individual banks have often lent beyond what IMF/IBRD consider advisable in the first place, so that the relationship is ambiguous. It is curious in this context to note that a central bank (insofar as IMF/IBRD can be considered as an embryo of one at the international level) is operated by controlling lenders (i.e. banks) rather than borrowers.

[55] Introduction to Thorp and Whitehead *op. cit.* It is important in this context, however, to make a distinction between 'Stanford' and 'Chicago' monetarism, which Thorp and Whitehead fail to do.

[56] Garcia and Sutin *op. cit.*

[57] For a good discussion of the policies proposed, agreed to and actually implemented, see the essays in Thorp and Whitehead *op. cit.* The irony is, of course, that a country's creditworthiness and bargaining position are strongest precisely when it does not need finance, and weakest when it does.

[58] The Mexican financial crisis of 1973–7 is a particularly good example of this – see C. Tello *La política económica de México, 1970–76* (Mexico 1979).

[59] This point is developed in E. V. K. FitzGerald 'The new international division of labour and the relative autonomy of the state: notes for a reappraisal of classical dependency' *Bulletin of Latin American Research* 1 1 (1981).

[60] Brazil in 1964–70, Peru 1968–75; Chile 1973–80 and Mexico 1940–65 are good examples of this. See A. Stepan *The state and society: Peru in comparative perspective* (Princeton 1978); Fitzgerald *Political economy of Peru.*

[61] T. Evers *El estado en la periferia capitalista* (Mexico 1979) p. 107.

[62] A. Dorfman 'Los nuevos grupos del poder y el sector industrial público' in J. Carrière *Industrialization and the state in Latin America* (Amsterdam 1979). See also F. L. Block 'Beyond relative autonomy: state managers as historical subjects' in R. Miliband and J. Saville (eds) *The Socialist Register, 1980* (London 1980).

[63] O. Rodríguez *La teoría del subdesarrollo de la CEPAL* (Mexico 1980).

[64] McKinnon *Money.*

[65] S. Brunhoff *The state, capital and economic policy* (London 1978).

25

A REAPPRAISAL OF THE ROLE OF PRIMARY EXPORTS IN LATIN AMERICA

Ernesto Tironi B.

It very often happens with countries – as with people – that the attention given to one particular issue or goal conceals events taking place in other related areas. Over the last two or three decades, Latin American countries have put great emphasis on diversifying their trade structures by increasing their exports of manufactures. However, little consideration has been given to the implications of the latter for trade in primary products, which still accounts for over four fifths of Latin America's total export revenue. This may explain why, notwithstanding significant success in diversifying the region's exports, its share within the world's total trade has fallen considerably over the last twenty years.

The purpose of this chapter is to analyze the evolution of Latin American commodity exports, and particularly their place in world trade, and to reappraise the strategy that has been followed in their regard. The chapter is organized in three sections. The first studies the evolution of Latin America's export diversification and of its share in world trade. Given the heterogeneity of Latin American countries and of the main export commodities, the second section disaggregates the figures by country and commodity in order to analyze to what extent we are dealing with a rather generalized or with a local phenomenon. The last section suggests an alternative strategy aimed at putting more emphasis on the possibility of a faster expansion of Latin America's primary exports.

Latin America in the world trade of primary exports

During the last two decades, the importance of Latin America within the world economy has increased as a consequence of its relatively faster economic growth. In fact, between 1960 and 1978 it expanded from 5 to 6 per cent of the world total, excluding the oil exporting companies.[1] Notwithstanding, the rate of growth of income per capita has been insufficient to satisfy the social needs of its population, and to diminish poverty to the extent that would seem possible, given the region's average income level and its human and natural resource endowment.[2]

The situation contrasts markedly with the economic performance of other developing regions similar to Latin America. Indeed, while the rate of growth of income per capita was 3.1 in Latin America during the last two decades, the non-oil-exporting developing countries of East Asia were growing at a rate of 5.3 per cent per annum.[3] In other words, Latin America increased its income per capita by 73 in those eighteen years, while the Asian figure was 150.

It is well known that the success of the East Asian developing countries has been associated with a very fast export growth, achieved by taking advantage of the expansion of world trade during the last two decades. Latin America, however, did not make use of that opportunity to the same extent. In contrast to what was happening in other developing regions, Latin America significantly reduced its share in world exports, from 8.5 per cent in 1960 to only 5 per cent in 1978. This comparatively low growth has been blamed mainly on an excessive concentration on primary products, the demand for which tends to grow less rapidly than that for manufactures. Nevertheless, during recent decades Latin America has been able to achieve a considerable diversification of the commodity composition of its exports.[4] Therefore, the explanation of its poor economic performance is either a still insufficient absolute level of trade diversification, or a diversification achieved concomitant with a very low rate of growth of the more traditional exports of primary products.

From the point of view of taking advantage of the opportunities offered by world trade, determining whether exports of different products grow fast or slowly must be judged in relation to the rate of growth of trade in those same commodities in the world as a whole. Table 20 shows the evolution of export diversification in Latin America as compared to other developing regions and to the developed countries. The table shows that diversification in Latin America has gone further than in any other region of the world. According to the World Bank's statistics and

Table 20 *Evolution of the composition of exports in Latin America and other regions, 1960–1978 (percentages)*

	Primary products			Oil			Manufactures		
	1960	1970	1978	1960	1970	1978	1960	1970	1978
Latin America	63	64	48	34	23	33	3	13	18
Asia	50	30	15	35	40	58	16	27	26
Africa	84	59	36	5	29	53	11	11	10
Developed countries	29	22	19	4	3	5	66	73	75
World total	38	28	21	10	9	14	51	61	61

Source World Bank *Commodity trade and price trends* (Washington DC 1980).

definitions, between 1960 and 1978 the share of manufactures within total exports increased from 3 to 18 per cent in Latin America, as compared to an increase from 16 to 26 per cent in Asia, and almost no change in Africa.

This fact would incline one to believe that Latin America has been able to increase its share in world trade, because it is well known that manufactured exports have grown much faster than primary products. Nonetheless, we have already seen that in fact this has not been the case, because the share of Latin America in world trade fell from 8.5 to 5.2 per cent between 1960 and 1978, according to the IMF figures. Excluding trade with and between the centrally planned economies, and according to the statistics of the World Bank, that share of Latin American trade fell from 6.1 to 4.2 per cent (see Table 21). The explanation of this result could be either that the rate of growth of Latin America's manufactured exports was lower than the world's average, or that it has not been higher by a big enough margin to compensate for the lower growth of primary exports.

Table 21   Growth of exports by sector in Latin America and other regions and shares in world exports, 1960–1978 (percentages)

	Latin America		Asia		Africa		Developed countries		World total	
	1960– 78	*1970– 8*	*1960– 78*	*1970– 8*	*1960– 78*	*1970– 8*	*1960– 78*	*1970– 8*	*1960– 78*	*1970– 8*
Primary products	9.2	13.9	9.1	17.9	7.2	10.5	10.9	15.8	10.1	15.2
Oil	10.8	23.6	20.0	35.0	28.7	36.8	14.6	23.1	17.4	29.3
Manu-factures	22.1	23.6	19.9	28.6	11.9	16.1	14.6	19.0	15.0	19.6
TOTAL	*10.8*	*18.1*	*16.7*	*28.7*	*12.4*	*17.4*	*13.8*	*18.5*	*13.9*	*19.7*
Share in world exports	*1960*	*1978*	*1960*	*1978*	*1960*	*1978*	*1960*	*1978*		
Excluding centrally planned economies	8.5	5.2	10.6	26.3	5.6	4.5	72.1	71.5		
Including centrally planned economies	6.2	4.1	7.6	8.2	6.0	9.5	77.9	82.2		

Source   World Bank *Commodity trade and price trends* (Washington DC 1980).

The available empirical evidence confirms the latter rather than the former hypothesis. The pertinent figures appear in Table 21 and show that in Latin America the rate of growth of manufactured exports is considerably higher than the world average, but the rate of growth of primary exports is lower. But since the latter are more significant than the former within Latin America's total exports, the rate of growth of overall exports is lower than the world's average. By contrast, in Asia the diversification towards manufactured exports was attained without letting the rate of growth of primary exports fall below the rate of expansion of such exports in the world as a whole.

Table 22 sheds further light on the relation between diversification and participation in world trade. We see that as a result of the faster growth of manufactured exports in Latin America, the region's share in world exports of manufactures rises from 0.5 per cent in 1960 to 1.2 per cent in 1970 and 1.5 per cent in 1978. What this table shows up vividly is the importance of the fall in the Latin American share of world oil exports. In fact, the fall in Latin America's share in world exports has been caused mainly by a lower rate of growth of its oil exports. This was happening even before the oil crisis of 1973. But it is important to note that that reduction is visible even when oil is excluded from the trade statistics. Therefore, the trend is not, or not only, a function of rising oil prices.

The previous analysis considers the situation aggregated across all Latin American countries and primary commodities. It is worth considering next whether the aggregate trends just mentioned were the result of the particular behaviour of only some countries and a few commodities, or whether they were more generalized.

Table 22   *Share of Latin America in world exports, by sector, 1960–1978 (percentages)

	1960	1970	1978
Primary products	14.1	13.4	12.1
Oil	29.1	14.5	10.2
Manufactures	0.5	1.2	1.5
TOTAL	8.5	5.7	5.2

Source   World Bank Commodity trade and price trends (Washington DC 1980).
* Excluding countries with centrally planned economies.

Trends by countries and commodities

Table 23 shows that the reduction in the share of primary products in each country's total exports was a generalized phenomenon that took place in all countries (except Paraguay) between 1960 and 1978. The number of countries in which primary products accounted for over 70 per cent of total exports fell from eleven to five in only four years (between 1970–2 and 1974–6). And consistent with this, the number of countries in which those commodities represented less than 50 per cent of total exports increased from three to seven.

Naturally, primary products are relatively more important for the smaller countries of the region: Bolivia, the Dominican Republic, Ecuador, Guatemala and Honduras. But it is interesting to observe that in the larger countries, such as Brazil and Argentina, those products also account for about 40 to 50 per cent of total exports. In the case of Mexico the proportion has increased in recent years, as a result of the expansion of oil exports.

The fall in the concentration of exports on primary products (excluding oil) has been fastest in Venezuela, Ecuador, Mexico, Uruguay and Brazil, in that order. But this has a different origin in the various countries. In the first three, trade diversification resulted from the rise of oil exports. In Brazil and Uruguay, by contrast, as well as in all other Latin American countries except Bolivia, diversification was a consequence of the faster expansion of manufactured exports. Between the early 1960s and the end of the 1970s, the reduction of the share of primary products within total exports was least accentuated in the cases of Peru, Bolivia, Colombia and Chile.

Table 23   Significance of primary products in total exports of each Latin American country, 1970–1976 (number of countries)

Primary products in total exports (percentages)	Number of countries* 1970–2	1974–6	Countries in each category in 1974–6
A Over 70	11	5	Bolivia, Dominican Republic, Ecuador, Guatemala and Honduras
B 50 to 70	7	9	Chile, Colombia, Costa Rica, El Salvador, Haiti, Nicaragua, Peru, Uruguay and Venezuela
C 40 to 50	2	4	Argentina, Brazil, Panama, and Paraguay
D Under 40	1	3	Jamaica, Mexico and Trinidad-Tobago
TOTAL	*21*	*21*	

Source   World Bank *Commodity trade and price trends* (Washington DC 1978).
* Excluding Cuba.

The evolution of Latin America's primary exports by commodity appears in Table 24. The first column shows that the main product exported by Latin America is oil, followed by coffee, sugar, copper and iron ore, in that order. These five commodities accounted for about two fifths of the region's total exports *c*.1976. But there are only eight commodities which represent more than 1 per cent of the region's total.

Table 24   Latin American, LDCs' and developed countries' shares in world exports of primary products, (PP) 1960–1977 (percentages)

Commodities and their share in LA's exports (1975–7)		Less developed countries						Developed countries	
		Latin America		Others		Total			
		1960	1975–7	1960	1975–7	1960	1975–7	1960	1975–7
1 Coffee	(9.5)	75.9	57.2	21.5	34.9	97.4	92.1	2.6	7.9
2 Cocoa	(0.8)	24.7	22.1	75.3	74.4	100.0	96.5	—	3.5
3 Tea	(0.1)	0.5	2.2	87.0	76.5	87.5	78.7	12.5	21.3
4 Sugar	(4.0)	54.2	23.6	20.4	23.8	74.6	47.4	25.4	52.6
5 Cotton	(1.5)	11.8	14.8	32.3	31.0	44.1	45.8	55.9	54.2
6 Rubber	(0.0)	0.5	0.3	79.8	95.8	80.3	96.1	19.7	3.9
7 Jute	(0.0)	0.0	0.1	97.6	95.7	97.6	95.8	2.4	4.2
8 Sisal	(0.1)	25.8	39.4	12.4	58.3	38.2	97.7	61.8	2.3
9 Copper	(2.8)	26.4	23.0	27.5	33.9	53.9	56.9	46.1	43.1
10 Tin	(0.5)	14.3	16.2	77.8	66.4	92.1	82.6	7.9	17.4
Subtotal 1–10	(19.4)	29.1	27.4	43.3	40.8	72.4	68.2	27.6	31.8
11 Bananas	(1.3)	79.4	75.3	14.2	21.9	93.6	97.2	6.4	7.3
12 Beef	(1.0)	28.2	12.3	1.4	1.1	29.6	13.4	70.4	86.6
13 Linseed	(0.2)	74.5	53.6	3.9	10.2	78.4	63.8	21.6	36.2
14 Timber	(0.4)	2.7	2.0	78.1	23.0	80.8	25.0	19.2	75.0
15 Bauxite	(0.6)	73.4	49.6	10.9	28.8	84.2	78.4	15.7	21.6
16 Manganese	(0.1)	23.0	16.0	47.1	33.7	70.1	49.7	29.9	50.3
17 Iron ore	(2.7)	22.6	24.8	17.4	14.8	40.0	39.6	60.0	60.4
18 Phosphates Rock	(0.0)	0.8	0.1	71.3	63.1	72.1	63.2	27.9	36.8
Subtotal 11–18	(25.7)	29.1	21.5	39.4	32.4	68.5	53.9	31.5	46.1
Petroleum	(19.8)	37.6	7.3	44.3	82.8	81.9	90.1	18.1	9.9
Other 15 PP	(5.3)	10.9	8.2	19.6	12.8	30.5	21.0	69.5	79.0
Main 33 PP	(50.8)	26.5	11.2	35.4	59.5	61.9	70.7	38.5	29.3
Other exports	(49.2)	1.8	3.2	4.5	6.1	6.3	9.3	93.7	90.7
TOTAL EXPORTS	**(100.0)**	**7.8**	**5.1**	**12.1**	**18.4**	**19.9**	**23.5**	**80.1**	**76.5**

Source IBRD *Commodity trade and price trends* (Washington DC 1973, 1977) table 2a.

The most significant facts revealed by this table are, in the first place, that Latin America has reduced its participation in the world's exports of *most* primary products considered individually. Moreover, these reductions have been larger within the markets of those primary products that are most important for the region: oil (from 38 to 7 per cent) coffee (from 76 to 57 per cent) and sugar (from 54 to 24 per cent). Latin America increased its share of world exports only in iron ore (from 23 to 25 per cent), and in three other commodities of very marginal significance for the region – tea, sisal and tin.

The second notable aspect revealed by Table 24, is that, in the case of most commodities except oil, Latin America did not lose its market to other developing countries, but to the developed countries. The larger losses occur in the share in world exports of sugar, as well as in oil seeds, timber, and minerals such as tin, manganese and bauxite. One of the main implications of this phenomenon, highlighted by Table 24, is that the industrialized countries have a share in the world's supply of primary products that is considerably higher than is commonly recognized, and that this share has *increased* during the last decades. In 1975–7, they controlled over half the exports of six of the eighteen main primary products traded worldwide (excluding oil). By contrast, in 1960 they had similar control over only three of those commodities. This obviously puts a limit on the capacity of less developed countries to achieve on their own a favourable reform of the international markets of primary products.

Alternative strategies for primary exports

The most important general conclusion of this analysis is that Latin America should give more attention to the prospects of trade in primary products. This does not imply abandoning the efforts to diversify exports. On the contrary, there is a need to maintain and even to increase that effort, but without necessarily neglecting the opportunity to profit from the region's comparative advantage in the production of primary products. Surely, without a more refined analysis, one could suggest as a rule of thumb that, at the very least, the region's share within the world's exports of commodities should be kept constant, given the abundance of natural resources in Latin America.

The main objection to this strategy is based on the argument that trade in primary products is not to the advantage of the exporting countries within the prevailing organization of international markets. For that reason, it is often argued that developing countries should *first* concentrate on changing the way in which those markets operate. In other words, the emphasis is placed on creating a new international economic order for the regulation of trade in primary products. The hypothesis suggested here is that developing countries – and Latin America in particular – should act at both levels simultaneously, because both are closely related. The point is that it is very difficult, if not impossible, to introduce reforms in primary product markets, if the countries that want and need those reforms are simultaneously reducing their market presence and bargaining power. The power of the country or region to affect the operation and institutional organization of markets depends on the *weight* that they have in controlling supply. And the latter is a function of their level of production.

During recent decades, Latin America has lost ground within world exports of primary products because its supply has been growing much less than in other regions. To that extent, its power to structure a new international economic order has also been falling. The alternative suggested here is to attempt to break that vicious circle by following a strategy aimed at re-establishing the pre-eminence of Latin America in the world markets of primary products, in such a way that the region's potential wealth in terms of its natural resource base can be reflected within present trade flows.

Moreover, it seems convenient to follow the strategy suggested here for two additional reasons. First, because during this coming decade the demand for primary products is expected to grow relatively more rapidly than in the past. Second, because political and economic conditions are not favourable to the success of an attempt by developing countries to create a new international economic order for primary products.

In relation to the first point, the World Bank has estimated that over the 1980s primary exports will grow at a rate only one third less than manufactures, while over the 1960s and 1970s the latter was nearly twice the former.[5] These trends arise mainly because the prospects for the expansion of manufactured exports in the future are less promising than in the past, as a result of increasing protectionism in the developed countries. On the other hand, the outlook for expanding trade in primary products with developing countries of other regions is becoming more auspicious. Thus, for example, the fast income growth of the South East Asian and the oil-exporting countries is opening up interesting new opportunities for Latin America. The World Bank estimates that during this coming decade the GNP of these regions will expand at an annual rate of over 7 per cent and 6 per cent per year respectively. These figures are more than twice the rate of growth expected in the industrialized countries. According to the same source, towards 1990 the four relatively more advanced countries of East Asia will by themselves account for over 27 per cent of all trade by developing countries, as compared to only 12 per cent in 1976.

This trend offers interesting opportunities for Latin America because the relatively advanced countries of South East Asia are comparatively poor in natural resources, while Latin America has a large endowment of the raw materials that those countries will need to expand their industrialization process.[6] The opportunities that are likely to arise in this respect in the 1980s will be similar to those that appeared towards the mid-1960s and 70s, with the emergence of Japan as a world economic power. Further analysis of the experience with Japan should encourage the Latin American countries to seek more favourable trade agreements with the present Newly Industrializing Countries (NICs). In particular, the Latin American countries should aim at exporting more elaborated or manufactured raw materials, as compared to those that are presently exported to the industrialized countries. Such arrangements should be more feasible with countries that are in a process of industrialization, such as the Asian ones, precisely because they have not yet completed the linkage of their industries from the final manufacturing stage through to the raw material processing stage. Therefore, since their industries have not yet been fully integrated backwards, there should not be as many vested interests and 'lobbying' groups that preclude the entry of more manufactured primary products to the markets of the industrialized countries.[7]

What is needed, therefore, are long-term agreements aimed at *sharing* the development of the primary product processing industries between the producing and consuming countries, according to comparative advantage. Explicit agreement might be called for, because in some cases it is necessary to 'jump' several stages of processing, instead of advancing through small steps. The reason is that transport costs are normally a strong impediment for trade in more manufactured primary products that have a small value-added margin over the raw material. This is, for instance, the case of wire rod as compared to refined copper.

It is worth noting that an expansion of trade between East Asia and Latin America had started to materialize by the end of the 1970s. Although Latin American exports to South East Asia are still a very small fraction of that region's total exports (1.5 per cent in 1978), the share doubled with respect to 1974. Exports grew at an annual rate of 45 per cent between 1974 and 1978, which is four times higher than the rate of growth of exports to the rest of the world. This has happened despite the fact that during this period Latin American-Asian trade has been restricted almost exclusively to two Latin American countries: Argentina and Chile.

With respect to what has been happening in the negotiations aimed at establishing a New International Economic Order, and especially in UNCTAD, the situation is sufficiently known as not to require further comment. Regarding the possibility that Latin America in particular could perhaps do something to break the stalemate, the prospects are not in fact very encouraging. There are ideological reasons that have led several countries in the region to stop defending traditional Latin American views on the unfairness of the present economic system. But in addition, the region's development over the last three decades has brought into being some structural economic changes that weaken the interest and power of Latin America in world forums. On the one hand, exports of primary products have, as we have seen, become less important for the region over the last twenty or thirty years, and on the other hand, this has not taken place homogeneously for all countries; with more heterogeneity the common base on which Latin America could act collectively has been eroded.

Notwithstanding, primary exports still have greater significance for Latin America than for any other region in the world. There is thus an imperative need for the countries in the region to reappraise the passive role that they have played recently, both in trade itself and in the negotiations aimed at making the indispensable reforms of the present international economic order.

Notes

[1] Inter-American Bank *Economic Report* (Washington DC 1980).

[2] CEPAL 'La pobreza en América Latina: situación, evolución y orientación de política', mimeo, E/CE AL/Proy. 1/1, 1970 (Santiago 1979).

[3] World Bank *World Development Report 1980* (Washington DC 1980).

[4] CEPAL *Políticas de promoción de exportaciones* (Santiago 1977); H. Chenery and D. Keesing 'The changing composition of developing country exports' World Bank Staff Working Paper no. 314 (Washington DC 1979).

[5] World Bank *World Development Report* (Washington DC 1980) table SA–4.

[6] E. Tironi B. 'Trade relations between the Latin American and Asian ADCs', Paper presented at 9th Pacific Trade and Development Conference, Seoul, Korea.

[7] M. Radetzki 'Where should developing country minerals be processed?' *World Development* v 4 (1977).

26

TRANSNATIONAL CORPORATIONS, COMPARATIVE ADVANTAGE AND FOOD SECURITY IN LATIN AMERICA

Christopher D. Scott

Introduction

In recent years there has been a rapid growth of empirical work on TNCs in the Latin American food industries.[1] While these studies provide much useful descriptive information, their contributions either to the theory of the transnational firms or to the analytic procedures for evaluating direct foreign investment are less well defined. This chapter examines certain criticisms of TNCs in one sector of the food industry, namely the processing of agricultural products for exports.[2] The analysis forms part of a more general search for a rigorous and relevant methodology for evaluating the impact of TNCs in the food industry on the host economy.

Foreign firms may affect these industries in four ways, but only the first case is discussed here:

(1) by direct investment in the food industries themselves;
(2) by licensing local producers to manufacture a foodstuff;
(3) by licensing a local producer to manufacture capital goods for the local food industry, which leads to embodied changes in food processing technology;[3]
(4) by directly exporting inputs to or importing the output from locally owned food firms.

Some blurring of these *a priori* distinctions occurs in practice, as when the direct foreign investment takes the form of a minority equity stake in a joint venture (with a local partner) which operates as the licensee of the foreign parent company, or where a foreign firm acts both as a local producer and as an overseas purchasing agency or broker for its parent company – for instance, United States broker-direct investors in the Mexican strawberry industry.[4]

Social cost-benefit analysis as an evaluative methodology

General assessments of food TNCs' activities in Latin America vary widely. At one extreme, the agribusiness approach of the Harvard Business School suggests that the positive contribution of such firms to the host economy is self-evident.[5] At the other extreme, both populists[6] and 'world systems' theorists[7] conclude that TNCs in the food industry have a negative effect on the welfare of the majority of the host country's population. However, neither of these positions will appear adequate to anyone entertaining the possibility that some types of direct foreign investment may be beneficial, while other types may not. In this case, an explicit, consistent and comprehensive methodology is required for distinguishing between desirable and undesirable investment projects. It might be argued that such a procedure already exists in the form of social cost-benefit analysis (SCBA), which has been successfully applied to the appraisal of foreign investment in food processing.[8]

SCBA has several strengths as an evaluative methodology. It remains the only technique that can reduce many of the different quantitative effects of foreign investment to a single criterion to which a coherent and consistent decision rule may be applied. Furthermore, it requires that the alternatives to direct foreign investment be explicitly identified. This is crucial, because the results of any evaluation will depend on what is assumed to occur in the absence of the TNC. In the case of the food industry in Latin America, any one of the following options may be relevant:

(1) importing the product;
(2) no domestic consumption or production because the good is non-tradable;
(3) production by a locally owned firm, in which case it should be stated whether the domestic firm is assumed to be publicly or privately owned;
(4) production by a joint venture with a specified domestic/foreign equity mix;
(5) another foreign firm is permitted to undertake the investment;
(6) production by the same foreign firm but subject to more stringent legal constraints imposed by the host government, for example the prohibition of certain promotional practices;
(7) banning domestic consumption and production of the product because the host government considers it socially undesirable.

Thus, if at the time a TNC wishes to make an investment there is no locally owned firm able (technically and/or financially) and/or willing (that is, prepared to take the risk) to undertake the project itself, then the effective *ex ante* alternatives to this direct foreign investment would be (1) if it was an importable (or potential exportable); (2) if it was non-tradable; (4) or (5) if another TNC was able and willing to undertake the investment. Options (6) and (7) are primarily relevant to *ex post* appraisals. Once a direct foreign investment has been made, additional information may become available regarding company practices or the product itself, which may lead the host government to reappraise the investment.

The failure to identify explicitly the presumed alternative to the presence of a TNC constitutes a major weakness of many empirical studies of direct foreign investment in the region's food industry. For example, the local manufacture of branded soft drinks such as Coca Cola is often criticized because of the low nutritional value of such beverages.[9] Leaving aside the fact that most bottlers are licensees rather than TNCs, the more desirable alternative which is implicitly assumed is to do without the product at all. This is acceptable so long as the critic admits that this is tantamount to placing soft drinks in the same category as banned drugs like marijuana and cocaine (though not tobacco). In this case, the argument should concern whether this specific abrogation of consumer sovereignty is justified. At this point, our putative critic might respond in one of two ways.

If he broadly accepts the framework of a mixed market economy within which to discuss matters of resource allocation, he might suggest that branded soft drinks should not be banned outright, but that he disapproved of the heavy advertising expenditure associated with these products, which weakens the concept of consumer sovereignty. This is a fair matter for debate, but what should be noted is that the implicit alternative is now (6) and not (7), that is, the introduction of legislation to encourage price rather than non-price competition amongst soft drinks manufacturers.

Alternatively, our critic may reject consumer sovereignty entirely, and visualize a social welfare function the arguments of which are not the individual welfare functions of each member of the population which depend on the consumption of leisure and material goods. In this case, an argument about the nutritional value of Coca Cola turns out to be the tip of an ideological iceberg, because the underlying substantive issue concerns the relative merits of markets (even if imperfect) and central planning as systems of resource allocation. In this case, the relevant alternative remains (7).

The explicit consideration of alternatives to a given investment project is thus an integral part of social cost-benefit analysis, and constitutes one of its major conceptual advantages. In the case of a *foreign* investment, the appraisal proceeds in two parts. In the first part, the net present value of the costs of producing a given level of output locally by a TNC is compared with the net present value of purchasing a similar volume of imports. If the latter exceeds the former, then the investment is considered socially desirable on cost-benefit grounds. The second part of the analysis is required because passing this initial test is a necessary but not sufficient condition for a host government to approve a direct foreign investment. It is not sufficient because domestic production by a locally owned firm or by means of a joint venture might be even more socially profitable than through a wholly foreign-owned affiliate of a TNC. This second stage of the appraisal allows the differential effects of the foreignness of a particular investment with respect to financing, technology and externalities to be isolated and quantified.

Although SCBA is a necessary element in appraising direct foreign investment in LDCs, it, in turn, is insufficient. This is because some major criticisms of TNCs concern not so much their foreignness as their role in integrating host economies with the world market in particular ways. The problem is seen not to be *foreign* capital, but capital in general. These criticisms may be equally relevant to locally owned firms, but they still need to be evaluated. However, to do so requires going beyond the effects of foreign investment, which are usually covered by SCBA. In this chapter, two such arguments are examined, both of which concern the role of TNCs in promoting the growth of export crop production through the establishment of local processing facilities. The first relates to the distribution of agricultural income, and the second to the issue of food security.

The food industries in Latin America
The food processing industries taken together constitute one of the principal activities in the manufacturing sector of Latin America.[10] In 1975 these industries generated net output of more than US $15,000 million and provided employment for more than two million persons.[11] However, the relative importance of food processing varies widely within the region. In 1973 food products, beverages and tobacco made up 15.4 per cent of manufacturing output in Brazil, 28.7 per cent in Colombia, 42.6 per cent in Ecuador and 72.1 per cent in the Dominican Republic.[12] Although not one of the fastest growing sectors of industry, the relatively labour-intensive nature of processed food production has meant that its contribution to the total increase in manufacturing employment continues to be significant.[13] Thus, between 1968 and 1975, food, beverages and tobacco accounted for 17.4 per cent of the overall rise in manufacturing employment in the region, which placed this branch second only to metal products, machinery and equipment with respect to incremental job creation in manufacturing industry.[14]

The food industries also enjoy a special qualitative importance for anyone concerned with poverty in less developed countries. In Rawls' terminology, staple foodstuffs are prime examples of social primary goods which are defined as 'things that every rational man is presumed to want'.[15] Recent discussion of 'basic needs' in less developed countries accords such foodstuffs a similar priority.

Studies of consumer behaviour in the region suggest that approximately half the expenditure of the mean urban household is on food and beverages, while this proportion reaches nearly 70 per cent in the case of the median urban household in the lowest (income) quartile.[16] The

Table 25　Distribution of TNC affiliates by food industry sector and sub-sector among Latin American countries, 1976 (number of affiliates)

Exports

	Meat packing & processing*	Fisheries	Fruit & vegetable processing*	Coffee processing	Cocoa & chocolate*	Tea*
Argentina	4	2	5	1	2	4
Bolivia	—	—	—	—	—	—
Brazil	6	2	13	4	4	2
Chile	—	2	2	1	1	—
Colombia	1	1	6	2	1	—
Ecuador	1	4	4	1	1	—
Mexico	5	5	14	2	5	3
Paraguay	1	—	—	—	—	1
Peru	—	3	4	1	—	—
Uruguay	2	1	1	1	1	—
Venezuela	6	1	13	1	4	2
Guyana	—	1	—	—	—	—
Surinam	—	1	1	—	—	—
El Salvador	1	1	2	1	—	1
Honduras	—	—	2	—	—	—
Guatemala	3	3	4	3	—	1
Panama	3	4	3	—	—	—
Costa Rica	—	1	6	1	—	—
Nicaragua	—	3	2	1	—	—
Dominican Republic	1	—	2	—	—	—
Bahamas	—	2	—	—	—	—
Jamaica	—	1	3	1	1	—
Barbados	—	—	1	—	—	—
Trinidad	—	—	—	1	1	—
Total	34	38	88	22	21	14

* This industry also supplies domestic markets; † this industry also supplies export markets; ‡ wheat and maize flour; § includes maize, palm, soya bean, sunflower, coconut, peanut and cotton seed.

Source Transnational corporations in food and beverage processing (United Nations Centre on Transnational Corporations, 1980).

special importance of food consumption is reflected in the use of nutritional intake levels as partial indices of human welfare, to be set alongside such indicators of economic growth and development as per capita incomes. In this regard, certain evidence suggests that 61 per cent of Latin American children under five were malnourished in the early 1970s, and that daily per capita consumption of protein declined in Argentina, Uruguay, Mexico, Paraguay, Colombia, Ecuador, El Salvador and Haiti between 1961 and 1971/3. By contrast, it is suggested that

Local market staples			Local market–branded goods				
Flour milling‡	Animal feeds†	Dairy production	Beer	Wines & distilled alcoholic beverages	Edible oils†‡	Soft drink concentrate	TOTAL
4	4	5	1	4	3	3	42
7	8	6	2	5	9	4	72
1	2	2	—	1	2	2	16
3	3	4	1	1	2	3	28
3	1	1	—	—	—	1	17
7	4	10	—	7	6	6	74
—	—	—	—	—	—	—	2
2	4	2	—	—	3	—	19
3	1	1	1	—	1	1	14
8	4	6	2	3	3	2	55
2	—	—	—	—	—	—	3
—	—	—	1	—	—	—	3
2	2	1	—	—	1	—	12
2	1	—	1	—	2	—	8
4	4	2	—	—	4	—	29
3	1	4	—	—	2	1	21
1	—	1	—	1	2	1	14
4	1	1	1	—	2	—	15
—	—	3	—	—	—	—	6
—	—	1	—	—	—	—	3
1	3	5	1	1	1	1	19
1	—	1	—	—	—	—	3
1	1	2	1	—	1	—	8
59	44	58	12	23	44	25	482

in 1975 5 per cent of the region's population 'consumed about 4,700 calories per capita per day or twice the minimum average requirement of 2,320 calories'.[17]

The rising share of merchandise imports composed of foodstuffs experienced by certain Latin American countries has also increased the political concern for 'food security' in certain quarters.[18] In some cases, this has led to apparently decisive shifts in policy to encourage a greater degree of self-sufficiency in basic foodstuffs – for instance, the establishment by the Mexican government of a National Food System (SAM).

It is difficult to estimate with precision the relative importance within the Latin American food industry of those branches processing locally produced foodstuffs for export. This is partly owing to the general paucity of data on the food industry, and partly to the fact that many processing firms supply both local and foreign markets. It is even more problematic to establish the significance of direct foreign investment in food export processing activities. However, Table 25, which has been constructed from data made available by the United Nations Centre on Transnational Corporations, indicates the approximate distribution of TNC affiliates in different branches of the Latin American food industry in 1976. It suggests that 217 affiliates, or 45 per cent of the total, were present in the six branches – meat packing and processing, fisheries, fruit and vegetable processing, coffee processing, cocoa and chocolate, and tea – where output is primarily destined for export.

Comparative advantage and the distribution of agricultural income

The first criticism of TNCs levelled under this heading is that the establishment of processing facilities for export crops has an adverse effect on the distribution of agricultural income in the host country.[19] Because of the unequal distribution of land, irrigation water and agricultural credit, only the richer farmers are able to cultivate the new crops, and it is they who obtain most of the benefits. The distribution of agricultural income changes in favour of the better-off, and so the theory of comparative advantage should be rejected as a principle of resource allocation on equity grounds.

There are several sources of confusion here. The theory of comparative advantage is concerned with *explaining* the pattern of trade between countries, and not with prescribing general rules for what a country *should* export or import. Given certain assumptions, it shows that (1) a unique (general) equilibrium will exist, and that (2) this equilibrium will be socially efficient, that is, it will maximize the value of national output, given relative prices. It does not claim to assess the equity of income distribution at all.[20] In principle, the government can achieve its equity objectives by designing a fiscal system which operates through lump sum taxes and transfers, and which would leave the efficiency optimum unchanged. In this particular case, farmers would pay a wealth tax based on the capitalized potential value of their land, and poor peasants and agricultural labourers with incomes below a certain level would receive direct income supplements.

Furthermore, this argument is not so much a criticism of TNCs as of imperfect capital markets in Latin American agriculture deriving from an unequal distribution of land, to which the appropriate solution is agrarian reform and improved access to credit for poor farmers.

But what is the evidence as to the distributional effects of export-led agricultural growth under the aegis of TNCs in food processing? Recent case studies suggest that these effects have varied widely among, and probably within, Latin American countries. The gains from trade have been most unequally distributed in those export sectors which correspond to plantation versions of the Lewis model. Thus, in the Dominican Republic, Gulf and Western increased sugar output at La Romana between 1963 and 1979, while the real wages of cane cutters may have fallen. This was made possible by the virtually unlimited supply of field labour from Haiti over this period.[21] In Panama, the average real product wage (that is, in terms of bananas) on the United Fruit (Brands) plantations rose by 3.8 per cent per annum between 1950 and 1974, while the average product of labour rose by 6.2 per cent per annum over the same period. This led to a decline in the wage share of gross export value from over 60 per cent to less than 40 per cent. In this case the crucial factor was disembodied labour-displacing technical change, which reduced employment on the foreign-owned corporate banana plantations in Costa Rica, Guatemala, Honduras and Panama from 75,249 persons in 1948 to 32,261 in 1976.[22]

Host country gains from TNC plantation exports are also affected by the extent of transfer pricing. Charges that exports were consistently undervalued, thereby reducing the industry's retained value (through lower business income tax payments), have been levelled both at Gulf and Western in the Dominican Republic and at the US corporations in the Central American banana industry.[23] This criticism is related specifically to the 'foreignness' of TNCs, which are assumed to have both an incentive and a capacity for price manipulation which locally owned firms are presumed to lack. In this case, free 'arms-length' trade is implicitly held up as the ideal, so the principle of comparative advantage itself is not being questioned.

Yet direct foreign investment of the enclave type is now the exception rather than the rule in Latin America. More common are TNC-owned processing plants which have backward supply linkages with medium-sized farms. In Brazil, where TNCs such as Anderson Clayton, Cargill and Continental Grain have a strong presence in soya processing, 30 per cent of the total area in soya beans in 1970 was on farms of less than 10 hectares, and 94 per cent of the labour input into the crop came from unremunerated family labour.[24] Although there are certain methodological difficulties surrounding the published data on agricultural incomes in Brazil, there is evidence of significant growth in the real incomes of small farmers and farm labourers since 1970. There is a strong positive correlation between average regional productivity and the household incomes of small farmers and farm labourers, and the southern region, where most of the soya is produced, is ranked second after São Paulo. For Brazil as a whole, the real casual rural wage rate rose by approximately 56 per cent between 1970 and 1977.[25]

TNCs which have invested in import-substituting activities have also established similar backward linkages with small and medium farmers. In the northern *sierra* of Peru an affiliate of Nestlé (PERULAC) has purchased fresh milk locally for its processing plant since 1947. Over this period the average annual milk delivery of intra-firm-supplies fell from 61 metric tons (in 1947) to 19 metric tons (in 1978), owing to the progressive incorporation of small farmers into the supply network. By 1979, 76 per cent of PERULAC's suppliers possessed on average only five cows each, yet they were responsible for 45 per cent of the milk delivered to the plant. Estimates of the growth of dairy farmers' incomes over this period are unavailable, but milk deliveries to the plant increased more than twentyfold, which indicates the importance of PERU-LAC for the expansion of peasants' cash revenues in the region.[26]

Therefore it is difficult to establish any general presumption that TNCs' investment in the processing of export crops or in import-substituting activities necessarily increases the relative inequality of rural income distribution, while it certainly raises total agricultural income. However, even if income distribution worsened as measured by some relative index of inequality, the situation with the TNC investment could still be Pareto-superior to the situation without it. Some groups have benefited, others have not, but no one is absolutely worse off than before. This last point is crucial, because if some groups are absolutely worse off, then (1) required compensation payments must be calculated and (2) some assessment of the likelihood of the gainers *actually* compensating the losers must be made.

Who might be worse off as a result of TNCs' promotion of export crops, and how might such a situation come about? Two possibilities may be identified. If a country's exports grow rapidly and it supplies a large share of the world market, and if the foreign price elasticity of demand for its exports is very low, then the country's net barter terms of trade could deteriorate sufficiently to leave its inhabitants worse off than before.[27] Since most Latin American countries are price takers in world markets, this case of immiserizing growth is not likely to be of general relevance. However, by 1975 Brazil had become the third largest soya bean exporter in the world, with 30 per cent of world trade in the commodity.[28] Since soya bean exports grew at 41 per cent per annum between 1968 and 1977 in Brazil, and agricultural products are generally held to have low short-run price elasticities of demand, the probability of immiserising growth is higher.[29] Nevertheless, given that soya beans only constituted 12 per cent of Brazilian merchandise exports in 1978, such an outcome is still unlikely.[30]

A second relatively common argument, associating the growth of agricultural exports with the reduced welfare of certain groups, goes as follows. An expansion in the acreage sown to export crops leads to a reduction in the area cultivated with locally consumed food staples. This decrease in domestic supplies of basic foodstuffs implies reduced domestic availability and hence a rise in their price. These price increases reduce the real wage of food deficit farmers unable to grow the new export crop, landless agricultural wage labourers and the urban poor. Such reasoning has been applied to the displacement of black beans by soya beans in Brazil during the 1970s,[31] while a similar debate surrounded the expansion of export crops in coastal Peru during and after the First World War.[32]

This 'crowding out' thesis appears plausible at first sight, but it contains several assumptions which need to be identified before its validity can be assessed. The supply of agricultural land (and other factors) is assumed fixed and fully employed before and after the expansion of exports, so the game is zero-sum. Accepting this, and given that the food staple is an importable (which is the case for black beans in Brazil), it is then necessary to distinguish between a price rise indicating a temporary shortage while the market readjusts to some exogenous change, and a permanent increase in price. Unless the importing country purchases a large share of total world imports of the food staple, it can buy more food imports at a constant price. In this situation, a rise in the price of the importable can only be a temporary frictional phenomenon following the leftward shift of the domestic supply curve of food, which leads to an unanticipated run-down in food retailers' stocks, who then face a short delay until increased food imports re-establish equilibrium at the unchanged previous price. Indeed, after consulting the primary source used by Lappé and Collins, it seems that it is precisely just such an 'immediate-run' market-clearing exercise that is being described.[33] Therefore, if domestic transport costs are ignored, the growth of export crop production would lead to a once and for all rise in domestic food prices only (1) under the large-country assumption, or (2) if increased food imports were unavailable for some reason – for instance, quotas levied on food imports, foreign exchange rationed by government and foodstuffs assigned low priority (which is unlikely); or (3) if a tariff were imposed on food imports.

However, if neither (1), (2) nor (3) hold, the domestic price of the food staple could rise in a sustained manner for certain groups if the internal costs of transport and distribution for imported food were greater than for an equal quantity of locally produced foodstuffs. Once these marketing costs are taken into account, it is possible that although the border price (c.i.f.) of imported food remains constant, the price facing certain consumers, particularly those in food deficit rural areas, will have increased. In this modified version the argument may have some substance, but there is little evidence to assess it empirically.

Free trade versus food security

It is often argued in the popular, not to say populist, literature on agribusiness that foreign firms through their promotion of export crops diminish the food security of the host country. The concept of 'food security' is elusive, and several senses of the term may be distinguished. *National* food security refers to a country's capacity to maintain current levels of aggregate food consumption in the face of unexpected reductions in food imports. Such reductions may be caused by foreign countries deliberately withholding food supplies for some reason, or by sudden shortfalls in foreign exchange earnings. Empirical measures of national food security might include

$$\left[\frac{\text{annual domestic food production}}{\text{annual food consumption}}\right]\% \text{ and } \left[\frac{\text{food stocks}}{\text{annual food consumption}}\right]\%$$

both of which attempt to indicate the significance of a temporary and unanticipated reduction in the volume of food imports on aggregate domestic food consumption. The higher the value of each index, the greater the degree of national food security.[34]

However, neither of these measures indicates the extent to which the poorest in society have 'secure' access to staple foodstuffs, nor whether those most at risk from malnutrition are able to obtain minimum food requirements. Therefore, *personal* food security may be defined as the minimum levels of nutritional intake required at different ages and physiological states (for example, pregnant or lactating mothers) to prevent long-term physiological damage to an individual. The precise determination of such nutritional minima has been the subject of intense debate for many years, but recent evidence does suggest that malnutrition in infancy can permanently stunt an individual's mental and physical development.[35] Given this notion of personal food security, we may pass finally to the concept of *group* food security, defined as the proportion of members of a given group having a nutritional intake less than the appropriate personal minimum at a given point in time. The relevant group could be all persons in the lowest quartile of the income distribution, all children under five or all pregnant and lactating mothers.

To what extent is specialization according to comparative advantage inimical to any of these concepts of food security? Two reasons may be given for limiting the degree of specialization below some static optimum in the interests of national food security. First, the United States is the dominant supply source for food imports into Latin America.[36] Given the domestic political importance of providing adequate food supplies to the increasingly urban population of the region, Latin American governments feel strategically vulnerable to the use of the 'food weapon' by the US for reasons of foreign policy which could lead to the disruption of their food imports – for example, President Carter's grain embargo on the USSR in 1980. For this reason, food security is increasingly being seen by governments in the region as an integral component of national security.

Second, a weaker argument against a rapid expansion of agricultural exports might be put forward based on the alleged adverse consequences of export instability for economic growth. A free trade policy, it is suggested, leads to a high degree of concentration in the commodity composition of domestic production and of exports. Reliance on a small number of export items will increase instability. This in turn will undermine national food security and reduce the country's aggregate growth rate in one of two ways. Under a flexible exchange rate and with no food subsidies, an unforeseen shortfall in export revenue will raise the domestic price of foodstuffs (an importable), as the exchange rate depreciates to re-establish equilibrium on the balance of trade. This leads to upward pressure on the nominal wage, as workers seek to maintain real wages. In a Lewis-type model, a rise in the modern sector's nominal wage is effectively a rise in the real product wage which capitalists have to pay. This reduces profits, and if desired investment is constrained by the supply of business savings in the modern sector, aggregate investment will fall and the aggregate growth rate will be reduced.

Alternatively, the government might prevent a sudden fall in export revenue leading to an increase in the domestic food prices. Under a flexible exchange rate, it could increase food subsidies to compensate for the depreciation of the local currency. However, this is likely to increase the budget deficit which is likely to lead to a general rise in domestic prices – that is, inflation. The government could also attempt to keep local food prices down by maintaining a fixed exchange rate. In this case, the trade deficit would need to be financed either out of reserves or from foreign loans. To the extent that a high level of reserves is maintained for this purpose, this reduces the mean rate of return on the nation's wealth, because gold and foreign currency reserves are by definition extremely liquid, and are, therefore, relatively low-yielding assets. If recurrent trade deficits are to be met through foreign loans, this could increase dependence on external financial sources such as the International Monetary Fund. The implicit alternative to a TNC-led expansion of agricultural export crops, leading to greater export instability, is a greater degree of national self-sufficiency in food, to be achieved through acreage quotas, production subsidies to domestic farmers or tariffs on imported foodstuffs.[37]

This argument is shaky both on theoretical grounds and with regard to the empirical evidence. In the first place, it is not clear why the costs of unexpected decreases in export revenue should necessarily outweigh the benefits of windfall increases in the value of exports. Yet the export instability argument assumes that such asymmetry exists. Other steps in the argument rest on firmer ground. It is true that the two most commonly used models of comparative advantage both predict high degrees of specialization under free trade, even in a multi-country, multi-commodity world. In the Ricardian model, it is still likely that a country will produce (and export) a single commodity, while in the Heckscher-Ohlin version it has been predicted that a maximum of two goods will be produced in any one national economy.[38] Although the inclusion of transport costs and specific factors of production may limit the degree of product specialization predicted, conventional trade theory does suggest that free trade will be associated with high levels of concentration in the commodity composition of both domestic production and exports.

There is also evidence that export commodity concentration is positively associated with export revenue instability, but the issue is still in debate. Assuming that high concentration does in general increase instability, will the presence of TNCs in the export sector aggravate or reduce such instability for a given level of commodity concentration? There are at least three reasons for believing that direct foreign investment may reduce instability.

First, in a national economy hosting TNCs in its export sector, it is not the instability of total export revenue that is important, but the instability of that proportion of total revenue which accrues to domestic factors (retained value). If export instability is caused by price fluctuations rather than by variations in export volume, then it is likely that retained value will be more stable than total revenue, with remitted profits acting as a buffer between them. When prices rise unexpectedly, although an increase in retained value may be assumed due to enlarged tax payments from corporate income tax and any taxes linked to export price levels, the major change will be remitted profits, which is the TNC affiliate's residual income. When prices fall suddenly, similar reasoning implies that this residual will fluctuate by more than retained value. Therefore the presence of TNCs in the export sector is likely to reduce the extent of export (retained) revenue instability for a given commodity concentration of exports, *ceteris paribus*.

Second, where the local TNC affiliate's operations form part of a vertically integrated structure of international production and distribution, the price of the export crop may be extremely stable over long periods of time. In his study of the Central American banana industry, Ellis showed that the coefficient of variation of the average annual f.o.b.

banana price was only 6.8 per cent between 1950 and 1974.[39]

Third, it will be recalled that a charge made against TNCs was that they promoted the substitution of export food crops for locally consumed basic staples. However, other things remaining equal, this will diversify the commodity composition of exports and increase the ratio of food exports to total exports. Massell's results show that a decrease in export commodity concentration and an increase in the food export ratio each reduce independently a country's export instability.[40]

The last link in this argument alleging that increased export instability leads to lower economic growth is the most controversial. Opinion on this topic has moved through 180 degrees, from early *a priori* views which considered export instability to be self-evidently harmful to growth, through a period when it was felt to have no effect on growth at all, to more recent contributions which have suggested that increased export instability may be associated with accelerated growth.[41] The theoretical approaches and empirical methodologies used by different authors vary widely, and the debate is still very much alive. However, it may be noted that one of the few studies to work with income growth on a per capita basis found that export instability had a significant negative effect on real per capita income growth rates of LDCs.[42]

Whether export instability has an adverse effect on per capita growth rates of food consumption in LDCs, or on either of the measures of national food security mentioned earlier, has not yet been investigated. Until such analysis is undertaken, it is not possible to reach any firm conclusions regarding the impact of sudden shortfalls in export revenue on the purchase of food imports compared with non-food imports.

Conclusions

This paper has examined an extremely limited number of arguments critical of the effects of TNCs which process export crops in Latin America. Many important issues relating to direct foreign investment in the food processing industries have not been discussed, for lack of space. These issues include the efficiency and equity consequences of production contracting between processors and growers, the impact of entry by TNCs on the market structure of individual food industries, and the role of TNCs in changing consumers' tastes in the region.

The main conclusions of the analysis may be summarized as follows:

(1) It is important to distinguish criticisms of TNCs based on their foreignness (which the application of two-stage social cost-benefit analysis can attempt to assess) from arguments critical of the practice of a certain entrepreneurial logic (that is, profit maximization) which locally owned firms may fully share with foreign firms.

(2) Much of the radical literature on TNCs in the food industry misunderstands the nature of the theory of comparative advantage. This

theory embodies an efficiency, not an equity, argument.

(3) The distributional effects of TNC-led agricultural export growth have varied widely among Latin American countries, depending on the technology employed and the nature of backward supply linkages.

(4) There is little evidence either of immiserizing growth or for the 'crowding out' thesis as a general consequence of TNC-led agricultural export growth in the region.

(5) The rapid increase of food imports into certain countries in recent years has led to a heightened awareness of strategic vulnerability to the United States as the world's major net exporter of foodstuffs.

(6) The evidence is insufficient to assess whether TNC-led agricultural export growth in the region has increased export instability, and if it has, whether such increased instability has reduced the growth rate of per capita food consumption or decreased national food security. The *a priori* arguments are not compelling.

(7) Specialization according to comparative advantage is not in and of itself inimical to target group food security. All depends on how export income is distributed, which is properly a matter for host government fiscal policy. Indeed, it is generally true that in Latin America as a whole, discriminatory government policies against domestic food agriculture, such as controlled prices and low public sector investment in rural areas, have contributed more to national and group food insecurity in the region than have the activities of TNCs.

Notes

[1] Major studies of TNCs in the Latin American food industries recently completed or in the process of completion include the project directed by Gonzalo Arroyo at the Centre de Recherche sur l'Amérique Latine et le Tiers Monde (CETRAL) and the studies coordinated by Raúl Trajtenberg and Raul Vigorito at the Instituto Latinoamericano de Estudios Transnacionales in Mexico City. In the United States there is a burgeoning radical populist literature on agribusiness which includes the work of Burbach and Flynn (specifically related to Latin America) and Lappé and Collins (relating to less developed countries generally). The recent report by the United Nations Centre on Transnational Corporations on TNCs and the food processing industries of developing countries also contains valuable information on Latin America. For an overview of the determinants of direct foreign investment in the Latin American food industries, see C. D. Scott *Transnational corporations and the food industry in Latin America: an analysis of the development of investment and divestment*, Working Paper no. 64, Latin America Program, Woodrow Wilson International Centre (Washington 1981).

[2] This paper follows the United Nations usage in defining transnational corporations as firms which own and control productive assets in two or more countries.

[3] For a study of foreign licensing to manufacture bread-making machinery in Latin America, see C. Cooper and P. Maxwell *Machinery and the transfer of technology to Latin America* (Washington 1975).

[4] E. Feder *Strawberry imperialism: an enquiry into the mechanism of dependency in Mexican agriculture* (Mexico 1978).

[5] R. Goldberg *Agribusiness management for developing countries: Latin America* (Cambridge 1974).

[6] R. Burbach and P. Flynn *Agribusiness in the Americas* (New York, 1980); Feder *op. cit.*

[7] A. G. Frank *Crisis in the Third World* (London 1981).

[8] D. Lal *Appraising foreign investment in developing countries* (London 1975); S. Lall and P. Streeten *Foreign investment, transnationals and developing countries* (London 1977).

[9] R. J. Ledogar *Hungry for profits* (New York 1975) pp. 111–26.

[10] The food processing industries include all forms of material transformation which a set of agricultural products (including livestock and fish) undergo between harvesting (or delivery to the slaughterhouse or netting) and emergence as a final edible good. Also included is the production of certain intermediate goods based on the utilization of by-products of food processing activities which are sold to manufacturers of non-foodstuffs, e.g. industrial alcohol sold by sugar mills to chemical plants, corn starch sold by grain mills to the paper industry. This definition is taken to exclude:
(1) any processing activities in the wholesale and retail segments of the food chain which are primarily concerned with distribution, e.g. supermarkets;
(2) commercial establishments which prepare and serve food directly to the public, e.g. restaurants;
(3) food processing activities within the household;
(4) processing of timber and fibres;
(5) agricultural production, except where TNCs own and control agro-industrial complexes which vertically integrate field and factory operations.
This definition of the food processing industries approximates the *United States Standard Industrial Classification (USSIC), Code 20 – Food and Kindred Products* (numerical list of manufactured products) 1978, and the *International Standard Industrial Classification (ISIC) Code 31 – Food, Beverages and Tobacco.*

[11] United Nations Centre on Transnational Corporations *Transnational corporations in food and beverage processing* (New York 1980) p. 182.

[12] United Nations Industrial Development Organization (hereafter UNIDO) *World industry since 1960: progress and prospects* (New York, 1979) p. 87.

[13] UNIDO *op. cit.* p. 68. Between 1960 and 1974 the unweighted average compound annual growth rate of output of food products, beverages and tobacco in Latin America was 5.2 per cent. This was higher than textiles, clothing and footwear, but approximately half the growth rate of the most rapidly expanding branches of manufacturing industry such as industrial chemicals and machinery.

[14] UNIDO *op. cit.* p. 240.

[15] J. Rawls *A theory of justice* (Oxford 1972) p. 302. Rawls argues that a general conception of justice requires that 'all social primary goods – liberty and opportunity, income and wealth, and the bases of self-respect – are to be distributed equally unless an unequal distribution of any or all of these goods is to the advantage of the least favoured'.

[16] P. Musgrove *Consumer behaviour in Latin America* (Washington 1978) pp. 130–1 and 161.

[17] Inter-American Development Bank *Nutrition and socio-economic development of Latin America* (Washington 1979) pp. 3, 18–19.

[18] World Bank *World Bank Development Report, 1981* (Washington 1981) p. 155. The most dramatic case is Mexico, where food imports as a proportion of total merchandise imports rose from 4 per cent in 1960 to 13 per cent in 1977.

[19] Burbach and Flynn *op. cit.* pp. 125–6; F. M. Lappé and J. Collins *Food first: beyond the myth of scarcity* (New York 1976) pp. 220–33.

[20] R. Caves and R. W. Jones *World trade and payments* (Boston, 3rd edn 1981) pp. 26–8, 98–102. Of course, trade models do predict changes in the pre-tax functional distribution of incomes as a result of opening a country to foreign trade.

[21] H. Frundt *Gulf and Western in the Dominican Republic: an evaluation* (New York 1979) pp. 13–16.

[22] F. Ellis 'The banana export activity in Central America, 1947–1976: a case-study of plantation exports by vertically integrated transnational corporations' (unpubl. D.Phil.

thesis, University of Sussex 1978) pp. 149, 151–60.

23 C. D. Scott *Tecnología, empleo y distribución de ingresos en la industria azucarera de la República Dominicana* (Santiago 1978) p. 12; Ellis *op. cit. passim.*

24 G. Muller *Les oléagineaux et l'expansion récente du soja au Brésil* (Paris 1979) pp. 175–7.

25 G. P. Pfeffermann and R. Webb *The distribution of income in Brazil*, World Bank Staff Paper no. 356 (Washington 1979) pp. 90–7. The rural wage series refers to cash earnings only. The authors suggest that although payments in kind were reduced, following the extension of labour legislation to the rural areas in the mid 1960s, these reductions were unlikely to have affected rural income trends in the 1970s.

26 M. Lajo Lazo 'The evaporated milk land: transnationals in the Third World food system shown with the example of Nestlé in Peru' (unpubl. mimeo) chap. 3, tables 3 and 7.

27 J. Bhagwati 'Immiserizing growth: a geometric note' *Review of Economic Studies* xxv 3 (1957/8).

28 Lappé and Collins *op. cit.* p. 250.

29 Muller *op. cit.* p. 163; W. Tyler *Advanced developing countries as export competitors in Third World markets: the Brazilian experience* (Washington 1980) pp. 18, 71.

30 The possibility of immiserizing growth should be distinguished from the Prebisch-Singer thesis concerning the secular deterioration of the commodity terms of trade of less developed countries. Bhagwati's model is more general in that it does not refer to any particular type of country (LDC or advanced economy) nor to any specific exportable (primary or manufactured product). It assumes growth in only one of two countries, while Prebisch assumed both centre and periphery growing simultaneously over time. Most important of all, immiserizing growth implies that a country is absolutely worse off, i.e., is on a lower community indifference curve, as a result of the fall in the commodity terms of trade. The Prebisch-Singer thesis does not imply this. It merely alleges that the commodity terms of trade of a primary exporting/less developed country will fall over time, but not necessarily by so much as to make the country absolutely worse off. Thus, the necessary and sufficient conditions for immiserizing growth to occur are more stringent than for a secular deterioration in the net barter terms of trade.

31 Lappé and Collins *op. cit.* pp. 223–4.

32 R. Thorp and G. Bertram *Peru, 1890–1977: growth and policy in an open economy* (London 1978) pp. 132–40.

33 *Latin America* x (1976) p. 326.

34 National food security might also be taken to mean local ownership and control of productive assets in processing foodstuffs for domestic consumption. However, the reasons for direct foreign investment in food processing to constitute 'food insecurity' are not self-evident.

35 A. Berg *The nutrition factor* (Washington 1973) pp. 9–13.

36 US Department of Agriculture *Agricultural Situation: Western Hemisphere Review of 1980 and Outlook for 1981* (Washington 1981). The value of United States agricultural exports (at current prices) to Latin America rose more than threefold between 1976 and 1980. In 1980 the value of these exports was over US $6,000 million. No other country or region of the world can substitute for the United States as the dominant net food exporter in the international food system in the foreseeable future.

37 H. Myint *The economics of developing countries* (London, 5th ed, 1980) p. 134. Myint suggests the subsidization of domestic food agriculture in order to promote infant industry.

38 Caves and Jones *op. cit.* pp. 87–9, 122–30.

39 Ellis *op. cit.* p. 156.

40 G. Massell 'Export instability and economic structure' *American Economic Review* 60 (1970) provides a definition of 'food' covering SITC categories O, 1 22, and 4 which includes soya beans, soya bean meal and soya bean oil, discussed above in the context of Brazil.

41 O. Knudsen and A. Parnes *Trade instability and economic development* (Lexington 1975); P. Yotopoulos and J. Nugent *Economics of development: empirical investigations* (New York 1976).

[42] C. Glezankos 'Export instability and economic growth; a statistical verification' *Economic Development and Cultural Change* xxi (1973).

27

Bibliography

This bibliography is intended to assist readers concerned with topics raised in this book that relate specifically to Latin America. For those interested in pursuing theories of imperialism, the annotated bibliography contained in R. Owen and B. Sutcliffe (eds) *Studies in the theory of imperialism* (London 1972) is admirable. Readers who wish to pursue questions of dependency will find the bibliography contained in an article by J. G. Palma ['Dependency: a formal theory of underdevelopment or a methodology for the analysis of concrete situations of underdevelopment?' *World Development* VI (1978)] most helpful.

Abbreviations

AER	*American Economic Review*
AHR	*American Historical Review*
BHR	*Business History Review*
CR	*CEPAL Review*
EHR	*Economic History Review*
HAHR	*Hispanic American Historical Review*
JAH	*Journal of American History*
JCH	*Journal of Contemporary History*
JEH	*Journal of Economic History*
JLAS	*Journal of Latin American Studies*
LAP	*Latin American Perspectives*
LARR	*Latin American Research Review*
NLR	*New Left Review*
TE	*El Trimestre Económico*
WD	*World Development*

Abrams, R. M. 'United States intervention abroad: the first quarter century' *AHR* (1974) pp. 72–102.

Adelman, I. and Morris, C. T. *Economic growth and social equity in developing countries* (London 1973).

Albert, B. *An essay on the Peruvian sugar industry 1880–1922* (Norwich 1976).

Albert, B. *South America and the world economy from independence to 1930* (London 1983).

Albert, B. and Henderson, P. 'Latin America and the Great War: a preliminary survey of developments in Chile, Peru, Argentina and Brazil' *WD* IX 8 (1981).

Althusser, L. *For Marx* (London 1969).

Amin, S. *Unequal development: an essay on the social formations of peripheral capitalism* (London 1976).

Anderson, R. W. 'The United States and Puerto Rico': a critique in R. G. Hellman and J. H. Rosenbaum (eds) *Latin America: the search for a new international role* (London 1975).

Baer, W. *Industrialization and economic development in Brazil* (Homewood 1965)

Baer, W. 'The economics of Prebisch and ECLA' *Economic Development and Cultural Change* x 2 (1962).

Baer, W. 'Import substitution and industrialization in Latin America; experiences and interpretations' *LARR* 1 (1972).

Baer, W. and Villela, A. V. 'Industrial growth and industrialization, revisions in the stages of Brazil's economic development' *Journal of Developing Areas* VII 2 (1972/3).

Bagú, S. *Economía de la sociedad colonial* (Buenos Aires 1949).

Bagú, S. *Evolución histórica de la estratificación social en la Argentina* (Buenos Aires 1961).

Bailey, D. C. 'Revisionism and the recent historiography of the Mexican Revolution' *HAHR* LVIII 1 (1978).

Baklanoff, E. N. 'External factors in the economic development of Brazil's centre-south, 1850–1930' in E. Baklanoff (ed.) *The shaping of modern Brazil* (Baton Rouge 1969).

Baran, P. *The political economy of growth* (New York 1960).

Barratt Brown, M. *The Economics of Imperialism* (London 1974).

Bauer, A. J. *Chilean rural society from the Spanish Conquest to 1930* (Cambridge 1975).

Bauer, A. J. 'Rural workers in Spanish America: problems of peonage and oppression' *HAHR* LIX 1 (1979) (and subsequent debate, Aug. 1979).

Bauer, A. J. 'The Church and Spanish American agrarian structures 1765–1865' *The Americas* XXVIII 1 (1971–2).

Bazant, J. *Alienation of church wealth in Mexico; social and economic aspects of the liberal revolution, 1856–1875* (Cambridge 1971).

Beckford, G. L. *Persistent poverty: underdevelopment in the plantation economies of the Third World* (New York 1972).

Benjamin, J. R. *The United States and Cuba: hegemony and dependent development 1880–1934* (Pittsburgh 1977).

Bergad, L. W. 'Agrarian history of Puerto Rico, 1870–1930' *LARR* XIII 3 (1978).

Bergquist, C. W. *Coffee and conflict in Colombia, 1886–1910* (Durham, North Carolina 1978).

Blaisier, C. and Mesa-Lago, C. (eds) *Cuba in the world* (Pittsburgh 1979).

Brading, D. *Haciendas and ranchos in the Mexican Bajío, León 1700–1860* (Cambridge 1978).

Brading, D. (ed.) *Caudillo and peasant in the Mexican Revolution* (Cambridge 1980).

Brito Figueroa, F. *Historia económica y social de Venezuela: una estructura para su estudio* (3 vols, Caracas 1966–78).

Brown, J. S. *A socio-economic history of Argentina 1780–1860* (Cambridge 1979).

Brunn, G. *Deutschland und Brasilien (1899–1914)* (Cologne 1971).

Bunge, A. E. *La economía argentina* (4 vols, Buenos Aires 1928–30).

Bunge, A. E. *Las industrias del norte: contribución al estudio de una nueva política económica argentina* (Buenos Aires 1922).

Calderón, F. R. *La república restaurada: la vida económica* (Mexico 1955).

Calderón, F. R. 'Los ferrocarriles' in D. Cosio Villegas (ed.) *Historia moderna de México* (Mexico 1965).

Cardoso, C. F. S. and Pérez Brignoli, H. *Historia económica de América Latina* (2 vols, Barcelona 1979).

Cardoso, F. H. *Ideologías de la burgesía industrial en sociedades dependientes (Argentina y Brazil)* (Mexico 1971).

Cardoso, F. H. *Estado y sociedad en América Latina* (Buenos Aires 1972).

Cardoso, F. H. 'Associated dependent development: theoretical and practical implications' in A. Stepan (ed.) *Authoritarian Brazil* (New Haven 1973).

Cardoso, F. H. 'The consumption of dependency theory in the United States' *LARR* xii 3 (1977).

Cardoso, F. H. *The originality of the copy: ECLA and the idea of development* (Cambridge, Working Paper no. 28, CLAS, 1977).

Cardoso, F. H. and Faletto, E. *Dependency and development in Latin America* (London 1979).

Chandler, A. D. 'The growth of the transnational industrial firm in the United States and the United Kingdom: a comparative analysis' *EHR* xxxiii 3 (1980).

Chilcote, R. H. and Edelstein, J. C. (eds) *Latin America: the struggle with dependency and beyond* (New York 1974).

Coatsworth, J. *The impact of railroads on the economic development of Mexico 1877–1910* (De Kalb 1981).

Coatsworth, J. 'Obstacles to economic growth in nineteenth-century Mexico' *AHR* (1978).

Collier, D. (ed.) *The new authoritarianism in Latin America* (Princeton 1979).

Collier, S. D. *Ideas and politics of Chilean independence, 1808–1833* (London 1967).

Conrad, R. *The destruction of Brazilian slavery, 1850–1888* (Berkeley 1972).

Consejo Latino Americano de Ciencias Sociales *La historia económica en América Latina* (CLACSO, Mexico City 1972).

Cortés Conde, R. and Gallo, E. *La formación de la Argentina moderna* (Buenos Aires 1967).

Cortés Conde, R. and Stein, S. (eds) *Latin America. A guide to economic history 1830–1930* (Berkeley 1977).

Cotler, J. *Clases, estado y nación en el Perú* (Lima 1978).

Cotler, J. and Fagen, R. R. (eds) *Latin America and the United States: the changing political realities* (Stanford 1974).

Cross, H. E. and Sandos, I. A. 'National development and international labour migration: Mexico 1940–1965' *JCH* xviii 1 (1983).

Cueva, A. *El desarrollo del capitalismo en América Latina* (Mexico 1978).

Dean, W. *The industrialization of São Paulo 1880–1945* (Austin 1969).

Dean, W. *Rio Claro: a Brazilian plantation system, 1820–1920* (Stanford 1976).

Deas, M. 'The fiscal problems of nineteenth-century Colombia' *JLAS* xiv 2 (1982).

De Kadt, E. (ed.) *Patterns of foreign influence in the Caribbean* (London 1972).

Denoon, D. *Settler capitalism: the dynamics of dependent development in the southern hemisphere* (Oxford 1983).

De Vylder, S. *Allende's Chile. The political economy of the rise and fall of the Unidad Popular* (Cambridge 1976).

Díaz Alejandro, C. F. *Essays on the economic history of the Argentine Republic* (New Haven 1970).

Di Tella, G. and Zymelman, M. *Las étapas del desarrollo económico argentino* (Buenos Aires 1967).

Dobb, M. *Studies in the development of capitalism* (New York 1963).

Domínguez, J. I. *Cuba: order and revolution* (Cambridge, Mass. 1978).

Domínguez, J. I. *Insurrection or loyalty: the breakdown of the Spanish American Empire* (Cambridge, Mass. 1980).

Domínguez, J. I. (ed.) *Cuba: internal and international affairs* (London 1982).

Domínguez, J. I. (ed.) *Mexico's political economy: challenges at home and abroad* (London 1982).

Domínguez, V. R. *From neighbour to stranger: the dilemma of Caribbean peoples in the United States of America* (New Haven 1975).

Dos Santos, T. *Dependencia y cambio social* (Santiago 1970).

Dos Santos, T. *Imperialismo y dependencia* (Mexico City 1978).

Dos Santos, T. 'The structure of dependence' *AER* lx 2 (1970).

Dos Santos, T. 'The crisis of development theory and the problems of dependence in Latin America' in H. Bernstein (ed.) *Underdevelopment and development: the Third World today: select readings* (Harmondsworth 1973).

Drake, P. *Socialism and populism in Chile 1932–52* (Urbana 1978).

Drosdoff, D. *El gobierno de las vacas (1933–56): tratado Roca-Runciman* (Buenos Aires 1972).

Duncan, K. and Rutledge, I. (eds) *Land and labour in Latin America: essays on the development of agrarian capitalism in the nineteenth and twentieth centuries* (Cambridge 1977).

Ebel, A. *Das Dritte Reich und Argentinien* (Cologne 1971).

Eisenberg, P. L. *The sugar industry in Pernambuco: modernization without change, 1840–1910* (Berkeley 1974).

Elkan, W. *An introduction to development economics* (London 1973).

Emmanuel, A. *Unequal exchange: a study in the imperialism of trade* (London 1972).

Emmanuel, A. 'Myths of development v. myths of underdevelopment' *NLR* 84 (1974).

Encina, F. A. *Nuestra inferioridad económica* (Santiago 1912).

Erickson, K. P. *The Brazilian corporative state and working-class politics* (Berkeley 1977).

Erickson, K. P. and Peppe, P. V. 'Dependent capitalist development, U.S. foreign policy and repression of the working class in Chile and Brazil' *LAP* iii 1 (1976).

Evans, P. *Dependent development. The alliance of multinational, state and local capital in Brazil* (Princeton 1979).

Fagen, R. R. (ed.) *Capitalism and the state in U.S. – Latin American relations* (Stanford 1979).

Falcoff, M. and Dockart, R. H. (eds) *Prologue to Perón. Argentina in depression and war 1930–1943* (Berkeley 1975).

Fausto, B. *A revolução de 1930* (São Paulo 1970).

Feis, H. *Europe the world's banker 1870–1914* (New Haven 1930).

Ferns, H. S. *Britain and Argentina in the nineteenth century* (Oxford 1960).

Ferrer, A. *The Argentine economy* (Berkeley 1967).

ffrench–Davis, R. and Tironi, E. (eds) *Latin America and the new international order* (London 1981).

Fiechter, G.–A. *Brazil since 1964: modernization under a military regime* (London 1975).

Fieldhouse, D. K. *The theory of capitalist imperialism* (London 1967).

Fieldhouse, D. K. *Unilever overseas: the anatomy of a multinational 1895–1965* (London 1978).

Finch, M. H. J. *The political economy of Uruguay since 1870* (London 1981).

Fishlow, A. 'Origins and consequences of import substitution in Brazil in E. Di Marco (ed.) *Essays in honour of Raúl Prebisch* (New York 1972).

Fitzgerald, E. V. K. *The state and economic development: Peru since 1968* (Cambridge 1976).

Fodor, J. and O'Connell, A. 'La Argentina y la economía atlántica en la primera mitad del siglo XX' *Desarrollo económico* XIII 49 (1973).

Foner, P. S. *The Spanish-Cuban-American War and the birth of American imperialism, 1895–1902* (2 vols New York 1972).

Forbes, I. L. D. 'German informal imperialism in South America before 1914' *EHR* XXXI 3 (1978).

Ford, A. G. *The gold standard, 1880–1914: Britain and Argentina* (Oxford 1962).

Ford, A. G. 'British investment and Argentine economic development, 1880–1914' in D. Rock (ed.) *Argentina in the twentieth century* (London 1975).

Foster–Carter, A. 'The modes of production controversy' *NLR* 107 (1978).

Frank, A. G. *Capitalism and underdevelopment in Latin America: historical studies of Chile and Brazil* (New York 1967).

Frank, A. G. *Latin America: underdevelopment or revolution* (New York 1969).

Frank, A. G. *Dependent accumulation and underdevelopment* (London 1978).

Fritsch, W. 'Aspectos da política econômica no Brasil: 1900–1914' in P. Nenhaus (ed.) *Econômia brasileira: uma visão histórica* (Rio de Janeiro 1980).

Furtado, C. *The economic growth of Brazil* (Berkeley 1963).

Furtado, C. *Economic development of Latin America: historical background and contemporary problems* (Cambridge 1977).

Gallagher, J. and Robinson, R. E. *Africa and the Victorians: the official mind of imperialism* (London 1961).

Gallagher, J. and Robinson, R. E. 'The imperialism of free trade' *EHR* VI 1 (1953).

Gallo, E. *Farmers in revolt: the revolutions of 1893 in the province of Santa Fé, Argentina* (London 1976).

Gallo, E. 'Agrarian expansion and industrial development in Argentina, 1880–1930' in R. Carr (ed.) *Latin American affairs*, St Antony's Papers no. 22 (Oxford 1970).

Gardner, L. C., La Feber, W. and McCormick, T. *Creation of the American empire* (London 1973).

Garrity, M. P. 'The multinational corporation in extractive industries: a case study of Reynolds Haitian Mines, Inc.' in S. W. Mintz (ed.) *Working papers in Haitian society and culture* (New Haven 1975).

Gerschenkron, A. *Economic backwardness in historical perspective* (Cambridge, Mass. 1962).

Giberti, H. C. E. *Historia económica de la ganadería argentina* (Buenos Aires 1961).

Girvan, M. *Corporate imperialism: conflict and expropriation: transnational corporations and economic nationalism in the Third World* (New York 1976).

Glade, W. P. *The Latin American economies: a study of their institutional evolution* (New York 1969).

Goldberg, R. *Agribusiness management for developing countries: Latin America* (Cambridge 1974).

González, L. *San José de Gracia: Mexican village in transition* (Austin 1974).

González Casanova, P. *Imperialismo y liberación en América Latina: una introducción a la historia contemporánea* (Mexico City 1978).

González Casanova, P. (ed.) *América Latina en los años treinta* (Mexico City 1977).

Gouré, L. and Weinkle, J. 'Cuba's new dependency' *Problems of Communism* XXI 2 (1972).

Graham, R. *Britain and the onset of modernization in Brazil, 1850–1914* (Cambridge 1968).

Griffin, K. *The political economy of agrarian change: an essay on the green revolution* (Cambridge, Mass. 1974).

Guerra y Sánchez, R. *Sugar and society in the Caribbean* (New Haven 1964).

Halperín Donghi, T. *Historia contemporánea de América Latina* (Madrid 1970).

Halperín Donghi, T. *The aftermath of revolution in Latin America* (New York 1973).

Halperín Donghi, T. ' "Dependency theory" and Latin American historiography' *LARR* XVII 1 (1982).

Hamilton, N. *The limits of state autonomy: post-revolutionary Mexico* (Princeton 1982).

Hansen, R. D. *The politics of Mexican development* (Baltimore 1971)

Harrison, R. J. 'Catalan business and the loss of Cuba, 1898–1914' *EHR* XXVII 3 (1974).

Hell, J. *et al. Der Deutsche Faschismus in Lateinamerika* (East Berlin 1966).

Hell, J., Katz, F. *et al. Lateinamerika zwischen Emanzipatia und Imperialismus* (East Berlin 1965).

Hilferding, R. *Finance Capital* (Vienna 1923).

Hilferding, R. *Boehm-Bawerk's criticism of Marx, with an introduction by P. M. Sweezey* (New York 1949).

Hilton, S. E. *Brazil and the great powers 1930–1939: the politics of trade rivalry* (Austin 1975).

Hilton, S. E. 'Vargas and Brazilian economic development, 1930–1945: a reappraisal of his attitude towards industrialization and planning' *JEH* XXXV 4 (1975).

Hirschman, A. O. *The strategy of economic development* (New Haven 1958).

Hirschman, A. O. *Journeys towards progress: studies in economic policy-making in Latin America* (New York 1963).

Hirschman, A. O. *A bias for hope* (New Haven 1971).

Hirschman, A. O. (ed.) *Latin American issues: essays and comments* (New York 1961).

Hobson, J. A. *Imperialism: a study* (London 1902).

Hoernel, R. 'Sugar and social change in Oriente, Cuba' *JLAS* x 1 (1978).
Holloway, T. *The Brazilian valorization of 1906: regional politics and economic dependency* (Madison 1975).
Holloway, T. *Immigrants on the land: coffee and society in São Paulo, 1886–1934* (Chapel Hill 1980).
Hughlet, L. J. (ed.) *Industrialization of Latin America* (New York 1946).
Humphreys, R. A. *Latin America and the Second World War* (2 vols. London 1981 and 1982).
Hunt, S. J. 'Growth and guano in nineteenth-century Peru' (unpubl. discussion paper, Princeton University, February 1973).

Ianni, O. *Industrialização e desenvolvimento social no Brasil* (Rio de Janeiro 1963).
Ianni, O. *A formação do estado populista na América Latina* (Rio de Janeiro 1975).
Ibarguren, C. *Juan Manuel de Rosas: su vida, su tiempo, su drama* (Buenos Aires 1930).
Irazusta, J. *Influencia económica británica en el Río de La Plata* (Buenos Aires 1963).

Jaguaribe, H. *Economic and political development: a theoretical approach and a Brazilian case-study* (Cambridge, Mass. 1968).
Jenkins, Rh. *Dependent industrialization in Latin America: the automobile industry in Argentina, Chile and Mexico* (New York 1977).
Jenkins, Rh, *Transnational corporations and industrial transformation in Latin America* (London 1984).
Joslin, D. *A century of banking in Latin America* (London 1963).

Karnes, T. L. *Tropical enterprise: the Standard Fruit and Steamship Company in Latin America* (Baton Rouge 1978).
Katz, F. *The secret war in Mexico: Europe, the United States and the Mexican Revolution* (Chicago 1981).
Katz, F. 'Labor conditions on haciendas in Porfirian Mexico' *HAHR* LIV 1 (1974).
Keith, R. (ed.) *Haciendas and plantations in Latin American history* (New York 1977).
Kellenbenz H. and Schneider, J. 'La emigración alemana a América Latina desde 1821 hasta 1930' *Jahrbuch* XIII (1976).
Kiernan, V. G. 'Imperialism, American and European: some historical comments' *Socialist Register* (1971).
Kindleberger, C. P. *Economic development* (London 1965).
Klaren, P. *Modernization, dislocation and Aprismo: origins of the Peruvian aprista party 1870–1932* (Austin 1973).
Knight, F. *The Caribbean: the genesis of a fragmented nationalism* (New York 1977).
Kuczynski, P.–P. 'Latin American debt' *Foreign Affairs LXI* 2 (1982–3).

Laclau, E. *Politics and ideology in Marxist theory: capitalism, fascism, populism* (London 1977).
Laclau, E. 'Feudalism and capitalism in Latin America' *NLR* 67 (1971).
Laclau, E. 'Modos de producción: sistemas económicos y población excedente aproximación histórica a los casos argentino y chileno' *Revista Latinoamericana de Sociología* v 2 (1969).
LaFeber, W. *The new empire: an interpretation of American expansion, 1860–1898* (Ithaca, 1961).
LaFeber, W. *The Panama Canal: the crisis in historical perspective* (New York 1978).

LaFeber, W. *America, Russia and the Cold War, 1945–75* (London 1976).

Landes, D. S. *The unbound Prometheus: technological change and industrial development in Western Europe from 1750 to the present* (Cambridge 1969).

Lang, J. *Portuguese Brazil. The King's plantation* (New York 1979).

Lebergott, S. 'The returns to U.S. imperialism, 1890–1929' *JEH* xi 2 (1980).

Leff, N. H. *Underdevelopment and development in Brazil* (2 vols. London 1982).

Lenin, V. I. *Imperialism: the highest stage of capitalism, a popular outline* (various edns, first published 1917; see Moscow 1966).

Levin, J. V. *The export economies: their pattern of development in historical perspective* (Cambridge, Mass. 1960).

Lewis, C. *America's stake in international investments* (Washington 1938).

Lewis, G. K. *Puerto Rico: freedom and power in the Caribbean* (New York 1963).

Lewis, G. K. *Main currents in Caribbean thought* (London 1983).

Lewis, W. A. *Growth and fluctuations, 1870–1913* (London 1978).

Linz, J. J. and Stepan, A. (eds) *The breakdown of democratic regimes: crisis, breakdown and reequilibration* (Baltimore 1978).

Lopez, A. and Petras, J. (eds) *Puerto Rico and the Puerto Ricans: studies in history and society* (London 1974).

Louis, W. R. (ed.) *Imperialism: the Robinson and Gallagher controversy* (New York 1975).

Love, J. L. 'External financing and domestic politics: the case of São Paulo, 1889–1937' in R. E. Scott (ed.) *Latin American modernization. Case studies in the crisis of change* (Urbana 1973).

Love, J. L. 'Raúl Prebisch and the origins of the doctrine of unequal exchange' *LARR* xv 3 (1980).

Loveman, B. and Davies, T. M. (eds) *The politics of antipolitics: the military in Latin America* (Lincoln 1976).

Lowenthal, A. F. *The Dominican intervention* (Cambridge, Mass. 1972).

Lowenthal, A. F. (ed.) *Armies and politics in Latin America* (New York 1976).

Lowenthal, A. F. 'The U.S. and Latin America: ending the hegemonic presumption' *Foreign Affairs* (1973).

Lozano, W. *La dominación imperialista en la República Dominicana 1900–1930* (Santo Domingo 1978).

Luxemburg, R. *The accumulation of capital, with an introduction by Joan Robinson* (London 1951).

Lynch, J. *The Spanish American revolutions: 1808–1826* (London 1973).

Lynch, J. *Argentine dictator: Juan Manuel de Rosas 1829–1852* (Oxford 1981).

Malan, P. S., Bonelli, R., de P. Abreu, M. and Pereira, J. E. C. *Política econômica externa e industrialização no Brasil (1939/52)* (Rio de Janeiro 1977).

Malloy, J. (ed.) *Authoritarianism and corporatism in Latin America* (Pittsburgh 1977).

Maluquer de Motes Bernet, J. 'El mercado colonial antillano en el siglo XIX' in J. Nadal and G. Tortella *Agricultura, comercio colonial y el crecimiento económico en la España contemporánea. Actos del primer coloquio de historia económica de España* (Barcelona 1974).

Mamalakis, M. J. *The growth and structure of the Chilean economy from independence to Allende* (New Haven 1976).

Mamalakis, M. J. 'The theory of sectoral clashes' *LARR* iv 3 (1969).

Mamalakis, M. J. 'The theory of sectoral clashes and coalitions revisited' *LARR* vi 3 (1971).

Manchester, A. K. *British pre-eminence in Brazil: its rise and decline; a study in European expansion* (Chapel Hill 1933).

Mariátegui, J. C. *7 ensayos de interpretación de la realidad peruana* (Lima 1928).

Martínez-Alier, J. *Haciendas, plantations and collective farms: agrarian class societies, Cuba and Peru* (London 1977).

Martins, L. *Pouvoir et développement économique. Formation et évolution des structures politiques au Brésil* (Paris 1976).

Mathew, W. M. *The House of Gibbs and the Peruvian guano monopoly* (London 1981).

Matos Mar, J. (ed.) *La crisis del desarrollismo y la nueva dependencia* (Buenos Aires 1969).

Matsushita, H. *Movimiento obrero argentino, 1930–1945: sus proyecciones en los origenes del peronismo* (Buenos Aires 1983).

Mattoon, R. M. 'Railroads, coffee and the growth of big business in São Paulo, Brazil' *HAHR* LVII 2 (1977).

May, E. *Imperial democracy: the emergence of America as a great power* (New York 1973).

Merrick, T. W. and Graham, D. H. *Population and economic development in Brazil: 1800 to the present* (Baltimore 1979).

Mesa-Lago, C. *Cuba in the 1970s: pragmatism and institutionalization* (Albuquerque 1974).

Mesa-Lago, C. *The economy of socialist Cuba. A two-decade appraisal* (Albuquerque 1981).

Meyer, J. *La révolution mexicaine 1910–1940* (Paris 1973).

Meyer, L. *Mexico and the United States in the oil controversy 1917–1942* (Austin 1977).

Meyer, M. and Wilkie, E. (eds) *Contemporary Mexico* (New York 1976).

Miller, R., Smith, C., Fisher, J. (eds) *Social and economic change in Peru* (Liverpool 1976).

Miller, R. 'Latin American manufacturing and the First World War' *WD* IX 8 (1981).

Mintz, S. W. *Caribbean transformations* (Chicago 1974).

Moreno Fraginals, M. *The sugar mill. The socio-economic complex of sugar in Cuba 1760–1860* (New York 1976).

Moreno Fraginals, M. *El ingenio* (3 vols Habana 1978).

Mörner, M. 'Comparative approaches to Latin American history' *LARR* XVII 3 (1982).

Morse R. (ed.) *The urban development of Latin America, 1750–1920* (Stanford 1971).

Moya Pons, F. *Manual de historia dominicana* (Santiago R.D. 1978).

Myint, H. *The economics of the developing countries* (London 1980).

Nicholls, D. *From Dessalines to Duvalier: race, colour and national independence in Haiti* (Cambridge 1979).

North, L. and Raby, D. 'The dynamics of revolution and counter-revolution: Mexico under Cárdenas, 1930–1940' *LARU Studies* II (1977).

Nurkse, R. *Problems of capital formation in underdeveloped countries* (Oxford 1960).

Nurkse, R. *Equilibrium and the world economy* (New York 1961).

O'Brien, P. J. (ed.) *Allende's Chile* (New York 1976).

Ohlin, B. *The course and phases of the world economic depression* (Geneva 1931).

Ospina Vásquez, L. *Industria y protección en Colombia, 1810–1930* (Medellín 1955).

Oszak, O. 'The historical formation of the state in Latin America; some theoretical and methodological guidelines for its study' *LARR* XVI 2 (1981).

Owen, R. and Sutcliffe, B. (eds) *Studies in the theory of imperialism* (London 1972).

Oxaal, I., Barnett, D. and Booth, D. (eds) *Beyond the sociology of development: economy and society in Latin America and Africa* (London 1975).

Palacios, M. *Coffee in Colombia, 1870–1970: an economic, social and political history* (Cambridge 1980).

Palma, G. 'Dependency: a formal theory of underdevelopment or a methodology for the analysis of concrete situations of underdevelopment?' *WD* vi (1978).

Paterson, T. (ed.) *American imperialism and anti-imperialism* (New York 1973).

Pélaez, C. M. *An economic analysis of the Brazilian coffee support programme, 1906–45; theory, policy and measurement* (Rio de Janeiro 1974).

Pélaez, C. M. *The state, the Great Depression and the industrialization of Brazil* (Ann Arbor 1975).

Pélaez, C. M. 'The theory and reality of imperialism in the coffee economy of nineteenth-century Brazil' *EHR* xxix 2 (1976).

Pélaez, C. M. (ed.) *Essays on coffee and economic development* (Rio de Janeiro 1973).

Pérez, B. H. 'The economic cycle in Latin American agricultural export economies 1880–1930' *LARR* xv 3 (1980).

Phelps, D. M. *Migration of industry to South America* (New York 1939).

Philip, G. *Oil and politics in Latin America: nationalist movements and state companies* (Cambridge 1982).

Pinto, A. *Chile: una economía difícil* (Mexico 1964).

Platt, D. C. M. *Trade, finance and politics in British foreign policy, 1815–1914* (Oxford 1968).

Platt, D. C. M. *Latin America and British trade, 1806–1914* (London 1972).

Platt, D. C. M. (ed.) *Business imperialism; an inquiry based on British experience in Latin America before 1930* (Oxford 1977).

Platt, D. C. M. 'The imperialism of free trade; some reservations' *EHR* xxi 2 (1968).

Platt, D. C. M. 'Economic factors in British policy during the "new imperialism"' *Past and Present* xxxix (1968).

Platt, D. C. M. 'Further objections to an "imperialism of free trade", 1830–60' *EHR* xxvi 1 (1973).

Platt, D. C. M. 'The national economy and British imperial expansion before 1914' *Journal of Imperial and Commonwealth History* ii 1 (1973).

Platt, D. C. M. 'British portfolio investment before 1870; some doubts' *EHR* xxxiii 1 (1980).

Platt, D. C. M. 'Dependency in nineteenth-century Latin America: an historian objects' *LARR* xv 1 (1980).

Portantiero, J. C. and Murmis, M. (eds) *El movimiento obrero en los orígenes del peronismo* (Buenos Aires 1969).

Potash, R. A. *El Banco de Avío de México: el fomento de la industria, 1821–1846* (Mexico City 1959).

Prado Jr, C. *História econômica do Brasil* (São Paulo 1953).

Prebisch, R. *The economic development of Latin America* (New York 1950).

Prebisch, R. *Change and development: Latin America's great task* (New York 1971).

Prebisch, R. 'A critique of peripheral capitalism' *CR* 1 (1976).

Prebisch, R. 'The Latin American periphery in the global system of capitalism' *CR* 13 (1981).

Prebisch, R. 'A historic turning point for the Latin American periphery' *CR* 18 (1982).

Quijano, A. 'Imperialism and the working class in Latin America' *LAP* III 1 (1976).

Radice, H. (ed.) *International firms and modern imperialism* (London 1975).

Remmer, K. L. and Mark, G. W. 'Bureaucratic-authoritarianism revisited' *LARR* XVII 2 (1982).

Reynolds, C. *The Mexican economy: twentieth-century structure and growth* (New Haven 1970).

Ridings, E. W. 'Class sector unity in an export economy; the case of nineteenth-century Brazil' *HAHR* LVIII 3 (1978).

Roberts, B. *Cities of peasants* (London 1978).

Rock, D. *Politics in Argentina, 1890–1930: the rise and fall of radicalism* (Cambridge 1975).

Rostow, W. W. *The stages of economic growth: a non-communist manifesto* (Cambridge 1960).

Rostow, W. W. *The world economy: history and prospects* (London 1979).

Rouquié A. (ed.) *Pouvoir militaire et société politique en République Argentine* (Paris 1978).

Roxborough, I., *Theories of underdevelopment* (London 1979).

Roxborough, I, O'Brien, P. and Roddick, J. *Chile: the state and the revolution* (London 1976).

Royal Institute of International Affairs *The republics of South America* (London 1939).

Safford, F. R. *The ideal of the practical: Colombia's struggle to form a technical elite* (Austin 1976).

Safford, F. R. 'Foreign and national enterprise in nineteenth-century Colombia' *EHR* XXXIX 4 (1965).

Safford, F. R. 'Bases of political alignment in Latin America' in R. Graham and P. Smith (eds) *New Approaches to Latin American History* (Austin 1974).

Sánchez-Albornoz, N. *The population of Latin America: a history* (Berkeley 1974).

Scalabrini Ortiz, R. *Política británica en el Río de la Plata* (Buenos Aires 1957).

Schneider, J. 'Terms of trade between France and Latin America, 1826–1856: causes of increasing economic disparities?' in P. Bairoch and M. Levy-Leboyer (eds) *Disparities in economic development since the industrial revolution* (London 1981).

Schumpeter, J. A. *Capitalism, socialism and democracy* (London 1943).

Schumpeter, J. A. *Imperialism* (Oxford 1951).

Scobie, J. R. *Revolution on the pampas: a social history of Argentine wheat, 1860–1910* (Austin 1964).

Seidel, R. 'American reformers abroad: the Kemmerer missions in Latin America, 1923–1931' *JAH* XXXII (1972).

Serra, J. *El 'milagro' económico brasileño: realidad o mito?* (Buenos Aires 1973).

Silva Herzog, T. *Historia de la expropriación de las empresas petroleras* (Mexico City 1964).

Singer, H. W. 'Distribution of gain between investing and borrowing countries' *AER* XXX (1950).

Simonsen, R. C. *Evolução industrial do Brasil e outras estudos* (São Paulo 1973).

Skidmore, T. E. *Black into White: race and nationality in Brazilian thought* (New York 1974).

Skidmore, T.E. 'Workers and soldiers: urban labor movements and elite response in twentieth-century Latin America' in V. Bernard (ed.) *Elites, masses and modernization in Latin America, 1850–1930* (Austin 1979).

Smith, P. H. *Politics and beef in Argentina: patterns of conflict and change* (New York 1969).

Smith, R. F. *The US and revolutionary nationalism in Mexico 1916–1932* (Chicago 1972).

Solberg, C. *Immigration and nationalism, Argentina and Chile 1890–1914* (Austin 1970).

Spalding, H. *Organized labor in Latin America: historical case studies of urban workers in dependent societies* (New York 1977).

Stein, S. J. *Vassouras: a Brazilian coffee county, 1850–1900* (Cambridge, Mass. 1957).

Stein, S. J. and B. *The colonial heritage of Latin America: essays on economic dependence in perspective* (New York 1970).

Stein, S. J. 'Comment on D. C. M. Platt' *LARR* xv 1 (1980).

Stepan, A. 'The US and Latin America: vital interests and the instruments of power' *Foreign Affairs* LVIII 3 (1979).

Stepan, A. *The state and society. Peru in comparative perspective* (Princeton 1978).

Stolcke, V. and Hall, M. 'The introduction of free labour into São Paulo coffee plantations' *Journal of Peasant Studies* x 2/3 (1983).

Sunkel, O. *El marco histórico del proceso de desarrollo y de subdesarrollo* (Santiago 1970).

Sunkel, O. 'Big business and "dependencia" ' *Foreign Affairs* L 3 (1971).

Sunkel, O. and Paz, P. *El subdesarrollo latinoamericano y la teoría del desarrollo* (Madrid 1970).

Sweezey, P. M. *The theory of capitalist development: principles of Marxian political economy* (New York 1968).

Tavares, M. C. 'The growth and decline of import substitution in Brazil' *Economic Bulletin for Latin America* ix 1 (1964).

Thorp, R. (ed.) *Latin America in the 1930s: the role of the periphery in world crisis* (London 1984).

Thorp, R. and Whitehead, L. (eds) *Inflation and stabilization in Latin America* (London 1979).

Todaro, M. P. *Economic development in the Third World* (London 1981).

Topik, S. 'The evolution of the economic role of the Brazilian state, 1889–1930' *JLAS* xi 2 (1979).

Topik, S. 'State intervention in a liberal regime; Brazil, 1889–1930' *HAHR* LX 4 (1980).

Urquidi, V. L. and Thorp, R. (eds) *Latin America in the international economy* (London 1973).

Vázquez-Presedo, V. *El caso argentino: migración de factores, comercio exterior y desarrollo, 1875–1914* (Buenos Aires 1971).

Vernon, R. *The dilemma of Mexico's development: the roles of the private and public sectors* (Cambridge, Mass, 1963).

Vernon, R. *Sovereignty at bay: the multinational spread of U.S. enterprises* (London 1971).

Vernon, R. *Storm over the multinationals: the real issues* (London 1977).

Versiani, E. R. *Industrial investment in an 'export' economy: the Brazilian experience before 1914* (Institute of Latin American Studies, Working Paper no. 2, London 1979).

Villamil, J. (ed.) *Transnational capitalism and national development: new perspectives on dependence* (Hassocks 1979).

Villela, A. V. and Suzigan, W. *Government policy and the economic growth of Brazil, 1889–1945* (Rio de Janeiro 1977).

Wallerstein, I. *The capitalist world economy* (Cambridge 1979).

Weaver, F. S. *Class, state and industrial structure: the historical process of South American industrial growth* (Westport, Conn. 1980).

Whitehead, L. *The United States and Bolivia* (London 1969).

Wilkie, J. W. *Mexican revolution: federal expenditure and social change since 1910* (Berkeley 1970).

Wilkins, M. *The emergence of multinational enterprise: American business abroad from the colonial era to 1914* (Cambridge, Mass. 1971).

Wilkins, M. *The maturing of multinational enterprise: American business abroad from 1914 to 1970* (Cambridge, Mass. 1974).

Wilkins, M. 'Multinational corporations' *LARR* xvii 2 (1982).

Williams, W. A. *The roots of the modern American empire – a study of the growth and shaping of a social consciousness in a market-place society* (London 1974).

Winkler, M. *Investments of United States capital in Latin America* (Boston 1929).

Wirth, J. D. *The politics of Brazilian development, 1930–1954* (Stanford 1970).

Wolf, E. and Mintz, S. 'Haciendas and plantations in middle America and the Caribbean' *Social and Economic Studies* vi (1957).

Womack, J. 'The Mexican economy during the revolution, 1910–1920; historiography and analysis' *Marxist Perspectives* i 4 (1978).

Wright, T. P., Jr *American support of free elections abroad* (Washington 1964).

Wythe, G. *Industry in Latin America* (New York 1945).

INDEX

Africa, 3, 5, 6, 21; Latin America compared with, 2, 20; relations with Latin America, 85, 341, 703.

agrarian protest, 182; *see also* agrarian reform; agrarian structures; labour, rural.

agrarian reform, 4, 22, 24, 114–5, 117, 150, 178, 179, 488–9.

agrarian reform in Mexico, 272, 295, 297, 298, 302–8; compared with rest of Latin America, 304–5, 306–7; compared with Soviet collectivization, 295; and consumption, 306–7; and export earnings, 306–7; and production levels, 305–7; *see also* agrarian structures; popular agrarianism.

agrarian structures, 24–5, re-structuring, 97, 99, 114–5, 117, 178, 179–80, 287; *see also* factors of production, factor markets.

agribusiness, 403, 482–3, 496n.1.

agriculture, 96, 113, 125, 129, 131, 133–5, 181, 215, 231–49, 305–8, 482–99; capitalist/agrarian capitalism, 232–4, 238, 305–6, 431, *see also* agribusiness; cash-crop production, 96, 103–7, 145n.22, 210, 215, 459; colonization, 322–3, 360; income, 488–92, *latifundismo*, 294, 307–8; performance compared with industry, in Mexico, 306–7; plantations, 96, 178, 489, *see also* specific crops; production cycles, 97; productivity, 305–8; rural credit, 349, 488, *see also* banks/banking, mortgage banks;

sharecropping, 243–4; subsistence and semi-subsistence, 96, 100, 103–5, 106, 208, 232–4, relationship with capitalist agriculture, 232; and immigration, 210; and imported inputs, 330; and industrialization, 214–5, 274, 307–8; *see also* agrarian protest; agrarian reform; agrarian structures; agribusiness; labour, rural; land; landholding; landowners, large; mortgage banks; peasants; specific commodities; trade; transnational corporations.

aid, 400.

Alamán, Lucas, 136.

Alavi, H, 63.

Alberdi, Juan Bautista, 201.

Alessandri, Arturo, 331.

Allende, Salvador, 402.

Alliance for Progress, 4, 400.

Alschuler, Lawrence, 55.

Altamirano, J. 160.

Althusser, Louis, 17.

Alvarado, Salvador, 293, 297, 299.

American Federation of Labour – Confederation of Industrial Organizations, (AFL–CIO), 278, 359, 407.

Amin, Samir, 19, 41, 42, 453.

anarchism, 33, 176, 272, 278, 320; and the state; 278.

anarcho-syndicalism, 255, 272, 278.

Anglo-American War (1812–4), 95.

Anglo-Argentine Bank, 188.

Anglo-Brazilian Payments Agreement(s). 387, 391n.7.

Anglo-Uruguayan Trade and

and agriculture, 210; immigrants and working-class formation, 213; immigrant remittances, 349.

military, 18, 23, 274, as institution/bureaucracy, 271, 467; civil-military relations, 271, 434; developmentalism, 85, 271; education, 271, 360; equipment, 150; expenditure, 179; *golpes*, 52, 87, 114, 269, 435, 437, 441; ideology, 271; missions, 179, 271; professionalization, 179, 271, 277; reform, 271, 360–2; rule/dictatorship, 52, 87, 269, 287, 342, 348, 353–7, 405, 417, 443, technology; 271; *see also* industrialization.

Minas Gerais, 202, 205, 216.

minerals, 55, 151, 153, 178, 458; *see also* individual commodities.

mineworkers, 278.

mining/mineownership, 95–6, 97, 102–3, 105, 107–9, 113, 128, 139–40, 143, 149, 153, 167, 175, 178, 294, 298, 303, 319–21, 329.

Miranda, Miguel, 408, 409.

modernization, theories of, 97–8, 99.

monetarism, 402, 452, 453, 455, 456, 457, 458, 464, 465–6, 468; monetarist alliance, 461; *see also* tripod alliance (banking).

monetization, 128–9, 208–14, 222; demonetization, 138.

money supply, 109–10; *see also* currency; individual countries.

Montero, Juan Estéban, 331.

Monterrey, 433.

Montevideo, 255, 256, 257, 258, 259, 260, 261, 262, 264.

Montevideo Waterworks Company, 194.

Morelos (state/province), 62.

Moreno Fraginals, Manuel, 97.

mortgage banks, 156, 184, 185–6, 188–9, 193, 349, 488.

Múgica, Francisco, 296.

multilateralism, 382, 384, 440.

Muñoz, Oscar, 321.

Myint, Hla, 24.

Nacional Financiera, 299.

Nahum, Benjamin, 257–8.

Napoleonic Wars, 95, 130, 132, 146n.50.

narcotics, 484.

nationalism, 4–5, 16, 18, 52, 53, 57, 71, 99, 296–300, 303, 358, 397, 405–8, 465; and dependency; 29, 52, *see also* economic nationalism; *indigenismo*.

nationalization/expropriation, 34, 251, 263, 264, 388, 393n.25, 461.

national schools of historiography, 177, 199, Argentina, 270, 367–8; Brazil, 284, 434–5; Chile, 161, 284; Colombia, 116; Dominican Republic, 340, *see also* Mexican Revolution, historiography of.

natural resources, 408, 462, 472, 478; wastage, 270.

nazism, 271, 405.

négritude, 270.

neo-colonialism, *see* business imperialism; dependency; *laissez-faire* imperialism; informal empire; transnational corporations.

neutralism, 412; in Argentina, 412.

new authoritarianism, 52.

New Deal, 9, 272, 301, 409.

'new' economic history, 199, 200, 224n.3.

Newfarmer, R., 45, 435.

'new' imperialism, 6, 367.

New International Division of Labour (NIDL), 280, 403, 415–27, 452, 468.

New International Economic Order (NIEO), 18, 280, 475.

New Left Review, 50, 51.

Newly Industrializing Countries (NICs), 479–80.

New Plan, German, 383.

New Right, 18.

New Spain, *see* Mexico.

New York money market, 251, 374, 381.

Nicaragua, 88, 272, 361.

Niemeyer, Sir Otto, 382, 389.